The Working Class in American History

Editorial Advisors
David Brody
Herbert G. Gutman
David Montgomery

THIS BOOK BELONGS TO:
Ann & Bill Kemsley

Books in the Series
The Working Class in American History

Worker City, Company Town: Iron and Cotton-Worker Protest in Troy and
Cohoes, New York, 1855–84
DANIEL J. WALKOWITZ

Life, Work, and Rebellion in the Coal Fields: The Southern West Virginia Miners,
1880–1922
DAVID ALAN CORBIN

Women and American Socialism, 1870–1920
MARI JO BUHLE

Lives of Their Own: Blacks, Italians, and Poles in Pittsburgh, 1900–1960
JOHN BODNAR, ROGER SIMON, AND MICHAEL P. WEBER

Working-Class America: Essays on Labor, Community, and American Society
EDITED BY MICHAEL H. FRISCH AND DANIEL J. WALKOWITZ

Eugene V. Debs: Citizen and Socialist
NICK SALVATORE

American Labor and Immigration History, 1877–1920s: Recent European
Research
EDITED BY DIRK HOERDER

Workingmen's Democracy: The Knights of Labor and American Politics
LEON FINK

Electrical Workers: A History of Labor at General Electric
and Westinghouse, 1923–60
RONALD W. SCHATZ

The Mechanics of Baltimore: Workers and Politics
in the Age of Revolution, 1763–1812
CHARLES G. STEFFEN

The Practice of Solidarity: American Hat Finishers
in the Nineteenth Century
DAVID BENSMAN

The Labor History Reader
EDITED BY DANIEL J. LEAB

The Labor History Reader

Edited by Daniel J. Leab

The Labor History Reader

University of Illinois Press   *Urbana and Chicago*

This book is printed on acid-free paper.

Library of Congress Cataloging in Publication Data

Main entry under title:

The Labor history reader.

(The Working class in American history)
Essays taken from periodical Labor history.
1. Labor and laboring classes—United States—His-
tory—Addresses, essays, lectures. 2. Trade-unions—
United States—History—Addresses, essays, lectures.
I. Leab, Daniel. II. Labor history (New York, N.Y.)
III. Series.
HD8066.L32 1985   331′.0973   84-16326
ISBN 0-252-01197-X (cloth)
ISBN 0-252-01198-8 (paper)

Contents

Acknowledgments

Labor History has been a collective effort since its inception, and while it is not possible to list individually all those who have toiled on its behalf, there are some who must be publicly thanked.

The journal owes a great debt to the Tamiment Institute, which has generously supported *Labor History* since it began publication. Moreover, there have never been any strings tied to that support, the Tamiment Institute always allowing the journal a free editorial rein. All the members of the Tamiment Institute board have proven to be loyal supporters of *Labor History* but the late Ben Josephson, the late Stephen C. Vladeck, and Myron Kolatch deserve special mention. Each, while serving as secretary of the Institute, has always been available for consultation and support.

It should be noted that over the years the journal's editorial board members have read manuscripts, solicited articles, and suggested new ways to deal with a multifaceted, constantly evolving subject. There has been a remarkable continuity of membership, and there have been but two board chairmen: Richard B. Morris and Sidney Fine have served with ability, energy, and intelligence. My predecessors, Norman Jacobs and Milton Cantor, deserve much credit for their diligent service in establishing *Labor History* as *the* journal in the field.

Also to be given a rousing vote of thanks is Gladys Feig, who has run the day-to-day operations of the journal for nearly twenty-five years with skill and devotion.

In the preparation of this *Reader* I was immeasurably aided by the efforts of the current board, especially David Brody, Sidney Fine, and Herbert G. Gutman. Thanks are also due to Richard L. Wentworth, the director of the University of Illinois Press, and to Susan L. Patterson, as well as other staff members, who have worked with me in an efficient and extremely helpful fashion.

Finally, may I please end on a personal note and express my thanks to my wife Katharine Kyes Leab, who has lived with *Labor History* for over a decade . . . and never, well hardly ever, complained about the demands made by this journalistic interloper.

Daniel J. Leab

Foreword

Since the appearance of its first issue in 1960, *Labor History* has invited the submission of manuscripts pertaining to all aspects of American labor history. As the journal now states, its pages are open to manuscripts dealing with "specific unions and . . . the impact of labor problems upon ethnic and minority groups, the nature of work and working class life, theories of the labor movement, biographical portraits of important labor figures, . . . foreign labor movements that shed light on American labor developments, and radical groups . . . as they relate to American labor history." Over the years the managing editors and editorial board members have been receptive to articles reflecting both the "old" labor history and the "new," and they have not limited the articles accepted to those conforming to a particular point of view. Their only concern has been the quality and relevance of the manuscripts submitted. The selections that follow are typical of the articles that have appeared in *Labor History* during its first twenty-five years.

In addition to articles and book reviews, *Labor History* has regularly published notes and documents of interest to students of American labor history. Although its central concern is American labor history, the journal also reviews books dealing with the labor history of other countries.

Labor History, from the start, has provided information on archival sources available for the study of American labor history. The fall 1982 issue of the journal was an archival issue that consisted of institutional reports "co-ordinated and edited" by Philip P. Mason. In 1967 *Labor History* began publishing an annual American labor history bibliography that followed the format of Maurice Neufeld's *A Representative Bibliography of American Labor History* (1964). The annual *Labor History* bibliographies and the Neufeld bibliography are to be consolidated into a single bibliography that is scheduled for publication in 1984.

Some issues of *Labor History* have focused on a single aspect of American labor history. The summer 1969 issue was devoted to blacks and the American labor movement; the summer 1974 issue consisted of a series of articles on working-class culture; and the winter 1979-1980 issue was primarily concerned with women and work. The subject of the winter 1978 issue, for which Maurice Neufeld was guest editor, was Philip Taft, a founder of *Labor History* and for many years an editorial board member. In the spring of 1968 *Labor History* published a supplementary issue, edited by Jack Barbash, that was comprised of articles dealing with David Dubinsky and the International Ladies' Garment Workers' Union.

Labor History was published only three times a year during its first nine years. It became a quarterly in 1970. Norman Jacobs was the first managing editor. Milton Cantor succeeded Jacobs in 1964, and Daniel J. Leab, the present managing editor, assumed the position ten years later. Richard Morris was chairman of the editorial board from 1960 to 1976, when I succeeded him.

In the ensuing pages, Richard Morris discusses the founding of *Labor History,* and David Brody and Herbert G. Gutman, current editorial board members, introduce the articles that follow. The authors of the articles were each allowed a few words to update their pieces, and these appear in the section called "Afterthoughts."

Sidney Fine

Preface

As a legal and social historian I came to the field of labor history by uncovering so much litigation concerning free workers and indentured servants buried in the minute books and file papers of inferior court records in the era when court cases went unprinted. My interest had always been on "the village Hampden" and the "mute inglorious Milton," as my first serious work, *Studies in the History of American Law* (1930), had demonstrated. That study was rather quickly followed by my *Select Cases of the Mayor's Court of New York City, 1674-1784* (1935), which dealt with numerous issues of seamen's wages and a variety of suits involving labor.

I was now off and running on my *Government and Labor in Early America,* a ten-year study based on some 20,000 inferior court cases of the colonial and Revolutionary years. This study, published in 1946, was followed by a number of discrete essays on quasi-slavery and white servitude in the pre–Civil War years.

All this is by way of explanation of how a historian with the many-sided interests that I possess became so inextricably involved in the founding of *Labor History.* A coincidence of events in the 1950s contributed. J. B. S. Hardman, veteran labor journalist, had found it necessary to discontinue *Labor and Nation* after a run of half a dozen years or so. During its brief life it offered to the labor historian a rich variety of essays and documents. But the Hardman experiment seemed to prove that a labor history journal as such could not succeed.

When I was elected president of a newly formed group called Labor Historians, I shared the group's feeling that the time had come for a renewed study of labor, utilizing new approaches and techniques and revivifying the field. If anything, the concern in the subject was heightened by the passing of Selig Perlman, virtually the last member of that distinguished group of historians and economists who had collaborated with John R. Commons in his seminal volumes on the labor movement in the United States. Labor Historians talked a good deal about a magazine and offered a small supplement of up-to-date labor history information as a step in that direction.

It was now time for a new series of investigations. The New Deal had given the labor movement a tremendous fillip, and postwar problems of labor and unionism had become a matter of national focus. Americans, like the French Annales group, were beginning to revolt from "court and trumpet" history.

It was the good fortune of Labor Historians that they were able to join forces with the Tamiment Institute. That partnership made possible the publication of a new journal in the field, one that commanded the immediate attention of labor specialists nationwide. In the late 1950s a joint conference of members of Labor Historians with officers of Tamiment Institute was held at the old Tamiment headquarters at the Rand School. Present were Ben Josephson, Norman Jacobs, John Hall, and myself, among others. Out of the conference came an expression of deep interest on the part of the Tamiment Institute to underwrite a labor history publication, with no strings attached. Immediately thereafter, according to my own files, Norman Jacobs and I canvassed virtually the entire field of labor historians, both in departments of history and economics, as well as in trade unions and trade union publications.

The result, the first issue of *Labor History*, made its appearance in the winter of 1960. Announced as a three-times-a-year effort, it had occasionally been ambitious and issued additional volumes, as in the case of the David Dubinsky supplement. It is now a quarterly. I had the honor of serving as chairman of a distinguished editorial board, whose members were Daniel Bell of Columbia University; Walter Galenson, then at the University of California; Maurice Neufeld of the School of Labor and Industrial Relations at Cornell University; Brendan Sexton of the United Automobile Workers; and the late Philip Taft of Brown University. A rotating group, it enlisted other scholars of standing in the field. My own tenure was much longer than originally intended, but in 1976 I bowed to the pressures imposed by the American Revolution Bicentennial to resign from the board, but with deep regret and cherished memories of shared planning with a dedicated group of scholars.

That first issue of *Labor History* appeared under the editorship of Norman Jacobs, whom we had enlisted part-time from his editorial services on *The New Leader,* with John Hall as associate editor. The first issue departed from traditional parameters, for it presented the problems of labor from the point of view of big business. I am referring to the article by John A. Garraty, "The United States Steel Corporation Versus Labor: The Early Years." Other articles dealt with the origins in World War I of early New Deal labor policy and the radical labor movement (Philip Taft's "The I.W.W. in the Grain Belt" and Archie Green's "The Death of Mother Jones").

Labor History made a bold bid for articles, though initially Jacobs found that there was little available in the field. Indeed, the initial importance of *Labor History* is that it stimulated research on the part of college professors and their graduate students. Within a relatively few years *Labor History* had acquired an impressive backlog of often first-rate pieces and was undoubtedly the major single factor in the enormous generation of interest in the field, interest continually demonstrated at meetings of national and regional historical sessions.

After Jacobs retired from the editorship, a task — really full-time, in fact — that he had assumed at considerable sacrifice and acquitted with distinction, we were successful in persuading Milton Cantor of the University of Massachusetts, a historian who was both a generalist and a distinguished labor buff, to undertake the assignment for some dozen fruitful years. An indefatigable searcher after talent among the younger generation of labor historians, the Cantor years added considerable scope in topics and contributors to the journal. In turn, the present editor, Daniel J. Leab, as readers of issues of recent years can attest, has maintained the quality and variety of contributions and helped *Labor History* attain worldwide recognition as the standard reference journal in the field of American labor relations.

As the journal has now passed the quarter century, two points should be made. *Labor History*'s continuity, unparalleled in the history of American journals in the field, owes much to the continued financial support of the officers of the Tamiment Institute, principally of the late Ben Josephson, and its loyal and growing list of subscribers, a list impressive for a journal of its specialized nature.

Second, *Labor History* has continued to stimulate research in history and economics. Sixteen pages of *Labor History* were required to list all of the articles published in the field in the single year 1981. The journal continues to represent in its pages the more recent trends in its field — emphasis on the lives of workers apart from the trade union movement and examples of the new radical school of labor historians. It is preparing the groundwork for a rich corpus of labor history rivaling the achievements of the brilliant constellation of contemporary English scholars and the Annales school.

Today the subject of labor history is alive and prospering, and in no small part due to the fact that this journal has provided an available publication medium for scholars, often unknown and unrecognized, who have fresh research to contribute and something new to say.

Richard B. Morris

Introduction

This collection celebrates the first twenty-five years of *Labor History.* During those years, the journal published some 400 articles. This surely constitutes the richest concentration anywhere of contemporary scholarship in American labor history. A serious student could get an unrivaled education in the subject by devoting several months to reading all those articles. Now that would be a true celebration of the journal's achievement! Life being what it is, this volume offers the next best thing — a representative sampling of the most prolific and inventive quarter century of scholarship in American labor history.

The collection can be read in two ways. One is to follow the chronological order in which the essays are presented in this book. Read in this sequence, the essays constitute a kind of history of American labor, not a comprehensive or continuous history, but rather a series of deep probes — case histories, explorations of major lines of development, discussions of important problems of interpretation and methodology. Most readers, certainly those who come upon this book in a college course, doubtless will read it profitably in this way. It will, for the most part, have a long and useful life as an important supplement to lectures and survey texts in American labor history.

There is, however, a second kind of chronology contained in this book. If one thinks about the order in which these essays were written (rather than about the chronology of the events they describe), much can be learned about the recent historiography of American labor. The opening essay surveys that subject as it seemed in 1978. In the intervening years the vitality of labor history has risen still higher: at present it stands as one of the most innovative and active fields of research in American history. That historiographical essay provoked a sharp response from Professor James O. Morris (see pp. 17-26). He felt, not without some cause, that the emphasis on "new" tendencies had cast in too unfavorable a light the more traditional work in labor history. As one considers this collection, a somewhat different perspective on the relationship between "old" and "new" begins to emerge. In these essays the tendencies merge and fertilize each other, rather than breaking into open conflict.

By the criterion of subject matter, this collection falls substantially in the traditional vein; the essays deal with strikes, unions, labor relations, labor radicalism, politics, and law. The explanation for this is quite mundane and practical. *Labor History* is the mainstream journal in the field: it naturally attracts work that can be clearly labeled as "labor history." The "newer" topics tend to cut across fields, and hence to find their way into a variety of other journals (see, e.g., the citations to chapter 1). Yet, if the subject matter seems traditional, the *treatment* ever more sharply breaks with what had been the norm for the institutional economists who had largely monopolized the earlier writing of labor history. At the very least, there is a sharp upgrading in the craftsmanlike qualities of research and writing. This is entirely evident, for example, in Sidney Fine's essay on "Frank Murphy, the Thornhill Decision, and Picketing as Free Speech." But, beyond that, many of even the earliest essays adopt a quite different orientation from that associated with institutional labor history.

The oldest essay, dating back to 1961, deals with a wave of strikes on the railroads. If the topic seems traditional, the way it is perceived is quite new. "The strikes revealed certain explosive elements in the social structure of post-bellum America." And the strikers were able to draw on broad support from within their communities. These perceptions foreshadow central concerns of the new labor history: what were the sources of working-class self-activity? What were the values of local community before the triumph of industrial capitalism? Next, by order of publication, comes Alfred Young's 1964 essay on the rivalry between Federalists and Jeffersonians for the allegiance of New York mechanics in the 1790s. Young explains the Jeffersonian success by probing the mind of the mechanics and, in so doing, observes in popular republican ideology a theme that would become central to the new labor history. Melvyn Dubofsky's 1966 essay traces western labor radicalism to the embittering experiences of the hardrock miners of the Western Federation of Miners. Paul B. Worthman's 1969 essay explores the interracial basis of early trade unionism in Birmingham, Alabama. In these essays (and others in the group as well), a palpable shift in orientation has occurred: not the events and institutions themselves, but what they reveal about their rank-and-file participants has become of central concern.

Nearly half of these essays appeared between 1961 and 1972. Then there is a four-year gap, no doubt inadvertent on the part of the selecting editor, but revealing nonetheless of a notable historiographical leap. The second group is no longer exploratory; it moves with a sure hand to apply new approaches to labor-history subject matter. First in this group is David Montgomery's landmark "Workers' Control of Machine Production in the Nineteenth Century" (Fall 1976). By looking at shop-floor relationships as they were experienced by skilled workers, Montgomery opened a rich new vein of investigation — the ongoing struggle of workers, rooted in specific shop-floor cultures, to maintain control over their working lives. The other essays in this second-generation group, although not as influential, clearly exhibit the marks of the new labor history. Its explanatory force is evident, for example, in James A. Henretta's critique of the assumptions underlying social-mobility studies, and in Gary B. Nash's emphasis on the resistance to industrial discipline in the failed experiment in textile manufacture in colonial Boston. Alice Kessler-Harris's and Nancy Gabin's essays sensitively apply the insights of women's history to the experience of working women. Daniel Nelson and Joshua Freeman, although writing very different kinds of essays, significantly advance the study of rank-and-file militancy of the industrial-union era beyond the celebratory treatment of earlier new-left historians. Finally, two of the essays make notable methodological contributions. By the superb use of a comparative approach, James Holt identifies employer resistance as the probable key to the differing histories of trade unionism in the British and American steel industries. Through intensive oral histories, Dale Newman discovers differing racial patterns of worker resistance in a southern textile town. It would be hard to find another group of essays that so fruitfully incorporates fresh approaches into the study of American labor history.

When scholarship is in ferment — as, thankfully, it is in this field — advances take place on many fronts. In the order of battle, *Labor History* occupies the center. From that position the journal has rendered an indispensable service: it has united the best of the old and the new and thereby raised the scholarly level of the entire field of American labor history. That is what these representative essays of the journal's first twenty-five years tell us. And, if we are not mistaken, that will continue to be the distinctive task of *Labor History* in the years to come.

David Brody
Herbert G. Gutman

The Labor History Reader

1

The Old Labor History and the New: In Search of an American Working Class

DAVID BRODY

In the first pages of his pioneering essay on "Work, Culture and Society in Industrializing America," Herbert Gutman set forth his intention of breaking out of the confining limits of trade-union history.[1] An entire generation of labor historians surely nodded in assent. If there has been any common point of agreement in the twenty years past, it has been that the proper study of labor history ought to be the worker, and not only his institutions. To the extent that we act on that conviction, we are writing what might be called "new" labor history. In large measure, of course, ours is merely a particular manifestation of the recent development of social history both in Europe and America. But the task of American labor historians does seem to pose special problems, partly inherent in the subject, partly of our own making. At long last, however, we are now making real headway toward a history of the American worker. American labor historians are, to start with, the victims of the history of our field. For more than half a century stretching well beyond World War II, the study of labor history was nearly the exclusive province of labor economists. Trained in the Wisconsin school of John R. Commons, they defined their field as the study of trade unionism and collective bargaining, and these boundaries they applied to their historical work no less than to contemporary problems. Compelling reasons kept the institutional economists from straying beyond those limits. For the pioneering Commons generation, there was the prideful sense of mission in what they were doing: by their institutional scholarship—central to which was history—

[1] *American Historical Review*, 78 (1973), 531-87.

Reprinted from *Labor History* 20 (Winter 1979), 111-26. This essay was first presented at the 1978 annual meeting of the Organization of American Historians in New York City.

they were contesting the primacy of classical economics in the academy and, in the outside world, its pernicious message that collective action by workers constituted an inadmissible interference with the free play of the market. The actual practice of labor economics, which involved close contact with trade-union leaders and often service in goverment and labor arbitration, maintained the narrow institutional perspective into succeeding generations. And, as with social scientists generally, there was always the tendency of labor economists to do the work they were trained to do.

The study of trade unionism of course always rested on assumptions as to the nature of the constituency. Only Selig Perlman, who was an exceptional practitioner of the Wisconsin tradition in many ways, tried to make those assumptions explicit. A speculative scholar with a wide-ranging knowledge of European history, Perlman was highly sensitive to the American conditions acting on working people, but his characterization of them was hardly more than a reasoning backward from his conception of job-conscious unionism. Perlman's prize student, Philip Taft, late in life took the master to task for expounding a group psychology of workers that was not grounded on empirical evidence and that "really does not help us to understand the behaviour of workers or employers."[2] But Taft, prolific scholar that he was, also never displayed any inclination to go beyond the study of trade unions. And it is my distinct impression that he considered those who did to be a lot of silly romantics. So the labor economists, for all that they contributed to our knowledge of the labor movement, left us otherwise nearly ignorant of the history of the American worker.

The historical profession itself was hardly blameless for the arrested state of labor history. Only when the profession was democratized after World War II by an influx of people with working-class and immigrant backgrounds did labor begin to become an acceptable subject of study. The sprinkling of graduate students who chose labor topics during the 1950s were intent on raising labor history to the level of excellence being achieved in other fields of American history. This involved, first of all, breaking out of narrow institutional and narrative history and opening

---

[2] Philip Taft, "Reflections on Selig Perlman," *Industrial and Labor Relations Review*, 29 (1976), 250.

the subject to the kind of multi-causal analysis we saw in the work of Handlin, Woodward, Hofstadter and others of that brilliant generation of American historians. It involved, secondly, applying to labor history the skills of the historical craft that were, on the whole, sadly lacking in the historical work of the labor economists. We have certainly succeeded in that enterprise. The scholarly superstructure for labor history is now impressive —major archives in Detroit, in Atlanta, at Penn State and elsewhere, a first-class journal, and active regional associations. The volume of scholarship has grown enormously: it took 25 pages of *Labor History* to list all the articles published in the field in 1977 not to speak of the additional space for the more than 50 PhD theses completed that year. And the better books of the last decade or so have certainly attained the standard of craftsmanship to be found in American history generally. The most recent example is Melvyn Dubofsky's and Warren Van Tine's *John L. Lewis,* which is in the best tradition of American biography and far-and-away the finest biography we have of an American labor leader. I suppose the appearance this year of Harold Livesay's short biography of Samuel Gompers in the Library of American Biography can be taken as the ultimate sign of the respectability labor has attained in American history.

But labor historians of my generation had not intended to settle for this conventional achievement. We wanted not only to write better history, but to change the focus of study so that labor history would become a history of workers. This was surely in David Montgomery's mind when he wrote about the labor movement of the 1860s, in Gutman's when he wrote his detailed studies of labor struggle in the 1870s, in Dubofsky's when he wrote on New York workers, and Irving Bernstein when he published *The Lean Years.* I would not want to underestimate what they did in the way of advancing ideas that have borne continuing fruit. But they faced enormous problems, both of evidence and of conceptualization. The first generation, in my view, was more successful at the practice of conventional skills than at breaking new ground. Perhaps that is just as well, since a standard of craft excellence has been established for future work in the field. The last decade, in any case, has seen an explosion of activity that is toppling the long-standing barriers to writing the history of the American worker.

One positive force is ideological in nature. Anyone who has had any dealings with English labor historians, for example, quickly becomes aware of a prevailing left-wing perspective among them. Labor history, Eric Hobsbawm has remarked, "is by tradition a highly political subject."[3] It had never been so in the United States, at least not in Hobsbawm's sense. From Commons onward, labor historians of the Wisconsin school identified themselves with "the pure-and-simple philosophy" of the labor movement. It was in fact, the special skill of a practitioner such as Philip Taft to be able to see the trade-union world from the inside. And the first generation of trained historians to enter the field on the whole fell within the liberal-pluralist spectrum that prevailed during the 1950s. The radicalizing events of the 1960s have changed all that. A radical perspective does not, of course, necessarily mean or require special attentiveness to the rank-and-file—witness the prolific work of Philip Foner or, of more recent origin, that of the corporate-liberal school. But a major thrust of the New Left clearly was in the direction of "history from-the-bottom up" and "history of the inarticulate."[4] The significance of this impulse, even if its original sources are spent, is in the determination it has given a younger generation of labor historians not to be distracted from the task of writing the history of workers. This commitment is probably of particular importance for the 20th century field, which is less well endowed with the kinds of influence encouraging 19th century working-class history. Given the conventional materials that grow richer every year and the fascinating problems still to be unravelled, anyone working on the 1930s or 1940s—as I can personally testify—is sorely tempted to deal with the events acting on workers rather than with the experience of the workers themselves. The fact that a hardy band of labor historians is working steadily at that lower level stems at least partly from the afterglow of the events of the 1960s.

The other primary stimulus of the new labor history, rich in the powers of insight as well as in the capacity to motivate, de-

---

[3] Eric J. Hobsbawm, "Labor History and Ideology," *Journal of Social History,* 7 (1974), 371.

[4] For a fuller statement of the impact of the New Left on labor history, see my review essay on Alice and Staughton Lynd's *Rank and File* in *Labor History,* 16 (1975), 117-26.

rives from England. No one needs to be told of the impact of E.P. Thompson's *The Making of the English Working Class* (1963), and, along with Thompson, of a brilliant constellation of historians—Hobsbawm, George Rudé, Brian Harrison and others— who spread before us dimensions of working-class experience scarcely dreamt of in American labor historiography. With the exception of Frederick Jackson Turner's frontier thesis, I cannot think of another historical statement such as Thompson's that has been so eagerly embraced or that has set off such a surge of scholarly activity. Among the Thompsonian insights transmitted to the American scene, the most fruitful seem to me to be threefold: first, the idea of an industrial morality rooted in evangelical religion, which is handled with great sensitivity in Paul Faler's dissertation on the Lynn shoemakers; [5] second, the meaning of 19th century labor politics and reformism, one of the richest themes, for example, in Alan Dawley's *Class and Community* (1976); and finally and perhaps most frequently observed, the habits and customs of pre-industrial work. Thompson has done more than map out a new terrain of working-class life for us to explore. By his own loving attention to the concrete and specific, he has helped legitimate the close, local study of workers that characterizes so much of the current research in American labor history. And by the example of his historical imagination—by his fertile effort to recreate an earlier world of working people— he has spurred an entire generation of American scholars to do likewise. Unfortunately, concreteness and imagination are the properties of Thompson's particular genius, and, while we may follow his example, we cannot expect to have his talent; we just have to do the best we can.

From the initial explorations following our English guides, we have now begun to strike out more independently along lines distinctive to the American experience. There is, for one thing, renewed interest in ethnic history. In the work of Virginia Yans-McLaughlin on the Italians of Buffalo,[6] for example, or John

---

[5] "Workingmen, Mechanics and Social Change: Lynn, Massachusetts, 1800-60" (unpublished PhD diss. Univ. of Wisconsin, 1971), chapts. 6, 7.

[6] "Patterns of Work and Family Organization: Buffalo's Italians," *Journal of Interdisciplinary History*, 2 (1971), 299-314. Also her essay, "A Flexible Tradition: South Italian Immigrants Confront a New Work Experience," in Richard L. Ehrlich, ed., *Immigrants in Industrial America* (Charlottesville, VA: Univ. of Virginia Press, 1977), 67-84.

Bodnar's research on the Slavs of Steelton, Pennsylvania,[7] we are
getting a fuller understanding of the ways ethnic characteristics
shaped the entry of immigrant workers into the American industrial world. And the studies of Bruce Laurie and Michael Feld-
berg on Philadelphia workers and the Kensington riots of 1844
reveal the depth of ethnocultural tensions that went counter to
class development.[8] Community study is offering a second fruitful
strategy for the new labor history. Gutman, of course, pioneered
this approach in some of his earlier work.[9] We have now begun
to explore more fully how workers fitted into their communities
because, on the one hand, the current research is so heavily involved in local history, and, on the other, because the cultural
aspects of working-class life we are seeking tend to be rooted in
the local community. The logic that leads to community study—
as well as the resulting benefits—can be seen, for example, in
Daniel Walkowitz' work on the iron molders of Troy, New York,
which starts out treating them as workers, then considers their
ethnic and associational activity, and finally reveals the web of
relationships with the police and government that made the
molders a powerful presence in Troy in the years after the Civil
War.[10]

A final strategy, also largely reflective of American industrial
experience, focuses on the shop floor. This approach divides into
two parts, one starting with the worker, the other with management. A provocative example of the first is David Montgomery's
recent article, "Workers' Control of Machine Production in the
19th Century," whose theme is the functional autonomy of skilled
machinists that was rooted in a workers' ethic of manliness.[11] If
this perspective was opened up for us by Thompson and Hobs-

---

[7] "Immigration and Modernization: The Case of Slavic Peasants in Industrial Amer-
    ica," *Journal of Social History*, 10 (1976), 44-71.
[8] Bruce Laurie, "The Working People of Philadelphia, 1827-1853" (unpublished
    PhD diss., Univ. of Pittsburgh, 1971); Michael Feldberg, "The Philadelphia Riots
    of 1844: A Social History" (unpublished PhD diss., Univ. of Rochester, 1970).
    Also, David Montgomery, "The Shuttle and the Cross: Weavers and Artisans
    in the Kensington Riots of 1844," *Journal of Social History*, 5 (1972), 411-46.
[9] "The Workers Search for Power: Labor in the Gilded Age," in H. Wayne Mor-
    gan, ed., *The Gilded Age: A Reappraisal* (Syracuse: Syracuse Univ. Press, 1963),
    47-101; "Class Status, and Community Power: Paterson, New Jersey," in Fred-
    eric Jaher, ed. *The Age of Industrialism* (New York: Free Press, 1968) 263-87.
[10] "Statistics and the Writing of Working Class Culture ... Iron Workers in Troy,"
    Labor History, 15 (1974), 416-60.
[11] *Labor History*, 17 (1976), 485-509. See also, e.g., Katherine Stone, "The Origin
    of Job Structures in the Steel Industry," *Radical America*, 7 (1973), 19-64.

bawm, Montgomery and some of his students are carrying it forward in time and making labor's struggle to protect its prerogatives and values a central issue in the age of the modern factory. The other side of the subject—the role of management—is very much in our own ball park. The key formulation here is Harry Braverman's. His *Labor and Monopoly Capital* (1974), which takes as its text Frederick W. Taylor's *Principles of Scientific Management,* is important above all because it reminds us that management, by its unceasing compulsion to rationalize the productive process, has played a potently aggressive part in determining the fate of the American worker. In his *Workers and Managers* (1976), Daniel Nelson has made a good start toward establishing the factory context in which the practice of modern management developed, although his analysis is not informed by Braverman's insight into Taylor's logic for controlling the worker on the job.

Shop-floor history opens up to us a vast field for research, not only because so much remains to be learned in the formative years, but also because, of all the aspects of working-class history, this is the one least confined by time. The struggle of workers to retain a degree of job satisfaction, of managers to subordinate them to a rationalized system of production, is a continuing story, and not one ending at any given stage of industrialism. Current research on electrical workers, auto workers, telephone operators, department store employees, and doubtless others unknown to me, suggest the richness of shop-floor research for 20th century labor history.

So far I have been considering the range of planned forays into new terrain. A great deal of additional information is now accumulating through the efforts of scholars who do not think of themselves as labor historians, that is to say, people whose starting point is not the worker, but political behavior, urban history, social mobility, demography, the family, women, and minorities. As the focus widens from elites to the "plain people"—to use Peter Knight's phrase—this research inevitably generates a vast body of data on workers. The new social history is providing us with a veritable cornucopia of information, although much of it is still of rather uncertain useability. I am hopeful that labor history will continue to profit more and more from the contributions of social historians.

For one thing, some of them are discernably being drawn into the study of work and workers. In fact, Elizabeth Pleck has recently made an explicit plea for an end to the unnatural separation of family and labor history, "as if families existed without workers and workers were devoid of families".[12] Two examples will have to serve to show the uses of this merger: Tamara Hareven's shrewd analysis of the influence of the family system of French Canadian cotton workers on recruitment and working patterns at the Amoskeag mill in Manchester, New Hampshire;[13] and, moving in the opposite direction, Susan Kleinberg's work on the impact of a basic-industry economy on the households of Pittsburgh.[14]

The benefits to labor history are also bound to accrue, in my opinion, simply as a function of the increasing sophistication of social history. Take, for example, the study of social mobility, which in its initial formulation has come under rather hot attack of late. Is occupation, without data on income and wealth, an adequate index of socio-economic standing? Does an occupational scale that is static and limited to a few gross categories measure anything worth measuring? And what is the point of tracing the social mobility of people who may not live by the ideology of opportunity in the first place? These problems, if they are taken as insuperable, lead to bleak conclusions as to the future of social-mobility research.[15] But they are not insuperable, or at the very least will lead to fresh discoveries that are bound to be of interest to labor historians.

The need for a more exact map of job structures has, for example, drawn attention to the economic setting and specific characteristics of particular occupations. A case in point is a recent article growing out of the Philadelphia Social History Project that explores the Philadelphia occupational structure over time and with attention to such factors as wage levels, working

---

[12] "Two Worlds in One: Work and Family," *Journal of Social History,* 10 (1976), 178-95.

[13] "Family Time and Industrial Time," *Journal of Urban History,* 1 (1975), 365-89.

[14] "Technology and Women's Work," *Labor History,* 17 (1976), 58-72.

[15] See, for example, James A. Henretta, "The Study of Social Mobility: Ideological Assumptions and Conceptual Bias," *Labor History* 18 (Spring, 1977), 165-78; Richard W. Fox, review of Thomas Kessner's *The Golden Door* in *The Chronicle of Higher Education* (May 23, 1977).

conditions, and relative opportunities for advancement. The by-product of this investigation—as a demonstration of the uses of the manuscript schedules of the Census of Manufactures for the detailed analysis of industrial change—would be highly important even if nothing of value emerged for social-mobility studies. But, on the contrary, the tentative conclusions are bound to stimulate further work, for they indicate the importance of relative job opportunity—i.e., whether a particular industry or region was expanding or not—in the determination of mobility rates.[16] And this, in turn, may provide a key to the much discussed matter of geographic mobility, i.e., that the high degree of movement was a direct, rational response to relative economic opportunity. The point is, in any case, that we are going to learn more about the jobs workers held and why they moved about. We can reasonably expect comparable advances on questions of popular ideology, ethnic and religious factors, income and wealth, all responsive to the problems raised by the study of social mobility, and all grist for the mills of the labor historians. It goes without saying, of course, that one of our major tasks will be to digest all this new information coming at us from many quarters and put it to our own uses.

In one respect, the new social history has already made its mark on our field. Only numbers can tell us much that we need to know about the history of workers. The point may be obvious, but we have been agile in avoiding it for many years. One of the persistent attractions of institutional history, I would suspect, has been that it offered an efficient way of dealing with aggregates of workers. As our attention has shifted to the workers directly, we are inevitably drawn into quantification, and our guides have been the social historians. In a study such as Dawley's which exploits the census manuscripts and city directories, the computer printouts provide us with a rich fund of information—the composition of the labor force, career lines, property ownership, family patterns—not accessible to us in the past. It can be instructive to compare two books covering similar ground—for instance, two excellent books on Milwaukee, Gerd Korman's *In-*

---

[16] Bruce Laurie, et al., "Immigrants and Industry: The Philadelphia Experience, 1850-1880," *Journal of Social History,* 9 (1975), 219-48; also, e.g., Anthony E. Broadman and Michael P. Weber, "Economic Growth and Occupational Mobility in 19th Century America," *Journal of Social History,* 11 (1977), 52-73.

dustrialization, Immigrants and Americanizers (1967) and
Kathleen Conzen's new *Immigrant Milwaukee* (1976)—to get a
sense of what statistics can bring to our grasp of labor history.
And this applies to quite traditional questions as well. The single
most striking finding in Dawley's book, for example, refers to
the identity of the Knights of St. Crispin. By the simple expedient
of comparing union membership lists with the names on the local
census tracts, Dawley discovered that the Crispins represented a
cross-section of Lynn factory workers and thereby knocked into
a cocked hat the long-standing characterization of the Knights of
St. Crispin as a movement of artisans resisting the factory system
and the incursion of green hands.

It seems likely, in fact, that the quantitative approach will
score its easiest successes in settling some of the traditional issues
of American labor history. Thanks to Jonathan Garlock, we have
now a data bank on the Knights of Labor that will enable us to
unravel some of the mystery that has so long surrounded the history of the Knights. Garlock's dissertation has made a good start
by dealing with such basic matters as the size and duration, occupational coverage (the importance of the miners is an especially notable discovery), and the geographic representation of the
Knights of Labor.[17] Warren Van Tine similarly has used quantitative data to give us a fuller understanding of the social origins
and careers of trade-union leaders in his *The Making of the
Labor Bureaucrat, 1870-1920* (1973). We very much need a
good quantitative study of strike activity in the 19th and early
20th centuries, such as has recently been done for European
workers. Most of the current statistical work, of course, is not
devoted to traditional problems, but to measuring the complex
dimensions of working-class life. Quantitative analysis has its
pitfalls, of course, hazardous if not competently done,[18] wasteful
if not vigorously exploited. But we should not complain. The
accumulation of the data, even if it is ill-used initially, is bound
ultimately to provide us with the means for attacking that range
of questions in labor history that can only be answered by
counting.

[17] "A Structural Analysis of the Knights of Labor" (unpublished PhD diss., Univ. of
Rochester, 1974).
[18] See, e.g., the critical review by Michael Katz of Dawley's *Class and Community*
in *Reviews in American History*, 5 (1977), 223-29.

Any discussion of quantification is likely to induce grumbling among labor historians working in the 20th century, for it reminds them that the stimuli to innovative work have been very unevenly distributed. The central statistical resource for 19th century research—the census schedules—are not available for the 20th century; ethnicity, community; working-class culture become increasingly submerged or dispersed in the modern urban world; and the guiding influence of the English historians and the new social history grows tenuous in the 20th century context.

So the modern labor historian is thrown more completely on his own resources. If community study grows unmanageable, he must perhaps turn to the individual plant or local union as the unit of intensive study. If conventional statistical sources cannot be used, he must explore what can be done with the vast bureaucratic record accumulated by employers, unions and the state from the 1930s onward. If the rich local and labor press of the 19th century peters out in the 20th, the labor historian may find equally specific evidence of what workers thought and experienced in public records, such as in the hearings of NRA boards and the NLRB, in certain kinds of union records—Robert Zieger, for example, has found the correspondence files of the AFL federal labor unions to be very rich—and, above all, in the oral testimony of surviving participants.[19] And if the well-established topics of 19th-century research become ever harder to identify and handle after 1900, there are other ways of defining the experience of workers in the 20th century—by the advent of consumerism in the 1920s, by unemployment in the 1930s, by rank-and-file militancy within the CIO, by the impact of World War II, by the massive entry of women into the labor force, and so on into contemporary times.

We have in Peter Friedlander's recent *The Emergence of a UAW Local* (1975) an example of the fruitful merging of a 19th century historiographical perspective—the specific influence Friedlander credits is Paul Kleppner's—with a modern research strategy that focuses on the industrial plant as the unit of intensive study and makes remarkable use of oral testimony. Friedlander's analysis turns on the ethno-cultural identity of the work-

---

[19] *Madison's Battery Workers, 1934-1952: A History of Federal Labor Union 1957* (Ithaca: NY State School of Industrial and Labor Relations, Cornell Univ., 1977), 8-13.

ers in his auto-parts plant, with the young Polish-American workers taking the role of union militants.

It remains to be seen how fruitful the cultural approach will be for a history of modern workers. From a number of different angles, in any event, a good deal of promising work is currently going on, especially among dissertation writers, that will surely lead to a fuller history of the American worker in the 20th century than seemed possible a decade or so ago. And it may well turn out that, precisely because these students have been left on their own, they will ultimately produce more interesting and imaginative work than will many of the students writing on the increasingly well-worn topics of 19th century labor history.

As all this research accumulates, we are going to have to start asking ourselves: what does it add up to? This was a question about which the labor historians of the Wisconsin School never had to bother their heads very much. They knew perfectly well where the bits and pieces of their research fitted. It was, of course, in the nature of institutional history to provide for its adherents a clear framework—and none was clearer than a trade union, with its well-defined structure and rules. And, on a larger scale, Perlman's *A Theory of the Labor Movement* performed the same function. Even when the specific analysis of the *Theory of the Labor Movement* fell into disrepute among labor scholars after World War II, they mostly did not doubt that Perlman had successfully captured the job-conscious character of the American labor movement. As we have pushed out beyond trade-union history, we have necessarily left the safe haven of Perlman's explicit framework.

Two features in our current work act powerfully against the construction of a new one. First is the narrow focus of our research, our devotion to intensive, local study of workers. The other is our acute sense of the complexity and variety of working-class experience, in which all lines of inquiry—family, ethnicity, mobility, technology and so on—converge into an intricate web of connections. All this is healthy, even essential to the purposes of the new labor history, but it does militate against any easy or obvious synthesis. To make clear our present situation, let me offer a simple proposition. We have several estimable surveys of American labor history that are based on the state of our knowledge as it was roughly a decade ago. Is anyone prepared to write a new survey based on what we presently know (or are likely to know in a few years) that will provide a comparably coherent and logical account of the history of American workers?

The Making of the English Working Class was going to be our future guide. The enormous enthusiasm that greeted Thompson's great book derived not only from our discovery of rich new dimensions to labor history, but equally from the expectation that, once we had accumulated a comparable body of information, we would then go on to write our own history of "The Making of the American Working Class."

Class, says Thompson, "is a cultural as much as an economic formation. . . ." He defines "the class experience" as "largely determined by the productive relations into which men are born— or enter involuntarily." And then: "Class-consciousness is the way in which these experiences are handled in cultural terms: embodied in traditions, value-systems, ideas, and institutional forms." The central event occurs "when some men, as a result of common experiences (inherited or shared), feel and articulate the identity of their interests as between themselves, and as against other men whose interests are different from (and usually opposed to) theirs." But Thompson is much less concerned with the productive relations leading to class identity than with its expression in the form of a working-class culture. Thompson's orientation may serve admirably in the English setting; certainly his followers think so. Thus Gareth Stedman Jones, who is seeking to push Thompson's analysis into the late 19th century, writes confidently of "the basic consistency of outlook reflected in the new working-class culture which spread over England after 1870." And further:

> The distinctiveness of a working-class way of life was enormously accentuated. Its separateness and impermeability were now reflected in a dense and inward-looking culture. . . .

Like Gareth Stedman Jones, we are busily gathering the evidences of American working-class culture. But can we share Jones' confidence of discovering for American workers a "basic consistency of outlook" and a "distinctive . . . way of life"?[20]

---

[20] "Working-Class Culture and Working-Class Politics in London, 1870-1900," *Journal of Social History,* 7 (1974), 498.

Consider, for example, Herbert Gutman's deservedly famous article, "Work, Culture and Society in Industrializing America," which is the most ambitious attempt we have yet got to generalize from a Thompsonian perspective. As with all Gutman's work, the essay is richly detailed and documented, and offers a superb survey of what was known roughly ten years ago about the work habits and values of the recruits to American industrialism—rural Americans in the earlier 19th century, artisans in the middle period, peasant immigrants at the end of the industrializing era—and about "pre-industrial" forms of collective behavior throughout the industrializing century. (If Gutman rewrote his essay today, of course, he would have a great deal more information to choose from.) What is most interesting (at least for purposes of this discussion) is the extent to which, despite its attentiveness to the cultural dimensions of American labor history, the essay actually represents a strategic retreat from Thompson's basic formulation. Class is, in fact, wholly jettisoned from Gutman's analysis. Instead, he relies on a distinction between culture and society drawn from social anthropology that has the effect of focusing his discussion down to a narrow band of working-class experience—the moment of contact between the industrial society and the newcomers bearing with them a pre-industrial culture.

By pointing to the repetition of an essentially identical experience by generation after generation of recruits to American industrialism, Gutman has certainly given us a fruitful observation into the specific history of American workers, but not one that can lead on to a working-class history in Thompson's meaning. Even within the narrow terms of which Gutman pitches his argument, in point of fact, the reliance on the idea of pre-industrial cultures raises problems not present in Thompson's study, which dealt with a settled population of working people—above all, the weavers—whose work habits and values were demonstrably antagonistic to the new industrial order into which they were inexorably drawn. For my purposes, in any case, the pertinence of Gutman's essay is to the larger point: that, for all we have learned from Thompson and his English colleagues, we cannot expect to develop a new synthesis of American labor history on the lines of *The Making of the English Working Class.*

It is possible, of course, to imagine a synthesis that does not rely on the notion of a unified working-class culture. One might, for example, employ a typological approach, classifying workers into subcultures by a variety of possible criteria.[21] An alternative approach, giving more scope to the imagination, might emphasize the divisive forces in American labor history. Undoubtedly there is a fertile mind at work somewhere playing with ideas of bipolarity, solidarity versus conflict, or some such. Or one might try to hang a comprehensive analysis on such a specific theme as ethnicity or community. My own feeling is that none of these approaches would wholly satisfy the requirements for a successful new synthesis of American labor history: first, defining the common ground applying to all American workers; second providing an element of continuity running from the opening chapter to the present; and third, encompassing the dynamic forces shaping the experience of American workers. For our particular history, it seems to me that those requirements can best be met by an economic approach, one that takes as its starting point, not culture, but work and the job, and broadens out from there.

I am struck by the many evidences of a perspective of this kind in the new labor history. This is, of course, pre-eminently the case in the shop-floor studies. But it holds also to some degree for the larger body of scholarship that focuses on working-class culture. The unifying element in Gutman's essay, after all, is work. Greater attention to the economic side of his subject might have strengthened Gutman's analysis in certain ways: by a less static depiction of the industrial system; by more specificity on the central point of the essay—what actually happened when pre-industrial people entered the factory world; and by a greater degree of discrimination between pre-industrial artisans and craft workers whose skills and experience sprang from the industrial revolution.

Scholars following in Gutman's footsteps have actually had a great deal to say about industrial development and job issues, and also about strike activity and labor organization. This is true, for example, of Alan Dawley, Daniel Walkowitz, and Thomas Dublin (in his study of Lowell cotton workers).[22] David Montgomery's

---

[21] E.g., Raymond Miller, "The Dockworker Subculture . . ." *Comparative Studies in Society and History,* 11 (1969), 302-14.

[22] "Women, Work and Protest in the Early Lowell Mills," *Labor History,* 16 (1975), 99-116.

analysis of workers' control of machine production also involves a large dosage of the subject matter of the old labor history: informal work rules turn into the shop agreements of trade unions and, as the struggle with management intensifies, what Montgomery calls "workers' consciousness" manifests itself in sympathy strikes and an impulse toward industrial unionism. The distinction drawn in this paper between trade-union history and the history of workers is of course an entirely arbitrary one, useful for analytical purposes, perhaps necessary to break the institutional shackles on labor history, but not a reflection of historical realities. In both the 19th and 20th centuries, the job concerns of American workers were largely bound up with, and sometimes observable to us only through collective activity and labor organization. The persistent intrusion of these subjects into the new labor history, the repeated discovery by individual scholars that they must see the workers they are studying in the context of job and industry, I take as evidence of the powerful logic behind an economic approach to the history of American workers.

If this sounds as if we are circling back to old Selig Perlman, I think in a sense we are. It was the special insight of pure-and-simple unionism (as Perlman saw it) to aim at securing the common economic ground on which workers of the most diverse loyalties and persuasions might unite. We can capitalize on that insight, not so as to write more institutional history, but for purposes of constructing a useable framework for our particular labor history. With a steady focus on men and women *at work,* we ought to be able to delineate the continuities and dynamic elements in that history. To refer back to the question of writing a new labor history survey that would incorporate all we presently know: if such a book is to be written, I think we will have to resort to an intellectual strategy very like what Samuel Gompers employed when he defined American pure-and-simple unionism.

What has just been said perhaps sounds more definite than I intend it to be. I mean to open up discussion, not close it off. What I am definite about is the need for discussion. It is high time we began to think actively about the principle reference points—the framework—in which to place our New Labor History.

COMMUNICATIONS

To the Editor:

It is much easier to comment on an article than it is to write one, much easier to criticize than to create. I therefore begin with warm congratulations to Professor Brody for having presented a most thoughtful historiographical article which lays out in broad strokes and with impressive knowledge where we have been and where we may be going with respect to the writing of American labor history. Not only have the boundaries of labor history changed greatly in recent years, but our writing about the change, its nature and meaning, has produced a rather large body of historiographical literature. Professor Brody carries the latter discussion well ahead not only by identifying some of the major sources and subject matter content of new labor history but also in focusing attention upon a possible new underlying synthesis of its results.

My comments will be supplementary in a limited way to Professor Brody's article as well as directly responsive to some of his thoughts and his language. I begin with some supplementary remarks on the origins of the new labor history. I will follow with some thoughts on three questions: (1) Is old labor history dead? (2) Which is better, the old history or the new? and (3) Can there be a new synthesis of the growing research results of our enlarged inquiry?

Professor Brody suggests two developments which account for the recent burst of labor history activity—the advent of the new left in the political conflict and confusion of the 1960s and the impact of a new scholarship in England pioneered by E. P. Thompson and others. E. J. Hobsbawm, perhaps most notable among the "others," has asserted that the resurgence of radical politics has been the greatest force producing new labor history, although he makes no effort in the piece I have examined to name any lesser forces. He believes this to be true of the United States as well as of Britain, West Germany, and Italy.[1] I have not done, and do not expect to do, the kind of careful research which would be a necessary preliminary to my making any priority analysis of causes in this matter, but I do not hesitate in making a more modest effort to identify other possible stimuli of new labor history than the two named above. It is important that this be done, for reasons which will become apparent. One of these additional stimuli derives from the generalization that many, though not all, intellectuals are, in free societies, *avante garde*. It is the new, the novel, the most unknown that offers them the greatest challenge and the prospect of the greatest self-fulfillment. Professional recognition, status, and salary and job improvement may also figure among the prospective rewards. As Hobsbawm has put it, although in another context entirely, "the nature of the academic profession is such as to put a premium on originality and fashionableness."[2]

Long before the 1960s the labor movement had become a well-entrenched, permanent, and successful part of the so-called "establishment." Some of the intellectuals who were serving the unions began to leave them in the 1940s and 1950s to escape what they considered a stifling bureaucracy enmeshed in a largely routine and uninspiring day-to-day existence. Little wonder that some of their academic counterparts, members of a new generation, should also have become disenchanted. Those who seek intellectual excitement are not always content, by their nature, to stay long after a major victory has been won.

However, some new labor historians have been diverted from the old not by the successes of a maturing labor movement but by its alleged failures which have, in turn, given them new hope for a new left appealing in part to the rank-and-file worker and also reviving many of the old debates on conservative trade unionism versus radical party politics. As Robert Zieger has commented, some intellectuals have recently looked upon unions as "locked

---

[1] E. J. Hobsbawn, "Labor History and Ideology," *Journal of Social History,* 7 (1974), 375.
[2] *Ibid.,* 379.

in a syndrome of apathy, decline, and accommodation."[3] Professor Brody seems to suggest (although I may misunderstand him) that the new left has so far fallen short of achieving a breakthrough in our understanding of labor history, although its encouragement of a new look continues to enliven the field.[4]

Labor historians, or at least those who write labor history, have also been increasing in numbers in recent years—if the growth of research output and the remarkable appearance of over a score of state and regional labor history societies are any gauge of the matter. In some small measure, perhaps numbers themselves have spurred a search for new areas of thought and work. After all, historians do need jobs, and one way to justify them is to expand the jurisdiction. Of course, to separate cause and effect so neatly is dangerous. Surely the interaction has also worked to some extent, and maybe even more so, in the reverse, namely new historians have been attracted by the new opportunities that new history itself has generated.

I would suggest that striking new veins of raw material in labor history may be traced in some degree to the drop of imperialist blood found in the veins of labor historians themselves. In other words, not only does new history justify one's existence and provide payment therefor, but it also satisfies a natural desire (among social scientists as well as historians) to grow and to become more important. Who, except a dedicated humanist, isn't impressed with "cliometrics" and the application of social scientific methods to the study of worker culture in past time?

In indirect and subtle ways, I think labor history has benefited from the ideas and findings of a generation of developmental economists. The labor literature of development has mushroomed with the increasing attention focused upon the human problems encountered in the widespread efforts to modernize "backward" societies since World War II. Vast problems of labor mobility, labor force recruitment, labor force commitment, and industrial "culture shock" have attracted much attention. An emphasis upon industrializing elites, their differing ideologies and values,

[3] Robert H. Zieger, "Workers and Scholars: Recent Trends in American Labor Historiography," *Labor History*, 13 (1972), 246.
[4] David Brody, "The Old Labor History and the New," *Labor History*, 19 (1979), 5-6, 17-18. See also Brody, "Radical Labor History and Rank-and-File Militancy," *Labor History*, 16 (1975), 117-126.

and upon industrial relations systems rather than upon unions and jobs alone was given a resounding send-off in the pioneering work of the Inter-University Study of Labor in Economic Development spearheaded by Clark Kerr, John Dunlop, Fred Harbison, and Charles Myers.[5] Any debt we owe the economists of development is, however, not nearly so great, relatively speaking, as that we owe the political economists of the Commons school. Let it be said that representatives of other disciplines, including history and social anthropology, have in their practical experiences and studies abroad, also enlarged the labor framework of analysis at home.

Finally, much of recent labor history has surely been the product of both a vast expansion of source materials and the training of many historians in the use of quantitative methods—each of which has operated, often independent of one another, to revitalize interest in and expand the boundaries of the field.[6]

In sum, I see in the resurgence and growth of American labor history the expression of many developments—behavioral, methodological, interdisciplinary, international and comparative, professional, and resource-related, as well as the pair of ideological influences noted by Professor Brody. Not all those whom I might call new historians have looked initially to E. P. Thompson as "our future guide,"[7] some of them were at work before the radicalizing events of the 1960s, and the terms "new" and "old" themselves antedated the 1960s by several years.

Is the old labor history dead? Not in the least, although one might draw such a conclusion from the unguarded, or perhaps deliberate, language used by some of those who have commented in recent years on historiographical trends. Perhaps I exaggerate Professor Brody's position on this point, but I conclude from his

---

[5] Clark Kerr, John T. Dunlop, Frederick H. Harbison, and Charles A. Myers, *Industrialism and Industrial Man* (Cambridge, MA, 1960). See also John T. Dunlop, *Industrial Relations Systems* (NY, 1958). The literature generated by these two ground-breaking studies is vast. What it reveals with respect to the clash between the values of a rural peasant society and those of an industrializing one is especially relevant to the work of some of the recent historians in American labor.

[6] Vaughn Davis Bornet, "The New Labor History: A Challenge for American Historians," *The Historian*, 18 (Autumn 1955), 1-24; Richard B. Morris, "American Labor History prior to the Civil War: Sources and Opportunities for Research," *Labor History*, 1 (1960), 308-318; Herman Kahn, "Some Problems in the Writing of Labor History," *Proceedings of the Industrial Relations Research Association, 1965*, 330-331.

[7] Brody, "The Old Labor History and the New," 16.

paper that he believes the "shift" he sees to the new history has virtually decimated the ranks of the institutional labor historians. Thus, he remarks that one of the attractions of union history *"has been* that it *offered* an efficient way of dealing with aggregates of workers." He continues by saying "our attention has shifted to the workers directly . . ."[8] Surely unions still offer a convenient way to study workers in the aggregate, and present tense, not past, would therefore be in order. To say that "our" attention has shifted allows the implication that everyone's has, and that would not be accurate either. No doubt the attention of many has so shifted.

What about those whose attention hasn't shifted? Are they all to be considered writers of old labor history because their subject is the union? If they apply quantitative methods to the study of labor organizations or if they study the process of unionization, leadership entrenchment, or manipulative practices, does either one of these variations from the traditional make their product new? Is there, in other words, an "old institutional" and a "new institutional" labor history? If there is, of what real significance is the distinction? If there is, what becomes of the other distinction between the old institutional history and the new history of the worker? What *is* old and what *is* new? If new were to be Marxist, then we would have a cut that might make sense, if not bring agreement. But apparently we do not have it. Despite his inclination to sub-title his paper "In Search of an American Working Class," Professor Brody ultimately concludes that "a unified working-class culture" offers no key to the study of American labor history.[9] Then there is the view that a lot of Marxist writing has included and still includes as much emphasis on the old institutional history as found in the Commons school literature.[10] Despite some recent efforts to merge the two strains, there is still an "old left" labor history and a "new left" labor history. Some of the "young Turks," in their devotion to the history of the worker, roundly attack the old left whose sins of neglect and omission they believe to be just as great as those committed by

---

[8] *Ibid.,* 12.
[9] *Ibid.,* 18-19.
[10] For example, see Thomas A. Krueger, "American Labor Historiography, Old and New: A Review Essay," *Journal of Social History,* 4 (1971), 281; Brody, "Radical Labor History and Rank-and-File Militancy," 117, 121-122.

non-Marxists.[11] One wonders, however, whether the stimulus here is to tell the story of the worker qua worker, to become personal and direct in writing labor history or, perhaps, to search for group power generated at the bottom.

In any event, there is still institutional history being written, and to be written. It is an important part of the whole. While some intellectuals have been turned off by union success or impelled for other reasons to blaze new trails, many have become excited by such relatively recent developments as the merger of the AFL and CIO, organized labor's informal alliance with the Democratic party (which J. David Greenstone has characterized as the single most important change in the structure of our political system in the twentieth century[12]), significant changes in the direction of white-collar predominance in the composition of the labor force, the new union militancy of professional and public employees, and the special union problems of blacks, other minorities, and women in a civil rights and equality-conscious society. Still others are digging around in the recently established union and company archives which now make the investigation of institutional subjects more remote in time so rewarding. What a pity it would be if we should neglect such history now.

Hobsbawm describes recent labor history as having expanded in scope and method, concedes that traditional labor history is still alive in societies with developed labor movements and that it has "enormous" tasks to perform elsewhere.[13] I venture to predict that there will be more, and in some ways more important, institutional labor history written in the United States in the future than there has been in the past. Organized labor has become much too big in numbers and much too influential in the political as well as economic life of the nation to be an unattractive subject for scholarly historical study. Labor history has evolved. It is well on the way toward becoming a major province of the historian. It has pushed out its boundaries, but it has not by any means abandoned the subject matter of its starting point.

Another question growing in part out of Professor Brody's

---

[11] Paul Faler, "Working Class Historiography," *Radical America,* 3 (No. 2, 1969), 57; Krueger, 281.
[12] J. David Greenstone, *Labor in American Politics* (NY, 1969), xiii-xiv.
[13] Hobsbawm, 377-378.

paper is related to the one just discussed, namely which is better (that is, more reliable, more insightful, more useful for understanding the past) the old or the new labor history? More inadvertently than by design, I suspect, Professor Brody leaves with me the distinct impression that what is new is "best." The old labor history is "narrow" and also "narrative." American labor historians are "the victims" of the Commons school and the labor economists. New labor historians want to write "better" labor history as well as write the history of workers. We should accept the insights into unionism provided by Perlman and others, "not so much to write more institutional history, but for purposes of constructing a useable framework for our [whose?] particular labor history." The new labor history is geared to the total culture, it is complex in content and method, and it is analytical not just descriptive.[14] Other commentators on the new labor history have also lapsed into invidious comparison of the old and the new or have made assertions, unfortunate I believe, that the new history repudiates, rejects, or replaces the old—all of which clearly conveys a self-judgment of new history superiority.[15] The terms "new" and "old" may, in the language preferred by some people, be nothing more than euphemisms for what they believe is "good" and what they believe is "poor" in the subject matter of labor history or in the ideological approach to its study.

What is narrow and narrative and what is broad, complex, and analytical? Saying something has never yet made it so. How does one demonstrate that a history of the AFL, of labor and politics, of trade union democracy, or of an outstanding labor leader is narrower than a study of workers (or a portion of them) in a local community, or worker ethnicity in a particular city, of labor mobility in a particular plant or local industry? Or is it the sum of the parts in each type of historical research upon which comparative judgment has been based? And is it defensible at all to suggest that the work of institutional historians as a group does not rise above description?—quite apart from the fact that the Commons school (and the Glockers and Barnetts at Johns Hopkins as well) considered themselves social scientists and wrote from a broad framework that still has some explanatory value.

---

[14] Brody, "The Old Labor History and the New," 1-2, 4, 13, 15-16, 19.
[15] See Zieger, 250, 254, 257-258, 260, and Faler, 56-57.

Does the vigor of the new scholarship depend in part upon favorable comparison with the old? Will not the best interests of the profession be served by accepting an essential unity of objective among all of us (to come to know the worker better), however loose the theoretical underpinnings may be? Two heads (or three or four of them) can be better than one without any single one of them being self-evidently better than any other.

Finally, a few words on whether we can expect a new synthesis of the growing research results of our expanded jurisdiction. Economists are prone to develop theories. They seem equally prone to disagree among themselves respecting the validity or universality of them, whether a theory of the labor movement, a theory of worker mobility, or a theory of wages. We usually discover that many such "theories," which certainly imply the finality and universality of scientific principle, turn out to be, at best, pretty good keys to a better understanding of complicated behavior and events discrete in time and place. With respect to the English labor historians, their new synthesis seems to be a product of both their radical political ideology and, fortunately for them, the peculiar nature of English pre-industrial and industrial history which apparently (I emphasize apparently because E. P. Thompson's work has been criticized even in England) did create a working class, a working class culture, and therefore a working class consciousness. Thus the E. P. Thompson synthesis—at least for the early history of the English working class. Unless I misread him, Professor Brody (perhaps others as well) sees little possibility of successful application of such class cultural analysis to the history of the American worker.[16]

Professor Brody concludes his paper with somewhat surprising comments on this subject for which I was not prepared but with which I, for the most part, agree. The distinction between worker history and union history, is he says, "entirely arbitrary" since the two so often go together. (I would add that the distinction between the old and the new is also arbitrary and that we might avoid a lot of unnecessary emotion and confusion by talking about the older and the more recent labor history.) He sees in much of the new history and the old a common concern for work and the job. In a limited but still important sense we are returning

---

[16] Brody, "The Old Labor History and the New," 18-19.

to Perlman, a finding he seems, however, to find a bit uncomfortable. Thus the search for something new which might be spun
around the worker and the job.[17] Little wonder that he should
see this parallel. After all, denominating the new history as the
history of the "worker" is itself an explicit recognition that work
and not religion, ethnicity, ideology, or a separate culture still
lies at the center of explanation.

However, I must confess, in all candor, that I do not see the
outlines of a new synthesis in anything so broad, so diverse, and
so vague as work undefined and unqualified. Moreover, it would
seem that labor historians have in recent times lost much of their
claim to the field of work and thus much of their ability to lead
or discipline thought about it. In addition to social historians,
others have "invaded" the field, some anew—industrial sociologists, social anthropologists, industrial psychologists, political
scientists, political sociologists, and, of course, labor economists.
All of these scholars approach the subject from different disciplinary backgrounds and with different loyalties, guiding principles,
and methodologies. What is wrong in a democratic pluralist society (which posits a larger consensus from which the entire
industrial relations system is derived) with an eclectic approach,
each group seeking its own truth? Any general synthesis of such
a huge inter-disciplinary concern for work and the job would not
appear likely. Nevertheless, the labor historian who would write
with full sophistication must at least become familiar with the
thought of others who now labor in the field with him.[18]

Even with respect to that labor history which is the product of
historians, we need to be quite explicit about how much of it
is the object of synthesis. All of it (older and more recent), only
the more recent, or only a part of the more recent? Put somewhat
differently, is the object to find a common analytical framework
for economic, political, social, and cultural labor history, or just
social and cultural, or just economic and political? There may

---

[17] *Ibid.*, 19-21.
[18] For a much earlier statement of this essential view, see Gerd Korman, "Discussion
[on Labor History]," *Proceedings of the Industrial Relations Research Association, 1965,* 353-354. A most interesting recent development which illustrates the
point being made is the formation, by a number of organizational and industrial
sociologists at Cornell's School of Industrial and Labor Relations, of a program
to study the history of producers' cooperatives in this country. They call themselves "The History Group, New Systems of Work and Participation."

be no greater prospect of a synthesis of the history of labor in our pluralist society than there is, to date at least, of the larger field of industrial relations—though some scholars still are seeking mightily to find the bridges that may connect labor history, labor economics, labor law, organizational behavior, and manpower studies.[19]

New York State School of Industrial   JAMES O. MORRIS
    and Labor Relations
Cornell University

To the Editor:

I find it is somewhat difficult to come to grips with Professor Morris' critique of my paper. This is at least in part because he seems to have misapprehended my purpose, which was, at the invitation of the program committee for the 1978 OAH meeting, to discuss the character and implications of the new American labor history. It was certainly not my intention to suggest the death of institutional labor history. The larger part of the scholarship produced today still falls into that category, as is evident to any reader of this journal, and much of it is interesting and important work. The kinds of questions Professor Morris poses, especially for the more recent period, will continue to attract the attention of students, including myself. I do plead guilty to making qualitative judgments, although not quite in the way that Professor Morris suggests. Contrary to his reading of the paper, it does distinguish along disciplinary lines between "old" and "new" institutional labor history. The crop of trained historians who entered the field after World War II—Professor Morris among them—did write better history than the departing generation of labor economists, and there is a rich and growing literature to prove it. I do not think the new-style labor historians are better in the same sense, i.e., as practitioners of the historical craft. But they have unquestionably added dimensions of complexity and scope hitherto not part of American labor history.

---

[19] For example, see Gerald G. Somers, ed., *Essays in Industrial Relations Theory* (Ames, IA, 1970).

Why should Professor Morris begrudge them credit for enriching the field? Perhaps our differences here are partly of philosophy, reflecting differing notions about the historian's responsibility for assessing contributions as they are made to the field. But I must say I find disturbing Professor Morris' penchant for assigning motives for the popularity of the new work—it is voguish, it is imperialistic and careerist, it is anti-trade union and anti-establishment. True or not (mostly not), who cares? The worthwhile questions are whether the new scholarship represents an honest engagement with serious issues and advances our understanding of American labor history.

Professor Morris has drawn me far from the ground that my paper was intended to cover. Mainly, I wanted to suggest the influences that are inspiring and shaping the new labor history. Professor Morris proposes others, especially developmental economics. If so, they were not evident to me in my reading of the literature. As to the matter of a new synthesis, this is not the place to argue the question of how far such an effort is likely to get; surely the effort ought to be made. Professor Morris should be assured, however, that I am not in the least "uncomfortable" with the idea of Perlman as the starting point of such a synthesis. That he should believe so makes me think that he could profitably turn his plea for intellectual openness upon himself. It had not occurred to me that I was suggesting that the new labor historians were establishing any proprietary claims over the field or held the only keys for unlocking the history of the American worker.

University of California, Davis   DAVID BRODY

2

The Study of Social Mobility: Ideological Assumptions and Conceptual Bias

JAMES A. HENRETTA

One unexamined legacy of "consensus" historiography to the first generation of quantitatively-oriented social historians has been the analysis of "social mobility." For the study of "mobility" reflects—even embodies—certain assumptions about the nature of human motivation and of social reality which achieved intellectual prominence during the 1950s and early 1960s. The ideological passions generated by the Cold War need not be recounted in detail; for present purposes it is sufficient to suggest that American scholars were influenced in their approach to social history by the sharp dichotomy posited in this period between "individualism" and "totalitarianism" and (in a more personal way) by the opportunities for rapid professional advancement in an expanding economy and in a growing system of higher education.

Thus, until the mid-1960s American historians did not, as a rule, examine social *structures* and the persistence of established cultural patterns (as Ferdinand Braudel and members of the *Annales* school were attempting in France). Nor did American historians investigate the process of *class* or *group* struggle and social *transformation* (as Marxist-oriented historians associated with the journal *Past and Present* were undertaking in the United Kingdom). Rather, they chose to utilize the concepts of individual "character structure," of "mobility," and of "modernization" in their study of past societies. Consciously or not, they assumed the primacy of individualist values throughout American history and proposed the universal emergence of these behavioral norms in a process of historical evolution from traditionalism to modernity.[1]

---

[1] Four influential studies which reflected these general assumptions were: David Riesman, *The Lonely Crowd: A Study of the Changing American Character* (New Haven, 1950); Daniel Lerner, *The Passing of Traditional Society: Modernizing the Middle East* (New York, 1958); Merle Curti, *et al., The Making of an American Community: A Case Study of Democracy in a*

Reprinted from *Labor History* 18 (Spring 1977), 165-78.

The utilization of contemporary concepts and methods does not always or inevitably lead to a biased interpretation of the past. Demographic analyses, for example, appear to be ideologically neutral, despite their present origin and current vogue. Historians may differ over the relative significance of population change in the historical process—its status as an "independent" variable—but the methodology itself is not in question.

The same cannot—or should not—be said about the analysis of "social mobility." The first difficulty stems from the inherently comparative nature of the concept itself; it is designed to measure how well an individual, an ethnic group, or a sexual caste performs in relation to another. The study of social mobility (which must not be confused with change during a life-cycle, geographic movement, or a general rise in living standards) thus becomes the investigation of the nature and the extent of equality within a society. Indeed, without inequality the concept of mobility has no meaning. A person or a group rises "above" another; some individuals succeed, others fail. Mobility presupposes the existence of inequality.[2]

More importantly, the existence of mobility may be used as the *justification* of inequality. Is a good society one in which there is equality of "condition," or should a community be judged on the basis of its commitment to the

> equality of opportunity, on the degree to which society permits all men and women to realize their full potential and to compete as equals for education, income, status, and power?[3]

Some analysts explicitly endorse the latter system of values. "The quality of the society as it is seen by the historian," writes Lawrence Stone,

> is determined by two quite different factors. The first is the proportion of the lower and middling classes who are able to filter through into the elite...

Frontier County (Stanford, 1959); Seymour Martin Lipset and Reinhard Bendix, *Social Mobility in Industrial Society* (Berkeley, 1959). A fine critique of the ethnocentric aspect of such analyses is Dean C. Tipps, "Modernization Theory and the Comparative Study of Societies: A Critical Perspective," *Comparative Studies in Society and History*, 15 (1973), 199-226.

[2] For a non-comparative definition of equality—as the moral worth inherent in each individual regardless of condition or achievement—see Dorothy Lee, *Freedom and Culture* (Englewood Cliffs, N.J., 1959), esp. 39-48.

[3] R. Menard, P. Harris, and L. Carr, "Opportunity and Inequality: The Distribution of Wealth on the Lower Western Shore of Maryland, 1638-1705," *Maryland Historical Magazine*, 69 (1974), 169; the authors do not endorse this set of values and their work suggests, in fact, that opportunity—equal or otherwise—stems primarily from the economic structure of the society rather than from an ideological commitment to equal competition.

> [and] the second factor is the method by which this infiltration occurs. Is it "sponsored mobility"...or is it "contest mobility," the chance product of prolonged and open competitive struggle?[4]

The bias in Stone's analysis does not stem from the assumption that all societies are characterized by inequality—a more or less well-grounded empirical statement—but from the normative implications which are conveyed to contemporary readers. The test of the "quality" of a society becomes the ability to "rise" above others in a free open competition, not the extent to which a culture offers all men and women the means to achieve a basic dignity and sense of identity. Historians who would follow Stone's example are not, in fact, "value-neutral" but have espoused a capitalist-individualist rather than (say) a socialist-communitarian set of preferences.

Even those historians who are aware of the ideological assumptions which suffuse the study of social mobility have found themselves trapped by the demands of the methodology. Numerical analysis is based on the fiction that the actions of different individuals or cultural groups are, epistemologically speaking, the same—that they are identical and discrete "entities" which can be compared with one another in a scientific manner. The reductionist tendencies of this approach are compounded by its demands in terms of energy and of time. It takes months—even years—of laborious and painstaking work to assemble and to code even a few pieces of occupational or residential information on a statistically-significant sample of the working population in a given town or county. The hours or days which might have been spent in reading diaries, newspapers, or letters—in discovering and then pondering the felt *meaning* of the lives and cultural values of the historical actors—are consumed instead by a quest for technical exactness and statistical finesse. All of those events which had immense personal significance to the working population (family tragedies and triumphs, recreational outings, collective movements) are routinely ignored in a one-dimensional presentation of occupational change and residential mobility. Consciousness and meaning have been usurped by data and diagrams.[5]

---

[4] Lawrence Stone, "Social Mobility in England, 1500-1700," *Past and Present*, 33 (1966), 21.

[5] "Stephen Toulmin has compared scientific thought to the activity of map making," writes Theodore Roszak (in *Where the Wasteland Ends; Politics and Transcendence in Postindustrial Society* [Garden City, N.Y., 1972], 410), but "to mistake maps for landscapes is to degrade every other way of knowing the world's terrain.... We forget that to map a forest means less than to write poems about it; to map a village means less than to visit among its

And to what end? After hundreds of pages which purport to demonstrate an "historic [upward] American mobility pattern," Stephan Thernstrom notes that it is precisely the "ideology of mobility" which constitutes the "prime justification for the acute economic and social inequalities that have in fact existed in a supposedly egalitarian society." This realization moves Thernstrom to confess that he will welcome the imminent termination of this pattern, for this might

> promote a reexamination of the opportunity ethic itself, a questioning of the fundamental principle that extreme disparities in command over resources are justifiable so long as they result from "fair" and "open" competition. Out of this process of questioning might emerge a richer and more humane conception of the just society.[6]

As this rather uneasy afterthought suggests, the study of social mobility bears directly upon the moral and philosophical foundations of liberal capitalist society. For it raises the inherent contradiction within this system between political and legal equality on the one hand and social and economic inequality on the other. "All men have essentially the same rights," James Fenimore Cooper wrote in 1838 in *The American Democrat*, "an equality which, so far from establishing that 'one man is as good as another,' in a social sense, is the very means of producing the inequality of condition that actually exists."[7] The profound political implications of this paradox had been grasped at the very birth of republican government in America by the Marquis de Chastelleux. "Every citizen," the French officer explained to Samuel Adams in 1780,

> ...every man who pays taxes, has a right to vote in the election of..."the Sovereign." All this is very well for the present moment, because every citizen is about equally well-off, or can become so in a short time; but the success of trade, and even of agriculture, will introduce riches among you, and riches will produce inequality of fortunes and of property.

The economic and social disparities that Cooper would accept as inevitable (indeed, as salutary), Chastelleux insisted on viewing as a central ethical weakness in the new society:

---

people; to map a sacred grove means less than to worship there. Making maps [Roszak concludes] may be absorbing and useful; it may take enormous intellectual talent and great training; but it is the most marginal way of knowing the landscape."
[6] Stephan Thernstrom, *The Other Bostonians: Poverty and Progress in the American Metropolis, 1880-1970* (Cambridge, 1973), 256, 260-61.
[7] James Fenimore Cooper, *The American Democrat* (1838, reprinted New York, 1956), 73.

whereever this inequality exists the real force will invariably be on the side of property; so that if the influence in government be not proportioned to that of property, there will always be a contradiction, a struggle between the form of government and its natural tendency; the right will be on the one side, and the power on the other.[8]

This discrepancy between "right" and "power" has never been successfully resolved by theorists of liberal capitalist democracy. Two centuries of experience have demonstrated that equality of opportunity does not produce equality of condition; that the systematic social inequality fostered by such opportunity perverts the meaning of political democracy; that it is a class-based ideology which works to the long-term advantage of the propertied classes. "The continued existence of liberal democratic states," C. B. McPherson has argued, stems not from their moral integrity but from "the ability of a possessing class to keep the effective political power in its hands in spite of universal suffrage," a process which "savors too much of deception to be an adequate basis for a moral justification of liberal democracy."[9]

When confronted by such value-laden historical questions, an author may—like McPherson—choose to become a "moral critic." If this function is eschewed, for a variety of personal, professional, or political reasons, the historian still has the obligation to clarify the questions at issue. Was there an "American ideal of equal opportunity" by the end of the eighteenth century, as Jackson T. Main argues at one point in *The Social Structure of Revolutionary America?* Or, as he somewhat incongruously suggests some pages earlier, was the ideal "kind of society" which most Americans "wished to create" one in which there was

an economic equality in which distinctions based on wealth should be minimized; and social equality, in which invidious discriminations would be abolished.[10]

There is little indication in Main's analysis that equality of opportunity and equality of condition are antagonistic rather than complementary ideals; that the choice between them is ideological in

---

[8] *Travels in North America....*, Intro. by Howard C. Rice, Jr. (Chapel Hill, 1963), I, 161.

[9] C. B. McPherson, *The Political Theory of Possessive Individualism: Hobbes to Locke* (Oxford, 1962), 274; *idem.*, "Politics: Post-Liberal Democracy?," in Robin Blackburn, ed., *Ideology in Social Science; Readings in Critical Social Theory* (N.Y., 1973), 17-31.

[10] Jackson Turner Main, *The Social Structure of Revolutionary America* (Princeton, 1965), 286, 236.

nature; or that different sections or classes of the American people might have preferred one definition of the "good society" to the other.

Nor is Thernstrom's more precise and more revealing description of historical reality completely satisfactory. Even if we assume that "it is not equality of *condition* but equality of *opportunity* that [all?] Americans have celebrated," it does not follow that the analysis of social mobility will "help us to gauge to what extent the ideal of equal opportunity was in fact realized."[11] For this formulation contains a number of questionable assumptions. Is it true that all cultural or racial or class groups "want" above all else to improve their economic position, to attain a higher standard of living, or to surpass the achievements of their parents or of other groups? If not, if these are *not* their prime aspirations, then to evaluate their lives in such terms is misleading if not completely absurd. Any valid analysis of historical experience must consider the expectations and goals of the actors themselves; to do otherwise is to interpret their lives in terms of an alien conceptual framework.

In fact, there is a significant amount of evidence which suggests that economic or social mobility was not *the* most important value for many Americans. Many eighteenth-century migrants to southeastern Pennsylvania, James T. Lemon has shown, placed communal values above economic ones. They did not move to the most fertile areas but preferred to live near kin or among those who shared their language or religion. Other settlers were content to "get along"; if greater work were required, they would choose *not* to "improve" their material condition. "He would rather live somewhere else," a German traveller reported after conversing with a Pennsylvania hill-farmer,

> ...he heard in Kentucky there was no real winter, and where there was not winter, he argued, people must work year in, year out, and that was not his fancy; winter, with a warm stove and sluggish days being indispensable to his happiness.[12]

Such preferences should not be judged as "laziness," for that is to impose the standards of an alternative system of work-discipline. Rather, this outlook should be seen as the manifestation of a distinct

---

[11] Thernstrom, 256.
[12] Quoted in James T. Lemon, *The Best Poor Man's Country: A Geographical Study of Southeastern Pennsylvania* (Baltimore, 1972), 85, and 43-49.

set of cultural values, one which was quite consistent with the seasonal, family-oriented pattern of work in an agricultural society (and which has retained its vitality, over many generations, in the much less compatible environment of the industrial factory).

Nor were such preferences for a cyclical and non-compulsive work routine necessarily inconsistent with the values contained in the Puritan Ethic. Ministers from Massachusetts to Virginia had urged their congregations to "labor" and to diligence in the business of their "lawful calling," but the prescribed ends of this Christian asceticism were moral and spiritual, not endless economic improvement and the accumulation of individual wealth.[13]

Such materialist and individualist values were accorded legitimacy only in the early decades of the nineteenth century, as part of the deliberate cultivation of the ideology of social mobility by certain groups within the population. In 1835, the Lancaster, Pennsylvania *Examiner and Herald* found a "want of individual enterprise" to be "as strange as it is unnatural."[14] Similar assumptions about the motive springs of human conduct had been articulated a decade earlier by Lewis Cass. "A principle of progressive improvement seems almost inherent in human nature...," the young politician wrote in 1827,

> we are all striving in the career of life to acquire riches, or honor, or power, or some other object, whose possession is to realize the day dreams of our imaginations; and the aggregate of these efforts constitutes the advance of society.[15]

Mrs. Trollope observed in *The Democratic Manners of the Americans* (1832): "The idea that his origin is a disadvantage, will never occur to the imagination of the most exalted of his fellow citizens... Any man's son may become the equal of any other man's son, and

---

[13] Edmund S. Morgan, "The Puritan Ethic and the American Revolution," *William and Mary Quarterly*, 3rd ser., 24 (1967), 3-43, traces some of the political implications of this outlook. The intellectual restraints placed on economic activity by this system of values are explored by J. E. Crowley in *This Sheba Self: The Conceptualization of Economic Life in Eighteenth Century America* (Baltimore, 1974), which unfortunately does not examine actual cultural behavior. Important analyses of the latter are D.C. Coleman, "Labour in the English Economy of the Seventeenth Century," in E. M. Carus-Wilson, ed., *Essays in Economic History* (London, 1962), II, 291-308; E. P. Thompson, "Time, Work-Discipline, and Industrial Capitalism," *Past and Present*, 38 (1967), 56-97; and Herbert Gutman, "Work, Culture, and Society in Industrializing America," *American Historical Review*, 78 (1973), 531-88.

[14] Quoted in Carlton O. Wittlinger, "Early Manufacturing in Lancaster County, Pennsylvania, 1710-1840," (unpub. Ph.D. diss., Univ. of Penna., 1953), 115.

[15] Quoted in Michael Paul Rogin, *Fathers and Children: Andrew Jackson and the Subjection of the American Indians* (New York, 1975), 207.

the consciousness of this is certainly a spur to exertion...."[16] Exertion, striving, enterprise, individual achievement as the key to (and the test of) "the advance of society"—here was a *new* ideology, the product of the historical convergence of Protestant socio-economic values and the material possibilities of an emergent industrial capitalism.

Like most new visions of reality, the ideology of social mobility and individual accumulation was initially the outlook of a distinct social group. Among the working population of the shoe-making center of Lynn, Massachusetts, for example, there was a sharp split between the non-drinking, self-improving, religious "mechanics" and a more easy-going group of shoemakers who felt (the mechanics alleged) that "every moral enterprise is absolutely beneath their notice."[17] The heirs of a pattern of work in which the consumption of alcoholic beverages was a normal expectation, part of the wage payment in fact, these tradition-oriented, irreligious shoemakers found themselves opposed not only by sober, industrious "mechanics" but also by the new entreprenueurial class of industrialists, the prime architects of the Temperance Crusade.

This social alliance between mechanics and entrepreneurs was a limited one, for the two groups held radically different economic beliefs. Most journeymen, master craftsmen, and storekeepers—the backbone of the "mechanic" shoe-making population—did not favor a social system based on large-scale production, a relentless search for profit, and upward social mobility. Their ideal, rather, was an economy in which independent workers could pursue a trade or an occupation, a "living" or "competency" which would allow them "to lay up for a day of want" and to provide adequately for their children.

These Lynn shoemakers resented both the new division of labor imposed on the industry by Quaker merchants and the enormous profits extracted by these entrepreneurs. "The gaudy places in which they now reside," one mechanic complained bitterly in 1844, have been "erected upon the very ruins of those cordwainers who have been sent to an untimely grave by this same system of grinders."[18]

---

[16]Frances M. Trollope, *The Democratic Manners of the Americans* (Smalley ed., N.Y., 1949), 121.

[17]Quoted in Paul Gustaf Faler, "Workingmen, Mechanics and Social Change: Lynn, Massachusetts, 1800-1860," (unpub. Ph.D. diss., Univ. of Wisconsin, 1971), 480.

[18]*Ibid.*, 344, 432, 346. For a concise statement see Paul Faler, "Cultural Aspects of the Industrial

These emotions were not those of envy but of disgust—they represented a repudiation of a new way of life and system of values. Within the same town, indeed within the shoe industry itself, there were three competing value systems, each the property of a distinct social group. And this diversity of aspirations and of behavior had a parallel in the social divisions within the agricultural population. As one Massachusetts observer noted in 1849:

> Farming may be so conducted as to be made profitable, or merely to afford a living or to run out the farm. Taking the land as it averages in this state, this depends more on the farmer than on the soil.[19]

Given the wide divergence among these definitions of "success" and of the ideal social order, is it valid to compare the experiences of these groups with one another along a one-dimensional scale of economic or social mobility? Most tradition-oriented shoemakers were content to pursue a tenuous year-to-year financial existence; they would trust to their children or to the charity of the town to provide for them in sickness or old age. Those workers with more prudent habits—in drink, leisure, and religion—and with a less transitory sense of time toiled and saved for the future, for a "competency" which would provide security for their old age and a respectable trade which they could pass on to their children. Neither of these groups extolled social "mobility" as a prime value; nor did they behave in ways that were consistent with its precepts. Only the Quaker entrepreneurs, and those that emulated their example, fashioned their lives according to the dictates of this acquisitive, change-oriented ideology. And yet the entire conceptual framework of the analysis of social mobility is predicated upon the universality of the values and goals of this white, upwardly-mobile, Quaker or Protestant middle-class. The inevitable result is to distort the meaning of the life-experience of other ethnic, racial, or class groups.

This conclusion emerges clearly from a close examination of Stephan Thernstrom's deservedly well-known monograph, *Poverty and Progress: Social Mobility in a Nineteenth Century City*. In undertaking this analysis of social mobility among the Irish laboring

Revolution: Lynn, Massachusetts, Shoemakers and Industrial Morality, 1826-1860," *Labor History*, 15 (1974), 367-94.

[19]Quoted in Clarence H. Danhof, *Change in Agriculture; The Northern United States, 1820-1870* (Cambridge, 1969), 134. For important cultural differences among the white agricultural population of eighteenth century Virginia, see Rhys Isaac, "Evangelical Revolt: The Nature of the Baptists' Challenge to the Traditional Order ....," *William and Mary Quarterly*, 3rd ser., 31 (1974), 345-368.

population of Newburyport, Massachusetts, between 1850 and 1880, Thernstrom did not intend to extol the ideology of social mobility. Indeed, the structure of his book seems to be designed to show how the "hegemonic" Protestant ruling class employed this rhetoric as an ideological weapon in order to perpetuate its power. Thernstrom's conclusions, moreover, served to undermine the validity of social reality as presented by this dogma; there was little social mobility among these poor workingmen, even when traced over two generations. Sentiment, structure, and conclusion notwithstanding, Thernstrom's methodology—his investigation of *Irish* life in terms of a "Victorian" middle-class system of values—nearly vitiated his analysis.[20]

It is a tribute to Thernstrom's abilities that the truth comes out nevertheless; the richness of the presentation ultimately overflows the biased and confining one-dimensional forms to provide us with an "inside" understanding of the Irish laboring experience in this mid-nineteenth century town. First of all, it is quite apparent that even articulate Roman Catholics, those most likely to interpret their own lives in terms of the ideology of social mobility, recognized the profound discrepancy between myth and reality. "Five or ten out of a hundred may rise in the world," an editorial in the Boston *Pilot* observed in 1855, "while ninety-five will live and die in the condition in which they were born."[21] Such perceptions would not cause ambitious Catholic men and women to lapse into passivity, but they would force an acute awareness of the tenuousness of success; there were too many poor for them to ignore the exceptional nature of their own condition.

Among the Irish laboring population itself, there is little evidence that either behavior or goals were shaped by the ideology of individual social mobility. To what use did these laboring women and men put the money they earned as canal or railroad workers, unskilled

---

[20]Stephan Thernstrom, *Poverty and Progress: Social Mobility in a Nineteenth Century City* (Cambridge, 1964; references are to the Atheneum edition, 1973). This book was both radical—in its exposition of a false ideological description of reality—and innovative, in its attempt to assess the actual historical experience of the Irish laboring population. Its historiographical significance has been much more conservative. Subsequent studies—including Thernstrom's *Other Bostonians*—have used this flawed ideological description as a methodological premise; and the quest for technical exactness and statistical finesse has become more important than an understanding of the lives and cultural values of the historical actors themselves.

[21]*Ibid.*, 79; a similar opinion is noted by Oscar Handlin, *Boston's Immigrants, 1790-1880; A Study in Acculturation* (1941; rev. and enl. ed., Cambridge, 1959), 87.

factory operatives, and domestic servants? Did they plan for their
own individual material advancement? For that of their children? Or
did they spend their meager wages in ways which suggest a very
different scale of values and aspirations? The answers to these
questions are not completely clear, but a tentative resolution may be
attempted. By tracing the "cash flow" in these poor Irish households, it is possible to watch economic "choices" being made and
thus to understand the cultural values of this immigrant population.

These Irish laborers (two-thirds of whom came from rural agricultural backgrounds) were deeply enmeshed in a kinship network. The strength and persistence of these "family" attachments
were affirmed by the steady flow of "remittances" sent back to
Ireland for the subsistence of relatives there or for their transportation
to America. During the so-called "Scourge of 1847" the Irish in
Boston sent back more than $200,000; while between 1851 and
1880, the Emigrant Industrial Savings Bank of New York remitted
$30 million to Ireland. Estimates for the overall total of remittances
vary widely (one, for the period from 1848 to 1864, is $65 million);
but their enormous size is not in doubt.[22] Nor is their significance.
Whatever their hopes for themselves, these migrants were not
atomistic individualists, with an intense and overriding goal of
self-advancement, but responsible participants in a trans-Atlantic
kinship network with strong family ties and communal values.

There were also—many of them—pious adherents of the Roman
Catholic Church. This spiritual faith was reflected in the material
support they rendered to the Church and to the schools which it
established for the religious education of their children. Between
1871 and 1879, for example, the Irish Catholics of Newburyport
raised more then $65,000. The total is less significant than the size of
some of the individual donations. Thernstrom is rightly impressed
that at least two dozen laborers contributed $50 apiece to this fund-
raising campaign at a time when male workers were earning approximately one dollar a day. Would this amount represent the savings of
six months? A year? It certainly was equal to the entire annual
income of many urban working women, seamstresses, shoebinders,
or laundresses.[23] That such hard-earned sums were given to the

[22] Handlin, *Boston's Immigrants,* 152 and Chap. II, note 100; Carl Wittke, *The Irish in America* (New York, 1956), 51.
[23] Thernstrom, *Poverty and Progress,* 176; Faler, "Workingmen," 324.

Church—and not "invested" in small businesses or loans—is eloquent testimony to the pervasiveness of the religious values brought from the old country and deliberately perpetuated in the new environment.

Savings that were neither remitted to Ireland nor entrusted to the care of the religious hierarchy were invariably placed in Savings Banks. These laborers had migrated to an urban, capitalist society, one with increasingly complex financial institutions; and they were inevitably drawn into this economic network. Participation in a capitalist economy did not necessarily imply an acceptance of the ruling ideology, however, especially when one worked as a wage laborer with few legal rights and no share in the "profits." Nor did the use of these savings institutions signify adherence to the creed of social mobility. These deposits were not used as "capital," as profit-making investments. Rather, savings were accumulated slowly over the years and then withdrawn in a lump sum for the purchase of a house. Like their peasant relations in Ireland, these laborers wanted security in their old age, a rent-free house to which they could retire. They were determined and calculating in this quest. They cut expenses to the bone in order to save; they sent their children out to work at an early age. And they were successful. Of the 287 Irish laborers who remained in Newburyport for at least ten years (so that Thernstrom could examine a part of their lives from decennial census returns), 145 managed to accumulate landed property.[24]

This "success" in one area of economic endeavor increased the chances of "failure" in others. Few of these men (47 of the 287) experienced occupational mobility; the great majority remained in the low status, low-paying manual occupations with which they had begun their working lives in America. Perhaps this was the result of discrimination and limited education; but it is equally likely that, to some degree, it was the product of deliberate choice. These laborers may have "preferred," on the basis of a half-conscious understand-

---

[24]Thernstrom, *Poverty and Progress,* Chaps. 4 and 5. The author labels this "property mobility," but is it not more accurate to describe this (as he indeed does at other points—pp. 162, 164) as a successful quest for "security and dignity"? This confusion—this felt need to describe *every* economic success in terms of "mobility" even when other terms better convey the goals of the historical actors—clearly illustrates the difficulty of "working backwards" from analyses of comparative social mobility in order to determine the reasons for differential performance among ethnic or racial groups. The assumption has already been made that "mobility" was the primary goal.

ing of their values, background, and prospects, to seek the security of a house rather than the uncertainty of a small business or a capital investment. In so doing, they also made decisions with respect to the possibility of significant occupational or educational mobility for the next generation: a "choice" had been made to use the wages of child-labor for the purchase of the family residence. This behavior was not "selfish" but "typical" for men and women from a tradition-directed society. In such environments, as David Riesman has noted, "The parents train the child to succeed *them*, rather than to 'succeed' by rising in the social system."[25] In a somewhat similar fashion, Italian-born husbands in Buffalo at the end of the nineteenth century removed their sons from school and sent them into the labor force, so that their wives and daughters would not have to work as domestic servants, outside of the protected sexual environment of the home.[26] However understandable in terms of cultural values, these parental decisions would live on in the constricted occupational lives of their children.

It is imperative that these choices also live on in historical accounts of the life-experiences of these working-class Irish and Italian families. They must not be partially hidden, nor denigrated, nor distorted by methodological approaches which measure and evaluate human behavior within the narrow culturally- and class-biased framework of social mobility analysis. The point of departure for the study of any cultural group must be its own values and aspirations.

These must, of course, be subjected to close scrutiny and detached criticism: Was heavy drinking among the Irish the result of their rural, pre-industrial cultural background, or was it intensified and fundamentally altered by the harsh realities of their migrant urban existence? Was their support of Roman Catholicism self-determined, in the full sense of the term or the product of domination and indoctrination by the religious hierarchy? When Judith O'Rourke declined to educate her children, advising her sons to "grow up honest good men, like them that's gone afore them, not ashamed of their station, or honest toil," was this a positive affirmation of a cultural ideal or a necessary rationalization of a desperate reality?[27]

---

[25] Riesman, 40.
[26] Virginia Yans McLaughlin, "Patterns of Work and Family Organization: Buffalo's Italians," *Journal of Interdisciplinary History*, 2 (1971), 307.
[27] Quoted in Handlin, *Boston's Immigrants*, 132. On Irish drinking see Handlin, 121, while for the

The answers to such questions are complex, for the relative influence exerted on people's lives by inherited traditions, by the contemporary environment, and by new values and ideologies is not easily apportioned. Nevertheless, it is within this matrix of competing goals and limited possibilities that a valid social history must be written: of individuals and groups attempting to make their *own* history, in circumstances not completely of their own choosing.

---

use of intoxicants by all social groups in American pre-industrial society see Faler, "Workingmen," 216-217, 266-268, 274-275; David Bertelson, *The Lazy South* (New York, 1967), 76, 106; Charles Francis Adams, *Three Episodes of Massachusetts History....* (Boston, 1892), II, 783-794.

3

The Failure of Female Factory Labor in Colonial Boston

GARY B. NASH

Writing in the 1790s, Alexander Hamilton and Tench Coxe, two of the promoters of American industrialism, offered the female poor of the northern cities a way out of indigency. Poor women and children, counseled Hamilton, "are rendered more useful by manufacturing establishments." Coxe added that "the portions of time of housewives and young women which were not occupied with family affairs could be profitably filled up" by intermittent labor in "the manufactories." Both of these early advocates of American industrialism saw women and children as the human material out of which a new American economy could be built.[1] But the idea was far from new. It was merely a refurbished version of a plan put into effect in Boston nearly a half century before by the little known United Society for Manufactures and Importation, later renamed the Society for Encouraging Industry and the Employment of the Poor.

As the latter name hints, it was not entrepreneurial capitalism that brought the first American factory into being in Boston; nor was economic diversification on the minds of Boston's leaders; or an attempt to free women from confining domestic roles.[2] It was poverty in frightening proportions and the concomitant es-

[1] Quoted in Mary Ryan, *Womanhood in America From Colonial Times to the Present* (New York: Franklin P. Watts, 1975), 102. Victor S. Clark noted this "direct descent from the Boston Society of American industrial corporations, particularly those engaged in making textiles." *The History of Manufactures in the United States*, Vol. 1, 1607-1860 (New York: McGraw Hill, 1929), 183.

[2] Some of the alternative interpretations of the movement toward women's factory labor in Europe are perceptively discussed in Joan W. Scott and Louise A. Tilly, "Women's Work and the Family in Nineteenth-Century Europe," *Comparative Studies in Society and History*, 17 (1975), 36-64.

Reprinted from *Labor History* 20 (Spring 1979), 165-88. The author wishes to express his grateful appreciation to John Murrin of Princeton Univ. and Cynthia Shelton of the Univ. of California, Los Angeles, for helpful criticisms of this article.

calating costs of poor relief that ushered in America's first experiment in factory production. And a momentous experiment it was, marking the beginning of a century-long rocky series of attempts to restructure the organization and rhythm of urban work. We label the process "the industrial revolution," but this is far too grandiloquent a term to describe the small, fumbling early attempts at exploiting the labor of impoverished women and children in the northern seaport towns at the end of the Colonial period.

We may say, at the risk of oversimplification, that it was war that put the first American woman into the first American factory. New England had always carried the brunt of the wars against the French in North America, and Boston, as the maritime center and the chief staging ground for most of the expeditions against the Papist enemy, had borne especially heavy burdens. While in Philadelphia and New York the legislatures avoided war taxes by authorizing only a few companies of provincial troops, Massachusetts sent large numbers of its men off to die of starvation and disease in futile Caribbean amphibious assaults against Spanish bases in 1740-1741, in the massive attack against Louisbourg in 1745, and in frontier fighting along the French-Canadian border. The colony's losses were staggering. Historians have made only tentative efforts to count up the fatalities but William Douglass, surveying the human wreckage in 1748 at the end of King George's War, believed that nearly one-fifth of the province's adult males lost their lives. Even if we cut this casualty estimate in half, we are left with a literal decimation of the province's income earners, especially those in the lower class where recruitment was concentrated. Reports of the widowing of Boston's population indicate the magnitude of the town's losses. In 1742, when a census was taken, town officials reported 1,200 widows, "one thousand whereof are in low circumstances." If these figures are accurate then a staggering 30 percent of the town's married women had no spouses to contribute to the support of their households. Three years after the war ended the tax assessors reported that Boston contained 1,153 widows "of which at least half are very poor." [3]

---

[3] Otis Little, *The State of the Trade in the Northern Colonies Considered* . . . (Boston, 1749), 8; William Douglass, *Summary, Historical and Political* . . . (2 vols.;

The social derangement caused by Boston's extraordinary contribution to the war effort can also be seen in the rapid decline of taxable polls during this period. They fell from 3,395 in 1738 to 2,972 in 1741, to about 2,660 in 1746. This loss of more than 700 taxables represented a stripping from the tax rolls of persons now too poor to pay anything into the public coffers. Before the attack on Louisbourg, some critics predicted that if Governor William Shirley's grand strategy failed, as they expected, "such a shock would be given to the province that half a century would not recover us to our present state." Ironically, the expedition had triumphed but in succeeding brought such human and financial devastation that the victory was lamented for years thereafter. The glory of bringing French Catholic power to its knees was slight comfort for hundreds of Boston families, for they had to reflect upon the victory in homes that were fatherless, husbandless, and dependent on charity for food and fuel. By war's end, Boston's economy had faltered badly, poor taxes had reached an all-time high, and town officials were desperately trying to cope with the unparalleled numbers of indigent residents, among whom widowed women and their dependent children were the most numerous.[4]

Various attempts were made to find remedies for the plight of the poor. The children of the poor were bound out to financially secure families. The dispossessed were warned out of town as they tramped into the city from outlying areas after the war. The affluent were exhorted to greater charitable contributions. Heartrending appeals for provincial tax relief were sent to the legislature. But none of these measures, though they may have helped,

---

London, 1760), I, 356, 510n, as printed in *Boston Independent Advertiser*, Feb. 8, 1748; William H. Whitmore, et al., *Reports of the Record Commissioners of Boston* (29 vols.; Boston, 1880-1902), XV, 369 (hereafter *Bos. Town Rec.*); *Boston Gazette*, Aug. 27, 1751, gives the total white population as 14,190. The rise of widowhood is also reflected in the inventories of estate. From 1736 to 1745, 11.7 percent of the decedents were widows but this climbed in the next two decades to 14.9 and 17.5 percent respectively. Since lower-class women are underrepresented in the inventories and since some lag can be expected before widows of King George's War would die, it seems likely that at least 25 percent of the town's adult women were widows. The inventories are in Suffolk County Courthouse, Boston.

4 For a table of taxable polls see Gary B. Nash, "Urban Wealth and Poverty in Pre-Revolutionary America," *Journal of Interdisciplinary History*, 6 (1976), 564; Thomas Hutchinson, *The History of the Colony of Massachusetts-Bay*, quoted in George A. Rawlyk, *Yankees at Louisbourg* (Orono, Maine: Univ. of Maine Press, 1967), 37; Nash 555-65.

could solve the problem. So in the end, men turned from the benevolent desire to help the poor to the idea that the poor should help themselves.

The roots of such an approach to poverty are very tangled. New England Puritans, like their Elizabethan forbears, had always maintained a hearty distaste for the dependent poor, especially those who were thought to prefer public alms to hard work and self-support. Cotton Mather put the matter plainly in 1695 when he wrote that "for those that Indulge themselves in *Idleness*, the Express Command of God unto us, is *That you should Let them Starve*."[5]

But by the 1740s it had become clear that the problem in Boston was not one of able-bodied persons who refused work, but persons for whom no work was available. On a very small scale, Boston had faced this problem as early as 1656, and by 1700 the selectmen had taken a tentative step toward a practice extensively employed in England—creating work-relief programs for the poor so that they would earn their own keep in facilities provided and supervised by public authorities.[6]

Many English writers had by this time abandoned an earlier view that economic recessions and depressed wages were the main causes of indigency and began to blame the poor themselves for their plight. The lower class, it was said, was naturally lazy and would work only when forced to do so by hunger and extreme poverty. Thus, it was argued, lawmakers who passed relief statutes with the best of intentions only cultivated dependency and encouraged sloth. William Petty, one of the most respected economic writers of the late seventeenth century, even promoted a scheme for perpetually maintaining an artificial famine by storing food in government granaries. Kept at the edge of starvation, the laboring classes would develop an urge to work that was

[5] *Durable Riches* (Boston, 1695); also see Mather, *Concio and Populum* (Boston, 1721), quoted in Stephen Foster, *Their Solitary Way: The Puritan Social Ethic in the First Century of Settlement in New England* (New Haven: Yale Univ. Press, 1971), 135, 137. Foster's discussion of poverty (127-52) in Boston and attitudes toward it is the best available.

[6] In 1656, a group of subscribers privately raised money to buy materials with which to set unemployed youths to work (Foster, 147). In 1700, the selectmen spent £500 (£390 sterling) for a "Stock to set the poor on work" (*Bos. Town Rec.*, VIII, 3). The work program in 1700 was the outcome of a law passed in the previous year for "setting the Poor to work in workhouses." (Albert B. Hart, ed., *The Commonwealth History of Massachusetts*, 4 vols. [New York: States History Co., 1928], II, 266-67).

constitutionally absent in them.[7]

Out of this new climate of thought came the public workhouse movement. By 1723, when workhouses were operating in almost every sizable English town, thousands of impoverished persons were taken off out-relief and forced to move from their homes. Taken to the workhouses, they were set to spinning flax, weaving linen, and picking oakum. It was hoped that through hard labor the poor would pay for their own support and in the process gain a taste for the rewards of industry and frugality. The workhouse would benefit the middle and upper classes by reducing the poor rates; it would aid the poor by reprogramming them for a more satisfactory way of life. Some English writers also recommended transferring the management of the poor to private corporations owned by investors who might turn a profit from appropriating the labor of the indigent, even as they rehabilitated them. The English workhouse became a cultural artifact of the early eighteenth century, an institution arising from a moral analysis of poverty and committed to reducing the taxpayers' load in maintaining the impoverished. John Bellers, a Quaker merchant of London, dignified these workhouses with the name of "colleges of industry" and a number of other authors with whom Bostonians were familiar, including Henry Fielding, William Temple, William Petty, Charles Davenant, and Bernard Mandeville, also pumped for the new system.[8]

In 1735, with poverty spreading, Boston undertook its first major experiment in working the poor. The town meeting decided to build a separate workhouse where the able-bodied poor would be segregated, relieved, and rehabilitated. Slowly over the next few years private subscriptions were solicited, about £900 sterling in all, and by 1739, the brick Workhouse on the Common opened its doors. Nineteen months later, an inspection committee reported that expenses had exceeded income by £466 to £360 sterling

---

[7] William Petty, *Economic Writings,* edited by Charles Hull (Cambridge: The Univ. Press, 1899), I, 274-75. Also see Dorothy Marshall, "The Old Poor Law, 1662-1795," *Economic History Review,* 8 (1937), 38-47.

[8] A. W. Coats, "Economic Thought and Poor Law Policy in the Eighteenth Century," *Economic History Review,* 2d Ser., 13 (1960-61), 46-50; Sidney and Beatrice Webb, *English Local Government From the Revolution to the Municipal Corporations Act, I: The Parish and the County* (London: Longmans and Co. 1906). For Bellers, see John Bellers, *Proposals for raising a College of Industry* (London, 1695), and *Essays about the Poor, Manufacturers, Trade, Plantations, and Immorality* . . . (London, 1699).

and that 48 adults and 7 children were employed in the house, mostly picking oakum, carding, and spinning. In 1742, 36 persons were in the house and the number from that point on does not seem to have exceeded fifty.[9]

Obviously, the overseers were not going to cure Boston's poverty problem by institutionalizing about 5 percent of the town's distressed persons. But why were so few persons ordered to the workhouse, which had attracted 126 donors and gained the approval of the town meeting and provincial legislature? The answer cannot lay in the incommodiousness of the building, for it was one of the largest structures in Boston. Two stories high and 140 feet long, it was capable of holding scores of impoverished, unemployed persons.[10] The difficulty, apparently, was that Boston's poor resisted being taken from their homes. In 1740, a visitor remarked that the overseers of the poor were "very tender of exposing those that had lived in a handsome manner; and therefore give them good relief in so private a manner, that it is seldom known to any of their neighbors." This statement provides us with a clue to why the Workhouse failed. Many of the poor were widows with young children. Many of them had lived decently, if not "handsomely," in the past. Hence, it is not difficult to understand that they would rebel at the notion of giving up their lodgings, however cramped and cold, and repairing to the Workhouse where poverty was compounded with indignity and their ties with friends and relatives, as well as neighborhood life, would be broken.[11]

---

[9] *Bos. Town Rec.* XII, 104-05, 111, 114, 116, 156, 159-62, 165-68, 172; Carl Bridenbaugh, *Cities in the Wilderness: Urban Life in America, 1625-1742* (New York: Knopf, 1955; orig. ed., 1938), 393; Foster, 147-48. The fullest account of the workhouse is in Stephen Edward Wiberly, Jr., "Four Cities: Public Poor Relief in Urban America, 1700-1775," (unpublished Ph.D. diss., Yale Univ., 1975), 88-98; *Bos. Town Rec.* XII, 273 for financial report. The 1742 count is in 3 Massachusetts Historical Society *Collections,* I, (Boston, 1846), 152. Even in 1768, when poverty expenditures were even greater, there were only 40 persons in the workhouse (Carl Bridenbaugh, *Cities in Revolt: Urban Life in America, 1743-1776* [New York: Knopf, 1971; orig. ed., 1955], 320.)

[10] *Bos. Town Rec.,* XII, 159-60. According to a census taken in 1756, the almshouse, which was completed in 1686 and was not nearly as large as the new workhouse, held 148 inmates in 33 rooms. City of Boston, Indentures, 1734-1757, City Clerk's Office, City Hall, Boston. A list of 126 subscribers to the workhouse fund is in *Bos. Town Rec.,* XII, 180-83. John Kern, "The Politics of Violence: Colonial American Rebellions, Protests, and Riots, 1676-1747" (unpublished Ph.D. diss., Univ. of Wisconsin, 1976), 233-34, identifies many of the subscribers as prerogative men.

[11] "Bennett's History of New England," *Proceedings of the Massachusetts Historical Society,* 5 (Boston, 1862), 116-17; Wiberly, who has analyzed the admissions

The most unfortunate of Boston's impoverished—the aged,
sick, crippled, and insane without families to care for them—had
no choice but to go to the Almshouse, as did about one hundred
Bostonians each year in the 1740s. Another forty or fifty persons
could be induced to go to the Workhouse, especially if they did
not have children or had been apprehended for prostitution or
other crimes. But most of Boston's poor women regarded themselves above such treatment and preferred to starve at home even
if the authorities decided to cut off out-relief and ordered them to
the Workhouse. These persons refused to brook the strict regimen
of the Workhouse, with its rules against free coming and going
and its provisions for bread and water diets for "wanton and las-
civious Behavior." Moreover, they must have found it ungenerous
that the selectmen allowed them only one penny out of every
shilling they earned—and that "to be disposed of by the Overseers
for their greater Comfort." Alarmed at the spiralling cost of relief
and affronted by the challenge to order and harmony that hundreds of pauperized and idle townspeople evoked, Boston's leaders erected a substantial building that they could not fill. The
Workhouse experiment failed because it underestimated the stub-
bornness of ordinary people, who had ways of defending themselves against attempts to alter their way of life.[12]

By 1748, Boston's leaders were ready to make another attempt
to deal with the widowed poor and their dependent children. If
they would not trade their mean lodgings for the Workhouse,
perhaps they could be persuaded to go to a "manufactory" during
the day where their labor would contribute to their own support
and lighten the taxpayer's burden. Thus was born the United
Society for Manufactures and Importation. Its subscribers intended to put the unemployed poor to work, halt the rise of property taxes, and perhaps even make a profit off the cheap labor of
poverty-stricken women and children.[13] Public authorities had

records of the Almshouse and Workhouse, shows that women and children outnumbered men about three or four to one (94-95).

[12] *Bos. Town Rec.*, XII, 234-41, for the rules of the Workhouse; Wiberly emphasizes
that the Workhouse was a financial failure, costing the town more per indigent
than outrelief (95-97).

[13] In its promotional pamphlet, *The Society for Encouraging Industry ... Articles of
Incorporation ... with a List of Subscribers* (Boston, 1748, reprinted 1754) it
was pointed out that "the most immediate Advantage" to be gained by the scheme
"is that which will arise" when "Many Thousands of the poor are taught to support themselves." A corollary benefit was that the price of labor—"so much

been unable to make the dependent poor self-supporting; now private hands were to have a try.

The supporters of the Society for Manufactures were drawn from the ranks of Boston's most successful merchants and entrepreneurs. They concluded that of the various kinds of work that might be done by women and children, spinning and weaving were the most feasible. This notion was especially attractive because Massachusetts annually imported from England cloth worth thousands of pounds. The production of cloth by the poor, it was thought, not only would end idle pauperism and reduce taxes but also would improve the province's balance of trade by cutting back on imports. And hopefully, it would turn a profit for the Society's investors. But what kind of cloth? Woolens seemed not to be the answer because, although they were widely used, sheep grazing was only marginally profitable in New England and it took considerable craft skill, certainly skill beyond the capacities of a shifting, casual labor force, to produce the worsted materials favored by city people in contrast to the rough homespuns country folk found adequate for their needs.[14] Linen was the alternative and had much to recommend it. Flax grew well from the middle colonies northward to New Hampshire and linen was also widely imported—to the value, according to contemporary estimates, of £20,000 to £60,000 per year. Thirty years before, a group of Scotch-Irish immigrants had demonstrated the art of spinning flax in Boston and set off a mild "spinning craze." These Ulster immigrants had remained only briefly in Boston before setting out for the New Hampshire frontier where they founded the town of Londonderry and soon proved that linen could be profitably produced.[15] More important, linen production had

and justly complained of"—will fall. A. P. Usher believed that the Society's name and their expressions of concern for the plight of the poor "were mostly an indirect way of expressing an ambition to make good use of cheap labor" (Hart, *Commonwealth History of Mass.,* II, 408). The most extensive published account, which is antiquarian but filled with useful documentary material, is William R. Bagnall, *The Textile Industries of the United States* . . . (Cambridge, MA: The Riverside Press, 1893), 28-37.

[14] In 1754, it was claimed that sheep were not widely raised in Massachusetts because of the long winters (*The Society for Encouraging Industry* . . . [Boston, 1754], 1) but Usher disputes this (*Commonwealth History of Mass.,* II, 407) and he is supported by the 1735 tax valuation which counted 130,001 sheep of at least one year's age. (Leonard Labaree, William B. Willcox, et al., *The Papers of Benjamin Franklin* [New Haven: Yale Univ. Press, 1959-], III, 440).

[15] Edward L. Parker, *The History of Londonderry* . . . (Boston: Perkins and Whipple, 1851), 36-39, 48-50. The author does not indicate when the linen industry began

been promoted in Ireland since the late seventeenth century and was now regarded there as the sure-fire method of curing urban poverty. Here, then, seemed to be the answer to the bundle of problems that had beset the town. As the successors to the United Society later pronounced, the "palliatives" of poor relief would be replaced by "a lasting and permanent Scheme, that may be expected to reach the Root of this Malady."[16]

Despite these optimistic hopes, nothing went easily for the organizers of the manufactory. The initial call for investors in 1748 brought only 36 subscribers and about £200 sterling—some indication of the chariness that many felt about the prospects of success. Linen weavers and loom builders could not be found in Boston and had to be advertised for abroad.[17] Nor were spinners available, for contrary to the conventional understanding of historians, urban women and children who could spin were the exception rather than the rule.[18] It took until December, 1750 to

---

but implies that the Londonderry settlers brought their wheels and looms with them. The linen production was apparently carried out as a home industry. In 1798, when the Boston plan became known, the Londonderry town meeting quickly passed an ordinance regulating carefully the quality of linen and putting a Londonderry label on all linen products of the town. It seems likely, in view of this protective measure, that they refused help to the Bostonians, either in teaching them how to build looms or showing them how to weave, bleach, and stretch linen. Such uncooperativeness was a form of economic protectionism but it may also have been a belated settling of scores, for when the Ulster immigrants arrived in Boston in five ships in the fall of 1718, the town refused to succor some 300 impoverished souls who had insufficient money and provisions to carry them through the winter. Parker, *Londonderry*, 37-38; *Massachusetts House Journals, 1718-1720* (Boston, 1921), 83, 106, for 150 bushels of Indian meal contributed to the immigrants by the General Court.

[16] *Society for Encouraging Industry* ..., 3. For the growth of the Irish linen industry, see George O'Brien, *The Economic History of Ireland in the Eighteenth Century* (Dublin: Maunsel and Co., Ltd., 1918), 189-207; and W. H. Crawford, "The Rise of the Linen Industry," in L. M. Cullen, ed., *The Formation of the Irish Economy* (Cork: 1969).

[17] Bagnall, 29-31. The Society was directly violating a 1749 act of Parliament which made the enticement of manufacturing artisans a criminal offense (David J. Jeremy, "British Textile Technology Transmission to the United States: The Philadelphia Region Experience," *Business History Review*, 47 [1973], 25-26).

[18] It is usually assumed that eighteenth-century women learned spinning and weaving as a matter of course. Edith Abbott, an authority on the subject, says that in the "latter half of the eighteenth century many women were regularly employed spinning at home for purchasers who were really commission merchants"; that "the most important occupations for women ... before the establishment of the factory system were spinning and weaving"; and that, although "it is impossible to make any estimate of the number of women who did such work ... it is quite safe to say that spinning for the household was a universal occupation for women ..." (Abbott, *Women in Industry: A Study in American Economic History* [New York: D. Appleton & Co., 1900], 19-20). But such statements are based primarily on the assumption that English practice was carried to America. The extensiveness of household spinning and weaving varied widely in the colonies. In rural areas they were probably extensive. But the absence of wheels and looms

lease a building, set up "sundry looms," and open several free spinning schools where pauper children were to be taught the art of the distaff and wheel.[19] By this time the United Society had reorganized and changed its name to the more benevolent sounding Society for Encouraging Industry and the Employment of the Poor.

To stir up enthusiasm for the opening of the manufactory, the Society published an extraordinary pamphlet on November 2, 1750. It had a cumbersome title—*A Letter from Sir Richard Cox, Bart. To Thomas Prior, esq.; Shewing from Experience a sure Method to establish the Linnen-Manufacture, and the Beneficial Effects it will immediately produce*—but inside the covers was an exciting tale of poverty and progress. Sir Richard was none other than the grandson of the former Lord Chancellor of Ireland and his tract, published in Dublin and reprinted in London in 1749, described a fifteen-year experiment to bring prosperity and peace to the vale of tears he found on the River Bandon, where the two tiny towns of Kinsale and Bandon-bridge lay. Cox had been horrified in 1733 to find that the natives of his inherited estate "had contracted such a Habit of Idleness" that they would not work and that their children had imbibed "their pernicious Example." Naked beggars roamed the streets, people lived from hand to mouth, houses tumbled down in disrepair, and hope was nowhere to be found. A well-meaning man, Sir Richard vowed to alter this dismal situation. Thus, he embarked on an industrial experiment, turning his estates into a social laboratory and study-

---

in the thousands of surviving Boston household inventories and the discussions about the need to establish spinning schools in 1718 and 1750 makes this clear. In 1720, a town-appointed committee recommended the founding of seven spinning schools for children, offered £300 (£126 sterling) on interest-free loan to anyone who would undertake to start such schools, and found no takers. In 1721 Daniel Oliver, a wealthy merchant, erected a spinning school at his own expense but little came of it (Bagnall, 17-18). In 1750, the Society advertised that "several Spinning Schools in this Town" would be opened shortly and children would be taught free (*Boston Evening Post,* Dec. 17, 1750).

[19] Edward Winslow, "The Early Charitable Organizations of Boston," *New England Historical and Genealogical Register,* 44 (1890), 100-103 reprints the initial list of subscribers, but incorrectly gives 1735 as the year when the United Society for Manufactures and Importation was established. This error is noted in Bagnall, 29. For importing Irish weavers and the opening of the manufactory, see *Boston Evening Post,* July 9, 1750, Dec. 10, 1750. The United Society may have leased a part of the workhouse, for the Manufactory was located, according to the Dec. 10 notice, on the Common "below the seat of Thomas Hancock," which fits the location of the workhouse. The Company's records show that the North School and two private houses were rented (Ezekiel Price Papers, 314, 317, Mass. Historical Society, Boston).

ing human motivation until he found the formula for putting everyone to work, from the oldest members of the community down to little children who had just "quit their Leading-Strings." It had taken time, but by 1749, when Sir Richard published the pamphlet in London, Kinsale and Bandon-bridge were thriving towns where prosperity and contentment had replaced poverty and despair. The key to it all was the manufacture of linen.[20]

The pamphlet, like most promotional tracts, was somewhat fanciful, for what is known about the history of the Bandon River villages in the mid-eighteenth century does not entirely confirm Richard Cox's description of economic progress. But the promoters of the Manufactory in Boston were not concerned with accuracy. They had convinced themselves that linen production would solve Boston's problems and they were doubtless glad to find such a glowing account of its success elsewhere. They had received it fortuitously from an old hometown boy, Benjamin Franklin, who had sent it to friends in Boston shortly after receiving it from his London scientific correspondent, Peter Collinson.[21] The pamphlet was quickly reprinted in Boston with a preface explaining that "The Circumstances of this Province, and those of Ireland, tho' not altogether similar, are in so many Respects alike. . . . " They trusted, said the Society's officers, that the public would be swayed to support the Manufactory, now almost ready to open.

The public that needed to be swayed, of course, was composed of the unemployed and impoverished members of the community. It is not probable that very many of them read the *Letter from Sir Richard Cox* but it is likely that most were privately urged by the Overseers of the Poor and the clergy to contribute themselves to the experiment. Their response was not gratifying. A few months after the manufactory opened its doors in 1751, notices

---

[20] *A Letter from Sir Richard Cox*. The quoted passages are from 7 and 16. Cox neglected to state that the impoverishment of many Irish towns was attributable to the Woolen Act of 1699, which placed prohibitive tariffs on woolens imported from Ireland to England. This accomplished the desired effect of crushing the Irish woolen industry, which was eventually replaced by linen manufacturing. For Cox, see *Dictionary of National Biography*, Leslie Stephens and Sidney Lee, eds., IV (London, 1917), 1339-40.

[21] *Papers of Franklin*, V. 233n-34n. According to Collinson, Franklin "proposed the same Plan to some Ingenious publick spirited Friends." I assume Collinson referred to friends in Boston, for Philadelphia had no sizeable poverty problem at this time. The Bostonians, of course, already had a linen production scheme underway.

appeared in the papers describing the sermon that Joseph Sewall preached at a public meeting of the Society. "It is earnestly wished by all Lovers of their Country," it was pleaded, that the poor "would exert themselves at this Time" by working in the manufactory. "Great Numbers of Persons," if they would step forward, might now be "useful both to themselves and the publick, who have heretofore been a dead Weight upon . . . this poor Town." Six months later the Society reported that 5,000 yards of linen per year was now being produced, two-thirds of it by women working for the Society. Though the number of yards produced looks impressive at first glance, it is in fact what about three weavers supplied by thirty spinners could produce annually. It was a pathetic output for a town whose pauper population approached one thousand souls.[22]

At the very time when the Society was reporting its limited progress in putting the indigent of Boston to work, smallpox struck the town. It descended so severely on the lower class that it "entirely destroyed the Linnen Manufacture." The Society's officers were determined to continue the experiment, however, for their town was deep in a commercial recession that compounded all her other troubles. At the root of this decay was the decline of shipbuilding—a keystone of the town's economy. At the end of the Anglo-French War in 1748 shipbuilding was struck by what one citizen called "a galloping consumption." This was the result not only of a decline in orders that accompanied the return of peace but the rise of satellite ports in eastern Massachusetts as shipbuilding centers.[23]

---

[22] *Boston Gazette*, Aug. 27, 1751; *Report of the Committee for the Society for Encouraging Industry* . . . (Boston, 1752). According to the Society's records, "1 loom will Employ 10 Spinners." Price Papers, #319. In March 1753 the Society claimed that 200 children had been taught to spin but their output must have been meager *(Boston Evening Post,* Feb. 26, 1753). I have found no good statistics on the output of linen weavers but E. P. Thompson reports that a farming weaver could produce 8½ or 9 yards per day and Richard Cox, who awarded prize money to the most productive weavers in his village reported 45 yards per week in 1747, 74 yards per week in 1748, and 121 yards per week in 1749. Three weavers, producing 32 yards per week each, would yield 5,000 yards in a year. Thompson, "Time, Work-Discipline, and Industrial Capitalism," *Past and Present,* #38 (1967), 71, Cox, *Letter from Sir Richard Cox,* 26-28.

[23] William Douglass, *Summary, Historical and Political* . . . (2 vols.; London, 1760), I, 540; *Bos. Town Rec.,* XIV, 221. In 1756 the selectmen claimed in a petition to the General Court that during one year in the recent past 14,000 tons of shipping had been built whereas after the war shipbuilding output fell to less than 3,000 tons. Petition of Town of Boston, Feb. 11, 1756, Massachusetts Archives, CXVII, 67-68, Statehouse, Boston.

Added to the loss of shipbuilding was an exodus of butchers, bakers, tanners, distillers, and glovers. According to the selectmen, many of these artisans fled the city because of onerous tax rates passed during the war and maintained in the postwar period in order to support a growing number of poor. Poverty bred poverty, for as the number of poor who had to be maintained grew, officials levied heavier taxes upon those who themselves were struggling to make ends meet. "Unless the heavy Burthen be lightened," complained town officials in 1758, "there will be no such Town as Boston."[24] In this situation many artisans apparently decided to try their luck in outlying towns where tax rates were far lower. The loss of many substantial taxpaying families only increased the burden on those who remained, leaving the selectmen to bray pathetically that adverse conditions had "carried away from us many of Our most Industrious, frugal and provident Inhabitants, who have left us a number of thoughtless Idle and Sottish Persons, who have very soon" become public charges.[25]

Operating amidst these adversities, the Society redoubled its efforts when the smallpox epidemic passed. Several hundred spinners resumed their work and four or five looms hummed away. Newspaper accounts printed encouraging comments.[26] Simultaneously, the Society's officers launched a campaign for subscriptions to erect a large new building and enlisted some of Boston's most prestigious ministers, including Samuel Cooper at Brattle Street Church and Charles Chauncy of the First Church, in the cause. The latter argued that because of the Society's praiseworthy efforts "some hundreds of Women and Children have . . . been kept at Work, whereby they have done a great deal towards supplying themselves with Bread, to the easing the Town of its Burthen in providing for the poor." Now was the time for wealthy Bostonians to come to the aid of their town by subscribing as much as possible toward building the new manu-

---

[24] *Bos. Town Rec.*, XIV, 220-22; Petitions of the Town of Boston, Feb. 11, 1756 and April 1758, Mass. Archives, CXVII, 55-68, 395-96.

[25] *Bos. Town Rec.*, XIV, 239-40. By the end of the epidemic only 174 of 15,684 inhabitants had not been infected, either through inoculation or involuntarily. More than 10 percent of the uninoculated sick had died and it seems probable that these were concentrated in the lower class where resistance to inoculation was strongest. John Duffy, *Epidemics in Colonial America* (Baton Rouge, LA: Louisiana State Univ. Press, 1953), 59-60.

[26] *Bost. Evening Post*, Feb. 26, 1753.

factory. Cooper, who was Boston's most accurate reflector of the growing economic philosophy of self-interest, made a naked appeal to the pocketbooks of the affluent. Nobody, he wrote, was "actuated by a kind of mad good Nature" that led him to devote himself "to the Gratification of others, without any concern or Relish for his own private Happiness." But Bostonians could simultaneously indulge their natural and legitimate "self-love" and support a public cause because the manufactory was designed to "advance our private interest" by lowering taxes and turning a profit while giving employment to the idle. Chauncy also looked the profit motive in the eye: "The only proper Question is, whether this is, a likely Scheme, under proper Cultivation, to counter-balance with Advantage, the Expence necessary in order to its taking Effect." [27]

Ministerial urgings, however, could unlock less than £200 sterling of Boston's mercantile wealth. Some merchants may have feared that textile production would cut into trade profits, for cloth was a major import item. Others may have questioned whether the manufactory could operate at a profit and they could point to the Society's own report, in March, 1752, that the operation was £500 in debt. Cooper also hinted at financial problems in 1753 when he urged the well-to-do not to weary of "doing well" in subscribing to the new building fund and predicted a "fair Prospect of *reaping*" in the future. [28]

Unable to attract enough private capital, the Society's officers turned to government and got the response they sought. In March, 1753 the Town Meeting voted to lend £130 sterling toward the construction of a new building and in June, Boston's representatives persuaded the General Court to impose a luxury tax on coaches, chariots, and other wheeled vehicles for five years in order to raise £1125 sterling more. Newly capitalized, the Society started afresh. Construction on a large building began in the spring of 1753 and the Linen Manufactory House on Tremont Street was ready by fall. To whip up enthusiasm for its opening,

---

[27] *Boston Post-Boy*, Feb. 12, 1752; Charles Chauncy, *The Idle-Poor Secluded from the Bread of Charity by the Christian Law* (Boston, 1752), 18-19; Samuel Cooper, *A Sermon Preached in Boston, New England, Before the Society for Encouraging Industry* . . . (Boston, 1753), 12-23.

[28] Price Papers, #311-13, 317; from 1753 to 1759 the Society raised another £900 sterling in donations and subscriptions; *Report of the Committee of the Society* . . . (Boston, 1752); Cooper, *A Sermon Preached*, 34.

the Society staged a spinning exhibition on the Common in August. "Near 300 Spinsters, some of them 7 or 8 years old and several of them Daughters of the best Families among us," reported the *Boston Gazette,* ". . . made a handsome Appearance on the Common." High upon a stage erected for the occasion sat a number of weavers, one at work at his loom.[29]

All of the bright hopes that the Linen Manufactory would rid Boston of its poverty problem were shattered within a few years after the new facility opened its doors. Boston's leading ministers continued to give annual promotional sermons and the number of looms in operation rose from nine in 1753 to 21 in 1757. But by 1758 operations at the Manufactory were grinding to a halt. When Thomas Barnard gave the annual sermon in September of that year, he noted that economic affliction was still growing in Boston and that the thousands of men being recruited for the French and Indian War would create an even greater need for putting women to work. His sermon ended on a plea that reveals that the linen chimera was about to end. He urged the Society's members to continue their work even "tho' you should lose on the Balance," for their losses would be recompensed in lower poor taxes and the knowledge that they were helping to banish idleness.[30] But nobody was listening. In the next year the General Court, which had been unable to meet the cost of the new Manufactory from the luxury tax receipts (doggedly resisted by the wealthy) ordered the building sold at auction in order to recover the costs. But who would buy a linen factory that would not

[29] *Bos. Town Rec,* XIV, 234-35; *Mass. Acts and Resolves,* III, 680-82; Most of the £2,246 expended in purchasing land and erecting the Manufactory House was advanced by Thomas Gunter, a Roxbury merchant, who was to be repaid from luxury tax receipts; "An account of the cost of the Linen Manufactory House...." Mass. Archives, LIX, 391-94, Statehouse, Boston, shows that most artisans and suppliers were paid in September, 1753. See also *Boston Gazette,* Aug. 14, 1753, quoted in Richard B. Morris, *Government and Labor in Early America* (New York: Harper Torchbooks, 1965), 517. The public spinning exhibition and the attempt to induce lower-class women to spin by using upper-class daughters as examples of this kind of civic duty were taken straight from Richard Cox's description of his Irish linen experiment.

[30] Barnard, *A Sermon Preached before the Society...* (Boston, 1758). In an appendix to the sermon, the "Committee of the Society" repeated the old pitch that linen production was unusually well suited for Boston's problem, for the "greatest Part of the Labour is done by Women and Children, who have no other Employment and can therefore work cheaper at this." They closed with a final plea for contributions so that the poor could "maintain themselves by their Industry, instead of their being maintain'd by others in Idleness, the Pest of Society, and the Mother of every Vice."

work? No bids were made and all the province could do was lease a part of its white elephant to two Boston weavers, John and Elisha Brown, who wanted to run their own textile enterprise.[31] Not until the British troops eyed it as a barracks in 1768 could anyone think of a use for the Linen Manufactory.

Why had the linen manufactory failed? Cheap labor, sufficient capital, and technology were the prime factors that had led to success in Scotland and Ireland and all seemed available in Boston. It was not for lack of money to erect a large building and equip it with looms, spinning wheels, hackling and bleaching equipment, and other necessary items that the Manufactory closed its doors in 1759. Nor was it for lack of labor, for weavers were obtained and hundreds of women and children taught to spin. During its existence, in fact, the Society produced more than 17,000 yards of cloth. Yet the enterprise failed financially because it could not produce linen as cheaply as it could be imported. In part, this may have been because, as the Society claimed, government subsidies were not provided as in Ireland. There were also the problems of synchronizing labor and procuring ample supplies of flax.[32] But much of the answer to the Manufactory's failure lies in the resistance of the supposed recipients of the Society's efforts. As in the case of the workhouse, the majority of women and children were reluctant to toil in the manufactory. They would spin at home, working as time allowed to produce what they could within the rhythm of their daily routine and accepting small piecework wages. But removal to an institutional setting, even for daytime labor, involved a new kind of labor discipline and separation of productive and reproductive re-

---

[31] By early 1756, the Society had received only £312 sterling from the carriage tax. Wiberly, 100. Gunter's involvement and subsequent attempts to recover his money can be followed in a series of petitions to and actions by the General Court in Mass. Archives, LIX, 281-294, 427-28, 431, 441-42, 452-57, 494-99, 509-10, and *Massachussetts House Journals,* XXXV, 56-57, 249, 262, 314; XXXVI, 48. Gunter began petitioning for recovery of his loan in June, 1758 but the House stalled for a year before deciding to put the Manufactory on the auction block. Elisha Brown had been hired by the Society to supervise operations in the early 1750s (Price Papers, #317).

[32] *Ibid.,* #314, 318; *Bos. Town Rec.,* XVI, 226-27; Thomas Barnard, in *A Sermon Preached . . .* (Boston, 1758), 23, admitted that linen was cheaper to import than weave domestically but asked his auditors to reject "the stale Objection, of the Cheaper Importation of Linen" in view of the social advantages to be gained. In their initial petition to the General Court for a provincial subsidy, the Committee of the Society wrote at length on the subsidies in Ireland that had launched the linen weaving industry there.

sponsibilities that challenged deeply rooted values. "The factory system," E. P. Thompson reminds us, "demands a transformation of human nature, the 'working paroxysms' of the artisan or outworker must be methodised until the man is adapted to the discipline of the machine." Boston's women, of course, were not asked to adjust to power-driven machinery. But in creating a methodical, day-long work situation, the Society was asking them to transform not only their traditional irregular work habits but to rearrange their maternal responsibilities in order to leave the home for work.[33]

To understand how extensively routinized labor in the manufactory might change the work experience of laboring-class women we need to apprehend how they previously contributed to the family economy. This is extraordinarily difficult, for we are operating not only in a vacuum of secondary literature concerning the work experience of pre-industrial American women in urban areas but are faced with a dearth of evidence on the day by day working life of the wives and daughters of artisans and laborers. But we do know from studies of England and France in this period that laboring-class women typically supplemented their husbands' wages because, in an economy where large numbers of people regularly lacked an adequate supply of food, this was absolutely necessary. Servanthood and manufactory labor were the two types of work most frequently performed by young, unmarried women in Europe, but married women resisted factory labor, preferring domestic manufacturing, especially spinning at home. Spreading rapidly in eighteenth-century European towns, domestic spinning helped the laboring poor to establish a viable family economy while at the same time allowing "women to fulfill what they defined as their primary role, their family duties."[34]

---

[33] E. P. Thompson, "Time, Work-Discipline, and Industrial Capitalism," 56-97 examines this problem brilliantly, although without distinguishing the special problems pertaining to women's work; Thompson, *The Making of the English Working Class* (London: Gollancz, 1963), 362.

[34] Patricia Branca, "A New Perspective on Women's Work: A Comparative Typology," *Journal of Social History,* 9 (1976), 133. I have also been guided by Olwen Hufton, "Women and the Family Economy in Eighteenth-Century France," *French Historical Studies,* 9 (1975), 1-22; Mary Lynn McDougall, "Working-Class Women During the Industrial Revolution, 1780-1914," in Renate Bridenthal and Claudia Koonz, eds., *Becoming Visible: Women in European History* (Boston: Little, Brown, Co., 1977), 255-79; Theresa M. McBride, "The Long Road Home: Women's Work and Industrialization," in *ibid.,* 280-95; and

We cannot transpose the European experience directly to Boston; but the wider context of the urban work experience of eighteenth-century women does provide insights into the world of Boston's women. As the wives of artisans, mariners, and laborers, they had probably always contributed to the family economy by helping in their husbands' shops, taking in washing, serving as seamstresses for middle- and upper-class families, and doing daytime domestic labor in the houses of the well-to-do. After the 1720s, when the economic security of laboring-class families was steadily underminded, supplemental income from wives and older daughters probably became even more imperative. Domestic service may have been particularly important because, unlike Philadelphia and New York, Boston lacked the substantial labor pool of female slaves and indentured servants who performed household work in those cities. New York in 1756 had 695 female slaves over sixteen years of age and 443 under that age—a total of 1,138 slave women to serve a white population of 10,768. Philadelphia in 1767 had about 600 female slaves and indentured servants for a white population of about 18,500 and families of means also had at their command a substantial pool of free, unmarried immigrant women who entered the city each year. Boston, by contrast, received only a trickle of poor Scots-Irish and German immigrants and contained only 301 black females and 16 Indian females in 1765 for a white population of 14,672.[35] Much of the demand for domestic labor, it seems certain, must have been filled by young, unmarried women and by the wives of lower-class men, especially if they were childless.

Older women with young children may have taken in boarders as a second major way of supplementing the family income. There is a striking difference in the number of people per house in Boston and in the other port towns in this period, and we can infer from this either that Boston families were larger or that many householders rented rooms and furnished board to tran-

Elizabeth H. Pleck, "Two Worlds in One: Work and Family," *Journal of Social History*, 10 (1976), 178-95.

[35] New York: Evarts B. Greene and Virginia D. Harrington, *American Population Before the Federal Census of 1790* (Gloucester, MA: P. Smith, 1966), 101; Philadelphia: Gary B. Nash, "Slaves and Slaveowners in Colonial Philadelphia," *William and Mary Quarterly*, 3rd Ser., 30 (1973), 246 for the total number of slaves and servants, one-third of whom were female; Boston: J. H. Benton, Jr., *Early Census Making in Massachusetts, 1643-1765 with a Reproduction of the Lost Census of 1765* . . . (Boston: C. E. Goodspeed, 1905), following 71.

sients, unmarried mariners, and other families from the ranks of
the laboring poor. In 1741 Boston had 9.53 persons per house
and in 1765 9.26 persons. This contrasts sharply both with Philadelphia, where there were 6.51 inhabitants per house in 1749
and 6.26 in 1760, and with New York, where there were 6.72
persons per house in 1753.[36] All of the data available to us indicates that the birthrate in Boston was lower than in the other
northern ports, for the mid-century wars took a fearful toll on a
generation of young males, leaving a surplus population of young
women whose child-bearing potential was cut short by the loss
of a husband or who remained single and childless altogether for
lack of marriageable men. Hence, it is reasonable to conclude that
the large number of persons per house in Boston, which exceeded
the New York and Philadelphia averages by about 50 percent,
primarily represents the taking in of single boarders and even
families. For many Boston women, especially widows, this may
have been the primary means of providing a family income.

Both in daytime domestic service and in maintaining boarders
Boston's poor widows, who represented the major problem for
the administrators of poor relief, had previously been able to
combine maternal responsibilities with intermittent work, which
brought a modest income but had to be supplemented with out-
relief. Factory labor, however, required a workplace that was far
less amenable to the discharge of women's familial responsibilities. Even when children of seven years and older were taken to
the factory to assist in preparing flax for spinning, the problem
of managing younger children remained. If spinning could be
done in the home, it could be fit into the maternal work life of
the woman; in the factory it could not.

---

[36] The census of 1765, cited in n. 35 above, indicates 1,676 houses in the city. In
1742 there were 1,719 houses. *Boston Town Rec.* XIV, 369-70. The ratios are
taken from Lemuel Shattuck, *Report of the Committee of the City Council Appointed to Obtain the Census of Boston for the Year 1845* (Boston, 1846), 54. The
ratio in New York has been calculated by extrapolating the population for 1753
from the censuses of 1749 and 1756 and dividing by the number of houses in
1753 as specified by Thomas Pownall, the governor of Massachusetts, in Lois
Mulkearn, ed., *T. Pownall, A Topographical Description of the Dominions of
the United States of America...* (Pittsburgh: Univ. of Pittsburgh Press, 1949),
44. For Philadelphia I have used the house count as given in John K. Alexander,
"The Philadelphia Numbers Game: An Analysis of Philadelphia's Eighteenth-
Century Population," *Pennsylvania Magazine of History and Biography*, 98
(1974), 324, and the population figures calculated in Billy G. Smith, "Death
and Life in a Colonial Immigrant City: A Demographic Analysis of Philadelphia," *Journal of Economic History*, 37 (1977), 865.

Evidence of resistance to the new work system is mostly indirect. No records are extant that show how many spinners and weavers worked in the Manufactory, although something may be inferred from the fact that in 1757 there were 21 looms and 60 spinning wheels in the building. Hundreds of spinners had been trained in the previous years and 21 looms would have required yarn from the wheels of several hundred of them. Many, it appears, had accepted the Society's suggestion that they work at home, or, to reverse the causality, had obliged the Society to accept this modification of the original plan. Even so, the preepidemic production level, which was hardly impressive, was not being met in early 1753, and later that year it was reported that almost as many people were spinning for themselves as for the Society. Boston's poor would spin and weave but they were less than enthusiastic about doing it within the confines of the Society's manufactory house. With their initial plan falling apart, the Society began offering free house rent and firewood to those who would weave linen cloth in their homes. Over the next few years, Boston's poor turned away from the Society. By 1760, according to the Society's records, twice as much cloth had been produced over the previous nine years for "Private persons" as for the Society, a reversal of the situation in the opening years of the experiment. Several merchants began to purchase privately produced cloth, and apparently most of the poor preferred to produce for the merchants as their domestic responsibilities allowed, rather than work for or in the Manufactory. A decade after the Manufactory failed, a town committee concluded that "the carrying on this Business in private families (as by experience has been found in Scotland & Ireland as well as among ourselves) where the spinning and weaving are done when they [the women] have no other Employ" was the only way to put textile production on a viable footing. If they had been "fully supported" by wages, women and children might have been induced to go to the manufactory. But since they could not live on the wages offered, about seven shillings per week for spinners, they preferred to stay at home, working at their wheels in their free time, selling their yarn to independent weavers, and counting on private and public relief to supplement their meager income.[37]

[37] The Society reported that 489 yards had been woven for them and 340 yards for

The resistance of these women is all the more remarkable given the pressure they were under from the town's leading figures, who were intent on making the linen manufactory succeed. This upper-class determination is most revealingly articulated in the sermons given at the annual meetings of the Society. Some of eastern Massachusett's best known clergymen—Charles Chauncy, John Barnard, Samuel Cooper, Thomas Barnard, Thomas Prince, Joseph Sewell, and Ebenezer Pemberton—gave these sermons, which were often prefaced with descriptions of the plight of the poor. Once expressed, however, sympathy was quickly followed by admonitions that the idle poor could no longer expect the town to support them. Years before, when economic opportunity was waning in Boston, Cotton Mather advised the poor to endure their poverty quietly, pray for those whose benefactions eased their distress, and "be willing to go to Heaven by the way of an Almshouse, when GOD shall assign you such a lodging. . . ."[38] Now the message from above became even harsher: work in the manufactory was being provided and the poor must accept it or expect to starve. In a sermon preached at the launching of the Society's new subscription drive in August, 1752, Chauncy took as his text the Christian Law: "Thus we commanded you, that if any would not work, neither should he eat." He decried "the Swarms of Children, of both Sexes, that are continually strolling and playing about the Streets of our Metropolis, cloathed in Rags and brought up in Idleness and Ignorance"; he decried the "lazy and indolent, who are both healthy and strong"; he warned against giving money to the idle poor, because charity of this kind, far from helping, would be

private persons ("Report of the Committee of the Society . . . ," *Boston Evening Post*, Feb. 19, 1753). In the quarterly report a year earlier, the Society noted that 1,772 yards had been produced, more than twice as much (*Report of the Committee for Encouraging Industry . . . Feb. 1752* [Boston, 1752]); *Boston Evening Post*, Feb. 19, 1753; Cooper, *A Sermon Preached*, 33; Memorial of Andrew Oliver et al. to the Governor and Council, May 1753, Mass. Archives, LIX, 381-83; Price Papers, #318. John Hancock and John Barrett were buying cloth procured from independent weavers and were thus competing directly with the manufactory (*ibid.* #329). In 1752, 72 percent of the cloth woven was for the Society (*Report of the Committee . . . Feb. 1752*); *Bos. Town. Rec*, XVI, 226-27. The Society's records show that spinners could process one hundred pounds of flax per year and were paid three shillings, nine pence (Massachusetts money) per pound (Price Papers, #322). This works out to 7.2 shillings a week (4.8 shillings sterling), not enough to buy food for even one person.

[38] Mather, *Some Seasonable Advice unto the Poor* . . . (Boston, 1712). The sermon was reprinted in 1726.

"a great Hurt to a Community." Samuel Cooper reiterated the emerging ideology that public out-relief or private charity for widows and their children was money "worse than Lost." The only justifiable charity, he pronounced, was that which was directed toward "an Employment for honest Poverty, [that] chases away moaping Idleness, and meager Want; and introduces cheerful Industry and smiling Plenty in their Stead."[39]

Inherent in these strictures was the threat of cutting off public relief and discouraging private charity, thus forcing impoverished women to adopt themselves to factory labor or go hungry. But such finger-wagging at the poor though it may have cheered propertied Bostonians who welcomed any work program that would bring taxes down, met with considerable resistance among the lower class. Widowed women had little reason to subscribe to the notion that they were "lazy" or "idle" or lived parasitically on "promiscuously" distributed charity or that their children needed to be "trained up, not only to endure but to love a constant Employment." Such allegations must have been deeply resented by those whose misfortunes were not of their own making. Many of them had recently contributed husbands to a Canadian expedition that had been sponsored by the governor and the wealthy merchants of the town in the face of widespread resistance. Now they heard it charged that their idle children would soon graduate "from picking of sticks to picking of Pockets" and thus must be taken to the manufactory to learn more suitable habits. It is clear from the declining production of cloth in the linen manufactory and its complete failure by 1759 that lower-class women stubbornly resisted the new ideology and institutions of poor relief. The most vulnerable, to be sure, submitted to the new factory work discipline. Impecunious migrants entering Boston, such as Henry Neal, his wife, and children, were

---

[39] Chauncy, *The Idle-Poor Secluded from the Bread of Christian Charity*, 9-17; also see Chauncy, *Industry and Frugality Proposed as the Surest Means to make Us a Rich and Flourishing People; And the Linen Manufacture Recommended As tending to promote These among Us* (Boston, 1753), especially 10; Cooper, *A Sermon Preached*, 23. Some of the older ideology regarding the poor, charging the rich with responsibility for alleviating the distress of the unfortunate, still persisted. The *Boston Gazette* (Aug. 27, 1751) reprinted an essay on poor relief from the *New York Gazette* in 1751 that urged people of means to buy from artisans and shopkeepers who had fallen upon hard times, even if it meant paying a bit more, and to sell the necessities of life to the poor below the prevailing rates.

hustled off to the Manufactory by the overseers of the poor and did not resist. Nor, perhaps, did young lower-class women, who could find no marriage partners in a town where the sex ratio had been badly skewed by war casualties. But many poor women refused to submit to a work routine that disrupted their way of life and split dual functions of laboring-class women—work and family—into separate spheres. Samuel Cooper's argument that factory labor would not only inculcate industriousness but would add something "to the innocent Gaiety and Sprightliness of Childhood" was not well received, we may imagine, in most lower-class Boston homes.[40]

Boston leaders had undertaken the first experiment in the American colonies in routinized labor involving large numbers of people in a single workplace outside the home. But the Linen Manufactory, the embryo of capitalistic industrial factories, was conceived more in desperation at the rising tide of poverty than in entrepreneurial striving. As in England, authorities in Massachusetts had moved beyond many countries in agreeing implicitly that people should not be allowed to starve. Now they reached out in their frustration at mid-century to grasp at a straw that had floated across the Atlantic.

Something of the ambivalence of Boston's authorities toward the new system of poor relief can be seen in the halting manner in which the manufactory operated. In sermon literature the clergy castigated "idleness" but they did not charge, as so frequently was the case in England, that it was voluntary. Yet once an opportunity to work had been provided, the clergy warned that widows and children must take their places in the cloth-making scheme and accept part of the responsibility for their indigency. Otherwise, public and private charity would be cut off.

Despite this hectoring, women resisted. Their recalcitrance, moreover, may have been fed by the reluctance of the overseers of the poor to suspend out-relief for those who were Boston born and bred. They had no compunctions about acting severely with the strolling poor who entered Boston, but with their own people they were far less ruthless than authorities in English towns. Appalled at conditions that they supposed applied only to Eu-

---

[40] Chauncy, *Industry and Frugality Proposed* . . . ,10; *Bos. Town Rec.*, XIX, 38; Cooper, *A Sermon Preached*, 33.

ropean cities, they could not bring themselves to deny aid to women who would not submit to factory work for meager wages. It was this lack of coercion by elected officials that allowed most of Boston's widows and children to remain in their homes, spinning as time allowed within their familial routines. At the same time, neither the town nor the province was willing to continue subsidizing an industrial experiment that had failed to produce a profit. So the linen manufactory collapsed. Boston's leaders had found a way of making work for the poor and unemployed but had not discovered how to adapt the work to the needs and values of those who were to do it.

4

The Mechanics and the Jeffersonians: New York, 1789-1801

ALFRED YOUNG

In 1789, on the eve of George Washington's inaugural, New York was a solidly Federalist town. In the Congressional election of 1789, the city chose a Federalist by a vote of 2,342 to 373; in the gubernatorial poll it voted against George Clinton, anti-Federalist Governor, 833 to 385.[1] And the mechanics of all ranks were overwhelmingly Federalist. They poured forth to celebrate Washington's inauguration just as they had marched in 1788 to celebrate ratification of the Constitution. They were active in nominating Federalists and they voted Federalist.[2] "Almost all the gentlemen as well as all the merchants and mechanics," Virginia's Senator Grayson observed in 1789 "combined together to turn [George Clinton] out" while the "honest yeomanry" alone supported him.[3] In 1790 anti-Federalists did not even go through the motions of nominating Assembly or Congressional candidates.

From 1789 to 1801 the major thrust of New York City politics was the effort of the anti-Federalists, then the Republicans, to win back the following they enjoyed in the immediate post-war years and establish a new one among the rapidly expanding electorate.[4] Of necessity this was an effort to win support among the mechanics.

For the old anti-Federalist leaders this was a formidable task. George Clinton, the party chieftain and governor since 1777, was an Ulster county lawyer and landholder whose reputation was built on his services in the Revolution as a staunch Whig, wartime governor

---

[1] *Greenleaf's New York Journal and Patriotic Register*, Apr. 9, 1789 (hereafter cited as *New York Journal*); [New York] *Daily Advertiser*, Apr. 27, 1789.

[2] In 1788 Federalist legislative and convention candidates were endorsed at meetings of master carpenters, and at a meeting of "the respectable mechanics and tradesmen," *Daily Advertiser*, Apr. 24, 28, 29, 1788.

[3] William Grayson to Patrick Henry, June 12, 1789, W. W. Henry, ed., *Life, Correspondence and Speeches of Patrick Henry* (3 vols., New York, 1891), III, pp. 389-95.

[4] For a brief survey, Sidney Pomerantz, *New York, an American City, 1783-1803* (Columbia University Studies in History, Economics and Public Law, No. 442, New York, 1938), chs. 2, 3.

Reprinted from *Labor History* 5 (1964), 247-76.

and foe of Tories.[5] Anti-Federalist political support came primarily from the independent small farmers of Long Island, the west bank of the Hudson and the upper Hudson valley.[6] In New York City the small circle of Clintonian leaders, while men of lowly origins, were all successful merchants, as their homes in the fashionable part of lower Manhattan attested.[7] John Lamb, for example, was Collector of the Port, a lucrative position;[8] Marinus Willett was the county sheriff;[9] Melancton Smith was busy with various speculations, some of them in William Duer's group.[10] Henry Rutgers was born to wealth which made him one of the city's largest landlords.[11] Only one officer of the General Society of Mechanics and Tradesmen, John Stagg, their old radical Whig compatriot, acted with the Clintonians; while the only artisan in their circle,[12] Ezekial Robbins, a wealthy hatter, was not even a member of the Mechanics Society.[13] They had, in fact, better connections among merchants than mechanics.

In 1791-92 when the Livingston family defected from the Federalists to form a coalition with the old anti-Federalists, they brought with them no special strength among the mechanics. They were city merchants and lawyers, and owners of tenanted estates in the upper Hudson valley. Indeed before the Revolution, in 1768-69, the Delancey faction had been able to win over mechanics against William Livingston of the famed "whig triumvirate,"[14] and in 1774-76 the radical

---

[5] E. Wilder Spaulding, *His Excellency George Clinton, Critic of the Constitution* (New York, 1938), chs. 7-12.

[6] E. Wilder Spaulding, *New York in the Critical Period, 1783-1789* (New York, 1932), chs. 5, 12. Forrest McDonald, *We The People. The Economic Origins of the Constitution* (Chicago, 1958), pp. 283-300.

[7] For the leaders see "Minutes of the Republican Society" (1788), John Lamb Papers, N.Y. Hist. Soc. and Box 5 of Lamb Papers, *passim*.

[8] Isaac Q. Leake. *Memoirs of the Life and Times of General John Lamb* (Albany, 1850), pp. 296-98, 351-55; *American State Papers, Miscellany*, I, pp. 57-58, 60-62, for Lamb's income as collector.

[9] Daniel E. Wager. *Col. Marinus Willet: The Hero of the Mohawk Valley* (Utica, 1891), pp. 45-47.

[10] Robin Brooks, "Melancton Smith, New York Anti-Federalist, 1744-1798" (unpub. doctoral diss., University of Rochester, 1964), ch. 2.

[11] L. Ethan Ellis, "Henry Rutgers," *Dictionary of American Biography* VIII, pp. 255-56; "Tax Lists or Assessments on the Real and Personal Property" (New York City, June, 1796), Ms, N.Y. Hist. Soc., in particular for the seventh ward.

[12] See Roger Champagne, "The Sons of Liberty and the Aristocracy in New York Politics, 1765-1790" (unpub. doctoral diss., University of Wisconsin, 1960), p. 481. For Stagg on Clinton's election committee, *New York Journal*, Apr. 2, 1789.

[13] "Minutes of the General Society of Mechanics and Tradesmen," Dec. 1, 1794, Dec. 23, 1795 (typescript at the office of the Society, New York City); for his house see James Wilson, *Memorial History of the City of New York* (4 vols. New York, 1891-93), III, pp. 150-52.

[14] Roger Champagne, "Family Politics versus Constitutional Principles: The New York Assembly Elections of 1768 and 1769," *William and Mary Quart.*, 3rd ser., XX

mechanic factions usually were at loggerheads with conservatives led
by Robert R. Livingston (senior and then junior), Philip Livingston
and John Jay and William Duane, related to the Livingstons by marriage.[15] The memory of Chancellor Robert R. Livingston's veto of the
charter for the General Society of Mechanics in 1785 was even
fresher.[16] Moreover Aaron Burr, the young lawyer sent to the United
States Senate in 1791 by the Livingstons and Clinton, in 1785 was the
only city Assemblyman who had voted against the charter.[17] Thus the
loose coalition that became the "republican interest" as far as New
York City politics went—the Clintons, the Livingstons and Burr—
were in reality three factions in search of a following.

They found this following in stages in a long uphill battle. Their
first victory did not come until the end of 1794 when they won the
Congressional seat by a vote of about 1,850 to 1,650.[18] They did not
win an Assembly election until 1797, and in the closing years of the
decade all the elections were nip and tuck. In the famous "battle of
1800"—the election that determined that the state's electoral votes
would be cast for the Jefferson-Burr ticket—the Republicans took the
assembly by 3,050 to 2,600 and squeaked through the congressional
race 2,180 to 2,090 votes. Not until 1801 did they win a majority of
the £100 freeholder electorate privileged to vote for Governor. Thus
even at the end of the Federalist era, New York was not quite a safe
Republican town; Federalists in defeat retained a sizable following.
Analysis of the election returns leads to the conclusion that the mechanics who in 1789 were overwhelmingly Federalist, by 1800-01 were
divided: most were Republican; a good number stayed Federalist. The
task, then, that confronts the historian is to explain how various segments of the mechanic population left the house of Federalism in response to the successive issues of the 1790s.

I

Through most of Washington's first administration, from 1789
through 1792, the honeymoon of mechanic Federalist and merchant

(1963), 57-79; Milton Klein, "William Livingston: American Whig" (unpub.
doctoral diss., Columbia University, 1954), chs. 13, 15.
15 Becker, New York, 1763-1776, passim.; Champagne, "Sons of Liberty," ch. 7 and pp.
439-40.
16 George Dangerfield, Robert R. Livingston of New York, 1746-1813 (New York, 1960),
p. 197; for the veto, Charles Z. Lincoln, ed., Messages From The Governors (Albany,
1909), II, (1777-1822), pp. 228-233.
17 Nathan Schachner, Aaron Burr: A Biography (New York, 1937), pp. 84-85.
18 The returns for this and subsequent elections are given below.

Federalist continued. The sources of Federalist popularity among mechanics were several. Federalists were the party of the Constitution; they also appeared as the party of the Revolution. The Tories in their camp took a back seat; Colonel Alexander Hamilton ran the party and it was not missed that John Laurence, their first Congressman, had married the daughter of the famed "Liberty Boy," Alexander McDougall.[19] Federalists were also the party of George Washington, an object of universal veneration while the city was the nation's capital in 1789-90. "Poor men love him as their own," said a character in a play by the New York dramatist, William Dunlap.[20] The fact that the city was the capital also helped; anti-Federalists complained that the Federalist "electioneering corps" included "the masons, stone cutters, the carpenters and the mortar carriers" employed in refurbishing city hall as Federal Hall.[21]

In drawing up slates at election time Federalists accommodated mechanics. In the 1789 election when mechanics and merchants each nominated an assembly ticket, Hamilton presided over a meeting of delegates from both groups which drew up a satisfactory coalition ticket.[22] Hamilton claimed, with apparent impunity, in *Federalist* Essay Number 35 that "Mechanics and manufacturers will always be inclined with few exceptions, to give their votes to merchants, in preference to persons of their own professions and trades. Those discerning citizens are well aware that the mechanic and manufacturing arts furnish the materials of mercantile enterprise and industry."[23] But just to make sure, for years Federalists ran one or more leading mechanics, including leaders of the General Society, on their annual assembly ticket.[24]

---

[19] Charles W. Spencer, "John Laurence," *Dictionary of American Biography,* VI, pp. 31-32.

[20] Cited in Martha Lamb, *History of the City of New York* (2 vols., New York, 1880), II, p. 352.

[21] "Civis," *New York Journal,* Apr. 9, 1789.

[22] Miscellaneous Notes and Memoranda for April, 1789, Alexander Hamilton Papers, N.Y. Hist. Soc.; for the nominations, *Daily Advertiser,* Apr. 8, ff, 1789.

[23] Jacob Cooke, ed., *The Federalist,* Essay 35, (Middletown, Conn., 1961), p. 219.

[24] The mechanics elected as Federalist Assemblymen and the year of their election were: 1789: Anthony Post, carpenter and President of the General Society; Francis Childs, printer of the Federalist *Daily Advertiser* and Vice President of the Society, and Henry Will, pewterer, an incorporator of the Society; 1790: William W. Gilbert, silversmith, and Will; 1791: John Wylley, tailor, and Will; 1792: Gilbert and Wylley; 1793: Robert Boyd, blacksmith, Richard Furman, painter and glazier and Jotham Post, either a druggist or carpenter; 1794: Furman and Post; 1795: Furman, Post and Alexander Lamb, a cartman; 1797: (ticket defeated); 1798: Furman; 1799: John Bogert, iron monger, Jacob Sherred, painter, Anthony Steenback, mason and

In their policies in the first Congress, Federalists made good on some of their promises during the ratification controversy. The city's mechanics petitioned for tariff protection at once, pointing out to their brethren that "foreign importations were highly unfavorable to mechanic improvement, nourishing a spirit of dependence, defeating in a degree the purpose of our revolution and tarnishing the luster of our character."[25] Congressman Laurence neatly balanced the interests of his constituency, pleading for higher duties on beer, candles, hemp, and cordage, (manufactured by the city's artisans), for lower duties on rum, madeira, and molasses, (imported by the West Indies merchants), couching the latter plea on behalf of the poor—"that part of the community who are least able to bear it."[26] Early in 1792 Congress passed another mildly protective tariff bill while the anti-Federalist position was sufficiently blurred for Hamilton to be able to claim that "this faction has never ceased to resist every protection or encouragement to arts and manufactures."[27]

Hamiltonian finance was generally supported in the city as in the state as a whole. Funding drew only a few whimpers of protest in the city; in fact it was John Stagg, the Clintonian mechanic, who helped squelch a petition that appeared among veterans on behalf of Madison's proposals for discrimination.[28] Assumption struck sparks only among the old anti-Federalist foes of "consolidation." While Hamilton's "Report on Manufactures" does not seem to have drawn any special accolades from mechanics, his overall performance as Secretary of the Treasury gave him a prestige that outlasted his party's. On his retirement in 1795 a group of building craftsmen offered to build him

Anthony Post, carpenter; 1800 and 1801, defeated; see New York Civil List (Albany, 1869 edn.), 130-148 for assemblymen; for identifications, see New York Directory (New York, annually) and "Minutes of the General Society of Mechanics and Tradesmen, 1785-1832," passim. For a published list of the members of the Society, Thomas Earle and Charles C. Congden, eds., Annals of the General Society of Mechanics and Tradesmen of the City of New York, 1785-1889 (New York, 1882), appendix.

25 A letter to the Mechanics Society of Boston in "General Society of Mechanics Minutes," at November 18, 1788; the petition is in American State Papers: Finance (Washington, 1832), I, pp. 8-9.

26 Joseph Gales and W. C. Seaton, eds, The Debates and Proceedings in the Congress of the United States, 1789-1824 (42 vols., Washington, 1834-56), 1st Cong., 1st sess., Apr. 14, 1789, 131, 133-34, 150, 153; Apr. 24, pp. 205-06. Hereafter cited as Annals of Congress.

27 An unpublished ms. fragment (1794) in Hamilton Papers, Lib. of Congress, Microfilm, also reprinted in Beard, Economic Origins, pp. 246-47.

28 Daily Advertiser, Feb. 3, 22, 1790. Stagg was active in putting down the movement in the Society of Cincinnati.

a house at their own expense,[29] and after his death in 1804 the General Society went into mourning for six weeks.[30]

The first sign of a serious mechanic alienation from the merchants came in 1791, when the General Society's new petition for incorporation was "treated with contemptuous neglect" by the state assembly which in the same session granted a charter to the Bank of New York, the merchants' favorite. Some of the old mechanic consciousness, last apparent in 1785-86 when the charter was first rejected, now revived. "Mechanics," said a writer in Greenleaf's anti-Federalist organ, "those who assume the airs of 'the well born' should be made to know that the mechanics of this city have equal rights with the merchants, and that they are as important a set of men as any in the community."[31] Another man pushed the issue further:

> Who will deny that a republican government is founded on democratic principles? . . . That the manufacturing interest, from its nature is, and ever will remain of the democratic denomination, none can deny. Why then incorporate large monied interests, and no democratic ones? Should we not have a wholesome check to the baneful growth of aristocratic weeds among us?[32]

In the Spring elections of 1791 the mechanics refused to go along with the merchants ticket, nominating instead a slate that included one of their officers and two leaders of the burgeoning Tammany Society. Four of their candidates won—"our motley city representatives," Robert Troup called them in his alarmed report to Hamilton.[33] And the following year the mechanics charter sailed through the legislature.

Once chartered, the Society grew from about 200 members in 1792 to about 600 in 1798, most of them master craftsmen. Chartered "only for charitable purposes" as the society regretfully explained, it occasionally made small loans to its members besides acting as a benefit

---

29 Griffith J. McRee, *Life and Correspondence of James Iredell* (2 vols. New York, 1857), II, p. 442.
30 Martha Lamb, "The Career of a Beneficent Enterprise," *Magazine of American History*, XX: 2 (Aug., 1889), 94. I have found no evidence of mechanic testimonials in a search through the Hamilton Transcripts, Col. Univ. Lib. I am indebted to Harold Syrett, Editor of The Hamilton Papers, for the opportunity to make use of the transcripts. Nor is there any such evidence in Broadus Mitchell, *Alexander Hamilton, The National Adventure, 1788-1804* (New York, 1962) or in John C. Miller, *Alexander Hamilton, Portrait in Paradox* (New York, 1949).
31 A Friend to Equal Rights, *New York Journal*, Mar. 30, 1791.
32 "Leonidas," *ibid.*, Feb. 22, 1792.
33 For nominations, *New York Journal*, Apr. 13, 16, 1791; *Daily Advertiser*, June 2, 1791; Robert Troup to Alexander Hamilton, June 15, 1791, Hamilton Transcripts, Col. Univ. Lib.

society.³⁴ And while it eschewed partisan politics, it nonetheless had the effect it anticipated of "uniting us as brethren in common interests."³⁵

Mechanics expressed some of this same spirit by flocking into the Tammany Society, described confidentially by its organizer as "a political institution founded on a strong republican basis whose democratic principles will serve in some measure to correct the aristocracy of the city."³⁶ Founded in 1789, it had 300 members by the Fall of '91; and perhaps 200 more by 1795, among whom mechanics were the most numerous. Its first chief Sachem was William Mooney, an upholsterer and paper hanger.³⁷ Its leaders stressed its democratic rather than its class character. Tammany "united in one patriotic band," William Pitt Smith of the Columbia faculty exclaimed, "the opulent and the industrious—the learned and the unlearned, the dignified servant of the people and the respectable plebeian, however distinguished by sentiment or by occupation."³⁸ The organization was not political, and its leadership at first was predominantly Federalist. But the fact that anti-Federalists were active in Tammany and the Assemblymen elected in 1791 were Tammany figures were both omens of its political potential.³⁹

The little appreciated "bank war" and "panic" of 1792 brought to a boil such disillusionment with the Federalist honeymoon as then existed.⁴⁰ After the Bank of the United States was chartered and a threat of a coalition of its New York branch with the Bank of New York loomed in 1791, there was a movement to charter a third bank led by "the disappointed in the direction of the existing banks," foremost among whom were the Livingstons.⁴¹ While the origins of the

³⁴ "Minutes of the General Society," *passim*. The usual loan was £100 or £150; on Mar. 2, 1796, the society had £500 on loan, on Mar. 7, 1798, £1250.
³⁵ A letter to the Mechanics Society of Providence, *ibid.*, at Nov. 7, 1792. For the charter see *Laws of the State of New York*, 13th sess.,ch. 26.
³⁶ John Pintard to Jeremy Belknap, Oct. 11, 1790 cited in Edwin P. Kilroe. *Saint Tammany and the Origins of the Society of Tammany* . . . (New York, 1913), pp. 136-37.
³⁷ Peter Paulson, "The Tammany Society and the Jeffersonian Movement in New York City, 1795-1800," *New York History*, XXXIV (1953), p. 50.
³⁸ William Pitt Smith, "An Oration Before the Tammany Society, May 12, 1790," *New York Magazine or Literary Repository*, I (1790), pp. 290-95, at 294.
³⁹ For the officers see *New York Directory* (1789-1792). Pintard was elected to the Assembly in 1790 and failed in 1791 when William Pitt Smith and Melancton Smith were elected. See *New York Journal*, Apr. 22, 1790, *Daily Advertiser*, June 2, 1791.
⁴⁰ Alfred Young, "The Democratic Republican Movement in New York State, 1788-1797" (unpub. doctoral diss., Northwestern University, 1958), ch. vii and Joseph S. Davis, *Essays in the Earlier History of American Corporations* (2 vols., Harvard Economic Studies, XVI, Cambridge, Massachusette, 1917), II, ch. 2.
⁴¹ Alexander Macomb to William Constable, Feb. 21, 1792, **Constable Papers, N.Y. Pub.**

venture were speculative, "men of all classes flocked" to subscribe to its stock, as Edward Livingston claimed in extolling its advantages to "persons of small capital" and victims of the lending "favoritism" of the Bank of New York.[42] Hamilton fought the new venture desperately; by March he knew that the "bank mania" was "made an engine to help the governor's [Clinton's] re-election."[43] In April the "prince of speculators," William Duer, Hamilton's recently resigned Assistant Secretary, collapsed, and the bubble inflated by speculation in bank stock, securities, and land burst. Duer brought down with him not only leading merchants like the Livingstons but a host of common folk from whom he had borrowed to the hilt: "shopkeepers, widows, orphans, butchers, carmen, gardeners, market women," a businessman recorded, "even the noted bawd Mrs. McCarty." All business, including that of construction, halted; and "the mechanics began to feel the effect of the failures."[44] Small wonder, then, that a mob of about 400-500 threatened Duer's life at the debtor's jail,[45] or that Republicans "made bitter use" of Hamilton's "attachment to Colonel Duer" in the elections.[46] In the gubernatorial poll of 1792 Clinton ran better than he ever had in the city, receiving 603 votes, to 729 for John Jay, or 44 per cent of the total.[47]

In the Congressional election late in 1792 William Livingston— elected previously as a Federalist Assemblyman—offered the Federalists their first national challenge. "That whore in politics," as a Hamilton's informant called him,[48] Livingston made a special appeal to the Mechanics Society for support, claiming to be responsible for their charter. He was also identified with an unsuccessful appeal to

Lib.; see also Seth Johnson to Andrew Craigie, Jan. 21, 1792, Craigie Papers, III, No. 70, Amer. Antiq. Soc.

42 Reported in Johnson to Craigie, Jan. 22, 1792, *ibid.*, No. 71; see also "Decius," *New York Journal*, Feb. 15, 1792 and a spate of articles, *Daily Advertiser*, Feb. 7-29, 1792, *passim.*

43 See Alexander Hamilton to William Seton, cashier of the Bank of New York, Jan. 18, 24, Feb. 10, Mar. 19, 21, 1791; the quotation is from James Tillary to Hamilton, Mar. 1, 1792, all in Hamilton Transcripts, Col. Univ. Lib.

44 Johnson to Craigie, Mar. 25, Apr. 18, 1792, Craigie Papers, III, Nos. 73, 76. Amer. Antiq. Soc.; *New York Journal*, Mar. 28, 1792.

45 Benjamin Tallmadge to James Wadsworth, Apr. 19, 1792, Wadsworth Papers, Conn. Hist. Soc. and ms. fragment [Apr. 1792], N.Y.C. Misc. ms., Box 14, N.Y. Hist. Soc.

46 James Watson to James Wadsworth, Apr. 3, 1792, Wadsworth Papers, Conn. Hist. Soc. and Johnson to Craigie, Apr. 15, 1792, Craigie Papers, III, No. 75 Amer. Antiq. Soc.

47 *Daily Advertiser*, June 2, 1792.

48 James Tillary to Hamilton, Jan. 14, 1793, Hamilton Transcripts, Col. Univ. Lib.; for Livingston, Wilson, *Memorial History of the City of New York*, III, pp. 79-80.

make New York City's appointive mayor elective.[49] In a cloudy campaign in which party lines were not clearly drawn, Livingston received 700 votes to 1,900 for the successful Federalist, John Watts.[50]

Through these minor political crises, the leaders of the Mechanics Society did not break with the Federalists. They turned down Livingston's plea for support; it was not only "repugnant to their objects to participate in elections," but he was "an improper person."[51] Similarly they refused to endorse Governor Clinton in 1792[52] or Melancton Smith when he successfully sneaked into the Assembly in 1791. In the Spring of 1793 several officers of the Mechanics Society, including Robert Boyd, the radical Whig blacksmith, were still on the Federalist assembly ticket giving the party an easy victory.[53] In short, at the end of the first Washington administration, despite a smouldering discontent with Federalism in the city, mechanics of the substantial sort and mechanics as a whole had not left the house of Federalism.

II

The parting of the ways came in Washington's second term, and the precipitant was Federalist foreign policy. The French Revolution was an initial stimulus in 1793. When the French frigate *L'Embuscade,* did battle with the English man of war *Boston* off Sandy Hook some nine boatloads of New Yorkers went out to cheer the French victory while on the shore fistfights broke out between "Whig" and "Tory" cartmen.[54] The arrival of Citizen Edmund Genêt prompted the first open mass meeting of the decade and a welcoming committee was formed whose secretary was White Matlack, a well-to-do brewer and iron manufacturer.[55] As a young doctor walked through the poor east side section, he heard "a dram shop full of Frenchmen singing 'Carmagnole.' The next shop I came upon some person was singing 'God

[49] *Journal of the Assembly of the State of New York,* 15th sess., 151; "Atticus," *New York Journal,* June 17, 1792.
[50] *New York Journal,* Feb. 20, 1793. Livingston was not endorsed by anti-Federalist or Republican leaders either for Congress or for the Assembly the following spring; see Philip Ten Eyck to John B. Schuyler, Apr. 3, 1793, Schuyler Papers, Misc., N.Y. Pub. Lib.
[51] "General Society Minutes," Jan. 9, 1793; *New York Journal,* Jan. 12, 1793.
[52] See the election committees in *New York Journal,* Feb. 25, Mar. 21, 1792.
[53] *Ibid.,* May 29, June 1, 1793.
[54] Alexander DeConde. *Entangling Alliance: Politics and Diplomacy Under George Washington* (Durham, N.C., 1958), pp. 269-70.
[55] *New York Journal,* Aug. 7, 10, 1793; Rufus King to Alexander Hamilton, Aug. 3, 1793, Charles King, ed., *The Life and Correspondence of Rufus King* (6 vols., New York, 1894-1900), I, p. 493.

Bless Great George' and which immediately procured a parcel of hearty curses upon his majesty from the rest of the company."[56]

Actually it was Britain and not France that proved the real catalyst. By early 1794, because the thin wall of Federalist tariff protection was not holding the line against the competition of British manufactures, craft groups once again dispatched petitions to Congress.[57] Then news of massive British depredations against American ships and of a British threat to renew Indian war electrified all classes; it brought the possibility of war to the state's unprotected frontier and the city's unprotected harbor. Thus Republican proposals—in Congress, Madison's old bill for discrimination against British shipping; in New York, Governor Clinton's demand to fortify the harbor and the Livingstons' strident cry for war—caught full sail the most violent wave of Anglophobia since the Revolution.[58] At a meeting sponsored by Republicans, White Matlack was the principal speaker and mechanics were so prominent that a Federalist satirist derided the "greasy caps" in a mock epic poem. At each good point made by a speaker, he jibed:[59]

> Hats, caps and leathern aprons flew
> And puffs of wondrous size and jerkins blue

In the same flurry of patriotism the city's Democratic Society came into being: its leaders were merchants and lawyers; its members, according to one of them, "are composed of and mingle with every class of citizens"; its meetings, according to a Federalist critic, were attended by "the lowest order of mechanics, laborers, and draymen."[60]

---

[56] Alexander Anderson, "Diary," Jan. 9, 1794, Ms., Columbiana Col., Col. Univ. Lib.; see also entries for July 31, Aug. 8, 1793.

[57] *Annals of Congress*, 3rd Congress 1st sess. Petitions were received from the following New York City artisans: manufacturers of hand bellows (Feb. 3, 417), nail manufacturers (Feb. 21, 458), hatters (Mar. 5, 478). From other cities petitions came from manufacturers of metal buttons, tobacco, hemp, nails, paint, bar iron, glass, hats, and hosiery, 482, 1023, 1131, 432, 256, 475, 452, 453, 456, 523, 522. For support for protection from Tammany, see *New York Journal*, Nov. 27, 1795.

[58] DeConde, *op. cit.*, ch. 3. John C. Miller, *The Federalist Era, 1789-1801* (New York, 1960), ch. 9.

[59] *New York Daily Gazette*, Mar. 4, 1794; "Acquiline Nimblechops," [psued.] *Democracy, An Epic Poem* . . . (New York, 1794), attributed, falsely, I believe, to Brockholst Livingston.

[60] William Woolsey to Oliver Wolcott, Jr., Mar. 6, 1794 cited in Eugene P. Link. *Democratic Republican Societies, 1790-1800* (Columbia Studies in American Culture No. 9, New York 1942), 94; "Address . . . by the Democratic Society of New York," May 28, 1794, Broadside, N.Y. Pub. Lib. Of 43 men known to be members of the Society, a very incomplete number, it has been possible to identify them as follows: merchants, 14; craftsmen, 12; public officials, 2; lawyers, 4; teachers, 2; unidentified, 13. For analysis of the comparable Philadelphia society in which 32.8% were craftsmen, see *ibid.*, pp. 71-73.

A dramatic change in city opinion was apparent in the Spring of 1794 when the Commissioners of Fortifications, headed by Governor Clinton, called for volunteer labor to erect a fort on Governor's Island.[61] For weeks, the Republican paper reported, "hardly a day has passed . . . without a volunteer party of fifty to one hundred" putting in a day's labor.[62] A British visitor described it vividly:

> Marching two and two towards the water side . . . a procession of young tradesmen going in boats to Governor's Island to give the state a day's work . . . drums beating and fifes playing . . . with flags flying. Today the whole trade of carpenters and joiners, yesterday the body of masons; before this the grocers, school masters, coopers and barbers; next Monday all the attorneys and men concerned in the law, handle the mattock and shovel the whole day, and carry their provisions with them.[63]

And of course he could have added more: The Democratic Society, Tammany, the General Society of Mechanics, "all the true Republican carpenters," "the patriotic Republican sawyers," "the patriotic sailmakers"—so they called themselves in the papers—the journeymen hatters, cordwainers, peruke makers, hairdressers, tallow chandlers, tanners and curriers; in short, it was the Constitutional parade of 1788 all over again but under different leadership. And there was also something new: the most recent immigrants to the city styling themselves "Irish laborers," "English Republicans," and the "patriotic natives of Great Britain and Ireland."[64]

The Republicans reaped a political harvest quickly. Early in April 1794, Chancellor Robert R. Livingston advised his younger brother, Edward, not to run again for the Assembly. "The mechanics and cartmen" were Federalist; "I find no class of people on which you can depend."[65] A few weeks later in elections held after the work on the fort had just begun, Federalists won but the Republican vote unexpectedly zoomed from a high of 500 in 1793 to a range of 1,200 to

---

61 "Proceedings of the Commissioners of Fortifications for the City of New York and its Vicinity," (1794-1795), Ms., N.Y. Hist. Soc.

62 *New York Journal*, May 10, 1794.

63 Henry Wansey, *The Journal of an Excursion to the United States of North America in the Summer of 1794* . . . (Salisbury, Eng., 1796), reprinted in Bayrd Still ed. *Mirror for Gotham* (New York, 1956), pp. 65-66. I have changed the order of several sentences.

64 See *New York Journal*, Apr. 26, 30, May 3, 7, 10, 24, 28, June 18, 21, 1794. See also I. N. P. Stokes, comp. *Iconography of Manhattan Isle* (6 vols., New York, 1915-1928), V, 1307.

65 Robert R. to Edward Livingston, Apr. 10, 1794, R. R. Livingston Papers, N.Y. Hist. Soc.

1,400.[66] Then in the Congressional poll of December 1794-January 1795 Edward Livingston risked a race against John Watts, the Federalist incumbent. A lawyer and city resident, a member of the aristocratic Hudson Valley family known as "Beau Ned" (the young dandy),[67] he was presented to the voters as "the poor man's friend," a "good Whig," and "a good Republican and true friend of the French." Watts was described as a "Tory," "a paper man," "an opulent merchant" and "a friend to British measures."[68] The year before, when Livingston ran for the Assembly, he received 214 votes; he now won 1,843 to 1,638.[69]

In this changing climate the General Society of Mechanics and Tradesmen shifted perceptibly. John Stagg, the Clintonian and radical Whig, was returned as President; later he presided at the public meeting at which Livingston was nominated.[70] At its Fourth of July dinner in 1794, the Society toasted "the republican societies of the City of New York"; the following year it accepted an invitation from the Democratic Society for a joint celebration of Independence Day with them, Tammany and the Coopers Society. A committee worked out the details of an observance that was repeated every year thereafter: a parade to a church (militia officers seated in front of the pulpit, the mechanics to the right of the center aisle, the Democrats to the left, Tammany and the Coopers off to either side aisle), a ceremony consisting of the reading of the Declaration of Independence followed by a patriotic oration by a Republican leader.[71] The typical mechanic could now be portrayed in Republican hues: he was, according to a writer in the Republican paper, a hard working man who eschewed high living, opposed the "haughty well born," saved to buy a lot in the suburbs for his old age, and enjoyed a family gathering at home where his children beat time to "Yankee Doodle" and "Carmagnole."[72]

---

[66] New York Journal, June 7, 1794.

[67] William Hatcher, Edward Livingston: Jeffersonian Republican and Jacksonian Democrat (Baton Rouge, 1940), ch. 1; Charles H. Hunt, Life of Edward Livingston (New York, 1964), chs. 1-3.

[68] William Miller, "First Fruits of Republican Organization: Political Aspects of the Congressional Elections of 1794," Penn. Mag. Hist. and Biog. LXIII (1939), 118-43; Young, op. cit., pp. 616-20.

[69] New York Journal, Feb. 7, 1795 cf. to returns, ibid., May 29, June 1, 1793.

[70] New York Journal, Nov. 26, 29, Dec. 3, 1794.

[71] New York Journal, July 5, 1794; "General Society of Mechanics Minutes," June 3, 24, July 1, 1795 and for the seating arrangements, June 7, 1798.

[72] "See to That," New York Journal, Dec. 27, 1794.

Thus, the first Republican breakthrough came in a revival of "The Spirit of 76." Over the next few years Republicans had great difficulty transferring this new strength, which came on a national issue, to state elections.[73] They were also unable to sustain mechanic Republicanism on national questions, as the vicissitudes of the Jay Treaty fight of 1795-96 illustrated. A "town meeting" protesting the treaty was attended by from 5,000 to 7,000 people. It was held at the noon lunch hour when, according to an irate Federalist, "our demogogues always fix their meetings in order to take in all mechanics and laborers—over whom they alone have influence."[74] The poorer workers were especially noticeable: cartmen with their horses, "the hodmen, and the ash men and the clam men," as were recent immigrants—Scotsmen, Irish, English and French.[75] When the vote was taken to damn the Treaty, according to one contemporary, "there was not a whole coat" among them. The Livingstons were "supported by a few of the principal citizens, the rest being made up of men of the lower class." Others claimed, however, that the leaders did not have "a majority of the lower class," or that several hundred sided with Hamilton.[76] By the Spring of 1796, after Washington signed the treaty and Republicans in the House threatened to hold up its enforcement, anti-treaty sentiment faded. Playing on the fear of war and threatening economic coercion, Federalists were able to collect some 3,200 signatures on a pro-Treaty petition.[77] Republicans by contrast turned out less than half of the previous year's opponents at a public rally, one-third of whom, a Federalist charged, "as is usually the case were negroes, sweeps, boys, Frenchmen, and curious people." The "merchants and traders," he insisted, and "the substantial mechanics" backed the Treaty.[78]

The claim was probably justified. In the Congressional election at the end of 1796 James Watson, a wealthy merchant, received the Fed-

---

73 For returns in the 1795 gubernatorial elections, *New York Journal,* June 3, 1795.
74 Benjamin Walker to Joseph Webb, July 24, 1795 in W. C. Ford, ed. *Correspondence and Journals of Samuel Bacheley Webb* (3 vols., New York, 1894), III.
75 Grant Thorburn, *Forty Years Residence in America* . . . (Boston, 1834), 37-40.
76 Seth Johnson to Andrew Craigie, July 23, 1795. Craigie Papers, III, No. 97, Amer. Antiq. Soc.; "Slash," *New York Journal,* July 25, 1795 for the remark about "not a wholecoat;" Benjamin Walker cited in footnote 74.
77 Alexander Hamilton to Rufus King, Apr. 24, 1796, Hamilton Transcripts, Col. Univ. Lib. For pressure by insurance underwriters, "Circular letter by Nicholas Low, Archibald Gracie and Gulian Verplanck, New York, May 3, 1796," Broadside, N.Y. Pub. Lib.
78 William Willcocks, a New York City Federalist Assemblyman, in *Albany Gazette,* May 2, 1796.

eralist nomination after four others had turned it down because, in Hamilton's words, "he had gotten a strong hold of most of the leading mechanics who act with us."[79] Edward Livingston recovered his lost ground to win a second term by a safe margin of 2,362 to 1,812 votes. But his vote, a contemporary accurately put it, came from wards "chiefly inhabited by the middling and poorer classes of the people."[80] Thus at the end of the second Washington administration the city's working population was split: the Federalists retained a good section of the "substantial mechanics" while the Republicans had the "middling and poorer classes" in an unstable constituency.

III

Republicans did not consolidate this foothold until they mastered the art of exploiting the class antagonisms of the poor, threats to the economic interests of particular crafts, and the aspirations of new immigrants.

Poverty in New York went hand in hand with population growth and economic progress.[81] The city, the worldy-wise LaRochefoucauld observed in 1796, "like all great towns contains at once more riches and more wretchedness than towns less populous and commercial."[82] A petition from one group of workers pointed out that "house rent, fuel, provisions and prices of everything necessary for the support of a family have been rising." In the winter of 1796-97 some 600 unemployed journeymen petitioned for public assistance because many "by reasons of large families" were "in want of sufficient fire and wood."[83] For newcomers housing was the worst problem. The upper-east side near the shore—the seventh ward—was the city's worst slum. As a doctor described it, it had "narrow, crooked, flat, unpaved, muddy alleys" filled with swamps, stagnant water, "little decayed wooden huts," some inhabited by several families; all was wafted by an intoler-

79 Hamilton to Rufus King, Dec. 16, 1796, Hamilton Transcripts, Col. Univ. Lib.
80 "Impartial History of the Late Election," New York Journal, Dec. 27, 1796; Argus, Jan. 20, 1797.
81 Pomerantz, op. cit., 199-225; Morris, Government and Labor in Early America, 200 ff.
82 F. A. F. de La Rochefoucauld-Liancourt, Travels Through the United States of America, in the Years 1795, 1796, 1797 (2 vols., London, 1799), II, p. 205.
83 "Petition of the Repackers of Beef and Pork to the State Legislature, Jan. 24, 1795," Misc., Ms., N.Y.C. No. 86, N.Y. Hist. Soc.; "Jehosphapet," [New York] Evening Post, Jan. 14, 1795; "To the Inhabitants of the City of New York," Argus, Jan. 14, 1797.

able stench from garbage piled in the streets, putrefying excrement at
the docks and a tan yard in their midst.[84] Understandably, when a
yellow-fever epidemic claimed 700 lives in the summer of 1795, it was
here that the toll was heaviest.[85]

Discontent bred of such conditions was ready for political exploitation. By 1795 there were 900 more voters in the £100 electorate for a
total of 2,100 but there were 2,300 more 40 shilling renters, or a total
of 5,000. Moreover, the poorer voters were concentrated in the newly-
built parts of town, the fifth and especially the seventh wards along
the East River, and the fourth and especially the sixth to the west
along the North (or Hudson) River. In the seventh, known as the
"cartman's ward," there were 870 40-shilling voters to 311 £100
voters; in the sixth the proportion was 1,298 to 223. Here was the
Republican potential.[86]

The pent-up class feeling erupted in the election of the Spring of
'96 which, as Hamilton put it, "in view of the common people . . .
was a question between the rich and the poor because of the 'vile affair
of whipping Burke and McCredy'."[87] Thomas Burk and Timothy
Crady—Federalists could not get their names straight—were ferrymen,
recent Irish immigrants who got into an altercation with Gabriel Furman, an arrogant Federalist alderman of the wealthy first ward. Accused of the crime of "insulting an alderman" they were tried without
due process before a court of three aldermen and a Federalist Mayor
intent upon making an example of the "impudent rascals," and were
sentenced to two months in jail (Burk got twenty lashes as well).

William Keteltas, a young Republican lawyer, took this case of the
"oppression of the innocent poor" to the State Assembly, demanding
impeachment of the city official.[88] After a Federalist committee exon-
erated them and Keteltas turned his guns on the Assembly, he was
called before the Bar of the House and asked to apologize. He refused

[84] Dr. Elihu Hubbard Smith, "Letters to William Bull . . . on the Fever" in Noah Web-
   ster, Jr., comp., *A Collection of Papers on the Subject of Billious Fevers* (New York,
   1796), pp. 66-74.
[85] Matthew Davis, *A Brief Account of the Epidemical Fevers* (New York, 1796), pp.
   58-67 for a list of the dead, 6, 16-17 for housing. For verification, Dr. Richard
   Bayley, *An Account of the Epidemic Fever* (New York, 1796), 59-66, 122 and
   Argus, Oct. 17, 1795.
[86] See Table 1, in introduction above; for the electoral census of 1795 by wards, see
   Supplement to the *Daily Advertiser*, Jan. 27, 1796.
[87] Hamilton to Rufus King, May 4, 1796, Hamilton Transcripts, Col. Univ. Lib.
[88] For a full account, Young, *op. cit.*, ch. 20; for a brief account, Pomerantz, *op. cit.*,
   pp. 263-68.

and was found guilty of contempt, whereupon the tumultuous crowd that had jammed the Assembly carried him off to jail in a handsome arm chair midst cries of "The Spirit of '76." An issue of class justice had been transformed into one of free speech. After a month of agitation from "the iron gate," Keteltas was released and escorted home by a cheering crowd. That was a Tuesday; on Friday Republicans nominated him as one of their twelve Assembly candidates. When Federalists mocked the "ragamuffins" who paraded for Keteltas, Republicans claimed them as "the men by whose mechanical labours the necessaries and conveniences of life are prdouced in abundance"; it was "such men as these [who] were the triumphant victors at Breed's Hill, at Saratoga, at Yorktown." The Federalists won, but the Republican slate hit its highest peak thus far.[89]

In the September 1796 municipal elections Republicans for the first time capitalized on local issues. The Common Council was in the hands of conservative Federalist merchants elected by a tiny handful of voters.[90] Republicans railed at the Mayor and Council for dispensing arbitrary justice, failing to curb forestalling in the markets, neglecting to keep the streets clean, and increasing expenditures and taxes. They elected two men, both of whom were disqualified on technicalities, then re-elected one of them, Jacob Delamontagnie, a secretary of the Democratic Society, by an even wider margin.[91]

Early in 1797 Republicans took up the cause of a single craft, the seventy-five members of the Association of Tallow Chandlers and Soap Makers, whose factories the state legislature ordered removed from the city proper to the outskirts of towns—on the grounds that their fumes were a cause of epidemic. The chandlers petitioned the Assembly. The Republican Brockholst Livingston became their counsel, and at their request Dr. Samuel Latham Mitchill, the Columbia scientist and Tammany orator, prepared a pamphlet-length treatise exonerating the chandlers' "pestilential vapors," blaming the fever on "septic acid vapors," his favorite theory.[92] The chandler issue boiled

89 *New York Journal*, Apr. 15, 19, 22, especially "A Dialogue Between an Old Tory and a Young Republican," *ibid.*, Apr. 22.
90 Pomerantz, *op. cit.*, pp. 64-76.
91 In the *New York Journal*, "An Elector," Sept. 20; "A Citizen," Sept. 22; "A Freeholder," Sept. 22; and an editorial paragraph, Sept. 29, 1796; for the contested election, Arthur Peterson, ed., *Minutes of the Common Council of the City of New York* (19 vols., New York, 1917), II, pp. 284-86; Pomerantz, *New York*, pp. 120-22.
92 For the petition, Assembly Papers, Box 5, No. 113, New York State Lib.; for news-

through March; in April the Republicans nominated Mitchill for the Assembly on a slate that included a tanner, a hatter, a sailmaker, and the two aldermen elected in the wake of the Keteltas affair. Federalists capitulated, endorsing half the Republican ticket, an unheard of event, and Republicans won their first Assembly election of the decade, their vote ranging between 1,600 and 2,100 to a scant 600 to 700 for the Federalists.[93] In 1800 Dr. Mitchill, the tallow chandlers' hero, was the successful Republican candidate to replace Edward Livingston in Congress.

Republicans also won over another group, the cartmen. Numbering more than 1,000 by 1800, they were known for their "quick tempers" and "mistreating their horses." Normally they chafed under the regulations of the city fathers.[94] In the ferryman affair a doggerel verse on broadside reminded the cartmen of their own trouble with Major Richard Varick:[95]

> He often sits upon a bench
> Much like unto a judge, sir.
> And makes the wretches bosom wrench
> To whom he owes a grudge sir.
>
> But now he does a great offense
> It is no thing to mock at
> He takes away the cartmen's pence
> And puts them in his pocket.

By 1798 the cartmen were Republican enough for the Federalists to gerrymander the outlying seventh ward ("the cartmen's ward") out of the city into the Westchester congressional district. In the 1799 Assembly elections Federalist merchants stood at the polls and "used all their influence with the cartmen" with some success.[96] The next year "Independent Cartman" appealed to his brethren not to submit again to such merchant pressure: who will do the work if not us?

---

paper accounts, *New York Journal,* Feb. 18, 23, Mar. 8, 11, 1797; Samuel L. Mitchill, *The Case of the Manufacturers of Soap and Candles in the City of New State Stated and Examined* (New York, 1797); Mitchill to Robert R. Livingston, June 9, 1797, Misc., ms., N.Y. Hist. Soc.; Livingston to Mitchill, July 18, 1797, R. R. Livingston ms., N.Y. State Lib.

[93] *New York Journal,* June 4, 1797.

[94] Kenneth and Anna M. Roberts, trans. and ed., *Moreau de St. Mary's American Journey (1793-1798)* (New York, 1947), pp. 124-25, and 127, 158-59, 162 for other observations on labor in the city; "Regulations of the Cartmen . . . 1795," Broadside, Lib. of Congress.

[95] "The Strange and Wonderful Account of a Dutch Hog," (New York, 1796), Broadside No. 7765, N.Y. State Lib.; Varick was Dutch for hog.

[96] Peter Jay to John Jay, May 3, 1799, John Jay Papers, Col. Univ. Lib.

"Will their puny clerks carry the burdens which we do?"[97] The cartmen resisted and as a result there were only eighteen cartmen in the
crowd when Hamilton, in 1801, appeared at a meeting of cartmen
and appealed to "my dear fellow citizens."[98]

From the mid-'90s on, Republicans also spoke in clear tones to the
city's new immigrants. Federalists were not without experience in
dealing with nationality groups politically.[99] But to the French, Scots,
English, and especially the Irish recent arrivals who ran up the cost
of charity at the alms house, hated England and allegedly brought in
yellow fever, Federalists were cool or hostile.[100] Republicans, by contrast, formed the "Society for the Assistance of Persons Emigrating
from Foreign Countries." They turned out en masse to welcome
Joseph Priestly and in their press, Irish and Scots could read reports
of struggles for liberty in their native lands.[101] Congressman Livingston, during the xenophobia of 1798 to 1800, eloquently opposed the
Alien Law, even introducing a petition from Irish aliens of New York,
and in the Assembly Aaron Burr fought the proposed constitutional
amendment to bar Federal office to naturalized citizens.[102] The political
fruits fell accordingly. "The poor Irish and French," one Federalist
was convinced, were enough to carry the sixth and seventh wards for
Jefferson in 1800.[103]

IV

In the closing years of the decade Republicans also picked up some
of the issues that from the 1780s on had been of concern to master me-

---

97 "An Independent Cartman," *Republican Watch-Tower*, Apr. 30, 1800 and in the same
   issue "To the Cartmen of New York," "To the Cartmen," by "Eighteen Hundred,"
   and report of a meeting; "Leonidas" *ibid.*, Mar. 14, 1801 claimed that only 1,150 of
   1,500 votes were cast in the 1800 election as a result of threats.
98 "A Cartman," *Republican Watch Tower*, Apr. 25, 1801.
99 To take the Germans as an example: In 1788 Federalists candidates were endorsed "at
   a very numerous meeting of Germans," (*Daily Advertiser*, Apr. 28, 1788); in 1790
   the German Society, claiming to be rebuffed by the merchants, offered support to the
   mechanics' ticket if they nominated a German (*New York Gazette*, Apr. 20, 1790).
100 See Alfred Young, "New York City in the Hysteria of 1798 to 1800" (unpub. Master's
   thesis, Col. Univ., 1947), pp. 92-101.
101 "Society for the Assistance of Persons Emigrating From Foreign Countries . . . June
   30, 1794," Broadside, N.Y. Hist. Soc.; for their constitution, *New York Journal*,
   June 25, 1794 and philosophy, Thomas Dunn, A.M. *A Discourse . . . October 21,
   1794 Before the New York Society . . .* (New York, 1794); for Priestley's Welcome,
   Edgar Smith, *Priestley in America, 1794-1804* (Philadephia, 1920), pp. 21-40.
102 *The Speech of Edward Livingston on the Third Reading of the Alien Bill* (Philadelphia, 1798) also in *New York Journal*, July 14, 1798; *Annals of Congress*, 5th Congress, 1st Sess., Feb. 12, 1799, p. 2884; Schachner, *Aaron Burr*, 152.
103 Phillip Livingston to Jacob Read, Feb. 23, 1801, reprinted in *Col. Univ. Quart.*
   XXIII (June, 1931), p. 200.

chanics. For one, they committed themselves to tariff protection. In the
General Society a committee headed by the Republican sailmaker,
George Warner, drafted a letter lamenting the growth of foreign in-
portations; they were "an influence highly unfavorable to mechanical
improvement, nourishing a spirit of dependence, defeating in a degree
the purpose of our Revolution, and tarnishing the luster of our national
character"—the very language was that used by Federalist mechanics
in 1789.[104] In 1801 a mass meeting of "the mechanics and manufacturers of New York City" sent a memorial to Congress beseeching the
"protecting hand of government."[105] As the reign of Jefferson approached, "A Song for Hatters" expressed the expectations of other
artisans:[106]

> Before the bad English Treaty,
> Which Jay with that nation has made
> For work we need make no entreaty
> All Jours were employed at their trade.
>
> Philadelphia she then had a hundred
> New York she had fifty and more
> In the first scarce the half can be numbered
> In the last there is hardly a score. . . .
>
> And what has occasion'd this failing,
> And caus'd us to fall at this rate
> 'Tis the English, whose arts are prevailing
> With our Great rulers of state. . . .
>
> When shortly in our constitution
> A Republican party will sway
> Let us all then throw in a petition
> Our grievance to do away . . . .

---

104 "General Society of Mechanics Minutes," Jan. 16, Feb. 6, Feb. 20, Mar. 6, Apr. 3,
1799 reprinted in Earle and Congdon. eds., *Annals,* pp. 241-42. The letter was
drafted, agreed to, and reconsidered at a special meeting, then rejected. Thus there
was a division in the society on the question which may also account for the first
recorded contest for officers, Jan. 4, 1800. The fact that George Warner, an active
Republican, was chairman of the drafting committee leaves no doubt as to the
Republican position.
105 *American Citizen,* Mar. 19, Mar. 21, Apr. 10, 1801. George Warner was secretary to
this committee; another petition was sent to the state legislature requesting bounties
for the production of sheep to encourage the wool industries, signed by a number of
Republicans, *American Citizen,* Feb. 14, 1801.
106 "A New Song," by J. C. [James Cheetham, hatter and co-editor of the paper],
Republican Watch-Tower, Feb. 21, 1801; for other evidence of Republican support
for manufactures, Minutes of the Tammany Society, Dec. 1, 1800, ms., N.Y. Pub. Lib.,
for a debate; *Argus,* Nov. 27, 1795 for a Tammany toast; *New York Journal,* Apr.
15, 1797, June 8, 1799.

That our party in Congress may now rule
Let each voter for liberty stir
And not be to England a base tool
When Jefferson aids us and Burr.

Republicans again took up the cause of freer banking facilities. But where the Livingstons' frontal assault of 1792 failed, Aaron Burr in 1799 managed the camouflaged Bank of Manhattan through the legislature with finesse.[107] While the new bank was primarily of concern to aspiring merchants, it is symptomatic of the mechanic interest in credit that some two dozen members of the Mechanics Society were among the charter stock subscribers.[108] The new bank, Republicans boasted, broke the "banking monopoly" and struck a blow at usury, an object of special contempt to many working class patrons of the city's money lenders.[109]

From 1797 on, Republicans also committed themselves clearly to direct representation of master mechanics on their assembly tickets. In 1798 they repeated their success of the previous year by running four artisans on their ticket; in 1799 they ran six new ones. Even the famous all-star slate Aaron Burr assembled for the battle of 1800 had a place on it for George Warner, sailmaker, Ezekial Robbins, hatter, and Phillip Arcularius, tanner.[110]

The inroads Republicans made among mechanics of all types was confirmed by Federalist tactics from 1798-1801. For a while during the "half war" with France and the "reign of terror," Federalists basked in a glow of X.Y.Z. patriotism as some mechanics turned against the Republicans—now the so-called "French party"—just as they had deserted

107 Beatrice Rubens, "Burr, Hamilton and the Manhattan Company," *Polit. Sci. Quart.,* LXXII (1957), 578-607 and LXIII (1958), pp. 100-125.

108 Bank of Manhattan, *A Collection of 400 Autographs Reproduced in Facsimilie from the Signatures of the Original Subscription Book of the Bank of Manhattan* (New York, 1919).

109 *New York Journal,* Jan. 8, Feb. 12, 15, 1800; "Philander, *American Citizen,* Apr. 28, 29, 1800; for a debate, "Minutes of the Tammany Society," Mar. 31, 1800, Ms., N.Y. Pub. Lib.

110 The mechanic candidates on the Republican ticket were: for 1797: Phillip Arcularius, tanner, Ezekial Robbins, hatter, and George Warner, sailmaker; for 1798: Arcularius, Robbins, Arthur Smith, mason and John Wolfe, boot and shoemaker; for 1799; Joshua Barker, manager of an air furnace, Ephriam Brasher, goldsmith, John Brower, upholsterer, Matthew Davis, printer, Benjamin North, carpenter and William Vredenbergh, grocer. For excellent details: Anne B. Seeley, "A Comparative Study of Federalist and Republican Candidates in New York City" (Unpublished master's thesis, Col. Univ., 1959). Of 16 Republican candidates of mechanic background nominated over the entire decade Mrs. Seeley found the tax evaluations of about half of them to be high, e.g., £1200 to 5850 and about half to be low, £100 to 400

the Federalists in 1794-95 as the British party. It was almost a second honeymoon of mechanic and merchant as the Mechanics Society toasted "Millions for defense, not one cent for tribute," Tammany substituted "Yankee Doodle" for "The Marseillaise," and mechanics paraded en masse in Washington's funeral cortege. But the Federalist attitude to Republican mechanics was by this time fatally ambivalent. Besides threatening mechanics with the loss of their jobs, they beat the nativist drums, challenging naturalized aliens at the polls and attempted to suppress the city's two Republican papers. At election time when they sought to woo mechanics, Republicans warned about "the avowed despisers of mechanics who may for a few days intermingle with honest men in order to deceive them."[111] Federalists also voted the poor from the alms house and courted free Negroes with promises of office holding and "enormous supplies of home crackers and cheese."[112] And in the election of 1800 when Hamilton was unable to induce men of "weight and influence" to run, he arranged an Assembly slate filled with unknown artisans: a ship chandler, a baker, a bookseller, a potter, a shoemaker, a leather inspector, and spoiled the image only by including Gabriel Furman "the man who whipped the ferrymen."[113] Federalist tactics thus can only be described as desperate and to no avail. Mechanic interest was unsurpassed in the voting in the Spring of 1800: "all business was suspended, even the workmen deserted the houses they were building";[114] yet Federalists lost the city.

The election returns for 1800 and 1801 indicate that the mechanics were preponderantly Republican yet were divided in their allegiances. The fact that there were two categories of voters—the £100 freeholders alone qualified to vote for Senators and Governor, and the 40 shilling renters allowed to vote only for Assemblymen—enables us to differentiate roughly the voting patterns of the various strata of mechanics. (see Table 3) First, about two thirds of the Republican vote—in 1800, about 2,200 of 3,100 votes; in 1801, 2,400 of 3,600 votes—came from the Assembly voters, the 40 shillings renters who in effect were the poorer mechanics, the cartmen, petty tradesmen and journeymen. Sec-

---

111 *Argus,* Apr. 20, 1799; see James Smith, *Freedom's Fetters. The Alien and Sedition Acts* (Ithaca, N.Y., 1956), pp. 204-220, 385-417; Young, "New York City in the Hysteria of 1798-1800," *passim.*
112 "To a Certain Man," *American Citizen,* Apr. 24, 1801.
113 Matthew L. Davis to Albert Gallatin, Apr. 15, 1800, Gallatin Papers, N.Y. Hist. Soc.; see also Robert Troup to Rufus King, Mar. 9, 1800, in C. King, ed., *Correspondence of Rufus King,* III, pp. 207-08.
114 Peter Jay to John Jay, May 3, 1800, Jay Papers, Col. Univ. Lib.

ondly, about one half of the total Federalist vote came from this same group—in 1800, 1,300 of their 2,600 votes; in 1801, 1,100 of 2,150 votes. Thirdly, Republicans also had significant support among the £100 freeholders who included the master craftsmen—43 per cent or 876 voters in 1800, 54 per cent or 1,266 voters in 1801. As a Republican editor proudly pointed out, this refuted the Federalist contention that Jefferson and Burr were supported only by "persons of no property."[115]

TABLE NO. 3

THE NEW YORK CITY ELECTIONS OF 1800 and 1801

| | 1800 | | | | 1801 | | | |
| | Asssembly | | Senate | | Assembly | | Governor | |
Ward	Rep.	Fed.	Rep.	Fed.	Rep.	Fed.	Rep.	Fed.
1	172	245	47	130	208	222	82	145
2	200	434	74	213	217	375	112	209
3	250	438	75	185	284	365	104	194
4	412	330	124	179	426	274	145	162
5	458	370	139	147	545	313	170	148
6	814	363	187	108	919	267	289	89
7	786	485	231	164	1052	353	364	145
Total vote	3092	2665	877	1126	3651	2169	1266	1090

Sources: for 1800, *American Citizen*, May 5, 1800; for 1801, *Republican Watch-Tower*, May 6, 1801.

Analysis of the returns by wards confirms this political division among both prosperous and poorer mechanics. In the sixth and seventh wards with the greatest proportion of poor voters and recent immigrants, where Republicans made their greatest effort to get out the vote,[116] they received more than half of their total city vote in 1800 and 1801. Yet Federalists also had a following here, 800 voters in 1800, reduced to 600 the following year. By contrast, the second and third wards at the bottom of Manhattan, the centers of the fashionable wealthy merchant residences,[117] through the entire decade gave the

[115] *American Citizen*, May 4, 1801; see also Aaron Burr to William Eustis, Apr. 28, 1801, Eustis Ms., Mass. Hist. Soc.
[116] For 1800 Matthew L. Davis to Albert Gallatin, May 1, 1800, Gallatin Papers, N.Y. Hist. Soc. Notices of meetings: *American Citizen*, Apr. 22, 25, 1800; Peter Jay to John Jay, May 3, 1800. Jay Papers, Col. Univ. Lib., John C. Miller, *Alexander Hamilton*, p. 512.
[117] Wilson, *Memorial History of New York*, III, 150-52, for a list of 250 homes assessed at over £2000 in 1798; Stokes, *Iconography of Manhattan Island*, V, p. 1374; Beard, *Economic Origins*, pp. 382-87, erred in lumping the first with the second and third; it was more mixed; see "Impartial History of the Late Election," *New York Journal*, Dec. 27, 1796, for comment that remains valid for 1800.

Federalists almost a two to one margin. The fourth and fifth wards, the midtown on both the west and east side, which were probably the most "middling" in the city, divided about evenly between the two parties. In 1802 Republicans confirmed the class basis of their support in the poorer wards when they divided the city into two congressional districts. They created their own safe district by placing the sixth and seventh wards in together with the fourth, giving the first, second, third and fifth wards to the Federalists in a district which also included Brooklyn and Richmond. Federalists did not even run a candidate in the Republican district, while Republicans ran one in the Federalist area with "no hopes of success."[118]

By 1800-01 Republican support among mechanics, it is reasonable to hypothesize, came from: 1.) master craftsmen and journeymen in many trades, especially the less prosperous ones; 2.) craftsmen as a whole in trades whose interests Republicans espoused, such as tallow chandlers and shoemakers; 3.) craftsmen in those trades most in need of protection from British manufacturers such as hatters and tanners; 4.) cartmen as a whole; 5.) newer immigrants, especially the Irish,[119] French[120] and to a lesser extent the Scots,[121] and English, 6.) mechanics who had been patriots in the Revolution and responded to the revival of the "Spirit of '76."

The numerically smaller following of the Federalists may well have come from 1.) the more "substantial mechanics" in many trades to whom Hamilton's appeal for the Federalists—as the party that brought "unexampled prosperity"—was meaningful;[122] 2.) craftsmen least in need of protection, such as the building trades; 3.) poorer tradesmen

118 Editorial, *American Citizen*, Apr. 30, 1802.
119 For Republican organizations among the Irish: for the United Irishmen of New York, *Time Piece*, July 6, Aug. 30, 1798 and *Argus*, Mar. 18, 1799; for "Republican Irishmen," *American Citizen*, July, 1800 and July 9, 1801; for Hibernian Provident Society, *Republican Watch Tower*, Mar. 18, 28, 1801; for Hibernian Militia Volunteers, Link, *op. cit.*, p. 184.
120 For the variety of political opinions among the French see F. S. Childs, *French Refugee Life in the United States: An American Chapter of the French Revolution* (Baltimore, 1946), pp. 70-75; *Moreau de St. Mary's American Journey, passim;* for a French newspaper of a Republican cast see George P. Winship, "French Newspapers in the United States from 1790 to 1800," *Bibliographic Society of America Papers*, XIV (1920), pp. 134-47.
121 For the Calendonian Society, decidedly Republican, see [New York] *Evening Post*, Dec. 22, 1794; *Argus*, Dec. 3, 1795; *New York Directory for 1796*, unpaged; for a conservative Scot's observations on the "hot characters" among his fellow migrants, Grant Thorburn, *Forty Years Residence*, pp. 23, 37-40, 92.
122 New York *Commercial Advertiser*, Apr. 11, 1801 and *An Address to the Electors of the State of New York* (Albany, 1801).

most closely dependent on and most easily influenced by merchants, such as the service trades; 4.) American-born mechanics and New England migrants who felt their status threatened by the influx of "foreigners";[123] 5.) new immigrants, anxious to differentiate themselves from their radical countrymen, especially the English;[124] and 6.) mechanics of a loyalist or neutralist background who were made uneasy by the revival of anti-Toryism.

V

The New York Republicans, it should be clear, did not become a labor party. The Clintons, Livingstons and Burrites, and other merchants, landholders, lawyers and office holders ruled the party. Moreover, they had the support of a substantial segment of the merchant community, although not the men at the apex of economic power in the city.[125] Nor did the mechanics become even an organized wing of the party, bargaining for nominations as they had with the Federalists early in the decade. Republicans always found a place for a few mechanics on their twelve-man Assembly slate and for many others on their electioneering committees. Mechanics were members, though not leaders, of the Democratic Society and leaders as well as members of the Tammany Society. George Warner, sailmaker, or Matthew Davis, printer,[126] were speakers at the annual Republican celebration of Independence Day; James Cheetham, a former hatter,[127] was influential as an editor and pamphleteer; and early in the 1800s a number of tanners were active enough to win a reputation as the "tannery yard clique" and "the swamp clique." But there was no assertive workingmen's faction among the Republicans as there would be in the Jacksonian era.[128] And me-

---

[123] See the toasts of a "Yankee Fraternity," *Daily Advertiser,* July 10, 1798.

[124] For a short-lived Federalist paper founded by a recent English migrant, John Mason Williams, see [New York] *Columbian Gazette* (April 4-June 22, 1799), especially the prospectus April 6 and valedictory, June 22.

[125] Alfred Young, "The Merchant Jeffersonians: New York as A Case Study," (unpub. paper delivered before the Miss. Valley Hist. Ass'n., Apr., 1954).

[126] Matthew Davis, while best known as Burr's amanuensis for *Memoirs and Correspondence of Aaron Burr,* was a printer, publisher of the short-lived [New York] *Evening Post* (1795), then co-publisher of [New York] *Time Piece* (1797). He was active in Tammany and the Mechanics Society, was the Independence Day orator in 1800, and the organizer of the Society for Free Debate (1798).

[127] James Cheetham, a recent English immigrant and a hatter by trade, became co-editor of *American Citizen* and *Republican Watch-Tower* (1801-ff), a leading pamphleteer and the first biographer of Thomas Paine (1809).

[128] Frank Norcross, *History of the New York Swamp* (New York, 1901), 8-11; Lee Benson, *The Concept of Jacksonian Democracy: New York as a Test Case* (Princeton, 1961); Walter Hugins, *Jacksonian Democracy and the Working Class: A Study of the New York Workingman's Movement, 1829-1837* (Stanford, 1960).

chanic support was as much the product of the courting by Republican politicians as it was of the demands of the labor movement.

Nor were Republicans put to the severe test of choosing between wage workers and master craftsmen in labor disputes. Republicans, it is apparent, were sympathetic to the craft organizations. They celebrated the Fourth with the Mechanics and Coopers Societies, pleaded the cause of the Association of Tallow Chandlers, and opposed the use of prison labor to manufacture shoes, an issue close to the hearts of cordwainers.[129] While there were a few strikes late in the decade, there was no trial of "a combination of labor" as "a criminal conspiracy" until 1809-10.[130]

Nonetheless Republican thought was unmistakably shaped by the party's mechanic constituency. There was, to be sure, a tinge of agrarianism to some Republicans: a glorification of the yeomanry among the upstate anti-Federalist leaders; an idealization of the rural virtues in the aristrocratic landholder Robert R. Livingston[131] (who signed his newspaper articles "Cato"); a contempt for the hateful city in the poet-editor, Philip Freneau.[132] But, understandably, Chancellor Livingston, who fearfully vetoed the Mechanics Society charter in 1785, praised the aggressive tallow chandlers in 1797 as "those respectable and useful citizens."[133] By the late 1790s, when Republican writers analyzed the political alignment of social classes, they found a place for mechanics in the Republican coalition. The concept might be that "farmers and mechanics & co" were the "laborers, men who produce by their industry something.to the common stock of commodity" opposed by the unproductive classes,[134] or it might be that "farmers, merchants, mechanics and common laboring men" have a "common interest" against "the great landholders and monied men."[135] The General Society of Mechanics and Tradesmen, for its part, found a place for a picture of a plowman on its membership certificate side by side with a house

129 "A Shoemaker," *American Citizen*, Apr. 23, 1801; "To the Shoemakers," *Republican Watch-Tower*, Apr. 22, 1801; "A Shoemaker to the Journeymen Shoemakers," *ibid.* Apr. 25; Report of the Commissioners of the Prison, *Albany Register*, Mar. 3, 1801.
130 Richard Morris, "Criminal Conspiracy and Early Labor Combinations in New York," *Polit. Sci. Quart.*, LVII (1937), pp. 51-85.
131 Robert R. Livingston, "Address to the Agricultural Society of the State of New York," *New York Magazine*, VI (Feb., 1795), pp. 95-102.
132 Lewis Leary, *That Rascal Freneau. A Study in Literary Failure* (New Brunswick, N.J., 1941), pp. 260-65, 275.
133 Robert R. Livingston to Samuel L. Mitchill, July 18, 1797, Livingston Ms., N.Y. State Lib.; for the veto see note 16 above.
134 "To Farmers, Mechanics and other Industrious Citizens," *Time Piece*, May 14, 1798.
135 "Scrutator," *New York Journal*, Apr. 19, 1797.

carpenter and a shipwright, all beneath a slogan "By Hammer and Hand All Arts Do Stand."[136]

Perhaps the New York Republican leaders, who were neither agrarian-minded nor commercial-minded in the strict sense, will be best understood as spokesmen for productive capital. Three of the four merchant presidents of the Democratic Society, for example, invested in such productive ventures as a linen factory, a thread factory, a mine and spermaceti candle works.[137] Chancellor Livingston, who is well known for promoting the steamboat, also experimented with manufacturing paper and reducing friction in millstones. "Mechanicks is my hobby horse," he told Joseph Priestley.[138] He was the President and Samuel L. Mitchill the Secretary of the Society for the Promotion of Agriculture Arts and Manufactures. Mitchill was also a pioneer in industrial chemistry, and sympathized with the goal of protection for American manufactures. He congratulated Hamilton on his "Report on Manufactures" in 1792; as Republican chairman of the House Committee on Commerce and Manufactures, in 1804 he sponsored a tariff program.[139]

New York Republicans also took up the social reforms favored by their mechanic constituents. Tammany, for example, at one dinner toasted in succession "the speedy abolition" of slavery, "a happy melioration of our penal laws" and "the establishment of public schools."[140] William Keteltas, the hero of the ferrymen's *cause célèbre*—when incarcerated in the debtor's prison—edited a paper, *Prisoner of Hope,* which pleaded the debtor's plight.[141] Edward Livingston, in his first

136 Lamb, "The Career of a Beneficent Enterprise," *op. cit.;* a membership certificate is on exhibit at the General Society, New York City.

137 Henry Rutgers established a "bleach-field and thread manufactory" (*Daily Advertiser,* May 12, 1791); James Nicholson was chairman of the New York Manufacturing Society (*New York Directory for 1790,* p. 135) and was interested in a textile venture (Joseph Garlick to Nicholson, Mar. 15, 1798, Misc. Ms., Nicholson, N.Y. Hist. Soc.); Solomon Simpson had an interest in the New York Iron Manufacturing Company, was part owner of a lead mine and a founder of the American Minerological Society and co-owner of a spermaceti candle factory (Morris Schappes, "Anti-Semitism and Reaction, 1795-1800" *Pubs. of the American Jewish Hist. Soc.* XXVIII, Part 2 [Dec., 1948], 115-16).

138 Dangerfield, *op. cit.,* pp. 284-289.

139 Lyman C. Newall, "Samuel Latham Mitchill," *Dictionary of American Biography,* VII, pp. 69-70; Mitchill to Hamilton, Dec. 3, 1792, Hamilton Transcripts, Col. Univ. Lib.; Joseph Dorfman, *The Economic Mind in American Civilization, 1606-1865* (New York, 1946), I, pp. 324-25.

140 *New York Journal,* "Extraordinary" page, Dec. 6, 1794; for the Mechanics Society reform sentiment see "Minutes of the General Society" July 1, 1795.

141 *Forlorn Hope,* Mar. 24-Sept. 13, 1800; for a rival debtor's paper also edited by a Republican, see *Prisoner of Hope,* May 3-Aug. 23, 1800.

term in Congress, began the reform of the criminal code, a subject that would become a life-long concern.[142] Contrary to the contention of some historians, Republicans also lent active support to abolition.[143] Reform was bi-partisan and several measures came to fruition when John Hay was governor, but the urban Republicans imparted a warm humanitarianism to a frosty anti-Federalism and a crusading egalitarian flavor to the genteel philanthropic humanitarianism of the city's merchants and ministers. Equally important Republican orators instilled the environmentalist concepts of the enlightenment that justified a permanent program of reform.[144]

Neither mechanics nor Republicans made much of an issue of political reform, especially during George Clinton's long tenure as governor from 1777-95. The restrictive suffrage provisions in the state constitution and its unique Council of Appointment and Council of Revision were occasionally discussed but not widely protested.[145] Typically, when Tunis Wortman examined the question of abolishing the property qualification to vote, in his political treatise of 1800, the city's leading democratic theorist contented himself with summarizing the pros and cons and ended by saying the question was "not decided."[146] In 1801, when Republicans sponsored the first constitutional revision convention, they permitted universal male suffrage in the election of delegates, but restricted the convention itself to reforming the Council of Appointment.[147]

After 1801, their mechanic constituency cautiously beckoned the Republicans towards reform on the municipal level where only freeholders of £20 or more were permitted to vote for Aldermen and the Mayor was appointed. For a while Republicans were content to broaden suffrage in their own way. Wortman as county clerk was

---

142 *Annals of Congress,* 4th Cong., 1st Sess., pp. 254-55, 257, 304-07, 1394.
143 See Young, "Democratic Republican Movement," pp. 768-69.
144 Tunis Wortman, *An Oration on the Influence of Social Institutions Upon Morals and Human Happiness . . . before the Tammany Society May 12, 1795* (New York, 1796); and DeWitt Clinton, *An Oration on Benevolence Delivered before the Society of Black Friars . . . November 10, 1794* (New York, 1795).
145 I saw no signs of interest in suffrage reform in the Minutes of the Mechanics or Tammany, the toasts offered at their celebrations or in the expressions of the Democratic Society; for pro universal suffrage articles in *Time Piece:* "On Some of the Principles of American Republicanism," May 5, 1797; "Political Creed," Aug. 21, 1797; "Communication," Oct. 6, 1797; and "Universal Justice," Nov. 10, 1797.
146 Tunis Wortman. *Treatise Concerning Political Enquiry and the Liberty of the Press* (New York, 1800), pp. 195-97.
147 Jabez Hammond. *History of Political Parties in the State of New York* (2 vols., Cooperstown, 1846), I, ch. 6.

observed "running to the poll with the books of the Mayor's court under his arm, and with a troop of ragged aliens at his tail." He was also one of the organizers of "faggot voting," a process by which a group of propertyless Republicans were qualified to vote by the joint temporary purchase of a piece of real estate.[148] When the courts ruled out faggot voting, Republicans demanded that the voting qualifications be lowered at least to the 40 shilling leasehold requirement in Assembly elections; they also asked for the elimination of plural voting and voice voting and for the popular election of the Mayor.[149] By 1804 they won all but the last of these demands.[150]

It might be argued that Republicans did more within the framework of the existing political institutions to provide a greater place for mechanics. Like the old anti-Federalists, Republicans were generally distrustful of the wealthy. Unlike the anti-Federalists, who had confidence only in the yeomanry, Republicans included a role for mechanics among the *Means for the Preservation of Political Liberty,* as George Warner entitled his oration. The trouble, as this sailmaker put it, was that "tradesmen, mechanics, and the industrious classes of society consider themselves of too little consequence to the body politic."[151] Republicans defended the right of mechanics to scrutinize political affairs in "self-created" societies and to instruct their representatives at "town meetings." When Federalists mocked such pretensions, Republicans delighted in taunting them with their own epithets, signing their newspaper articles "one of the swinish multitude" or "only a mechanic and one of the rabble." Republicans also upheld the election of mechanics to public office against Federalist scoffers who "despise mechanics because they have not snored through four years at Princeton."[152]

The mechanic vote and viewpoint guaranteed that Republicans, in their political philosophy, would abandon the old anti-Federalist suspicion of the Constitution. For converts from Federalism like the Livingstons there was never any problem. Other Republicans straddled the constitutional question: Keteltas said he was "neither a Federal

---

148 John Wood, *A Full Exposition of the Clintonian Faction* (Newark, 1802), 20-21; Pomerantz, *op. cit.,* pp. 208, 134.

149 James Cheetham, *Dissertation Concerning Political Equality and the Corporation of New York* (New York, 1800).

150 Pomerantz, *op. cit.,* 133-145; Chilton Williamson, *American Suffrage From Property to Democracy 1760-1860* (Princeton, 1960), pp. 161-64.

151 George Warner. *Means for the Preservation of Public Liberty . . . delivered before the Mechanics, Tammany, Democratic and Coopers Societies, July 4, 1797* (New York, 1797), pp. 12-13.

152 *Argus,* Apr. 8, 1799.

nor anti-Federal."[153] Wortman, however, was tempted to revert to the old anti-Federalist view, and to indict the Federalists of '98. He began to collect materials for a book that would expose "the secret convention of 1787 and its members . . . , [and the] intrigues and artifices made use of, for the purpose of compelling the adoption of the constitution." But the book that appeared in 1800—Wortman's *Treatise Concerning Political Inquiry and the Liberty of the Press*—was a libertarian disquisition devoted to the Constitution and Bill of Rights.[154] Republicans could hardly have done otherwise, for their mechanic supporters were men who had paraded for the Constitution in 1788 or had since migrated to the new democracy in order to seek its blessings. To George Warner, the sailmaker and soldier, "the same American spirit which animated to the contest the heroes of the Revolution" prevailed in directing the national convention of '87 to the constitutional establishment of the liberty we at this day enjoy."[155] Thus the city's Republicans, like the mechanics, were both nationalistic and democratic in their outlook.

And now to return to the question posed in the introduction as to the character and continuity of the political conflict between the years 1774 and 1801. Beyond any question, in the 1790s the mechanics were important in New York City politics. Charles Beard's observation that "neither the Republicans nor the Federalists seem to have paid much attention to capturing the vote of the mechanics" was based on inadequate evidence. In the effort to construct the party conflict as one of "agrarianism" vs "capitalism," Beard did not allow a sufficient place for the mechanics to whom even Jefferson referred sympathetically as "the yeomanry of the city."[156] Carl Becker's projection of the conflict of the 1760s into the 1790s was misleading in another way.

---

[153] "A Dialogue Between 1776 and 1796," *New York Journal*, Jan. 29, 1796.
[154] Tunis Wortman to Albert Gallatin, Feb. 12, 1798, Gallatin Papers, N.Y. Hist Soc. For the book see Leonard Levy, *Legacy of Suppression, Freedom of Speech and Press in Early American History.* (Cambridge, Mass., 1960), pp. 283-89.
[155] Warner, *Means for the Preservation*, pp. 9, 19; in the same pro-constitution vein see Samuel L. Mitchill, *An Address . . . July 4, 1799* (New York, 1800), pp. 7, 20; Matthew L. Davis. *An Oration . . . July 4, 1800* (New York, 1800), 15; for a hint of the old anti-Federalist attitude, George Eacker, *An Oration . . . July 4, 1801* (New York, 1801), pp. 10-11, all delivered before the several societies.
[156] Beard, *op. cit.*, p. 466; Jefferson to Thomas Mann Randolph, May 6, 1793, Paul L. Ford, ed., *The Writings of Thomas Jefferson* (10 vols., New York, 1892-1899), VI, p. 241.

The implication of the continuity of mechanic allegiances—radical Whig to anti-Federalist to Jeffersonian—is insupportable. Mechanics who clearly were Federalist in 1788 remained safely Federalist until 1794 and the substantial mechanics a good deal longer, many of them through 1801 and beyond. Mechanics did not always behave as one unified class in politics. Nor can the Republicans be understood as a mechanic party if that was Becker's implication.

And yet Becker's thesis remains attractive. There was an intense struggle in New York City in the 1790s for "who shall rule at home," and if not strictly a class conflict, within it were the elements of a clash between "the privileged and the unprivileged" involving the mechanics as Becker suggested. The plot, dialogue and even character types of the 1790s bear a striking resemblance to the drama of the pre-Revolutionary era. Once again the battle cry that stirred the mechanics was British policy, the cause was American Independence, and the ideology was patriotism or "the spirit of '76." Other insistent mechanic demands thread through the last three decades of the century: for democratic participation, for social recognition, for protection for American manufactures. The new leaders of the 1790s, the Livingstons, resumed something of their pre-war position as aristocratic republicans at the head of the "popular party." The new mechanics' hero of the late 1790s, William Keteltas, was Alexander McDougall of 1769 all over again, a second "John Wilkes of America." The methods, too, were similar: the town meetings, the popular political societies, the churning printing presses. The symbolism of the July Fourth celebration perhaps completes the picture. Thus Jeffersonian Republicans of New York City, with due allowance for the rhetoric of politics, could claim that they were heirs to the "spirit of '76" and that the "revolution of 1800" was indeed the consummation of the Revolution of 1776.

5

Should Labor Have Supported Jackson?; Or Questions the Quantitative Studies Do Not Answer

EDWARD PESSEN

Twenty years ago I joined a number of my colleagues in Richard B. Morris's seminars in testing the validity of the labor thesis that had recently been put forward by Arthur M. Schlesinger, Jr.[1] Our approach to the problem was first to try to identify the working-class districts in such cities as Philadelphia, New York, Boston, and Newark, and then to consult the electoral data in order to determine the voting preferences of the laboring poor. In showing that most working men appeared to have voted against Andrew Jackson in most elections, we believed we were refuting Mr. Schlesinger's labor thesis.[2]

Schlesinger's *Age of Jackson* had argued that Jacksonian Democracy owed its success to the electoral support it received from urban working classes as well as to its following among the nation's yeomanry. Other features of the labor thesis were being challenged at the time by studies which questioned the authenticity of several of the Democracy's self-styled "labor" champions, Old Hickory's alleged sympathy for labor, and the closeness of the ties between Jacksonian Democracy and organized workingmen's groups.[3] Innocent as we were in the ways of statistical

---

*Paper presented at the Annual Meeting of the Organization of American Historians, April 18, 1969, in Philadelphia.

[1] Arthur M. Schlesinger, Jr. *The Age of Jackson* (Boston, 1945).

[2] William A. Sullivan, "Did Labor Support Andrew Jackson?" *Political Science Quarterly,* LXII (Dec. 1947), 569-580; Milton J. Nadworny, "New Jersey Workingmen and the Jacksonians," *Proceedings of the New Jersey Historical Society,* LXVII (July 1949), 185-198; *Walter Hugins, Jacksonian Democracy and the Working Class* (Stanford, 1960), 203-218; and Edward Pessen, "Did Labor Support Jackson?: the Boston Story," *Political Science Quarterly,* LXIV (June 1949), 262-274.

[3] Joseph Dorfman, "The Jackson Wage-Earner Thesis," *American Historical Review,* LIV (January 1947), 296-306; Richard B. Morris, "Andrew Jackson Strikebreaker," *ibid.,* LV (October 1949), 54-68; and Edward Pessen, "The Workingmen's Movement of the Jacksonian Era," *Mississippi Valley Historical Review,* XLIII (December 1956), 428-443.

Reprinted from *Labor History* 13 (Summer 1972), 427-37. Paper presented at the Annual Meeting of the Organization of American Historians, April 18, 1969, in Philadelphia.

procedure, our conclusions as to how workers voted were less than definitive.[4] Yet it appeared that we had either refuted the labor thesis in its entirety or at the least addressed ourselves to answering every question it had raised. There was one question we had overlooked, however. It happened to be the most interesting and important question Mr. Schlesinger had asked — one which he, of course, answered in the affirmative. The question· was: "*Should* labor have supported Jackson?"

It is not hard to understand why so many of us have bypassed this problem and others like it. Such questions are extremely difficult to answer. Even to discuss them sensibly requires vast and detailed knowledge of the actual policies of the Jacksonian or whatever other Administration is under consideration. Such knowledge cannot be confined to measures directly related to labor or to the economic interests of labor. Working men, like men of other classes, are affected significantly by policies that may be devoid of economic content. Only a most crude economic determinism would insist that labor's true interest in a given political act be measured by a type of hedonistic calculus which would establish whether the act in question moved toward maximizing wages, minimizing hours, or optimizing conditions. Young scholars will understandably hesitate before tackling a job they may modestly doubt that they have the erudition to handle.

Their older brethren may find such questions too likely to evoke a subjective response. We of this age of relativism know better than did our comrades of an earlier, more optimistic era that honest men will never agree as to what was good for labor or for any other economic or social class. Some of us may be suspicious, too, of any historical study that appears lacking in clinical detachment. In speaking of the past, ministers and moralists advise men what they ought to have done. Historians tell men what they did and — if with less certainty — why they did it and to what effect.

For whatever the reasons, many Jacksonian scholars then and now have preferred to deal with questions that can be answered by head counts. Such projects are satisfying in a number of ways. They are rela-

---

[4] Robert T. Bower observed that my own study had failed to note that Jackson's voting support in wards of low assessed valuation of property had steadily increased; "Note on 'Did Labor Support Jackson?: the Boston Story,'" *Political Science Quarterly*, LXV (September 1950), 441-444. Bower himself did not see that the Jackson vote also rose in wealthy wards. Using only the factor of assessed valuation, Bower failed to establish a significant correlation, let alone a causal relationship, between wards of low assessment and a preference for Jackson, to support his contention that the Boston evidence showed that labor did support Old Hickory.

tively easy to do. They may take a lot of time and also help induce blindness, yet they are not mentally taxing, certainly not for that stage in which the researcher proceeds to tick off the evidence of whatever it is he is looking for. When the evidence is new, each additional piece of it adds to the sense of worth felt by the man accumulating it. For he knows that he is doing something no one else before him has ever done. Modest though his contribution may be, it is beyond argument a contribution. The data are hard, their usefulness certain, there to serve other historians, whatever their persuasion. Where insights or interpretations may have undeserved reputations in their own time and be dismissed later as pretentious nonsense, the table of objective evidence on the voting or other behavior of this or that class will stand impervious to the ravages of time, its value intact. And where the research designs have been sensible, empirical evidence has often provided answers of the highest historical value. Earl Hamilton's innovative discussion of the early modern world's "price revolution" was based on the list he compiled of the changing prices paid for certain goods by a few hospitals in Spain.

Fritz Redlich has said of the "new economic history" — the at times forbidding and esoteric blending of econometrics and traditional economic history devised a little over a decade ago by *enfants terribles* in and out of the Harvard Graduate School of Economics — that it not only measures but that it *comprehends* by measuring. This is not necessarily an indictment. Where the data speak clearly someone obviously has had the sense to ask a good question.

Jacksonian issues have been illuminated in recent years by quantitative studies. There is nothing new in such studies, of course. Charles Beard did them. His contemporaries, Arthur C. Cole and Dixon Ryan Fox, relied heavily on them in their fruitful investigations of the Whig Party in the South, and the political parties of New York State in the Jacksonian era.[5] The something new in the work of such modern researchers as Charles G. Sellers, Jr., Grady McWhiney, John Vollmer Mering, Lee Benson, and Thomas B. Alexander and his associates, who have gone over the same ground examined by Cole and Fox, is how much more painstaking the newer investigators have been.[6] In a sense,

---

[5] Charles A. Beard, *An Economic Interpretation of the Constitution of the United States* (New York, 1913); Arthur C. Cole, *The Whig Party in the South* (New York, 1914); Dixon Ryan Fox, *The Decline of Aristocracy in the Politics of New York, 1801-1840* (New York, 1919).

[6] Thomas B. Alexander, Kit C. Carter, Jack R. Lister, Jerry C. Oldshue, and Winfred G. Sandlin, "Who Were the Alabama Whigs?" *Alabama Review*, XVI (January 1963),

the fundamental methodology of recent times continues to be what it was a half century ago. Heads are still being counted — if in greater numbers and according to a system of classification that divides or breaks them down into many more subgroups than was the case earlier. It would be carrying relativism too far to regard the contemporary methodology as merely a function of a transitory age preoccupied with the computer, an age whose ways are doomed to be superseded. It seems clear that the modern method is not only different from but superior to the old. Some of the questions it has asked may be less sweeping than were older ones but the answers are more firmly grounded in reality. Much of the most important new information we have acquired about the Jacksonian era since the end of World War II is the product of the new empiricism.

For an age many of whose scholars seem convinced that they have sharply repudiated Beard's simplistic equation of men's economic holdings with their political beliefs, we continue to show an amazing interest in the wealth and social status of party leaders. Detailed investigations have been conducted into the socio-economic backgrounds and positions of congressional representatives, national figures, top- and middle-grade major party leaders in the states, municipal candidates, and even municipal poll watchers. As might have been expected, the evidence has revealed variations in the situation of party activists. Florida's top Whigs were somewhat wealthier than their Jacksonian counterparts. A similar distinction prevailed in Missouri. In the latter State large slaveowners were decisively Democratic, tavern keepers overwhelmingly so. The burden of the modern studies, however, is the marked similarity in status as well as the atypical wealth enjoyed by leaders of the Whig and Jacksonian parties.[7] The traditional belief that Jacksonian civil service appointees

---

5-19; Thomas B. Alexander, Peggy Duckworth Elmore, Frank M. Lowery, Mary Jane Pickens Skinner, "The Basis of Alabama's Ante-Bellum Two-Party System," *ibid.*, XIX (October 1966), 243-276; Charles G. Sellers, "Who Were the Southern Whigs?" *American Historical Review*, LIX (January 1954), 335-346; Grady McWhiney, "Were the Whigs a Class Party in Alabama?" *Journal of Southern History*, XXIII (November 1957), 510-522; John Vollmer Mering, *The Whig Party in Missouri*, (Columbia, 1967); and Lee Benson, *The Concept of Jacksonian Democracy: New York as a Test Case* (Princeton, 1961).

7 Among the studies that make these points are Arthur W. Thompson, *Jacksonian Democracy on the Florida Frontier* (Gainesville, 1961); Mering, *op. cit.;* Benson, *op. cit.*, Herbert Doherty, *The Whigs of Florida* (Gainesville, 1961); Alexander and associates, "Who Were the Alabama Whigs?"; McWhiney, "Were the Whigs a Class Party in Alabama?"; William B. Hoffman, *Andrew Jackson and North Carolina Politics* (Chapel Hill, 1958); Paul Murray, *The Whig Party in Georgia, 1825-1853* (Chapel Hill, 1948); Herbert Ershkowitz, "New Jersey Politics During the Era of Andrew Jackson, 1820-1837," (New York University Doctoral Dissertation, 1965); Edwin A. Miles, *Jacksonian Democracy in Mississippi* (Chapel Hill, 1960); Harry R. Stevens, *The Early*

were typically commoners has also been exposed as a myth by a diligent empiricist.[8]

These modern disclosures demolish the old notion that the party of Clay was commanded by an aristocracy of wealth, in contrast to a Democracy led by plebeians: one more point scored against the old Progressive version of Jacksonian politics and its Schlesingerian supplement. If, however, the political beliefs and actions of individuals are not determined by their material situations, how much is our understanding of politics enhanced by new socio-economic information concerning the status of party leaders?

Not that such evidence is irrelevant. That the leaders of Caesar's party were neither of the partriciate nor the poor, is important information. Insight into the nature of that or any other party is deepened by familiarity with the kind of social or economic types who composed it. If Beard is passé, it is not because economic factors have lost their significance. Skepticism is due rather to his thin research, the *excessive* importance he attributed to wealth as a clue to political behavior, and his doctrinaire dedication to a particular interpretation of the significance of mercantile as against landed wealth. While an individual's wealth may not determine his politics, the political behavior of a group whose members share a similar economic situation, is influenced by that situation. Any historian under the impression that economic factors can now be discounted as an influence on voting because many studies indicate that voters' denominational or other non-economic affiliations seemed more decisive than economic factors in accounting for their voting behavior, is laboring under a false impression. That the correlation between a given group's religious characteristics and its political choice is greater than the correlation between its economic status and its voting habits, does not preclude the possibility that the group's electoral preference was due in part to economic considerations in the minds of its members.

Socio-economic data on party leaders remains valuable. Yet it does not answer the most important questions about party: what was the nature of the party's *behavior?* what principles were revealed by the party's *actions?* what was the *consequence* of these actions?

Jacksonian Party in Ohio (Raleigh, 1957); and Milton Henry, "Summary of Tennessee Representation in Congress from 1845 to 1861," *Tennessee Historical Quarterly,* X (June 1951), 140-148.

[8] Sidney H. Aronson, *Status and Kinship in the Higher Civil Service: Standards of Selection in the Administration of John Adams, Thomas Jefferson, and Andrew Jackson* (Cambridge, 1964).

Joel Silbey has painstakingly gathered evidence on the voting behavior of Whig and Democratic Congressmen for the decade after 1841.[9] Silbey shows — if it needed showing — that head counts can be applied to party actions as well as to the status of the actors. It is no criticism of his valuable contribution to note that it settles for reporting the congressional votes. Its modest attempt at historical evaluation is confined essentially to noting that party loyalty better than sectional interest explains the major party voting blocs that developed in response to the issues of the day.

The historical method that counts heads has been applied most widely to the study of voting behavior. We have studied the voting of the rich and the poor, and as a sign of our growing emancipation from Marx and Beard and our fascination for Freud and Jung, have lately taken to measuring the political choices of distinctive personality types. Lee Benson and his able graduate student, Ronald P. Formisano, breaking away from the earlier preoccupation with the socio-economic status of voters, have drawn correlations between particular ethnic groups, religious denominations, and men of unique life style, on the one hand, and Whig or Democratic voting, on the other, for New York State and Wayne County, Michigan.[10] Richard P. McCormick's quantitative studies of voting have shown that Andrew Jackson's candidacy attracted no particularly mighty outpouring of voters to the polls. His investigation of New York and North Carolina elections during the Jacksonian era demonstrates that voters in these states did not vote by class: poorer voters were divided in their party preferences almost precisely as were their wealthier neighbors.[11] In a number of other states, certain counties in election after election reported exactly the same distribution of votes between the major parties despite changes in the socio-economic situation within the counties. The unchanging party voting percentages obviously downgrade the significance of voters' material conditions as explanation of their electoral choices.

John Vollmer Mering and Donald B. Cole have used electoral statis-

[9] Joel H. Silbey, *The Shrine of Party: Congressional Voting Behavior, 1841-1852* (Pittsburgh, 1967)

[10] Benson, *op. cit.;* Ronald P. Formisano, "The Social Bases of American Voting Behavior, Wayne County, Michigan, 1837-1852, As a Test Case" (Wayne State University Doctoral Dissertation, 1966).

[11] Richard P. McCormick, "New Perspectives on Jacksonian Politics," *American Historical Review,* LXV (January 1960), 288-301; and McCormick, "Suffrage Classes and Party Alignments: A Study in Voter Behavior," *Mississippi Valley Historical Review,* XLVI (December 1959), 397-410. Also see Charles G. Sellers, "The Equilibrium Cycle in Two Party Politics," *Public Opinion Quarterly,* XXIX (Spring 1965), 16-38.

tics from Missouri and New Hampshire, respectively, to draw detailed portraits of the kind of county that was either attracted to or alienated by the Democracy. Economics had much to do with it but the choice of party was not a simple function of a community's wealth or poverty. Closeness to rivers; ties with other communities; the presence of a number of churches, particularly those of evangelical tendency; a sizable population; an educated citizenry; a general atmosphere of vitality — these and not "aristocratic" leanings or wealth per se — were the characteristic traits of anti-Jacksonian towns.[12] And, of course, a number of us, Mr. Cole included, have disclosed that workers showed no special attachment to the party of the Hero.

Rich men, on the other hand, were heavily anti-Jacksonian. It had been surmised that the more or less equal wealth enjoyed by the leaders of New York's Democratic and Whig parties indicated that New York's men of wealth were equally divided in their political preferences. Frank Otto Gatell has recently indicated that this was not so for New York City.[13] The overwhelming preference shown by rich men in the Metropolis for Whiggery by no means demonstrates that overwhelming fears of the Democracy accounted for it. Yet any correlation between wealth and Whig voting appears to confirm an earlier view of Jacksonian parties. On the other hand, New York City was not the whole country. According to Alexandra McCoy, one of Lee Benson's students, Wayne County's rich men were pro-Whig by a much smaller margin than were New York's plutocracy. In Michigan the evangelical religion of substantial men was found a much surer clue to their Whiggery than was their wealth.[14]

These studies of voting are for the most part of high value. It is in no sense a criticism of them to suggest, however, that they leave important things unsaid. That moralistic types opposed the Jacksonian party does not explain why they did so. Interestingly, in opposition to the explanation that the anti-Jacksonian voting of wealthy evangelicals was due more to their religious beliefs than to their social position, the leading student of the Protestant "Benevolent Empire" attributes the political

---

[12] Donald B. Cole, "The Presidential Election of 1832 in New Hampshire," *Historical New Hampshire*, XXI (Winter 1966), 32-50; Mering, *op. cit.*

[13] Frank Otto Gatell, "Money and Party in Jacksonian America: A Quantitative Look at New York City's Men of Quality," *Political Science Quarterly*, LXXXII (June 1967), 235-252.

[14] Alexandra McCoy, "Political Affiliations of American Economic Elites: Wayne County, Michigan, 1844, 1860, as a Test Case" (Wayne State University Doctoral Dissertation, 1965).

position of its wealthy leaders to the Democracy's banking policy.[15] That moralistic anti-latitudinarians found the reputed Jacksonian affinity for drink and high living distasteful does tell us something about the *reputation* of the Democracy and of the mental set of some of its opponents. In my judgment it does not provide us with the most important information about the party.

A similar point can be made about almost all of the quantitative studies of voter behavior. They throw a useful if indirect light on the mood of the voter. They suggest the contemporary reputation of the parties. The latter information is by no means insignificant, since what men of a time think is so may be as important as the historical actuality. (Relativists understand that this actuality can never be known.) What the empirical studies do not do is to evaluate the actual performance of party — precisely the supreme task of the historical craft to all but narrative historians.

An unfortunate consequence of overvaluing the affinity between a party and a given class of voters is the tendency to draw unwarranted conclusions from the disclosed relationship. That Jackson's — or any other — party won support from workers would not make it the "workers' party" even had the support in question been overwhelming. Workers or members of any other occupational category who might unite as a class behind a candidate might do so for the wrong reasons. Being human, voters are prone to misconstrue events. In an age of patent demagogy the Democracy's claim that it championed the common man — seemingly confirmed by its rival's less than astute assertion that the Jacksonians were indeed a revolutionary *canaille* — could convince many voters that charge and counter-charge were true, at least in part. In the face of such propaganda, have-nots — or men who believed themselves have-nots — could easily conclude that the maligned party was truly theirs. Yet neither florid rhetoric nor poor peoples' illusions can transform an opportunistic party into a radical one.

We do not yet know why voters vote as they do. All we know is that their motives are complex and that irrational factors seem to play a part.[16]

---

[15] Clifford S. Griffin, *Their Brothers' Keepers: Moral Stewardship in the United States, 1800-1865* (New Brunswick, N. J., 1960), 55-57.

[16] See Edward N. Saveth, "American History and Social Science: A Trial Balance," *International Social Science Journal*, XX (No. 2, 1968), 319-330, for its informed discussion and excellent notes on this and related issues. Richard Hofstadter has written that the "rationalistic bias," according to which political man votes in order to advance his economic interests as he understands them, "has very largely broken down in our own time . . . partly because of what has been learned through public opinion polling

Statisticians note that a correlation between voters of a particular characteristic and a given party does not establish a causal relationship.[17] To repeat, even if we were to learn how to explain a man's behavior in the polling booth, we still should not have come any closer to understanding the performance of the party he votes for. What we would then know definitively would be the mind of the voter and the impact that the party — or the reputation of the party — has made on it.

The essential point of the labor thesis is that the Jacksonian party earned or truly deserved labor support. Elsewhere I have tried to show at some length why Democratic behavior did not warrant such support.[18] If Mr. Schlesinger put forward a highly imaginative argument for his view, he did so in the judgment of many of his critics because he was compelled to. The evidence itself appears to point in another direction. Plato, too, had been forced to extremes of ingenuity as would any man who tried to demonstrate that since concerns of the flesh impair thought, thinking is better done when the flesh is no more! It must be admitted, however, that the positive effect of Mr. Biddle's Bank on the workingman's dollar was not quite as demonstrable as is that of a functioning physical organism on a brain's ability to conceptualize (though R. C. H. Catterall, Thomas P. Govan, Walter Buckingham Smith or Bray Hammond would perhaps not have agreed).[19]

Of course scholars have not forsaken other than quantitative approaches to history. Much of the most interesting modern work on the politics of the Jacksonian era has been the interpretive discussion of its issues. Friend and foe alike to Mr. Schlesinger's argument, and the men who recently have bypassed it and moved consideration of the subject to a new plateau, have engaged in a historical debate of high level, marked not least by its ability to command the interest of the non-specialist.[20]

---

and depth psychology;" "Fundamentalism and Status Politics of the Right," *Columbia Forum*, VIII (Summer 1965), 24.

[17] See V. O. Key, Jr. *A Primer of Statistics for Political Scientists* (New York, 1959).

[18] Edward Pessen, *Jacksonian America: Society, Personality and Politics* (Homewood, 1969), chapters 10-12.

[19] R. C. H. Catterall, *The Second Bank of the United States* (Chicago, 1902); Thomas P. Govan, *Nicholas Biddle, Nationalist and Public Banker* (Chicago, 1959); Walter Buckingham Smith, *Economic Aspects of the Second Bank of the United States* (Cambridge, 1953; and Bray Hammond, *Banks and Politics in America from the Revolution to the Civil War* (Princeton, 1957), are economic studies which emphasize the Bank's positive contributions to the economy. For a recent book that focuses on the political aspects of the Bank struggle, see Robert V. Remini, *op. cit.*

[20] Examples of original and insightful analysis would include John William Ward, *Andrew Jackson, Symbol for an Age* (New York, 1955); Marvin Meyers, *The Jacksonian Persuasion* (Stanford, 1957); Glyndon G. Van Deusen, "Some Aspects of Whig Thought

I hope that I have not given the impression that what I call the head count approach is in any sense a bad thing. My belief is that it has been widely used heretofore to answer questions that are not of the highest significance to the historian. In some cases it has served as a substitute for what should be the main activities of the historian's calling: the vivid narrative recounting of what happened and the discussion of why it happened and what its consequences were. It is paradoxical that at that point in time when historians, like their co-workers in other scholarly fields, have grown increasingly aware of the complexity if not the unattainability of truth and the unavoidable subjectivity of those who pursue it, a historical methodology should flourish whose unspoken assumption seems to be not only that truth exists "out there," but that it is not so elusive after all. We can somehow grasp it and do so by a quantitative approach. A nice example of human unwillingness to be unduly influenced by theoretical assurances of hopelessness! Like the character in Samuel Beckett's *Waiting for Godot,* who *knows* that everything is meaningless yet happily tries on new hats, the head counters are practicing existentialists. More power to them! (Or should I say, to us? since this essay is a digression from a quantitative study I am doing on the social backgrounds and origins of the Jacksonian era's wealthy men.) Most of us head counters are doubtless well aware that if discrete truths can be achieved by empiricism, the larger Truth is resistant to it.[21]

Rather than propose the setting aside of the method whose recent uses I have questioned, I would urge its continued refinement and ask its practitioners to give thought to possible new applications. Certainly our understanding of party behavior and its consequences would be enlarged

and Theory in the Jacksonian Period," *American Historical Review,* LXIII (January 1958), 305-322; Gene Wise, "Political 'Reality' in Recent American Scholarship: Progressives versus Symbolists." *American Quarterly,* XIX (Summer 1967), 303-328; Lynn L. Marshall, "The Strange Stillbirth of the Whig Party," *American Historical Review,* LXXII (January 1967), 445-468; Major L. Wilson, "The Concept of Time and the Political Dialogue in the United States, 1828-48," *American Quarterly,* XIX (Winter 1967), 619-644; Frank Otto Gatell, "Sober Second Thoughts on Van Buren, the Albany Regency, and the Wall Street Conspiracy," *Journal of American History,* LIII (June 1966), 19-40; Richard H. Brown, "The Missouri Crisis, Slavery and the Politics of Jacksonianism," *South Atlantic Quarterly,* LXV (Winter 1966), 55-72; and Mary E. Young's essays on the Indian issue: "The Creek Frauds: A Study in Conscience and Corruption," *Mississippi Valley Historical Review,* XLVII (December 1955), 415-439; and "Indian Removal and Land Allotment: The Civilized Tribes and Jacksonian Justice," *American Historical Review,* LXIII (October 1958), 31-45. Of course the quantitative studies by Lee Benson and the other scholars I have cited earlier also contain their share of original and provocative analysis.

21 For an informal discussion of the quantitative method in history, its achievements, possibilities and limitations, see William O. Aydelotte, "Qualification in History," *American Historical Review,* LXXI (April 1966), 803-825.

by the devising of procedures that could enable us to establish quantita-
tively the effects of party policy on the American population as a whole
or on particular segments of it.

Perhaps, too, we can imitate our imaginative brethren of the new
economic history. Where Mr. Fogel posited an America without railroads, to test the validity of the thesis that stressed their indispensability
to the antebellum economy, perhaps Jacksonian scholars can measure the
hypothetical consequences of measures that were never enacted.[22] I can
still recall being charmed as a graduate student by Allan Nevins' dramatic utterance, that the most fascinating statement in history is: "It
might have been." Let a bold spirit among us carry our art into the age
of surrealism, hypothetico-deductive models, and metahistory by writing
a history of things that never were. What would connect this poetic enterprise to the realms of science and reality would be its reliance on an
analytic method that measured the likely consequences of a rejected historical proposal and compared them with the effects of policy that was
actually followed. One can foresee a future doctoral dissertation done
in this spirit: "The Political and Economic Effects of the Overriding of
Andrew Jackson's Bank Veto."

---

[22] Robert W. Fogel, *Railroads and Economic Growth: Essays in Econometric History* (Baltimore, 1964).

6

Workers' Control of Machine Production in the Nineteenth Century

DAVID MONTGOMERY

"In an industrial establishment which employs say from 500 to 1000 workmen, there will be found in many cases at least twenty to thirty different trades," wrote Frederick Winslow Taylor in his famous critique of the practices of industrial management which were then in vogue.

> The workmen in each of these trades have had their knowledge handed down to them by word of mouth.... This mass of rule-of-thumb or traditional knowledge may be said to be the principle asset or possession of every tradesman....[The] foremen and superintendents [who comprise the management] know, better than anyone else, that their own knowledge and personal skill falls far short of the combined knowledge and dexterity of all the workmen under them.... They recognize the task before them as that of inducing each workman to use his best endeavors, his hardest work, all his traditional knowledge, his skill, his ingenuity, and his good-will—in a word, his "initiative," so as to yield the largest possible return to his employer."[1]

Big Bill Haywood put the same point somewhat more pungently, when he declared: "The manager's brains are under the workman's cap."[2]

Both Taylor and Haywood were describing the power which certain groups of workers exercised over the direction of production processes at the end of the nineteenth century, a power which the scientific management movement strove to abolish, and which the Industrial Workers of the World wished to enlarge and

---

[1] Frederick Winslow Taylor, *The Principles of Scientific Management* (Norton Library Edition, New York, 1967), 31, 32.
[2] William D. Haywood and Frank Bohn, *Industrial Socialism* (Chicago, n.d.), 25.

Reprinted from *Labor History* 17 (Fall 1976), 485-509. The research for this study was assisted by a Fellowship from the John Simon Guggenheim Memorial Foundation.

extend to all workers. It is important to note that both men found
the basis of workers' power in the superiority of their knowledge
over that of the factory owners. It is even more important to note
that they were referring not to "pre-industrial" work practices,
but to the factory itself.

The richly impressive work of Herbert Gutman in this country,
E.P. Thompson in England, and others[3] has already unveiled to
us the profound changes forced by the advent of industrial capitalism upon people's values and expectation, work habits, and sense
of time, as well as the persistence with which working people
clung to their traditional, spasmodic, task-oriented styles of work
and to a social code which was less tightly disciplined, less
individualistic and less exploitative than that which industrialization was imposing upon them. These studies have directed our
attention to the experiences of the first generation of industrial
workers, or, in the case of Gutman's conception, to the persistence of that "first-generation" experience over more than a
century of American life.

My concern here, however, is not with the encounter of industrial with "pre-industrial" ways, but rather with the patterns of
behavior which took shape in the second and third generations of
industrial experience, largely among workers whose world had
been fashioned from their youngest days by smoky mills, con-
gested streets, recreation as a week-end affair and toil at the times
and the pace dictated by the clock (except when a more or less
lengthy layoff meant no work at all).[4] It was such workers, the

[3] Herbert G. Gutman, "Work, Culture, and Society in Industrializing America, 1815-1919,"
    American Historical Review, LXXVIII (June, 1973), 531-88; E.P. Thompson, "Time,
    Work-Discipline, and Industrial Capitalism," *Past and Present*, XXXVIII (Dec., 1967),
    56-97; E.J. Hobsbawm, "Custom, Wages and Work-load in Nineteenth-Century Industry,"
    in Hobsbawm, *Labouring Men* (London, 1964), 344-70; Gregory Kealey, "Artisans Respond
    to Industrialism: Shoemakers, Shoe Factories and the Knights of St. Crispin in Toronto,"
    Canadian Historical Association, *Historical Papers* (June, 1973), 137-57; Paul G. Faler,
    "Workingmen, Mechanics and Social Change: Lynn, Massachusetts, 1800-1860" (unpub-
    lished Ph.D. diss., Univ. of Wisconsin, 1971); Bruce C. Laurie, "The Working People of
    Philadelphia, 1827-1853" (unpublished Ph.D. diss., Univ. of Pittsburgh, 1971); David
    Montgomery, "The Shuttle and the Cross: Weavers and Artisans in the Kensington Riots of
    1844," *Journal of Social History*, V (Spring, 1972), 411-46.
[4] The question of industrial generations has been treated in American history largely in terms of
    leaders. See David Montgomery, *Beyond Equality: Labor and the Radical Republicans,
    1862-1872* (New York, 1967), 197-229; Warren R. Van Tine, *The Making of the Labor
    Bureaucrat: Union Leadership in the United States, 1870-1920* (Amherst, 1973), 1-32. For
    more fundamental social analyses, see Leopold H. Haimson, "The Russian Workers'
    Movement on the Eve of the First World War," unpublished paper, presented at the American
    Historical Association convention, 1972; Michelle Perrot, *Les ouvriers en grève: France
    1871-1890* (Paris, 1974), I, 312-95.

veterans, if you will, of industrial life, with whom Taylor was preoccupied. They had internalized the industrial sense of time, they were highly disciplined in both individual and collective behavior, and they regarded both an extensive division of labor and machine production as their natural environments. But they had often fashioned from these attributes neither the docile obedience of automatons, nor the individualism of the "upwardly mobile," but a form of control of productive processes which became increasingly collective, deliberate and aggressive, until American employers launched a partially successful counterattack under the banners of scientific management and the open shop drive.

Workers' control of production, however, was not a condition or state of affairs which existed at any point in time, but a struggle, a chronic battle in industrial life which assumed a variety of forms. Those forms may be treated as successive stages in a pattern of historical evolution, though one must always remember that the stages overlapped each other chronologically in different industries, or even at different localities within the same industry, and that each successive stage incorporated the previous one, rather than replacing it. The three levels of development which appeared in the second half of the nineteenth century were those characterized by 1) the functional autonomy of the craftsman, 2) the union work rule, and 3) mutual support of diverse trades in rule enforcement and sympathetic strikes. Each of these levels will be examined here in turn, then in conclusion some observations will be made on the impact of scientific management and the open shop drive on the patterns of behavior which they represented.

The functional autonomy of craftsmen rested on both their superior knowledge, which made them self-directing at their tasks, and the supervision which they gave to one or more helpers. Iron molders, glass blowers, coopers, paper machine tenders, locomotive engineers, mule spinners, boiler makers, pipe fitters, typographers, jiggermen in potteries, coal miners, iron rollers, puddlers and heaters, the operators of McKay or Goodyear stitching machines in shoe factories, and, in many instances, journeymen machinists and fitters in metal works exercised broad discretion in the direction of their own work and that of their helpers. They often hired and fired their own helpers and paid the latter some fixed portion of their own earnings.

James J. Davis, who was to end up as Warren Harding's Secretary of Labor, learned the trade of puddling iron by working as his father's helper in Sharon, Pennsylvania. "None of us ever went to school and learned the chemistry of it from books," he recalled. "We learned the trick by doing it, standing with our faces in the scorching heat while our hands puddled the metal in its glaring bath."[5] His first job, in fact, had come at the age of twelve, when an aged puddler devised a scheme to enable him to continue the physically arduous exertion of the trade by taking on a boy (twelve-year old Davis) to relieve the helper of mundane tasks like stoking the furnace, so that the helper in turn could assume a larger share of the taxing work of stirring the iron as it "came to nature." By the time Davis felt he had learned enough to master his own furnace, he had to leave Sharon, because furnaces passed from father to son, and Davis' father was not yet ready to step down. As late as 1900, when Davis was living at home while attending business college after having been elected to public office, he took over his father's furnace every afternoon, through an arrangement the two had worked out between themselves.[6]

The iron rollers of the Columbus Iron Works, in Ohio, have left us a clear record of how they managed their trade in the minute books of their local union from 1873 to 1876. The three twelve-man rolling teams, which constituted the union, negotiated a single tonnage rate with the company for each specific rolling job the company undertook. The workers then decided collectively, among themselves, what portion of that rate should go to each of them (and the shares were far from equal, ranging from 19¼ cents, out of the negotiated $1.13 a ton, for the roller, to 5 cents for the runout hooker), how work should be allocated among them, how many rounds on the rolls should be undertaken per day, what special arrangements should be made for the fiercely hot labors of the hookers during the summer, and how members should be hired and progress through the various ranks of the

[5] James J. Davis, *The Iron Puddler: My Life in the Rolling Mills and What Came of It* (Indianapolis, 1922), 91.

[6] *Ibid.*, 85, 92-3, 96, 114, 227. The issue of promotion of helpers to puddlers' furnaces provoked strikes by helpers against puddlers in the 1870s. See John H. Ashworth, *The Helper and American Trade Unions* (Baltimore, 1915), 83, 93-4.

gang.[7] To put it another way, all the boss did was to buy the equipment and raw materials and sell the finished product.

One cannot help being impressed by the fact that the Columbus iron rollers were conducting the operations of the firm in precisely the way J.T. Murphy and the Sheffield Workers' Council demanded that shop stewards should operate British industries in 1918, the union contracting with the employer to do the whole job, then performing that job without interference from employers.[8] But to make that analogy is to run too fast. The iron rollers of Columbus were not raising revolutionary demands, but pursuing commonplace practices. On the other hand, the practices themselves were both historically quite new (a "pre-industrial" iron roller is a contradiction in terms), subject to incessant attacks by employers, and defended by the craftsmen's own disciplined ethical code.

Three aspects of the moral code, in which the craftsmen's autonomy was protectively enmeshed, deserve close attention. First, on most jobs there was a stint, an output quota fixed by the workers themselves. As the laments of scientific management's apostles about workers "soldiering" and the remarkable 1904 survey by the Commissioner of Labor, *Regulation and Restriction of Output,* made clear, stints flourished as widely without unions as with them.[9] Abram Hewitt testified in 1867 that his puddlers in New Jersey, who were not unionized, worked 11 turns per week (5 1/2 days), made three heats per turn, and put 450 pounds of iron in each charge, all by arrangement among themselves. Thirty-five years later a stint still governed the trade, though a dramatic improvement in puddling furnaces was reflected in union rules which specified 11 turns with five heats per turn and 550 pounds per charge (a 104% improvement in productivity), while some nonunion mill workers followed the same routine but boiled bigger charges.[10]

---

[7] Minute Books, Lodge No. 11, Rollers, Roughers, Catchers and Hookers Union (Columbus, Ohio), July 14, 1873-April 28, 1876 (William Martin Papers, University of Pittsburgh library).

[8] Ernest Mandel, ed., *Contrôle ouvrier, conseils ouvriers, autogestion, anthologie* (Paris, 1970), 192-97. See also Carter Goodrich, *The Frontier of Control* (New York, 1921).

[9] Frederick Winslow Taylor, "Shop Management," *Transactions of the American Society of Mechanical Engineers,* XXIV (1903), 1337-1456; U.S. Commissioner of Labor, *Eleventh Annual Report,* "Regulation and Restriction of Output" (Washington, 1904).

[10] United Kingdom, Parliament, *Second Report of the Commissioners Appointed to Inquire into the*

Stints were always under pressure from the employers, and were often stretched over the course of time by the combined force of competition among employers and improving technology. In this instance, productivity under union rules expanded more than three per cent annually over three and half decades. But workers clung doggedly to the practice, and used their superior knowledge both to determine how much they should do and to outwit employers' efforts to wring more production out of them. In a farm equipment factory studied in 1902, for example, the machine shop, polishing department, fitting department and blacksmith shop all had fixed stints, which made each group of workers average very similar earnings despite the fact that all departments were on piecework. In the blacksmith shop, which unlike the others had no union rule fining those who earned too much, workers held down the pace by refusing to replace each part they removed from the heaters with a cold one. They emptied the heaters entirely, before refilling them and then waited for the new parts to heat up.[11] Similarly, Taylor's colleague Carl Barth discovered a planer operator who avoided exceeding the stint while always looking busy, by simply removing the cutting tool from his machine from time to time, while letting it run merrily on.[12]

"There is in every workroom a fashion, a habit of work," wrote efficiency consultant Henry Gantt, "and the new worker follows that fashion, for it isn't respectable not to."[13] A quiver full of epithets awaited the deviant: 'hog,' 'hogger-in,' 'leader,' 'rooter,' 'chaser,' 'rusher,' 'runner,' 'swift,' 'boss's pet,'[14] to mention some politer versions. And when a whole factory gained a reputation for feverish work, disdainful craftsmen would describe its occupants, as one did of the Gisholt turret lathe works, as comprised half "of farmers, and the other half, with few exceptions, of horse thieves."[15] On the other hand, those who held fast to the carefully measured stint, despite the curses of their employers and the lure of higher earnings, depicted themselves as

Organization and Rules of Trades Unions and Other Associations (Parliamentary Sessional Papers, 1867, xxxii c3893), 2; "Restriction of Output," 243.
[11]"Restriction of Output," 198-99.
[12]U.S. Commission on Industrial Relations, *Final Report and Testimony Submitted to Congress by the Commission on Industrial Relations* (64th Cong., 1st sess., Washington, D.C., 1915), 893-94.
[13]Henry L. Gantt, *Work, Wages, and Profits* (second revised edition, New York, 1919), 186.
[14]"Restriction of Output," 18.
[15]P.A. Stein to *Machinists' Monthly Journal,* XV (April, 1903), 294.

sober and trustworthy masters of their trades. Unlimited output led to slashed piece rates, irregular employment, drink and debauchery, they argued. Rationally restricted output, however, reflected "unselfish brotherhood," personal dignity, and "cultivation of the mind."[16]

Second, as this language vividly suggests, the craftsmen's ethical code demanded a "manly" bearing toward the boss. Few words enjoyed more popularity in the nineteenth century than this honorific, with all its connotations of dignity, respectability, defiant egalitarianism, and patriarchal male supremacy. The worker who merited it refused to cower before the foreman's glares—in fact, often would not work at all when a boss was watching. When confronted with indignities, he was expected to respond like the machinist in Lowell, who found regulations posted in his shop in 1867 requiring all employees to be at their posts in their work clothes when the first bell rang, to remain there until the last bell, and to be prevented from leaving the works between those times by locked doors:

> Not having been brought up under such a system of slavery, [he recalled,] I took my things and went out, followed in a few hours by the rest of the men. Thinking perhaps that it might be of some benefit to the rest, I remained with them on the strike. They went back to work with the understanding that the new rules should not apply except in regard to the doors being locked. A few days after I went for my pay and it was politely handed me without the trouble of asking for it.[17]

Finally, "manliness" toward one's fellow workers was as important as it was toward the owners. "Undermining or conniving" at a brother's job was a form of hoggish behavior as objectional as running more than one machine, or otherwise doing the work that belonged to two men. Union rules commanded the expulsion of members who performed such "dirty work," in order to secure employment or advancement for themselves. When the members of the Iron Heaters and Rollers Union at a Philadelphia mill learned in 1875 that one of their brothers had been fired "for dissatisfaction in regard to his management of the

[16]See"What One Trade Has Done," *John Swinton's Paper*, March 23, 1884. *Cf.*, Peter N. Stearns, "Adaptation to Industrialization: German Workers as a Test Case," *Central European History*, III (Dec., 1970), 303-31.
[17]Massachusetts Bureau of Statistics of Labor, *Report of the Bureau of Statistics of Labor for 1871* (Boston, 1871), 590-91.

mill,'' and that another member had ''undermined'' the first with the superintendent and been promised his rolls, the delinquent was expelled from the lodge, along with a lodge member who defended him, and everyone went on strike to demand the immediate discharge of both excommunicates by the firm.[18]

In short, a simple technological explanation for the control exercised by nineteenth-century craftsmen will not suffice. Technical knowledge acquired on the job was embedded in a mutualistic ethical code, also acquired on the job, and together these attributes provided skilled workers with considerable autonomy at their work and powers of resistance to the wishes of their employers. On the other hand, it was technologically possible for the worker's autonomy to be used in individualistic ways, which might promote his own mobility and identify his interests with those of the owner. The ubiquitous practice of subcontracting encouraged this tendency. In the needle trades, the long established custom of a tailor's taking work home to his family was transformed by his employment of other piece workers into the iniquitous ''sweat shop'' system.[19] Among iron molders, the ''berkshire'' system expanded rapidly after 1850, as individual molders hired whole teams of helpers to assist them in producing a multitude of castings. Carpenters and bricklayers were lured into piece work systems of petty exploitation, and other forms of subcontracting flourished in stone quarrying, iron mining, anthracite mining, and even in railroad locomotive works, where entire units of an engine's construction were let out to the machinist who filed the lowest bid, and who then hired a crew to assist him in making and fitting the parts.[20]

Subcontracting practices readily undermined both stints and the

[18] Associated Brotherhood of Iron and Steel Heaters, Rollers and Roughers of the United States, ''Report on Communications. The Year's Term Having Closed July 10th, 1875,'' Feb. 25, 1875. For more on ''dirty work'' and ''one man-one machine'' rules, see Amalgamated Association of Iron and Steel Workers, *Proceedings* (1877), 52, 75; ''Restriction of Output,'' 101-05, 226-27.

[19] On the origins of ''sweating'' in the needle trades, see Conrad Carl testimony, U.S. Congress, Senate Committee on Education and Labor, *Report of the Committee of the Senate upon the Relations between Labor and Capital* (Washington, D.C., 1885), I, 413-21; Louis Lorwin, *The Women's Garment Workers* (New York, 1924), 12-23.

[20] Ashworth, 67-72; Robert A. Christie, *Empire in Wood: A History of the Carpenters' Union* (Ithaca, N.Y., 1956), chapt. 5; Paul Worthman, ''Black Workers and Labor Unions in Birmingham, Alabama, 1897-1904,'' *Labor History*, X (Summer, 1969), 374-407; Jacob H. Hollander and George E. Barnett, *Studies in American Trade Unionism* (New York, 1912), 147-48; *The Iron Age*, LXXXXI (Jan. 30, 1913), 334; *Machinists' Monthly Journal*, XVI (April, 1904), 321.

mutualistic ethic (though contractors were known to fix stints for their own protection in both garment and locomotive works), and they tended to flood many trades with trained, or semi-trained, workers who undercut wages and work standards. Their spread encouraged many craftsmen to move beyond reliance on their functional autonomy to the next higher level of craft control, the enactment and enforcement of union work rules. In one respect, union rules simply codified the autonomy I have already described. In fact, because they were often written down and enforced by joint action, union rules have a visibility to historians, which has made me resort to them already for evidence in the discussion of autonomy per se. But this intimate historical relationship between customary workers' autonomy and the union rule should not blind us to the fact that the latter represents a significant new stage of development.[21]

The work rules of unions were referred to by their members as "legislation."[22] The phrase denotes a shift from spontaneous to deliberate collective action, from a group ethical code to formal rules and sanctions, and from resistance to employers' pretentions to control over them. In some unions the rules were rather simple. The International Association of Machinists, for example, like its predecessors the Machinists and Blacksmiths' International Union and the many machinists' local assemblies of the Knights of Labor, simply specified a fixed term of apprenticeship for any prospective journeyman, established a standard wage for the trade, prohibited helpers or handymen from performing journeymen's work, and forbade any member from running more than one machine at a time or accepting any form of piece work payment.[23]

Other unions had much more detailed and complex rules. There were, for example, sixty-six "Rules for Working" in the by-laws of the window-glass workers' Local Assembly 300 of the Knights of Labor. They specified that full crews had to be present "at

---

[21]*Cf.*, Benson Soffer, "A Theory of Trade Union Development: The Role of the 'Autonomous' Workman," *Labor History*, I (Spring, 1960), 141-63.

[22]The Typographers still call their rule book the Book of Laws. See Selig Perlman, *A Theory of the Labor Movement* (New York, 1928), 262-72; Seymour Martin Lipset, Martin A. Trow, and James S. Coleman, *Union Democracy* (Garden City, N.Y., 1962), 160-226.

[23]"Restriction of Output," 101-08; Charles B. Going, "The Labour Question in England and America," *Engineering Magazine*, XIX (May, 1900), 161-76; Hollander and Barnett, 109-52.

each pot setting," that skimming could be done only at the beginning of blowing and at meal time, that blowers and gatherers should not "work faster than at the rate of nine rollers per hour," and that the "standard size of single strength rollers" should "be 40x58 to cut 38x56." No work was to be performed on Thanksgiving Day, Christmas, Decoration Day or Washington's Birthday, and no blower, gatherer or cutter could work between June 15 and September 15. In other words, during the summer months the union ruled that the fires were to be out.[24] In 1884 the local assembly waged a long and successful strike to preserve its limit of 48 boxes of glass a week, a rule which its members considered the key to the dignity and welfare of the trade.[25]

Nineteenth-century work rules were not ordinarily negotiated with employers or embodied in a contract. From the 1860's onward it became increasingly common for standard *wages* to be negotiated with employers or their associations, rather than fixed unilaterally as unions had tried earlier, but working rules changed more slowly. They were usually adopted unilaterally by local unions, or by the delegates to a national convention, and enforced by the refusal of the individual member to obey any command from an employer which violated them. Hopefully, the worker's refusal would be supported by the joint action of his shop mates, but if it was not, he was honor bound to pack his tool box and walk out alone, rather than break the union's laws. As Fred Reid put the point so well in his description of nineteenth-century Scottish miners' unionism: "The strength of organised labour was held to depend upon the manliness of the individual workman."[26]

On the other hand, the autonomy of craftsmen which was codified in union rules was clearly not individualistic. Craftsmen were unmistakably and consciously group-made men, who sought to pull themselves upward by their collective boot straps. As unions waxed stronger after 1886, the number of strikes to enforce union rules grew steadily. It was, however, in union legislation against subcontracting that both the practical and ideological

---

[24] *By-Laws of the Window Glass Workers, L.A. 300, Knights of Labor* (Pittsburgh, 1899), 26-36.
[25] "What One Trade Has Done," *John Swinton's Paper*, March 23, 1884.
[26] Fred Reid, "Keir Hardie's Conversion to Socialism," in Asa Briggs and John Saville, eds., *Essays in Labour History, 1886-1923* (London, 1971), 29. See also Montgomery, *Beyond Equality*, 142-53; David A. McCabe, *The Standard Rate in American Trade Unions* (Baltimore, 1912).

aspects of the conflict between group solidarity and upwardly mobile individualism became most evident, for these rules sought to regulate in the first instance not the employers' behavior, but that of the workers themselves. Thus the Iron Molders Union attacked the "berkshire" system by rules forbidding any of its members to employ a helper for any other purpose than "to skim, shake out and to cut sand," or to pay a helper out of his own earnings. In 1867, when 8,615 out of some 10,400 known molders in the country were union members, the national union legislated further that no member was allowed to go to work earlier than seven o'clock in the morning.[27] During the 1880s the Brick Layers' Union checked subcontracting by banning its members from working for any contractor who could not raise enough capital to buy his own bricks. All building trades unions instructed their members not to permit contractors to work with tools along side with them. The United Mine Workers limited the number of helpers a bituminous miner could engage, usually to one, though the employment of several laborers by one miner remained widespread in anthracite mines through the first World War. The Carpenters and the Machinists outlawed piece work altogether, for the same purpose. The Amalgamated Iron and Steel Workers required the companies to pay helpers directly, rather than through the craftsmen, and fixed the share of tonnage rates to which helpers were entitled.[28] All such regulations secured the group welfare of the workers involved by sharply rejecting society's enticements to become petty entrepreneurs, clarifying and intensifying the division of labor at the work place, and sharpening the line between employer and employee.

Where a trade was well unionized, a committee in each shop supervised the enforcement in that plant of the rules and standard wage which the union had adopted for the trade as a whole. The craft union and the craft local assembly of the Knights of Labor were forms of organization well adapted to such regulatory activities. The members were legislating, on matters on which they were unchallenged experts, rules which only their courage and solidarity could enforce. On one hand, the craft form of organiza-

---

[27]*Proceedings of the Eighth Annual Session of the Iron Molders' International Union* (Philadelphia, 1867), 10, 14, 40-41; Ashworth, 36, 38, 68.
[28]See above, note 20.

tion linked their personal interests to those of the trade, rather than
those of the company in which they worked, while, on the other
hand, their efforts to enforce the same rules on all of their
employers, where they were successful, created at least a few
islands of order in the nineteenth-century's economic ocean of
anarchic competition.

Labor organizations of the late nineteenth century struggled
persistently to transform workers' struggles to manage their own
work from spontaneous to deliberate actions, just as they tried to
subject wage strikes and efforts to shorten the working day to their
conscious regulation. "The trade union movement is one of
reason, one of deliberation, depending entirely upon the voluntary
and sovereign actions of its members," declared the executive
Council of the AFL.[29] Only through "thorough organization," to
use a favorite phrase of the day, was it possible to enforce a
trade's work rules throughout a factory, mine, or construction site.
Despite the growing number of strikes over union rules and union
recognition in the late 1880s, the enforcement of workers' standards of control spread more often through the daily self-assertion
of craftsmen on the job than through large and dramatic strikes.

Conversely, strikes over wage reductions at times involved
thinly disguised attacks by employers on craftsmen's job controls.
Fall River's textile manufacturers in 1870 and the Hocking Valley
coal operators in 1884, to cite only two examples, deliberately
foisted severe wage reductions on their highly unionized workers
in order to provoke strikes. The owners' hope was that in time
hunger would force their employees to abandon union membership, and thus free the companies' hands to change production
methods.[30] As the treasurer of one Fall River mill testified in
1870: "I think the question with the spinners was not wages, but
whether they or the manufacturers should rule. For the last six or
eight years they have ruled Fall River."[31] Defeat in a strike
temporarily broke the union's control, which had grown through

[29]Samuel Gompers, "The Strike and Its Lessons," in John Swinton, *A Momentous Question. The
    Respective Attitudes of Labor and Capital* (Philadelphia and Chicago, 1895), 311.
[30]See Philip T. Silvia, Jr., "The Spindle City: Labor, Politics and Religion in Fall River,
    Massachusetts, 1870-1905" (unpublished Ph.D. diss., Fordham Univ., 1973), chapt. 3; Jon
    Amsden and Stephen Brier, "Coal Miners on Strike: The Transformation of Strike Demands
    and the Formation of the National Union in the U.S. Coal Industry, 1881-1894," forthcoming
    in *The Journal of Interdisciplinary History;* Andrew Roy, *A History of the Coal Miners*
    (Columbus, Ohio, 1902), 220-242.
[31]Massachusetts Bureau of Statistics of Labor, *Report, 1871,* 55.

TABLE I
Strike Trends, 1881-1905

Year	Number of Strikes (1)	Workers Involved (000) (2)	Per Cent Wage Strikes (3)	Per Cent Ordered By Unions (4)	Per Cent Sympathy- Strikes (5)	Number Sympathy- Strikes (6)
1881	471	101	79.8	47.3	0.8	2
1882	454	121	75.4	48.5	0.9	3
1883	478	122	77.2	56.7	0.6	2
1884	443	117	74.1	54.2	2.0	6
1885	645	159	72.9	55.3	3.1	20
1886	1432	407	63.0	53.3	2.9	37
1887	1436	273	54.8	66.3	4.7	71
1888	906	103	55.2	68.1	3.8	34
1889	1075	205	59.0	67.3	6.1	67
1890	1833	286	50.9	71.3	9.9	188
1891	1717	245	48.9	74.8	11.5	204
1892	1298	164	50.4	70.7	8.9	117
1893	1305	195	58.8	69.4	4.5	62
1894	1349	505	63.7	62.8	8.8	120
1895	1215	286	69.6	54.2	0.6	7
1896	1026	184	57.6	64.6	0.6	7
1897	1078	333	66.2	55.3	0.7	9
1898	1056	182	63.0	60.4	0.8	9
1899	1797	308	59.4	62.0	1.5	29
1900	1779	400	59.0	65.4	1.5	29
1901	2924	396	46.6	75.9	2.4	71
1902	3162	553	51.2	78.2	2.6	87
1903	3494	532	51.5	78.8	2.4	88
1904	2307	376	42.2	82.1	3.7	93
1905	2077	176	44.5	74.7	2.7	61

Sources: The number of strikes and the number of workers involved (1 and 2) are taken from U. S. Commissioner of Labor, *Twenty-First Annual Report* (1906), 15. Wage strikes as a per cent of all strikes (3) is from J. H. Griffin, *Strikes* (1939), 76. The percentage of strikes ordered by unions, the per cent of all strikes represented by sympathetic strikes, and the number of sympathetic strikes (4, 5, and 6) are from Florence Peterson, *Strikes in the United States, 1880-1936* (1937), 32, 33.

steady recruiting and rule enforcement during years which were largely free of work stoppages.

The third level of control struggles emerged when different trades lent each other support in their battles to enforce union rules and recognition. An examination of the strike statistics gathered by the U.S. Commissioner of Labor for the period 1881-1905 reveals the basic patterns of this development.[32] Although there had been a steady increase in both the number and size of strikes between 1881 and 1886, the following 12 years saw

---

[32]See Table One.

a reversal of that growth, as stoppages became both smaller and increasingly confined to skilled crafts (except in 1894). With that change came three important and interrelated trends. First, the proportion of strikes called by unions rose sharply in comparison to spontaneous strikes. Nearly half of all strikes between 1881 and 1886 had occurred without union sanction or aid. In the seven years beginning with 1887 more than two-thirds of each year's strikes were deliberately called by a union, and in 1891 almost 75 per cent of the strikes were official.

Secondly, as strikes became more deliberate and unionized, the proportion of strikes which dealt mainly with wages fell abruptly. Strikes to enforce union rules, enforce recognition of the union, and protect its members grew from 10 per cent of the total or less before 1885 to the level of 19-20 per cent between 1891 and 1893. Spontaneous strikes and strikes of laborers and factory operatives had almost invariably been aimed at increasing wages or preventing wage reductions, with the partial exception of 1886 when 20 per cent of all strikes had been over hours. The more highly craftsmen became organized, however, the more often they struck and were locked out over work rules.

Third, unionization of workers grew on the whole faster than strike participation. The ratio of strike participants to membership in labor organizations fell almost smoothly from 109 in 1881 to 24 in 1888, rose abruptly in 1890 and 1891 (to 71 and 86 respectively), then resumed its downward trend to 36 in 1898, interrupted, of course, by a leap to 182 in 1894.[33] In a word, calculation and organization were the dominant tendencies in strike activity, just as they were in the evolution of work rules during the nineteenth century. But the assertion of deliberate control through formal organization was sustained not only by high levels of militancy (a persistently high propensity to strike), but also by remarkably aggressive mutual support, which sometimes took the form of the unionization of all grades of workers within a single industry, but more often appeared in the form of sympathetic strikes involving members of different trade unions.

Joint organization of all grades of workers seemed most likely

[33]John H. Griffin, *Strikes. A Study in Quantitative Economics* (New York, 1939), 107. A splendid discussion of the increasing role of calculation in nineteenth-century strikes may be found in Perrot, *Les ouvriers en grève*, I, 101-180; II, 424-85, 574-606.

to flourish where no single craft clearly dominated the life of the workplace, in the way iron molders, brick layers, or iron puddlers did where they worked. It was also most likely to appear at the crest of the waves of strike activity among unskilled workers and operatives, as is hardly surprising, and to offer evidence of the organizational impulse in their ranks. In Philadelphia's shoe industry between 1884 and 1887, for example, the Knights of Labor successfully organized eleven local assemblies, ranging in size from 55 to 1000 members, each of which represented a different craft or cluster of related occupations, and formulated wage demands and work rules for its own members. Each assembly sent three delegates to District Assembly 70, the highest governing body of the Knights for the industry, which in turn selected seven representatives to meet in a city-wide arbitration committee with an equal number of employers' representatives. Within each factory a "shop union" elected by the workers in that plant handled grievances and enforced the rules of the local assemblies, aided by one male and one female "statistician," who kept track of the complex piece rates.[34]

There is no evidence that local assemblies of unskilled workers or of semi-skilled operatives ever attempted to regulate production processes themselves in the way assemblies of glass blowers and other craftsmen did. They did try to restrict hiring to members of the Knights and sometimes regulated layoffs by seniority clauses. For the most part, however, assemblies of operatives and laborers confined their attention to wages and to protection of their members against arbitrary treatment by supervisors.[35] On the other hand, the mere fact that such workers had been organized made it difficult for employers to grant concessions to their craftsmen at the expense of helpers and laborers. Consequently, the owners were faced simultaneously with higher wage bills and a reduction of their control in a domain where they had been accustomed to exercise unlimited authority.

[34] Augusta E. Galster, *The Labor Movement in the Shoe Industry, with Special Reference to Philadelphia* (New York, 1924), 49-57.

[35] See, for example, the agreement between Carpet Weavers' National Assembly No. 126, K. of L. and E. S. Higgins & Co., in New York Bureau of Statistics of Labor, *Fourth Annual Report, 1886* (Albany, 1887), 256. Much more research is needed on the demands of unskilled workers, but note the sharp contrast in the types of demands presented by craftsmen and laborers when each group met separately during the Bethlehem Steel Strike. U.S. Congress, Senate, *Report on the Strike at the Bethlehem Steel Works* (Senate Document No. 521, Washington, D.C., 1910), 26-32.

Moreover, workers who directed important production processes were themselves at times reluctant to see their own underlings organized, and frequently sought to dominate the larger organization to which their helpers belonged. A case in point was offered by the experience of the Knights of Labor in the garment industry, where contractors were organized into local assemblies of their own, supposedly to cooperate with those of cutters, pressers, tailors, and sewing machine operators. Contractors were often charged with disrupting the unionization of their own employees, in order to promote their personal competitive advantages. Above all, they tried to discourage women from joining the operators' assemblies. As the secretary of a St. Louis tailors' local assembly revealed, contractors who were his fellow Knights were telling the parents of operators that "no dissent [sic] girl belong to an assembly."[36]

On the other hand, the experience of the Knights in both the shoe and garment industries suggests that effective unionization of women operatives was likely to have a remarkably radicalizing impact on the organization. It closed the door decisively both on employers who wished to compensate for higher wages paid to craftsmen by exacting more from the unskilled, and on craftsmen who were tempted to advance themselves by sweating others. In Philadelphia, Toronto, Cincinnati, Beverly, and Lynn both the resistance of the manufacturers to unionism and the level of mutuality exhibited by the workers leapt upward noticeably when the women shoe workers organized along with the men. Furthermore, the sense of total organization made all shoe workers more exacting in their demands and less patient with the protracted arbitration procedures employed by the Knights. Quickie strikes became increasingly frequent as more and more shoe workers enrolled in the Order. Conversely, the shoe manufacturers banded tightly together to destroy the Knights of Labor.[37]

In short, the organization of all grades of workers in any

[36] Abraham Bisno, *Abraham Bisno, Union Pioneer* (Madison, 1967), 77-78, 135-37; John W. Hayes Papers (Catholic University of America), LA 7507, LA 2567, LA 10353. The quotation is from Gustive Cytron to John Hayes, Nov. 1, 1893. Hayes Papers, LA 10353. See Ashworth, *passim,* on the domination of helpers' unions by locals of craftsmen.
[37] Galster, 55-57. See also Alan C. Dawley, "The Artisan Response to the Factory System: Lynn, Massachusetts, in the Nineteenth Century" (unpublished Ph.D. diss., Harvard Univ., 1971); Kealey, 145-47; James M. Morris, "The Cincinnati Shoemakers Lockout of 1888," *Labor History,* XIII (Fall, 1972), 505-19.

industry propelled craftsmen's collective rule making into a more aggressive relationship with the employers, even where it left existing styles of work substantially unchanged. The other form of joint action, sympathetic strikes, most often involved the unionized skilled crafts themselves, and consequently was more directly related to questions of control of production processes. When Fred S. Hall wrote in 1898 that sympathetic strikes had "come so much in vogue during the last few years,"[38] he was looking back on a period during which organized workers had shown a greater tendency to walk out in support of the struggles of other groups of workers than was the case in any other period in the history of recorded strike data. Only the years between 1901 and 1904 and those between 1917 and 1921 were to see the absolute number of sympathetic strikes approach even *one-half* the levels of 1890 and 1891.

There were, in fact, two distinct crests in the groundswell of sympathetic strikes. The first came between 1886 and 1888, when a relatively small number of disputes, which spread by sympathetic action to include vast numbers of workers, caught public attention in a dramatic way. The Southwest railways strike of 1886, the New York freight handlers dispute of 1887, and the Lehigh coal and railroad stoppages of 1888 exemplified this trend. None of them, however, primarily involved control questions, in the sense they have been described here.

The second crest, that of 1890-92, was quite different. It was dominated by relatively small stoppages of organized craftsmen. In New York state, where the Bureau of Labor Statistics collected detailed information on such stoppages until 1892 (and included in its count strikes which were omitted from the U.S. Commissioner of Labor's data because they lasted less than a single day or included fewer than six workers), the number of establishments shut by sympathetic strikes rose from an average of 166 yearly between 1886 and 1889 to 732 in 1890, 639 in 1891, and 738 in 1892. Most of them involved the employees of a single company, like the 15 machinists who struck in support of the claims of molders in their factory or the four marble cutters who walked out to assist paper hangers on the same site. A few were very large.

---

[38] Fred S. Hall, *Sympathetic Strikes and Sympathetic Lockouts* (New York: Columbia University Studies in History, Economics and Public Law, No. 26, 1898), 29.

When New York's cabinet makers struck to preserve their union in 1892, for example, 107 carpenters, 14 gilders, 75 marble cutters and helpers, 17 painters, 23 plasterers, 28 porters, 12 blue stone cutters, 14 tile layers and helpers, 32 upholsterers, 14 varnishers, 149 wood carvers, and others walked out of more than 100 firms to lend their support.[39]

Eugene V. Debs was to extoll this extreme manifestation of mutuality as the "Christ-like virtue of sympathy," and to depict his own Pullman boycott, the epoch's most massive sympathetic action, as an open confrontation between that working-class virtue and a social order which sanctified selfishness.[40] It is true that the mutualistic ethic which supported craftsmen's control was displayed in its highest form by sympathetic strikes. It is equally true, however, that the element of calculation, which was increasingly dominating all strike activity, was particularly evident here. As Fred S. Hall pointed out, sympathetic strikes of this epoch differed sharply from "contagious" strikes, which spread spontaneously like those of 1877, in two respects. First, the sympathetic strikes were called by the workers involved, through formal union procedures. Although figures comparing official with unofficial strikes are not available, two contrasting statistics illustrate Hall's point. The construction industry was always the leading center of sympathetic strikes. In New York more than 70 per cent of the establishments shut by sympathetic action between 1890 and 1892 were involved in building construction. On the other hand, over the entire period of federal data (1881—1905) no less than 98.03 per cent of the strikes in that industry were called by unions.[41]

Second, as Hall observed, the tendency toward sympathetic strikes was "least in those cases where the dispute concerns conditions of employment such as wages and hours, and [was] greatest in regard to disputes which involve questions of unionism—the employment of only union men, the recognition of the union, etc."[42] The rise of sympathetic strikes, like the rise of

---

[39] New York B. L. S., *Report, 1890,* 936-49, *Report, 1891,* Part II, 732-45; *Report, 1892,* 124-39.

[40] Debs, "Labor Strikes and Their Lessons," in Swinton, *Momentous Question,* 324-25.

[41] U. S. Commissioner of Labor, *Twenty-First Annual Report* (Washington, D. C., 1906), 21-2, 33-4, 81-2. The calculation of the percentage of New York sympathetic strikes involving the building trades are my own, from the New York B. L. S. data.

[42] Hall, 33.

strikes over rules and recognition, was part of the struggle for craftsmen's control—its most aggressive and far-reaching manifestation.

It is for this reason that the practice of sympathetic strikes was ardently defended by the AFL in the 1890s. Building trades contracts explicitly provided for sympathetic stoppages. Furthermore, at the Federation's 1895 convention a resolution carried, directing the Executive Council to "convey to the unions, in such way as it thinks proper, not to tie themselves up with contracts so that they cannot help each other when able." The Council itself denied in a report to the same convention that it opposed sympathetic strikes. "On the contrary," it declared, "we were banded together to help one another. The words union, federation, implied it. An organization which held aloof when assistance could be given to a sister organization, was deserving of censure," even though each union had the right to decide its own course of action.[43]

On the other hand, not all unions supported this policy by any means. Under the right conditions it was just as possible for work processes to be regulated by the rules of a craft union which stood aloof from all appeals to class solidarity, as it was for an individual craftsman to identify his functional autonomy to his employer's interests through subcontracting. Precisely such a solitary course was proudly pursued by the locomotive engineers and firemen. In general, where a union was strong enough to defy its employers alone and where no major technological innovations threatened its members' work practices, it tended to reach an accommodation with the employers on the basis of the latter's more or less willing recognition of the union's work rules.

Two examples will suffice. One appeared in stove molding, where eight years of protracted strikes and lockouts followed the National Stove Founders' Defense Association's 1882 denunciation of the "one-sided cast-iron rules" of the Molders' Union, from which it envisaged "no appeal except through a bitter struggle for supremacy." But the molders' indispensable mastery of the art of casting satiny smooth stove parts, their thorough organization, and their readiness to strike again and again enabled

---

[43] E. Levasseur, *The American Workman* (Baltimore, 1900), 237-39; Hall, 102-03. The quotations from the AFL are in Hall, 102-03.

the Molders Union to prevail with little help from other unions. In 1890 the employers' Defense Association signed a national trade agreement, which provided for arbitration of all disputes and tacitly accepted the union's authority to establish work rules.[44] In sharp contrast to machinery molders, who often joined machinists, boiler makers, and other metal tradesment in strikes, participation by stove molders in sympathetic strikes was practically unheard of.

Similarly, brick layers and stone masons proved eminently capable of defending themselves, seldom found their rules seriously challenged, and consequently felt little need for joint action with other trades, except during campaigns for shorter hours. The forceful but conservative form of craft control which they represented is evident not only in the refusal of the Bricklayers' and Masons' International Union to send representatives to New York City's Board of Walking Delegates or to affiliate with the AFL, but also in the reluctance of its members to engage in sympathetic strikes. Between 1890 and 1892 only four New York firms were shut by bricklayers and four by stone masons in sympathetic actions. By way of contrast, during the same three years sympathetic strikes by carpenters in that state closed 171 firms and similar stoppages by cloakmakers another 152.[45]

Furthermore, employers in many industries banded together in the early 1890s to resist sympathetic strikes, union rules and union recognition with increasing vigor and effectiveness. Sympathetic lockouts were mounted by employers' organizations to deny striking workers alternative sources of employment or financial support. Legal prosecutions for conspiracy in restraint of trade, including use of the Sherman Anti-Trust Act against the Workingmen's Amalgamated Council of New Orleans for the city-wide sympathetic strike of 1892, and court-ordered injunctions provided supplementary weapons. In this setting, unionized craftsmen suffered a growing number of defeats. Whereas less than 40 per cent of the strikes of 1889 and 1890 had been lost by the workers, 54.5 per cent of the strikes of 1891 and 53.9 per cent of

---

[44]Hollander and Barnett, 226-31. The quotation is on p.226. The trade agreement is reprinted on pp. 230-31.
[45]John R. Commons, *Trade Unionism and Labor Problems* (First Series, Boston, 1905), 66-7; Philip Taft, *The A.F. of L. in the Time of Gompers* (New York, 1957), 25, 29, 251. On sympathetic strikes in New York, see above, note 39.

those of 1892 were unsuccessful. This level of defeats was by far the highest for the late nineteenth century, and would not be approached again until 1904.[46] The losses are all the more remarkable when one recalls that these were record years for union-called strikes (as opposed to spontaneous strikes), and that throughout the 1881 to 1905 period strikes called by unions tended to succeed in better than 70 per cent of the cases, while spontaneous strikes were lost in almost the same proportion. The explanation for the high level of defeats in calculated strikes of 1891 and 1892 lies in the audacity of the workers' demands. Official strikes over wages remained eminently successful. The fiercest battles and the bitterest losses pivoted around union rules and recognition and around sympathetic action itself.

Consequently trade unionists began to shy away from sympathetic strikes in practice, despite their verbal defenses, even before 1894. The statistical appearance of a crescendo of sympathetic strikes in 1894 followed by an abrupt collapse is misleading. Hall suggests that crafts other than the building trades were becoming hesitant to come out in sympathy with other groups, especially with workers from other plants, from 1892 onward. Although the New York data ends that year, it seems to bear him out in an interesting way. The total number of sympathetic strikes in New York was as great in 1892 as it had been in 1890. On the other hand, 67 per cent of those strikes had been in the building trades in 1890, as compared to 69 per cent in 1891 and 84 per cent in 1892. One wishes the figures had continued, so as to reveal whether the small numbers of such strikes after 1895 were confined to construction. In any event, even in 1892 more than 100 of the 120 establishments outside of the building trades which were hit by sympathetic strikes were involved in a single conflict, that of the cabinet makers. And the workers ultimately abandoned that battle in total defeat. In this context the resurgence of such strikes in 1894 appears as an aberration. Indeed, the Pullman boycott and

---

[46]Hall, 36-51, 70-78; John T. Cumbler, "Labor, Capital, and Community: The Strugle for Power," *Labor History*, XV (Summer, 1974), 395-415; Almont Lindsay, *The Pullman Strike* (Chicago, 1942), 122-46, 203-73; Edwin E. Witte, *The Government in Labor Disputes* (New York and London, 1932), 26-31, 61-82; Gerald G. Eggert, *Railroad Labor Disputes: The Beginnings of Federal Strike Policy* (Ann Arbor, 1967), 81-191; United States v. Workingmen's Amalgamated Council of New Orleans, et al., 54 Fed. 994 (1893); Florence Peterson, *Strikes in the United States, 1880-1936* (Washington: U.S. Dept. of Labor Bulletin No. 651, Aug., 1937), 34.

the bituminous coal strike together accounted for 94 per cent of the establishments shut by sympathy actions in the first six months of that year.[47]

In short, historians have, on the whole, been seriously misled by Norman J. Ware's characterization of the period after the Haymarket Affair as one of "Sauve qui peut!"[48] As craftsmen unionized, they not only made their struggles for control increasingly collective and deliberate, but also manifested a *growing* consciousness of the dependence of their efforts on those of workers in other crafts. They drew strength in this struggle from their functional autonomy, which was derived from their superior knowledge, exercised through self-direction and their direction of others at work, and both nurtured and in turn was nurtured by a mutualistic ethic, which repudiated important elements of acquisitive individualism. As time passed this autonomy was increasingly often codified in union rules, which were collectively "legislated" and upheld through the commitment of the individual craftsmen and through a swelling number of strikes to enforce them. Organized efforts reached the most aggressive and inclusive level of all in joint action among the various crafts for mutual support. When such actions enlisted all workers in an industry (as happened when women unionized in shoe manufacturing), and when they produced a strong propensity of unionized craftsmen to strike in support of each other's claims, they sharply separated the aggressive from the conservative consequences of craftsmen's autonomy and simultaneously provoked an intense, concerted response from the business community.

In an important sense, the last years of the depression represented only a lull in the battle. With the return of prosperity in 1898, both strikes and union organizing quickly resumed their upward spiral, work rules again seized the center of the stage, and sympathetic strikes became increasingly numerous and bitterly fought. Manufacturers' organizations leapt into the fray with the open shop drive, while their spokesmen cited new government surveys to support their denunciations of workers "restriction of output."[49]

---

[47]Hall, 37-8.

[48]Norman J. Ware, *The Labor Movement in the United States, 1860-1895* (New York and London, 1929), xii.

[49]Clarence E. Bonnett, *Employers Associations in the United States: A Study of Typical*

On the other hand, important new developments distinguished the first decade of the twentieth century from what had gone before. Trade union officials, who increasingly served long terms in full-time salaried positions, sought to negotiate the terms of work with employers, rather than letting their members "legislate" them. The anxiety of AFL leaders to secure trade agreements and to ally with "friendly employers," like those affiliated with the National Civic Federation, against the open shop drive, prompted them to repudiate the use of sympathetic strikes. The many such strikes which took place were increasingly lacking in union sanction and in any event never reached the level of the early 1890s.[50]

Most important of all, new methods of industrial management undermined the very foundation of craftsmen's functional autonomy. Job analysis through time and motion study allowed management to learn, then to systematize the way the work itself was done. Coupled with systematic supervision and new forms of incentive payment it permitted what Frederick Winslow Taylor called "*enforced* standardization of methods, *enforced* adoption of the best implements and working conditions, and *enforced* co-operation of all the employees under management's detailed direction."[51] Scientific management, in fact, fundamentally disrupted the craftsmen's styles of work, their union rules and standard rates, and their mutualistic ethic, as it transformed American industrial practice between 1900 and 1930. Its basic effect, as Roethlisberger and Dickson discovered in their experiments at Western Electric's Hawthorne Works, was to place the worker "at the bottom level of a highly stratified organization," leaving his "established routines of work, his cultural traditions of craftsmanship, [and] his personal interrelations" all "at the mercy of technical specialists."[52]

Two important attributes of the scientific management movement become evident only against the background of the struggles

---

Associations (New York, 1922); Commons, *Trade Unionism and Labor Problems, passim;* "Restriction of Output."

[50] See Van Tine, 57-112; Mark Perlman, *The Machinists: A New Study in American Trade Unionism* (Washington, D.C., 1956), 20-36, 48-50.

[51] Taylor, 83.

[52] F. J. Roethlisberger and W. J. Dickson, *Management and the Worker: Technical vs. Social Organization in an Industrial Plant* (Cambridge: Harvard University Business Research Studies, No. 9, 1934), 16-17. *Cf.,* Harry Braverman, *Labor and Monopoly Capital: The Degradation of Work in the Twentieth Century* (New York and London, 1974).

of nineteenth-century craftsmen to direct their own work in their own collective way. First, the appeal of the new managerial techniques to manufacturers involved more than simply a response to new technology and a new scale of business organization. It also implied a conscious endeavor to uproot those work practices which had been the taproot of whatever strength organized labor enjoyed in the late nineteenth century. A purely technological explanation of the spread of Taylorism is every bit as inadequate as a purely technological explanation of craftsmen's autonomy.[53]

Second, the apostles of scientific management needed not only to abolish older industrial work practices, but also to discredit them in the public eye. Thus Taylor roundly denied that even "the high class mechanic" could "ever thoroughly understand the science of doing his work," and pasted the contemptuous label of "soldiering" over all craft rules, formal and informal alike.[54] Progressive intellectuals seconded his arguments. Louis Brandeis hailed scientific management for "reliev[ing] labor of responsibilities not its own."[55] And John R. Commons considered it "immoral to hold up to this miscellaneous labor, as a class, the hope that it can ever manage industry." If some workers do "shoulder responsibility," he explained, "it is because certain *individuals* succeed, and then those individuals immediately close the doors, and labor, as a class, remains where it was."[56]

It was in this setting that the phrase "workers' control" first entered the vocabulary of the American labor movement. It appeared to express a radical, if often amorphous, set of demands which welled up around the end of World War I among workers in the metal trades, railroading, coal mining, and garment industries.[57] Although those demands represented very new styles

[53]For basically technological interpretations of scientific management, see David Landes, *The Unbound Prometheus* (New York, 1969), 290-326; Samuel Haber, *Efficiency and Uplift: Scientific Management in the Progressive Era, 1890-1920* (Chicago and London, 1964); Hugh G. J. Aitken, *Taylorism at Watertown Arsenal: Scientific Management in Action, 1908-1915* (Cambridge, Mass., 1960).
[54]U. S. Congress, House of Representatives, *Hearings before the Special Committee of the House of Representatives to Investigate the Taylor and other Systems of Shop Management* (3 vols., Washington, D.C. 1912), 1397.
[55]Brandeis, "Brief before the I.C.C., January 3, 1911," in Daniel Bloomfield, *Selected Articles on Employment Management* (New York, 1922), 127.
[56]John R. Commons and others, *Industrial Government* (New York, 1921), 261.
[57]See Arthur Gleason, "The Shop Stewards and Their Significance," *Survey,* XLI (Jan. 4, 1919), 417-22; Carter Goodrich, "Problems of Workers' Control," *Locomotive Engineers Journal,* LVII (May, 1923), 365-67, 415; Evans Clark, "The Industry Is Ours," *Socialist Review,* IX (July, 1920), 59-62; David Montgomery, "The 'New Unionism' and the Transformation of

of struggle in a unique industrial and political environment, many of the workers who expressed them could remember the recent day when in fact, the manager's brains had been under the workman's cap.

Workers' Consciousness in America, 1909-1922,'' *Journal of Social History,* VII (Summer, 1974), 509-29.

7

Trouble on the Railroads in 1873-1874: Prelude to the 1877 Crisis?

HERBERT G. GUTMAN

"Strikes," complained the New York *Railroad Gazette* in January 1874, "are no longer accidents but are as much a disease of the body politic as the measles or indigestion are of our physical organization."[1] Between November 1873 and July 1874, workers on the Pennsylvania system and at least 17 other railroads struck.[2] Engineers, firemen, brakemen, and track hands as well as shopmen and ordinary laborers resisted wage cuts, demanded salary due them, and opposed such employer practices as blacklisting and the use of iron-clad contracts. None of these disputes was so dramatic or important as the general railroad strike in 1877, but together they prophetically etched the outlines of that violent outburst. The strikes also revealed certain explosive elements in the social structure of post-bellum America. Seemingly pathetic and seldom lasting more than a week or two, the significance of the strikes lay not in their success or failure but rather in the readiness of the strikers to express their grievances in a dramatic, direct, and frequently telling manner. Even though the workers were mostly without trade union organization or experience, they often exerted a kind of raw power that made trouble for their employers. Most of the 1873-1874 disputes, furthermore, took place in small railroad towns and in isolated semi-rural regions where small numbers of workers often could marshall surprising strength. The social structure and ideology in these areas often worked to the advantage of the disaffected workers. Large numbers of non-strikers fre-

---

[1] "The Strike," *Railroad Gazette*, Jan. 3, 1874, p. 4.

[2] Between November 1873 and June 1874 workers struck on the following railroads: the East Tennessee, Virginia, and Georgia, the Philadelphia and Reading, the Pennsylvania Central, the New Jersey Southern, the New York and Oswego Midland, the various eastern divisions of the Erie Railroad system, the Boston and Worcester, the Delaware, Lackawanna, and Western, the Louisville Short Line, the Allegheny Valley, and the Chicago and Alton.

Reprinted from *Labor History* 2 (1961), 215-35.

quently sided with them. Though the railroad operators put down almost all the strikes, they faced difficulties that they were unprepared for and that taxed their imaginations and their energies.

Even though the railroad industry was probably the largest single employer in the country when the 1873 depression started, most railroad workers were without unions of any kind.[3] The track hands, switchmen, firemen, and brakemen had no union. A small number of machinists employed in certain repair shops belonged to the Machinists' and Blacksmiths' International Union, but the large majority of shopmen and stationary hands were not union members. Most conductors also were free of union ties, for the Locomotive Conductors' Brotherhood was a weak union. Founded in 1868, it had only 21 locals five years later.[4] Only the engineers had an effective union in 1873, the Brotherhood of Locomotive Engineers. Almost 10,000 engineers, employed on nearly every major trunk line, belonged to the Brotherhood. Led by Grand Chief Engineer Charles Wilson, the Brotherhood enforced written contracts on a number of lines, published a monthly magazine, and maintained a well-managed accident and insurance program.[5] At the same time, the absence of trade unions

---

[3] The railroad system had grown enormously by 1873. Only 9,201 miles of track were used in 1850, but in the next ten years this figure had more than tripled. By 1873 slightly over 70,000 miles existed. In the four years between 1869 and 1873 more than 24,000 miles were built. Not counting clerks, Pennsylvania had about 18,000 railroad workers in 1870. Nearly 30,000 men worked for the Ohio roads in 1873. See, for examples, American Iron and Steel Association, *Annual Report to December 31, 1874* (Philadelphia: Chandler Printers, 1875), 75-77; Pennsylvania Bureau of Labor Statistics, *First Annual Report, 1872-1873* (Harrisburg: Benjamin Singerly, 1874), 407-408; Ohio Bureau of Labor Statistics, *First Annual Report,* 1877 (Columbus; Nevins and Myers, 1878), 281-283.

[4] *Brotherhood of Locomotive Engineers' Monthly Journal,* VII (December, 1873), 598. Examples of the strength of the Machinists' and Blacksmiths' International Union in the Indianapolis repair shops appear in the *Indianapolis Daily Sentinel,* Dec, 27, 1873-Jan. 10, 1874.

[5] Charles Wilson, a conservative trade unionist, rejected labor reform and politics, did not allow union members to cooperate with other non-railroad workers, opposed strikes, stressed matters such as sobriety, and believed that workers and employers shared a common interest. Under Wilson's leadership, the BLE worked closely with the American Railway Association, an organization of employers. Local lodges could not strike without his permission on pain of expulsion. Many engineers, especially in the west and the south, opposed his policies, but in 1873 his position seemed unassailable. See, for examples, *Brotherhood of Locomotive Engineers' Monthly Journal,* VII (November, 1873), 508; "List of Sub-divisions," *ibid.,* VII (December, 1873), 612-616. Wilson's views of other labor leaders such as Robert Schilling, John Fehrenbatch, and William Saffin are found in "The Missouri Strike," *ibid.,* VII (September, 1873), 408. See also George McNeil, ed., *The Labor Movement: The Problem of Today* (New York: M. W. Hazen, 1891), 321-332 and John R. Commons and others, *History of Labour in the United States,* II (New York: The Macmillan Co., 1918), 63-66.

among most railroad workers was no proof of their satisfaction with their jobs and their employers, for they voiced numerous grievances.[6]

During the early months of the depression, many railroads hastily adjusted to the drop in freight and passenger traffic. The New York Central Railroad, for example, discharged 1400 shopmen in New York City, and Jersey City, an important eastern rail terminus, listed thousands of unemployed workers by early November 1873. Railroads in every region—the Union Pacific, the Missouri, Kansas and Texas, the Louisville and Nashville, and the Lake Shore and Michigan Southern, to cite only a few examples—cut wages. A number of financially pressed roads also withheld wages.[7] In a number of instances, furthermore, the companies added insult to injury when they instituted their new wage policies. Knoxville officials of the East Tennessee, Virginia, and Georgia Railroad told their employees of a 20 per cent wage cut the day before it went into effect.[8] On November 30, the various divisions of the Pennsylvania system announced that the wages of engineers and firemen would fall 10 per cent the next day. The Pennsylvania violated a written agreement drawn up with the Brotherhood of Locomotive Engineers in 1872, for that contract fixed a wage

---

[6] Railroad workers had numerous grievances. They often complained that employers withheld wages from them for several weeks or even months. Certain Wisconsin roads made them trade in company-owned stores. Pennsylvania workers at the large Susquehanna Depot repair shops of the Erie Railroad said that many of the "best and oldest" workers were discharged "without assigned cause" and that "utterly unskilled" laborers received the same wages as some skilled mechanics. Engineers and firemen on the Pennsylvania system charged that when engines were damaged the workers paid the repair cost regardless of the cause. "If you don't pay the damages," company officials reportedly told complaining engineers, "we'll discharge you." Many engineers lost as much as 3 months of work every year because company officials did not supply them with new engines when their cabs were in repair. After listing a number of grievances, one engineer declared, "If I fall sick and am even absent for an hour from the engine I am docked the time, while the company can throw me off just as many hours as they choose." "We get paid so much a day for every day we are on a run," said another engineer. "They pay us by the 'run' not by the day . . . A day is 12 hours and from our point of view there are 14 days in the week." See *Workingman's Advocate*, Feb. 21, 1874; "Resolutions of the Susquehanna Depot, Pa., Strikers," n.d., printed in *ibid.*, March 14, 1874; "Interviews with unidentified locomotive engineers," n.d., *Chicago Tribune*, Dec. 29, 1873 and *Chicago Times*, Dec. 31, 1873. See also the discussion of conditions of work in Robert V. Bruce, *1877: Year of Violence* (Indianapolis: Bobbs-Merrill, 1959), 42-47.

[7] Examples of the severe amount of unemployment among railroad workers are found in the *Workingman's Advocate*, Oct. 11, 18, 25, Nov. 22, 29, Dec. 30, 1873; *Chicago Times*, Oct. 31, Nov. 10, Dec. 3, 5, 24, 1873; *Philadelphia Inquirer*, Nov. 5, 1873. The New Jersey Southern Railroad, a major link between Philadelphia and New York, in serious financial trouble, withheld $40,000 of back wages (*New York Times*, Jan. 14, 15, 1874).

[8] Knoxville dispatches, *Cincinnati Commercial*, Nov. 5, 7, 1873; *Chicago Times*, Nov. 6, 7, 1873.

scale that could not be altered by either side without prior notice or joint consultation. After the firm's announcement, therefore, the Union sent a special committee to J. N. McCullough, the system's western superintendent. McCullough brushed the committee aside, fired its members, and issued an order that forbade leaves of absences to other engineers who sought to discuss the matter with him. When angered engineers threatened to strike, McCullough, aware of the thousands of unemployed railroad men, announced, "Let them strike, I can't help it. If it is to be a strike, strike it must be."[9]

Most of the 1873-1874 strikes revealed the power of the railroad workers to disrupt traffic on many roads. Engineers, firemen, and machinists on the East Tennessee, Virginia, and Georgia Railroad demanded fewer hours in place of a wage cut in November 1873, but the Knoxville company turned them down. After the men left work, they removed coupling pins from many freight cars so that master mechanics, non-striking engineers, and new hands could not move them. No serious violence occurred, but for several days only mail trains left Knoxville.[10] New Jersey Southern Railroad workers tore up sections of track, disabled locomotives, and cut telegraph wires. Where track was removed, they posted signals to prevent accidents. Anxious to collect $40,000 of back wages, the men publicly denied responsibility for these depredations. Still, conditions on the New Jersey line remained chaotic and trains did not run in mid-January and early February 1874.[11] Soon after, track hands on the New York and Oswego Midland Railroad, who wanted five months' back pay, spiked switches

[9] J. D. Layng, Assistant General Manager, Pennsylvania Railroad Company, Pittsburgh, to A. J. Poole, Chairman, Committee of Locomotive Engineers, Jan. 20, 1872, and AJP and 19 representatives of the various divisions of the Pennsylvania Central Railroad, "Agreement with the Company," n. d., printed in the *Indianapolis Daily Sentinel,* Dec. 28, 1873; Richmond, Indiana, dispatch, *Chicago Tribune,* Dec. 31, 1873; A. J. Poole, "For the Indianapolis Engineers, Resolutions Unanimously Adopted on Dec. 27, 1873," *Indianapolis Daily Sentinel,* Dec. 28, 1873; Peter M. Arthur, "Speech . . . at the Atlanta Convention, 1874," *Brotherhood of Locomotive Engineers' Monthly Journal,* VIII (November, 1874), 584-585; "Interview with J. N. McCullough," Pittsburgh dispatch, *Chicago Times,* Dec. 28, 1873.

[10] R. A. B., Knoxville correspondent, *Cincinnati Gazette,* n. d., reported in *Chicago Tribune,* Nov. 8, 1873; *Cincinnati Commercial,* Nov. 5, 7, 1873; *Chicago Times,* Nov. 6, 7, 1873; Manufacturer to the editor, n. d., *Cincinnati Commercial,* Nov. 7, 1873; P. M. Arthur, "Address . . . to the Citizens of Knoxville . . . Dec. 16, 1874"; *Brotherhood of Locomotive Engineers' Monthly Journal,* IX (January, 1875), 33-34.

[11] *New York Times,* Jan. 14, 16, 1874; *Railroad Gazette,* Jan. 24, 1874, p. 31; *Philadelphia Inquirer,* Jan. 16, 1874.

and tore up sections of track near Middletown, New York.[12] In April 1874, 250 section hands struck the Louisville and Nashville Railroad for the same reasons. Freight trains did not run for a time, and the company told of switches tampered with and water tanks ruined.[13] Brakemen, switchmen, and track hands on the western New York division of the Erie Railroad also stopped trains. The strike centered in Hornellsville, where the Erie made important connections with other railroads. The workers allowed Erie trains to enter the town but would not let them leave. Within 24 hours, trains from three lines crowded the area. The strikers let mail trains pass but removed the brakes from passenger and freight cars. According to one report, 75 freight trains and 5 passenger trains with 1000 persons were detained for two days.[14]

The Lehigh Valley Railroad's coal line from Pittston, Pennsylvania, to Waverley, New York, was in similar difficulty in March 1874. On condition that wages would improve when rail traffic picked up, its workers had accepted a 10 per cent wage cut in December 1873. The company, however, reneged, and 250 men, all the employees except the engineers, struck. Congregating in Waverley, they set brakes, removed brake wheels, switched track, and allowed only mail trains to pass. They escorted stranded passengers to the depot and politely carried their baggage, moved into stalled railroad cars and raised an American flag over their new "home," and visited local hotels and taverns to prevent excessive drinking among the workers. For several days, the workers controlled local affairs. An observer noted, "No threats of violence are made—no disorderly conduct is feared—no drinks [are] allowed. . . . The property of the company is being guarded with as much care and zeal as if it were their own." Nevertheless, when officials ran a coal train over the Delaware, Lackawanna, and Western Railroad's tracks, strikers met it, unhooked its cars,

---

[12] *Railroad Gazette,* Feb. 14, 1874, p. 48.

[13] *Cincinnati Commercial,* April 18-26, 1874.

[14] The brakemen protested after the railroad, in an economy move, dropped one of every four brakemen on a train crew, and the switchmen and track hands complained about a wage cut and a simultaneous order to pay rent "for the shanties in which many of them lived along the railroad line." Details are found in *Railroad Gazette,* March 7, 1874, p. 87; Hornellsville dispatch, *Chicago Tribune,* March 7, 1874; "Strikes—Riot—Revolution," *Woodhull and Claflin's Weekly,* March 14, 1874, pp. 8-9.

and threw the coupling pins into a canal nearby.[15]

Shop workers and repair mechanics in the large Erie Railroad shops in Susquehanna Depot, a northeastern Pennsylvania town, also struck in late March 1874. They had many grievances against the corporation but especially complained about its failure to pay regular wages. More than 1000 of them left work on March 25, and they attracted nationwide attention. "Susquehanna is the subject of talk the country over," wrote the *Scranton Times*. The *Chicago Times* called the walkout "one of the most startling incidents that ever occurred in Pennsylvania."[16]

After electing a Workingmen's Committee to manage their affairs, the workers seized control of the repair shops. "Bells were rung" and "a mammoth steam whistle was blown." The men forced company officials from the shops, and within 20 minutes the entire works was cleared and "under the complete control of the men." Temperance committees visited tavern owners and asked them to close. For the moment, the strikers allowed trains through the city but warned Erie officials that they would halt traffic unless they were paid within 24 hours and the firm introduced a regular pay day, time and a half for overtime work, and a decent apprenticeship system. Instead of paying the men, the managers fired the strike leaders and said wages would be offered at a future unspecified time. On March 27, therefore, the workers made good their threat. "As fast as trains arrived," an Erie official wrote, strikers "proceeded to disable the locomotive by removing portions of the machinery." At least 45 engines were switched into a roundhouse. Passenger and freight cars were left on track nearby, but mail cars were let through the town. For a few days, rail business remained stalled in Susquehanna Depot. Although a number of prominent citizens found the strikers "quiet and orderly,"

---

[15] *Philadelphia Inquirer*, Jan. 14, March 6, 1874; *Philadelphia Bulletin*, Jan. 14, 1874; *Scranton Times*, March 5, 11, 1874; *Chicago Tribune*, March 5, 1874; *Railroad Gazette*, March 14, 1874, p. 94.

[16] The Erie Railroad frequently waited six or eight weeks before paying its employees. Most of the shopmen had worked three-quarters time during the early months of the depression, and in early March they struck and demanded a regular pay date. The company agreed to pay them on the fifteenth of each month, and the strike quickly ended. When March 15 came, the men were put off until March 25, and on that day the Erie managers again announced a postponement. See *Workingman's Advocate*, March 14, 1874; *Scranton Republican*, March 30, 1874; *Scranton Times*, March 28, 1874; *Chicago Times*, April 2, 1874; Pennsylvania Bureau of Labor Statistics, *Ninth Annual Report*, 1880-1881, III (Harrisburg: Lane S. Hart, 1882), 309-310.

the agitated shopmen indisputably controlled the Erie Railroad's valuable properties.[17]

Disgruntled engineers and firemen on the western divisions of the Pennsylvania Central Railroad also stopped trains. Acting without the permission of Charles Wilson, western members of the Brotherhood of Locomotive Engineers secretly planned a general strike and invited the firemen to join them in December 1873. A surprise walkout started at noon on December 26. About 3000 engineers and firemen simultaneously quit in many western cities. They struck in large cities such as Chicago, Pittsburgh, Cincinnati, Louisville, Columbus, and Indianapolis as well as smaller Ohio and Indiana towns such as Dennison, Alliance, Crestline, Logansport, and Richmond and affected almost the entire western division of Pennsylvania system, including the Pittsburgh, Fort Wayne, and Chicago Railroad, the Little Miami Railroad, the Pittsburgh, Cincinnati, and St. Louis Railroad, and the Jeffersonville, Madison, and Indianapolis Railroad. Ohio's *Portsmouth Tribune* called the dispute "the greatest railroad strike" in the nation's history.[18]

The suddenness of the strike paralyzed traffic on most of the Pennsylvania's divisions for several days. Stranded passengers filled the Pittsburgh Union Depot and loaded freight cars piled up in yards

---

[17] The behavior of the strikers was quite revealing. When Erie officials refused to allow mail cars through alone, the strikers telegraphed postal authorities in Washington and lodged a complaint against the firm. The Assistant Postmaster-General thanked the strikers for "facilitating the transportation of the United States' mails." Another time, as an express train drew up toward the city, the Erie Division Superintendent met it and ordered the engineer to drive through Susquehanna Depot at full speed and "in spite of hell." Filled with 300 passengers, the train dashed into the city at an excessive speed and stopped at the rail depot. Beyond the city to the west was a loose rail that could have derailed the entire train. "The Workingmen's Committee knew this," explained the *Scranton Republican*, "and . . . two of their *(sic)* number boarded the engine at the depot and in spite of the engineer and (Supperintendent) Thomas stopped the train." Thomas drew a revolver on the strikers, but he was seized and disarmed, and a warrant was issued for his arrest. See *Scranton Republican*, March 30, 1874; "Statement of James C. Clarke," Third Vice-President, Erie Railroad, *New York Tribune*, April 9, 1874; Adjutant General of Pennsylvania, *Annual Report*, 1874 (Harrisburg: Benjamin Singerly, 1875), 18-20, 23.

[18] The Indianapolis branch of the Brotherhood of Locomotive Engineers, for example, publicly criticized the Pennsylvania Railroad for its "oppressive and tyrannical" practices toward men who had "exerted themselves to work for the interest of the company." Though the engineers and firemen openly attacked the company, none publicly mentioned the strike before it actually began. See *Portsmouth Tribune*, Dec. 27, 1873; *Cincinnati Commercial*, Dec. 26-29, 1873; *Chicago Times*, Dec. 26-29, 1873; *Indianapolis Daily Sentinel*, Dec. 26-31, 1873; Charles Wilson, "To All Members of the Brotherhood," n. d., *Brotherhood of Locomotive Engineers' Monthly Journal*, VIII (January, 1874), 28-30.

nearby. Huge crowds gathered in depot yards in all the affected cities and, egged on by strikers, hooted at workers and company officials who tried to run the trains. In Indianapolis, for example, a noisy crowd jeered loudly as a superintendent manned the locomotive of a Vincennes-bound train. Cincinnati supervisory personnel found it hard to hire new engineers and firemen. Repair shops in many of these cities also closed.[19]

The most serious trouble occurred in Logansport, Indiana, a small rail terminal north of Indianapolis, where 200 engineers, firemen, and train hostlers halted the traffic on the Pittsburgh, Cincinnati, and St. Louis Railroad. The men gathered in the depot yards, uncoupled coaches and freight cars, pulled non-strikers from their cabs, and tampered with engines and boilers. They fixed one engine so that it could run only backwards. A non-striking engineer was hit with a stone. Even though the sheriff swore in special deputies and arrested 15 men and the mayor pleaded with the strikers to allow the trains through, company officials found it impossible to conduct their business. When an excited non-striker drove an express train through the city at a hazardous speed and in violation of state and local law, furthermore, he was arrested. Crowds continued to jam the depot yards, and trains remained still.[20]

In most cities, the strike was less effective than in Logansport. Still, for at least two or three days only mail trains regularly traveled the 3000 miles of struck road. Passenger trains manned by non-strikers, company officials, and master mechanics occasionally left one or another of the struck depot yards but few freight trains moved. The engineers and firemen, however, had uneven strength. In some cities, such as Pittsburgh and Chicago, they were quickly put down. In Cincinnati, Louisville, and Columbus, they held out for a week or two. Indianapolis engineers appealed to the traveling public, "We are not ready to sell our labor . . . for a price that would virtually close the doors of our educational institutions against our children and com-

---

[19] See, for many details on the early effects of the strike, *Pittsburgh Post*, Dec. 27, 1873; *Cincinnati Commerical*, Dec. 27, 28, 1873; *Chicago Tribune*, Dec. 27, 28, 30, 1873; *Indianapolis Daily Sentinel*, Dec. 26-31, 1873; *Chicago Times*, Dec. 27, 28, 1873.
[20] *Indianapolis Daily Sentinel*, Dec. 27, 28, 29, 1873; *Cincinnati Commercial*, Dec. 27, 29, 1873; *Chicago Times*, Dec. 27, 1873; *Chicago Tribune*, Dec. 29, 1873. The stoned engineer told a reporter that his assailant, a fireman named J. Hogan, "had no companionship with the Logansport strikers. (Interview with Charley Miller, *Chicago Times*, Dec. 31, 1874).

pel them to begin a life of drudgery without the first rudiments of
a common school education." Striking Cincinnati engineers explained,
"We assure you that we intend to fight it out on this line if it takes
all winter and summer, too."[21]

The strike was not without a number of violent incidents. Railroad officials everywhere accused the men of throwing switches, cutting telegraph lines, derailing trains, threatening and stoning non-
strikers, disengaging engines, and putting "soap or oil in water tanks
to explode engines." In Cincinnati, they blamed the strikers after an
express train jumped the track a few miles east of the city. After a
former official of the Indianapolis branch of the Brotherhood of Locomotive Engineers shot a non-striking engineer in the arm as latter drove
a train out of the city, the companies charged the union with foment-
ing violence. Company spokesmen also reported numerous threats
against working engineers and said non-strikers feared to return to
work.[22]

Publicly counseling against violence, the striking engineers and
firemen rejected the charges of the railroad companies. The Cincinnati strikers offered a reward for information concerning the derail-
ment and then blamed it on a cowardly non-striker, who jumped from
the express engine after he erroneously threw an air brake. The strikers accused the railroads of hiring "immoral, drunken, rowdy, and
incompetent" engineers, who had been discharged previously by the
same firms, as strikebreakers. Indianapolis engineers offered a reward
for the arrest of those who caused violence and even asked the permission of their employers to guard railroad property against possible
destruction. The managers refused and instead armed those men who
remained loyal. The strikers then offered to "stand or fall by the
verdict of an impartial tribunal" and insisted that certain persons
committed "unlawful depredations and charge the same to the engi-

21 Division 11, B. L. E., "To the Public," n. d., *Indianapolis Daily Sentinel,* Dec. 31,
1873; Little Miami Railroad Division Engineers, "To the Commuters on the Little
Miami Division of the Pennsylvania Central Railroad and the Public in General,"
n. d., *Cincinnati Enquirer,* Jan. 1, 1874. See also E. Price, First Assistant Engineer,
Little Miami Division, B. L. E., Lodge 34, to Brother Committeemen, n. d., *loc.
cit.* Price gave the *Enquirer* the names of "scab" engineers in his letter and urged
his fellow-strikers to hang posters everywhere so that the public would learn of the
incompetent skills of these "scabs."
22 See, for examples, *Chicago Times,* Dec. 27, 1873; *Chicago Tribune,* Dec. 30, 1873;
Cincinnati Commercial, Dec. 28, 29, 1873; *Indianapolis Daily Sentinel,* Dec. 28,
29, 30, 1873.

neers and firemen in the hope of turning public opinion against us and in favor of the railroad companies."[23]

In each of these strikes, the workers disrupted traffic and made other kinds of trouble. The character of their behavior closely paralleled events that would take place in the summer of 1877. Commenting on the seizure of railroad property and the halting of trains in 1873-1874, *Railroad Gazette* insisted that the workers were in "flat rebellion, not simply against the companies . . . but against the law of the land." Such behavior was "a defiance to every law-abiding citizen." The trade journal explained:

> Imagine a servant girl disconnecting the water and gas, putting the range out of order . . . locking up the kitchen, and coolly declaring that there shall be no cooking in the kitchen till she gets her pay and the right to two "afternoons out" weekly.

Charging the strikers with criminal and violent acts, most urban newspapers supported the *Railroad Gazette* and advised "swift, decided, and exemplary" punishment.[24]

---

[23] The scant and often contradictory nature of the evidence makes it impossible to establish responsibility for the acts of violence. The *Cincinnati Enquirer*, no friend to strikers, said that "a large amount of terrorism existed in the minds of [railroad] managers." (*Cincinnati Enquirer*, Jan. 16, 1874. See also *Coopers' New Monthly*, I [January, 1874], 13-14) Jerry Bush, who shot the non-union engineer in Indianapolis, was held in $3000 bail, but no trial record has been found. (Indianapolis dispatch, *Chicago Tribune*, Dec. 30, 1873). Samuel Marchbanks was arrested for cutting down telegraph wires near Dennison, Ohio, but no information has been located about his occupation or his motive. (Cadiz, Ohio, dispatch, *Cincinnati Commercial*, Feb. 23, 1874). There is suggestive but incomplete data concerning the Cincinnati derailment. In mid-January 1874, the Cincinnati railroad companies announced that several private detectives had studied the incident and that 7 firemen and an engineer from Zenia, Columbus, and Cincinnati were partners to the "crime." Accused of "conspiracy," planning to pour soap and lye into boilers and engines, and throwing the switch that derailed the express, the men faced jail sentences of from 7 to 21 years if convicted. One of them, Daniel Harvey, a fireman, confessed and implicated the other six. Henry Lewis, the supposed ringleader, was defended by a prominent Ohio State Senator, W. P. Reed. The railroad officials pleaded in Harvey's behalf and said the others had misled him. No record has been found of the outcome of the trial. (*Ibid.*, Jan. 16, 1874; *Cincinnati Enquirer*, Jan. 16, 21, March 14, 1874).

[24] "Railroads Seized by Strikers," *Railroad Gazette*, April 4, 1874, p. 122; "The Railroad Strike," *Philadelphia Bulletin*, Dec. 27, 1873. See also the editorials in *Philadelphia Inquirer*, Dec. 27, 1873; *Cincinnati Commercial*, Dec. 28, 1873; *Chicago Times*, Dec. 30, 31, 1873; *Chicago Tribune*, Dec. 28, 1873; extracts from editorials in *Louisville Courier and Journal*, n. d., *Cincinnati Inter-Ocean*, n. d., *Cincinnati Times*, n. d., and other western and southern newspapers reprinted in the *Indianapolis Daily Sentinel*, Dec. 30 and 31, 1873. Certain newspapers such as the *New York Times* and the *Chicago Tribune*, however, took a more conciliatory approach and especially criticized those roads that failed to pay their workers on time. "Men who are starving for the want of wages," observed the *Times*, ". . . cannot be expected to be always reasonable." "They are dependent on their wages for bread," wrote the

Evidence of community support for the 1873-1874 railroad strikers also suggested a parallel with the later 1877 events.[25] Engineers and firemen from the Alabama and Chattanooga Railroad refused to run idle Knoxville trains during the East Tennessee, Virginia, and Georgia Railroad strike.[26] The strikers on the New Jersey Southern Railroad found local support in and near Manchester, New Jersey, and even though the railroad pleaded for state and even federal intervention in its behalf, the New Jersey legislature made back wages a first lien on the receipts of railroads in receivership.[27] During the Lehigh Valley Railroad dispute, Erie Railroad workers brought the strikers provisions, and many Waverley citizens also supported them.[28] When 400 freight depot hands in New York City demanded pre-depression wages and special overtime rates from the Erie Railroad, a Catholic priest encouraged them.[29] Similarly, striking brakemen on the Chicago and Alton Railroad were aided by Bloomington, Illinois, citizens in June 1874.[30]

During the Pennsylvania Central dispute, the disaffected engineers and firemen also found a good deal of sympathy from non-strikers. An Indianapolis militia officer complained that the Logansport authorities were helpless because the "public" actively sided with the railroad workers. He also found that the Indianapolis troops sent

---

Chicago Tribune of the Susquehanna Depot strikers. "The remedy of a law-suit is a mockery to a starving man or, in this case, a starving community." While critical of the Erie Railroad, these same newspapers and others still supported the Pennsylvania governor when he sent militia to allow the trains to run again. See, for examples of this moderately critical attitude, New York Times, March 29, 31, 1874; Chicago Tribune, March 30, 1874. See also Cleveland Leader, March 31, 1874; Philadelphia Bulletin, March 30, 1874.

25 Evidence of the character of community support for workers during other industrial disputes at the start of the 1873 depression can be found in Herbert G. Gutman, "Two Lockouts in Pennsylvania, 1873-1874," The Pennsylvania Magazine of History and Biography, LXXXIII (July, 1959), 322-325 and "An Iron Workers' Strike in the Ohio Valley," The Ohio Historical Quarterly, LXVIII (October, 1959), 357-358, 361, 363, 365-369.

26 Knoxville dispatches, Chicago Tribune, Nov. 8, 1873; Chicago Times, Nov. 6, 7, 1873; Cincinnati Commercial, Nov. 6, 7, 1873.

27 New York Times, Jan. 24, Feb. 20, 1874; Railroad Gazette, Jan. 31, Feb. 21, 1874, pp. 40, 66. The strike finally ended when the workers signed an agreement under which the road's receivers would lease the road so that the net earnings of the line could be applied to the payment of back wages as a first lien.

28 Scranton Times, March 11, 1874.

29 New York Times, March 21, 22, 23, 25, 26, 27, 29, 1874; Chicago Tribune, March 24, 1874.

30 Ibid., June 3-6, 1874; Chicago Times, June 3-6, 1874.

to Logansport had no heart in their work and wanted to go home. A Dennison, Ohio, resident repudiated charges that local strikers behaved like "drunken rioters" and insisted that the Steubenville militia, sent to put down "violence" in Dennison, was embittered over its task. Cincinnati socialists demonstrated in support of the strikers, and in Columbus, non-striking engineers promised the strikers half of their wages. Enthusiastic numbers of Indianapolis workers defended and even aided the strikers. Local trade unions, such as the Iron Molders' Union, the Carpenters' and Joiners' Union, and the Indianapolis Trades' Assembly, commended their "pluck against acts of tyranny," and the Indianapolis Typographical Union, after urging the strikers "to resist the unjust demands of this [railroad] monopoly to the bitter end," voted them $300. Members of the Machinists' and Blacksmiths' International Union in the Indianapolis repair shops refused to fix damaged Pennsylvania engines, and John Fehrenbatch, the union's national president, visited the city and defended the engineers and firemen.[31]

The Indianapolis strikers also attracted substantial backing from the non-laboring population. The mayor, a prominent local judge, and several members of the city council attacked the Pennsylvania Railroad. General Daniel Macauley, who had just returned from Logansport where he headed the Indianapolis militia and restored order, joined other local dignitaries who "extended their sympathies to the engineers" and encouraged "them in their efforts to break up the monopoly which has been oppressing them." Letters in the local press generally favored the strikers: one asked if the railroad officials were "gods that mortal men dare not speak to?" The *Indianapolis Daily Sentinel*, a Democratic newspaper, called the railroads an "oligarchy ...more powerful...than the absolutism of the Napoleons." Hark-

[31] Daniel Macauley, Logansport, to Gov. Thomas A. Hendricks, Indianapolis, Dec. 29, 1873; DM, Logansport, to the Mayor and Sheriff, Logansport, n. d.; Mayor S. L. McFadden, "A Proclamation," n. d.; and other details printed in the *Indianapolis Daily Sentinel*, Dec. 29, 30, 31, 1873; Resolutions of the Printers' Union, the Carpenters' and Joiners' Union, the Iron Molders' Union, the Machinists' and Blacksmiths' International Union, and the Indianapolis, Trades' Assembly, printed in *ibid.*, Jan. 2, 4, 7, 1874; John Fehrenbatch's visit is described in *ibid.*, Jan. 3, 1874; and the *Chicago Tribune*, Dec. 31, 1874; the Dennison details are revealed in H. B. Keffer, Dennison, to the editor, Dec. 30, 1873, *Cincinnati Commercial*, Jan. 3, 1874. See also *Indianapolis Daily Sentinel*, Dec. 29, 1873 and Jan. 11, 1874; *Chicago Times*, Dec. 30, 1873; *Chicago Tribune*, Dec. 29, 30, 1873.

ing back to Jacksonian concepts, the *Sentinel* blamed the strike on "the great interests" and "the grasping and imbecile management of the great corporations."[32]

Many of Susquehanna Depot's 8000 inhabitants, although dependent on the Erie Railroad whose shops dominated the local economy, also supported and aided the strikers. When railroad officials announced the dismissal of the strike leaders and demanded that M. B. Helme, the Lackawanna County sheriff, organize a posse and drive the shopmen from the railroad's properties, Helme refused to act until the strikers received all the wages due them. Soon after, when Helme and a 35-man posse arrived near the shops, the strikers refused to talk with them unless they came disarmed. Helme surrendered their arms to the strikers, who then allowed the police to stay in the shops and "preserve order." Local law enforcement authorities also thwarted the company's importation of 200 "special police" from New York and New Jersey. Scranton reporters called these 200 men "a gang of ruffians of the no-profession-in-particular class." Together with a number of strikers, Sheriff Helme intercepted the strangers outside of the town, disarmed them of their "billies and revolvers," and, after threatening their arrest, shipped them back home.[33]

At the same time, other local citizens supported the strikers. A prominent officer in the state militia told Governor John Hartranft that the shopmen had "the sympathy of nearly if not all the citizens of the town." As a result, a friend of the Erie company exploded, "The Commune could do no more." "Public sympathy is with the men," wrote the *Scranton Times*, "and '*vox populi vox dei*' is a fairer law than many of our statutes embody." When Governor Hartranft agreed to send troops, leading local citizens, including a justice of the peace, a town burgess, an assistant postmaster, and a physician, assailed his decision. Why, asked one critic, were troops needed if the strikers were "quiet [and] orderly and the mails ... allowed to run?" A petition signed by a majority of the city's prominent residents charged Hartranft with "supporting the interests of a corporation against our own citizens, who ask nothing but their hard-earned

32 *Indianapolis Daily Sentinel,* Jan. 3, 4, 5, 8, 1874.
33 *Scranton Times,* March 29, 1874; *Scranton Republican,* March 30, 1874; "Statement of J. C. Clarke," *New York Tribune,* April 9, 1874.

wages." "In the name of humanity," the petitioners asked him to withdraw the soldiers.[34]

In neighboring Scranton, the *Times* and the *Republican* backed the shopmen, too. Admitting that their seizure of property was illegal, the *Times* still defended the workers:

> The law is an uncertain, tedious, and expensive means of reaching a powerful corporation. It was an insult to these men to retain their wages upon which most of them were dependent for their bread—bread for their families. "The laborer is worthy of his hire" and he should have it.

To withhold his wages was "an insult . . . to his dignity as a citizen and to his worth as a workman." "An insulted man," the *Times* concluded, "don't [*sic*] think about law and legal redress . . . Erie has wronged its labor grossly and got its blow."[35]

The popular support afforded the strikers expressed itself in many ways. Citizens housed marooned Erie passengers. A local minister preached a severe Sunday sermon against the Erie company. After the state troops arrived, many merchants refused to sell them provi-

---

[34] *Scranton Republican,* March 30, 1874; S. H. Daddow, Scranton, to the editor, March 30, 1874, *ibid.,* March 31, 1874; *Scranton Times,* March 31, 1874. General E. S. Osbourne, Susquehanna Depot, to Gov. J. F. Hartranft, Harrisburg, March 29, 1874, printed in Adjutant General of Pennsylvania, *Annual Report,* 1874 (Harrisburg: Benjamin Singerly, 1875), 20; ESO, Wilkes-barre, to Major-General James Latta, Harrisburg, Oct. 1, 1874, *ibid.,* 23-24; W. H. Telford Susquehanna Depot, to Gov. JFH, Harrisburg, March 28, 1874; WHT, S. Mitchell, A. M. Falkenberg, C. Ovidor, and Dr. Leslie, Susquehanna Depot, to JFH, Harrisburg, March 29, 1874; petition enclosed in Burgess William J. Falkenburg, Susquehanna Depot, to JFH, Harrisburg, March 29, 1874; *ibid.,* 18-20. A copy of the petition also appeared in the *Scranton Republican,* March 30, 1874. The petitioners told the governor: "The peace of this community is not disturbed, and the sheriff has been assured by the strikers that if any arrests are to be made, they will assist him if called upon." The petitioners also protested "against the employment of troops under the command of the paid counsel of the company," William Jessup, "in whose interests they are to be used." Hartranft, however, insisted that troops were necessary. He accused the shopmen of trying to "obtain their rights by violence" and not respecting "the laws of the country." "As an individual," Hartranft explained, "I may sympathize with your people in their misfortune in not receiving prompt payment of their dues, but as the chief Executive of this State, I can not allow creditors . . . to forcibly seize [the] property of their debtors and hold it without due process of law. . . . Whenever the laws of this Commonwealth shall provide that the employees of a railroad company may suspend all traffic upon it, until their wages are paid, I will acquiesce, but I cannot do so while the law refuses to contemplate any such remedy. . . ." (Gov. JFH, Harrisburg, to WHT, Susquehanna Depot, March 28, 1874; JFH, Harrisburg, to WHT, Susquehanna Depot, March 29, 1874; and JFH, Harrisburg, to WJF, Susquehanna Depot, March 29, 1874 printed in Adjutant General of Pennsylvania, *op. cit.,* 20-21.)

[35] *Scranton Times,* March 31, 1874. See also editorials in *Scranton Republican,* March 30, 31, 1874.

sions, and some soldiers suffered "for want of food." The *Susque-hanna Depot Gazette* accused the troops of stealing cigarettes and liquor and called them "Molly Maguires," who insulted citizens and created "forty times more disturbance than the strikers." Among the militia itself, a large majority were reported in sympathy with the shopmen. In light of all this hostility toward the Erie Railroad, it was not surprising that company officials bitterly complained of the "bad advice . . . certain citizens of this place" gave the workers.[36]

The railroad strikes in 1873-1874 created a number of difficulties for management. In many of the strikes, the employers learned that they had a rather tenuous hold on the loyalties of their men. Some-thing was radically wrong if workers could successfully stop trains for from two or three days to as much as a week, destroy property, and even "manage" it as if it were their own. The law itself seemed insufficient. *Iron Age* called for new legislation modeled after the English Master's and Servant's Act and prohibiting "surprise" strikes. *Railroad Gazette* suggested an even harsher remedy: the strikers were "ignorant and violent," had no respect for "law," and deserved only "bayonets."[37]

Except in the Hornellsville strike, the railroad companies declined to compromise with the strikers.[38] Unemployment was especially severe in the industry during the early months of the depression. In many instances, therefore, the companies brought in new workers. When 500 Buffalo freight handlers, brakemen, carpenters, painters, and track hands struck for back wages as well as a regular pay day, Erie Railroad officials simply fired more than half of them.[39] Dis-affected Chicago and Alton Railroad brakemen also lost their jobs.[40] In New York City, after 400 freight depot hands struck against the Erie Railroad, the company hired Italian and German workers. Hun-

---

[36] *Scranton Times,* March 30, 31, 1874; *Scranton Republican,* March 30, 31, 1874; *Susquehanna Depot Gazette,* n. d., reprinted in *ibid.,* April 8, 1874; J. C. Clarke, Susquehanna Depot, to President Lucius D. Robinson, New York, March 30, 1874, printed in *Scranton Times,* April 1, 1874.

[37] *Iron Age,* Jan. 8, 1874, pp. 16-17, "Railroad's Seized by Strikers," *Railroad Gazette,* April 4, 1874, p. 122.

[38] *Ibid.,* March 7, 1874, p. 87; *Chicago Tribune,* March 7, 1874; *Woodhull and Claflin's Weekly,* March 14, 1874, pp. 8-9.

[39] *Railroad Gazette,* March 14, 21, 1874, pp. 94, 100; *Chicago Tribune,* March 4, 5, 6, 1874; *New York Times,* March 6, 1874; *Scranton Times* March 6, 1874; *Locomotive Engineer's Advocate,* March 14, 1874 reprinted in *Workingman's Advocate,* March 21, 1874.

[40] *Chicago Times,* June 3-7, 1874; *Chicago Tribune,* June 3-7, 1874.

gry unemployed Italians also replaced discontented tunnel builders on a Delaware, Lackawanna, and Western Railroad project near Hoboken, New Jersey. Most of them had been "unemployed for a long time because of hard times" and "manifested great eagerness to begin work."[41] New engineers and firemen also took the jobs of many strikers on the Pennsylvania Railroad system. In Crestline, Ohio, a small railroad town where many workers lived, company officials ordered them "to surrender unconditionally to the company's order or . . . leave the services of the road for all time." The *Indianapolis Daily Sentinel* found that widespread unemployment dealt a "death blow" to the engineers and firemen.[42]

If it proved difficult to bring in new workers, the railroad managers used other techniques to defeat the strikers. In one instance, according to the engineers, the Pennsylvania Central tried to halt mail trains so as to force federal intervention against the strikers.[43] More common employer instruments were the blacklist and the iron-clad contract. Before striking New York City freight depot workers could return, they had to pledge never to join a union or strike.[44] During the East Tennessee, Virginia, and Georgia Railroad strike, the company fired all workers belonging to ". . . any league, body, organization, or combination which instigates . . . acts of disorder, violence, and wrong." At the same time, representatives of 20 southern roads met in Chattanooga and unanimously decided not to hire workers discharged for "insubordination or combination to stop the operations on any road by intimidation or interference with others willing to work." These companies also drew up a list of proscribed workers and circulated it throughout the region.[45] When the strikers, led by the engineers, sought a compromise, they were ordered to surrender their union charter. Twenty-two of them, who signed an iron-clad contract, publicly declared:

We now acknowledge that we have been beaten, and that we were in

[41] William Jessup, New York, to the editor, April 1, 1874, *Workingman's Advocate,* April 11, 1874; *New York Times,* March 21, 22, 23, 24, 25, 26, 27, 29, 1874; *Chicago Tribune,* March 24 1874.
[42] *Indianapolis Daily Sentinel,* Jan. 5, 14, 1874; *Chicago Tribune,* Dec. 31, 1873; *Chicago Times,* Dec. 30, 1873; *Cincinnati Commercial,* Dec. 31, 1873.
[43] *Indianapolis Daily Sentinel,* Dec. 31, 1873 and Jan. 1, 1874; *Chicago Times,* Dec. 29, 1873.
[44] *New York Times,* March 21, 22, 23, 25, 26, 27, and 29, 1874; *Chicago Tribune,* March 24, 1874.
[45] Knoxville dispatches, *Chicago Times,* Nov. 7, 8, 1873.

error. . . . We have withdrawn from the organization known as the
"Brotherhood of Locomotive Engineers," and if you think proper to
employ us again, we will work for you as faithfully as we ever did before,
notwithstanding the reduction in wages. . . .[46]

Leaders of the strike against the Pennsylvania system also were blacklisted. The *Chicago Times* found men returning to work after they
learned that the company had "marked some of the bell-wethers . . .
of this strike for the shambles." Some strikers, such as the Columbus
men, held out in the hope of "forcing the employment of even the
leaders," but the company's threats proved effective. The company sent
the names of the strike leaders "through the length and breadth of the
country." Although the Brotherhood of Locomotive Engineers warned
of a bitter "conflict," the workers on the Pennsylvania Railroad remained quiet until the violent uprisings of 1877.[47]

State militia put down some of the more truculent strikers.
Troops went to Dennison, Ohio, and Logansport, Indiana, during the
Pennsylvania Railroad dispute. On the second day of the strike, Indiana Governor Thomas A. Hendricks answered an appeal for aid
from the Logansport sheriff and sent two companies of militia. Led
by General Daniel Macauley and armed with breech-loading repeater
rifles, the soldiers guarded the depot, tracks, and trains. They accompanied trains leaving the city and quieted "large crowds of excited
men." Though some railroad workers "proffered their sympathy" to
Macauley, he arrested a number of strikers, swore in special deputies,
had Hendricks send a detachment of Indianapolis city police, and
convinced the Logansport mayor to issue a riot proclamation that
ordered citizens "to their several homes or places of business in order
that peace . . . be preserved." Within a few days, the militia and police
restored normal traffic and left Logansport.[48]

In Susquehanna Depot, state troops also were used. After Sheriff M. B. Helme refused to ask Governor John Hartranft for militia,

[46] The entire correspondence between the engineers and the railroad officials is found in
the *Brotherhood of Locomotive Engineers' Monthly Journal,* VII (December, 1873),
579-580 and *ibid.,* IX (January 1875), 33-34.

[47] *Chicago Times,* Dec. 29, 30, 31, 1873; *Cincinnati Commercial,* Jan. 3, 1874; *Indianapolis Daily Sentinel,* Jan. 3, 1874; *Brotherhood of Locomotive Engineers' Monthly
Journal,* n. d., reprinted in the *Coopers' New Monthly,* I (July, 1874), 14.

[48] The correspondence between the Logansport sheriff and mayor, General Macauley, and
Governor Hendricks is found in the *Indianapolis Daily Sentinel,* Dec. 28, 29, 30, 31,
1873 and Jan. 4, 1874. For other details see *ibid.,* Dec. 27, 1873-Jan. 5, 1874;
Chicago Times, Dec. 30, 1873; *Chicago Tribune,* Dec. 30, 1873.

William H. Jessup, the Erie's lawyer in Susquehanna Depot and a ranking officer in the Pennsylvania National Guard, telegraphed the governor that "a mob of 1000 have seized the railroad trains, stopped the mails, and are causing terror." Jessup asked for 700 soldiers. Hartranft reminded Jessup that only the sheriff could ask for militia and rejected his plea. A day later, amid unsubstantiated "rumors" that Sheriff Helme had been "bribed" by the railroad firm to "betray" the shopmen, Helme publicly ordered the strikers to let the passenger trains through. He advised them that the road would pay them back wages and then discharge them. The shopmen agreed to allow the trains to move. Yet, when it *appeared* that they were stalling, Helme wired Hartranft to send 1500 soldiers armed with "plenty of ammunition." Dispatching the Wilkes-Barre militia, Hartranft told its commanding officer, "Use every effort to restore order without bloodshed. Suppress the riot, disperse the rioters, and afford security and protection to the owners of property in its lawful use."[49]

Even though prominent citizens protested, Susquehanna Depot soon became an armed camp. Major-General E. S. Osbourne, the head of the Wilkes-Barre militia, admitted that the shopmen were "not disposed to commit violence," but he asked Hartranft for more troops, and the Governor sent the Philadelphia First Regiment. Special trains supplied by the region's coal railroads brought the Philadelphia soldiers, and Susquehanna Depot, a town of 8000, was patrolled by 1800 soldiers and an artillery group with 30 pieces of cannon. The militia took over the railroad properties and worked closely with company officials. Martial law was proclaimed, and no one could walk on company property without a special pass. Erie Vice-President James C. Clarke fired all the workers and promised them their wages after the trains left town. The shopmen let several loaded passenger trains through, but hesitated about the freight trains. At the same time, they overwhelmingly rejected the company's terms of settlement and asked it to rehire them all. "I shall run the road," Clarke telegraphed

---

[49] The correspondence between Jessup, Helme, and Hartranft, as well as the communications to the militia leaders, is printed in Adjutant General of Pennsylvania, *Annual Report*, 1874 (Harrisburg: Benjamin Singerly, 1875), 17-18, 22. See also *Scranton Republican*, March 30, 1874. The Erie Railroad took a false public position regarding its request for state troops. According to James Clarke, who issued a statement that appeared in the *New York Tribune* of April 9, the company did not ask for troops until Saturday, March 28, after the strikers had reneged on their promise to let all trains through the city. Jessup's telegrams, however, are dated March 27, 1874.

President Lucius Robinson in New York. "I am through [with] compromise. I have offered everything but the right of the company to operate its own property subject to the laws which created it."[50]

The strikers remained firm for a few more days, but it was to no avail. Twelve hundred shopmen paraded the streets and demanded to be rehired. But the company paid and discharged all of them. The militia formed "a cordon of bayonets on both sides of the depot and track for half a mile" while the men were paid off. Clarke announced that 400 new workers were needed. No strike leader was to be taken back, and only family men with suitable references were advised to apply for jobs. At first, the strikers held off, "determined to stick to their resolution of 'work for all or none'." The company thereupon announced that unless some of the old hands accepted its terms the shops would move to Elmira. A number of business people and other residents, undoubtedly fearing that the local economy would collapse without the repair shops, turned against the shopmen and formed a committee of 60 to protect the railroad's interests. "They see," wrote the *Scranton Republican,* "that unless they keep the shops running their businesses will be ruined." The leader of these businessmen was a local politician, who a few days before had protested to Governor Hartranft when he sent the militia. Now, he furnished the Erie Railroad's counsel with the names of leading strikers for possible criminal prosecution. When the shops reopened on April 1, 406 old hands showed up. In the end, the company took back all but 150 of the strikers. It denied work to the leaders of the strike, who left the town in search of jobs. Clarke insisted that only those men "interested in the success and welfare of the community in which they lived" were rehired. By effectively combining military power (which cost the Pennsylvania taxpayers $25,000 because the soldiers received salary for half a month although they served only five or six days) with economic coercion, the Erie restored its position in Susquehanna Depot.[51]

---

[50] The vote by which shopmen rejected the company offer was either 476-11 or 478-48. Details on the events after the troops arrived are found in Adjutant General of Pennsylvania, *op. cit.,* 20, 23-24; *Scranton Republican,* March 30, 31, 1874; *Scranton Times,* March 30, 1874; J. C. Clarke, Susquehanna Depot, to L. Robinson, New York, March 30, 1874, printed in *ibid.,* April 1, 1874.

[51] *Ibid.,* April 1, 2, 1874; *Scranton Republican,* April 2, 1874; "Statement of J. C. Clarke," *New York Tribune,* April 9, 1874; *Chicago Times,* April 1, 1874; Adjutant General of Pennsylvania, *op. cit.,* 24-27; Pennsylvania Bureau of Labor Statistics, *Ninth Annual Report,* 1880-1881, III (Harrisburg: Lane S. Hart, 1882), 309-310; *Army and Navy Journal,* May 2, 1874, p. 653.

Several brief but pertinent observations may be made about the 1873-1874 railroad strikes. First, local discontent sparked the strikes; they were neither centrally directed nor national in scope. Two of the strikes involving engineers, in fact, were condemned by the head of the Brotherhood of Locomotive Engineers, who publicly assailed the strikers and advised other workers to replace them.[52] Secondly, the ability of workers in so many different towns and regions to stop trains and "take over" railroad properties as well as the degree of public support tendered these men indicates that certain institutional and ideological factors added to the strength of the workers and temporarily, at least, weakened the power of the employers and created additional obstacles for them to surmount. The sympathy the workers found in Waverley, Manchester, Indianapolis, Logansport, and Susquehanna Depot often came from property owners, who supported the strikers even though their spontaneous protests (the response to

---

[52] Wilson ran into difficulty after he attacked the striking engineers on the East Tennessee, Virginia, and Georgia Railroad and on the Pennsylvania Railroad. The leaders of other national unions called him a friend of "scabs" and "unjust employers," and they blamed him for the defeat of the workers. The *Iron Molders' Journal* labeled him "a grand corporosity." During the Pennsylvania Railroad strike, Wilson publicly announced: "No dishonor will be attached to any man who accepts a situation from Pennsylvania Railroad during the present strike." Engineers in Columbus, Louisville, and other cities denounced him, but the urban press and business weeklies said he was a model labor leader and not "molded . . . on the European plan." After the Pennsylvania strike ended, Wilson continued his attack on the strikers and argued that "strife between labor and capital" could but be ended by "civil war." Enraged Pittsburgh engineers published an eight-page monthly, the *Locomotive Engineers' Advocate*, which sharply attacked his policies, and, finally, in February 1874, he was removed from office by the nearly unanimous vote of delegates to a special convention of the B. L. E. Peter M. Arthur, who was to dominate the union for the next quarter of a century and give it a distinctly conservative flavor, replaced him as the "reform" candidate. Wilson's behavior in the two strikes is found in *Chicago Times*, Nov. 9, 1873; CW, "Remarks," *Brotherhood of Locomotive Engineers' Monthly Journal*, VII (December, 1873), 379-380; "Law and Order," *Iron Molders' Journal* (December, 1873), pp. 165-166; CW to the Public, *Cleveland Herald*, n. d., reprinted in the *Chicago Tribune*, Dec. 29, 1873; CW to the Associated Press, *Cincinnati Commercial*, Dec. 29, 1873; *Chicago Times*, Dec. 31, 1873; *Indianapolis Daily Sentinel*, Jan. 6, 1874; "The Strike and the Brotherhood," *Railroad Gazette*, Jan. 3, 1874, pp. 4-5; *Cleveland Leader*, Jan. 12, 1874. Criticism of Wilson is found in *Workingman's Advocate*, Dec. 27, 1873-Jan. 3, 1874; *Machinists' and Blacksmiths' Journal*, n.d., reprinted in *ibid.*, Feb 7, 1874; *Coopers' New Monthly*, I (January, 1874), 13-14; *Iron Molders' Journal* (January, 1874), p. 200. Wilson's defense is presented in CW, "General Statement," *Brotherhood of Locomotive Engineers' Monthly Journal*, VII (January, 1874), 29-30; CW to the editor, *Cleveland Leader*, Jan. 5, 1874; CW and E. S. Ingram to the Members and Officers of the BLE, *Railroad Gazette*, Feb. 21, 1874, pp. 59-60. The later attack on Wilson is found in L. B. Greene, "To the Brotherhood," *Brotherhood of Locomotive Engineers' Monthly Journal*, VIII (February, 1874), 86; "The Locomotive Engineers," *Iron Molders' Journal* (February 1874), 243-244 and *ibid.* (March, 1874), 273. Wilson's removal is described in *Cleveland Leader*, Feb, 21-28, 1874 and *Chicago Tribune*, Feb. 21-28, 1874.

deeply felt grievances and the absence of experienced trade union leadership) were extreme and often violent. Not unusual, for example, was the attitude reflected in an editorial in the *Scranton Times* during the strike on the Pennsylvania system:

> Labor is the great moving power of the world and has the same right to unite for its own advancement that capital has to mass itself for the aggrandizement of the few who control it. . . . [If the railroads] have the right to reduce the wages of workmen, the workmen themselves have the right to dissolve the partnership and take their labor out of the firm. Capital and labor together earn a certain profit which should be equitably divided.[53]

In many small towns in the 1870's, and in sharp contrast to the larger cities of that time, the discontented worker still was viewed by his fellow citizens as an individual and was not yet the stereotyped "labor agitator," who so often stirred an automatically negative reflex from his more fortunate observer. The support tendered these railroad workers in 1873-1874, furthermore, was not unique to the structure and reputation of that industry. Similar attitudes shaped the behavior of non-industrial property owners during conflicts that involved coal miners and iron, textile, and glass workers in the 1870's.[54]

Finally, even though the troubles that railroad operators faced in 1873-1874 were small and insignificant compared with those that developed in July 1877, the same essential patterns of behavior that were widespread in 1877 were found in the 1873-1874 strikes. Three and a half years of severe depression ignited a series of local brush fires into a national conflagration that seared the conscience as well as the confidence of the entire nation. The 1877 railroad strikes are put into their proper historical context only when measured against the events that took place in 1873-1874.

---

[53] *Scranton Times,* Dec. 31, 1873.

[54] Supporting data is found in the articles by the author cited in footnote 25. See also Herbert G. Gutman, "Social And Economic Structure and Depression: American Labor in 1873 and 1874," unpublished Ph.D., University of Wisconsin, 1959, v-xvii, 1-203.

8

Adolph Strasser and the Origins of Pure and Simple Unionism

H. M. GITELMAN

In a recent article entitled "On the Origins of Business Unionism"[1] Philip Taft has argued that the earlier view of Selig Perlman—that business unionism was developed by a group of trade union leaders in the 1870s and 1880s—is essentially incorrect. Professor Taft has convincingly demonstrated that salient elements of the philosophy of business unionism had existed throughout the nineteenth century and were more or less indigenous to American soil.

The present article had originally been prepared for publication before the appearance of Professor Taft's article. My own interpretation differs from his on the point that while I agree that the ideas of business unionism had been "in the air" for some time, I believe they required an agent for their codification and transmission. It was not until the precepts of business unionism (herein referred to as "pure and simple unionism") had been made explicit as a formula for trade-union stability and development that business unionism itself became an important, and finally a dominating, influence upon the course of American labor history. Even in the light of Professor Taft's revision, it would not be fruitful to analyze the labor movement in terms of its devotion to pure and simple unionism until the post-Civil War era.

Professor Perlman erred in neglecting the data which Professor Taft summarily presents in this article. Moreover, he failed to demonstrate concretely how the union leaders he named—Adolph Strasser, P. J. McGuire and J. P. McDonnell—accomplished the transition from socialism to pure and simple unionism. The present article deals with the transformation of the key personality in this story, Adolph Strasser. Both McGuire and McDonnell played subsidiary roles at best. McGuire

[1] *Industrial and Labor Relations Review,* Vol. 17, No. 1 (Oct. 1963).
Reprinted from *Labor History* 6 (Winter 1965), 71-83.

was still a socialist in the mid-1880s, and McDonnell was a newspaper publisher without an effective trade-union base. Strasser, in contrast, arrived at an explicit formulation of pure and simple unionism first, and because of his trade-union base was in a position from which he could, and in fact did, influence the entire labor movement.

Throughout most of the nineteenth century the American labor movement was confronted by two crucial problems: how to survive in a hostile environment; and what role to play in American life. The rise of the national union, an organic response to the nationalizing trends in the economy, resolved the first of these problems; the emergence of pure and simple unionism as an ideological creed resolved the second. The fact that both problems were resolved at about the same time and by the same people has led many writers to conclude that the two riddles were in reality one. Yet there is no reason why the objectives of an organization cannot be viewed as separate from its structure and operating methods.

Pure and simple unionism may be defined as that variety of trade unionism which limits its activities to servicing the *immediate* needs of its members through collective bargaining and political action, and without more than an indirect regard for the following: the structure of, or the distribution of power within, the society in which such unionism exists; the long-range interests of union members, regardless of how those interests are defined; and the welfare of workers who do not belong to the organization, except for those who readily fall within the recognized jurisdiction of a union but have not yet been organized.

In a simplified but often used sense, pure and simple unionism relates exclusively to the ends to which unionists put their political activities. The purpose of collective bargaining—to win the most advantageous employment conditions possible under prevailing circumstances—was rarely questioned by nineteenth-century unionists nor is it questioned today. The question was what, if any, were labor's political goals to be?

The simplification involved in such a view lies in its neglect of alternative methods and aims of working-class action which were suggested during the nineteenth century and which were not encompassed by collective bargaining and political action. These were co-operation and communal association. While these alternatives had some support among various groups of workers, unionists among them, they were comparatively unimportant next to the vexing question of the political-social role of the labor movement.

The debate within the labor movement over pure and simple unionism began in the movement's infancy in the 1820s.

> In Philadelphia, in 1828, the first Trades' Union was formed in this country, and one clause of its constitution excluded all political action; but, judging that the object of the Union could not be obtained without its taking part in politics, many members diverged from it and established what was called the "Working Men's Party," and, from that moment, as it advanced the Union retrograded. . . . The same cause . . . would produce the same effect [today].[2]

This debate continued throughout the remainder of the century. It may be seen in the proceedings of the National Labor Union (1866-72), in those of the Federation of Organized Trades & Labor Unions (1881-86), as well as in those of the American Federation of Labor.[3]

In one important sense this debate was never truly resolved. Pure and simple unionism became the accepted creed of most American unionists by 1890, but the advocates of reform unionism carried on in one form or another: as socialist borers from within, as syndicalist rivals from without, as Progressives, and later as industrial unionists. It is not stretching the point too far to suggest that this debate continues even today, though in a somewhat abbreviated form, in the ideological differences which separate George Meany and Walter Reuther.

The man who derived the principle of pure and simple unionism in an explicit form, and who in a very direct way was responsible for its wide acceptance by American unionists, was Adolph Strasser. Out of an admixture of Marxism, British trade-union precedents and American trade-union experience, he developed a long-sought-after set of operating procedures and a trade-union philosophy which placed American unionism on a firm foundation and at the same time gave it a conception of the role it should play in society.

---

[2] Statement by delegate English during a debate on the use of the word "politics" at the Trade Union National Convention held in New York City, 1834. John R. Commons, et al. (eds.) *A Documentary History of American Industrial Society,* (New York: 1958) Vol. VI, p. 215.

[3] *Ibid.,* Vol. IX, p. 135: *Report of the First Annual Session of the Federation of Organized Trades & Labor Unions,* 1881, pp. 19 and 24: *Report of Proceedings of the 14th Annual Convention of the American Federation of Labor,* 1894, pp. 14f.

Strasser came to the United States in 1872, at the age of twenty-eight. Before his arrival it seems very likely that he sojourned in England for a time, for he soon spoke fluent English, revealed a high degree of familiarity with the working methods of British trade unionism, and understood those elements of socialist thought current only in the British section of the First International.[4] These last two attributes were to play a fundamental part in shaping his thinking about the role of American trade unions.

On establishing himself in New York City, Strasser became active in the American Section of the First International and in the union of his trade, the Cigar-Makers' International Union (C.M.I.U.). The American Section of the International was—as it had been from its inception—small, faction-ridden, and in composition and outlook more German than American. The energies of its members were more often devoted to internal disputations over ideology and discipline than to active participation in the affairs of the day.[5] Late in 1873 Strasser was among a group of socialists who joined hands with a group of native American reformers and radicals for the purpose of protesting against rising unemployment and economic distress. The climax of this agitation was the Tompkins Square Riot of January 13, 1874; and partly because their participation had been outside the discipline of the American Section, Strasser and his cohorts were expelled from the organization.[6]

Strasser and P. J. McGuire[7] then proceeded to organize their own socialist organization, the Social Democratic Workingman's Party.

---

[4] G. D. H. Cole, *Socialist Thought, Marxism and Anarchism 1850-1890.* Volume II of *A History of Socialist Thought* (London: 1954), pp. 94-95.

[5] Both parties to the ideological disputes within the American Section, being primarily German, were influenced by German intellectual traditions. One group was loyal to Karl Marx and, in consequence, looked with some favor upon trade unionism; another was loyal to the teachings of Ferdinand Lassalle, who viewed trade unionism with scorn and favored political action. These lines were not hard and fast. It could and indeed did happen that a Marxist led a group of Lassalleans against the Marxist leadership and was expelled from the Section. Schism in this instance, however, owed to a dispute over internal discipline, not over ideology. *Letterbook of the North American Central Committee, International Workingmen's Association* (Wisconsin State Historical Society). See also, Samuel Bernstein, *The First International in America* (New York: 1962).

[6] "F. Bolte to all Sections" April, 1874, *Letterbook.*

[7] McGuire was to follow the same route as Strasser—from socialism to pure and simple unionism—in the course of building the Brotherhood of Carpenters & Joiners. Their paths crossed many times in the period 1873-86 and they were to cooperate in organizing the A. F. of L. McGuire retained socialist leanings for a much longer time. For his tragic end, see Robert Christie, *Empire in Wood* (Ithaca: 1956).

With Strasser as its executive secretary, the Workingmen's Party was to face the same variety of factionalism as had beset the American Section, though with a significant difference. Whereas in the American Section the dispute over trade-union versus political socialism had led to the expulsion of members, in the Workingmen's Party it led to the virtual expulsion of leaders.

It is of considerable significance that the Workingmen's Party, unlike the American Section of the First International, attracted to its ranks a number of native Americans who were familiar with American trade unionism and with the eight-hour movement.[8] It was in this party that Strasser made his first acquaintance with American thinking on subjects which his German comrades believed were uniquely their own.

A little more than a year after the organization of the Workingmen's Party, Strasser headed a committee which met with representatives of the American Section in an unsuccessful effort to reunify the socialist movement. In April 1876, the two delegations resumed merger talks and reached an agreement. This agreement was formalized at the "Unity Convention" in Philadelphia in July 1876.[9]

Two weeks before the Unity Convention, Strasser called upon the members of his Party to debate and redefine their objectives.

> It is . . . of greater importance to discuss how this union of the whole working class shall be achieved on a sound basis. On this point many divergent opinions are held which need to be clarified in order to prevent the movement from having an ill-effect on the entire Labor Movement by conflict within its own ranks.

Having called for a debate, he clearly stated his own position.

> The working class pays attention primarily to those things which may be achieved immediately: provision of jobs, high wages, short working-time, support in case of unemployment and illness. [In support, he cited part of the agenda of the forthcoming annual convention of the Blacksmith's Union.]
>
> Those who do not pay much attention to these matters but fight primarily

---

[8] Among them were: Ira Stewart, George McNeill, Jesse H. Jones, E. M. Chamberlain, all members of the National Eight Hour League; Albert R. Parsons and Thomas J. Morgan, Chicago socialists and trade unionists; John T. Elliott and George Block New York socialists, the former being subsequently the founder of the Paper-Hangers Union and the latter of the Bakers Union. *The Labor Standard* (New York), Apr. 29, June 10, Sept. 16, and Dec. 16, 1876. (This paper was the official organ of the Social Democratic Workingmen's Party.)

[9] *Proceedings of the Union Congress* (New York: Workingmen's Party of the U. S., 1876).

for the abolition of wage labor have not fully grasped the idea of
modern socialism.

[He then cited Dühring and Marx]

Many people wonder why the American worker has not achieved in one
decade these results [the eight-hour day] for which the British worker
has been fighting since 1830. They do not understand that the lack of
centralization of the trade-unions in this country . . . is to blame. . . .
The eight-hour working day can be achieved only by mass organization
and development of powerful trade unions. [For confirmation, he turned
to the *Communist Manifesto*.] . . . Therefore, I will admonish the
Congress on the Unity of Workers taking place in Philadelphia: The main
tasks of the American Socialists in the near future consists in the strong
and energetic promotion of the organization and centralization of the
trade unions.[10]

Apart from revealing his familiarity with socialist and trade-union
literature, in this early article Strasser clearly indicated the sources of
his views on trade-union objectives and tactics. He looked upon the
pursuit of short-run material objectives as consonant with current American trade-union interests as well as with the teachings of Duhring
and Marx. One such objective, the eight-hour day, seemed paramount,
and it would be realized only when trade-union advocates became
unified in a national trade-union center. The importance of the eight-
hour day was attested to by American trade-union experience, by the
writings of Marx, and by the experiences of British unionism.

Viewed in retrospect, it is ironic that Strasser should have been so
strongly influenced by that element of Marxist thought which was, to
Marx himself, more a political expedient than a theoretical necessity.
In the mid-1860s Marx had lavished compliment after compliment
upon the British labor movement for its success in winning such
material improvements as the eight-hour day. He had done this with
the aim of wooing the British movement into the First International.[11]
Whether Marx truly believed in the ability of trade unions to stem the
forces of capitalist exploitation significantly is unimportant in this context. What is important is that Strasser, reinforced by his knowledge
of British and American trade-union preference for such short-run

10 *Social Demokrat* (New York) July 9, 1876. This paper was one of the official
organs of the Workingmen's Party of the United States.
11 *Address and Provisional Rules of the International Working Men's Association*
(London: 1924). A. Lozovsky, *Marx and the Trade Unions* (New York: 1935),
p. 24.

gains as the eight-hour day, was acting as a faithful Marxist when he supported a principle which was to become central to the concept of pure and simple unionism.

Since most of the delegates to the Unity Convention of 1876 were Marxists, the views expressed by Strasser in the above article were fully accepted. The organization of trade unions was to be the first task of the newly created Social Labor Party (shortly to be rechristened the Workingmen's Party of the United States). Only where it was strong enough at the local level "to exercise a perceptible influence" was the party to enter political contests. In the event that there were successful candidacies, those elected were to concentrate on such measures as improved conditions of the workers: the eight-hour day, sanitary inspection, the establishtment of bureaus of labor statistics, the prohibition of child labor, etc.[12]

Unfortunately, the ideological unanimity achieved at the Convention was not acceptable to the German faction within Strasser's own party. Whereas Strasser stressed the primary importance of trade unionism, most of the German rank-and-file members held political action more important. Whereas Strasser had agreed to the ultimate desirability of political action—at some time in the future, when the party had more chance of success—most of the German rank-and-file members wanted to engage immediately in political campaigns.[13] This division resulted in Strasser's ejection from a position of leadership. By the time debate over the priorities to be accepted by the party had concluded, he was being stigmatized in the socialist press as a red-baiter.[14] Party leadership was transferred to the political activists and the membership, with some slight success, rushed into the political campaigns of late 1876 and 1877.[15]

At this point late in 1876, Strasser still considered himself a socialist. His views on how socialism was to be achieved, first through trade-union organization and then through political action, led only to his deposition from party leadership, not to his disaffection from socialism;

---

[12] *Proceedings of the Union Congress.*

[13] *Social-Demokrat,* July 16, 1876 (articles by G. Winter and H. LeMaire); Aug. 6, 1876 (articles by "B.K."); Aug. 20, 1876 (article by J. Schaefer); Sept. 3, 1876 (article by J. Schaefer).

[14] *Ibid.,* Oct. 29, 1876.

[15] George A. Schilling, "The Labor Movement in Chicago," in *The Life of Albert Parsons,* edited by Lucy Parsons (Chicago: 1903); and Edward B. Mittleman, "Chicago Labor in Politics, 1877-1896," *Journal of Political Economy* Vol. 28, No. 5, (May, 1920).

this he made quite clear in a concluding letter to the debate he had initiated:

> The workers who have thought a little about the Socialist Movement will realize that sectarianism is doomed to death. Where are the followers of St. Simon, R. Owen, Fourier, Cabet, and Weitling? These people had such an influence on the Labor Movement. They ignored and condemned Trade Unionism emerging from real needs and conditions. The same will hold true with all organizations which do not see their tasks as to centralize and organize the pure proletariat movement.
>
> The trade unions are the natural and only justified Labor Party [and they] have to struggle for the daily bread if they do not want to be doomed to death. If this struggle will be centralized and vigorously fought, then it will lead to a revolutionary change of society.[16]

Having been denied leadership in the socialist movement, Strasser was now free to devote his energies to the development of trade unionism. Indeed, at the moment he was losing his standing in the movement, he was rising to leadership in his own union, the C.M.I.U. In August 1876, after having served the union as an organizer, he was elected its second vice-president. In October 1877, he was elected president, a position he would hold for the next fifteen years.

The union whose leadership he now took over was a shambles. Its membership had steadily declined since the onset of the 1873 depression and by 1877 had dropped to 1,016. Strasser was determined to rebuild and to restore the union to a place of importance in the cigar trade. Equipped with little more than a conviction that trade unionism was a necessary prelude to socialism, he set about his work.

Although small, the union was not easy to lead. The reforms Strasser proposed were expensive and too daring for many of its members. The rank and file balked at higher dues, at the creation of a benefit system, at the equalization of funds among locals, and at the centralized control of strikes. At each hurdle Strasser coaxed and cajoled, educating the members by detailed accounts of how such reforms had strengthened British trade unions.[17] On more than one occasion

---

16 *Social-Demokrat,* Sept. 24, 1876.
17 The pages of the *Cigar Makers Official Journal,* which Strasser edited, were regularly taken up with detailed accounts of how such and such a reform worked within the Amalgamated Society of Engineers or the Amalgamated Society of Carpenters. These were the British unions upon which Strasser relied most heavily for precedent. The *Journal* also carried news of Trade Union Congress happenings. See also, Theodore Glocker, "The Structure of the Cigar Makers' Union" in J. H. Hollander and G. E. Barnett (eds.) *Studies in American Trade Unions* (New York: 1906).

he forced reforms through with the support of his own local union, the largest in the International.

In large measure these reforms achieved the desired effects: the union's membership grew steadily; the drop-out rate of members was considerably lowered; and the strike performance of the union improved.[18] Of equal consequence was the effect the fight for these reforms had upon Strasser. He had assumed the leadership of the C.M.I.U. as an avowed Marxist. It was as a Marxist that he justified the pursuit of short-run material goals, his imitation of British trade-union internal procedures, and his support of the proposal for a national trade union center. The membership grudgingly accepted these first two points and warmly supported the third. But when the pursuit of short-run goals necessitated political rather than economic action, a strong rank-and-file opposition developed. Here some background information will help clarify this point.

Introduction of the cigar mold in the early 1870s had made it possible for unskilled workers to enter the cigar trade for the first time. Cigar manufacturers in New York City, the center of the trade, had been quick to capitalize upon this innovation. Large numbers of recently arrived Bohemian families were recruited, quartered in company-owned tenement houses, and put to work—men, women and children—manufacturing cigars. C.M.I.U. locals struck against this practice but were unable to halt its spread, and skilled German cigar-makers helplessly watched their job opportunities and wage rates decline.[19]

Once it became apparent that strike action was futile, Strasser resorted to two tactics. First was the introduction of a union label to help all sympathetic workingmen distinguish between union-made and tenement-made cigars. Secondly an appeal was made to federal and state legislatures for aid. Strasser, in 1878, attempted to have Congress prohibit the manufacture of goods in living quarters.[20] When this failed, he turned to the New York State legislature for relief. In

---

[18] Membership climbed from 1,016 in 1877 to 12,790 in 1881. The drop-out rate declined as follows:
    1877-79, 11 for every 12 recruits
    1879-80,   1 for every 3 recruits
    1880-81,   1 for every 4 recruits
[19] See, Appendix entitled: "Cigar-Makers' International Union" in George E. McNeill (ed.) *The Labor Movement: The Problem of To-day* (Boston: 1887), especially p. 589. This article was probably written by Strasser.
[20] *Paterson Labor Standard,* Nov. 3, 1878.

1880, 1881, and 1882 bills were introduced which would have outlawed tenement manufactures on grounds that the health of the operatives was being impaired. But these bills either failed to gain passage
or were lost in the courts on constitutional grounds.[21]

The debate within the union over Strasser's internal changes had
stirred up some dissent, but the issues involved were open to differences of opinion and had not led to the formation of an opposition
bloc. The attempt to win political support for an anti-tenement work
bill was, however, clearly an ideological matter, and socialists within
the union viewed Strasser's legislative efforts as a sell-out to bourgeois
politicians. From their point of view, support of the socialist party
alone was the duty of every worker and working-class leader.[22]

As a result of this disagreement over policy, a group of rank-and-
file members, all of them loyal to the Socialistic Labor Party, organized an internal union opposition. By late 1881 this opposition had
become so powerful that it was able to capture the largest local in the
C.M.I.U. From this vantage point the party loyalists were capable of
harassing Strasser and limiting the freedom of his activities.

Strasser, however, was not prepared to accept this challenge to his
authority. Fully convinced that "the workingmen are led by success,
no matter how it is accomplished . . ."[23] "the Prussian" (as he was
called) nullified the election and placed a loyal partisan at the head
of the local. The party socialists then had little choice but to leave the
C.M.I.U. and, with the S.L.P.'s moral support, established their own
organization—the Progressive Cigar-Makers Union.[24]

Strasser and his former socialist comrades now stood in open opposition. Whatever vestiges of socialist thinking remained in Strasser's
mind, they were subordinated to the needs of the present conflict. He
turned the union label to use against socialist-made cigars in the same
way it was used against tenement-made cigars. Where the opportunity

---

[21] *Cigar Makers Official Journal* (New York), Feb. 10, 1880, Oct. 10, 1881, Apr. 15,
1882, June 15, 1882, Feb., March, 1883, Feb. 1884.

[22] *Ibid.*, May 15, 1882. A leaflet issued by the Strasser faction (which was led by
Samuel Gompers) included the following statement in its defense of the legislative effort to end the tenement system: "It is a cigar makers issue, pure and
simple. . . ." This is the earliest use of the phrase that I have encountered.

[23] *Ibid.*, Sept. 10, 1880.

[24] *Progress* (New York) Aug., 1882. This was the official organ of the Progressives.
Documents relating to the split appear in *Fifteenth Convention Proceedings,*
C.M.I.U. 1883, printed in the *Cigar Makers Official Journal,* Sept. 1883, Supplement. The convention agreed that Strasser had acted unconstitutionally but exoner-
ated him because the action was justified by "extraordinary necessities" (p. 13).

presented itself, he ordered C.M.I.U. men to replace members of the Progressive Cigar-Makers Union.[25] In these ways he sought to undermine and destroy his opposition.

Apart from ending Strasser's intellectual affiliation with socialism, the conflict within the C.M.I.U. produced the last attribute of pure and simple unionism: non-partisan political action. So long as Strasser had accepted socialism, he also accepted the notion that trade unions would one day become strong enough to support a socialist party and elect socialist candidates to office. His flirtation with the regular parties had been necessitated by the fact that the socialist party was not yet strong enough to help in the fight against tenement-house cigars. But now the socialist party was an enemy; he accused it of provoking the split which had occurred, and no longer had to rationalize his political activities. The C.M.I.U. would turn to whomever would aid it and in return would promise its political support.[26]

Thus, by 1883 Strasser had arrived at a definition of unionism which, both in terms of its operations and its objectives, seemed to fit his American experience and British precedent. The structural achievement had been accomplished largely by imitating British practices, and while the C.M.I.U. was by no means alone in building a strong national union at the time, it succeeded so well that it served as the model for a number of other unions (e.g., the Brotherhood of Carpenters and Joiners, and the Bakers Union).[27]

The objectives of the "new" unionism were limited to short-run material gains—advances purely and simply in the interests of union members—achieved through collective bargaining and political action. Questions such as the fate of capitalism and the ultimate arrival of a cooperative commonwealth would be left to theorists and visionaries.

> We have no ultimate ends. We are going on from day to day. We are fighting only for immediate objects. . . . We are all practical men.[28]

---

[25] *The Journal of United Labor* (Philadelphia) Dec. 1883, p. 609; *John Swinton's Paper* (New York) Jan. 10, 1886.

[76] *Cigar Makers Official Journal,* Sept. 1883, Supplement. Strasser recommended the following political-action scheme to the convention: 1.) public meetings to influence the press and public opinion; 2.) petitions to legislators; 3.) private letters to legislators; 4.) thorough canvass of the legislature; 5.) oral and printed arguments before legislative committees; 6.) organized effort to defeat those voting against the bill; and 7.) endorsement of those voting for passage of the bill.

[27] Glocker, *op. cit.*

[28] Strasser in testimony before the Senate Committee on Education and Labor, *Report of.* . . . (Washington: G.P.O., 1885) Vol. I, p. 460. (Testimony was given in 1883.)

This position had been reached by examining American trade-union experience and by first supporting and ultimately rejecting Marxism. Although the long-run projections of Marxism were finally rejected, the short-run goals were left untouched. To this extent, American pure and simple unionism can be directly tributed to Marx.

Though Strasser abandoned socialism, he—like so many of his contemporaries—could not entirely rid himself of long-run views on the destiny of trade unionism. As the years wore on, the never-precise dimensions of a co-operative commonwealth blurred and lost their importance.[29] Strasser's abandonment did not, however, imply an immediate or complete acceptance of capitalism. Though he was prepared to turn to the capitalist state legislature on occasion, Strasser appears to have retained a sense of mistrust toward bourgeois politicians for some time. This sense of mistrust partly explains his reticence to rely upon the state for benefits which might well be provided by each national union—and which might bind members more closely to the union.[30] It is in this light that we must understand why he chose to establish such programs as sick benefits and out-of-work benefits within the C.M.I.U., in preference to lobbying for state-sponsored sickness, accident, and unemployment benefit plans.[31]

Conclusion

Lloyd Ulman has demonstrated that the development of strong national unions dedicated to pure and simple aims took place more or less simultaneously within a number of unions contemporary with the C.M.I.U.[32] The significance of the emergence of such unionism within the C.M.I.U., however, is two-fold. First, it developed in the course of ideological dispute, so that of necessity its meaning was made explicit and, therefore, it emerged as an explicit formula for trade-

---

[29] At its 1885 convention, the C.M.I.U. voted to endorse a co-operative commonwealth. As late as 1887, Strasser suggested that co-operation was the end goal of the labor movement. *Cigar Makers Official Journal,* Oct. 1885, May 1887.

[30] On the role of internal benefits see: *Cigar Makers Official Journal* Jan. 15, 1883; June 1883, Jan. 1885; and Strasser's presidential address to conventions, Oct. 1880, Oct. 1881, Sept. 1883.

[31] By 1891, having met with success in efforts to have state legislatures protect the union's label against counterfeiting, Strasser appears to have lost his wariness of bourgeois politicians. *Cigar Makers Official Journal,* Oct. 1891.

[32] Lloyd Ulman, *The Rise of the National Trade Union* (Cambridge: 1955).

union development only from the C.M.I.U. This formula was transmitted to other unions and to unions yet to be organized. Second, given Strasser's role in the organization of the A.F.L., and his placement of Samuel Gompers as its leader, the doctrine of pure and simple unionism received both a national platform and a national spokesman.

9

Trade Unionism in the British and U.S. Steel Industries, 1880-1914: A Comparative Study

JAMES HOLT

From the 1880s to the First World War, trade unions grew and flourished among British steelworkers. In the U.S. steel industry, on the other hand, trade unionism lost ground rapidly after 1892 and all but disappeared. By 1914 the British steel industry was heavily unionized and the initial steps had been taken towards the creation of a single national organization embracing most of the major trade unions in the field. Meanwhile, in America, the open shop had become the rule in steelmaking. It would be an exaggeration to suggest that these contrasting patterns typified trade union development in the two countries, since it was in this period that the national unions and the American Federation of Labor became firmly established in the United States. Nevertheless the fate of the trade unions in the U.S. steel industry may reasonably be seen as an extreme example of a general trend. Compared with Britain and most other industrialized capitalist countries, the unionized proportion of the non-agricultural labor force remained low in the United States before the 1930s, and until that time trade unionism was peculiarly weak in America's mass production industries.

The relatively slow growth of trade unionism in the United States is an important subject in itself, but it takes on added significance when considered in the light of political developments. In Britain, Australia, New Zealand, and Scandinavia, trade unions launched political labor movements which ultimately achieved national power. Elsewhere trade unions were created by or closely associated with strong socialist parties. The absence of a nationally powerful socialist or political labor movement in the United States may be explained in part by factors quite indepen-

Reprinted from *Labor History* 18 (Winter 1977), 5-35.

dent of trade union development, such as the peculiar nature of American political institutions, but it seems probable that the comparative weakness of American socialism is associated in some way with the slow and painful growth of the trade unions in the United States. This study deals with industrial organizations only, and focuses on a single industry, but the aim is to throw some light on a more general question, *viz.:* why, in broad comparative terms were industrial and political organizations of manual workers so weak in the United States during the late 19th and early 20th centuries?

There are many aspects of trade union organization that might usefully be considered in a comparative study, depending on the ultimate purpose of the inquiry. Here the focus is on contrasting patterns of growth and decline, and subjects such as the structure of union government, dues, benefits, and rules of membership are dealt with only as they appear to bear on the major question. A full narrative history of the various unions involved has not been attempted either, but a brief outline of the major institutions and developments under study is necessary and will serve as an introduction to the discussion that follows.

In Britain steelworkers were organized by several trade unions with overlapping jurisdictions, a pattern typical of British industry.[1] First of the important unions in the field was the Amalgamated Malleable Ironworkers of Great Britain which was founded in 1862 and reorganized in 1867 as the Associated Iron and Steelworkers of Great Britain. The Ironworkers' Union, as it was generally known, began its life as an organization of puddlers and skilled rolling mill hands in the wrought iron industry, but as steel supplanted wrought iron, the Ironworkers began taking in steelworkers. At least some Bessemer converter men were represented by the Ironworkers as early as the 1860s, and skilled rolling mill hands in the steel industry, especially those in Northeast England, gradually assumed a prominent place in the union's affairs.[2] Yet

---

[1] The standard history of trade unionism in the British iron and steel industry is Sir Arthur Pugh, *Men of Steel, by one of them: a chronicle of 88 years of trade unionism in the British Iron and Steel Industry* (London, 1951). There are useful chapters on labor and trade unionism in J. C. Carr and W. Taplin, *History of the British Steel Industry* (Oxford, 1962), and brief but illuminating sections in H. A. Clegg, Alan Fox and A. F. Thompson, *A History of British Trade Unions Since 1889, Vol. I: 1889-1910* (Oxford, 1964).

[2] *The Ironworkers' Journal*, No. 244, July 1883, No. 245, August 1883, No. 300, March 1888, No. 303, June 1888, No. 304, July 1888, No. 314, May 1889.

though it was flexible enough to survive the transition from wrought iron to steel, the Ironworkers' union remained throughout its existence a complacent and conservative organization. It largely ignored the interests of the unskilled, made no effort to establish itself in Scotland or Wales, and showed no interest in the rapidly growing number of open hearth furnace workers. Early in its existence, the Ironworkers' leaders committed the union to formal conciliation and arbitration procedures as a wage fixing device and to a sliding scale of wages based on the selling price of iron and steel products. By accepting this system, the Ironworkers acquiesced in automatic wage cuts whenever prices fell, and although this may have been a necessary condition for the union's survival in its early years, "its intrinsic advantages," in the words of Clegg, Fox, and Thompson, "were obvious only to employers."[3] Membership of this undynamic organization fluctuated between 5,000 and 8,000 during the 1890s and the first decade of the 20th century.[4]

More important in the long run was the British Steel Smelters' Amalgamated Association which was founded by Scottish open hearth furnace workers in 1886, and which soon spread its activities to England and Wales. In its early years the Smelters' union concentrated on the skilled men working open hearth furnaces. For these men it succeeded in winning the abolition of the contract system of wages and in negotiating tonnage (piece) rates which covered most of the open hearth industry by 1890.[5] Lesser skilled men working around the open hearth furnaces were excluded from the union altogether by some branches in the early years and throughout the 1890s the Smelters had difficulty retaining the loyalty of the "gas producer men." These workers were paid like laborers by daily rather than tonnage rates and frequently complained that their interests were being ignored by the Smelters.[6]

[3] Clegg, Fox and Thompson, *British Trade Unions*, 204.
[4] Except where stated otherwise, figures for British trade union membership have been taken from The Board of Trade, Labour Department, *Report on Trade Unions in 1889*, Cd. 442, and *Report on Trade Unions in 1903-1904*, Cd. 2838.
[5] British Steel Smelters' Amalgamated Association (cited hereafter as B.S.S.A.A.), *Monthly Report*, No. 18, Oct. 31, 1890.
[6] B.S.S.A.A., *Report of Proceedings of Triennial Conference July 26-28, 1894*, 183; *Monthly Reports*, No. 85, May, 31, 1896. No. 117, Jan. 31, 1899; Sidney & Beatrice Webb Collection, London School of Economics Library, Collection E, Section A. Vol. 23, 170, 172.

However the Smelters' redoubtable secretary, John Hodge, later a Labour M.P. and cabinet minister, worked consistently to broaden the basis of the union. In 1894 Hodge negotiated a scheme for amalgamation with the Scottish Millmen, but it was rejected overwhelmingly by the membership. When negotiations with the Ironworkers for amalgamation also led to nothing, the Smelters began recruiting rolling mill hands. By 1900 the Smelters were also welcoming the unskilled into their ranks. In 1899 a new class of membership was established for these men whose dues were fixed at one quarter of those of first class members.[7]

Though ably led and highly successful in one branch of the industry, the Smelters' union grew only slowly until the late 1890s. Then, in 1899, the collapse of the South Wales, Monmouthshire, and Gloucestershire Tinplate Workers' Union enabled the Smelters (among others) to move in and recruit a large number of Welsh tinplate workers. Membership more than doubled (from 4,605 to 9,976) in that year. An organizing drive in Sheffield in 1907 reaped another rich harvest of new members. By then the Smelters represented over 15,000 workers, its capital assets stood at 76,000 pounds, and two of its paid officials, John Hodge and John McPherson, sat in Parliament.[8]

In Scotland rolling mill hands formed their own union in 1888, known as the Associated Society of Millmen and after 1895 the Amalgamated Society of Steel and Iron Workers. In the early 1890s, the Millmen attempted to establish branches in England but failed to make significant progress there or to persuade the stronger Smelters to amalgamate with them. An arbitration agreement entered into with employers covered only four out of seven Scottish mills in 1892 and the Millmen compensated for their relatively weak position in the rolling mills by taking in wrought iron and foundry workers. By 1900, membership had risen to over 9,000 but it declined in subsequent years.[9]

Two societies of blastfurnacemen amalgamated in 1887 to form

---

[7] B.S.S.A.A., *Monthly Reports.* No. 42, Oct. 1892, No. 43, November 1892. No. 60, April 20, 1894, No. 68. Oct. 31, 1894. No. 81, Jan. 31, 1896. No. 123, July 31, 1891; *Conference Reports*, 1889, 1891, 1894; *Constitution and Rules of the British Steel Smelters' Amalgamated Association*, revised, 1898.

[8] B.S.S.A.A., *Monthly Reports*, Nos. 117-122, Jan.-June 1899, May 31, 1907, Dec. 31, 1907.

[9] Associated Society of Millmen, *Monthly Reports*, No. 10, March 1891, No. 11, April 1891, *Royal Commission on Labour*, C—6795—IV (1892) Q.S. 15916, 15925, 15938, 15989-15994; Clegg, Fox and Thompson, *British Trade Unions*, 207.

a national organization which became the National Federation of Blastfurnacemen in 1892. Its membership grew from 4,544 in 1895 to nearly 9,000 in 1904. In Wales, the Amalgamated Association of Iron and Steel Workers and Mechanics of South Wales and Monmouthshire, described by Clegg, Fox and Thompson as a "company union," had 3-5000 members throughout the period 1892 to 1904. Several unions of enginemen, cranemen, and firemen organized these specialized trades in the steelworks and the general laborers' unions organized some of the unskilled workers in the industry. In addition to all of these there were a number of smaller local unions in the industry.[10]

Clearly the pattern of trade union organization in the British steel industry down to 1910 was complicated and confused in the extreme. Rolling mill hands for example were organized by the Ironworkers, the Smelters, and the Millmen, and unskilled laborers in the steel industry were divided among even more organizations. In 1911, however, serious negotiations aimed at the amalgamation or federation of all of the major unions in the steel industry were opened. Eventually there emerged in 1917 the Iron and Steel Trades Confederation which embraced all of the important unions except the Blastfurnacemen.[11]

Between 1897 and 1913 total membership in British iron and steel trade unions rose from about 30,000 to approximately 80,000. It is impossible to calculate precisely what "density" (i.e., proportion of workers in the industry) this figure represented, since census reports lumped together workers engaged in the manufacture of iron and steel with some who worked *with* the metals, including foundrymen. It is also impossible to work out how many steelworkers belonged to the several trade unions which organized other groups of workers as well. Nevertheless it can safely be concluded that trade unionism was very strong in the British steel industry by the outbreak of the First World War and was still growing stronger.

In the American steel industry, only two labor organizations were of any great significance in the late 19th and early 20th centuries. These were the Amalgamated Association of Iron,

---

[10]J. Owen, *Short History of the National Union of Blastfurnacemen, 1878-1953* (Middlesbrough, 1953), 19; Clegg, Fox and Thompson, *British Trade Unions,* 210-212.
[11]Carr and Taplin, *British Steel Industry,* 284-288.

Steel and Tin Workers (The A.A.), and the Knights of Labor. The A.A. was formed in 1876 when the United Sons of Vulcan, composed of iron puddlers and boilers, joined forces with several smaller unions of rolling mill hands and other skilled iron workers. Membership of the A.A. rose from 3,755 in 1877 to 16,003 in 1882, declined to 5,702 in 1885 and climbed again to a peak of 24,068 in 1891. After its crushing defeat in the Homestead strike of 1892, the A.A. lost ground steadily and never regained its former strength.[12]

Throughout the period in which it was a large and powerful organization, the A.A. was dominated by iron workers, and especially by puddlers and boilers. Each year, delegates to the union's annual convention drew up elaborate scales of prices for the boiling, puddling, heating, and rolling of wrought iron, and when endorsed by the convention these scales were presented to the ironmasters. As in Britain, the ironworkers based their scales on the selling price of the products they made (i.e., they were sliding scales) but unlike the British Ironworkers' Union, the A.A. rejected arbitration as a method of settling disputes. Differences between the A.A. and the employers sometimes led to strikes or lockouts, and the union was not always victorious in these struggles. In general, however, the A.A. established a powerful position in the iron industry and claimed to control three quarters of the iron mills in the United States by 1891.[13]

The A.A. began as an "exclusive" organization, confining membership to the skilled men in the iron and steel industries. Yet as early as 1877 the union's president was deploring the tendency of boilers to exclude their "helpers" from A.A. lodges, despite their eligibility for membership, and union leaders were constantly warning members that it would be dangerous to exclude lesser

---

[12] Easily the best book on labor in the U.S. steel industry is David Brody, *Steelworkers in America: the Non-union Era* (Cambridge, Mass., 1960), though as the title indicates, it deals mainly with the period after 1892 and ignores the Knights of Labor entirely. An excellent contemporary work is John A. Fitch, *The Steelworkers*, Vol. III of *The Pittsburgh Survey*, edited by Paul V. Kellogg (New York, 1911), which contains a brief history of trade unionism and labor relations down to the date of publication. On the Amalgamated Association, see also Jesse S. Robinson, *The Amalgamated Association of Iron, Steel and Tin Workers* (Baltimore, 1920); Carroll D. Wright, "The Amalgamated Association of Iron and Steelworkers", *Quarterly Journal of Economics*, VII (July, 1893), 400-432. For membership figures in the A.A. see Robinson, *Amalgamated Association*, 21.

[13] Commonwealth of Pennsylvania, Secretary of Internal Affairs, *Annual Report*, Part II, *Industrial Statistics*, Vol. 15, (1887), Official Document No. 12, G.7; Amalgamated Association of Iron and Steelworkers, *Proceedings*, 6th Annual Convention (1891), 570.

skilled men. New categories of workers were added to those eligible for membership at almost every convention after 1876 until by 1882 it took almost an entire page of the constitution to list them all. By 1890 the membership provisions had been simplified to include simply "all men working in and around rolling mills, steel works, nail, tack, spike, bolt and nut factories, pipe mills, and all works run in connection with the same, except laborers, the latter to be admitted at the discretion of the subordinate lodges to which application is made for membership." As with the British Steel Smelters then, the trend was towards a more broadly based membership including more and more of the lesser skilled men.[14]

The ironworkers of the A.A. viewed the rise of steel production in the United States with apprehension. In 1885, the national officers suggested reducing scales with the exception of those covering mills making steel nails, the object being "to deal a blow at steel nails that will kill them and enforce [the] return to iron nails, thereby employing our boilers again...[and stopping] the introduction of steel in general to supercede iron." Unfortunately for the A.A., the main effect of this policy seems to have been to drive the nailers out of the union rather than steel out of the nail industry, and obstructionist tactics of this sort were not attempted again; at least not on any systematic basis. Instead, the A.A. encouraged steelworkers to join the union and formulate their own scales. In December 1887 a meeting of delegates from all the steel lodges in the A.A. was held to draw up scales for steel, and at the 1888 convention a steel workers' committee was established to consider the proposals. Yet in 1891 steel delegates at the annual convention complained that few of the delegates understood their industry, and that the four lodges representing Bessemer converting departments at the meeting were all working on different scales.[15]

Coverage of the skilled steel workers by the A.A. was never

[14]A.A., *Proceedings,* 2nd Convention (1877), 50, 12th convention (1887), 1917-1918, 13th convention (1888), 2352, 14th convention (1889), 2685-2687, 15th convention (1890), 3031. Changes in the membership rules of the A.A. can be traced through copies of its constitution located in the William Martin Papers, University of Pittsburgh Libraries, Special Collections.
[15]William T. Hogan, *Economic History of the Iron and Steel Industry in the United States,* (Lexington, Mass., 1971), Vol. 1, 228-229; A.A., *Proceedings,* 2nd Convention (1877), 56, 4th Convention (1879) 223, 10th Convention (1885), 1577, 13th Convention (1888), 2337, 16th Convention (1891), *National Labor Tribune,* Dec. 3, 1887.

more than patchy. Several major steel producing firms, such as the Cambria and Bethlehem companies never recognized the union at any stage. Nevertheless the A.A. made significant progress in the steel industry until its disastrous defeat at Homestead in 1892 as a brief survey of the union's history in the nation's two major steelmaking districts, Pittsburgh and Chicago, shows. The major mills concerned in the Chicago area were the North Chicago mills, the South Chicago mills, and the Joliet mill, which were all operated after 1889 by the Illinois Steel Company. In the Pittsburgh area the major mills concerned were the Edgar Thompson, Homestead, and Duquesne, all ultimately owned by the Carnegie company. During the 1890s the Carnegie and Illinois Steel companies were the largest steelmaking firms in the United States.

In the early 1880s, the A.A. had reason to feel reasonably satisfied with its progress in the steel mills of both Chicago and Pittsburgh. Although an A.A. lodge at the Edgar Thompson had been suspended in 1877 when its members had signed an ironclad oath, two lodges were successfully established there in 1882-83. Two lodges were also established at Homestead soon after that plant opened in 1881 and won recognition after a bitter and violent strike in 1882. An A.A. lodge was formed in North Chicago in 1881, two were organized at South Chicago in 1883-84, and Joliet boasted five A.A. lodges in the early 1880s.[16]

Most of this ground was lost in 1884 and 1885 when the industry was depressed and the union weakened by internal dissension. At North Chicago the A.A.'s one lodge folded up when the mill lay idle for six months. At South Chicago, the men left the A.A. and joined the Knights of Labor when the A.A. refused to admit a lodge of blastfurnacemen. All the A.A. lodges at Joliet collapsed at least for a time during 1885. At Carnegie's Edgar Thompson mill, the A.A. lodges lost both recognition and their (unusual) eight hour shifts when the company closed the mill for an extended period, announced the introduction of labor-saving machinery that would supposedly cost many jobs, and began to

---

[16]2nd Convention (1877), 43, 7th Convention (1882), 806-807, 9th Convention (1884), 1341. *National Labor Tribune,* April 1, 1881, Jan. 14, Feb. 11, Feb. 18, March 4, March 16, March 25, 1882; June 23, 1883, August 18, August 25, 1883; March 22, 1884, August 24, 1884. Commonwealth of Pennsylvania, Secretary of Internal Affairs, *Annual Report,* Part III, *Industrial Statistics,* Vol. 10 (1881-1882), 171-175.

recruit non-union labor. Only at Homestead, of the mills under discussion, did the A.A. retain lodges in good standing in August 1885, and there the number of lodges had fallen from three to two during the previous year.[17]

This vacuum was filled to some extent by the Knights of Labor in the mid-1880s. At the Edgar Thompson, assemblies of Knights had co-existed and co-operated with A.A. lodges until 1884, and survived there till 1888 when they too were driven out by the Carnegie company. Whether the Knights represented any of the skilled men formerly belonging to the A.A. at the Edgar Thompson after 1884 is not clear, but at both North and South Chicago and elsewhere the Knights certainly took in dropouts from the A.A. In other cases assemblies of Knights represented lesser skilled workers who were excluded from the A.A. Unfortunately it is not possible to tell from the surviving records which form of recruitment was more important to the growth of the Knights in the iron and steel industries in the 1880s. In any case it is clear that the Knights were for a short period a force to be reckoned with in iron and steel. In Allegheny county alone there were 17 local assemblies of iron and steel workers recorded in 1886, most of them recently formed. Until 1886, relationships between the A.A. and the Knights at the national level were at least cordial. Grand Master Powderly was invited to the A.A.'s annual convention that year where he invited the union to affiliate with the Knights. The proposal was overwhelmingly rejected by the A.A. lodges in December however and the following two years brought a flood of complaints by A.A. men about encroachments by the Knights and several bitter jurisdictional disputes.[18]

In 1887 a National District Assembly of iron and steel workers (D.A. 217) was formed by the Knights but this time the organization was in decline in the industry as it was in the country as a

[17] A.A., *Proceedings*, 9th Convention (1884), 1341, 10th Convention (1885) 1545-47, 11th Convention (1886), 1741, 1748; *National Labor Tribune*, August 24, 1884, August 23, 1885, Dec. 18. 1884, Feb. 14, 1885, March 28, 1885; Pittsburgh *Chronicle-Telegraph*, Dec. 18, 1884.

[18] Information on the number of Knights of Labor local assemblies in iron and steel was drawn from *The Knights of Labor Data Bank*, compiled by Jonathan Garlock with the help of N. C. Builder. For a description of this project see *Historical Methods Newsletter*, VI (Sept. 1973), 149-160. Fitch, *Steelworkers*, 115. A.A., *Proceedings*, 11th Convention (1886), 1748, 1794 12th Convention (1887), 2052-2053, 13th Convention (1888), 2448. *National Labor Tribune*, Dec. 22, 1883, April 24, 1886, June 5, 1886, June 19, 1886, Dec. 18, 1886, Dec. 25, 1886, Feb. 26, 1887, March 12, 1887, April 28, 1887, June 25, 1887, Nov., 5, 1887, Feb. 11, 1888, June 30, 1888.

whole. D.A. 217 never became firmly established and by 1890 the Knights no longer posed any serious threat to the A.A. which had regained much of the ground lost since 1885. At Joliet two lodges were reorganized in 1885-86 and four had been established by 1890. The men who had been organized by the Knights at North Chicago in the mid-1880s came back to the A.A. in a body in 1888 and the new lodges remained in existence well into the 1890s. In 1891, two A.A. lodges were re-established at South Chicago and the local Vice President declared that the mammoth Illinois Steel Company was now "pretty well organized." At Homestead, where the A.A. had hung on during the lean years of the 1880s the number of lodges increased from two in 1885 to four in 1887 to seven in 1891. On the other hand the A.A. never recaptured the Edgar Thompson after its defeat there in 1885 and several attempts to organize the Duquesne mill, which opened in 1889, were defeated.[19]

On the eve of the Homestead strike, the strength of trade unionism in the U.S. iron and steel industry overall was in some respects greater than it was in Britain. The 24,000 members of the A.A. in 1892 must have represented a greater proportion of the total workforce than the 21,000 who belonged to the various British unions at this date.[20] Moreover the British unionists were divided among several unions, the largest with 7,800 members, whereas the Americans were combined in one apparently powerful organization. On the other hand the A.A.'s strength lay chiefly in the declining iron trade and no branch of the U.S. steel industry was covered by the kind of industry-wide agreement that John Hodge had negotiated for the open hearth furnace workers at least for Scotland and North-east England.

The defeat of the A.A. in the infamous Homestead strike, a familiar story which will not be repeated here, was a staggering

[19]*The Commoner and Glassworker*, Jan. 28, 1888; A.A., *Proceedings*, 11th Convention (1886), 1743-44, 12th Convention (1877), 1921, 13th Convention (1888), 2448, 14th Convention (1889), 2612-13, 15th Convention, (1890), 2995, 3065, 16th Convention (1891), 3337, 3542; 17th Convention (1892). 3974-3975, 3859, 3955-56. 18th Convention (1893). 4368-70; *National Labor Tribune*, Jan. 16, 1886, Sept. 11, 1886, Nov. 26, 1887, June 16, 1888, Oct. 6, 1888, March 30, 1889, June 8, 1889, July 20, 1889, April 12, 1890, May 3, 1890, Feb. 7, 1891, Aug. 13, 1892.
[20]Comparable figures on the number of men employed in the two industries are unavailable but since total production figures for iron and steel were similar in Britain and the U.S. in the early 1890s, and the British industry was known to have been the more labor intensive of the two, it follows that the British labor force must have been larger than the American, and the proportion unionised lower.

blow to the union. It meant that the A.A. had lost control of all three of the Carnegie Company's great steel mills in the Pittsburgh area. Without some say in Pittsburgh there could be no prospect of a nationwide scale agreement for steel. Furthermore Homestead was one of the best organized steel mills in the United States in 1892 and the workers there had fought long and hard after the company had provoked them into a contest. Nevertheless they were overwhelmingly defeated and lost everything. Union morale plummeted as a result. Most important of all, the Homestead struggle demonstrated that a great corporation could refuse to negotiate with a strong trade union, use the most oppressive strike-breaking tactics available, and ignore the flood of adverse publicity which resulted. Despite heavy criticism from politicians and the press, the Carnegie company refused to budge an inch at Homestead and followed up its victory by instituting a system of blacklists and industrial spying to ensure that unionism never raised its head in the company's mills again.[21]

The A.A. retained its lodges in the Chicago mills after 1892 and was recognised in a number of finishing mills around the country throughout the 1890s, but it was clearly on a downhill path after Homestead. Defeat by the newly organized U.S. Steel Corporation in 1901 was merely the *coup de grâce*. After 1892 the U.S. steel industry was run largely on open shop lines, a state of affairs which persisted until the 1930s.

*   *   *   *   *

Why did the A.A. fail where the British steelworkers' unions succeeded?[22] According to Selig Perlman, "the fragility so characteristic of American labor organizations has arisen in the main...from the lack of class consciousness in American labor."[23] A weak sense of class solidarity has in turn been attributed by different historians to various aspects of the eco-

---

[21] The story of the Homestead strike is probably more familiar than any other labor dispute in U.S. history. See Brody. *Steelworkers,* 53-56; Edward W. Bemis. "The Homestead Strike," *Journal of Political Economy,* II (1893-94), 369-396; J. B. Hogg, "The Homestead Strike of 1892" (unpublished Ph.D. diss., Univ. of Chicago, 1943).

[22] Ideally, this question should be asked of the Knights of Labor as well as the A.A. The reason for ignoring the Knights is simply the disappointing dearth of source materials on the Knights in the steel industry.

[23] Selig Perlman, *A Theory of the Labor Movement* (New York, 1928), 162.

nomic and social order in America, each of which will be considered as it applies to the workingmen on the steel industry.

Most historians of American labor have emphasized the impact of mass migration from Europe on the wage-earning class in the United States. It has often been argued that particular nationality groups, especially the "new" immigrants from Southern and Eastern Europe were "poor union material" because they were accustomed to low living standards and hence developed modest material aspirations, or because they were used to paternalistic patterns of authority, or because they saw themselves as transient residents of the United States who would shortly return to their homes in Europe, or simply because they were cowed into submissiveness by the sheer novelty of the new environment. A different, though related argument is that mass migration created such an ethno-cultural mixture among American wage-earners that co-operation and even communication between the various groups was rendered difficult if not impossible. What mattered, according to this view, was not so much the cultural characteristics of particular immigrant groups but the rivalries and tensions that emerged from the mixing together of several different ethno-cultural groups.[24] How do these themes fit the case of the steel-workers in the United States?

In 1890 the 142,588 men who labored in the U.S. iron and steel industry included 79,053 native born Americans, 5,778 colored Americans, and 57,574 foreign born whites. Of the latter the overwhelming majority (43,816) came from the British Isles and Germany. There is at least one piece of evidence which suggests that American employers saw the ethno-cultural diversity of their employees as a blessing and deliberately fostered it in order to build up a compliant workforce. "My experience has shown", wrote Captain William Jones, the famous superintendent of Carnegie's Edgar Thompson plant, to E. V. McCadness in a much quoted letter of February 1875, "that Germans and Irish, Swedes, and what I denominate 'Buckwheats'—young American country boys, judiciously mixed, make the most effective and tractable force you can find." Englishmen, "great sticklers for high wages

---

[24] For general discussions of the impact of immigration on American labor, see Perlman, 168-9; Henry Pelling, *American Labor* (Chicago, 1960), 210-213; Lloyd Ulman, *The Rise of the National Trade Union* (Cambridge, Mass., 1955), 23-26.

and strikes,'' were above all to be avoided. It would be interesting to know whether other American employers shared Captain Jones's view and attempted this "judicious mixture" of their workforce, but if so, the policy cannot be adjudged a success. Unionism, as we have seen, spread through the American iron and steel industry during Captain Jones's lifetime about as fast as it was spreading in Britain during the 1880s, and Captain Jones's own Edgar Thompson plant spawned both A.A. lodges and Knights of Labor Assemblies while he was in charge there. Perhaps rivalries and distrust between Germans, Swedes, Irish and American-born workers inhibited the growth of unionism in the steel industry but other than Captain Jones's letter, I have found no evidence to support the contention.[25]

During the 1890s there was a massive influx of immigrants from Southern and Eastern Europe into the labor force of the U.S. steel industry, especially Slavs (chiefly Poles, Slovaks, and Croations) and Hungarians. In his study of Slavic workers in the anthracite coalfields of Pennsylvania, Victor Greene has argued persuasively that these new immigrants did not prove to be "poor union material" but on the contrary became solid and militant supporters of the United Mineworkers of America (UMW). By the time the Slavic workers entered the American steel mills in large numbers there was not much of a union left to be loyal to, but there is scattered evidence suggesting that when industrial disputes did occur in the steel industry the Slavic workers were "more tenacious in their hold upon their right to organize even than the Americans...."[26]

On the other hand there can be no doubt that the impact of the Slavic-Hungarian immigration on the workforce in steel as a whole was profoundly divisive. Greene's account of the anthracite coalfields makes it clear that the Slavic workers there encountered strong nativistic hostility, and labor leaders were among those

[25] U.S. Immigration Commission, *Reports: Immigrants in Industries.* Vols. 8 and 9 (Washington, 1911), 23; Jones quoted in Bridge, J. H., *The Inside History of the Carnegie Company* (New York, 1903), 81.
[26] U.S. Immigration Commission, *Reports*, Vols. 8 and 9, 193; Victor R. Greene, *The Slavic Community on Strike: Immigrant Labor in Pennsylvania Anthracite* (Notre Dame, Indiana, 1968); U.S. House of Representatives, Committee on Investigation of the U.S. Steel Corporation, *Hearings*, 8 Vols., 62nd Congress, 2nd Session (1911-1912), Testimony of John A. Fitch, Vol. 4, 2917; U.S. Senate Committee on the Employment of Armed Bodies of Men for Private Purposes, *Report 1280*, 52nd Congress, 2nd Session (1892-1893), 42-43; Brody, *Steelworkers*, 260-261.

who lobbied for legislation restricting the employment of immigrants in the mines. In the steel mills there is ample evidence that "Hunkies," "Polaks," etc., were despised and discriminated against by older-established groups and that ethno-cultural divisions and tensions were pervasive features of milltown life from the 1890s onwards.[27]

Nevertheless nativism did not prevent the U.M.W. from recruiting the new immigrants in the Pennsylvania coalfields and the A.A. might well have done the same, had it had the opportunity, for by 1890 it was moving away from the craft exclusiveness of its early years. The critical point is that the A.A. was drawn into battle by the Carnegie company at Homestead in 1892 and delivered a knockout blow at a time when the influx of "new" immigrants had scarcely begun. The most that can be said about the impact of the Slavic-Hungarian migration on the fortunes of the A.A. therefore, is that it may conceivably have made a very bad situation even worse.

In this context it is important to recognize too that the labor force in the British steel industry was not without its internal divisions, including ethno-cultural ones. In Wales, John Hodge had to struggle against Welsh hostility towards all outsiders and with workers who spoke only the Welsh language. In Lancashire, another steel-making region, P. F. Clarke has described the rift between the English and Irish communities as "the most basic and persistent feature of social and hence political life in the region." Much the same could be said of Scotch/Irish divisions in the west of Scotland where Hodge attributed the loss of at least one strike to Protestant/Catholic rivalries.[28]

Another divisive force among wage-earners, the rift between highly-paid skilled "labor aristocrats" and poorer lesser skilled workers, was almost certainly more intense in Britain than in the United States at least until the arrival of the new immigrants in America. In both countries the steel unions were launched and built up by the skilled men, initially on an exclusive basis. In Britain, however, the wage differentials between skilled and unskilled were greater than they were in America where common

---

[27]Greene, *Slavic Community*, 111-121; Fitch, *Steelworkers*, 147-148.
[28]John Hodge. *From Workman's Cottage to Windsor Castle* (London, 1931) 118, 282-83; P. F. Clarke. *Lancashire and the New Liberalism* (Cambridge, 1971). 37; Patrick McGeown, *Heat the Furnace Seven Times More* (London, 1967), 15.

labor was scarcer and consequently more expensive.[29] The wages of first hand melters, who dominated the Smelters, "stood out like skyscrapers in a town of two-storey buildings" and these men were often arrogant in their dealings with the less favored men who worked with them.[30] Discontent among the lesser skilled steelworkers in Britain led to internal disputes within the Smelters and occasional secessions.[31] It was also a source of inter-union rivalry. The bitter and drawn-out struggle between the Iron-workers and the Steel Smelters at the Hawarden Bridge Works in 1909-1910, for example, arose from a dispute between the day wage men who belonged to the Smelters and the skilled tonnage rate men who were members of the Ironworkers.[32]

Jurisdictional disputes were not unknown in the U.S. steel industry of course. The A.A. faced formidable competition from the Knights in the late 1880s and had to cope with rival organiza-tions of nailers in the 1880s and finishers in the 1890s. At the time the A.A. received its knockout blow in 1892, however, it faced little serious competition from organizations within the world of unionism. By contrast, several organizations competed for the same classes of steelworkers in Britain, and the records of the Smelters show that they were constantly at odds with the other unions on both minor and major issues.[33] All things considered, it is difficult to make much of the proposition that internal disunity was a primary cause of the relative weakness of the A.A. as against its British counterparts.

A lack of class consciousness among American workers also "owes a great deal," according to Henry Pelling, "to the factor of high wages, which has enabled American workers to exhibit many of the same consumption and behavior patterns as those of other social groups." In a somewhat similar vein, Perlman has

---

[29]Mosely Industrial Commission to the U.S.A., *Reports of the Delegates* (Manchester, 1903), 16; B.S.S.A.A., *Monthly Report*, Nov. 30, 1907, 753.

[30]McGeown, *Heat the Furnace*, 23, 94.

[31]*R. C. on Labor*, (1892), Q.s 16369-16380; B.S.S.A.A., *Monthly Reports*, No. 31, Nov. 1891, 465, No. 36, April 30, 1892, 555, No. 120, April 30, 1898, No. 94, Jan. 31, 1902, No. 39, Oct. 31, 1902, 424-425, *Special Report on the Fourth Annual Conference of Delegates*, July, 1891, 331; Webb Collection, Collection E, Section A, Vol. 23, p. 214.

[32]For an account of the Hawarden Bridge Works dispute, see Carr and Taplin, *British Steel Industry*, 282-284.

[33]Sidney Pollard, *A History of Labour in Sheffield, 1850-1939*, (Liverpool, 1959), 172; Associated Society of Millmen, *Monthly Report*, No. 2, May 1890, 24; B.S.S.A.A., *Monthly Reports*, No. 123, 31 July 1899, 189, No. 126, 31 Oct. 1899, 288, No. 2, Feb. 1900, 64, No. 4, 30 April 1900, 163, 170, No. 5, 31 May 1900, 201-206.

argued that "the American employer has, in general, been able to keep his employees contented with the conditions, determined by himself, on which they individually accepted employment," and this, according to Perlman, was a primary cause of "the want of inner cohesiveness" in American labor organizations. Whatever the impact of high wages and good working and living conditions on class consciousness in general, however, the idea that they inhibit trade union growth is not especially persuasive. All over the capitalist world, trade unions emerged first among better paid workers and usually developed most rapidly in periods of economic boom. If trade unions were comparatively weak in the United States, where real wages were high, they were unusually strong in the late 19th century Australia, another high wage country.[34]

In the case of British and American steelworkers, it is not easy to determine with any degree of precision just how real wages compared in the late 19th century. The skilled men in both countries were paid by piece rates and it is difficult to find out how these translated into actual earnings. Furthermore estimates of comparative real wages rest on the construction of comparable cost-of-living indices, and this is a very complex task.[35] Contemporary observers, however, were united in the opinion that the unskilled men in America were better paid, both in monetary and real terms, than those in Britain, and most thought that skilled American steelworkers were better paid also.[36]

Though their earnings were high, both by U.S. and world standards, the American steel workers were forced to accept long

---

[34]Pelling, *American Labor*, 221; Perlman, *Labor Movement*, 154.

[35]In *A Century of Pay: the Course of Pay and Production in France, Germany, Sweden, the United Kingdom and the United States of America, 1860-1960* (London, 1968), E. H. Phelps-Brown and Margaret H. Browne came to the "remarkable" conclusion that average real wages in the United States did not draw ahead of British ones till after 1900, but they show that their conclusions would have been radically different if they had followed Paul Douglas's cost of living index for the United States rather than A. Rees's. See 163-165.

[36]In 1907 John Hodge claimed that skilled British steelworkers were better paid than their American counterparts but this should probably be regarded as a boast designed to impress his American audience rather than a judicious assessment. See B.S.S.A.A., *Monthly Report*, Nov. 30, 1907, 753. For other estimates of steelworkers' wages in Britain and America see T. H. Burnham and G. O. Hoskins, *Iron and Steel in Britain, 1870-1930* (London, 1943), 194; J. Stephen Jeans (ed.), *American Industrial Conditions and Competition: Reports of the Commissioners Appointed by the British Iron Trade Association to Enquire into the Iron, Steel and Allied Industries of the United States* (London, 1902), 55; U.S. Commissioner of Labor, *6th Annual Report*, 1890 (Washington, 1891), 287-470; Commonwealth of Pennsylvania, Secretary of Internal Affairs, *Annual Report*, Part 3, Industrial Statistics, Vol. 12 (1884), Legislative Doc., No. 7.

periods of unemployment and frequent wage cuts as a matter of course. Round the clock shift work, the twelve hour day, and the seven day week were normal practices. Industrial accidents, often fatal, were frequent in the steel industry and working conditions were extremely unpleasant. Pittsburgh, Roy Lubove has noted, has been compared to hell more frequently than any other American city, and it was the heat and the arduous, dangerous work of the steel industry which earned it this unsavoury reputation. British steel workers were amazed when they learned in 1907 that their American counterparts were frequently driven to work by their wives in buggies, but American steelworkers were well aware of the enormous profits earned by companies like Carnegie's, and can hardly have believed that high wages were anything less than their due. When John Fitch studied the skilled steelworkers of the Pittsburgh region in 1907-1908, he found them "resentful and bitter toward their employers." No comparable study exists for the 1880s or 1890s but it is difficult to believe that the decline of the A.A. was rooted in a deep sense of contentment among the steelworkers.[37]

More difficult to measure and evaluate is the impact of social and geographic mobility on British and American manual workers generally, and on steelworkers in particular. Recently Stephan Thernstrom and other American scholars have begun to provide us with a clear picture of just how fast and in what ways American workers accumulated property, rose or fell on the occupational ladder, and moved from place to place.[38] Obviously these matters have a direct bearing on the question of class consciousness and group solidarity. Unfortunately, census returns, the most important source of data for the American studies, do not provide the same wealth of information about property holdings, earnings and occupations for Britain as America, and in any case are only available to scholars for England and Wales to 1871.[39]

---

[37] Roy Lubove, *Twentieth Century Pittsburgh: Government, Business, and Environmental Change* (New York, 1969). I: James Kitson. "Iron and Steel Industries of America," *Contemporary Review*, LIX (May 1891), 629; Charles R. Walker, *Steel: The Diary of a Furnace Worker* (Boston, 1922), 145-157; U.S. House of Representatives, Investigation of U.S. Steel Corp., Hearings, 2911; Brody, *Steelworkers*, Ch. 2; B.S.S.A.A., *Monthly Report*, No. 7, July 31, 1901, 252; Fitch, *Steelworkers*, 233.

[38] See Stephan Thernstrom, *The Other Bostonians: Poverty and Progress in the American Metropolis, 1880-1970* (Cambridge, Mass., 1973), for an outstanding example of this work and a discussion of other literature in the field.

[39] Problems of using British census data are discussed at length in E. A. Wrigley (ed.), *Nineteenth*

If some statistical method exists for isolating steelworkers from the rest of the population in Britain and tracing their geographic and social progress in this period, I have failed to discover it. It seems probable that faster rates of economic growth in the United States provided greater opportunities for social advancement and the *embourgeoisement* of workers there. On the question of geographic mobility, however, we know that rates of rural exodus, urbanization, and migration abroad were very high in 19th century Britain, and that British steelmaking centers were rapidly growing, highly mobile communities. Middlesbrough, for example, the Pittsburgh of Northeast England had a population of 154 in 1831, 18,892 in 1861, 55,788 in 1881, and 91,302 in 1901. In the early 20th century Lady Bell described the population of Middlesbrough as "recruited by the incessant influx of fresh workers into the town of which a great part is forever changing and shifting, restlessly moving from one house to another, or going away altogether in the constant hope that the mere fact of change must be an improvement." In general, the social and geographic mobility of steelworkers in Britain and America remains a murky subject and whether American steelworkers were a more volatile group, socially and geographically, than British ones remains unknown and possibly unknowable.[40]

For one vital class of British steelworkers, the open hearth melters who formed the hard core of the Steel Smelters' union, geographic mobility was certainly impeded by the system of promotion which developed in that branch of the industry. Promotion from chargewheeler to third hand melter to second hand melter to first hand melter was by seniority *within the firm*. A first hand melter who left his job to take up a position elsewhere started at the bottom again. Since, in 1892, a first hand earned about £5-£10 per week, a second hand two-thirds of this, a third hand one-half of the first hand's wage, and a chargewheeler about four shillings and sixpence per day, the incentive to stay in one place was obviously strong. Evidence bearing on promotion practices in the U.S. steel industry is hard to find but it would have been entirely out of character for American employers to accept

Century Society: Essays in the Use of Quantitative Methods for the Study of Social Data (Cambridge, 1972).
[40]Lady Hugh Bell, *At the Works*, (London, 1907), 9,11.

this kind of restriction on their ability to hire and promote workers at will. It may be that skilled men in the U.S. steel industry moved about more than British open hearth melters and that the stability of A.A. lodges suffered as a result. However we are faced with a chicken and egg problem here. Promotion by seniority was something which the Steel Smelters imposed on the employers and their ability to do this may have reflected other sources of strength.[41]

Even more elusive are questions relating to the spirit of labor/management and class relationships generally in Britain and the United States. According to Louis Hartz the failure of socialism in the United States owes less to the "objective movement of economic forces" than to the absence of a feudal tradition in America. If there is anything in the view that Americans were peculiarly lacking in a "sense of class" for reasons unconnected to the economic situation, then this could help explain the relative weakness of trade unionism in the United States. Whatever value one places on Hartz's theory, it is true that European visitors frequently commented on the relative openness and ease with which American workingmen approached and were approached by their employers and managers. Men like Superintendent Jones of the Edgar Thompson prided themselves on the good personal relationships they maintained with their men. Could it be that trade union development was hindered by the fact that workingmen sensed less social distance between themselves and their bosses than British workers?[42]

It is difficult to be sure but the answer is probably not. However easy relationships between employer and employee were on a day to day basis, the fundamental conflict of interest between capital and labor was too obvious to be ignored. When industrial disputes did break out in American steel plants as for example at Homestead in 1881 and 1892, Bethlehem in 1883, and Duquesne in 1889, the employers commonly refused to recognize the union, sacked union leaders, evicted strikers from company houses, called in non-union labor from far afield, and generally used every weapon at their disposal in order to defeat the men. Violence was far more

[41]McGeown, *Heat the Furnace*, 8; Webb Collection, Collection E., Section A, Vol. 23, 179.
[42]Louis Hartz, *The Liberal Tradition in America*, (New York, 1955), 6 and *passim*: I have discussed Hartz's thesis in "Louis Hartz's Fragment Thesis," *New Zealand Journal of History*, VII (April, 1973), 3-11.

common in U.S. labor relations generally and in the U.S. steel industry in particular than it was in Britain. Though the relationship between manager and men might be "somewhat freer" a visiting British unionist wrote of the U.S. steel industry in 1903, "it is not better than in this country...." Managers might be more approachable personally but wage disputes were settled "in the jingo spirit."[43]

All of the points under discussion so far, ethno-cultural and other divisive forces within the workforce, wages and working conditions, rates of social and geographic mobility, and the spirit of worker/management relations are related to the question of trade union strength and weakness in a similar fashion; all have a bearing on class consciousness and group solidarity. Yet there is good reason to doubt whether the collapse of the A.A. in the U.S. was caused by a comparative lack of class or group consciousness on the part of American steelworkers. The greatest single blow to the fortunes of the A.A. occurred at Homestead in 1892 where not only the A.A. lodges but the entire workforce demonstrated a high degree of group consciousness and solidarity. Though there are cases recorded of A.A. lodges simply folding up, usually during periods when mills lay idle for long periods, another common pattern was a head-on clash between the employers and the A.A. over the right to organize, followed by a lengthy and bitter stoppage, ending in a victory for the employers and the open shop.

Of course some of the A.A.'s defeats may have come about in whole or in part because the workers lacked sufficient solidarity, or because there were large numbers of non-union men willing to take the place of strikers in any dispute. One reason for the A.A.'s failure to organize the Duquesne plant was undoubtedly the fiercely anti-union policies adopted by the management, but the union's leaders also complained that the men there lacked the necessary spirit to maintain a successful strike.[44] The record of industrial disputes in the U.S. steel industry during the 1880s makes nonsense of the notion that the workforce was so utterly

---

[43]For the strike at Bethlehem in 1883, see *National Labor Tribune*, July 7, 1883, July 21, 1883, Sept. 1, 1883; Commonwealth of Pennsylvania, Secretary of Internal Affairs, *Annual Report*, Part 3, Industrial Statistics, Vol. II (1882-1883), 135. For the conflicts at Homestead and Duquesne, see sources cited in notes 16, 18 and 21. Mosely Commission, *Reports*, 49.
[44]A. A., *Proceedings*, 17th Convention (June 1892), 3956.

divided or intrinsically contented that it lacked any will for collective action at all, but it is conceivable that, for one reason or another, group consciousness was comparatively weaker among American than British steelworkers.

It should be noted, however, that apathy and lack of militancy were not unknown among British steelworkers. The complaints of A.A. leaders that the men at Duquesne lacked solidarity and union discipline are little different in kind from dozens of items in the Monthly Reports of the British Steel Smelters about the same time.[45] In Britain, as in America, steelworkers had often to be prodded into paying union dues, maintaining branches, and staying loyal in difficult strike situations. Whole steel-making regions remained almost untouched by unionism in Britain until well into the 20th century, Sheffield being a notable case in point.[46] In summary, it remains uncertain whether American steelworkers possessed less of a sense of group solidarity than British steelworkers or not, and this is surely not the most obvious explanation for the total collapse of the steelworkers' unions in the United States.

Whether or not it was more difficult to persuade American than British steelworkers to join or support a trade union, the very structure of U.S. trade unionism may have inhibited efforts to recruit union members in the American steel industry. In both countries the first unions to enter the field were ironworkers' organizations, dominated by the puddlers and rollers of wrought iron. In Britain, as we have seen, the Ironworkers' union recruited some steelworkers in some regions but never threw itself into a vigorous recruitment campaign throughout the industry. Other organizations, notably the Steel Smelters sprang up to take on these tasks, and although the existence of several different unions within the British steel industry produced jurisdictional confusion and inter-union squabbles, it also ensured that efforts to expand union membership did not lapse. Rivalry may even have encouraged vigorous efforts at recruitment.

In America, on the other hand, the concept of one union per trade was fiercely defended by the national unions and formed the

---

[45]See, for example, B.S.S.A.A., *Monthly Report,* Oct. 1887, No. 4, April 30, 1900, No. 6, June 30, 1900, *Report of Second Biennial Conference,* Jan. 1889. Also see *Ironworker's Journal,* No. 234, Sept. 1882, 2.

[46]B.S.S.A.A., *Monthly Report* No. 4, 30 April 1901, 141.

very cornerstone of the American Federation of Labor's policies after its formation. "Dual unionism" was perceived as an unmitigated evil by union leaders in the United States and any effort to establish a rival organization within the jurisdiction of an existing union was bitterly resisted with the full backing of the AFL. The challenge of the Knights of Labor to the national unions in the 1880s may account in part for the American unions' obsession with jurisdictional purity, and other more general explanations have been put forward by labor historians.[47] Whatever the reasons, the impact was significant and in some ways unhelpful to the cause of unionism in the American iron and steel industry. The A.A. claimed the sole right to organize skilled steelworkers in the United States and after 1886 could back up its claim with an AFL charter. Yet throughout the 1880s and 1890s it remained primarily an ironworkers' union and a Pittsburgh-centered organization. Since the main sources available to the historian for the study of the A.A.'s activities are the union's own *Proceedings*, and its official organ, the *National Labor Tribune*, it is difficult to be sure whether the A.A. neglected the interests of steelworkers, especially those outside the Pittsburgh area, or not. Obviously, union spokesmen did not advertise their leaders' failings. It is clear from these official publications, however, that the wrought iron industry was overwhelmingly the center of the union's concern in the late 19th century.

There were also cases where steelworkers expressed or demonstrated dissatisfaction with the A.A., as for example in Chicago during the mid-1880s, when several lodges seceded and joined the Knights of Labor. The Chicago steel mills were later re-organized by the A.A. but in the interval Carnegie had driven first the A.A. and then the Knights from the Edgar Thompson plant, arguing that lower wage rates in Chicago forced him to cut costs in Pittsburgh and reject the men's demands. The *National Labor Tribune* blamed the Knights for allowing this situation to develop, but it was the failure of the A.A. to maintain the loyalty of the Chicago steelworkers that had allowed the Knights to move in there in the first place. It seems possible, then, that the unionization of American steelworkers was hindered by the Pittsburgh

---

[47] Ulman, *National Trade Union*, 362–363; Perlman, *Labor Movement*, 163-164.

ironworkers' dominating role in the national union's affairs.[48]

So far attention has been concentrated on what might be termed "internal" factors affecting trade union growth: characteristics of the unions themselves, their members, and their potential membership. It is also necessary to consider "external" factors: i.e., aspects of the economic, social, and political setting within which the men labored and the unions organized. Obviously enough these were not identical in Britain and America.

Every British steelman, whether employer or employee, who inspected the steel mills of the United States from the 1880s onwards, and every American observer of the British steel industry was struck by the rapid pace of technical change in the American industry and the increasing obsolescence of British manufacturing techniques.[49] Technical developments in some cases rendered traditional skills, such as iron puddling, completely obsolete. In other cases the degree of skill required by a workman to perform a particular manufacturing operation was severely reduced. Since semi-skilled workmen were easier to replace than highly skilled tradesmen, such changes weakened the bargaining power of the trade unions concerned. Could it be that the collapse of the A.A. came about in whole or in part because technical change had undermined the importance of its members' skills; skills which remained critical in the technically less advanced steel mills of Britain?[50]

It should be noted first of all, that the impact of technical developments on the skills of steel workers was not uniform in all branches of the industry. In some, the main impact of technical innovation was to reduce the amount of physical labor required rather than the skills. This was true of the blastfurnaces, for example, and also of the open hearth furnaces, where the major innovation in this period was the introduction of mechanical

[48] A. A., Proceedings, 9th convention (1884), 1320, 1341, 11th Convention (1886), 1741, 1748, 12th Convention (1887), 2052-2053, 13th Convention (1888), 2448; National Labor Tribune, April 7, April 14, April 28, 1888.

[49] Mosely Commission, Reports, 41; D. L. Burn, The Economic History of Steelmaking, 1867-1939 (Cambridge, 1940), 183-218; Jeans, American Industrial Conditions, 317; Fitch, Steelworkers 140; William Garrett, "A Comparison Between American and British Rolling Mill Practice," Journal of the Iron and Steel Institute, LIX (1901), 101-145; Henry H. Howe, "Notes on the Bessemer Process," XLVIII (1890), 101-145; B.S.S.A.A., Monthly Report, No. 6, June 30, 1901; Frank Popplewell, Some Modern Conditions and Recent Developments in Iron and Steel Production in America (Manchester, 1906).

[50] In Steelworkers in America, David Brody argues that the A.A.'s "fatal weakness" was its dependence on its members' skills. See Ch. 3.

methods for charging furnaces. How much skill was required of an open hearth steel worker at this time is difficult to determine, since employers and employees differed on the question. In 1902 Charles Schwab of U.S. Steel claimed he could train a "fairly intelligent agricultural laborer" to be a steel melter in six to eight weeks. Ten years earlier James Riley of the Steel Company of Scotland had made much the same claim in strikingly similar language. A man "off the fields" he said, could be turned into a melter "within three months." Union men, on the other hand claimed that operating open hearth furnaces required a great deal of skill and long experience, and when strikes were in progress, they almost invariably claimed that substitute labor was producing "messes" and ruining the furnaces. Whatever the truth, the major change in the period involved the replacement of manual by mechanical labor and the degree of skill required cannot have varied significantly between Britain and American.[51]

In the American rolling mills too the amount of physical labor required was greatly reduced by mechanization but in this case it is also true that the introduction of automatic mechanical devices reduced the importance of the roll hands' skills. Even union officials admitted as much.[52] It was in rolling mill practices that the British lagged farthest behind their U.S. competitors, and it is probable that the impact of technical change on the position of the American rolling mill hands made the A.A. comparatively easier to defeat and destroy than the British unions. American employers certainly did use the threat of technical innovation to force the workforce into submission. In December, 1884, for example, the Carnegie Company shut down the Edgar Thompson plant for an indefinite period and paid off all hands. Shortly afterwards, Pittsburgh newspapers reported that when the mill reopened using new automatic rolling equipment it would require 1600 fewer men. Faced with this situation and news that the company's agents were recruiting non-union labor outside the district, some

---

[51]For Schwab's statement, see Jeans, *American Industrial Conditions,* 62; for Riley's, see Webb Collection, Collection E, Section A, ,Vol. 23, 1841; for other views of the question see McGeown, *Heat the Furnace,* 94-95; Charles Reitell, *Machinery and Its Benefits to Labor in the Crude Iron and Steel Industries* (Menasha, Wisconsin, 1917), 23; for assertions that non-union labor could not manage open hearth furnaces, see Hodge, *Workman's Cottage,* 122; B.S.S.A.A., *Monthly Reports,* No. 6, Nov. 30, 1889, No. 32, Dec. 31, 1891, No. 69, Jan. 31, 1895, No. 96, April 30, 1897.

[52]See the testimony of A. A. President Weihe, Senate Committee on the Employment of Armed Men, *Report,* 202.

A.A. men deserted the union and signed new contracts on the employers' terms. Subsequently the A.A.'s two lodges at the Edgar Thompson disbanded.

Another feature which distinguished the British from the U.S. steel industry was the much larger scale of corporate organization in America. As early as 1878 the ten active U.S. Bessemer steel plants were producing, on average, one and a half times as much steel as their British counterparts. Faster growth within individual plants and horizontal mergers, such as that which produced the Illinois Steel Company in 1889, increased the disparity between the sizes of the largest British and American firms. By 1892 the Carnegie and the Illinois Steel Companies had annual capacities of over one million tons of steel. As late as 1905 the ingot capacity of the largest British firm was somewhat less than half of this figure.[53]

For trade unions, large firms have their advantages, but they are more difficult to organize initially if they are determined to resist, as many of the American companies were.[54] Multiplant operations, such as Carnegie's, after 1883, and the Illinois, after 1889, were particularly difficult opponents for the unions since these companies could maintain full production and profitable operations in non-union plants while strikes were in progress elsewhere. Carnegie used this tactic successfully during the Homestead struggle of 1892 and the gigantic U.S. Steel Corporation was able to squeeze what life remained out of the A.A. with similar methods in 1901. At the conclusion of the Homestead strike, the *National Labor Tribune* editorialized on this point: "If, on July First, it had appeared reasonably possible that the [Carnegie] company would stick to the contest, regardless of cost in cash," the editors wrote, "then the issue would have been solved without a contest, for there was no workman of the A.A. but who knows that no labor organization under the sun could contend successfully against such immense resources as were at the disposition of the Carnegie company on July 1." Certainly the resources controlled by the Carnegie company dwarfed those of any British steel firm at that date and the contrast was even more

[53] Peter Temin, *Iron and Steel in Nineteenth-Century America: an Economic Enquiry* (Cambridge, Mass., 1964), 137; Hogan, *Economic History of the Iron and Steel Industry in the United States*, Vol. 1, 235; Burn, *Economic History of Steelmaking*, 229.
[54] For a discussion of this point see Ulman, *Rise of the National Trade Union*, 37-42.

marked after the formation of U.S. Steel in 1901.[55]

Perhaps more important than the enormous size of the great American companies was the sheer determination with which so many of them resisted efforts to unionize their mills, or in the case of the Carnegie company, drove unions out of divisions that were already organized. Whereas bitter struggles over union recognition were commonplace in the U.S. steel industry during the 1880s and 1890s, the principle of unionism was rarely an issue in the British industry during this period. There were employers who refused to deal with unions, John Hodge remarked, in a tone more of sorrow than anger, but clearly for Hodge the determined anti-union management represented more of an irritant than a serious threat to the growth and survival of his union. On the whole, according to Hodge, "the employers are entitled to credit for always having played cricket."[56]

Why was it that British employers were more willing to tolerate the existence of unions in their mills than their American counterparts? Surely not because they felt any positive enthusiasm for the unions. When Sidney Webb interviewed James Riley, manager of Scotland's largest steel-producing firm in 1892, Riley spoke bitterly about the obstructive tactics of both the Smelters and the Millmen and down-graded the value of the skill of their members. Yet Riley played a leading role in the establishment of conciliation and arbitration machinery for the Scottish iron and steel industry and his public stance towards the unions was invariably conciliatory. In this respect he typified the attitudes of British steelmasters towards the trade unions in the years when Carnegie's men were driving the unions out of their Pittsburgh mills.[57]

Perhaps American employers were emboldened by the knowledge that they controlled vast resources and that rapid technical change was undermining the scarcity value of skilled workmen. If there is anything in the notion that American workmen lacked the solidarity and capacity for organization of the British, then this too could have encouraged U.S. employers to resist the emer-

---

[55]Brody, *Steelworkers*, 59; *National Labor Tribune*, Nov. 26, 1892.
[56]Hodge, *Country Cottage*, 91, 284; B.S.S.A.A., Annual Conference of Delegates, July 1891, *Report*, 382.
[57]Webb Collection, Collection E, Section A, Vol. 23, 184-185; for examples of Riley's public dealings with one union see Associated Society of Millmen, *Monthly Reports*, August 31, 1890, Jan., Feb., and March 1891.

gence of trade unions. In other words, the attitudes of employers
may not have been an independent variable in this situation but a
function of other factors already discussed. Yet it seems unlikely
that British employers were dissuaded from adopting more
strongly anti-union policies by fear of the intrinsic fighting
strength of the unions they dealt with or lack of confidence in
their own resources, since the occasional anti-union employer in
Britain demonstrated from time to time that determination and
strong arm tactics could work as well in Glasgow as in Pittsburgh.
Two examples will illustrate this point.

In 1889 the Millmen's union, which was recognized by most of
the steel companies in Scotland, established a branch with about
30 members at a plant called Clyde Bridge. The management
refused to recognize the union and dismissed the union men. A
strike ensued, supported, according to the union, by most of the
workforce. But the owner, one James Neilson, recruited enough
non-union labor to keep the mill operating and boarded them
inside the mill gates. After 19 weeks the strike was called off by
the Millmen and Clyde Bridge remained a non-union mill until
about 1904.[58]

Just ten years after the Millmen's defeat at Clyde Bridge, the
Steel Smelters, by this stage a well-established union which was
recognized by most of the major employers in Britain also ran up
against the Neilsons, this time at the Mossend works in Scotland.
In August, 1889, the Smelters established a branch at Mossend
which had been non-union until that time. Management responded
by dismissing the branch secretary and about 20 other union
members. Attempts to negotiate a settlement failed and a strike
was called for October 21. The company hired non-union labor to
keep their plant running and evicted strikers from company-owned
houses, but the union fought back with picketing, "meetings,
games, concerts, dances, football matches, etc." Over 400 men
were supported with strike pay and the assistant secretary of the
union, John T. McPherson, spent several months almost constantly at Mossend directing the struggle and addressing meetings.
Throughout 1900 the Smelters' *Monthly Report* carried encouraging stories from Mossend assuring members that morale re-

---

[58]B.S.S.A.A., Third Annual Conference of Delegates, *Report*, Jan. 2-3, 1890, 88; *Monthly Reports*, Sept. 30, 1889, April 30, 1903, August 31, 1904; *R.C. on Labor* (1892), Qs. 15963,
15989-994; Pugh, *Men of Steel*, 217-8.

mained high among the strikers despite police harassment and the management's blandishments. Blackleg labor was alleged to be so inefficient that the firm would soon be driven into bankruptcy. Yet after 18 months of solid effort and the expenditure of over £13,000 (the union's total assets in Jan. 1901 were valued at £25,000) the Smelters admitted defeat and called off the strike.[59]

Why did other more important British steel-producing firms not emulate the Neilsons of Clyde Bridge and Mossend and throw their much greater resources into the fight against unionism? This is a critical question but one that is extremely difficult to answer given the paucity of surviving evidence. Since the British steel industry never suffered a major confrontation between unions and employers, there was no great incentive to discuss problems of labor relations in public. Strikes and lockouts such as those at Mossend and Clyde Bridge were small scale affairs receiving little or no attention in the general press, and trade publications such as the *Iron and Coal Trades Review* discussed labor relations in only the most general terms. Some company records survive but these consist mainly of minutes from meetings of Boards of Directors and they contain little or nothing about managerial attitudes towards unions. Thus the records of the Steel Company of Scotland tell us that Mr. Riley, the manager, reported on the meeting between employers and unionists at Newcastle in 1889, but they do not tell us *what* he reported, how the meeting was arranged, or what deliberations, if any, went on among employers before this crucial meeting occurred.[60]

All that can be done is to suggest some possible explanations for the attitudes of the British steelmasters. First of all, a general survey of British labor history reveals that British trade unions had to fight stubbornly, on both the industrial and political fronts, for the right to exist, before they were generally accepted as legitimate institutions. By the last quarter of the 19th century, however, many of the critical battles had been fought and won. In the United States, industrialism, the industrial proletariat, and the industrial union appeared much later. The violent resistance of many American employers to unionism in the late 19th century

---

[59]B.S.S.A.A., *Monthly Reports*, Nos. 124 *et seq,* Aug. 31, 1899 - April 30, 1901.
[60]I am grateful to Mr. Derek Charman, Archivist of the British Steel Corporation and Professor P. L. Payne of the University of Aberdeen who made it possible for me to look at a broad range of surviving steel company records in Britain.

may simply have reflected the relative novelty of the "labour problem" in the United States and perhaps should be compared with the activities of British employers in the era of the Combination Acts or the great lockouts of the 1850s. In 1892 the British economist, W. J. Ashley, thought it "...very apparent that the feeling of the comfortable classes in America is still in the same stage as that reached by the like classes in England a quarter of a century ago."[61]

One remark of James Riley to Sidney Webb may provide another clue to the differing attitudes of British and American employers towards unions. He had been accused by other employers, Riley said, of being unduly kind to the unions, in order to protect the political career of his company chairman, Sir Charles Tennant who at one time represented a Glasgow constituency in Parliament as a Liberal.[62] Though a direct link between the political aspirations and labor policies of individual employers was no doubt unusual, the influence of political pressures on labor relations is always critical, and the fact that manual workers formed a much larger proportion of the total population in Britain than in the United States meant that, even though partially disfranchised, the British working class was politically more potent. The frequent recourse of American state governments to the use of the National Guard in labor disputes, nominally to maintain law and order but usually in practice to protect non-union labor, President Cleveland's employment of federal troops to crush the American Railway Union in 1894, and the politicians-be-damned attitude of the Carnegie company during the Homestead contest, are all indications of the vulnerability of American trade unions to a hostile political environment in the late 19th century.

*   *   *   *   *

It has not proved possible to provide easy or conclusive answers to all of the questions raised in this study. On several significant aspects of the subject the evidence is scanty and conclusions can be no more than tentative. Nevertheless, at least one salient point does emerge. Though the conditions and aspirations of steel-

[61]W. J. Ashley. "Methods of Industrial Peace," *Economic Review*, II (1892), 311.
[62] Webb Collection, Collection E, Section A, Vol. 23, 185.

workers, and the structure and leadership of their organizations may have had something to do with the contrasting fortunes of the steelworkers' unions in Britain and America, the most striking difference between the two situations concerns the behavior of employers rather than employees. In both countries, the impulse to organize was present among steelworkers but in one, most employers offered little resistance to union growth while in the other they generally fought back vigorously.

It may be that the truculent attitude adopted by so many American employers was encouraged by the attitudes of their employees and the tactics of the unions. If evidence suggesting that American steelworkers lacked the solidarity of British ones is less than compelling, it must be conceded that there could be an element of truth in the proposition. The dominating position of ironworkers in the one union with AFL jurisdiction in the U.S. steel industry is also a factor which must be taken into account when considering the disintegration of trade unionism there. But if union morale and group solidarity are to be stressed we must consider the odds against which the A.A. struggled, surely enough to dampen the spirits of the most ardent union man. When the Carnegie company closed down the Edgar Thompson plant for an indefinite period and let it be known new machinery would cost hundreds of jobs in the mill, it is not surprising that many unionists lost heart and signed on for work on the company's terms. When neither the united resistance of the workforce nor protest of press and politicians could dissuade the management at Homestead to settle for anything less than the complete eradication of the union from the mill, who can wonder that the A.A. lost members rapidly? The determination to resist the growth of trade unions by employers who possessed vast financial resources, who controlled a rapidly changing technology, and who were uninhibited by political constraints, may not have been the only reason for the collapse of unionism in the American steel industry, but it is surely the most important one.

A comparative study of some other industry common to Britain and the United States, or unionization among American and German steelworkers would undoubtedly produce a different emphasis. Still, many of the points made here about the U.S. steel industry do have a broader application. Rapid rates of technological change were characteristic of American industry in this period. Domination of national markets by a small number of very large firms was also much more typical of the United States than Britain. Though the standard work on British trade unions talks of an "employers' counter-attack" on the unions in the 1890s, the goals of the British employers were limited and their tactics generally timid when compared to those of many American employers at that time. The victories of British employers over the boot and shoe workers' union in 1895 and the engineers in 1897, for example, led not to the institution of the open shop in those industries but merely to restrictions on the unions' powers to impose restrictive practices.[63] The impact of an unsympathetic political environment on the outcome of labor disputes, so evident during the Homestead struggle, affected unions generally.

The weakness and political conservatism of the American labor movement in the late 19th and early 20th centuries have often been seen primarily as the product of a lack of class consciousness among American workingmen. In the United States, it is suggested, class lines were more fluid and opportunities for advancement more rapid than in European countries like Britain, where, according to Perlman, "the hierarchy of classes keeps labor together by pressure from the top." Perhaps so, yet as Perlman also acknowledges, in some ways the American workingman was more rather than less oppressed than his British counterpart. The retreat of so many American union leaders from a youthful socialism to a cautious and conservative "business unionism" may have reflected less a growing enthusiasm for the economic and political status quo, than a resigned acknowledgement that in a land where the propertied middle classes dominated politically and the big corporations ruled supreme in industry, accommodation was more appropriate than confrontation.[64]

---

[63]Clegg, Fox, and Thompson, *British Trade Unions*, 161-168, 201-205.
[64]Perlman, *Labor Movement*, 155-62, 164.

10

Black Workers and Labor Unions in Birmingham, Alabama, 1897-1904

PAUL B. WORTHMAN

Southern industrial development at the end of the nineteenth century drew thousands of black workers to the region's cities and towns, where many of the migrants became an integral part of the South's industrial labor force. Historians have drawn attention to the organization of these and Northern black workers by the Knights of Labor and other unions during the 1880s and early 1890s.[1] Later efforts to organize black workers, especially in the South, have too often been ignored, however, because most historians dealing with relations between black workers and trade unions have concentrated on the racial hostility of white workers, and the exclusionary and racially restrictive policies of various trade unions.[2] Exclusive emphasis on the labor move-

---

[1] Sidney Kessler, "The Negro in Labor Strikes," in *Midwest Journal*, VI:2 (Summer 1954), 16-35; Frederic Myers, "The Knights of Labor in the South," in *Southern Economic Journal*, VI:2 (April 1940), 479-485; C. Vann Woodward, *Origins of the New South, 1877-1913* (Baton Rouge, 1951), 229-234; Sterling D. Spero and Abram L. Harris, *The Black Worker: The Negro and the Labor Movement* (New York, 1931), 40-45; Roger W. Shugg, "The New Orleans General Strike of 1892," in *Louisiana Historical Quarterly*, XXI:2 (April 1938), 559-563; Robert Ward and William Warren Rogers, *Labor Revolt in Alabama: The Great Strike of 1894* (University, Alabama, 1965); F. Ray Marshall, *Labor in the South* (Cambridge, Mass., 1967), 21-24, 60-70; W.E.B. Du Bois, *The Negro Artisan* (Atlanta, 1902), *passim;* Herbert Gutman, "The Negro and the United Mine Workers," in Julius Jacobson, ed., *The Negro and the American Labor Movement* (Garden City, N. Y., 1968), 49-127.

[2] A vast amount of literature examining the failure of the American Federation of Labor and national trade unions to organize black workers at the beginning of the twentieth century is available. Herman D. Bloch, "Labor and the Negro, 1866-1910," in *Journal of Negro History*, L:3 (July 1965), 163-184; Philip S. Foner, *History of the Labor*

Reprinted from *Labor History* 10 (Summer 1969), 375-406. The author is indebted to Yale University for a travel grant which made much of the research for this article possible. I am also grateful to C. Vann Woodward, Mark Leiserson, and Edwin Redkey for their critical reading of an earlier version.

ment's abandonment of black workers during the early years of the twentieth century has obscured the complex relationships which existed among black workers, white workers, and trade unions, and has led to the neglect of tensions and conflicts in the labor movement and in the South which helped shape those relationships.[3] Evidence from Birmingham, Alabama, indicates that despite the rapid spread of racial conflict at the beginning of the twentieth century, the heritage of interracial cooperation in the Knights of Labor and in Populist campaigns lingered among many white and black workingmen. Within trade unions, moreover, no monolithic attitude towards black workers existed. While some national labor leaders opposed organizing Negroes, others favored such a policy. In addition, since most black workers labored in unskilled jobs, union relations with them were determined not merely by racial attitudes, but also by a particular union's outlook towards organizing the unskilled. C. Vann Woodward pointed out in *Origins of the New South* that the evolution of post-Civil War Southern society involved a tangled web of economic and political conflicts and alliances with industrial laborers as well as agrarian Populists often seeking to overcome racial animosities in order to challenge the hegemony of Southern industrialists.[4] Between 1897 and 1904 the growth of Birmingham's labor movement stimulated new efforts at interracial workingmen's cooperation and the organization of black workers.

Exploitation of the rich coal and iron reserves of northern Alabama, which began after the Civil War rapidly transformed this agrarian region into one of the most important industrial centers in the United

---

Movement in the United States, II (New York, 1955), 347-361, and III (New York, 1964), 233-255; Gerald Grob, "Organized Labor and the Negro Workers, 1865-1900," in *Labor History,* I:1 (Spring 1960), 164-176; Herbert Hill, "In the Age of Gompers and After: Racial Practices of Organized Labor," in *New Politics,* IV:2 (Spring 1965), 26-46; Marc Karson and Ronald Radosh, "The American Federation of Labor and the Negro Worker, 1894-1949," in Jacobson, ed., *Negro and the Labor Movement,* 155-187; Bernard Mandel, "Samuel Gompers and the Negro Workers, 1886-1914," in *Journal of Negro History,* XL:1 (January 1955), 34-60; F. Ray Marshall, *The Negro and Organized Labor* (New York, 1965), 14-33, and *Labor in the South,* 3-19, 29-36; Herbert Northup, *Organized Labor and the Negro* (New York, 1944), *passim;* Spero and Harris, *The Black Worker, passim;* Philip S. Taft, *The AF of L in the Time of Gompers* (New York, 1957), 308-317, and *Organized Labor in American History* (New York, 1964), 665-670; French E. Wolfe, *Admission to American Trade Unions* (Baltimore, 1912), 117-134.

[3] As Herbert Gutman recently suggested, where a particular national or local union did not explicitly exclude black workers, "local 'traditions,' particular notions of 'self-interest,' the conflict between racial attitudes and the egalitarian emphasis of much trade union ideology, and numerous other influences as yet unstudied shaped the behavior and the attitudes of Negro and white workers." Gutman, *op. cit.,* 117.

[4] Woodward, *op. cit.,* 175-290.

States.[5] Delayed by the depression of the 1870s and harassed during the remainder of the century by periodic economic setbacks, the growth of Alabama's mineral district was nothing short of phenomenal. In 1870 only eighty-one manufacturing establishments employing 500 people existed in the area. One mine had seven workers who irregularly turned out coal for local use. By 1900 almost 700 manufacturing establishments, capitalized at more than $25 million, employed 16,000 workers and made products valued at $30 million. Three hundred mines employing 18,000 miners produced over ten million tons of coal and iron ore. The district's coke ovens, first built during the 1870s, turned out more than two million tons of coke, and blast furnaces produced over one million tons of pig iron. Subsidiary industries like iron foundries, machine shops, rolling mills, cast-iron pipe factories, and a newly-erected steel plant added to the industrial production of the region. As a result of consolidation, expansion, and diversification, by the end of the nineteenth century several large firms, led by the giant Tennessee Coal, Iron and Railroad Company, controlled the district's economy. The return of prosperity in 1897 sparked an economic boom for these firms and for the region which lasted seven years and led many people to look forward confidently to the city's emergence as the nation's iron and steel capital.[6]

Alabama's coal and iron production gave birth to numerous mining villages and industrial communities. The largest of these new towns was Birmingham, laid out in 1871 in an old cornfield at the anticipated junction of two railroads. By 1880 the young city had a population of 3,800. Twenty years later the population had increased ten times, and by 1910, with further migration and the incorporation of surrounding suburbs, Birmingham's population exceeded 130,000. Jefferson County, the heart of Alabama's mineral district, contained only 12,345 people

[5] Ethel Armes, *The Story of Coal and Iron in Alabama* (Birmingham, 1910) is still the best account of Alabama's industrial development before World War I. The "Birmingham District" consists of Jefferson, Walker, Bibb, and parts of Tuscaloosa and Shelby counties. Before and during the Civil War coal mining and manufacturing developed in the southern part of Shelby County, which is not really a part of the "district." Statistical information about the district is based on Jefferson, Walker, and Bibb counties.

[6] Armes, *op. cit.*, 461-472; U. S. Census: *Manufactures: Ninth Census, 1870,* Vol. III, 392, *Tenth Census, 1880,* Vol. III, 88-89, *Eleventh Census, 1890,* Part I, 334-339, *Twelfth Census, 1900,* Part II, 8-13, Part IV, 39-78, *Mining: Tenth Census, 1880,* Vol. V, 642-644; American Iron and Steel Association, *Statistics of the Foreign and American Iron Trade,* 1874, . . . -1910 (Philadelphia, 1874-1910) ; Alabama Inspector of Mines, *Report, 1910* (Montgomery, Alabama, 1910), 3.

in 1870; within ten years the figure had doubled. By 1900 it approached
150,000 and by 1910 more than 226,000 people lived in Jefferson
County.[7] The steady migration of new people, and the region's rapid
transition from agriculture to industry, destroyed the area's social
fabric, forcing people to adjust almost overnight to a complex urban
and industrial environment.[8]

Birmingham's growing industrial labor force dramatically altered
the composition as well as the size of the district's population. For the
first time large numbers of foreign-white and black workers came to the
region. In 1870 only one percent of the white population in the district
and in Jefferson Country was foreign-born or of foreign parentage.
Twenty years later, however, the proportion of first- and second-generation immigrants in the total white population had increased to fourteen
percent in the district, eighteen percent in Jefferson County, and twenty-
five percent in Birmingham.[9] In industrial occupations the proportion
was even greater. As indicated in Table 1, forty-two percent of the white
miners in the state and thirty-eight percent of the white iron and steel

TABLE I
Employment in Mining and Iron and Steel Industries in Alabama
By Race and Nativity, 1890 and 1900[10]

| | Mining | | | | Iron and Steel | | | |
	1890		1900		1890		1900	
Total White	4279	100%	8163	100%	1410	100%	2440	100%
Native White: Native Born	2487	58%	5984	73%	877	62%	1717	70%
Foreign Born White	1492	35%	1573	19%	321	23%	351	15%
1 or Both Parents For. Born White	300	7%	606	7%	212	15%	372	15%
Colored	3687	46%	9735	55%	1749	55%	4439	65%
Total Workers	7966	100%	17898	100%	3159	100%	6879	100%

[7] U. S. Census, *Population: Ninth Census, 1870*, Vol. I. 11, *Tenth Census, 1890*, Part I,
451, *Twelfth Census, 1900*, Part I, 573.
[8] The impact of the rapid development of industrial and mining communities in Alabama
during the last quarter of the nineteenth century can profitably be compared with
similar developments and their impact in the middle-west and mountain west. See
Herbert Gutman, "The Worker's Search for Power: Labor in the Gilded Age," in
H. Wayne Morgan, ed., *The Gilded Age: A Reappraisal* (Syracuse, 1963), 38-68, and
Melvin Dubofsky, "The Origins of Western Working Class Radicalism, 1890-1905,"
in *Labor History*, 7:2 (Spring 1966), 131-155.
[9] U. S. Census, *Population: Ninth Census, 1870*, Vol. I, 303, *Eleventh Census, 1890*, Part
I, 480, 610, *Twelfth Census, 1900*, Part I, 647. While the proportion of the foreign-
born in the *total* population was low, an assessment of the role of the European
immigrants in Birmingham society can more properly be understood by considering
the proportion of first and second generation immigrants in the *white* population.

workers were of immigrant stock in 1890. Even though the depression of the 1890s slowed the migration of foreign-born workmen into Alabama and intensified the migration of Southern whites to the mineral district, in 1900 first- and second-generation immigrants still made up twenty to thirty percent of the white population in the city and county, and in the mining and iron and steel industries. These large numbers of foreign workers, an ever-increasing number of whom came from Southern European countries after 1897, did not share traditional Southern habits and patterns of thought and complicated the problems of adjusting to industrialism and rapid population growth. Often difficult to control, less moved by appeals to white solidarity, and sometimes linked to Northern-based trade unions, they were an important influence in the development of new social and industrial relationships among the district's growing population.[11]

Even more important than the migration of foreign workers for such relationships was the influx of black labor into the district during the last quarter of the nineteenth century. Before the founding of Birmingham only ten percent of the district was black. By the end of the century, Negroes made up thirty-five percent of the population in the district, and forty percent in Jefferson County and in the city of Birmingham.[12] In 1870 fewer than 2,500 black people lived in Jefferson County, and only 5,000 in the district. Thirty years later, however, 67,000 blacks lived in the Birmingham district—57,000 of them in Jefferson County and 16,500 within the city limits of Birmingham. As the economy expanded, the black worker's role in the industrial labor force expanded with it. In 1880 only 163 of the district's 389 miners were black.[13] As Table 1 points out, despite the influx of white miners, by 1900 the number of black miners had increased 600 percent and more than one-half of the state's miners were black. In the iron and steel industry black workers were even more dominant, making up

---

[10] U. S. Immigration Commission, *Immigrants in Industries: Bituminous Coal Mining & Iron and Steel* (Washington, 1911), IV, 142-161, VII, 125-126.

[11] Foreign-born and second-generation immigrants, particularly coal miners, were often leaders in the labor movement in Alabama. In addition, several contemporary commentators noted that foreign workers in Alabama were often less hostile to cooperation with Negroes than native whites. Richard L. Davis to Editor, *United Mine Workers' Journal*, November 25, 1897 (hereafter *UMW Journal*), and *Immigrants In Industries: Bituminous Coal Mining*, IV, 196-200.

[12] U. S. Census, *Population: Ninth Census, 1870*, Vol. I, 11, *Twelfth Census, 1900*, Part I, 573.

[13] Compiled from U. S. Census, Tenth Census, 1880, Manuscript Census Schedules, Bibb, Jefferson, Walker Counties, Alabama.

sixty-five percent of the industry's workmen. The district's population thus had to answer not only questions about industrial relations, but also about race relations.[14]

Birmingham employers had never hesitated to hire black workers as a source of cheap, tractable labor. Testimony before a Senate committee investigating capital-labor relations in 1883 revealed that, despite complaints about the shiftlessness and irregularity of their black employees, industrialists were well-satisfied with their alleged docility and willingness to work for low wages.[15] After a series of strikes in the 1890s and the introduction of technological changes which made possible greater utilization of unskilled labor, Birmingham industrialists increased their use of black labor. Companies began to employ black craftsmen in preference to whites in the expansion and improvement of their plants.[16] The Tennessee Coal and Iron Company employed Negroes exclusively at several of its mines, promising them "a chance to demonstrate . . . whether there is intelligence enough among colored people to manage their social and domestic affairs . . . without the aid or interference of the white race."[17] The Louisville and Nashville Railroad, after a strike of white firemen in 1893 and of white switchmen, two years later, turned over almost all the brakemen, switchmen, and firemen jobs in its Birmingham division to non-union Negroes as a bulwark against the white railroad brotherhoods.[18] Except for the L&N, however, few firms during these years paid much attention to programs designed to obtain the loyalty of their black laborers. Although the high labor turnover reduced efficiency and increased labor costs, most companies merely relied on the ease with which they could recruit additional black labor, and depended on the racial divisions which separated black workers from white to keep their employees from rebelling.[19]

---

[14] By 1900, forty-three percent of the males over twenty-one-years old in the district were black. U. S. Census, *Twelfth Census, 1900: Population,* Part I, 442.

[15] U. S. Senate Committee on Education and Labor, 49th Congress, 2nd Session, *Testimony Before the Committee to Investigate the Relations Between Capital and Labor* (Washington, 1885), III, 47, 290, 483.

[16] Birmingham *Labor Advocate,* August 21, 1897, March 19, 1898, June 3, 17, 1899 (Hereafter *Labor Advocate*).

[17] Birmingham *Daily News,* April 20, 1894; *Proceedings of Joint Scale Convention of Coal Operators and District 20, UMW, 1903, and Arbitration Proceedings* (Birmingham, 1903), 226-268.

[18] File #63298, "Re-examination of Employees on Train Service Rules: Colored Switchmen and Brakemen," General Manager's Office, Louisville and Nashville Railroad Archives, Louisville, Kentucky.

[19] Material in the file on "Colored Brakemen and Switchmen" in the L&N archives reveals

As race relations in Alabama deteriorated generally at the end of the nineteenth century, racial divisions between Birmingham's workingmen intensified. Efforts to use Negroes as scapegoats in order to reconcile whites estranged by the Populist crusade of the 1890s led to disfranchisement of the state's black population in 1901, and with it to an extension of segregation, discrimination, and racial violence.[20] When Richard L. Davis, a Negro member of the United Mine Workers' Executive Board, visited Birmingham in the winter of 1897-1898 to encourage organization of the district's coal miners, he reported that "The one great drawback is the division between white and colored." Racial segregation was so extensive, he observed, that at post offices "the white man and the colored man cannot get his [sic] mail from the same window." Even in coal mines, Davis found, "while white and colored miners worked in the same mines, and maybe even in adjoining rooms, they will not ride even on a work-train with their dirty mining clothes on together."[21]

Racial prejudice among Birmingham workers sometimes broke out into open conflict as white workingmen attempted to eliminate the economic competition from black workers by barring them from certain trades. Railroad firemen and trainmen unsuccessfully attempted to pressure the L&N and other Alabama railroads into eliminating Negroes from train crews.[22] Birmingham's white bricklayers, carpenters, machinists, and telephone linemen engaged in strikes against the employment of Negroes between 1899 and 1901.[23] In 1899 employees at a Walker County cotton mill drove black workmen out of town after they had begun work around the factory.[24] Even union membership did not insure acceptance from white workers. When a black bricklayer transferred from a Denver local to Birmingham in 1899 and began work on a union job, the white bricklayers struck against his employment.

---

some efforts to provide YMCA's and other social clubs for black trainmen. On the later establishment of welfare work by coal and iron companies see Spero and Harris. *op. cit.* 246-247.

[20] Woodward, *op. cit.,* 321-368, *Strange Career of Jim Crow* (New York, 1957), 49-95; Malcolm Cook McMillan, *Constitutional Development in Alabama, 1798-1901: A Study in Politics, the Negro, and Sectionalism* (Chapel Hill, 1955), 233-248.

[21] Richard L. Davis to Editor, *UMW Journal,* February 10, 1898.

[22] See for examples *Railroad Trainmen's Journal,* XVII:8 (August 1900), 678; *Locomotive Firemen's Magazine,* 33:3 (September, 1902), 428; File #63298, "Colored Switchmen and Brakemen," L&N RR Archives.

[23] *Labor Advocate,* June 3, 17, 1899, July 29, 1899, January 18, 1901; Birmingham *News,* April 6, 1901.

[24] Jasper *Mountain Eagle,* May 19, 1899.

When the Negro continued work, the local filed charges against him for strikebreaking and forced him out of the union.[25]

Antagonism of white workers, coupled with the lure of jobs provided by white employers, naturally left black workers suspicious of white workingmen and their labor organizations. Since the ante-bellum period many black men had looked to upper-class whites to protect them from the assaults of white workers. Despite the dislocations of freedom and industrialism this traditional alliance retained strong appeal. Negro spokesmen in the Birmingham district, supported by frequent appearances by Booker T. Washington and William H. Councill, denounced cooperation between white and black wage-earners and urged the district's black workers to "maintain peaceful and friendly relations with the best white people of the community . . . who give our race employment and pay their wages."[26] Reverend William McGill, editor of the *Hot Shots*, probably spoke for several ministers when he urged "Every colored laborer [to] strive to make friends with his employer." If a dispute arose, the worker should "take whatever wages the company offered." The black worker who "puts in full time, saves his money, puts it to good use, has no cause to strike, nor sympathize with those that do strike," McGill insisted.[27] Labor organizers, another minister warned his followers, were "trifling, ungrateful soreheads who are going around poisoning the minds of the ignorant masses against wealth."[28]

In the midst of this climate of hostility and suspicion between Birmingham's black and white workingmen, the American Federation of Labor and national trade unions launched their Southern organizing campaigns.[29] The return of industrial prosperity in 1897 brought with

[25] "Case No. 6: Giddens vs. Union No. 1 Alabama," in *37th Annual Report of President and Secretary of the Bricklayers and Masons' International Union, 1902* (North Adams, Mass., 1902), 173-180.

[26] Birmingham *Hot Shots*, July 23, 1908. Washington and Councill often travelled into the Birmingham district to speak. Visits of Washington were reported in Birmingham *Age-Herald* (Hereafter *Age-Herald*) April 1, 1899, May 19, 1906, June 11, 1906, Birmingham *News*, September 20, 1902, January 31, 1903, *Negro Enterprise*, November 19, 1904. Visits of Council were reported in Birmingham *News* January 2, 1901, September 19, 1902, *Age-Herald* May 18, 1900, *Ensley Enterprise*, January 28, 1905. For an excellent analysis of both Washington's and Councill's attitudes toward labor unions and employers, see August Meier, *Negro Thought in America, 1880-1915* (Ann Arbor, 1966), 100-118, 209-210. For the close relations between prominent Birmingham ministers and industrialists see Horace Mann Bond, *Negro Education in Alabama: A Study in Cotton and Steel* (Washington, 1939), 168-170.

[27] *Hot Shots*, August 17, 1899, March 2, 1905, April 15, 1905, July 23, 1908.

[28] Birmingham [Negro] *Free Speech*, June 20, 1903.

[29] American Federation of Labor, *Report of Proceedings, Eighteenth Annual Convention, 1898* (n.p., 1898), 89-90, 93-100; Leo Wolman, *The Growth of American Trade*

it strong, stable, national trade unions and the revival and expansion of trade union activity. These unions undertook, directed, and financed organizing campaigns across the country, including the South, in an effort to minimize sectional wage differentials in various industries. Craft unions, as well as Knights of Labor locals, had existed in Birmingham since 1878 and had achieved enough strength by the early 1890s to form a city trades council with twenty-five locals and to host the 1891 A.F.L. national convention.[30] The depression of the 1890s decimated the labor movement in Birmingham. At the end of the nineteenth century, however, organizers from a number of unions, including the bricklayers, carpenters, machinists, molders, boilermakers, iron and steel workers, miners, as well as the A.F.L., appeared in Birmingham to revive locals which had collapsed during the depression and to found new ones.[31] Thirty-one locals with 6,000 members were represented in the Birmingham Trades Council by the end of 1900, and within two more years the number had grown to over sixty locals with more than 20,000 members, including District 20 of the United Mine Workers' of America representing 8,000 miners.[32]

Despite the general climate of racial hostility in Alabama, relations between trade unions and Birmingham's black workers were still undetermined at the end of the nineteenth century. While many national labor leaders ignored black workers or equivocated about organizing them, and several craft unions adopted racially restrictive membership policies which barred Negroes, in at least a dozen unions, including some of the exclusionary ones, officers and members argued that effectively organizing the South depended upon the inclusion of black workers.[33]

Unions, 1880-1923 (New York, 1924), 33; Taft, *The AF of L in the Time of Gompers*, 95-111.

[30] Holman Head, "The Development of the Labor Movement in Alabama Prior to 1900" (Unpublished Master's thesis, University of Alabama, 1955); See also *Journal of United Labor*, August 15, 1880 and *National Labor Tribune*, January 4, 1878.

[31] *American Federationist*, VI:3-VII:6 (May 1899-June 1900), lists activities of organizers in Birmingham. Also *Age-Herald*, May 14, 24, 1899; Birmingham *News*, February 26, 1900, October 17, 1901; *Labor Advocate*, August 5, 1899, April 8, 1901; *Iron Molders' Journal*, 38:9 (September 1902), 603.

[32] *Labor Advocate*, April 8, 1901, August 2, 1902.

[33] Appeals for the organization of Negroes fill union journals and the reports of proceedings of labor conventions. *Iron Molders' Journal*, 35:1 (November 1899), 590-592, 36:5 (May 1900), 283-284; *Machinists' Monthly Journal*, IX:21 (March 1897), 61-63; *Railroad Trainmen's Journal*, XV:11 (November 1898), 912-914, XVI:9 (September 1899), 620-621, XX:10 (October 1903), 790-791; *Locomotive Firemen's Magazine*, 31:1 (January 1901), 112; *Blacksmith's Journal*, IV:2 (February 1903), 11; *The Carpenter*, 23:1 (January, 1903), 3, 23:9 (September 1903), 5; *Bricklayer and Mason* V:1 (February 1902), 8, IX:1 (February 1906), 3; *37th*

Both the egalitarian principles of the labor movement and the self-interest of white workers, they insisted, dictated that Southern Negroes not be left unorganized. "We are banded together in our grand Brotherhood for the purpose of elevating the condition of our entire craft, regardless of color, nationality, race or creed," the editor of *The Carpenter*, the journal of the United Brotherhood of Carpenters and Joiners, asserted in 1903.[34] The Negro carpenter, he added, "must be brought into our fold in order that his hours of toil will be reduced and his wages raised, and thus his white brother will be given an opportunity to raise his own standing to the level of his brother in the East and West." The president of the Bricklayers and Masons' Union, disturbed that racial discrimination impeded the organization of Southern bricklayers, urged that "every opportunity [be] given our colored brothers to earn a livelihood as union members instead of driving them into the non-union ranks or a hostile organization to be used against us."[35] Although by 1900 Samuel Gompers accepted racially exclusive unions into the A.F.L. and sanctioned segregated city labor councils, he also urged that unless black workers were organized and befriended by trade unions they would "not only be forced down in the economic scale," but would be "used against any effort made by us for our economic and social advancement, [and] race prejudice will be made more bitter and to the injury of all."[36] Rarely conscious of the needs of black workers and frequently racist in his public statements when referring to them, Gompers nevertheless warned Henry Randall, the Federation's Birmingham organizer, that "The Negro workers must be organized in order that they may be in a position to protect themselves and in some way feel an interest with our organized white workmen, or we shall unquestioningly have their undying enmity."[37] The failure of Southern railroad trainmen to

Annual Report . . . Bricklayers and Masons' International Union, 1902 (North Adams, Mass., 1902), 152-153; International Union of Hod Carriers and Building Laborers, 5th Annual Convention, *Proceedings, 1907* (Norfolk, Virginia, 1907), 41; Amalgamated Association of Iron, Steel and Tin Workers, *Amalgamated Journal*, May 11, 1905; *United Mine Workers' Journal*, February 7, 1895, and letters quoted in Gutman, "The Negro and the United Mine Workers", 49-127; American Federation of Labor, 17th Annual Convention, *Proceedings, 1897* (Nashville, 1897), 36; *American Federationist*, VIII:4 (April 1901), 118-120; International Car Workers, *Proceedings, 1905*, as quoted in Spero and Harris, *op. cit.*, 65.

[34] *The Carpenter*, 23:1 (January 1903), 3.
[35] *Bricklayer and Mason*, IX:1 (February 1906), 5.
[36] American Federation of Labor, 20th Annual Convention, *Proceedings, 1900* (Louisville, 1900), 12-13.
[37] Samuel Gompers to H. N. Randle [sic], March 19, 1903, Samuel Gompers Letterbooks, Library of Congress, Washington, D. C.

bar Negroes as job competitors even convinced the editor of the *Railroad Trainmen's Journal* that only by organizing black trainmen and committing them to the defense of common standards of wages and hours could white trainmen improve their working conditions. "It is humiliating, no one will take kindly to it, . . ." he pleaded, "but unless the Negro is raised, the white man will have to come down."[38]

Implementing these views depended not merely on convincing union leaders of the desirability of organizing black workers, but also on the response to such proposals from white workingmen in the South. Railroad trainmen and many other white union members in Birmingham did not, in fact, take kindly to admitting Negroes to their unions. Some protested to their union journals that they would "never accept the Negro as their equal," and threatened that they could not "entertain the idea of complying with the oath we take if the Negro is admitted to our brotherhood."[39] A white fireman on the L&N who opposed any effort to improve black firemen's wages argued that "If he were getting our wages, he would then be on our plane."[40] The city's union bricklayers, as previously noted, refused to work with a black union bricklayer who transferred to the city in 1899, and Birmingham's union carpenters, despite their complaints about non-union Negro competition, ignored the request of black carpenters in the city for organization in 1902.[41] As will be discussed later, when national unions which supported the organization of black workers stood firm, they often found that they could overcome objections from white locals. More important, though, these protests did not represent the thinking of all of Birmingham's white unionists.

In spite of mounting hysteria by Alabama's white supremacists, there were white workingmen in Birmingham at the beginning of the twentieth century who not only supported organization of black laborers, but also encouraged such organization. The city's labor newspaper, the *Labor Advocate,* advised Birmingham unions to "Obliterate the Color Line," and to recognize that "the common cause of labor is more im-

[38] *Railroad Trainmen's Journal,* XVI:9 (September 1899), 880, and XVII:8 (August 1900), 678.
[39] *The Carpenter,* 23:4 (April 1903), 5; *Locomotive Firemen's Magazine,* 22:2 (February 1897), 125-126. For examples of other protests from Birmingham see *Railroad Trainmen's Journal,* 17:6 (June 1900), 499-510, and *Iron Molders' Journal,* 44:4 (April 1908), 287-288, 577-578.
[40] *Locomotive Firemen's Magazine,* 30:3 (March 1901), 440-441.
[41] *The Carpenter,* 23:1 (January 1903), 3.

portant than racial differences." Even when whites and blacks organized in an integrated union, its editor insisted that "it is a response to conditions to which there is no other solution," and urged white workers to "accept the inevitable with ready grace and strive to better the conditions of the Negro by every means, knowing that in doing this is the only way to better [your] own condition."[42] Although some of Birmingham's white bricklayers had resisted the employment of a Negro union member in 1899, a year later the local secretary of the International Union of Bricklayers and Masons wrote the editor of his journal that the arrival of their organizer would "wake up the colored man and show him that he must join the I.U.—and when we get them [sic] in this will be one of the best union towns in the United States."[43] In response to assertions that black laborers would not remain loyal to the union even if admitted, a white railroad fireman on the L&N replied that "my experience with the Negroes shows me that they are easily organized, and when organized they will stick to their lodges as long as the average member of any other order."[44] A white painter concurred: "Anyone who will study the character of the Negro," he wrote, "will agree that he will stick to his union."[45] Although Richard Davis was discouraged by racial prejudice in the Birmingham district, he nevertheless found "a number of good men both white and colored" among miners he met who deplored the prejudice.[46] One miner, writing to the *Labor Advocate* to support its position on organization of black workers, appealed to district unions not to leave black laborers to "the tender mercies of the sweatshops," and insisted that "the only question for consideration is, Will Organized Labor admit the black man, not only thereby benefiting him, but adding strength to organization?"[47]

In addition to the question of whether labor unions would admit Negroes, there was also the question of whether Negroes would join these organizations. Despite the demands of prominent Negroes that black workers remain diligent, dependent, and docile, other, less well-known black men encouraged black wage-earners to organize. References to organizational meetings in Negro churches indicated that at

[42] *Labor Advocate*, April 2, 1898, April 27, 1901.
[43] John Ellison to Editor, *Bricklayer and Mason*, III:3 (June 1900) 10.
[44] Pat Filburn to Editor, *Locomotive Firemen's Magazine*, 31:1 (January 1901), 112.
[45] Birmingham painter to Editor, Brotherhood of Painters, Decorators, and Paperhangers *Journal*, March 1903, quoted in *The Carpenter*, 23:4 (April 1903), 7.
[46] Richard Davis to Editor, *UMW Journal*, January 6, 1898.
[47] W. T. Westbrook to Editor, *Labor Advocate*, June 30, 1900.

least some of the influential churchmen disagreed with one of their number who referred to labor organizers as "false prophets."[48] Richard Davis reported that he met one Negro minister in Birmingham, W. M. Storrs, who "had the manhood to attend a meeting . . . and speak a kind word for organized labor."[49] A letter from a white miner praised the Negro Odd Fellows and Reverend J. M. Morton in his camp for supporting the union.[50]

More active than churchmen in aiding organizing efforts were black workers who became union officials.[51] Some served as delegates to state and national labor conventions where they regularly sponsored resolutions advocating more black organizers for the South in general and Birmingham in particular.[52] Others became salaried organizers. In a society often hostile to black militancy their organizing activities occasionally subjected them to violence from racially hostile whites. Silas Brooks, vice-president of the Alabama United Mine Workers' (U.M.W.) district organization from 1898 to 1900, was stoned and beaten in one town while organizing miners in 1900, for example. A white mob led by a mining company official attacked both B. L. Greer, a successor of Brooks as vice-president, and a white organizer in 1903, "heaped various indignities upon them, some of which were too repulsive to print," and chased them out of Walker County. A year later, a white mob at a remote mining camp again attacked Greer when he arrived to organize the miners. These experiences did not seem to dampen the enthusiasm of Brooks or Greer for the union. Only a week after losing the district election for vice-president in 1900, Brooks urged black unionists to show no animosity towards their "white brethern," and to beware of any "outside influences" trying to separate them. In subsequent years, he remained an important organizer in the union and in the labor movement in Alabama. First elected vice-president of U.M.W. District 20 in 1902, Greer served until 1908, frequently visiting mining camps in Walker County to organize black and white miners. When he retired

[48] Birmingham *Free Speech,* April 25, 1903, June 20, 1903; *Labor Advocate* April 13, 1901.
[49] Richard Davis to Editor, *UMW Journal,* January 6, 1898.
[50] Peter Tidwell to Editor, *Labor Advocate,* March 5, 1898.
[51] Little is known about Birmingham Negroes who encouraged black workers to join unions—or about the men who joined. The particular experiences which drew them to the labor movement are unknown. Their relations with other Negroes and whites during Reconstruction, Populism or the coal miners' upheavals of the 1880s and 1890s, their experience with slavery, their length of residence in the district, their employment pattern, their family status, their age, are all unknown but important facts which could illuminate much of Alabama's labor history during this period.
[52] *Labor Advocate,* April 20, 1901, May 7, 1904, May 6, 1905; See note 33.

to a government job as mail carrier, the *Labor Advocate* praised him as
"one of the best known colored men in the district."[53] Greer and other
black labor leaders undoubtedly did much to counter the anti-union
sentiments of prominent Negroes, and probably were more influential
among the black masses than more publicized figures like Booker T.
Washington and Reverend William McGill.[54]

Black workers in the Birmingham district were organized most successfully by the U.M.W. Victory in the midwestern coal fields in 1897
strengthened the U.M.W. and enabled it to turn its attention to the
organization of Alabama and West Virginia mines whose growing competition threatened the gains won in midwestern states. The Mine
Workers' commitment to the organization of black miners, carried over
from Knights of Labor locals and developed in the midwest during the
early 1890s, did not lessen in Alabama. The need to prevent Birmingham Negroes from serving as strikebreakers in Illinois, Ohio, Kansas,
and Colorado mines made their organization a practical necessity.[55]
Perhaps most important to the U.M.W.'s success in organizing Alabama's black miners, however, was its structure as an industrial union.
Most of the 6,000 Negroes who worked in the coal mines at the beginning of the twentieth century were employed by sub-contractors or
as laborers by white and occasionally black miners.[56] This subcontracting

---

[53] Birmingham *News*, December 8, 10, 13, 1900; *Labor Advocate*, August 15, September 19, 26, October 3, 1903, June 2, 1908; *Age-Herald*, August 12, 1903. Six men were arrested for the assault on Greer and the white organizer, Joseph Hallier, in 1903. The U. S. Commissioner dismissed the charges when he ruled that Hallier was a citizen of Wales and thus could not sue in federal courts for deprivation of his civil rights, and that "lack of evidence" precluded a case against these six men for attacking Greer. The UMW appealed the decisions to the Federal District Court where Judge Thomas G. Jones, former governor and railroad attorney, sustained the dismissal on the grounds that conspiracy to interfere with an attempt to establish a labor organization was not infringing any right guaranteed by the Constitution and was thus not protected by law. Jasper *Mountain Eagle*, May 11, 1904.

[54] For evidence of a different reaction among Birmingham Negroes which also indicates a gap between Booker Washington and the black masses see Edwin S. Redkey, "Black Exodus: African Emigration Movements Among American Negroes, 1890-1910" (forthcoming, Yale University Press, 1969).

[55] Gutman, "The Negro and the United Mine Workers," 46-110.

[56] U. S. Census, *Twelfth Census, 1900: Occupations, Part* I, reported 9,735 blacks among 17,898 miners in Alabama. *Annual Report of State Board of Alabama Inspector of Mines, 1900* (Montgomery, 1900), lists 12,881 *coal* miners. Contemporaries esti-mated that of the 5,000 iron ore miners, at least 80% were black, which means that approximately 5,800 Negroes, or 40%, of the state's coal miners were Negro. See J. H. McDonough memorandum, February 11, 1908, in Booker T. Washington Papers, Principal's Office Correspondence, 1908, Library of Congress, Washington, D. C. Report of an Alabama House of Representatives Mining Investigating Committee, in *Birmingham State-Herald*, January 26, 1897, describes most of the mining camps in the district in January 1897, and its estimates of black miners in each camp indicate about 35% at that time.

system divided miners and mine laborers along occupational as well as racial lines, and many miners who employed laborers saw little benefit to be derived from organization. Since not only miners but laborers and other workmen employed at the mines could belong to the U.M.W., however, the union could overcome the occupational and racial divisions which separated most of Alabama's black mine workers from white miners by bringing all of them into the union.[57]

Alabama miners were receptive to an interracial union. The Knights of Labor locals of the 1880s and the statewide miners' organization of the early 1890s had collapsed by the end of the nineteenth century, but local miners' organizations in several camps still existed, many of them with black officers and members.[58] After the state's miners voted to affiliate with the national United Mine Workers' organization in November 1897, these locals became the nucleus of U.M.W. organizing activity in the state. U.M.W. organizers' reports in 1898 and 1899 testified to "great enthusiasm for union among the colored brethern."[59] The district president rejoiced that black miners were "fighting to join" the union when eighty-five percent of 280 black miners at an isolated previously unorganized camp in Tuscaloosa County enlisted after his first visit.[60] By the beginning of the twentieth century, Negro membership in the Alabama U.M.W. was widespread. Although precise membership statistics by race are non-existent, there is no reason to doubt the claims of contemporaries that in 1900 probably thirty-five to forty percent of the 6,500 members of District 20 were black and, by 1904, that more than one-half of the 13,000 U.M.W. members in the state were black miners.[61]

---

[57] Richard L. Davis to Editor, *UMW Journal,* February 10, 1898; *Birmingham State-Herald,* April 13, 1897; *Labor Advocate,* April 13, 1901, October 14, 1905. In addition to subcontracting, Alabama's infamous convict lease system complicated organizational efforts. By 1900 coal operators leased more than 1,500 state and county convicts per year to work in the mines. These convict miners, about fifty per cent of whom remained in the district after their release, were an important source of labor during, and after, their sentences. Alabama State Board of Convict Inspectors, *Biennial Report, 1900, 1902* (Montgomery, 1900, 1902); Shelby Harrison, "A Cash Nexus for Crime," in *Survey,* XXVII (4 January 6, 1912), 1541-1556.

[58] Ward and Rogers, *op. cit.,* 23-58; *Labor Advocate,* July 31, October 2, 1897, February 5, 1898.

[59] *Labor Advocate,* February 5, October 29, 1898, April 29, July 12, 26, 1899.

[60] *Labor Advocate* April 1, 1899.

[61] Total membership statistics for UMW District 20 for 1898-1907 published in *Labor Advocate,* June 14, 1907. Forty percent of the delegates to the 1900 District Convention were identified as Negro, from *Labor Advocate,* June 27, 1900. Unfortunately, no indication of the delegates' race appears in subsequent lists of delegates published in the *Labor Advocate.* William Fairley, UMW Executive Board Member,

An active administrative role in the state's U.M.W. organization over-
came initial Negro distrust of the miners' union. In every U.M.W. local
in Alabama with black members, whether all-black or integrated—such
as the local at Pratt City, the largest U.M.W. local in the country by the
early twentieth century—black miners served as officers: as presidents
and vice-presidents, as members of executive boards and grievance committees, as checkweighmen, and as delegates to the district and national
conventions. Some camps whose living conditions were almost completely segregated met at integrated union halls, heard reports from
black officers, and elected black men as local committeemen and as convention delegates. Even at camps with racially separate locals, black and
white representatives served on grievance committees and as checkweighmen together.[62] At district conventions as well as local meetings
black officers spoke from the same platforms as whites, delivered committee reports and, as the proceedings make clear, even chaired the meeting at district conventions. To guarantee continued black representation
in leadership posts, certain positions were allocated for black members.
These included the vice-presidency of the district organization and of
integrated locals, three of the eight positions on the district executive
board, and places on every union committee, whether functional or ceremonial. The satisfaction of black miners with this arrangement was
shown when some white miners introduced a plan, at the 1902 district
convention, to choose district officials by popular vote instead of having
convention delegates elect them. The black delegates, according to the
Birmingham News, "seem to think that if the officers were selected by
popular vote they would not have as many officers as they now have."
With the aid of the leadership they helped defeat this proposal.[63]

Black delegates at district conventions were not merely passive sub-
ordinates of white members and leaders, but actively participated in
committee discussions and floor debates. They often differed with white
miners—not only about such matters as whether to appropriate funds
to support a Birmingham exhibit at the St. Louis World's Fair in 1904,

---

and former president of District 20, testified before the 1903 Coal Arbitration Commission, that one-half the district's members were black. *1903 Coal Arbitration Commission Proceedings,* 239.
[62] *Labor Advocate,* December 17, 1898, July 15, 1899, June 23, 1900, July 2, 1901, June
28, 1902, June 13, 1904.
[63] Birmingham *News,* December 11, 1902. See also *News,* December 15-20, 1903; *Labor
Advocate,* May 21, 1898, February 11, 1899, June 23, 1900, March 6, 1901, December
19, 1903, June 17, 1905.

but also on the important issue of wage demands.[64] Even the presence of national president John Mitchell at an early District 20 convention in 1900 did not stifle Negro initiative. Although Mitchell, and the district president, supported a request from the coal operators that they be heard before the convention conducted any business, two black delegates were among those who objected, and the convention, forty percent of which was Negro, defeated the resolution to admit the operators. Mitchell also supported the request of the Birmingham Trades Council that the miners endorse a resolution stating that U.M.W. members would give their business only to union workmen. When Negro vice-president Silas Brooks objected to the resolution and made a "strong speech" declaring that the mine workers should not endorse it since the Trades Council and some of its affiliates discriminated against Negroes, Mitchell protested that as a member of the A.F.L. executive board he could assure black delegates that no A.F.L. affiliate barred Negroes. The black miners refused to be deceived and got the convention to table the resolution.[65]

Information about the organizational activities of other trade unions in Birmingham during this period is scarce, but material available indicates that the United Mine Workers was not alone in organizing urban black workers. In 1901 Birmingham's Negro barbers secured a charter from the national union with the approval of the city's white barbers.[66] The plasterers' union inaugurated black men into an integrated local which lasted throughout the decade.[67] Birmingham's building laborers, first organized in 1899 as an A.F.L. local, affiliated with the International Hod Carriers and Building Laborers' Union in 1903. With the support of other building trades organizations in the city, by 1905 it commanded $2 per-eight-hour day for its sixty members with time-and-one-half for overtime and double-time for Sunday work.[68] The Bricklayers and Masons' union, with black members in other locals in both the North and South, encouraged the Birmingham chapter to admit black bricklayers, and in 1904 a Negro organizer from Atlanta visited

[64] *Labor Advocate,* June 18, 1903, June 18, 25, 1904.
[65] *Labor Advocate,* June 23, 30, 1900; Birmingham *News,* June 22, 25, 1900, July 3, 1901.
[66] *American Federationist,* VIII:9 (September 1901), 378.
[67] "A White Friend of the Workingman," to Editor, *Birmingham Journal,* June 22, 1911; Du Bois, *op. cit.,* 162.
[68] *American Federationist,* VI:7 (September 1899), 171; International Hod Carriers and Building Laborers' Union of America, 2nd Annual Convention, *Report of Proceedings,* (1904 Sayre, Penn.,* 1904), 33; *Age-Herald,* December 27, 1905.

TABLE II
Employment in Selected Occupations in Birmingham, By Race, 1900[69]

Occupation	Total Workers	Black Workers	Per Cent Black	Per Cent Black to All Black Listed
Building Trades				
Plasterer	33	25	75.8%	.7%
Brickmason	130	36	27.7	.9
Carpenter	585	94	16.8	2.6
Plumber	32	5	15.6	.1
Painter	94	6	6.4	.1
Electrician	33	. . . .	. . . .	. . . .
Mechanics				
Blacksmith	122	27	22.2%	.6%
Printer	56	4	7.1	.1
Boilermaker	81	4	4.9	.1
Molder	142	2	1.4	.1
Sta. Engineer	82	1	1.2	. . . .
Tinner	34	. . . .	. . . .	. . . .
Puddler	89	. . . .	. . . .	. . . .
Heater & Roller	28	. . . .	. . . .	. . . .
Machinist	379	. . . .	. . . .	. . . .
Harnessmaker	13	. . . .	. . . .	. . . .
Carriagemaker	7	. . . .	. . . .	. . . .
Railroad Employees				
Brakeman	14	87	70.5%	2.3%
Locomotive Fireman	154	87	56.5	2.3
Switchman	51	16	31.4	.4
Railroad Repair Shop	179	7	3.9	.2
Flagman	93	1	1.1	. . . .
Conductor	146	. . . .	. . . .	. . . .
Locomotive Engineer	236	. . . .	. . . .	. . . .
Streetcar Driver	70	. . . .	. . . .	. . . .
Service				
Barber	169	105	61.1%	2.9%
Shoemaker	99	49	49.0	1.5
Tailor	44	9	20.5	.3
Factory Operatives				
Bottling and Brewing	43	4	9.3%	.1%
Avondale Cotton Mill	154	3	1.9	.1
Other	233	3	1.3	.1
Other: Unskilled				
Drayman and Teamster	355	271	80.9%	7.3%
Laborer—not spec.	3472	2844	81.9	77.1
TOTAL—INDUSTRIAL	7412	3691	49.8%	100%

[69] Compiled from *Birmingham City Directory, 1901.* Although city directories are uneven, and undoubtedly failed to count large number of people, those ignored are likely to be heavily weighted towards unskilled black laborers. Consequently, the proportion of black laborers in the industrial labor force is probably even higher. If the "service" category is eliminated, moreover, the proportion of black laborers to all black "industrial" workers would be almost 90%.

The occupations used are the same as those used in the city directory. Laborers are generally not otherwise specified, although sometimes an employer is listed. The seemingly low numbers of iron and steel workers is explained by the fact that many

the city to work among the city's black brickmasons.[70] After Birmingham's white carpenters ignored a request from the city's black carpenters for union membership, the United Brotherhood of Carpenters and Joiners appointed a Birmingham Negro organizer in 1903. When the Birmingham local objected, the editor of *The Carpenter* informed it that "as far as our Brotherhood is concerned the drawing of the color line should be stopped at once and for all time." Additional pressure must have been exerted, for the following year a Negro carpenters' local existed in Birmingham, its members working at union scale, participating in the meetings of the powerful Carpenters' District Council, and marching under the union banner in the annual Labor Day parade.[71] These locals, which were generally segregated, covered few black workers, and probably left them still powerless to protect their jobs. Despite these limitations, the locals nevertheless at least represented some effort by skilled craft unions to reconcile the egalitarian principles of the labor movement and the need to control the job competition of Southern black workmen with the mounting climate of racial hatred and with their own exclusionist tendencies.

Bringing Birmingham's black workers into the labor movement depended not so much on organization of the trades as on organization of the unskilled. As indicated in Table 2, the city's black industrial wage-earners worked predominantly as common laborers by 1900. Black workers employed at coke ovens, blast furnaces, iron foundries, steel mills, and railroad shops in Birmingham and in other industrial communities in the district were almost all common laborers. But the craft union structure of the American labor movement at the beginning of the twentieth century impeded organization of unskilled workers. Committed to preserving union autonomy and protecting the interests of the skilled minority, few craft unions attempted to organize semi-skilled or unskilled workers—of any race or nationality.[72] The American Federation of Labor tried to take up the slack by organizing unskilled

of the furnaces and steel plants were located outside the city limits. A discussion of the changing numbers of workers in various occupations and the changing racial composition of these occupations from 1880 to 1914 is part of a work now in progress on "The Development of an Industrial Labor Force in Birmingham, Alabama."

[70] Du Bois, *op. cit.,* 162; *83th Annual Report . . . of Bricklayers and Masons' International Union, 1903* (North Adams, Mass., 1903), 116; Whether black bricklayers were inducted into a local in Birmingham is not clear. See *Bricklayer and Mason,* X:1 (February 1907), 3.

[71] *The Carpenter,* 23:1 (January 1903), 3; 23:4 (April 1903), 6-7; *Labor Advocate,* May 21, 1904, September 9, 1905.

[72] Foner, *op. cit.,* III, 174-218.

laborers into Federal Labor Unions directly affiliated with the A.F.L., but these locals were never of any importance and remained "the neglected stepchildren of the American labor movement."[73] Without a national union to bargain for them, without funds to sustain them when on strike, and subject to raids by craft unions, Federal Labor Unions could not protect their members' interests. Yet for a brief period at the beginning of the twentieth century, in Birmingham as in other cities of the country, these unions brought unskilled workers into the American labor movement.

Between 1899 and 1904, when financial stringency forced the A.F.L. to curtail its organizing efforts throughout the country, the Federation devoted as much attention to organizing Birmingham's black unskilled laborers as it did to organizing the city's skilled workmen. The Federation's Southern organizer visited Birmingham in May 1899, and most of his effort was directed toward black laborers. "Some objection has been raised," the Birmingham *Age Herald* noted, "but the leaders of organized labor recognize that negro labor, which works side by side with white labor, will necessarily hold the latter back, unless they—the blacks—are themselves organized."[74] Before leaving Birmingham the organizer had founded locals of coke workers, ore miners, furnace laborers, and draymen.[75] During the next several years Gompers urged A.F.L. organizers in Birmingham to "make friends of the colored man," and appointed several black men as special organizers.[76] By 1904, as listed in Table 3, thirteen more locals of unskilled black laborers had been organized in the district. Except for periods in which the unions were seeking recognition, membership in these locals was generally small. Moreover, although some locals showed signs of stability, few lasted more than two years, and by 1904 all but the iron ore miners, iron pipe workers, and building laborers had collapsed. But during these years, in addition to more than 2,000 black workers who joined the A.F.L. locals, 6,000 black miners in the U.M.W., and an unidentified number of black workers in craft union locals and in locals directly affiliated with the A.F.L. It meant that at least 8,000 black workers in the Birmingham district belonged to labor organizations during the first

[73] Quoted in *ibid.*, 200.
[74] *Age-Herald*, May 24, 1899.
[75] *Age-Herald*, May 15, 1899; *American Federationist*, VI:3, 4, 7, 10 (May, June, September, December 1899), 59, 89, 171, 253-254; *Labor Advocate*, August 5, 12, 1899.
[76] Gompers to H. N. Randle [sic], March 19, 1903, Gompers Letterbooks.

years of the twentieth century. "A lot of colored men here in our juris-diction would like to become [sic] into the A.F. of L.," Negro organizer William Downey observed in 1904. "They are coming to the light of Organization fast and see what an elevation it is to them." Henry Randall, the Federation's organizer, asserted confidently that same year that, given more assistance by the A.F.L., he could organize all 4,000

TABLE III
Black AFL Locals in Birmingham, Alabama, District, 1899-1904[77]

Union	Year Org.	Maximum Number Members Identified
Furnacemen No. 7564, Bessemer	1899	647 (1900)
Coke Workers No. 7576, Bessemer	1899	118 (1900)
Coke Workers No. 7577, Johns	1899	120 (1900)
Iron Pipe Workers No. 7581, Bessemer	1899	100 (1905)
Team Drivers No. 167, Birmingham	1899	c.200 (1900)
Laborers No. 7575(?), Bessemer	1899	66 (1900)
Iron Ore Miners No. 19, Birmingham	1899, 1903	700 (1904)
(later locals No. 10, No. 13 Western Fed. of Miners, May 1904)		
Building Laborers No. 7174	1899	50 (1904)
(later No. 72, I.H.C.B.L.U., 1904)		
Stone Cutters, Birmingham	1899	. . . .
Iron Pipe Workers, Blocton	1899	. . . .
Furnacemen's No. 8359, Oxmoor	1900	40 (1900)
Furnace Workers No. 8051, Woodward	1900	. . . .
Core Makers, Birmingham	1900	. . . .
Coke Workers, Birmingham	1901	. . . .
Coke Workers No. 9648, Thomas	1902	. . . .
Rolling Mill Helpers No. 10592, Birmingham	1902	144 (1903)
		c.2185
Bessemer Central Labor Council	1900	1080 (1900)
Birmingham Central Labor Council	1903	(20 locals—1903)

[77] All of the locals listed, except the Team Drivers and Core Makers, were taken from the monthly lists of "Charters Issued" in the *American Federationist*, 1899-1904. The Team Drivers and Core Makers—as well as most other locals—were identified from Birmingham or Bessemer newspapers. Membership figures for most locals were difficult to obtain. Where a local's Federal Labor Union number was available the A.F.L.'s monthly financial statements, published in the *American Federationist*, could usually be used to compute membership by dividing the total monthly tax collected from the local by the A.F.L.'s monthly per capita tax. Unfortunately, dues were not always collected every month, and statements of per capita tax collected were often unclear about what time period the payment represented. The other major source of membership information was newspaper articles. Although these usually estimated union membership, where possible to check their figures with computations from the *American Federationist* they turned out to be substantially accurate. The estimated membership for Team Drivers #167 is based upon reports of a Colored Drayman's Association in the Birmingham *News*, January 5, 6, 1900, to which "almost every colored man driving a dray" allegedly belonged. The membership figures presented in Table 3 which are derived solely from newspaper reports are only the number of workers reported as union members and are not the number of workers participating in a strike, which was usually a much higher figure.

black iron ore miners and thousands of other black common laborers in
the Birmingham district. And the head of the district's Negro labor
council even suggested to Gompers that the cooks and washerwomen
in the area could be unionized.[78]

Birmingham industrialists and other spokesmen of the New South
frequently advertised the docility and tractability of their black labor,
but a series of strikes by newly-organized black laborers in 1899 and
1900 demonstrated that these unskilled workers, like their counterparts
in the mines, were prepared to resist the "place" assigned to them by
their employers. Coke workers' strikes against the Tennessee Coal and
Iron Company in 1899 erupted into violence. When a group of deputies
attempted to disperse striking workers, they found the strikers "willing
to resort to bloodshed before allowing the white officers of the law
to arrest them." Hidden behind coke ovens, 250 strikers ambushed the
deputies and killed two of them before being routed. Only the forced
departure of "several carloads" of black workers returned the situation
to normal.[79] The company's treasurer complained that coke worker
strikes throughout the summer and fall continued to "make life a burden." When the company tried to fire the leaders of a Bessemer local,
the newly-organized workers struck for their reinstatement, "even
though their wages were advanced a week before" and despite an
agreed-upon one-year moratorium on strikes, the T.C.I. treasurer noted
incredulously. The company's refusal to reinstate the discharged leaders
led the strikers to try to burn the company's quarters.[80] When Bessemer's
cast iron pipe firm refused to recognize the newly-chartered A.F.L.
local in 1899 and fired the committeemen who appealed for recognition,
300 pipe workers quit. They convinced 200 black strikebreakers brought
in to replace them to leave their jobs and forced the company to import
non-union white men, which a city newspaper reported they "had no
trouble getting at $1.75 per day." But newspapers, in the following
months, still reported incidents of strikers firing on company workmen.[81]
Seven months later, 647 blast furnace workers at the T.C.I. plant in

---

[78] W. H. Downey to Gompers, quoted in Gompers to H. N. Randall, February 1, 1904,
Gompers Letterbooks; Speech of Henry Randall in *Age-Herald*, May 7, 1904;
Gompers to J. E. Smith, August 11, 1904, Gompers Letterbooks.
[79] *Birmingham State-Herald*, March 28, 29, 1899.
[80] James Bowron Diaries, October 3, 1899, and James Bowron, "Autobiography," I,
407-408, 477, University of Alabama Library, University, Alabama.
[81] *Bessemer Weekly,* October 28, November 18, 25, December 16, 1899; *Labor Advocate,*
November 25, December 2, 1899; *American Federationist,* VI:10 (October 1899), 261.

Bessemer, all members of a recently-organized A.F.L. local, struck for a wage increase, semi-monthly pay days, the right to choose their own doctor, and recognition of their union. They persuaded hundreds of imported strikebreakers to return home and kept the furnaces closed for four months. The strike was finally settled after Samuel Gompers responded to an appeal from the Birmingham Trades Council and threatened the company that he would urge workmen throughout the country to boycott Bessemer unless T.C.I.'s manager met with a committee of the strikers to settle their grievances.[82]

The most disruptive strike during these two years occurred at the iron ore mines of Red Mountain on the Birmingham city limits. Few labor situations in Alabama rivalled that at these mines for sheer injustice. The ore was dug by subcontractors who hired laborers at 65¢ per day. Commissary prices were reputed to be the highest in the district, and housing conditions the worst. When hired, the men were compelled to agree to purchase all their supplies at the companies' commissaries and if, at the end of the month, their total purchases had lagged, their pay was docked. Whether or not they lived at the camps, at least 50¢ per month was deducted from each man's wages for rent. By the beginning of the twentieth century over eighty percent of the workers around the mines, and almost all of the laborers in the mines, were Negro. In April 1899, 350 ore miners struck one of the mines for several weeks. In May the A.F.L. organizer inducted sixty miners from the all-black camp at Ishkooda into a newly-chartered local. Two months later, when a union committee demanded a $12\frac{1}{2}$¢ per-day wage increase, the Robinson Mining Company, subcontractors from T.C.I., fired them. Seventy-five miners quit immediately, and within the next few days all 1,000 black miners in the camp struck. Although Reverend McGill's *Hot Shots* praised the Robinson Mining Company "for standing for the right," and insisted that the "best elements" in the camp had returned to the job, only fifty-three of the strikers were reported at work six weeks after the strike began, and scattered incidents of violence against strikebreakers and guards erupted throughout the summer. Despite Gompers' appeals, company officials refused to meet the strikers' demands or to recognize the union. Since many

[82] *Bessemer Weekly,* June 16-30, 1900; *Bessemer Workman,* June 20, 1900; Bessemer *Herald-Journal,* September 18, 1900; Birmingham *News,* June 15-20, 29, July 16, September 18, 1900; Gompers to John Dowling, October 20, 1900, Gompers to J. C. Wilson, October 20, 1900, Gompers Letterbooks.

strikers refused to return to work, production lagged until the Tennessee Company, itself trying to obtain a regular output, took over the operation in 1901. Although improving living and working conditions, the company did not destroy union sentiment. Three years later more than 700 black iron ore miners joined locals affiliated with the Western Federation of Miners (W.F.M.), and although these lapsed when the Ishkooda camp was closed in 1905, when T.C.I. reopened the camp in 1907, Negro organizer William Downey claimed that if the A.F.L. would support an organizing campaign he could bring 1,200 to 1,500 ore miners in this camp and thousands in other camps into unions.[83]

These militant black laborers, and most other organized black workers in the district, were in segregated locals, but they were not isolated from the labor movement in Birmingham and in Alabama. As previously indicated, black miners in the U.M.W. participated actively in union affairs and district conventions. The Birmingham Trades Council inducted black delegates from the U.M.W. in 1900 and in the following three years also accepted representatives from the city's Negro barbers' local, the Negro carpenters, and from at least one of the Negro coke workers' locals.[84] The Trades Council remained integrated until 1903, even though the American Federation of Labor permitted the formation of segregated central labor organizations in 1900. In 1903, the Bessemer Negro Central Labor Council merged with Birmingham's black locals to form a Colored Central Labor Council with twenty affiliated unions. Although no longer represented in the Trades Council the black labor organizations continued to participate in the city's annual Labor Day parades, the chief activity of the Trades Council. These annual affairs were an important ceremony in which the district's union workers demonstrated their numbers and solidarity. The ceremonial nature of these occurrences should not obscure both the actual and symbolic importance of participation by black union members. Representatives of black skilled and unskilled unions marched under their union banners

[83] *Labor Advocate,* February 4, May 27, June 24, July 1-28, 1899; *Alabama Miner* (Jasper), July 22, 1899; *Oakman News,* July 21, 1899; *Bessemer Weekly,* April 15, June 17, 1899; *Hot Shots,* August 17, 1899; Birmingham *News,* January 19, 1900, April 11, 1899; Gompers to John Robinson, June 30, 1900, Gompers to Charles Bryant, June 30, 1900, Gompers to W. H. Downey, February 25, 1907, Gompers Letterbooks; *American Federationist,* X:2, 3, 9 (February, March, September 1903), 106, 185, 953, XIV:8, 10 (August, October 1907), 566, 796; Western Federation of Miners, *Miners' Magazine,* VI:57 (July 28, 1904), 15, first lists two Alabama locals of iron ore miners with their officers, and continued to list them through 1906, although by the end of 1905 they had probably lapsed.
[84] Birmingham *News,* August 13, 1900; *Labor Advocate,* March 3, 1901, September 5, 1903.

in every parade between 1900 and 1905 presenting, the *Labor Advocate* once observed, "a most credible appearance and preserving perfect order."[85]

Alliance between Alabama's black and white wage-earners during these years went well beyond joint participation in Labor Day parades. The major vehicle for racial cooperation was the Alabama State Federation of Labor. Formed in 1900, it sought to unite unions and central labor councils throughout the state in one powerful organization which could present a united front in labor's demands for favorable political action. It also encouraged further organization of the state's industrial workers, and attempted to rally support for strikes and boycotts. At its peak membership in 1904, the Federation claimed 235 local affiliates and nine central labor bodies, with a paid up membeership of 33,000 workers. During its first five years the Federation was dominated by locals from the United Mine Workers. William Kirkpatrick, a former U.M.W. district president, was the State's Federation's president three of these years and several other officers were also U.M.W. members. The Mine Workers racial policies thus became the racial policies of the Alabama Federation of Labor. At the first convention, Silas Brooks, then vice-president of District 20, warned delegates who might be inclined to ignore black workers that if the Alabama labor movement excluded Negroes, they would side with their employers when the state's white workers struck. Just one month before the state's constitutional convention met to disfranchise Alabama black voters, the labor convention demonstrated its racial attitude by selecting Brooks 1st vice-president and J. H. Bean, a Selma Negro carpenter, 2nd vice-president. "The only thing that remains," the *Labor Advocate* triumphantly proclaimed, "is for the colored race to wake up to the benefits of unionism and embrace the opportunity offered."[86]

The Alabama Federation of Labor, like the state's United Mine Workers, included black men in leadership positions during the first five years of the twentieth century. Among the five vice-presidents elected annually two or three each year were Negro. Every convention committee included black members. Despite disfranchisment, even the

[85] *Labor Advocate,* September 10, 1904; Birmingham *News,* September 5, 1904; *Age-Herald,* September 6, 8, 1903; *Labor Advocate,* September 1, 1900, August 30, 1902, September 5, 1903, August 20, September 10, 1904, September 16, 1905.
[86] *Labor Advocate,* April 27, 1901. See also April 20, 1901, May 7, 1904, April 15, May 16, 1905; Birmingham *News,* April 18, 1901.

political arm of the State Federation, the United Labor League, had
black vice-presidents in 1903 and 1904. In 1906, five years after the
state's Negroes were disfranchised, the League elected two Negroes to
a newly-formed committee designed to get out the vote for candidates
favorable to labor.[87] Committed to the organization of the state's black
workers, the Federation several times appealed to the A.F.L. to send
salaried organizers to Alabama who would "devote their entire time
and ability" to organizing black laborers. David Williams, the Federation's secretary and former vice-president of the Birmingham local of
the Amalgamated Association of Iron, Steel and Tin Workers, declared that Alabama's wage-earners must "lay aside all malice and
prejudice against color, creed, or nationality, and as we are all wage-
earners under the same banner of trades unionism, let us all work with
one end in view."[88]

Although the admission of black workers to labor unions and the
militancy of many of these black unionists conflicted with increasingly
strident demands in the state for Negro subordination, black workers
and their unions received aid and encouragement not only from white
union members, but occasionally from other elements in the white community. When, for example, Bessemer's blast furnace workers struck in
1900, the *Bessemer Weekly,* although feeling the strike untimely in the
face of returning prosperity, conceded the legitimacy of the strikers' demands and urged the company to comply with them. Bessemer's Manufacturers and Merchants Association, faced with continuing shutdown
of the city's blast furnaces, sent its executive committee to the company
superintendant to ask him to settle the strike by recognizing the strikers'
union. When he refused to compromise, the association called on the
head of the Birmingham Trades Council to mediate. Although the furnaces remained closed for four months because of this walkout, and
incidents of violence sometimes broke out, the city's newspapers and
the Manufacturers and Merchants Association denounced company
officials, not the strikers, for their intransigence.[89] During the iron ore
miners' strike in 1899, Bessemer merchants, angered at the commissary
policy which deprived them of a lucrative trade, supplied the strikers for
several weeks. The *Bessemer Weekly,* "though generally not believing

[87] *Labor Advocate,* September 8, 1900, April 28, 1901, April 26, 1902, May 9, 1903, May
7, 1904, May 6, 1905, January 13, 1905; Birmingham *News,* April 27, 1906.
[88] *Labor Advocate,* May 9, 1903; April 25, May 2, 1903, May 6, 1905.
[89] *Bessemer Weekly,* June 16, 23, 30, 1900; Bessemer *Herald-Journal,* September 18, 1900.

in strikes," condemned the company for the miserable conditions in its camps and endorsed the strikers' demands. A petition from Bessemer and Birmingham merchants urged the Robinson Mining Company to give the strikers higher wages, regular payments, and "cash, not rations like slaves." A gun-battle between strikers and guards erupted at the end of July, when strikers fired into a boarding house containing strike-breakers, killing two of them. A coroner's jury, after sitting for three weeks and hearing 135 witnesses, implicated twenty-five men in the assassinations, but an all-white grand jury refused to indict most of them. Only one of the black strikers ever came to trial, and although the state claimed to have "an excellent case," an all-white Bessemer jury acquitted him.[90]

During this time of increased racial conflict in Alabama, black membership in the United Mine Workers and in locals affiliated with the A.F.L. and the State Federation of Labor of course met with opposition. When the state's labor leaders stood firm, however, they discovered that despite the mounting tide of segregation they could still gain acceptance for interracial labor organizations. At Birmingham's 1901 U.M.W. district convention, for example, owners of the hall used for meetings objected to the presence of black delegates and ousted the convention. William Kirkpatrick, U.M.W. district president, informed the city merchants who owned the hall that "The Negro could not be eliminated. He is a member of our organization and when we are told that we can not use the hall because of this fact then we are insulted as an organization." Convention delegates denounced Birmingham merchants, voted to hold their next meeting in Bessemer, and recommended to their locals that all trade be withdrawn from the city until they received an apology. Under the threat of losing considerable business from the district's miners, Birmingham's merchants apologized for the "oversight and misunderstanding." Such discourtesies, they promised, would not be repeated in future years.[91]

A similar incident occurred the following year at the State Federation of Labor convention in Selma. City officials refused to supply a decent hall for the delegates because of the presence of black delegates. But convention officials resisted this effort to force them to draw the color

---

[90] *Bessemer Weekly*, June 17, 1899, Birmingham *Arbitrator*, August 2, 1899, January 18, 1900; *Labor Advocate*, July 21, 1899; Birmingham *News*, January 19, 1900.
[91] Birmingham *News*, July 3, 1901.

line. "Rather than see one accredited delegate, black or white, thrown out of this convention," a member of Birmingham's typographical union asserted, "I would go to the woods and hold this meeting." This return to nature was not necessary, however, for both the city's streetcar company and the United Confederate Veterans offered the use of their halls after the convention threatened to leave the city.[92] The following year, at the annual convention held in Bessemer, the interracial State Federation was more favorably received by the city. At a smoker given by "Bessemer citizens," the Federation's black vice-president joined the mayor and the white president of the Federation on the platform to address the guests. At the end of the convention, several black delegates arose to thank Bessemer's citizens for their hospitality and courtesies.[93]

Alabama's labor leaders, led by the U.M.W., also resisted opposition from white workingmen to the organization of black workers and their incorporation into the state's labor movement. In 1900 the U.M.W. used the Birmingham Trades Council's request for a boycott of non-union work by the district's miners to secure an investigation of the discriminatory practices of the Trades Council and some of its affiliates. After a "lively discussion," during which several Trades Council members walked out, representatives of the U.M.W. convinced the Council to rescind its prohibition against Negroes, and to enroll delegates from black locals.[94] Some white delegates to early State Federation conventions also objected to the Federation's racial policies. After the Selma convention in 1902 they urged their locals to withdraw from the organization unless it expelled its black members. Within a few months after the convention only sixteen locals, most of them miners' organizations, remained in the Federation. The officials, however, refused to relent in their policy of admitting black workers. "A great many unions throughout the state did not seem to understand the question and desired the separation of the races," Federation president Kirkpatrick recalled in 1905. As he had done with the Birmingham Trades Council in 1900, Kirkpatrick pointed out to these locals that "the American Federation of Labor did not discriminate between creed, color or nationality," and insisted that "it was just as necessary to organize the colored workers at it

[92] *Labor Advocate,* April 26, 1902, quoted in Francis Sheldon Hackney, "From Populism to Progressivism in Alabama, 1890-1910" (Yale University Ph.D. dissertation, 1966), 221.
[93] *Labor Advocate,* May 2, 9, 1903.
[94] Birmingham *News,* August 13, 1900. See *Supra,* 18, above.

was to organize the whites."[95] Whether these arguments were compelling or not, the Federation had persuaded most of the secessionists to return the following year. Delegates from ninety-nine locals, thirty more than the previous year, attended this 1903 convention. Included among them, and participating actively in the convention proceedings, were black delegates from unions of ore miners, coal miners, coke workers, furnace-men, rolling mill helpers, hod carriers, and carpenters in Birmingham, as well as from locals in Mobile, Montgomery, Selma, Anniston and other cities in the state.[96]

The growing strength and success of Alabama's labor movement, coupled with an economic recession in the Birmingham district in 1903 and 1904, led to employer assaults in those years which severely tested the interracial alliance and helped destroy unionism in Birmingham. In 1904 the district's furnace companies, which operated about sixty per-cent of Alabama's coal mines, refused to renew their contracts with the U.M.W. and annnouced their intention to operate their mines on an open shop basis. Over 9,000 miners, probably half of them black, struck. Led by the Tennessee Coal and Iron Company, the companies resorted to their usual policies of importing Negro strikebreakers, sending out large forces of deputies to intimidate miners, and trying to split the white and black miners by offering Negroes the best places in the mines if they would return to work. A black miner from the Blue Creek region, however, promised that "there is no idea entertained by the colored members [of] . . . deserting the union."[97] The president of the Tennes-see Company predicted that over eighty percent of the black miners would be back at work in less than a month, but four months after the walkout began less than fifty of 2,000 black strikers in the Pratt City mines, for example, had returned; and when, two years later, the strike was finally called off, only 300 of the 9,000 strikers had gone back to work at the mines which had been struck. Striking Negro miners con-vinced many imported black strikebreakers to desert the coal companies, and the U.M.W. contributed over $1 million to support strikers and their families, both white and black. Continued coal output in convict mines, and the importation of Southern European immigrants from

---

[95] *Labor Advocate,* April 15, 1905.
[96] *Labor Advocate,* April 25, May 2, 1903.
[97] *Labor Advocate,* October 1, 1904. The strike can be followed in the *Labor Advocate,* Birmingham *News,* and *Age-Herald* from June through November 1904, when news began to taper off as the companies succeeded in reopening enough mines to obtain about thirty percent of normal output.

Pennsylvania and West Virginia mines and from the immigration station at Ellis Island, enabled the coal operators to maintain high enough
production levels to outlast the union, and sixteen months after the
strike began the U.M.W. admitted defeat and called it off.[98]

Struggle with the coal operators was renewed in 1908 when these
immigrants joined with other white and black miners to resist wage
cuts and to attempt to re-establish the union. Aided by the governor
and the state militia, the operators responded by seeking to destroy the
remains of the mine workers' organization. Vigilante committees, made
up of leading citizens of Birmingham antagonistic to the union, har-
rassed and intimidated both black and white strikers, insisting that they
would not "tolerate the organization and striking of Negroes along with
white men." Train loads of imported strikebreakers were kept under
armed guard to prevent any intimidation by or contact with the strikers.
State militia broke up the interracial tent camp which housed striking
miners. In the face of the opposition of the state government and the
destruction of the miners' tent camp, the U.M.W. called off the
strike. The coal companies refused to rehire most of the white miners,
who were thus forced to leave the state. Led by T.C.I., Alabama's coal
companies initiated welfare programs to secure the loyalty of their
black employees and to upgrade their efficiency. By the end of 1908
U.M.W. membership in Alabama had dropped from 18,000 in the
midst of the strike to 700.[99] Only the destruction of the union, however,
destroyed black membership in the U.M.W. For a decade black miners
had stuck to the interracial union and cooperated with the white members. The U.M.W., a Negro school principal, himself a member of the
union, lamented shortly after the collapse of the 1908 strike, "has done
more for the colored man than all the secret orders combined."[100]

The racial principles of the Alabama Federation of Labor were also
tested in 1904. The previous year the Rolling Mill Helpers and Laborers' Union at the Republic Iron and Steel Mill in Birmingham had
sent a committee to the mill's general manager to appeal for union
recognition and a wage increase of ten cents per day. When the general

---

[98] Birmingham *News,* August 24, 1904, April 11, 1906; United Mine Workers' Executive
Board Minutes, August 24, 1904, August 1, 1906, in UMW National Executive Board
Minutebooks, UMW National Headquarters, Washington, D. C.; *Immigrants in
Industries: Bituminous Coal Mining,* IV, 142-161, 197-198, 215; Justin Fuller, "The
History of the Tennessee Coal, Iron and Railroad Company" (University of North
Carolina Ph.D. dissertation, 1966), 278.
[99] Spero and Harris, *op. cit.,* 358; Woodward, *Origins of the New South,* 363-364.
[100] B. H. Dillard to Editor, *Labor Advocate,* September 4, 1908.

manager fired the committee and threatened to fire every man who remained in the union, all 144 members of the union struck, closing the mill for two weeks. Samuel Gompers, A.F.L. organizer Henry Randall, State Federation president Kirkpatrick, and J. E. Smith, head of Birmingham's Central Labor Council, all urged the strikers to stand firm. Although the Republic Iron Company offered the men a fifteen-cents per day wage increase, five cents more than they were asking, the strikers refused to return to work without recognition of their union, even though Randall now advised them to accept the wage increase and forget about recognition. The company then brought in enough laborers to reopen the mill, and despite the objections of Gompers and Theodore Shaffer, national president of the Amalgamated Association, the skilled steel workers at the mill, members of the Amalgamated, returned to work with the strikebreakers. The walkout dragged on for fifteen months, at which time the black laborers finally returned to the mill and asked for their jobs back.[101]

The Amalgamated's action and the failure of the strike did not dampen the Alabama Federation of Labor's support for the organization of black workers. When Thomas Freeman, president of the Rolling Mill Helpers, complained to the Federation's convention in 1904 that the Amalgamated's return to work "with scabs and blacklegs to defeat the Helpers and Laborers . . . [was] not unionism," convention delegates agreed. Although the issue ostensibly revolved around a conflict between white and black workers, the predominantly white convention of Alabama workingmen sent resolutions to Gompers and to Shaffer denouncing the actions of white Amalgamated steel workers, and appealing to them not merely to use their "best efforts to organize the common laborers of the Birmingham district," but to take "immediate steps to bring about closer relationships between organized mechanics and organized laborers when they work in the same mill or place."[102] To wage-earners who belonged to the Alabama Federation of Labor and to the state's United Mine Workers, the labor movement was an instrument for the cooperation of all workers, skilled and unskilled, white and black. "I may dig coal on one entry and the black man on

---

[101] Most of the episode is taken from Samuel Gompers' letters. Gompers to H. N. Randall, July 11, 21, August 12, October 6, 1903, Gompers to Thomas Freeman, July 11, 21, 1903, Gompers to T. J. Shaffer, July 11, 1903, Gompers Letterbooks. See also *Labor Advocate*, July 4, 1903, May 7, November 19, 1904, May 6, 1905.

[102] *Labor Advocate*, May 7, 1904.

another some distance away, yet we work together," a white miner observed in 1900. "You may work in one shop and he in another, yet you work together; you may work in a rolling mill and he may fire the engine that runs on the rail you forged into shape, yet you work together."[103] During the early years of the twentieth century, this vision permeated Alabama's labor movement, encouraging organization of the state's black workers, and resisting the spread of racial conflict in Alabama and the growth of exclusiveness in trades unions.

Despite the appeal of the Alabama Federation, the Amalgamated Association refused to take any action about cooperating with black laborers in Birmingham steel mills. When the union's president, T. J. Shaffer, personally appealed to the 1905 Amalgamated convention to organize unskilled workers in the Republic steel mill in Birmingham, the convention ignored his request.[104] The Amalgamated's animosity towards black laborers in Birmingham, however, cannot be understood solely in terms of racial prejudice. In steel mills in other sections of the country the Association remained just as adamant about not cooperating with unskilled immigrants.[105] To most Amalgamated members, and to most craft unionists, the primary purpose of the labor movement was to provide job security for skilled workmen. Their unions' exclusionist racial policies were part of a larger program designed to protect them against competition from unskilled workers and to preserve the domination of skilled workers in the labor movement. The triumph of this position, not the racial hostility of Alabama's white workers or the apathy of the state's black workers, prevented successful organization of Birmingham's black workers at the beginning of the twentieth century.[106]

The collapse of Negro labor unions in Birmingham after 1904 was also caused by lack of support from the American Federation of Labor. As the Alabama Federation recognized, bringing Birmingham's black workers into labor unions depended upon the willingness of the American labor movement to commit organizers and money to this project. For five years, the A.F.L.—like the U.M.W.—had supported the organization of Alabama's black industrial laborers. In 1904, however, the Federation was in retreat from the organization of unskilled labor

---

[103] W. T. Westbrook to Editor, *Labor Advocate,* June 30, 1900.
[104] *Amalgamated Journal,* May 11, 1905.
[105] David Brody, *Steelworkers in America: The Non-Union Era* (Cambridge, Mass., 1960), 120-146.
[106] Spero and Harris, *op. cit.,* 53-56.

throughout the country. Committed to protection of its craft union members, its treasury depleted by a drop in membership and by the costs of defending itself against employer counteroffensives being mounted in every section of the nation, the A.F.L. could not expand its organizing efforts among Birmingham's black workers, as the Alabama Federation of Labor requested; rather, after 1904, it was forced to reduce them. Federal Labor Unions throughout the country collapsed, and in Birmingham the locals of black workers disappeared.[107]

Consequently, Birmingham's trade union strength rapidly declined after 1904. The United Mine Workers struggled unsuccessfully to defend itself against coal operators' efforts to destroy unionism in the Alabama coal fields, and other unions desperately attempted to protect their hard-won gains from employers who sought to crush unions. As unions lost ground, Alabama's interracial labor movement evaporated. The Alabama Federation of Labor turned its attention from the organization of black laborers to a political alliance with the Farmers' Union. Discrimination and racial hostility, no longer held in check by cross-pressures from the state's labor movement, came to the fore among white workers. Yet, for a brief period in the Birmingham district at the beginning of the twentieth century, the state's labor movement, struggling to overcome both craft union exclusiveness and growing racial conflict in Alabama, organized thousands of black workers and challenged the industrialists' ability to use racial hostility to discipline the class antagonisms of the New South.

---

[107] Foner, *op. cit.*, III, 32-33; Wolman, *op. cit.*, 33-34; Gompers to H. N. Randall, June 19, 1904, Gompers to Andy Marx, June 13, 1907, Gompers Letterbooks.

11

The Origins of Western Working-Class Radicalism, 1890-1905

MELVYN DUBOFSKY

Fifty years ago the labor economist and historian Louis Levine (Lorwin) explained the origins of the radical unionism and syndicalism which the Lawrence textile strike of 1912 had brought to the American nation's attention. Rather than viewing American syndicalism as the product of a few inspired individuals or as a sudden decision to imitate French ideas and methods, Levine insisted that working-class radicalism could only be understood by a proper examination of United States economic and political developments. He wrote: "The forces which drove American toilers to blaze new paths, to forge new weapons and to reinterpret the meaning of life in new terms were the struggles and compromises, the adversities and successes, the exultation and despair *born of conditions of life in America.*"[1] Unfortunately, in the half century since Levine's seminal article, too few historians have chosen to investigate his hypothesis. The field has been left to labor economists more concerned with the nature of industrial relations and the internal history of individual trade unions than with the dynamics of historical change.[2] This paper will apply the historical method and research into

---

[1] Louis Levine, "The Development of Syndicalism in America," *Political Science Quarterly,* XXVIII (Sept., 1913), 451-479. Italics added.

[2] Even among labor economists there have been few substantial works dealing with Western working-class developments. Vernon Jensen's *Heritage of Conflict: Labor Relations in the Nonferrous Metals Industry Up To 1930* (Ithaca, 1950) is by far the best of

Reprinted from *Labor History* 7 (Spring 1966), 131-54. A version of this article ("The Role of the Environment: The American West and Labor Radicalism") was read at a session on American Labor History sponsored by the Labor Historians' Association at the Mississippi Valley Historical Association Convention in April 1964. The present version has benefited from the trenchant critiques of session commentators Mark Perlman and Gerd Korman. I am also indebted for research assistance and suggestions to two of my former graduate students, Michael L. Johnson and Clyde Tyson, and to my colleagues at Northern Illinois University, Charles Freedeman and Kenneth N. Owens, for their helpful comments on the original paper.

unused or seldom used documents to analyze the forces which impelled the working class in a part of the American West to adopt socialism and syndicalism.

At the outset several concepts require clarification. By the American West, I mean the metals-mining area stretching from the northern Rockies to the Mexican border, and particularly the states of Colorado, Idaho, and Montana. By radicalism, I mean, not murder or mayhem,[3] but a concept of social change and a program for altering the foundations of American society and government, which was proscripted ultimately from the Marxian indictment of capitalism. This paper makes no pretense, however, of offering an exegesis on the theoretical foundations of Western working-class radicalism or of its decline and fall; instead it simply seeks to comprehend why, within a particular historical, social, and economic context, a group of American workers found radicalism relevant.

During the Populist and Progressive eras (1890-1917) when radical-

---

such books and is indispensable to any student of the subject, particularly for its insights into the process of industrial relations and the evolution of the W.F.M. But it suffers from a lack of historical perspective and the failure to use the papers of public officials in the West and other individuals involved in the area's labor conflicts. Equally indispensable to a student of the subject are the relevant sections in Selig Perlman's and Philip Taft's *History of Labor in the United States, 1896-1932,* (New York, 1935), 169-281. Here again historical perspective is limited to Turner's insights about the frontier, and local newspapers and trade union journals provide the bulk of sources. Of less use is Benjamin M. Rastall's "The Labor History of the Cripple Creek District," *Bulletin of the University of Wisconsin, No. 198; Economic and Political Science Series Volume 3, No. 1,* (Madison, Wis., 1908), which, while providing solid information about the labor war in Cripple Creek, is strongly biased against radical labor organizations and thus accepts at face value many of the employers' charges against the WFM. A more recent, similar, but superior work by an historian, Robert W. Smith, is *The Coeur D'Alene Mining War of 1892: A Case Study of an Industrial Dispute,* (Corvallis, Oregon, 1961). Actually, it is an unrevised 1935 doctoral dissertation, which still refers to Perlman's and Taft's work of the same year as the most recent and authoritative interpretation of labor developments in the Mountain West, and thus also falls into the Turnerian trap. The two best treatments of the I.W.W., Paul Brissenden, *The I.W.W.: A Study of American Syndicalism,* (New York, 1957 ed.) and John G. Brooks, *American Syndicalism: The I.W.W.,* (New York, 1913), are both dated and contain only the briefest treatments of the Western origins of working-class radicalism. Robert F. Tyler, "The I.W.W. and the West," *American Quarterly,* XII (Summer, 1960), 175-187, is more concerned with investigating the views of the I.W.W. held by Eastern literary figures and dilettantes than with the actual Western origins of syndicalism, which he tends to devaluate.

3 During industrial conflicts the American West produced more than its share of murder and mayhem. Harry Orchard, the siege at Bull Hill, and the Everett Massacre cannot be ignored; John Dos Passos can excite the reader with wild tales of Wobblies acting in the American pioneer spirit [*U.S.A.* (New York, 1937) and *Midcentury,* (Cambridge, Mass., 1961)], and Stewart Holbrook can fabricate a "Rocky Mountain Revolution," [*The Rocky Mountain Revolution,* (New York, 1956)]. But of greater importance to the historian is an understanding of the sources of Western working-class radical economic, social, and political doctrine.

ism took root among Western workers, reform crusades — middle-
class and lower-class, urban and rural, moderate and militant, conservative and revolutionary — challenged the classic capitalist order. This
order, described fifty years earlier by Marx and Engels, was dying
throughout the industrial world, the United States included; and social
groups struggled to control or shape the economic order to come. None
were sure of the future, but all wanted it to accord with their concept
of a just and good society. In America many options *appeared* to exist,
for in 1890 and 1900 the triumph of the modern corporation and the
corporate state was still in the future. And Western workers were
among those Americans who opted for an alternative to the capitalist
order.

At this time the American Federation of Labor, with its conservatism
and "pure and simple" policies, dominated organized labor. Its original
competitor, the Knights of Labor, had declined and died; Populism had
failed to cement a farmer-labor alliance; and in the East the immigrant
needle trades' workers had not yet built stable, semi-industrial, socialist
organizations offering an alternative to the AFL craft unions. Western
workers, however, presented a direct and radical challenge to AFL
hegemony. Around the Western Federation of Miners (W.F.M.) rallied
America's radical dissidents, those dissatisfied with things as they were
— with McKinley, Roosevelt, Bryan and the political parties they
represented, with Samuel Gompers and craft unionism, and especially
with corporate capitalism.

Nowhere was the economic and social change which produced American radicalism in the late nineteenth century so rapid and so unsettling
as in the mining West. There, in a short time, full-blown industrial cities
replaced frontier boom-camps and substantially capitalized corporations
displaced grub-staking prospectors. The profitable mining of refractory
ores (silver and gold) and base metals (lead, zinc, and copper) required
railroads, advanced technology, large milling and smelting facilities,
and intensive capitalization. "The result," in the words of Rodman
Paul, "was that [by 1880] many mining settlements were carried well
beyond any stage of society that could reasonably be called the frontier.
They became, instead, industrial islands in the midst of forest, desert,
or mountain . . ."[4] During the 1890s and 1900s, with continuing eco-

---

[4] Rodman W. Paul, *Mining Frontiers of the Far West, 1848-1880,* (New York, 1963),
    9-10, 137-138, 195-196, is by far the best scholarly account of the urban-industrial

nomic growth, mining communities moved still further beyond the frontier stage. Corporations such as William Rockefeller's Amalgamated Copper Company and the Phelps-Dodge Company consolidated the copper industry; other large corporations exploited the lead and silver mines; and the American Smelting and Refining Company and the United States Reduction and Refining Company apparently monopolized the refining and smelting of ores.[5]

As early as 1876, Colorado, though still sparsely settled and far removed from the nation's primary industrial centers, had been colonized by corporations and company towns. In Leadville, for example, the population increased from 200 in 1877 to 14,820 in 1880, by which time Leadville was a primary smelting center. Cripple Creek, the famous Colorado gold camp, surpassed Leadville. Beginning in 1892 when it was hidden in the wilderness, the Cripple Creek region changed overnight into an industrial fortress. By 1900 Cripple Creek advertised its 10,000 inhabitants, three railroads connecting the region to the outer world, and trolleys and electric lights serving the district's own needs. Domestic and foreign capital rushed to exploit Colorado's opportunities. Between 1893 and 1897, 3,057 new mining corporations were organized, each of which was capitalized at over one million dollars. By 1895 all Colorado's larger cities boasted mining exchanges, and the Colorado Springs Mining Exchange handled over 230 million mining shares valued at over $34 million in 1899.[6]

Montana followed the Colorado pattern. Its production of ores, valued at $41 million in 1889, made it the nation's leading mining state. Butte, the copper capital by that time, had a population of 30,000, three banks with deposits in excess of $3,000,000, an adequate public school system, four hospitals, two fire companies, newspapers, and water, gas, and electric companies. Its wealthier classes lived in elegant homes and worked in handsome business residences; its miners and mill-men received over $500,000 monthly in wages, and over 100 smoke stacks poured out their residue night and day in what was hardly a frontier

---

transformation of the Mountain West and proves decisively the irrelevance of old Turnerian terminology.

[5] The changing nature of mining and smelting processes, and their increasing corporate concentration can best be followed in *Report of the Industrial Commission on the Relations and Conditions of Capital and Labor Employed in the Mining Industry*, (Washington, 1911), XII, 191-618, *passim*.

[6] Percy S. Fritz, *Colorado: The Centennial State*, (New York, 1941), 304, 311-312, 367; Robert G. Athearn, *High Country Empire: The High Plains and Rockies*, (New York, 1960), 267-268.

environment.[7] Idaho, on a lesser scale, repeated Montana's and Colorado's development.[8]

In their mill and smelter towns, their shoddy company houses and stores, their saloons, and their working class populations, the cities of the Mountain West bore a distinct resemblance to their Eastern industrial counterparts.[9] The speed of the transition from a primitive to a more mature economy, from the village to the city, combined with the great instability of a mining economy, had important social consequences.[10] Rapid economic growth, instead of bringing prosperity and contentment, brought unrest, conflict, violence, and radicalism.

Those workers who filled the young industrial cities of the West shared a tradition of union organization, a common language, and a certain amount of ethnic similarity. Miners had organized unions by the 1860s on the Comstock Lode. When that area's mines played out, its miners moved on to new lodes in Idaho, Colorado, and Montana, carrying the union idea with them.[11] While in some mining districts the foreign-born outnumbered the native Americans, no great ethnic division separated foreigners from natives. In most mining communities the dominant foreign nationalities were of Irish, English (mostly Cornishmen), and Canadian extraction.[12] The foreign-born, particularly the Cornishmen (better known as "Cousin Jacks") and the Irishmen, were professional miners, and many of their native American counterparts had

---

[7] *The Works of Hubert Howe Bancroft*, XXXI, "History of Washington, Idaho, and Montana, 1845-1889," 752n, 755n, 763-764, 769; Joseph K. Howard, *Montana: High, Wide, and Handsome*, (New Haven 1943), 83-84.

[8] *Works of Bancroft*, XXXI, 572; Merrill D. Beal and Merle W. Wells, *History of Idaho*, (New York, 1959), I.

[9] Most historians of the region agree on its urban and industrial character by the 1890s. "The very concentration of miners' cabins, crowded together in an area of highly concentrated wealth automatically provided an urban type of living." Athearn, *High Country Empire*, 77; *Works of Bancroft*, XXXI, 752n, 755n, 769; Fritz, *Colorado*, 367, Paul, *Mining Frontiers*, 68-69.

[10] The same authorities agree upon the speed of the change, which can be charted in the federal census returns from 1890 to 1910 for the mining counties and smelter cities of the Mountain West. U.S. Census Office, *Compendium of the Eleventh Census: 1890* (Part I, Population), (Washington, D.C., 1892), 478, 481, 496, 541, 559; *Idem.*, *Twelfth Census of the United States Taken in the Year 1900* (Population Part I), (Washington, 1901), 495-496, 499, 511, 648, 664, 739-741, 744, 768; U.S. Bureau of the Census, *Thirteenth Census of the United States Taken in the Year 1910*, "Population," II (Washington, 1914), 216-227, 228, 430, 432, 1156, 1158-1159. For the rapidity of the social and economic change in Montana, see Howard, *Montana*, 4-5. On the destabilizing effects of rapid economic growth see Mancure Olson, Jr., "Rapid Growth as a Destabilizing Force," *Journal of Economic History*, XXIII (December, 1963), 529-552; and Carter Goodrich's comments in *Ibid.*, 553-558.

[11] For the early origins of miners' unions in California and Nevada see Paul, *Mining Frontiers*, 69-70, 94-95; Jensen, *Heritage*, 10-18.

[12] The census figures cited above also reveal the ethnic characteristics of the Mountain States' mining and smelting centers. Every district in Colorado, Idaho, and Montana

forsaken prospecting and striking it rich for the steadier returns of wage labor.[13] Furthermore, the Western mining centers shared with mining communities throughout the world the group solidarity derived from relative physical isolation and dangerous, underground work.

At first, owing largely to the ethnic composition of Western mining communities and to the reliance of local merchants and professionals upon the patronage of miners, workers and local businessmen were not split into hostile camps. Local businessmen and farmers often supported the miners in their struggles for union recognition and higher wages. In Idaho's mineral-rich Coeur d'Alene, the local inhabitants — farmer and merchant, journalist and physician, public official and skilled worker — sympathized with striking miners. A leading Idaho attorney and Democratic politician, Boise's James H. Hawley, from 1892 to 1894 defended indicted strikers, referred to them as friends and allies, and importuned President Cleveland to provide several with patronage positions.[14] East of the Continental Divide in Montana, mine

---

had, unlike other American industrial cities, a native-born majority. Furthermore, the foreign-born came predominantly from the British Isles, including Ireland, and Scandinavia, and were hardly representative of the more recent waves of immigration altering the United States' ethnic complexion. An unusually large number of foreign-born were also naturalized citizens. Paul (*Mining Frontier*, 122, 182) found that by the 1870s Cornishmen and Irishmen predominated among the foreign-born miners. Emma F. Langdon, a union sympathizer and a participant in the 1903-04 Cripple Creek Civil War, saw the local miners, who were mostly native-born plus German, Swedish, and Irish immigrants, as more difficult to subdue than the Italians and Hungarians employed in Eastern coal mines. *The Cripple Creek Strike* (Denver, 1904-05), 34. In the Coeur d'Alenes in 1899, 132 of 528 imprisoned miners were native-born, the remainder being of greatly varying nationalities; and 208 of the foreign-born were naturalized citizens. United States Congress, 56th: 1st Session, *Senate Document* No. 24, "Coeur d'Alene Mining Troubles," 13. For other estimates of the ethnic complexion of Western mining communities, see the testimony of union officials and mine and smelter managers in *Capital and Labor Employed in Mining*, 313, 377, 485, 572, 588, 595. The overwhelmingly Anglo-Saxon origins of the W.F.M.'s local and national leadership becomes obvious when one looks at the names listed in the monthly union directory published in the *Miners Magazine*.

[13] Paul (*Mining Frontiers*, 69-70, 94-95, 122, 182) points out that as mining became more complex and costly, Irish and Cornish professionals replaced American amateurs. John Calderwood, the first union leader in Cripple Creek, had entered coal mines at the age of nine and later attended mining school. Holbrook (*Rocky Mountain*, 74) notes that Ed Boyce, W.F.M. president from 1897 to 1903, worked as a professional miner from 1884 until his election to the presidency in 1896, and his successor, Charles Moyer had been a skilled worker in the Lead, South Dakota smelter complex. *W.F.M., Proceedings of the Eleventh Convention* (1903), 17; May A. Hutton, *The Coeur d'Alenes—Or A Tale of the Modern Inquisition in Idaho*, (Denver, 1900), 53-54. Furthermore, there is every reason to believe that mine and smelter operators preferred skilled, professional workmen to "pioneers" or "frontiersmen," and that wage differentials would attract European and Eastern miners to the American West.

[14] The testimony of Coeur d'Alene residents in *Capital and Labor in Mining*, 389-546, *passim*, reveals the community support won by striking miners; James H. Hawley to H. F. Brinton, Esq. Nov. 1, 1892; Hawley to George A. Pettibone, Nov. 15, 1892,

and smelter owners, battling among themselves, wooed their labor forces with promises of union recognition, higher wages, the eight-hour day, and improved working conditions.[15] And even Bill Haywood admitted that in Colorado's Cripple Creek district prior to the 1903-04 civil war, miners and businessmen associated with each other, belonged to the same fraternal societies, and were bound together by ethnic ties.[16]

Into these urban communities the modern corporation intruded to disrupt the local peace and to drive a wedge between the workers and their non-working class allies. The 1890s was an uneasy decade for American businesses, and for none more so than mining, milling, and smelting enterprises. The falling price of silver, the depression of 1893, the repeal of the Sherman Silver Purchase Act, and the inherent instabilities of extractive industries made mine owners and smelter operators anxious to reduce production costs and consequently less tolerant of labor's demands. Mining corporations formed associations to pressure railroads by threatening to close down mining properties and cease shipments until rates declined. But capitalists found it easier to make the necessary savings by substituting capital for labor.[17]

Technological innovations increased productivity, but in so doing diluted labor skills and disrupted traditional patterns of work. While technological change did not as a rule decrease total earnings, it tended to lower piece rates and to reduce some formerly skilled workers to

Hawley to Pettibone, January 3, 1893; Hawley to Patrick F. Reddy, March 20, 1893; Hawley to J. F. Poynton, April 29, 1893; Hawley to Pettibone, May 4, 1893; Hawley to Poynton, October 17, 1893; Hawley to Reddy, February 5, 1894, James H. Hawley Letterbooks, Idaho State Historical Society; R. Smith, *Mining War of 1892*, 38-40; Hutton, *Coeur d'Alenes, passim.*

15 F. Augustus Heinze to Michael McCormack, President, Butte Miners' Union, June 12, 1900, in *Miners Magazine*, I (July, 1900), 47, 49; *Ibid.*, II (Jan., 1901), 12-13; Butte *Reveille*, May 23, 1904, 8, June 6, 1904, 5. The *Reveille*, which was the Butte Miners' Union's official paper was owned at various times by the union, by Heinze, and by the Amalgamated Copper Company. It is one of the better printed sources from which to follow the tangled Butte story. Cf. Jensen, *Heritage*, 298.

16 Stenographic Report of Advisory Board Appointed by Governor James H. Peabody to Investigate and Report upon Labor Difficulties in the State of Colorado and More Particularly at Colorado City, in Hawley Papers, describes best the anxiety of Cripple Creek district businessmen and mine owners to settle labor disputes equitably with their workers, and the friendlier attitude of local business and capital as compared with national interests in Colorado City symbolized by the United States Smelting and Reduction Company. Cf. *Capital and Labor in Mining*, 389-564, *passim; Bill Haywood's Book: The Autobiography of William D. Haywood*, (New York, 1958), 117-128.

17 B. Goldsmith to Simeon G. Reed, June 6, 1887; Reed to Victor M. Clement, March 29, 1889; Clement to Reed, November 23 and December 2, 1889, in Simeon G. Reed Papers (Microfilm, Idaho State Historical Society); Job Harriman, "The Class War in Idaho," *Miners Magazine*, V (October 8, 1903), 8; *Haywood's Book*, 80-81; R. Smith, *Mining War of 1892*, 24-35.

unskilled laborers (and thus lowered their earnings).[18] Since the mining enterprises competed in a common market, all the Western mining areas experienced similar pressures on piece rates and established skills.[19] In Bill Haywood's hyperbolic words: "There was no means of escaping from the gigantic force that was relentlessly crushing all of them beneath its cruel heel. The people of these dreadful mining camps were in a fever of revolt. There was no method of appeal; strike was their only weapon."[20]

Thus in 1892 Coeur d'Alene miners revolted against technological change, corporate concentration, and a recently organized Mine Owners' Association. Supported by local citizens, the community's newspapers, and local officials, miners appeared on the verge of success when their capitalist opponents, aided by state and federal authorities, outflanked them. Federal troops crushed the labor revolt, imprisoning union leaders and prominent non-union local residents alike. Strike leaders, while awaiting trial in prison, brooded about their recent experiences and the future of Western mining communities. Then and there in an Idaho prison, they decided to create a new labor organization, joining together the separate miners' unions in Idaho, Montana, Colorado, California, Nevada, and the Southwestern territories. Upon their release from prison, they called a convention, which met in Butte in 1893 and established the Western Federation of Miners.[21]

By 1893 the mining West, as shown above, had passed well beyond the frontier stage and the working class' emerging radicalism was hardly the response of pioneer individualists to frontier conditions. The W.F.M. did not consist mostly of men who had been prospectors and frontiersmen; it was not "permeated with the independent and often lawless spirit of the frontier"; nor did its radicalism result from a lack of respect for the social distinctions of a settled community, or a disregard by labor for the "elementary amenities of civilized life," or the absence of farmers, a neutral middle class, and others who might keep matters within bounds.[22] Perlman and Taft, and their disciples,

---

[18] The sources cited above describe fully the impact of technological change.

[19] The testimony of mine owners and mill and smelter managers in *Capital and Labor in Mining, passim.* covers the pressures common to all such enterprises in labor and product markets.

[20] *Haywood's Book,* 80-81.

[21] R. Smith, *Mining War of 1892* is the fullest account of the conflict and its relation to the founding of the WFM. Cf., J. Harriman, "The Class War," *Miners Magazine,* V (October 22, 1903), 9-12, (Nov. 5, 1903), 13; V. Jensen, *Heritage,* 25-37.

[22] The quotations cited above come from Foster Rhea Dulles, *Labor In America,* (New York, 1949), 209; Louis Lorwin, *The American Federation of Labor,* (Washington,

have in fact reversed the dynamics of social change in the Mountain West. The violent conflicts which they so fully described came, not on an undeveloped Western frontier but in a citadel of American industrialism and financial capitalism. Perlman's and Taft's "class war without a class ideology" resulted from a process of social polarization not from an absence of middle groups, and consequently brought Marxian class consciousness. After 1910 farmers and others did not suddenly settle the area to blur sharp class distinctions and end the class war. The Ludlow Massacre occurred in 1914, Butte erupted into violent industrial warfare from 1914-17, and the bitter Colorado County coal wars developed still later — in the 1920s.

Violent conflict came not from the "general characteristics of the frontier" or "quick on the trigger" employers and employees but from the general nature of early industrialism.[23] Western working-class history is the story not of the collapse of social polarization but of its creation. Prior to the triumph of corporate capitalism, Western workers retained numerous allies among local merchants, professionals, farmers, and party politicians. The interesting historical feature is the manner in which corporate executives separated labor from its quondam allies, and polarized society and politics to the disadvantage of the worker. The remainder of this paper will demonstrate that class war in the West created a class ideology, and that that ideology was Marxist because the Mountain West from 1890 to 1905 followed the classic Marxian pattern of development.

*   *   *   *   *   *   *

The Westerners' radicalism derived quite directly and naturally from the forces which had successfully refashioned American society. To-

D.C., 1933), 84-85; Charles A. Madison, *American Labor Leaders*, (New York, 1950), 264; Selig Perlman, *A History of Trade Unionism in the United States*, (New York, 1922), 213; Idem., *A Theory of the Labor Movement*, (New York, 1949), 227; Perlman and Taft, *Labor in the U.S.*, 169, 178, 189; Fred Thompson, *The I.W.W.: Its First Fifty Years*, (Chicago, 1955), 9.

23 It seems strange to seek to explain violent conflict in the Mountain West in Turnerian terms when at the very same time in the "settled, civilized" East, open warfare prevailed at Homestead, in Chicago during the Pullman Strike, and even later in Lawrence, Massachusetts and Paterson, New Jersey. It seems equally foolish to account for the creation (in the Mountain West) of private armies in frontier terms, when Eastern employers and even workers did likewise. The coal and iron police appeared in Pennsylvania, not Montana; Colorado employers and workers may have utilized Western "desperados" and gunmen but employers and workers in New York's garment industry made ample use of similar services provided by the metropolis' gun-slingers and club wielders. Such violence and conflict, wherever it erupted, seems more a characteristic of the early stages of industrialism than of any peculiar geographical environment.

gether with other individuals and groups forced by corporate capitalism
to the bottom of the economic and social ladder, miners asserted their
claim to a more decent treatment and a better place in the American
system. They joined the Knights of Labor, crusaded with the Populists,
and eventually united with Eastern socialists. Western workers wedded
to the utopianism of the Knights, allured by the promise of Populism,
and victimized by the corporation could not rest content with the "pure
and simple" unionism of Samuel Gompers.

The local miners' unions which coalesced to form the W.F.M. in
many cases had simply dropped their Knights of Labor affiliation without shedding the Knights' essential spirit and carried with them the
fundamental idea of the Knights, "the unity of all workers." Although
many miners may have joined the Knights of Labor simply to gain
better conditions or job security, many certainly became imbued with
that organization's spirit of solidarity and its antipathy to capitalism.
While the Knights vanished in the East, their organization had a marked
rebirth in the Mountain West. Montana labor papers reported in 1894
that their State's Knights of Labor were advancing at a rate not attained
in years and were ready to lead laborers into the Populist crusade.[24]
On the other side of the Bitterroot range in Idaho, former Grand
Master Workman, J. R. Sovereign, editor and publisher of the Wallace
Tribune — the Coeur d'Alene miners' union official publication — was
amalgamating the Knights, Populism, and the W.F.M.[25] As late as 1903
a W.F.M. member from Slocan, B. C., wrote to the Miner's Magazine:
"Now there are thousands of old-line K. of L.'s in the W.F. of M. and
the unsavory acts of the A.F. of L. officials have not been all together
forgotten . . ."[26]

W.F.M. members learned their political lessons in Populist schools.
Unlike other areas of the nation where Populism was primarily an
agrarian protest and labor, organized and unorganized, declined over-

---

[24] Butte Bystander, January 20, 1894, 2, January 27, 1894, 1, April 21, 1894, 2, May 5,
    1894, 2, September 1, 1894, 2; The Populist Tribune, January 20, 1894, 6; The
    Montana Silverite, April 20, 1894, 4.
[25] Capital and Labor in Mining, 389-390, 531-532, 537; Butte Bystander, April 21, 1894,
    3; Hutton, Coeur d'Alenes, 70.
[26] Anonymous, Slocan, British Columbia Miners Union to Editor, Miners Magazine, III
    (April, 1902), 30-31; Ibid., I (February, 1900), 28; Haywood's Book, 30-31;
    Fritz, Colorado, 368. For the principles of the Knights, which must have rubbed
    off on some of the Western members, see P. Brissenden, IWW, 32; Gerald Grob,
    Workers And Utopia (Evanston, Ill., 1961), 34-137, passim.; Norman Ware, The
    Labor Movement in the United States, 1860-1895 (New York, 1959), passim.

tures from farm organizations for a political alliance, Populism in the Mountain West was a working-class movement and labor organizations courted farmers.[27] Thus politics and Populism intruded at the early conventions of the W.F.M. The 1893 founding convention, meeting before panic and depression swept the West, considered the necessity of united political action. The 1895 convention, convened during the depths of depression, gave its endorsement and ". . . undivided support to the party [Populist] advocating the principles contained in the Omaha platform."[28] Mining districts across the Mountain West elected miners' candidates to local office on labor or Populist tickets. And on occasion working-class Populists held the balance of power in state-wide elections. Western miners, like farmers elsewhere, learned that politics paid.[29]

Although free silver was obviously an important Populist attraction in the Mountain West, miners, unlike their employers, demanded sweep-

---

[27] In Montana the major Populist newspapers were labor journals and reading them makes clear the working-class nature of Montana Populism. State Labor conferences and Populist conventions often met at the same time in the same city and passed resolutions supporting and complimenting each other. Butte *Bystander*, January 20, 1894, 2, February 24, 1894, 1; The Silver Bow (Butte) Trades and Labor Assembly called for all lower class groups to unite at the polls. "The farmer must join hands with the wage earners of all classes. . . . The people's party is organized by those from the humble walks of life to destroy monopoly and give equal and exact justice to all." *Bystander*, October 1, 1894, 1; The Populist State Committee Chairman was an official of the American Railway Union and party candidates in Silver Bow County were mostly union members. *Bystander*, October 3, 1894, 2, October 8, 1894, 2; In 1895 the separate labor parties in Montana amalgamated to obtain more effective political action and issued a call to the state's farmers; "We . . . appeal to the farmers of Montana to organize into some form of union . . . and send delegates to the States Trades and Labor Council, in order that we may mutually aid and assist each other in the great struggle to emancipate labor from . . . industrial slavery." *Bystander*, November 26, 1895, 2-3, December 3, 1895, 2; In Anaconda, the local Populist paper, the *Populist Courier*, was edited by a member of the W.F.M. and the Knights of Labor; the Missoula paper, the *Montana Silverite*, was the official journal of the local AFL unions and always emphasized labor reforms before free silver. *Silverite*, June 22, 1894, 1, August 3, 1894, 7, August 31, 1894, 1, February 1, 1895. 1. November 29, 1895, 1; *The Populist Tribune* (Butte) also was primarily a labor paper, January 20, 1894, 1, April 21, 1894, 1, May 5, 1894, 4, June 30, 1894, 8, June 16, 1894, 5, February 24, 1894, 5; In Idaho's Coeur d'Alenes local labor groups were indistinguishable from the Populists, and Ed Boyce, W.F.M. president, was a power in the party and a Populist representative in the state assembly. Testimony of J. R. Sovereign and Sheriff James D. Young in *Capital and Labor in Mining*, 405, 437, 531-532, 537. The *Pueblo Courier*, the official WFM organ in Colorado, was also a Populist political sheet.

[28] *Bystander*, June 2, 1894, 1, May 21, 1895, 3; *Montana Silverite*, May 24, 1895, 1.

[29] The James H. Hawley Papers show clearly the dependence of the Democratic party in Idaho on the support of working-class Populists in the Coeur d'Alenes; Populist Governor "Bloody Bridles" Waite of Colorado was elected largely through the efforts of working-class supporters and always promptly paid his debts. The full strength of working-class Populism is revealed in the election statistics for the mining counties in W. Dean Burnham, *Presidential Ballots, 1836-1892* (Baltimore, 1955), 306-317, 366-367, 600-601; Edgar E. Robinson, *The Presidential Vote, 1896-1932*, (Palo Alto, 1934), 150-154, 174-177, 256-260.

ing political and economic reforms. If free silver had been the only manifestation of Western working-class political radicalism, it could have found an outlet in the Republican or Democratic parties as well as the People's party.[30] The western workers instead supported a radical Populism — sometimes cranky, sometimes funny — which was the industrial counterpart of C. Vann Woodward's Southern Alliancemen and Norman Pollack's Midwestern agrarians.[31] Consequently, after the failure of the Populist coalition with Silver Democrats and the defeat of Bryan, W.F.M. president Ed Boyce, speaking at the union's 1897 convention, denounced the free silver fraud and informed his audience: "The silver barons of the west are as bitter enemies of organized labor as the gold bug Shylock in his gilded den on Wall Street. . . ." Boyce then called for more intelligent and effective political action, a call which could lead in only one direction — toward the Socialist party.[32] As the AFL turned away from socialism and political action to the narrower path of "pure and simple" trade unionism,[33] the Western Federation moved toward socialism, political action, and the broad road of radical unionism.

---

[30] All political parties in the Mountain West were officially for free silver but this similarity tends to cloak important, qualitative differences. For example, mine owners were not as committed to free silver as popular legend implies. Weldon B. Heyburn, attorney for the Coeur d'Alene Mine Owners' Association and himself a mining speculator, led the Gold Republicans in Idaho. Claudius O. Johnson, "The Story of Silver Politics in Idaho, 1892-1902," *Pacific Northwest Quarterly* XXXIII (July, 1942), 283-296; Elmer Ellis in his study of Henry More Teller, the Colorado Silver Republican, discovered the same tendencies. He found free silver sentiment waning among mine owners by 1894 as they recognized the hard economic facts of life; and he emphasizes that Fred Dubois, leader of Idaho's Silver Republicans, would not consider a coalition with Populism because simple silverites differed with Populism on all issues except free silver. Most wealthy mine owners had drifted into the more conservative Republican party by 1899. "It seems almost impossible in this State (Colorado) for any man with an independent fortune to refrain from allying himself with the Republican party." Governor Charles S. Thomas to William Jennings Bryan December 22, 1899, quoted in Elmer Ellis, *Henry Moore Teller: Defender of the West* (Caldwell, Idaho, 1941), 237, 248, 325.

[31] The Mountain States Populists endorsed all the usual planks including free silver, nationalization of telephones, telegraphs, railroads, and mines as well as specific labor reforms such as legal eight-hour day, sanitary inspection of workshop, mill, and home, employers' liability, and abolition of contract system on public works, and abolition of sweating system. *Montana Silverite,* November 29, 1895, 1; *Bystander,* February 24, 1894, 1, May 14, 1895, 2. On the radical content of Midwestern and Southern Populism, see Norman Pollack, *The Populist Response to Industrial America* (Cambridge, Massachusetts, 1962) and C. Vann Woodward, "The Populist Heritage and the Intellectual," *The American Scholar* XXIX (Winter, 1959-60), 55-72; *Tom Watson: Agrarian Rebel* (New York, 1938).

[32] Quoted in *Bystander,* May 15, 1897, 1.

[33] The movement of the AFL toward less radical political action can best be followed in *The American Federationist,* I-III (1894-1896) and in the convention debates for 1893-1896 contained in *Proceedings of the American Federation of Labor, 1893-1896* (Bloomington, Illinois, 1906).

Initially, however, the W.F.M., except for its unusual concern with Populism and politics, appeared much like any other trade union. It waged strikes to protect wages, reduce hours, or gain union recognition, not for the co-operative commonwealth. So famous an American radical as "Big Bill" Haywood, during his early years as an officer of the Silver City, Idaho local, concerned himself not with the coming revolution but with enrolling all working miners in the union. Nowhere do the minute books of Haywood's local, which he kept, hint of a future revolutionist.[34] Ed Boyce, the union leader most responsible for transforming the W.F.M. into the cynosure of left-wing socialists, initially bore no taint of radicalism. During its first four years, 1893-1896, the W.F.M. seemed a rather ordinary trade union waging a losing battle against corporations and depression; in 1896 the organization was weaker and numbered fewer members than at its birth in 1893. Then the W.F.M. revived.[35] And with apparent success came not conservatism or self-satisfaction but radicalism and revolutionary ardor.

The W.F.M.'s radicalism was buried deep in the organization's conscious and unconscious past. The Knights of Labor had contained an obvious utopian tinge; Populism, while less utopian, nevertheless proposed for the America of the 1890s a meaningful radical alternative. Many miners remained at heart Knights and Populists. Given the proper circumstances and the necessary motivation, both strains came alive in the W.F.M. The Western Federation transformed the naive idealism of the Knights and the native radicalism of the Populists into a brand of radicalism shared by socialist workers throughout the industrial world.

The Western Federation began as an open, inclusive union and became more so. "Open our portals to every workingman, whether engineer, blacksmith, smelterman, or millman . . .," President Boyce advised the union convention in 1897. "The mantle of fraternity is sufficient for all." Three years later Boyce expanded his concept of fraternity: "We will at all times and under all conditions espouse the cause of the producing masses, regardless of religion, nationality or

---

[34] Minute Books, Silver City, Idaho, Miners' Union, Local 62, Bancroft Library, University of California, Berkeley.

[35] The growth of the Union can be followed in correspondence and reports in the *Miners' Magazine,* especially the union directory published regularly, which grew much longer between 1900 and 1903. See particularly, II (June, 1901), 20-24, and IV (July, 1903), 28, in which the Executive Board reported that since the 1902 convention, which indorsed independent political action and progressive unionism, WFM membership increased by one-third to reach its peak.

race, with the object of arousing them from the lethargy into which they have sunk, and which makes them willing to live in squalor. . . ."[36] With Boyce and the W.F.M., commitment to solidarity and fraternity became more than platform oratory; the Western organization epitomized in philosophy and practice the spirit of industrial unionism.

Boyce's presidency also established economic and political radicalism as union policy. In his presidential inaugural speech, he directly challenged Gompers' approach to industrial relations and working-class organization. Speaking of his experience at the 1896 AFL convention, Boyce remarked: ". . . surely it is time for workingmen to see that trades unionism is a failure."[37]

One might well ask, as Samuel Gompers himself wondered, what prompted the leader of a growing labor union to declare trade unionism a failure. And the answer might be that Boyce arrived at his conclusion not on theoretical or philosophical grounds but on the basis of the miners' union's actual experience in dealing with corporations. Even before the W.F.M. appeared, miners had discovered the weakness of ordinary trade unions facing employers allied with state and federal authorities. And after its founding in 1893 events in Idaho and Colorado illustrated further the weaknesses inherent in a "pure and simple" trade union. Weakness drove the Western miners toward radicalism, and radicalism apparently resulted in strength and success.

Twice in the Coeur d'Alenes, in 1892 and 1899, miners' unions were impotent against concentrated capital and hostile state and federal forces. Although miners at first elicited sympathy and support from the local middle class, controlled municipal and county offices, and published the community's leading newspapers, their local power proved insufficient. Mine owners, organized in an employers' association, influenced the Governor, maintained their own newspaper just across the state line in Spokane, and kept their own judge in the Idaho federal district court to hand down sweeping injunctions. When injunctions failed to end strikes and state militia proved inadequate and unwilling to repress strikers, Idaho's chief executives, responding to mine owners' pleas, requested federal troops.[38] The reaction of mine owners and state

---

36 *Bystander,* May 15, 1897, 4; *Miners Magazine,* I (January, 1900), 16-18 V (October 22, 1903), 5: *Haywood's Book,* 71; Jensen, *Heritage,* 70-71.
37 *Bystander,* May 15, 1897, 1; cf. *AFL Proceedings,* 1896, 59.
38 Governor Norman Willey to Senator George Shoup, July 5, 1892; Willey to President Benjamin Harrison, June 24, 1892, Governor's Letter books and Correspondence, (Microfilm, Idaho State Historical Society).

officials was frightening in its implications. Idaho's Attorney-General, for example, demanded of his state's congressional delegation: "The mob must be crushed by overwhelming force"; and to implement his objective, he suggested the use of Gatling guns and howitzers.[39] The Governor and other state officials, counselled by the Mine Owners' Association, demanded the permanent presence of federal troops in northern Idaho to prevent future troubles and protect citizens against guerilla warfare.[40]

Idaho's mine owners and state officials did not desist until they had crushed the miners' unions. In 1899, again abetted by federal troops, they incarcerated workers and strike sympathizers in the infamous bull-pen and denied employment to union miners. Some of those who had defended the self-same miners in 1892 now turned against them. James H. Hawley, together with his junior associate, William Borah, prosecuted the union leaders he had defended in court seven years earlier. His one-time warm political friends had become dangerous criminals. Hawley also engaged in the extracurricular practice of organizing a company union. "No matter how it [the court case] goes," he wrote to his law partner, "we will win our fight by breaking the power of the Union."[41] The corporations had finally succeeded in polarizing Idaho politics and society.[42] Against this type of activity, the W.F.M. and particularly President Boyce, a former Coeur d'Alene miner, found strict trade union tactics unavailing.

The W.F.M. learned the same bitter lesson in Colorado. With the

---

[39] Attorney-General George H. Roberts to Senators Fred Dubois and George Shoup, July 12, 1892; Roberts to Dubois, July 13 and 14, *ibid.*

[40] Willey to Charles W. O'Neil, July 15, 1892; A. J. Pinkham to Senators Dubois and Shoup, July 19, 1892; Willey to President Harrison, July 27, 1892, *ibid.*

[41] Between 1894 and 1899, the W.F.M. had rebuilt its strength in the Coeur d'Alenes and had fully organized most of the area's mines, with the exception of the most important, the Bunker Hill and Sullivan. The Bunker Hill's intransigent management made labor conflict inevitable, setting the stage for the 1899 debacle and the eradication of the W.F.M. from the Coeur d'Alenes. James H. Hawley's letters to this younger law partner, Will Puckett [June 19, 21, 27, 29, July 2, 13, 1899 (Hawley Papers)] reveal the Boise attorney's new-found detestation of the W.F.M. and his flirtation with the Mine Owners' Association, which was paying the cost of the prosecution. Cf. Pinkerton Reports to Governor Frank Steunenberg, June 24-25, July 2-3, 1899, Steunenberg Papers (Microfilm, Idaho State Historical Society); James H. Hawley, *History of Idaho*, I (Chicago, 1920), 250-255.

[42] After 1899, the Mine Owners' Association successfully organized a company union (thus denying employment to W.F.M. members), exerted political coercion on their workers, and attempted to employ Borah as their political manager. M. A. Folsom to William A. Borah, May 7, 1902, Borah Papers (Idaho State Historical Society, Microfilm); Pinkerton Report to Governor Frank Steunenberg, July 6, 1899, Steunenberg Papers; Testimony of Joseph MacDonald, Manager, Helena-Frisco Mine, *Capital and Labor in Mining*, 484; M. A. Hutton, *Coeur d'Alene*, 133-134.

aid of a Populist Governor, "Bloody Bridles" Waite, they had defeated a mine owners' private army in 1894. But two years later with a Republican in the State House, mine owners obtained the state militia to break a strike in Leadville.[43] After the unsuccessful Leadville strike of 1896, the W.F.M. made the crucial shift to the left in politics and practice.

As the union moved further left, Colorado's Mine Owners' Association prepared to turn to its own advantage American fear of radicalism and socialism. In 1902 mine owners formed a state-wide organization to combat unions with money, propaganda, and Pinkertons. Simultaneously they enlisted the aid of local businessmen and professionals previously allied with the miners. Again the process of social polarization came relatively late and was consummated on the initiative of the larger corporate interests. By February 24, 1903, Boyce's successor as president of the W.F.M., Charles Moyer, informed union members: "We are being attacked on all sides at this time by the Mill Trust and Mine Owners' Association."[44]

W.F.M. officials, although on the defensive, tried to negotiate with Colorado employers. During a dispute with Colorado City mill and smelter operators, Moyer emphasized that the purpose of the W.F.M. was to build, not destroy—to avoid by all honorable means a war between employer and employee. But Haywood, at the same time, probably described the W.F.M.'s position more accurately: " . . . We are not opposed to employers, and it is our purpose and aim to work harmoniously and jointly with the employers as best we can under this system, and we intend to change the system if we get sufficiently organized and well enough educated to do so."[45] In brief, union leaders separated long-term from immediate goals: in the short-run they barely differed from the AFL, but the America they desired for the future was vastly different from and hardly acceptable to the AFL or to the American business community.

Corporate interests in Colorado, like corporations elsewhere in America, would have no compromise with labor for the short run or the

---

[43] 58th Congress; 3rd Session, *Senate Document No. 122*, "A Report on Labor Disturbances in the State of Colorado, from 1880 to 1904" (Washington, 1905), 75-85, 87-101; *Bystander*, September 24, November 26, 1896, February 7, 1897; Rastall, *Cripple Creek*, 37-43; Jensen, *Heritage*, 41-53, 57-59.

[44] *Miners Magazine*, III (January, 1902), 22-23, III (May, 1902), 15-18, IV (February, 1903), 1-3; *W.F.M. Convention Proceedings*, 1902, 17; *American Labor Union Journal*, March 5, 1903, 1; Jensen, *Heritage*, 88-95.

[45] Testimony of Moyer and Haywood, Governor Peabody's Advisory Board, 80, 81, 84, 109, 118.

long run. Company attorneys callously viewed labor as another commodity to be bought and sold in the market place; and company managers denied to unions, the state, and the public the right to intervene in company affairs.[46] Between management's deepest commitments and W.F.M. objectives, compromise was impossible; thus a delicately balanced *modus vivendi* collapsed and a miniature civil war erupted in Colorado's Cripple Creek district in 1903-04.

The W.F.M.'s now clear desire to abolish the prevailing economic system turned previously moderate employers against the union. Employers *might* tolerate and bargain with a labor organization prepared to accept the *status quo,* but not one dedicated to the abolition of capitalism. Nation-wide corporations, local businessmen, and state and national officials united to rid the West of working-class radicalism. Martial law gripped Colorado's mining districts. Military officers made, administered, and executed the law, flaunting with impunity established courts.[47] The W.F.M. Executive Board declared a state of open war in Colorado in December 1903 but still maintained its willingness to compromise: "The W.F. of M. has at all times been ready and willing to go more than half way in meeting the Mine Operators of the State, and use every honorable means to bring a close to this conflict, that has left scars upon the welfare and prosperity of every citizen of the State."[48] Though the W.F.M. preferred negotiation, employers, aware of their unity and strength, crushed the union in Colorado.

*   *   *   *   *   *

Industrial conflicts in the Coeur d'Alenes, Leadville, and Cripple Creek convinced W.F.M. leaders of the need to convert their organization from an industrial union concerned with wages and jobs, into an advocate of revolutionary change and socialism. The W.F.M. had been formed after the first Coeur d'Alene conflict. After the 1896 Leadville debacle, Boyce castigated Gompers and the AFL, called upon union miners to join rifle clubs, and demanded a more radical brand of politics.[49] Then, as both Democrats and Republicans turned against labor and allied with corporate interests while middle-class friends

---

[46] *Ibid.,* 170, 158-195.
[47] "Report on Labor Disturbances in Colorado," 115-282; *Miners Magazine,* IV-V (1903-1904) contains full coverage on the Colorado conflict as seen by the W.F.M.; Jensen, *Heritage,* 127-155.
[48] *Miners Magazine,* V (December 10, 1903), 6.
[49] *Bystander,* May 15, 1897, 4; *Miners Magazine,* I (June, 1900), 41.

deserted it, the W.F.M. became more radical as well as more politically conscious. The organization's adoption of Marxian Socialism (1900-03) finally completed the process of social polarization in the urban-industrial centers of the Mountain West as the W.F.M. lost the remainder of its local middle-class allies. Simultaneously, for the same reasons, the Western labor organizations came into overt conflict with Gompers and the AFL.

Western hostility to Gompers was of long standing, as he had not been forgiven for destroying the Knights of Labor and neglecting the Populists. As early as 1894, when John McBride defeated Gompers for the AFL presidency, the Western Federation's official paper exulted: " . . . good riddance of bad rubbish," and later it accused Gompers of belonging "to that class of leaders which is fast being relegated to the rear—a narrow-minded, self-seeking, and trouble breeding element."[50] During the 1896 Leadville conflict, when AFL assistance to striking miners proved negligible, Boyce and Gompers debated the deficiencies of the AFL and the advantages of radical unionism. Gompers warned Boyce against breaking with the AFL and bringing grief to the house of labor, while Boyce informed the AFL leader that Western workers were 100 years ahead of their Eastern comrades. Thus the W.F.M. at its 1897 convention withdrew from the AFL, to which it had belonged for only a year, and established a rival regional labor organization.[51]

The W.F.M.'s Executive Board in 1898, following similar attempts by Montana's State Trades and Labor Council, invited all Western unions to attend a meeting in Salt Lake City to organize the Western Labor Union.[52] A loyal AFL man described the new Western labor organization to Gompers as " . . . only the Western Federation of Miners under another name. . . . Boyce dominated everything. . . . Boyce's influence with the miners is unquestionably strong. The majority believe him sincerely, and all of them fear to oppose him."[53]

---

50 *Bystander*, December 22, 1894, 2, May 7, 1895, 2.
51 Ed. Boyce to Samuel Gompers, March 16, 1897, Gompers to Boyce, March 26, 1897, Boyce to Gompers, April 7, 1897, Gompers' Statement May 1, 1897 all printed in United States Senate, 56th Congress; 1st Session, *Senate Document No. 42*, "Labor Troubles in Idaho," 8-13; for an uncritical defense of the AFL position see Philip Taft, *The A.F. of L. In The Time of Gompers* (New York, 1957), 150-152.
52 The Salt Lake Meeting was the culmination of a labor conference called in Chicago September 27, 1897 by Eugene Debs to rally all radical labor unionists and believers in solidarity and industrial unionism. *Bystander*, October 16, 1897, 1, November 20, 1897, 2, November 27, 1897, 1; *Miners Magazine I* (January, 1900), 24-26.
53 Walter MacArthur to Gompers, May 20, 1898 quoted in Taft, *AFL In Time of Gompers*, 153. MacArthur's impressions about the miners' sincere belief in Boyce's radicalism

Western workers, during the Salt Lake meeting, stressed their desire
to escape conservative unionism and demanded an industrial, educational, and political organization, uncompromising in policy and
" . . . broad enough in principle and sufficiently humane in character to
embrace every class of toil, from the farmer to the skilled mechanic, in
one great brotherhood."[54] The new Western Labor Union insisted that
industrial technology had made trade-union methods obsolete and left
the working class but one recourse: " . . . to take up the arms of a
modern revolutionary period . . . the free and intelligent use of the
ballot." Thus in 1900 the W.L.U.'s newspaper endorsed the socialist
ticket, and its 1901 convention adopted a preamble and platform denouncing American government, "the very foundations of which is
crumbling to decay, through the corruption and infamy of the self-
constituted governing class. . . ." The W. L. U. professed to be ready to
spill every drop of its blood at the point of a bayonet rather than submit
to further capitalistic aggressions.[55] If the W.L.U. intended to frighten
conservative America, it succeeded.

The differences between the AFL and Western labor grew. Even those
W.F.M. members who favored union with the AFL did so as Western
missionaries, not as true believers in Gompersism; they insisted that
in the face of united capital, labor must do likewise or fail. "We must
try to teach our benighted brothers in the 'jungles of New York' and
[in] the East what we have learned here in the progressive, enterprising
West."[56] This attitude, which represented the more conservative ele-

---

contradicts John McMullen's (leader of W.F.M. conservatives) assertion that the
majority of W.F.M. members were neither radicals nor socialists. Jensen, *Heritage*, 189.

[54] Butte *Reveille*, May 14, 1901, 1; Butte *People*, November 9, 1901, 1; *Miners Magazine*,
II (February, 1901), 31-33.

[55] *Reveille*, September 18, 1900, 6, September 4, 1900, 3, April 23, 1901, 4, April 9, 1901,
4, June 11, 1901, 2.

[56] Press Committee, Local 89, Gilman, Colorado to Editor, December 27, 1901, *Miners
Magazine*, III (February, 1902) 42-43. Another rank and filer seeking a rapprochement
with Eastern labor, criticized pure and simple trade unionism and called upon both
the AFL and the WLU to give way before a new national organization based upon
solidarity and free transfer between craft and craft. He concluded: "If we ever unite
with the East on these broad lines the West must give way first. If we don't they
will continue to place the burden on us and the Western Labor Union." M. F. Coll,
to Editor, *Miners Magazine*, III (April, 1902), 25-26. Of course, I must agree with
Perlman and Taft (*History of United States Labor*, 214-215, 217) that local conditions had something to do with Western dualism, but to concentrate on geographical
peculiarities is to overlook what were real ideological differences. Western workers,
as shown above, had radical backgrounds. They had engaged in partisan political
activity and would continue to do so, and they supported industrial unionism of a
strong social reformist nature. While Western short-run objectives—higher wages,
reduced hours, etc.—did not differ basically from those of AFL unions, their long-run
aims and their avowed opposition to time contracts flaunted basic AFL principles.

ments of the W.F.M., could lead only to conflict. Suddenly AFL organizers appeared in the previously neglected Mountain States to compete with their W.L.U. counterparts.[57] In Denver, AFL organizers tried to destroy W.L.U. locals. Insisting that it had only attempted to organize the unorganized within its territory, the W.L.U., through its Executive Board, informed the AFL that it was too busy battling corporations to seek a fight with another labor organization. "If the officers and members of organized labor will do their duty, the Western Federation of Miners, the Western Labor Union included, there is a broad field for all while ninety per cent of those who toil remain unorganized."[58]

Instead of submitting to the AFL's demands,[59] Western workers became more aggressive. They carefully catalogued the indignities which the W.F.M had borne with extreme patience, but warned: ". . . there comes a time in the history of all such imposition when patience ceases to be a virtue, and this juncture for the Western Federation of Miners has now arrived."[60] In the spring of 1902, when the AFL sent two delegates to the W.F.M. convention urging re-affiliation with the Federation, the W.F.M.'s journal commented: "The Western Federation of Miners and the Western Labor Union are ready to join forces with any labor organization that offers a remedy, but they don't propose to be led like sheep into a slaughter pen to await the butcher's knife without a struggle." Thus the W.F.M., instead of dissolving the W.L.U. and returning to Gompers' waiting arms, transformed the W.L.U. into the American Labor Union and more firmly embraced socialism.[61]

The American Labor Union, considered by Paul Brissenden the climactic development in the evolution of industrial unionism of the political-socialist type,[62] appeared too radical and too revolutionary for some socialists. While party leaders welcomed the A.L.U's endorsement, they deprecated its war upon the AFL, compared the A.L.U. to

[57] In the past the AFL had made no attempts to organize Western workers, thinking it an unpromising possibility. John B. Lennon to Frank Morrison, August 8, 1898, AFL Papers (State Historical Society of Wisconsin); but by 1901 AFL organizers were busy in Denver and other Mountain States cities. Butte *People*, November 16, 1901, 1, November 30, 1901, 1.

[58] *Ibid.*, December 21, 1901, 7; *Miners Magazine*, II (December, 1901), 4-8, III (January, 1902), 10-11.

[59] Disbandment of all "dual" unions in Denver, abolition of W.L.U., and W.F.M. re-affiliation with AFL.

[60] *Miners Magazine*, III (March, 1902), 38-42, (April, 1902), 2-5; Butte *People*, February 12, 1902, 5, March 17, 1902, 1.

[61] *Miners Magazine*, III (June, 1902), 4, 14-16; *The Labor World*, May 19, 1902, 5, June 2, 1902, 1-2, June 9, 1902, 1, 5; *American Labor Union Journal*, November 20, 1902, 1, 4.

[62] Brissenden, *IWW*, 45-46.

DeLeon's infamous Socialist Trades and Labor Alliance, and refused to acknowledge its existence as a recognized national labor organization.[63] The socialist left, however, immediately rose to defend the Westerners. Debs characterized Western labor as militant, progressive, liberal in spirit, with a class-conscious political program. "The class-conscious movement of the West," he wrote, "is historic in origin and development and every Socialist should recognize its mission and encourage its growth. It is here that the tide of social revolution will reach its flood and thence roll into other sections, giving impetus where needed and hastening the glorious day of triumph."[64]

Clearly little room for compromise existed between Western radicals and Eastern labor leaders. The AFL could not allow its Western competitor to enter national organizing territory without suffering potential losses. By the same token, the A.L.U., a declared enemy of capitalism, could not inch closer to the AFL, whose leader it accused of being controlled absolutely by capitalism.[65] Instead the Western radicals defied Gompers, continued to organize the unorganized of the West, and made threatening gestures east of the Mississippi and even of the Hudson. "We believe that the time has arrived when our organization should say in no uncertain language to this band of disruptionists [AFL leaders], 'hands off'," the W.F.M.'s Executive Board announced at the end of 1902. "We have no desire to interfere with their organization and demand that they discontinue their efforts to create disruption in our ranks."[66]

The more radical the W.F.M. became, the more it grew, and the more popular its president became among Western workers. By 1900 the W.F.M. had won the warm backing of Debs, who became more enthusiastic as the Western organization heightened its political consciousness and radicalism. In January 1902, Debs, accepting an invitation to address the coming convention, responded: "I have always felt that your organization is the most radical and progressive national body in

---

[63] G. A. Hoehn, "The American Labor Movement," *International Socialist Review*, III (January, 1903), 410-411; *The Labor World*, August 8, 1902, 3; *Miners Magazine*, III (December, 1902), 33-42; Ira Kipnis, *The American Socialist Movement, 1897-1912* (New York, 1952), 144-145; Nathan Fine, *Labor and Farmer Parties in the United States, 1828-1928* (New York, 1928), 277-278.

[64] Eugene V. Debs, "The Western Labor Movement," *International Socialist Review*, III (November, 1902), 257-265.

[65] *American Labor Union Journal*, October 23, 1902, 2.

[66] *Ibid.*, November 6, 1902, 1, January 1, 1903, 4; *The Labor World*, July 11, 1902, 3, June 5, 1903, 2, July 3, 1903, 1; *Miners Magazine*, III (November, 1902), 23-24, IV (January, 1903), 40-41.

the country, and I have it in my mind that it is to take a commanding part, if it does not lead, in the social revolution that will insure final emancipation to the struggling masses." The 1902 convention made Debs still happier by formally endorsing socialism, founding the American Labor Union and proclaiming, in Boyce's farewell address, "Trade unions have had a fair trial, and it has been clearly demonstrated that they are unable to protect their members."[67]

While union leaders were most responsible for converting the W.F.M. into a socialist organization, the rank and file exhibited no strong reservations about such radicalism, for in a labor organization more democratic than most, ideologically-equivocal officials would have been removed. When Boyce retired, his successor, Charles Moyer, was equally committed to socialism. Moyer immediately reaffirmed the W.F.M.'s commitment to independent political action in "a determined effort to bring about such a change in our social and economic conditions as will result in a complete revolution of the present system of industrial slavery." He found politics and socialism no bar to union growth and in fact claimed that radicalism was responsible for growth in the number of locals and members.[68] Correspondence to the W.F.M.'s journal from rank and filers also showed a heavy preponderance in favor of independent political action and socialism.[69] While the political views of the majority of W.F.M. members are unclear, a significant, literate, and articulate union group certainly evinced an abiding concern for a radical transformation of American society.

* * * * * *

---

[67] *WFM, Convention Proceedings,* 1902, 8-10; *Miners Magazine,* III (July, 1902), 23-33; Debs' quotes are in *ibid.,* III (January, 1902), 16, IV (February, 1903), 37-39.
[68] *WFM, Convention Proceedings,* 1904, 202-203; *Miners Magazine,* IV (July, 1903), 4-5.
[69] While there is apparently no way to quantify the political sentiments of W.F.M. members and thus dispute exists as to the extent of radicalism and socialism in the union, the available evidence suggests strong socialist leanings. The mining-smelter areas, especially Butte and Denver, were the strongest socialist regions in the Mountain West and among the strongest in the nation. The letters-to-the-editor column of the *Miners Magazine* was open to all variety of opinions, even those opposed to official WFM policy, but the bulk of the letters from rank and filers and local unions endorsed either socialism or other forms of independent political action. The testimony of labor leaders and rank-and-file hard-rock miners before a government commission showed overt hostility to capitalism and explicit endorsement of public ownership of the basic means of production. *Capital and Labor in Mining,* 213-214, 246, 255, 362-363. As late as 1906, W.F.M. rank and filers refused to co-operate with the AFL's political programme because it was based on employer-employee harmony. William H. Pierce, Secretary, Randsburg, California Miners' Union to Frank Morrison, July 30, 1906; R. D. Mitchell, John McClunes, David M. Speare, Phoenix, B.C., Miners' Union Committee to Samuel Gompers, August 4, 1906, AFL Papers. An observer to the Cripple Creek labor war and WFM sympathizer, Emma Langdon, pointed out the anti-capitalist bias of the local miners. *Cripple Creek Strike,* 283.

Politics and socialism, however, did not by themselves bring the new dawn. Local battles were won but the employers allied with the older parties controlling state and national governments seemed to be winning the war. "Pure and simple" trade unionism may have failed but seemingly so had socialism. Consequently, just as Populism gave way to socialism and the W.L.U. to the A.L.U., socialism was to give way to syndicalism and the A.L.U. to the I.W.W.

The W.F.M. in 1904, admitting the failure of its two previous attempts at dual unionism, tried for a third time with the Industrial Workers of the World. Much in the same way that the W.L.U. and the A.L.U. had been the Western Federation in disguise, the I.W.W. for two years was simply the Western Federation plus a smattering of fellow-travelers.[70] Though W.F.M. and I.W.W. broke sharply in 1907, the Western Federation could not fully deny its progeny. To an earlier generation of less sophisticated, more provincial Americans, Wobblies appeared the greatest threat to the established order—in short, "a clear and present danger."

The foundation of the Industrial Workers of the World seemed to confirm a prophecy made by Friedrich Engels in 1893. "In America, at least," he wrote, "I am strongly inclined to believe that the fatal hour of capitalism will have struck as soon as a native American working class will have replaced a working class composed in its majority by foreign immigrants."[71] The men who created the I.W.W. were by and large native Americans, or the most Americanized immigrants, committed to interring capitalism in America.[72] In a sense, as Engels prophesied, the most radical working-class movement in American history, the one most feared by capitalists and government officials, came not for alien radicals but from native revolutionaries. And today it remains well worth asking, why?

Though no simple and complete answers are at hand, some facts are apparent. The American West, through an unique conjunction of circumstances produced the conditions most conducive to radical unionism.

---

[70] Brissenden, *IWW*, 57-228, *passim;* Jensen, *Heritage*, 160-196.

[71] Quoted in Pollack, *Populist Response*, 84.

[72] See above, p. 5 for WFM ethnic characteristics. An examination of the trial transcripts (U.S. v. W.D. Haywood, *et. al.*) of the 1918 Chicago Wobbly trials shows that of the I.W.W. leaders who testified about nationality and citizenship over half were citizens, one-third of whom were native-born, and nearly a majority of the aliens came from Great Britain, Ireland, and Canada.

This region's industrialism altered social and economic arrangements more rapidly and drastically than elsewhere in America. Modern technology and corporate capitalism advanced too quickly for smooth adjustment; the rapid pace of economic growth resulted in individual failures and frustrations, social breakdowns, and mob violence. Seeking to stabilize competition, rationalize work processes, and reduce costs, Western corporations encountered a labor force less tractable than the uprooted and ethnically-divided immigrants of the East. The American West, like early industrial England, produced militant and destructive working-class demonstrations. Mining corporations and smelting companies could only control and discipline their workers with assistance from state and federal authorities. The alliance between corporate capitalism and government, which succeeded in polarizing Western society, convinced Western workers that the American nation suffered from grave political and social disorders which could be cured only through revolutionary action. Their past, their experiences, and their hopes for the future shaped Western miners into radicals and revolutionaries.

In a larger sense, however, the development of radical unionism and the emergence of syndicalism in the American West was hardly unique. Simultaneously, thousands of miles removed geographically and farther away socially and spiritually, Italian and French labor organizations declared for syndicalism.[73] The origins of radical unionism in America, France, or Italy thus must be sought in the process of capitalist growth and the larger trends transforming the industrial world. Today we need fewer vague generalizations about the uniqueness or significance of the American frontier and more intensive studies of social and economic structures in the capitalist, industrial, and urban American West. We also need comparative studies placing American labor history in the broader context of world-wide economic history, where all workers, regardless of nationality, tasted the fruits, both bitter and sweet, of the capitalist order.

---

[73] Val R. Lorwin, *The French Labor Movement,* (Cambridge, Massachusetts, 1954), 29-40; Maurice F. Neufeld, *Italy: School for Awakening Countries,* (Ithaca, 1961), 336-338, 352-354.

12

The Passaic Strike of 1912
and the Two I.W.W.s

MICHAEL H. EBNER

The great textile strike of 1926, which has given Passaic, New Jersey,
a significant place in American labor history, was the final, most tragic
act in a fourteen-year saga of industrial disruption in this North Jersey
city. Three major strikes against Passaic's dominant industry, worsted
manufacturing, had preceded it. The first, the subject of this study,
began in March 1912, and soon attracted national attention because of
the involvement of the Industrial Workers of the World.

For several years, beginning in 1909, the I.W.W., or Wobblies, had
been active in several Eastern states; and in January 1912 it had turned
militant attention to the textile workers at Lawrence, Massachusetts, in
a strike which dramatized its ambitious plan to organize Eastern industrial centers. One month later the silk weavers struck at Paterson, five
miles north of Passaic, and the strike soon spread to Passaic where it
became a battleground for conflicting factions of the I.W.W.[1]

Passaic was a rising industrial city by 1912. The arrival of the worsted
manufacturers to the city, beginning in 1889, had been paralleled by
an influx of immigrants. By 1910, when Passaic ranked fourth nationally
in the production of worsted, 52 percent of its 54,773 inhabitants were
foreign-born whites. Four of every five came from Southeastern Europe
or Russia, and most flocked to the worsted mills for jobs. Probably nine-

---

[1] To date the lone scholarly study is: Philip C. Newman, "The I.W.W. in New Jersey,"
(unpublished master's thesis, Columbia University, 1940). His findings are more
readily available in "The First I.W.W. Invasion of New Jersey," *Proceedings,* New
Jersey Historical Society , Vol. 58, No. 4, (October, 1940), 268-283. All references
hereafter are to the latter. My disagreements with the study by Newman are elaborated
upon in subsequent footnotes.

Reprinted from *Labor History* 11 (Fall 1970), 452-66. The author wishes to express his
gratitude to Professor William H. Harbough of the University of Virginia for his advice
in preparing this essay.

tenths of these immigrants settled near the mills, in a section called
"The Eastside," while the Italians alone clustered in a colony near the
center of Passaic.[2]

Prior to 1912 Passaic had been free of mass labor unrest.[3] The United
Textile Workers (U.T.W.), an affiliate of the American Federation of
Labor, showed little disposition to expand its membership there.[4] On
the eve of the 1912 strike, indeed, mills hands in the city were completely unorganized. As a result, the I.W.W. regarded Passaic as unusually fertile ground.

The I.W.W. role in Passaic must be studied in the context of the
internal dissension and suspicion that had plagued it since its founding
convention of 1905.[5] A prime factor was Daniel DeLeon, whose dog-
matism and arrogance were responsible for splitting every major organization in which he participated over his long career.[6] He broke with
the Wobblies in 1908, contending that only if an informed proletarian
union such as the I.W.W. subordinated itself to a political action organization, such as his Socialist Labor Party (S.L.P.), could progress be
made toward reaching a workingmen's utopia. Such a proposition was
anathema to direct-actionists within the I.W.W., who condemned
political action as a palliative when used exclusively in the struggle to
attain the working-class's revolutionary goals. As an official Wobbly

---

[2] *Thirteenth Census of the United States,* Vol. 3, *Population, 1910,* (Washington, 1913),
153, and *Report of the Immigration Commission,* Vol. 17, (Washington, 1911),
315-316.

[3] Brief strikes had occurred as early as 1893 in Passaic's worsted mills, but none resembled
that of 1912, or thereafter, in either magnitude or duration. For an overview of the
situation which the industrial force of the city confronted see Jay Michael Hollander,
"Prelude to a Strike," *Proceedings,* New Jersey Historical Society, Vol. 79, No. 3,
(July, 1961), 161-168, and Martin C. Mooney, "The Industrial Workers of the
World and the Immigrants of Paterson and Passaic, N.J., 1907-1913," (Unpublished
M.A. thesis, Seton Hall University, 1969), 12-44. My doctoral dissertation now in
progress, "Industry & Society in Passaic, New Jersey, 1855-1912: The Paradox of
Quantity and Quality in Post-Civil War City-Building," treats this aspect in further
detail.

[4] David J. Saposs, *Left Wing Unionism, A Study in Radical Politics and Tactics,* (New
York, 1926), 138, writes that after the initial attempt of the United Textile Workers
to organize at Passaic, as well as Lawrence and Paterson, the union lost interest. Henry
Streifler, "Textile Workers Organize," *American Federationist,* (June, 1912), 474-475,
affords some idea of the U.T.W. mentality. Also consult Marion Dutton Savage,
Industrial Unionism in America, (New York, 1922), 250-251.

[5] Don K. McKee, "Daniel DeLeon:: A Reappraisal," *Labor History,* Vol. 1, No. 3, (Fall,
1960), 273. The early career of DeLeon is best examined by Howard H. Quint, *The
Forging of American Socialism: Origins of the Modern Movement,* (Columbia, S.C.,
1953), Chapter 5, 142-147.

[6] In 1896 he forced a split in the Socialist Labor Party which culminated in the formation
of the rival Socialist Party six years later. Thereafter DeLeon's name became synonom-
ous with the S.L.P. and its satellites, although the party was really little more than
a front for his doctrines.

chronicler wrote, the leaders understood after 1907 that "a fight must be made to keep the I.W.W. from becoming a tail to DeLeon's kite."[7] DeLeon's opponents, then, controlling the 1908 convention, barred him as a delegate, ostensibly for improper credentials. And when they struck the political-action phrase from the I.W.W. Preamble, his supporters bolted from the convention, joining him in a new, rival organization. Refusing to give up the name *Industrial Workers of the World,* the DeLeonites established headquarters in Detroit and became known as the Detroit I.W.W. The original organization, with offices in Chicago, was referred to as the Chicago I.W.W.[8]

In any event, the 1912 Passaic strike was one of those rare instances when the Detroit I.W.W. successfully challenged its Chicago rival.[9] While the Chicago faction was involved at Lawrence early in 1912, the DeLeonites entrenched themselves in several North Jersey cities, including Paterson. Indeed, Rudolph Katz, a DeLeon lieutenant, had been trying to organize a Detroit I.W.W. local there since 1910.[10] Paterson silk weavers, meanwhile, had been striking intermittently since November 1911 under U.T.W. direction. Finally, in late February 1912 the Detroit I.W.W. gained leadership of the strikers as 5,000 left work,[11] and thereby fulfilled the prophecy of one of its officials, who after an "agitational tour" of New Jersey in January 1912 had written: "The I.W.W. will make itself felt in Paterson and vicinity. . . ."[12]

Two weeks after the strike began at Paterson, a walk-out occurred in Passaic. Five hundred weavers struck Forstmann & Huffman Mills in

[7] Fred Thompson, *The I.W.W., Its First Fifty Years, 1905-1955,* (Chicago, 1955), 37.
[8] Joseph R. Conlin, *Bread and Roses Too, Studies of the Wobblies,* (Westport, Conn., 1969), 62, contends that: "It was a power struggle between two groups. . . . Both sides publicly espoused the same ideology." Another perspective on the split of 1908 is offered in Melvyn Dubofsky, *We Shall All Be; A History of the Industrial Workers of the World,* (Chicago, 1969), 136-140.
[9] According to Paul F. Brissenden (*The I.W.W., A Study of American Syndicalism,* New York 1957, second ed., second printing), 247), the other strikes led by the Detroit I.W.W. were at Paterson and Easton, Pennsylvania.
[10] For a biographical sketch of Katz see, Solon DeLeon, "Personals," *The Survey,* Vol. 28, No. 21, (August 28, 1912), 677. The author was the son of Daniel DeLeon.
[11] Philip S. Foner, *History of the Labor Movement in the United States,* Vol. 4, *The Industrial Workers of the World, 1905-1917,* (New York, 1965), 353-354, provides the best published account of the 1912 phase of the over-all Paterson strike of 1912-1913. Although Foner considered an impressive array of sources, he did not utilize Lawrence Schliefer, "Prelude to the Paterson General Silk Strike of 1913," (unpublished M.A. thesis, Fairleigh Dickinson University—Rutherford, 1963), esp. 42-43; curiously, however, Schliefer fails to cite the studies done two decades earlier by Newman. A full-scale study of the Paterson strike remains to be undertaken.
[12] The secretary-treasurer of the Detroit I.W.W. wrote this after touring several Eastern cities in January 1912. See, *Industrial Union News,* February 1912, which was the official national organ of the Detroit faction. (I am indebted to the State Historical Society of Wisconsin for allowing me to borrow it on microfilm.)

Passaic and nearby Garfield on the very first day, after management rejected their demand for a uniform daily wage of three dollars. Mill officials, according to a local newspaper, expected "little or no trouble" in warding off a serious strike, but fifty worsted weavers at Gera Mills walked out the next day, and by March 19 nearly 1,600 textile workers were idle.[13]

A Federal commission studying immigrant labor in Passaic around 1910 had reported: "This labor is cheaper than any to be found in the vicinity; it is not organized; it is tractable."[14] *The Survey,* a progressive journal of social workers, strongly criticized the wage system that prevailed in Passaic's worsted industry.[15] Rudolph Katz sarcastically quipped, "The Botany Mill in Passaic—there is no place in the United States or the Chinese empire where wages are lower in comparison with the amount of work produced."[16] But after investigating such claims, the *Newark Evening News* concluded that they were exaggerated, and the *Passaic Daily News,* which was usually sympathetic to the strikers' cause, concurred.[17] Finally, an agent of the state immigration commission verified the findings of the Newark paper.[18] But a wage analysis of the industry reveals that while Passaic wages compared favorably with national averages in the textile industry, they were still far below daily earnings in such industries as rubber, glass, boots, shoes, and leather.[19]

From the beginning, then, Detroit I.W.W. organizers worked among the strikers, although it cannot be precisely determined what role they played before the strike began.[20] On March 13, the evening preceding the strike, Henry Zahler, an agent of the Paterson local, had addressed

---

[13] *Passaic Daily Herald,* March 13 & 14, 1912, hereafter cited as *PDH; Passaic Daily News,* March 13, 19 & 20, 1912, hereafter cited as *PDN.* (Both are available in The Forstmann Public Library of Passaic.) Hereafter, unless otherwise noted, all newspaper citations are for the year 1912.

[14] *Report of the Immigration Commission,* 335.

[15] "A New Jersey Weaver, A Budget and a Gospel of Revolution," *The Survey,* Vol. 28, No. 7, (May 18, 1912), 289-291.

[16] *Final Report and Testimony Submitted to Congress by the Commission on Industrial Relations,* Vol. 3, Senate Document No. 415, 64th Congress, 1st Session, (Washington, 1916), 2478.

[17] As quoted in *PDN,* April 17.

[18] *Report of the Commission of Immigration of the State of New Jersey,* Appointed Pursuant to the Provisions of Chapter 362 of the Laws of 1911, (Trenton 1914), 75.

[19] Albert Rees, *Real Wages and Manufacturing, 1890-1914,* (Princeton, 1961), Table 13, 44-55. This table is based in part on studies of statistics on the state of New Jersey.

[20] *Thirty-fifth Annual Report,* The Bureau of Statistics of Labor and Industries of New Jersey for the Year Ending October 31st, 1912, (Camden, 1913), 227. Newman ("The First I.W.W. Invasion . . .," 281) specifically commented that before March 14 organizers were active in Passaic. He failed, however, to cite his sources, leading me to believe that he accepted the Bureau's account cited above at face value.

disgruntled mill hands in a Passaic hall.[21] To be sure, professional organizers such as Zahler influenced the strikers to escalate their demands beyond the quest for higher pay. "The principal feature of the demands besides an increase in wages," said one strike leader, "is the recognition of the 'shop committee'."[22]

On March 20, Boris Reinstein stepped onto the stage center. Passaic papers for this day reported for the first time that one "Mr. Rheinstein" was speaking at meetings of the Detroit I.W.W.[23] A Russian immigrant who had fled the Tsar's police, Reinstein came to the United States in 1901 and settled at Buffalo where he operated a drug store. There he joined DeLeon's S.L.P., and soon became a party leader. Fluency in English, Polish, German, and Russian prepared him for his future role at Passaic.[24] Two days after arriving in the city, Reinstein claimed that the I.W.W. had appropriated the name of his union. He soon became the central figure in the strike, tangling with anyone whom he considered an enemy of the working class—sheriffs, municipal officials, mill owners, Big Bill Haywood and the Chicago I.W.W., and even some of the strikers![25]

Passaic's strike, unlike that at Lawrence, never reached industry-wide proportions.[26] At best, workers in an entire department within a particular mill would simultaneously walk out. The weavers proved especially willing to follow Detroit's I.W.W. organizers. This faction established strike headquarters in the heart of the immigrant district and developed standard procedures. A rally, presided over by an organizer such as Reinstein or Zahler, would be held on the evening before a specific group of mill hands planned to submit its list of demands to management. Representatives of participating groups would exhort their countrymen, in their native tongue, to follow DeLeon's teachings and refrain from violence against management. At the first such assembly, speeches were delivered in Polish, Hungarian, Italian, German, and Ruthenian. The next morning a delegation of workers

[21] *PDH,* March 14; *Testimony Submitted by the Commission on Industrial Relations,* Vol. 3, 2638.

[22] *PDH,* March 22.

[23] *PDH,* March 20.

[24] Reinstein returned to Russia in 1917, and remained there as a functionary in various government and party capacities. In 1922, he returned briefly to the United States as an emissary to the secret Communist Party conclave at Bridgeman, Michigan. See, Theodore Draper, *The Roots of American Communism,* (New York, 1957), 148-149. Rumor has it that Reinstein was executed in Moscow during the 1938 purge.

[25] *PDN,* March 22; *PDH,* March 25; and, *Industrial Union News,* May.

[26] For an account of the strike at Lawrence consult, Donald B. Cole, *Immigrant City, Lawrence, Massachusetts, 1845-1921,* (Chapel Hill, 1963), 177-194.

would present the group's demands to management; if it refused to accede, a strike began.[27]

At first the mill owners regarded the walkout lightly. Nevertheless, Reinstein claimed that Forstmann & Huffman would only discuss terms with their employees *after* they had returned to work, and the company did actually shut down its operation on March 25. "We shall keep the mills closed several weeks to give them a chance to cool off," the president of the firm announced. The unrest, he added, was caused by agitators "from the West." Meanwhile, the *Passaic Daily News* editoralized that, because wages were so low in the city, management must consider the strikers' demands "in a proper spirit," lest there be violence.[28]

The walkout received encouragement on March 26, when Botany Worsted Mills's owner rejected the demands of 400 of the company's 1,000 weavers. Two days earlier the company's superintendent had boasted, "We have never dealt with unions and never will." And the day before the walkout Botany was reported ready to hear grievances from all employees not represented by outside interests. Then, when the weavers left the mill on the morning of March 26, violence flared for the first time and six were injured, including four women. The conservative New York *Herald* even compared this incident in intensity to the riots at Lawrence.[29] Charging "ruffianism," *Industrial Union News,* the national organ of the Detroit I.W.W., placed the blame on Botany's private detectives. Meanwhile, the *Passaic Daily News* urged, in a rare front-page editorial, that detectives and municipal police should be "extremely cautious" thereafter. "Jersey Strikers Slugged by Thugs," was the headline of the Socialist Party's *The Call* of New York.[29] The Commission in Industrial Relations in effect confirmed the charge. In its final report, the Commission found that violence such as that at Botany was in fact caused by the "stronger party"—management.[30]

The climax of the strike came on March 29, fifteen days after it had begun, when approximately 40 percent of the 9,590 textile workers in Passaic area worsted mills were idle.[31] "The streets in the Eastside Sec-

[27] Savage, *op. cit.,* 254, stresses the importance of ethnic unity in the textile unions. Also see, *PDN,* March 19 & 20; and, *PDH,* March 14, 15 & 20.
[28] *PDN,* March 14 & 28; *PDH,* March 25; and, *The Call* (New York), March 25-28. (*The Call* is on microfilm at Tamiment Institute Library, New York City).
[29] *PDH, PDN, The Call, NY Herald,* March 25-27; also, *Industrial Union News,* May, dispatch dated March 26, Passaic. Cole (*op. cit.,* 179-183) notes that the strike at Lawrence was "not unusually violent." Nevertheless, one cannot deny that the city was the symbol of labor unrest at the time.
[30] *Final Report of the Commission on Industrial Relations,* (Washington, 1915), 140.
[31] The number of textile workers in the Passaic area, 9,590, was the figure given in, *Thirty-*

tion of Passaic have the appearance of one of New York's busy streets,"
the local press reported. Yet the city remained calm, perhaps because
of the mayor's admonitions to strikers and mill owners alike.[32]

The Detroit I.W.W.'s control of the strike went almost unchallenged
by its Chicago rival until March 27, when the Lawrence walkout ended.
To be sure, James P. Thompson, the general organizer for the Chicago
I.W.W.'s textile section, had been in Passaic on March 19 and 23.[33]
But the two I.W.W.s clashed four days later, when Edmondo Rossoni,
a New York-based agitator allied with the Chicago faction (and later
a leader in Mussolini's fascist labor federation), urged the strikers to
coerce those still working into joining them. At a rally of the same day
sponsored by the Detroit faction about sixty Italian men and women
bolted from the hall, objecting to the DeLeonist policy of non-violence
that a fellow countrymen advocated. "What are we going to do to
win?," they chanted. "We must use violence to get the others out. . . ."
A similar incident occurred when Boris Reinstein told an audience that
included many Italians, "You must not listen to any talk of physical
violence. . . ."[34]

Another factor, and probably a more important one, in the Italian
revolt against the Detroit I.W.W. was the news from Lawrence. More
than any other ethnic group there, the Italian workers had supported
the Chicago I.W.W. Unquestionably, victory in Lawrence inspired
Italian dissidents in Passaic. A group of them told the Passaic press that
upon leaving work they had been assured by union leaders that a wage
increase would be forthcoming within a week. After two weeks, however, their goal still had not been realized; so they had begun to urge
direct-action tactics in the hope of attaining it. Their response to the
Chicago I.W.W. was heightened on March 29, when Boris Reinstein
removed Frank Pless Domo, who was competing with him for leadership, as the treasurer of the Detroit faction's Passaic local. Domo had
been elected on March 15, and viewed his rival, who had arrived at
Passaic four days later, as an interloper. Clearly, Reinstein blundered in
ousting him. For no matter what the issues, he should have understood
the cost of alienating a segment of the immigrant community. Now

---

fifth Annual Report, 238. Reinstein reported that 4,000 were out, see *PDN*, March 29.
The New York Times, March 27, estimated that between 3,500-4,000 were idle. Of
course it should be recalled that the number included non-strikers who had been
forced out of work when mills closed.
[32] *PDH*, March 25 & 27.
[33] *PDH*, March 20 and *PDN*, March 23.
[34] *PDH* and *PDN*, March 28-29.

national prejudices had been aroused, and they overshadowed the real problem of winning the strike.[35]

Rumors began to circulate that a settlement was pending at the time that the Chicago I.W.W. became involved. "A citizen who has been working for a strike agreement" stated the *Passaic Daily Herald* on March 28, "reports a settlement in the next few days advantageous to all the workers." The terms, it was rumored, included an industry-wide wage increase and a pledge from the companies that they would not discriminate against workers who had joined the I.W.W.

Apparently the "citizen" working to end the strike was the city's postmaster. Revealing himself in a letter-to-the-editor, he liberally praised the strikers and manufacturers alike, urging that good will prevail. The mill owners, he stated, had assured him that they would match the pay raise given at Lawrence, although they would not recognize what he termed "non-resident agitators." Henry Zahler replied that the shop committees would have to be recognized before any settlement on wages was agreed upon. To this demand the *Passaic Daily News* responded with a prudent editorial cautioning the strikers not to be completely uncompromising. Also, the Botany superintendent toured his firm's mill, in what the press termed a demonstration of good faith, to hear the grievances of those still working. He promised that their demands for increased wages and better working conditions would be met within one week.[36] But such professions ignored the shop committee issue, which the striker leaders so ardently championed.

Several factors, therefore, converged at the beginning of April, which would determine the strike's ultimate success or failure. First, the Detroit I.W.W., which had directed the strike from the start, was losing control. Next, the Chicago I.W.W. seemed to afford disgruntled strikers such as the Italians an alternate route to victory. Finally, the concession which management was apparently about to offer meant that the strike leaders so ardently championed.

Beginning on March 29, the local press repeatedly charged that immigrant strikers were being deceived by the I.W.W. The newspapers alleged that the proposals of the manufacturers were being misrepresented in non-English speeches at strike rallies. Also, some mill officials

---

[35] The day after the removal of Domo more than 500 Italians met with James P. Thompson to form a local of the Chicago I.W.W., but from available evidence it cannot be determined whether the local was really organized. See, *PDH* & *PDN*, March 29-April 1.

[36] *PDH* and *PDN*, March 28-30. The letter was on the front page rather than the editorial page, where letters normally appeared in the *PDH*.

charged—probably accurately—that in some instances employees were
not reporting to work because they had been intimidated by the strikers.
The *Passaic Daily News* correctly observed that "there seems to be more
or less trouble among the strikers themselves."[37]

Two days later, on April 1, Gera Mills and Forstmann & Huffman
Company announced that all their employees who returned to work the
next morning would receive a 5-10 percent pay hike. Both companies
also pledged that they would not discriminate against workers who had
joined the union, but their spokesmen declared that neither shop committees nor unions would be recognized. In addition, Forstmann &
Huffman warned that should any of their striking employees not return, "we shall be forced to fill their places with other workers." Boris
Reinstein replied vituperatively, charging that the strikers must be dealt
with collectively, or "they will stay on strike until the companies come
around to this point of view."[38]

The strikers failed to respond to management's terms. Indeed, they
turned out in large numbers early on the morning of April 2 to protest
against these terms. "We will not return until the shop committee is
recognized," claimed a strike leader—which statement, *The Call* of
New York contended, gave the mill owners "the jolt of their lives."[39]
By forcing at least two of the struck companies to offer any settlement
at all, the Detroit I.W.W. had gained in prestige. Such gains were important; for, in addition to the battle against the mill owners, a struggle
of growing proportion was now being fought within the ranks of the
strikers.

During the first week of April, the Chicago I.W.W. made a bold
attempt to wrest strike leadership from its rival. In addition to James
P. Thompson, who had come to Passaic a week earlier, Big Bill Haywood now briefly lent his talents to the cause. Haywood was already
notorious. "A good talker and equipped with a personality just sufficient
to shake the red flag, and gather others to cheer it,"[40] he had, since
1909, devoted much of his time to the immigrant masses in the Eastern
industrial centers.[41] His career, one historian has written, led the public
to view him as "the very epitome of all that was dangerous about

[37] *PDN*, March 30.
[38] *PDH*, April 1; *The New York Times* and *The Call*, April 2.
[39] *PDN*, April 2 and *The Call*, April 4.
[40] Hezekiah N. Duff, "The I.W.W.'s: What They Are and What They Are Doing," *Square Deal*, Vol. 10, (May, 1912), 299.
[41] Dubofsky, *op. cit.*, 233, and Joseph R. Conlin, *Big Bill Haywood & The Radical Union Movement*, (Syracuse, 1969), 130-147.

radicalism."[42] Noting his arrival, the *Passaic Daily News* commented that, "flushed with his success at Lawrence, Haywood came here like a conquering hero. . . ." He spoke only once during the strike, to a meeting of immigrant workers, a majority of them Italian, at Garfield on April 2.[43] "Organize like they did [at Lawrence]," Haywood told them, "and stand by each other no matter what happens and they won't be able to break your strike. . . ."[44]

Without exaggeration the *Passaic Daily News* reported that "the coming of Haywood has spread a general feeling of alarm." Both local dailies editoralized against him and the Chicago I.W.W.[45] Within three days after his Garfield speech, strikers skirmished twice with police cordons at the Forstmann & Huffman mills. But the *Daily News* belittled as "grossly exaggerated" an Associated Press dispatch reporting a "serious clash."[46]

But the second incident at Garfield, on April 5, was quite serious. After Charles Rothfisher, editor of the Chicago I.W.W.'s Hungarian-language newspaper, had addressed a group in his native tongue, a riot of sorts did take place. When order was restored, after a volley of rifle shots had been fired over the strikers' heads, one sheriff's deputy was found to be seriously hurt, having been hit by a rock. Strikers had also been injured, as the police had liberally used clubs to subdue them.[47] When Rothfisher was convicted for inciting violence and sentenced to ten days in jail, his plight won sympathetic notice in the radical press as far away as Seattle.[48]

The *Passaic Daily Herald,* after the first incident, had urged editorially that area police "act with firmness." The county sheriff read the plea literally. He proclaimed the so-called Riot Act of New Jersey in effect on April 4 to prevent the Chicago faction from holding further assemblies in Garfield. Barred in Garfield, the direct-actionists planned

---

[42] Morris Schonbach. *Radicals and Visionaries: A History of Dissent in New Jersey,* (Princeton, 1964), 56.

[43] *PDN,* April 3. But, Newman writes ("The First I.W.W. Invasion . . .," 283), again without documentation: "The outbreak was hardly a day old when William D. Haywood and several other organizers of the Chicago I.W.W. appeared on the scene and attempted to wrest the leadership away from the Detroit faction"; this, however, remains unfounded.

[44] *PDH,* April 2; *PDN,* April 3; and, *Solidarity,* April 20. The latter was the official organ of the Chicago I.W.W. in the East. ((It is available at the Library of Congress.)

[45] *PDH* and *PDN,* April 3.

[46] *PDN,* April 3 and *PDH,* April 4.

[47] *PDH,* April 5 and *The New York Times,* April 6.

[48] In an article which revealed that conservative newspapers had no monopoly on distorting news, the Western organ of the Chicago I.W.W., *Industrial Worker,* April 11, commented that Rothfisher had been jailed in *Passaic* for his efforts among the *silk* workers. (This newspaper is on microfilm at the Tamiment Institute Library.)

to move across the county line into Passaic, which one of their number called "the camp of the enemy." Passaic's director of public safety was reported ready to close all the city's meeting halls, but before he could act Boris Reinstein and James P. Thompson confronted each other at a rally sponsored by the Detroit I.W.W. Thompson told the audience: "Stand together now while under the fire of the enemy. Win this fight for a living wage and when it is over and settled join whichever union you wish." Reinstein was quoted as having approved cooperation with his rival, but the following day he "vehemently" denied this. Perhaps more than anything else, Passaic citizens feared that the two factions might battle each other in their city, clouding its image. The president of the local pastor's association offered his organization's help in working for a solution to the strike. The Board of Commissioners even considered, but finally rejected, a bid from a public relations agency which wanted to write *undistorted* news releases about the city. Such fears proved to be unwarranted, however, inasmuch as the week ended without the arrest of a single striker in the city, much less any violence.[49]

Although Passaic remained relatively calm, the out-of-town press tended to distort news of the strike.[50] The *Newark Evening Star* had an especially broad coverage of events at Passaic. That newspaper was the mouthpiece of former United States Senator James Smith, Jr., an outspoken opponent among state Democratic leaders of the presidential hopes of Governor Woodrow Wilson of New Jersey.[51] Certainly, if the *Evening Star* had succeeded in invoking public fears of a battle between the two I.W.W.s in Passaic, Governor Wilson would have encountered a delicate situation that might possibly have tarnished his national image.[52]

[49] *PDH*, April 3-4 and *PDN*, April, 5-6.
[50] For instance, "Labor Controversies," *The Independent*, Vol. 72, No. 3006, (New York, April 11, 1912), 761. According to this article, "There have been riots at Passaic, New Jersey, where striking silk workers are being led by William D. Haywood."
[51] Arthur S. Link, *Wilson, he Road to the White House*, (Princeton, 1947), 169n., confirms that the *Evening-Star* was favorable to Smith. On April 3, for instance, the *Evening-Star* carried a picture of Haywood entitled, "William D. Haywood, Who Is Leading the Passaic Strike." Also, a picture of Haywood, Thompson, Rothfisher, and Domo appeared in several newspapers as credited to the *Evening-Star*, such as *PDH*, April 15. Later it also appeared in H. S. Randolph, "The I.W.W.," *Common Cause*, Vol. 1, No. 5, (May, 1912), 3.
[52] This possibility was raised by Rudolph Katz in 1914, and may be found in *Testimony Submitted by the Commission on Industrial Relations*, Vol. 3, 2478. On April 1, Smith had openly announced his support for the principal rival of Governor Wilson, Champ Clark of Missouri. Immediately thereafter, Smith initiated two months of political manuevers aimed at embarassing Wilson in New Jersey. But the Governor won the New Jersey primary on May 28, gaining twenty of the twenty-four convention delegates. See, Link, *op. cit.*, 424-426. Schleifer, *op. cit.* 39, notes that in July, 1912,

The anti-Wilson camp had a real and growing issue. The publicist Justus Ebert wrote in *Solidarity*, the voice of the Chicago faction in the East, of Reinstein's complicity against the direct-actionists in Passaic. Ebert may have exaggerated the details, but his conclusions seem plausible. Another report in *Solidarity* stated that Reinstein was "working in collusion with the police," and this charge similarly carried more truth than fantasy. Indeed, after the second incident at Garfield, on April 5, Reinstein had met with Passaic's director of public safety to discuss the presence of Bill Haywood in the city. The director was quoted as saying after that conference that "Haywood and his men will not be allowed in Passaic." That very day, in fact, James P. Thompson informed the press that he was unable to rent a hall there. From so-called "authentic sources" it was learned that if Thompson or Haywood attempted to speak in the city they would be arrested, while the local police chief boasted that "Haywood's people would have the time of their lives to get a hall in Passaic." Thompson threatened to challenge the Passaic authorities, claiming that Governor Wilson, "with his political ambitions," could hardly afford to deny the I.W.W. "the right of free speech."[53]

Boris Reinstein's action proved to be another attempt on his part to preserve his position as leader, but again he had merely succeeded in dividing the ranks. Not only did he unduly alarm municipal officials, he also alienated the Socialist Party's Passaic local, which previously had maintained neutrality in the fight between the rival Wobbly factions. This local had a considerable following at the time, and even published a weekly newspaper, *The Issue*.[54] Its membership convened on April 7 to consider the existing situation, and it decided to withdraw all support from the Detroit I.W.W. unless Reinstein agreed to cooperate with the Chicago faction. Reinstein replied negatively, thereby losing the support of Passaic's Socialists.[55]

The Call of April 8 included a report that dealt yet another blow to

---

Governor Wilson did meet with a delegation of strike leaders from Paterson regarding the jailing of Katz over an incident that had taken place in that city. Wilson told them that he was powerless to deal with the case.

[53] *PDH*, April 5; *PDN* and *The Call*, April 6; and, *Solidarity*, April 20.
[54] I have been unable to locate copies of *The Issue*. Evidence of the Socialist Party's local area strength was seen in the general election of 1911, when the party gained over 5% of the total Passaic County vote and thus, as provided by state law, became an official political party with the right to have a line on the ballot. See, *PDH*, November 14, 1911.
[55] *PDN*, April 8-10; *Industrial Union News*, May, dispatch dated April 9, Passaic; and, *The Call*, April 9.

Reinstein's reputation. James P. Thompson accused him of aiding the
mill owners, when he urged the director of public safety to ban the
Chicago faction from Passaic. (The restraining order was rescinded at
the time that *The Call* article circulated around Passaic.) The director
of public safety admitted that Boris Reinstein had originally influenced
him regarding the reputation of Big Bill Haywood. Reinstein himself
confessed to counselling the police that the Chicago I.W.W. advocated
violence. Justus Ebert rightly concluded in *Solidarity* that Passaic
manufacturers were bent on smashing the Wobblies. They disliked
Haywood, Thompson, and the Chicago faction more than Detroit's because they advised the workers on how to organize rather than because
they advocated violence.[56]

Increasing factionalism diminished the strikers' hopes. Their walkout
was now in its declining stage, nearly a month after it had begun. The
Passaic Daily News once again editorialized, in bold print, "It is high
time for the operators to consider this situation from the standpoint
of justice. . . ." But the strike was suffering from lack of direction. A
group of weavers reached a settlement with Forstmann & Huffman,
disregarding the advice of Boris Reinstein. The next day, however,
Reinstein claimed that the 5-15 percent wage increase constituted a
compromise victory. But the staid *New York Times* thought differently:
"unless William D. Haywood . . . comes here quickly and whips the
strikers into line the strike of the mill workers here is broken." Reinstein, however, remained outwardly optimistic, contradicting those who
claimed that the strike had already been lost.[57]

The Detroit I.W.W. never regained the allegiance of the strikers in
Passaic; and attempts to do so through parades and free meals failed
to curb the growing disenchantment. Italian and Hungarian strikers,
for instance, voiced their disapproval of Reinstein, and meetings sponsored by agents of the Chicago I.W.W. drew larger audiences than
those of the Detroit faction. Although Reinstein continued to speak of
progress, the strikers were returning to work in greater numbers. By
April 22, only two companies were still affected by the strike. "As far
as Passaic is concerned," the police chief concluded, "the textile strike
is about over." Reinstein admitted as much on April 25, and the next
day he urged the remaining strikers to return to work. But when queried

---

[56] *The Call*, April 8-9; and, *Solidarity*, April 13. Also consult Josdeph Conlin, "The
I.W.W. and the Question of Violence," *Wisconsin Magazine of History*, Vol. 51, No.
4, (Spring, 1968), 316-326.
[57] *PDN*, April 10-11; *PDH*, April 10-12; and *The New York Times*, April 11.

by the press he refused to rule the strike a failure: "Well, I count it a compromise victory, but if the strikers stuck together as I often told them, they would receive still more of an increase and better conditions." On May 3, Reinstein departed from Passaic, leaving behind a final reminder to the workers that they should stick together.[58]

Industrial Union News blamed the collapse of the strike on "the dirty work of that mean, contemptible conglomeration of slummists— the Chicago I.W.W." Conversely, *Solidarity* attacked the Detroit faction, especially "drugstore keeper Boris Reinstein," who had allowed the strike to "fizzle out."[59] But the newspaper of Passaic's Socialist Party local, *The Issue,* touched on the critical shortcoming of Reinstein's leadership when it charged that he had been more concerned with defeating Bill Haywood than with concentrating on the strikers' goals.[60] In short, Reinstein had continued to fight the battle Daniel DeLeon lost at the 1908 convention of the I.W.W. Indeed, the New Jersey Bureau of Statistic's summation was perhaps the strike's most accurate epitaph: "The wage loss as reported by several concerns amount to $119,000, and as all returned to work under practically the same conditions . . . the entire movement was a very costly failure."[61]

Passaic workingmen suffered most during this strike. Some workers lost three weeks of wages. All the hands of Forstmann & Huffman, Gera Mills, and the New Jersey Worsted Spinning Company were locked-out for at least one week, even though some did not support the strike. Little evidence remains that would shed light on the post-strike attitude of the workingmen, but certainly a sense of frustration is evident as early as the last week in March. Passaic and Garfield workers were idle a total of 116,675 days in 1912 due to strikes; in 1913, the number plummeted to forty. Even during the mammoth strike of 1913 in nearby Paterson, the workers of Passaic and Garfield remained on their jobs.[62]

How might the strike have ended more profitably for the workers? To attribute its failure to the entry of the Chicago faction would seem to be a mistake. Even before James P. Thompson began agitating, striker

---

[58] *The New York Times,* April 10; *The Call,* April 10-11; *PDH,* April 10. 16, 17, 26 and May 4; *PDN,* April 10-13, 16, 18, 23, 25; and *Industrial Union News,* May 4.
[59] *Industrial Union News,* June & *Solidarity,* May 11.
[60] Article from *The Issue* (no date given), as reprinted by *Solidarity,* May 11.
[61] *Thirty-fifth Annual Report,* 238.
[62] *Ibid.,* 268; and, *Thirty-Sixth Annual Report,* The Bureau of Statistics of Labor and Industries of the State of New Jersey for the Year Ending October 31st, 1913, (Paterson, 1914), 312.

dissatisfaction over the role of Boris Reinstein was evident. For dissenters such as Frank Pless Domo and his fellow Italians, the Chicago I.W.W. provided an alternate course. But no sooner had the direct-actionists gained a toehold in Passaic and Garfield, than Reinstein resorted to the very scare tactics which future opponents of the Wobblies would utilize. Reinstein, as the dominant force of the Detroit I.W.W. in Passaic, clearly foreclosed the possibility for even a temporary united front of the rivals. Thus, Thompson, sensing defeat, openly stated in the waning days of the strike, "I will not interfere or bother with the strike in Passaic."[63]

But adept leadership was essential if the immigrant masses in the East were to be successfully organized. Boris Reinstein, however, like so many in the radical union movement, did not possess talents adequate for the task which he took on in Passaic. He did, to be sure, arouse the workers in the worsted industry for the first time. But he lacked the sensibility for a more pragmatic approach that would yield permanent economic benefits for more than 9,000 textile hands.[64] Nevertheless, it would be rash to conclude that an alliance of the two I.W.W.s in Passaic would have spelled victory. Economic necessity, in the form of four weeks without wages, compelled even the most dedicated striker to return to work. It is difficult to deny, in the final analysis, that Reinstein complicated an already complex situation when he deviously attempted to undermine the opposition.

In spite of the immediate defeat, the 1912 strike at Passaic did have some influence on the minds of the strikers. The lessons learned educated them for future protest efforts. Many of the methods of the I.W.W.s introduced in 1912 were apparent in the strikes at Passaic in 1916, 1919 and 1926.[65]

---

[63] *PDH*, April 11, and *The Call*, April 12.

[64] Saposs, *op. cit.*, 142-143, 154-163.

[65] See, for instance, Savage, *op. cit.*, 250-264; and, Morton Siegel, "The Passaic Textile Strike of 1926," (unpublished doctoral dissertation, Columbia University, 1952), *passim:* and, Esther Liberman, "The Influence of Left-Wing Radicalism in Paterson Silk Strikes of 1912-1913 and the Passaic Woolen Strike of 1926," (unpublished undergraduate honors essay, Brooklyn College — C.U.N.Y., May, 1963; on deposit in New Jersey Collection of Rutgers University Library — New Brunswick), *passim.* (I join the growing list of historians who now are indebted to Mrs. Liberman for allowing them to photocopy her manuscript.)

13

Organizing the Unorganizable:
Three Jewish Women and Their Union

ALICE KESSLER-HARRIS

Women who were actively engaged in the labor struggles of the first part of this century faced a continual dilemma. They were caught between a trade union movement hostile to women in the work force and a women's movement whose participants did not work for wages. To improve working conditions for the increasing numbers of women entering the paid labor force, organizers painstakingly solicited support from labor unions that should have been their natural allies. At the same time, they got sympathetic aid from well-intentioned women with whom they otherwise had little in common. The wage-earning women who undertook the difficult task of organizing their co-workers also faced yet another problem: they had to reconcile active involvement in labor unionism with community traditions that often discouraged worldly roles.

Understanding how women who were union organizers experienced these tensions tells us much about the relationships of men and women within unions and throws into relief some of the central problems unionization posed for many working women. It also reveals something of what feminism meant for immigrant women. Evidence of conscious experience, frequently hard to come by, exists in the papers of three women who organized for the International Ladies Garment Workers Union: Pauline Newman, Fannia Cohn, and Rose Pesotta. All were Jews working for a predominately Jewish organization. Their careers span the first half of the twentieth century. Taken together, their lives reveal a persistent conflict between their experiences as women and their tasks as union officers. Their shared Jewish heritage offers insight into the ways

Reprinted from *Labor History* 17 (Winter 1976), 5-23. This paper is a revised draft of one presented at the Conference on Class and Ethnicity in Women's History, SUNY, Binghamton, Sept. 21-22, 1974. The author gratefully acknowledges the generous support of the Louis H. Rabinowitz foundation.

women tried to adapt familiar cultural tradition to the needs of a new world.

Like most of the women they represented, Newman, Cohn and Pesotta were born in Eastern Europe. Cohn and Newman emigrated as children before the turn of the century, Pesotta as a teenager in 1913. In the United States, poverty drove them to the East Side's garment shops. There they worked in the dress and waist industry, a rapidly expanding trade in which Jewish workers predominated until the 1930s, and in which women made up the bulk of the work force.[1]

Their experience was in many ways typical. Among immigrant Jews in New York, Philadelphia, Boston, and other large cities only the exceptional unmarried woman did not operate a sewing machine in a garment factory for part of her young adult life.[2] In the old country, where jobs were scarce, daughters were married off as fast as possible. In America they were expected to work, for the family counted on their contributions. Many young girls emigrated as teenagers to go to an uncle or older sister who would help them to find a job so that a part of their wages could be sent back to Europe.[3] The wages of others helped to pay the rent, to buy food and clothing, to bring relatives to America, and to keep brothers in school. An eldest daughter's first job might mean a larger apartment for the family—"a dream of heaven itself accomplished." [4] When they married, young women normally stopped working in the

[1] In 1913, 56.56% of the workers in the industry were Jews and 34.35% were Italian. 70% or more were women. See Hyman Berman, "Era of the Protocol: A Chapter in the History of the International Ladies Garment Workers Union, 1910-1916" (unpublished PhD diss. Columbia Univ., 1956), pp. 22 and 24. Jewish women were much more likely to be working inside a garment shop than were Italian women who often preferred to take work home. 53.6% of all employed Jewish women were in the garment industry in 1900. Nathan Goldberg, *Occupational Patterns of American Jewry*, (N.Y., 1947), p. 21. The relative proportion of women in the garment industry declined between 1900 and 1930. In addition to dresses and waists, women were heavily employed on kimonos, housedresses, underwear, children's clothing, and neckwear. Melvyn Dubovsky, *When Workers Organize: New York City in the Progressive Era*, (Amherst, 1968), p. 73 ff has a good description of conditions in the garment industry.

[2] The industry was characterized by the rapid turnover of its employees. In 1910 about 50% of the dress and waist makers were under 20 years old. The best estimate is that less than 10% of the women working on dresses and waists were married. See U.S. Senate, 61st Congress, 2nd Session. *Abstracts of the Report of the Immigration Commission*, Doc. #747, 1911, Vol. II, p. 336; Berman, p. 23.

[3] The proportion of women in the Jewish immigration between 1899 and 1910 was higher than in any other immigrant group except the Irish. See Samuel Joseph, *Jewish Immigration to the U.S., 1881-1910* (N.Y., 1914), p. 179. This can be accounted for in part by the high proportion of family emigration, and in part by the numbers of young women who came to America without their parents, to work. Rose Pesotta, Rose Cohn, Emma Goldman fall into this category.

[4] Unpublished autobiography #92, YIVO archives. See also #160, p. 8; Etta Byer, *Transplanted People* (Chicago, 1905), p. 28.

garment shops. As in the old country, they were still expected to contribute to family income. Married women often took in boarders, helped in their husbands' businesses, or ran small shops.

A combination of factory work before marriage and the expectation of a different kind of paid labor afterwards, presented problems for Jewish women, who, like Newman, Cohn, and Pesotta wanted to take advantage of the new world's possibilities. Women who earned wages could dream of self-sufficiency.[5] Adolescents hoped that the transition to America would bring about a previously unknown independence and offer them new and different roles. Rose Pesotta (the name had been changed from Peisoty) arrived in America in 1913, aged 17. She had left Russia, she said, because she could "see no future for [herself] except to marry some young man ... and be a housewife. That [was] not enough.... In America a decent middle class girl [could] work without disgrace."[6]

Expectations of independent self-assertion were frustrated when marriage intervened and women were confined to more restricted roles. But aspirations towards upward mobility may have provided the death blow. The legendary rapidity of Jewish economic success perhaps did women a disservice by encouraging husbands to deprive their wives of the limited economic roles marriage permitted—contributing, incidentally, to the American version of the "Jewish mother." Yet the hard physical labor required of women who worked for wages at the turn of the century led them to escape from the work force as soon as possible. A folk song, reportedly first sung in Eastern Europe at the turn of the century, and later heard in New York's sweat–shops records one woman's wish for a husband:

> Day the same as night, night the same as day.
> And all I do is sew and sew and sew
> May God help me and my love come soon
> That I may leave this work and go.[7]

Women who hoped they would soon marry and leave the shops joined trade unions only reluctantly and male union leaders thought them poor candidates for membership.[8]

---

[5] Flora Weiss, interview in Amerikaner Yiddishe Geschicnte Bel-Pe, YIVO archives, June 15, 1964, p. 4. See also Anzia Yezierska, *Bread Givers* (N.Y. 1932), p. 28.

[6] Rose Pesotta, *Bread Upon the Waters* (N.Y.: 1944), p. 4. The novels of Anzia Yezierska, who arrived in America from Russian Poland in 1901, beautifully express these aspirations. See *Bread Givers; All I Could Never Be* (N.Y., 1932); *Arrogant Beggar* (Garden City, N.Y., 1927); and her semi-fictional autobiography: *Red Ribbon on a White Horse* (N.Y., 1950).

[7] Ruth Rubin, *A Treasury of Jewish Folksong*, (N.Y., 1950), pp. 43, 97.

[8] See for example, Rose Schneiderman as quoted in "Finds Hard Job unionizing Girls whose Aim is

To choose a militant and active future among a people who valued marriage and the family as much as most Eastern European Jews did must have been extraordinarily difficult.[9] Women who chose to be continuously active in the labor movement knew consciously or unconsciously that they were rejecting traditional marriage. In her autobiography, Rose Schneiderman, just beginning a career in the Women's Trade Union League, recalls her mother warning her she'd never get married because she was so busy.[10] One woman organizer, who did marry, made the following verbatim comment to an interviewer who asked her about children: "I wouldn't know what to do with them. First of all I never . . . we were very active, both of us, and then the unions. I don't think I . . . there were always meetings . . . so we had no time to have children. I am sorry now. . . ." [11] Even after so many years, her discomfort at talking about her unusual choice was apparent. Despite difficulties, many in the first generation of immigrants, Newman and Cohn among them, did not marry and there are numerous examples of women whose marriages did not survive the urge to independence. Rose Pesotta divorced two husbands, and anarchist Emma Goldman and novelist Anzia Yezierska one each before they sought satisfying lives outside marriage.

These women were not entirely outside the pale, for while on the one hand, American-Jewish culture urged women into marriage, that culture's injunction to self-sufficiency encouraged extraordinary militancy. In this respect Jewish women may have been luckier than most. They came from a class conscious background in which competitive individualism and the desire to make it in America was only one facet. A well-developed ethic of social justice was equally important and played its part in producing perhaps the most politically aware of all immigrant groups. Socialist

---

to Wed," New York *Telegram,* June 18, 1924; Julia Stuart Poyntz, "Marriage and Motherhood," *Justice,* March 18, 1919, p. 5; Matilda Robbins, "My Story," unpublished manuscript, Matilda Robbins collection, Wayne State University Archives of Labor History, p. 38. Mechanics of organizing women are illustrated in Alice Kessler-Harris, "Where Are All the Women Unionists?", *Feminist Studies,* III (Fall, 1975), 92-110.

[9] Although the same tensions existed for women of other cultural backgrounds, one does not always get the impression that non-Jewish women were quite so torn. Mary Kenney, for example, continued to be active after she married John O'Sullivan. The most prominent Jewish women who remained active after marriage married outside their ethnic group. Anna Strunsky Walling and Rose Pastor Stokes are two examples. In some ways Emma Goldman's life acted out the protest many women must have felt but expressed in more limited ways. See Blanche Wiesen Cook, "Emma Goldman and Crystal Eastman," unpublished paper delivered at the Organization of American Historians meeting, April 1973.

[10] Rose Schneiderman with Lucy Goldthwaite, *All for One* (N.Y., 1967), p. 50.

[11] Interview with Pearl Halpern in Irving Howe collection, YIVO (undated), p. 8.

newspapers predominated in the Yiddish-speaking Lower East Side. Jews were well represented in the Socialist Party at the turn of the century and were among the best organized of semi-skilled immigrants.[12] On the Lower East Side, as in Europe, women absorbed much of their community's concern for social justice.[13] A popular lullabye provides a clue to the extent to which women experienced a prevailing class consciousness:

Sleep my child sleep,
I'll sing you a lullabye
When my little baby's grown
He'll know the difference and why

When my little baby's grown
You'll soon see which is which
Like the rest of us, you'll know
The difference between poor and rich.

The largest mansions, finest homes
The poor man builds them on the hill
But do you know who'll live in them?
Why of course the rich man will!

The poor man lives in a cellar
The walls are wet with damp
He gets pain in his arms and legs
And a rheumatic cramp.[14]

There is no way of knowing whether Cohn, Newman or Pesotta knew that song, but it is likely that they sang the following tune:

No sooner in my bed
Than I must up again
To drag my weary limbs
Off to work again

To God will I cry
With a great outcry!
Why was I born
To be a seamstress, why?

Should I once come late
'Tis a long way

---

[12] Report of the Immigration Commission, Vol. 11, p. 317, indicates that in 1910 23.9% of Jewish men belonged to trade unions as opposed to 14% of Italian men.
[13] See for example unpublished autobiography, #160, YIVO, pp. 8 and 12.
[14] Rubin, *A Treasury of Jewish Folksong*, p. 23.

They dock me straight off
A full half-day!

The machines are old
The needles they break
My bleeding fingers—
Oh, how they ache!

I've nothing to eat
I'm hungry all the day
They tell me: forget it
When I ask for pay! [15]

Like the women who sang them, the songs had travelled to America,
steerage class. In the garment shops of the Lower East Side, they could
sometimes be heard over the noise of the machines, reflecting always the
conscious desire of working women not only to get out of the shops but to
make life in them better.

Faced with the exploitative working conditions characteristic of the
early twentieth century United States, many women turned naturally to
unionism. The ILG, founded and nurtured by socialist Jews from New
York's Lower East Side, offered an appropriate organizing agency, and
early expressions of enthusiasm indicate something of its romantic appeal.
"I think the union is like a mother and father to its children. I'd give my
whole life for the union," said one young woman in 1913.[16] Half a century
after she joined the union in 1908 an eighty-year-old woman wrote to
David Dubinsky, the ILG's president, "And I still have my membership
book of that year. And I will keep it with reverence until the end of my
days." [17] Another recalled her experience on the picket line: "I felt as if I
were in a holy fight when I ran after a scab." [18]

It could be said of the early 1900s that Jewish women courted the
unions that should have been courting them. Rose Schneiderman solicited
the signatures of 25 capmakers before the union would acknowledge them
or provide aid.[19] Her friend, Pauline Newman, recalled that when she and

[15] *Ibid.,* p. 97. These songs, with their hope of escape, should be compared with the hopeless and
agonized verse of Morris Rosenfeld. See *The Teardrop Millionaire and other poems* (N.Y., 1955),
pp. 14, 19.
[16] "Manhattan's Young Factory Girls," The New York *World,* March 2, 1913.
[17] Lillian Mallach to David Dubinsky, December 18, 1964, Glicksberg, mss., YIVO.
[18] Weiss, YIVO, p. 11. The same woman recorded the influence the legend of Mother Jones had
had on her, p. 20.
[19] Schneiderman, *All for One,* p. 49. Officially, ILGWU policy was to organize whoever was in the
shop, regardless of sex. It was easier in practice to discriminate against women since they were
often employed in sex-segregated jobs.

her friends "organized a group, we immediately called the union . . . so that they could take the members in and naturally treat them as they would treat any member who joined the union. Our job was to attract women which men were not willing . . . to do." [20] But unions did not treat women even-handedly. During a capmakers strike, for example, when married men got strike benefits amounting to $6.00 per week, women, even those who supported widowed mothers and young siblings, got nothing.[21]

Women who had had to struggle to create and enter trade unions, who were baited, beaten, and arrested on picket lines, and who had already rejected traditional roles sought help from other women, identifying their problems as different from those of male workers. Large numbers indicated their need for organization by participating in spontaneous strikes. Workers on women's clothing (largely female) tended to strike without union support more than half again as many times as workers on men's clothing (largely male).[22] In the early years of organizing, attacks against other women often elicited support from co-workers. Clara Lemlich, whose proposal to strike sparked the 1909 uprising of 20,000 in the dress and waist trade, had been badly beaten by thugs. A woman who had participated in the Chicago garment strike of 1911 recalled that violent attacks against other female strikers had persuaded her not to return to work until the strike was won. As she and her fellow workers were negotiating with their employer to call a halt to the strike, they heard a terrific noise. "We all rushed to the windows, and there we [saw] the police beating the strikers—clubbing them on our account and when we saw that we went out." [23] A sense of female solidarity joined the oppressed together. A 1913 striker who said she was "in good" at her job refused to work without a union "for the sake of those that didn't have it good." [24] In jail women strikers passively resisted when their captors tried to separate them.[25]

Yet solidarity among women was limited by ethnic and class antagonisms that persistently interfered with the best efforts of organizers, and of which the organizers themselves were often guilty. Organizers repeatedly complained that their work was hampered by ethnic conflict among

[20] Pauline Newman, Interview, Amerikaner Yiddishe Geshichte Bel-Pe, June 26, 1965, YIVO, p. 19.
[21] Schneiderman, *All for One*, p. 61.
[22] Isaac Hourwich, *Immigration and Labor: the Economic Aspects of European Immigration to the United States* (N.Y., 1922), p. 373. These figures are for the period from 1880-1905.
[23] *Life and Labor* February 1911, p. 52.
[24] "Manhattan's Young Factory Girls," The New York *World*, March 2, 1913.
[25] Weiss, YIVO, p. 28.

women. Jewish women thought they were superior unionists. They treated non-Jews in the garment shops suspiciously complaining, for example, that Polish women would listen to their speeches quietly and then report them to the boss.[26] Italian women were felt to be unreliable allies, and fear that they would not join in a strike sometimes hindered other garment workers from going out.[27] In the 1909 uprising, Italian and Jewish women, divided by language barriers, met separately. The ILG, without an Italian-speaking organizer, selected women to harangue the Italians in English daily until the Italians agreed not to desert the strike.[28] Julia Poyntz, the ILG's first educational director, used the pages of *Justice,* its official journal, to argue in 1919 that "our Italian sisters who are still suffering from the age long seclusion of women in the home need a long and serious education to enable them to function intelligently as members of the working class in the shop and in the political field." [29]

"American" women, as the organizers persistently called them, were hardest of all for Jewish women to unionize. It was a necessary assignment in order to prevent some shops from undercutting the wages of others, enabling them to charge lower prices for finished goods. But it was dreaded by Jewish organizers who saw "shickses" as at best indifferent to unionism, and more often as strike breakers and scabs.[30] Success at organizing "Americans" evoked unconcealed glee. Pauline Newman wrote to Rose Schneiderman from Massachusetts that they had "at last succeeded in organizing an English-speaking branch of the waist makers union. And my dear not with ten or eleven members–but with a good sturdy membership of forty. Now what will you say to that!" [31] Long after most Jewish women were comfortable within unions, Rose Pesotta complained that she was having a "hell of a job" with the Seattle workers she had been sent to organize. They were, she said, the "100% American white daughters of the sturdy pioneers. They are all members of bridge clubs, card clubs, lodges, etc. Class consciousness is as remote from their thoughts as any idea that smacks with radicalism." [32] Women from such an ethnic background

[26] Faigele Shapiro, Interview, Amerikaner Yiddishe Geshichte Bel-Pe, August 6, 1964, YIVO, p. 9.

[27] Constant D. Leupp, "Shirtwaist Makers Strike," in Edna Bullock, ed., *Selected Articles on the Employment of Women* (Minneapolis, 1919), p. 126.

[28] Louis Lorwin, *The Women's Garment Workers: A History of the International Ladies Garment Workers Union* (N.Y., 1924), p. 156.

[29] Julia Stuart Poyntz, "What do you do with Leisure," *Justice,* February 22, 1919, p. 13.

[30] Unpublished autobiography, #160, YIVO, p. 13.

[31] Pauline Newman to Rose Schneiderman, September 20, 1910. Rose Schneiderman Collection, Tamiment, Box A94. Hereinafter referred to as P.N. and R.S. respectively.

[32] Rose Pesotta to David Dubinsky, February 6, 1935, Rose Pesotta Collection, New York Public Library, General Correspondence. Hereinafter referred to as R.P.

could severely inhibit the success of an organization drive. Pesotta complained that she could not call a strike as women would not picket. "No one will stand in front of the shop . . . as they will be ashamed. Not even the promise of getting regular strike benefits moved them." [33]

Isolated from the mainstream of the labor movement and divided from other working women who came from less class conscious backgrounds, Jewish women gratefully accepted help from middle class groups like the Women's Trade Union League. But the financial and moral support of the WTUL came at a price.[34] Jewish women had been nurtured in the cradle of socialism, and for them, alliances with other women were largely ways of achieving a more just society. Many middle class members of the WTUL, in contrast, held that political, social, and biological oppression of women was the major problem. They saw labor organization among women as a way of transcending class lines in the service of feminist interests.

Contemporary testimony and filtered memory agree that the WTUL provided enormously valuable organizing help.[34] Yet the tensions were not easily suppressed. Rose Schneiderman, working for the WTUL in 1911 needed reassurance from a friend: "You need not chide yourself for not being able to be more active in the Socialist Party. You are doing a much needed and splendid work." [35] And it was always clear to those who continued to work for the union that the women of the WTUL had only limited access to and limited understanding of the Jewish labor movement. "Remember Rose," wrote Pauline, "that no matter how much you are with the Jewish people, you are still more with the people of the League. . . ." [36] And again, Pauline comforted her friend: "They don't understand the difference between the Jewish girl and the gentile girl. . . ." [37]

Neither the trade union nor solidarity from other women offered adequate support to the exceptional women who devoted themselves to organizing. How did they choose between the two? And at what cost? They worked in a lonely and isolated world, weighing the elements of their

---

[33] Jennie Matyas to R.P., February 25, 1935.

[34] See Weiss, YIVO, p. 32 for one encomium. For the WTUL side of the story see Nancy Schrom Dye, "Creating A Feminist Alliance: Sisterhood and Class Conflict in the New York Women's Trade Union League, 1903-1914," paper presented at the Conference on Class and Ethnicity in Women's History, SUNY, Binghamton, September 22, 1974; and Robin Miller Jacoby, "The Women's Trade Union League and American Feminism," *Feminist Studies*, III (Fall, 1975), 126-140.

[35] "Joe" to R.S., November 8, 1911. R.S., A94.

[36] P.N. to R.S., April 17, 1911. R.S., A94.

[37] P.N. to R.S., February 9, 1912. R.S., A94.

success against the conflict and tension of their lives. They were not typical of rank and file union women, nor symbolic of others' lives. The three female ILG organizers I have selected, each chose not to conform to traditional patterns and to pursue what for women was an extraordinary lifestyle. Their particular struggles crystallize the tensions other women faced, and more easily resolved in the service of a familiar destiny. As their relationship to the union is filled with conflict so their attitudes towards women reflect the way feminism is experienced by working women. Their lives illustrate a continuing uncertainty over the sources of their oppression.

Pauline Newman became the ILG's first female organizer in the aftermath of the "Great Uprising" of 1909. She had a stormy relationship with the union until she settled down in 1913 to work for the Joint Board of Sanitary Control—a combined trade union and manufacturers unit designed to establish standards for maintaining sanitary conditions in the shops. Fannia Cohn worked for the union from 1919 to the end of her life. For most of that time she was educational director though she also served as an executive secretary and briefly as a vice president. Rose Pesotta (some 10 years younger than the other two) became a full time organizer in 1933 and a vice president of the union in 1934. She remained active until 1944 when she returned to work in the shops.

Their lifestyles varied. Pauline Newman, warm, open and impulsive, had a successful long-term relationship with a woman with whom she adopted a baby in 1923. Fannia Cohn lived alone—a sensitive, slightly irritable woman, concerned with her ability to make and retain friends. Rose Pesotta married twice and afterwards fell in love with first one married man and then another. Cohn and Newman called themselves socialists. Pesotta was an anarchist. No easy generalization captures their positions on women, or their relationships to the union. But all felt some conflict surrounding the two issues.

From 1909 to 1912 just before she went to work for the Joint Board, Newman vacillated between the union and the middle class women of the WTUL. Frequently unhappy with a union that often treated her shabbily she nevertheless continued to work for them throughout her life. "I cannot leave them," she wrote in 1911, "as long as they don't want to accept my resignation." "Besides," she rationalized a few months later, "they are beginning to realize . . . women can do more effective work than men, especially where girls are involved." [38] Yet later that year she angrily

[38] P.N. to R.S., April 17, 1911 and P.N. to R.S., August 9, 1911. R.S., A94.

severed her connection with the ILG for which she had been organizing in Cleveland. "They wanted me to work for *less* than the other organizers get," she wrote angrily to her friend Rose Schneiderman, "and while it was not a question of the few dol[lars] a week with me, I felt that I would lower myself before the others were I to go out on the price offered to me. . . ." Her anger increased as the letter continued to describe the women selected by John Dyche, the union's executive secretary, to replace her: "Well they too are not bad looking, and one is rather liberal with her body. That is more than enough for Dyche." [39] Two months later she was still angry. ". . . The International does not give a hang whether a local lives or dies . . . ," she wrote to Rose.[40] And several weeks after that: "I for one would not advise you to work for any Jewish organization." [41] But within a few months she was back at work again for the ILG.

She had little choice. Though she disliked the union's attitude towards women, she had equal difficulty relating to the middle class women who were potential non-union allies. Not that she disagreed with them on the women's issues: she was more than sympathetic. An ardent supporter of the ballot for women, she could not, she said later, recall any woman (save for Mother Jones) "in any of our organizations who was not in favor of getting the vote." Like her friends she was convinced that the ballot would "add greatly to our effectiveness for lobbying or sponsoring labor legislation." [42] Moreover, she not only willingly accepted aid and support from women who were not workers but she actively solicited it, even quoting Christ in order to induce church women to help garment workers.[43] To gather support for striking corset workers in Kalamazoo, Michigan in 1912, she visited women's clubs. When local officials and the mayor had been unable to help resolve the strike she "decided that the best thing to do would be to ask the ladies who wear corsets not to buy that particular brand." [44]

Yet the task of reconciling class and feminist interests exhausted her. "My work is horrible," she complained from Detroit a few months before

[39] P.N. to R.S., November 14, 1911. R.S., A94. Three months later, the ILG fired the new organizers and Pauline crowed "I tell you, Rose, it feels fine when you can say to a secretary of an International to 'go to hell with your job together' and after have the same man beg you to work for them again!" P.N. to R.S., February 22, 1912. R.S., A94.

[40] P.N. to R.S., January 17, 1912. R.S., A94.

[41] P.N. to R.S., February 9, 1912. R.S., A94.

[42] Newman interview, YIVO, pp. 21 and 22. See also P.N. to R.S., May 17, 1911, R.S., A94, where Newman expresses sadness at not being able to attend a conference to discuss the "woman problem." "You must tell me about it in your next letter."

[43] P.N. to R.S., April 11, 1910. R.S., A94.

[44] Newman interview, YIVO, p. 2.

the Kalamazoo strike. "The keeping sweet all the time and pleading for aid from the 'dear ladies' and the ministers is simply sickening." [45] Her greatest praise went to the St. Louis, Missouri WTUL. It was, she said, "a strictly working class organization in spirit as well as in action." When she sent off an article praising it to the WTUL journal, *Life and Labor*, Margaret Dreier Robbins suppressed it.[46] Newman, in a remarkable letter to Rose Schneiderman written in 1911, explored her feelings about the effect of the WTUL on women workers. Mrs. Robbins, she noted, "has made all the girls of the League think her way and as a consequence they do not use their own mind and do not act the way they feel but the way Mrs. R. wants them to." She frowned at the League's Saturday afternoon teas (which served "a glass Russian Tea") and disapproved of giving the girls folk dancing lessons. "It is of course very nice of her," conceded Newman, "but that is the instinct of charity rather than of unionism." [47]

Her disagreements were not simply matters of style. She was more than willing to give way when she thought a well-spoken woman could influence a stubborn manufacturer. But she thought it bad strategy to raise issues of morality when they threatened to interfere with negotiations over wages and hours. It may have been true, she argued, that a factory owner's son and his superintendent had taken liberties with female employees: "There is not a factory today where the same immoral conditions [do] not exist. . . . This to my mind can be done away with by educating the girls instead of attacking the company." [48]

Caught between the union and middle class allies, Newman called for help—a pattern repeated by other women involved in the labor movement. Her letters to Schneiderman are filled with longing: "all evening I kept saying if only Rose were here . . . ;" and with loneliness: "No matter how good the people are to me, they do not know me as yet." [49] At times one can only guess at the toll her job took. She wrote repeatedly of trying to "get away from the blues" and complained, "I am just thrown like a wave from one city to another. When will it end?" [50] Respite came at last in the form of the Joint Board of Sanitary Control. With the struggles to organize behind her she could spend her energies improving working

[45] P.N. to R.S., March 5, 1912. R.S., A94.
[46] P.N. to R.S., November 7, 1911. R.S., A94. Newman had already had a similar experience with the *Ladies Garment Worker* (*Justice*'s predecessor) which mutilated an article on the League she had written for them.
[47] P.N. to R.S., December 1, 1911. R.S., A94.
[48] P.N. to R.S., July 11, 1912. R.S., A94.
[49] P.N. to R.S., October 19, 1910 and April 11, 1910. R.S., A94.
[50] P.N. to R.S., October 29, 1911 and November 7, 1911. R.S., A94.

conditions for women in the factories.

Feelings of displacement and the need for support may have preceded the drive by women members of ILG's Local 25 to create first an educational department and then a vacation retreat. The men in the union had no patience with the demands at first. One active woman recalled the men's snickers: "What do the girls know–instead of a union they want to dance." [51] But the women persisted, insisting that the union would be better if the members danced with each other. The women proved to be right. By 1919 Unity House, as the vacation home was called, had moved to quarters capable of sleeping 900 people and two years later Local 25 turned it over to a grateful International.

Unity House may have symbolized a growing solidarity among working class Jewish women. In any event, the feminism of ILG members seems to have become a problem for just at the peak of its success, *Justice,* the Union's official journal, began to attack middle class women. Could it have been that some union leaders feared that working women were seeking alliances with others of their sex and would eventually cease to identify their interests with those of working men? "Women who work," an editorial intoned early in 1919, are not like "that type of woman, who to her shame be it said, is less a person than a thing." [52] Increasingly *Justice*'s writers insisted that working women had it in their own power to defend themselves. When female pickets faced attacks by gangsters, *Justice* insisted that the solution was in the hands of the strikers themselves. It urged women to "take a little trip down to City Hall and get the vote that will put these fellows out of business." [53] Julia Poyntz, *Justice*'s writer on women's affairs, was adamant that middle class women no longer interfere with their sisters. "The interests of the women of the working classes are diametrically opposed to those of the middle classes. . . ." [54] A month later she attacked a Women's International League for Peace and Freedom conference for virtually excluding working women and their problems.[55] Although the journal continued to solicit support for the WTUL and the ILG continued to send women to the Bryn Mawr Summer School, attacks did not cease. A 1923 article protested the absence of working women at a conference on women in industry: "The ladies who employ domestics came to Washington to speak about higher wages, shorter hours, and

[51] Shapiro interview, YIVO, p. 17.
[52] "On Lightheaded Women," *Justice,* March 8, 1919.
[53] Julia Poyntz, "The Unity Corner," *Justice,* March 29, 1919, p. 3.
[54] "The Problem of Life for the Working Girl," *Justice,* February 1, 1919, p. 3.
[55] *Justice,* March 15, 1919, p. 5.

better working conditions for their help. The domestics, of course, or their representatives were not invited." [56]

It was just in this period that Fannia Cohn climbed to a position of authority in the ILGWU. In many ways she was fully aware of women's issues. In 1919, in the aftermath of a successful shirtwaist strike, she pleaded for tolerance from male union members. Recalling the militancy of the young female strikers she wrote: "Our brother workers in the past regarded with suspicion the masses of women who were entering the trades. They did everything to halt the 'hostile army' whose competition they feared." [57] Wasn't it time, she asked, finally to accept fully the women strikers who had so often been jailed and beaten. An ardent supporter of the Bryn Mawr Summer School and a regular contributor to the WTUL, Cohn had friendly relations with many of its officers.[58] In 1926 she protested the absence of women's names on a list of anti-war petition signatures, and later she was to fire off a rapid telegram insisting that Anne Muste be included in a tribute offered to her husband.[59] Her experiences strike familiar chords. She complained of the difficulty of holding independent views from the men she worked with but noted "It is still more painful to have women, too, assume a similar attitude toward their sex." [60] She laughed with a friend whose husband was called by his wife's surname ("let men have the sensation of changing their lifelong name for a new one"), and supported Mary Beard's proposed world center to preserve a record of women's achievements.[61]

Cohn's strong empathy for women's feelings surely derived from her own uncomfortable experiences in the ILG. Theresa Wolfson, later to become a well-known economist and an expert on the problem of working women, glimpsed this suffering in 1923. "Never have I realized with such poignancy of feeling," she wrote to her, "what it means to be a woman

---

[56] B. Maiman, "Conference on Women in Industry," *Justice,* January 19, 1923, p. 4.

[57] Fannia Cohn, "With the Strikers," *Justice,* February 22, 1919.

[58] Fannia Cohn to R.S., January 24, 1929, Fannia Cohn papers, New York Public Library, Box 4; see also E. Christman to F.C., October 2, 1915, F.C., Bx. 1.

[59] James Shotwell to F.C., December 31, 1926, F.C., Bx. 1; F.C. to James Maurer, March 6, 1931, F.C., Bx. 5.

[60] F.C. to Helen Norton, February 9, 1932, F.C., Bx. 5. The rest of the letter reads in part: "It hurts me also to know that while 'men' frequently come to each others' assistance in an emergency, 'women' frequently remain indifferent when one of their own sex is confronted with a similar emergency. Of course, a woman is expected to assist a man in his accomplishments, but she (the woman) is forced in her aspirations—in social and economic field—to struggle along. She is compelled to depend upon her own resources, whether this be material, moral or intellectual."

[61] F.C. to Dorothea Heinrich, February 3, 1937. F.C., Bx. 5; F.C. to Mary Beard, January 23, 1940. F.C., Bx. 5.

among men in a fighting organization as last Monday when I heard your outcry and realized the stress under which you were working." [62] In a letter she hesitated at first to mail, Cohn shared some of her angry frustration with a woman who taught at Brookwood Labor College. Cohn had urgently requested the college's faculty to make two studies of union women for her. The faculty had repeatedly postponed the request. "I wonder whether they would treat in the same manner, a 'man' who would find himself in a similar position . . ." she wrote. "The labor movement is guilty of not realizing the importance of placing the interest of women on the same basis as of men and until they will accept this, I am afraid the movement will be much hampered in its progress." [63]

Despite the anguish caused by her male colleagues and her strong sympathy with women's causes, Cohn came down on the side of the labor movement when a choice had to be made. She rejected a request to segregate men and women workers in evening classes: "I am a great believer that men and women working together in the labor movement or in the classroom have much to gain from each other." [64] In 1925 she appealed to William Green, the AFL's president, "not as an officer speaking for her organization [but as] a woman trade unionist" protesting conferences called by ladies. "When the deplorable conditions of the unorganized working woman are to be considered," she objected, "a conference is called by many ladies' organization who have no connection with the labor movement and they are the ones to decide 'how to improve the conditions of the poor working woman.'" [65] A year and a half later she regretfully refused an invitation to attend a WTUL conference on working women, cautioning the delegates to "bear in mind that it is very difficult nowadays to even organize men and they should remember that in proportion there are not enough men organized in our country as yet." [66] On the question of protective legislation for women, Cohn only reluctantly sided with the middle class reformers who favored it: "I did not think the problem of working women could be solved in any other way than the problem of working men and that is through trade union organization, but considering that very few women are as yet organized into trade unions, it would be folly to agitate against protective legislation." [67]

---

[62] Theresa Wolfson to F.C., November 19, 1923. F.C., Bx. 1.
[63] F.C. to Helen Norton, February 9, 1932. F.C., Bx. 5.
[64] F.C. to Evelyn Preston, September 21, 1923. F.C., Bx. 4.
[65] F.C. to Wm. Green, March 6, 1925. F.C., Bx. 4.
[66] F.C. to R.S., October 5, 1926. F.C., Bx. 4.
[67] F.C. to Dr. Marion Phillips, September 13, 1927. F.C., Bx. 4.

These contradictory positions were not taken without inner struggle. Cohn knew well the sacrifice she was making to stay in the labor movement. "Did you ever think of the inner pain, worry and spiritual humiliation . . . ?" she lamented in 1922.[68] Her remedy, like Newman's, was close friendship. "You know that I . . . must be in constant touch with my friends," she wrote. "If I can't have personal contact then the medium of letters can be employed." [69] Or again, "To satisfy my own inner self, I must be surrounded by true friends . . . [who] never for a moment doubt my motives and always understand me thoroughly." [70] Cohn found refuge in the education department of the ILG where she could continue the battle and yet remain sheltered from the worst of the storm.

Rose Pesotta took no shelter and asked no quarter. By 1933 when she began full-time organizing for the ILG, it had become clear to many that women, married and unmarried, were in the work force to stay and the ILG willingly committed both money and resources to organizing them.[71] Membership campaigns no longer focused on the East Coast cities. In the garment centers of the Far West and in places like Buffalo and Montreal, Jews took second place to Mexican, Italian, and "American" women. But Pesotta was a Russian Jew who worked for a still Jewish union and, like her predecessors, she suffered the turmoil of being a woman in ambivalent territory. Sent by the ILG to Los Angeles in 1933, she moved from there to organize women in San Francisco, Seattle, Portland, Puerto Rico, Buffalo, and Montreal before she became involved with war mobilization.

None could question her awareness of women's particular problems. Persuaded by the argument that there were no women on the union's General Executive Board, she accepted a much-dreaded nomination for Vice President. "I feel as if I lost my independence," she confided to her diary.[72] She often berated the union leadership for its neglect of women: "our union, due to the fact that it has a WOMAN leader is supposed to do

---

[68] F.C. to Theresa Wolfson, May 15, 1922. F.C., Bx. 4.

[69] F.C. to Evelyn Preston, September 9, 1922. F.C., Bx. 4; see also F.C. to E.P., February 19, 1924.

[70] F.C. to Theresa Wolfson, May 15, 1922. F.C., Bx. 4.

[71] Fannia Cohn, "A New Era Opens for Labor Education," *Justice,* October 1, 1933, p. 9. The article may be more hopeful than real. Cohn said in part ". . . the women strikers, many of whom were married and their younger sisters, too, increasingly realized that no longer do they want a strong union as a temporary protection for themselves but as a permanent safeguard for their present and future families." There is no question, however, that the industry's workers were increasingly drawn from married women and older women.

[72] R.P., diary, June 9, 1934, Rose Pesotta Collection, New York Public Library. In her autobiography, *Bread Upon the Waters,* p. 101, Pesotta wrote that "the voice of a solitary woman on the General Executive Board would be a voice lost in the wilderness."

everything, organizing, speechmaking, etc., etc." [73] She was not shy about asking for courtesies that men might have had trouble obtaining. Women who earned meager wages could not be expected to pay even modest union initiation fees, she urged at one point. At another, she demanded that ILG pay not only the expenses but make up the lost income of a Spanish woman elected to attend the biennial ILG convention.[74] And she knew the advantages of solidarity among women, making personal sacrifices to "win the support of the ladies who might some day be of great help to the girls." [75]

Repeatedly, however, Pesotta and her fellow West Coast organizers sacrificed the feminist issues in the interests of generating an enthusiastic and loyal membership. To keep striking women happy they agreed to double strike benefits before Easter Sunday "for the girls to buy something." [76] When newly organized women brought their husbands to discussion meetings, the men were made welcome.[77] In 1933, Pesotta compromised to the extent of abandoning the negotiating process to men and confining her own activities to organizing women because "our late President Schlesinger once told your humble servant to stop this kind of business and go home and get married. I hate to hear that from an employer." [78] Her perspectives were not always those of other women. While WTUL officials were praising the NRA codes, Rose Pesotta condemned them. Organizing in Seattle and witness to how badly the codes were abused, she complained "the women are satisfied that the N.R.A. gave them 35 hours and better wages, why pay dues to a union that does nothing for the workers?" [79]

Pesotta carried the scars of the woman organizer. "A flitting happy little whirlwind," her friends called her. It was an image that did not fit. "Nobody knows how many cheerless, sleepless nights I have spent crying

[73] R.P. to Rae Brandstein, April 9, 1934.

[74] R.P. to David Dubinsky, April 26, 1934.

[75] R.P. to David Dubinsky, March 3, 1934. Pesotta on this occasion stayed in a YMCA because it was "respectable."

[76] R.P. to Jennie Matyas, April 16, 1935.

[77] R.P. to Paul Berg, February 15, 1934.

[78] R.P. to David Dubinsky, September 30, 1933. Pesotta's snippy attitude comes through in the rest of that letter. "Now, my dear President, you will have to come across with the help we need namely; financial, moral and the representative for a week or two. After we'll pull this through you will come to visit these whores and I am confident that you will see with your own eyes that enthusiasm is not such a bad thing after all."

[79] Rose Schneiderman called the codes "the Magna Charta of the working woman" and characterized them as "the most thrilling thing that has happened in my lifetime." New York Evening Journal, October 24, 1933, p. 15 (clipping in R.S., A97); R.P. to David Dubinsky, February 1, 1935.

in my loneliness . . . ," she confided to her diary.[80] Unlike Newman and Cohn, she sought solace in men and depriving herself of close women friends exacerbated her isolation. Tormented by the gossip of her female colleagues she struggled with her self-image. Occasionally she confessed "I feel so futile . . . ," or sorrowed "everybody has a private life. I have none." [81] In an effort to avoid entangling herself with a married man she exiled herself to Montreal in 1936. It was no use. She wrote from there to her lover: "Why must I find happiness always slipping out of my hand . . . I'm sinking now and who knows where I will land." [82] For ten years, Rose Pesotta battled against police alongside her union colleagues. Then she returned to the comparative peace of the garment shop from which she had come.

By the middle 1930s, with unionism apparently secure and the ILG's membership expanding rapidly, it looked as though women might at last begin to raise issues peculiar to them within the confines of the union. Fannia Cohn wrote a play in 1935 which raised critical issues. Intended for presentation at union meetings, it described a husband and his "intellectually superior" wife. Both worked, but, because the wife had to devote her evenings to caring for the home, the husband rapidly developed more interests and became increasingly discontented with his spouse. The wife, wrote Cohn, brought with her the resentment and "the protest of a woman worker, wife and mother against an economic condition that compels her to work days in the shop and evenings at home." [83] Chivalry, Rose Schneiderman had said, "is thrown away" when a girl enters the factory or store: "Women have to work and then are thrown on the dust heap the same as working **men**." [84] Working men were by no means chivalrous in 1935, but enough women had been organized in the ILG so that the union, no longer afraid of imminent disintegration and collapse, could lend an ear to the women's issues. Perhaps in consequence the solidarity of women within the unions diminished.

Those who came before walked an uneasy tightrope—slipping first to one side and then to the other. Tempted sometimes by the money and

---

[80] R.P., diary, November 3, 1931.

[81] R.P., diary, February 24, 1934, March 12, 1934, August 9, 1934.

[82] R.P. to Powers Hapgood, February 21, 1937.

[83] F.C. to Jess Ogden, June 25, 1935, F.C. A second play described how two sisters, both of whom worked, nevertheless waited on their brother at home because they had to atone for earning less than he did.

[84] Quoted in a clipping entitled "Says Chivalry stops at Door of Workshop," from an unidentified newspaper, 1912. R.S., A97.

support of middle class women, at others by the militance of a changing labor union leadership; alternately repelled by "ladies" and repeatedly hurt by their union's male leadership, women who tried to organize their sisters were in a precarious position. They were not feminist—they did not put the social and political rights of women before all else. They did draw strength and support from the solidarity of women inside unions and outside them. Their lives illustrate the critical importance of "female bonding" and of female friendship networks. Newman and Cohn, who had particularly strong relationships with women and who managed to find relatively passive roles within the union, maintained their relationship with the ILG far longer than Pesotta who relied on men for support and who stayed in the front lines of battle. All were class conscious, insisting that the class struggle was preeminent. When their class consciousness and their identification as women conflicted, they bowed to tradition and threw in their lot with the working class.

14

Affluence for Whom? — Another Look at Prosperity and the Working Classes in the 1920s

FRANK STRICKER

Our picture of economic life in the United States in the 1920s has been remarkably constant. From Frederick Lewis Allen's popular *Only Yesterday* (1931) to Ellis Hawley's recent (1979) history of the American People and their institutions from 1917 to 1933, the 1920s appear as a time of "unparalleled plenty." From 1923 to 1929, "the prosperity band-wagon rolled down Main Street." The real earnings of workers "shot up at an astonishing rate" and "unemployment largely disappeared." To be sure, income distribution worsened, but the share going to workers "was enough to produce the world's first excursion into mass affluence."[1]

There was, apparently, a shift in consumer spending toward durables like automobiles and appliances. One historian noted that by the end of the decade there was one car for every 4.5 persons and "only a half a million fewer cars than there were married couples with separate households." It seemed to follow, as John Hicks and William Leuchtenburg have agreed, that "al-

---

[1] Quotations from the following: Frederick Lewis Allen, *Only Yesterday: An Informal History of the 1920s* (New York, 1964), 133; William E. Leuchtenburg, *The Perils of Prosperity, 1914-1932* (Chicago, 1958), 178; Ellis W. Hawley, *The Great War and the Search for Modern Order: A History of the American People and Their Institutions, 1917-1933* (New York, 1979), 81. See also W. Elliot Brownlee, *Dynamics of Ascent: A History of the American Economy* (New York, 1974), 264-265.

Reprinted from *Labor History* 24 (Winter 1983), 5-33. The author thanks for their help the librarians at California State University, Dominguez Hills, and the many colleagues who read drafts of this paper, especially Deborah Schopp and Gary Nash.

most everyone owned a car." Utopia had arrived: "the bread and butter problems of survival of earlier decades were now replaced for a majority by the pursuit of happiness in the form of the traditional minority pursuits of wine, women and song." This flight into fantasy is only a slight exaggeration of the way the 1920s is often recalled in the historical consciousness.[2]

There have been, of course, other images of the decade. An early alternative, born in the Great Depression, was the Brookings Institution's *America's Capacity to Consume* (1934), which emphasized the poverty of most Americans. Recently historians have attacked the assumption that new appliances and household conveniences actually cut down on labor time in housework. In his history of the American worker from 1920 to 1933, Irving Bernstein concluded that the 1920s were golden "only for a privileged segment of the population." And Robert Ozanne demonstrated that wage increases in the 1920s were relatively small.[3]

But on the whole labor historians have done little to revise accepted views of the 1920s by analyzing wage and family income data. Not surprisingly, the paradigm that dominates the historiography of the period has not been shaken. Typically, writers admit that income distribution worsened and that there were "sick" industries and "sick" regions. Farming, coal mining, textiles, and sometimes railroading, shipping, shipbuilding, and shoe and leather production are mentioned.[4] But these sick

---

[2] Jim Potter, *The American Economy Between the World Wars* (New York, 1974), 47; Leuchtenburg, 194; John D. Hicks, *Republican Ascendancy, 1921-1933* (New York, 1960), 112; and for the final quotation in the paragraph, Potter, 48.

[3] Maurice Leven, Harold G. Moulton, and Clark Warburton, *America's Capacity to Consume* (Washington, DC, 1934), hereafter cited as Brookings; Irving Bernstein, *The Lean Years: A History of the American Worker, 1920-1933* (Baltimore, 1966); Robert Ozanne, *Wages in Practice and Theory: McCormick and International Harvester, 1860-1960* (Madison, 1968); Heidi Irmgard Hartmann, "Capitalism and Women's Work in the Home, 1900-1930" (unpublished PhD diss., Yale Univ., 1974), 227-253. See also James R. Green, *The World of the Worker: Labor in Twentieth-Century America* (New York, 1980), 111, which claims that workers experienced a 26 percent gain in real income; and compare David Brody, "The Rise and Decline of Welfare Capitalism," in John Braemen, Robert H. Bremner, and David Brody, eds., *Change and Continuity in Twentieth-Century America* (Columbus, 1968), 147-178, which, on 161 argues that wages "rose insignificantly during the 1920s," with Brody, *Workers in Industrial America, Essays on the Twentieth Century Struggle* (New York, 1980), 48-81, which, on 62, claims that real earnings slowed their increases in the war period and exhibited a "genuine upward trend" from 1922 to 1929.

[4] Leuchtenburg, 193-194; Hawley, 87-88; and Allen, 133-134.

industries and the regions which suffered because of them (the South and New England in particular) are segregated from the dominant history of the period as exceptions.

The prosperity thesis is rarely supported with detailed evidence. Sometimes the thesis is based on accepting at face value statements made in the decade—a decade whose politicians and business leaders had their own reasons for announcing a "new era" of rising American living standards. Much of the case is built on aggregate statistics about income, consumption, and output. Certainly those statistics are impressive. The real Gross National Product (GNP) increased by 39 percent from 1919 to 1929, real per capita GNP by 20 percent, and personal disposable income per capita by 30 percent.[5] Personal consumption expenditures rose in all categories, but especially in the areas of services and durables. Radios, vacuum cleaners, and electric toasters flooded the market. The flow of durables to consumers (in 1929 dollars) annually averaged $4.29 billion from 1909 to 1918 and $7.06 billion from 1919 to 1928, an increase of 65 percent. Auto registrations almost tripled in nine years (from over eight million in 1920 to over twenty-three million in 1929).[6]

The home and its furnishings appeared to be undergoing a revolution. The percentage of households with inside flush toilets jumped from 20 to 51 percent between 1920 and 1930, of households with electric lighting from 35 to 68 percent, and of homes with radios from zero to 40 percent. Other items showed significant increases although by the end of the decade they were still found only in the homes of a minority: the percentage of homes with vacuum cleaners increased from 9 to 30, of families with washing machines from 8 to 24, and of families with mechanical refrigerators from 1 to 8.[7]

---

[5] *Historical Statistics of the United States: Colonial Times to 1970*, I (Washington, DC, 1975), 224, 211, hereafter cited as *HS*.

[6] Figures on the flow of durables are from Harold G. Vatter, "Has There Been a Twentieth-Century Consumer Durables Revolution?" *The Journal of Economic History*, 27 (Mar. 1967), 5. Other data on flow to consumers is in Robert Aaron Gordon, *Economy Instability and Growth: The American Record* (New York, 1974), 24. On auto registrations, *HS*, II, 716. For an ebullient statement from the period, see Christine Frederick, "New Wealth, New Standards of Living and Changed Family Budgets," *Annals of the American Academy of Political and Social Science*, 115 (Sept. 1924), 74-82.

[7] Stanley Lebergott, *The American Economy: Income, Wealth, and Want* (Princeton, 1976), 272-288, 355.

Data can also be advanced to show that progress extended beyond higher incomes and the acquisition of more consumer goods. Public expenditures on "free" services like schools and hospitals jumped; high school graduates as a percentage of persons seventeen years old increased from 16.3 (1920) to 27.5 (1929). Death rates continued to decline. The diet of the average American seemed more varied and nutritious. Leo Wolman asserted in 1929 that "there is no longer serious danger of shortage" in basic vitamins and minerals "in any class of the population, except as ignorance or carelessness may be the cause." [8]

All these "facts" may be true and yet misleading about how the average worker lived. Especially if incomes were unequally distributed, the mean average for all Americans tells us little about the living standard of the average working-class family. By one estimate, in 1929 the top 24 percent of all spending units made 50 percent of all expenditures on clothing, the top 20 percent made 50 percent of all expenditures on shelter, and the top 10 percent made 36 percent of all food expenditures and 50 percent of all expenditures on non-essential items like recreation, health, and education.[9] Notwithstanding these facts it is clear, 1) that during the 1920s while wages were generally at a higher level than before World War I, gains made during the decade, especially the long period of prosperity from 1923 to 1929, were not exceptional and in some cases non-existent; 2) that unemployment was much higher than we have been led to believe and a continuing worry for most workers; 3) that the wages of millions of workers—and perhaps a third of all non-farm *family* incomes—were at or below the poverty line in 1929; 4) that the lower sections of the working class, such as unskilled railroad workers, probably had insufficient incomes for a nourishing diet; and 5) finally, taking one vaunted symbol of the decade's prosperity, that the proportion of working-class families owning automobiles was probably less than half. In short, our picture of

---

8 On public expenditures, Leo Wolman, "Consumption and the Standard of Living," in *Recent Economic Changes in the United States, I, President's Conference on Unemployment* (New York, 1929), 15 ff.; on diet, Wolman, 25-51, and for the quotation, 47-48; high school graduates, *HS*, I, 379.
9 Data on consumption expenditures, Brookings, 85.

the 1920s as a period of prosperity for workers must be radically qualified.[10]

           *   *   *   *   *   *

If the wages of workers were higher in the 1920s than before
the war and if they increased steadily year-by-year, at least one
thrust of the prosperity view can be saved. Workers may not
have been living like the middle class, but they could have lived
at higher material levels every year. After all, was it not in this
decade that employers, living by the golden rule of high wages,
"agreed to pay high pay rates and to give lavish benefits"?[11]

As a matter of fact, wages and salaries were generally much
higher in 1929 than they had been in 1919 or 1914. Stanley
Lebergott's estimates of real annual earnings for all non-farm
employees (not just working-class occupations) show total increases of 25.6 percent over the period 1919 to 1929, and 10.5
percent for the period from 1923 to 1929.[12] Paul Douglas, in his
pioneering study on real wages in the US concluded that wage-
earners in transportation and manufacturing, after deductions
for unemployment, took home 27 percent more in real annual
earnings in 1926 than they had in 1914. Although these workers apparently reached a plateau in 1923-26, their annual earnings in the later year were 13.2 percent over 1919.[18] Albert
Rees' figures for hourly wages in manufacturing, when corrected
for price changes, show real gains of 12 percent from 1920 to
1929 and 5.8 percent from 1923 to 1929.[14] Real weekly earnings for production workers in manufacturing increased by 14.5
percent for the decade, 1919 to 1929, but gained only 4.7 percent in the era of prosperity, 1923 to 1929.[15]

---

[10] This article focuses on the working class broadly conceived. The working class in
1920 was about 20 percent of the labor force—a rough estimate based on
adding for 1920 the following categories of workers: clerical, sales, craftsmen
and foremen, operatives, private household workers, other service workers,
farm laborers and foremen, and laborers. The total is 30,677,000 workers or
72.7 percent of the labor force. Data from HS, I, 140-145.
[11] Mark Perlman "Labor in Eclipse," in Braeman, Bremner, and Brody, 122.
[12] Stanley Lebergott, Manpower in Economic Growth: The American Record Since
1800 (New York, 1964), 524.
[13] Paul H. Douglas, Real Wages in the United States, 1890-1926 (Boston and New
York, 1930), 463-464.
[14] Albert Rees, New Measures of Wage-Earner Compensation in Manufacturing,
1914-1957 (New York, 1960), Table 1, p. 3, divided by the Consumer Price
Index in HS, I, 210.
[15] HS, I, 170, divided by Consumer Price Index in HS, I, 210.

Table 1:   Changes in Real Earnings, 1914-1929

	A	B	C	D
	Real Hourly Wages in Manufacturing	Real Annual Earnings All Employees After Deduction For Unemployment	Real Annual Earnings Wage-earners in Manufacturing & Transportation, After Deduction for Unemployment	Real Weekly Production Workers, Manufacturing
1914-1926	+33.5%	+30.7%	+37.0%	+26.8%
1919-1926	+ 5.9%	+17.6%	+13.2%	+ 9.1%
1923-1926	− 0.1%	+ 3.5%	0%	− 0.2%
1914-1929	+41.4%	+39.5%	–	+33.0%
1919-1929	+12.2%	+25.6%	–	+14.5%
1923-1929	+ 5.8%	+10.5%	–	+ 4.7%

Sources: For Series A, Albert Rees, *New Measures of Wage-Earner Compensation in Manufacturing, 1914-1957* (New York, 1960), Table 1, p. 3, corrected for price changes according to the *Historical Statistics of the United States*, I (1976). 211. Series B, Stanley Lebergott, *Manpower in Economic Growth: The American Record Since 1800* (New York, 1964), 524. Series C, Paul H. Douglas, *Real Wages in the United States, 1890-1926* (Boston & New York, 1930), 463-464. Series D, *Historical Statistics of the United States*, I, 170, divided by the Consumer Price Index, 211.

Table 1 outlines changes in four series for specific time periods. A glance at the data suggests how complicated was the history of wages in the war period and the 1920s. There were substantial gains from 1914 to 1929, a conclusion apparently sustaining the views of the prosperity school. But closer examination reveals the necessity of distinguishing groups and periods. First, the category of "All Employees" (B) tells us little about blue-collar workers; the differences are especially large in the 1920s. Second, combining the war period and the 1920s distorts very large differences in wage behavior between a war-induced prosperity and a peacetime prosperity. Finally, the data show that during the "new era" (1923-1929), the real hourly and weekly wages of wage-earners in manufacturing advanced rather modestly. The period smack in the middle of the prosperity decade (1923-1926) even shows a decline, and for the whole of the "new era," as Robert Ozanne has pointed out, real hourly wages for all manufacturing workers increased only about 1 percent a year—less than in all but one of six other peacetime prosperity periods from 1865 to 1960 and far below the increases registered in the major war periods, 1914 to 1920 and 1940 to 1946. Real hourly manufacturing wages rose from 1923 to 1929 but just barely faster than the only weaker period (1905 to 1913) until recent times.[16]

Some workers fared less well than these general averages indicate. Real daily wage rates for farm labor in 1929 ($2.30) were almost exactly what they had been in 1914, fifteen years before. After climbing during the economic expansion of 1922-1923, they stagnated from 1923 to 1929.[17] The hourly wages of mule spinners in cotton textiles fell 16 percent from 1924 to 1929.[18] Anthracite and bituminous coal miners lucky enough to work a normal year lost 14.2 percent and 30 percent respectively in real annual wages from 1923 to 1929.[19] Massachusetts manufacturing workers made big gains of 13.3 percent from 1919 to 1927 in real annual earnings, but from 1923 to 1927 they gained next to nothing (0.16 percent). Printers and workers in rubber boots and shoes did well in the Bay State, but workers in leather, boots, shoes, cottons, woolens, paper and confections lost ground or gained relatively little.[20]

The millions of workers in these "sick" industries and regions might be pushed aside as exceptions, but the experience of workers outside the troubled areas was not always much better. Domestics gained a total of 1.96 percent from 1923 to 1929 in real annual earnings.[21] Hourly union rates in six building trades rose between 22 and 36 percent from 1923 to 1929. But not all skilled workers earned union rates, not all construction workers were skilled, and many did not work a full year. Construction

---

16 Ozanne, Table 1, p. 8.
17 *HS*, I, 468. See also Douglas 168, which shows that real annual earnings were less in 1926 than they had been in 1914. An abundance of labor and a "natural" decline in wages was noticed in California in 1924. See Carey McWilliams, *Factories in the Field: The Story of Migratory Farm Labor In California* (Santa Barbara, 1971), 189.
18 Leo Wolman and Gustav Peck, "Labor Groups in the Social Structure," in *Recent Social Trends in the United States, II, President's Research Committee on Social Trends* (New York, 1933), 815.
19 *HS*, I, 166.
20 "Wage Earners and Per Capita Earnings in Manufacturing in Massachusetts, 1919-1927," *Monthly Labor Review*, 29 (Sept. 1929), 174-176.
21 *HS*, I, 167.

workers as a whole for the same period increased their real annual earnings by 3.7 percent.[22] Common laborers in basic steel lost 0.7 percent in hourly earnings from 1923 to 1929; road labor gained only 2.2 percent in real hourly earnings for the same period; wages for common labor at International Harvester were stable after 1923. The real weekly earnings of female workers in manufacturing hardly moved from 1923 to 1929.[23]

Within particular industries and sectors as well as between different sectors, there were enormous variations in what happened to wages and salaries. It was not only in "sick" industries that workers did badly and some workers in sectors that were thought to be declining or stagnant did well. As one example, the following graph illustrates the disparities among selected categories of railroad workers in the long period of prosperity, 1923-1929. Workers as a whole and shop labor made moderate increases, but unskilled workers, who comprised almost a third of the total workers actually lost earnings over the period. The four operating crafts on passenger trains did very well, averaging increases of 11-14 percent in weekly earnings.

Of twenty-six manufacturing industries surveyed by the National Industrial Conference Board and shown in Graph 2 the real weekly earnings of workers in fifteen categories increased more and those of workers in eleven categories increased less than the average for all workers (6.1 percent). Of the eleven catgeories that made a poor showing, five can be connected with the troubled apparel industry, but the other six (three foundry categories, iron and steel, rubber, and furniture) were not generally thought to have been sick industries.

We have seen that some workers did very well in the 1920s, among them more privileged railroad workers, skilled construction workers, printers, and workers in the hosiery and knitwear

22 Union rates in Robert Christie, *Empire in Wood: A History of the Carpenters' Union* (Ithaca, NY, 1956), 331-332; all workers in construction, *HS*, I, 166.
23 Bernstein, 66; Wolman and Peck, "Labor Groups in the Social Structure," 816; Ozanne, 51; National Industrial Conference Board, *Wages in the United States, 1914-1929* (New York, 1930), 104. For other industries see *Wages and Hours of Labor in the Boot and Shoe Industry, 1910 to 1930*, Bureau of Labor Statistics Bulletin No. 551 (1932); *Wages and Hours of Labor in the Motor Vehicle Industry, 1928* (1929), BLS Bull. No. 502; *Wages and Hours of Labor in the Iron and Steel Industry: 1929*, BLS Bull. 513 (1930); Douglas, 124-127; Bernstein, 67; *Wages and Hours of Labor in the Slaughtering and Meat-Packing Industry, 1929*, BLS Bull. No. 535 (1931).

Graph 1: Changes in Average Real Weekly Earnings of Selected Categories of Railroad Workers, 1923 through 1929

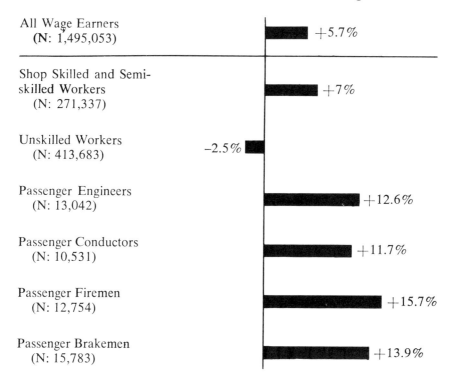

All Wage Earners
(N: 1,495,053)   +5.7%

Shop Skilled and Semi-
skilled Workers
(N: 271,337)   +7%

Unskilled Workers   -2.5%
(N: 413,683)

Passenger Engineers   +12.6%
(N: 13,042)

Passenger Conductors   +11.7%
(N: 10,531)

Passenger Firemen   +15.7%
(N: 12,754)

Passenger Brakemen   +13.9%
(N: 15,783)

Source: National Industrial Conference Board, *Wages in the United States, 1914-1929* (New York, 1930), 180, 182, 183, 185, 188, 191, 194.

industry. White-collar workers also gained. Each of eight groups of white-collar workers (Table 2) made big gains in annual real earnings in the 1920s, partly because their money earnings did not drop (or dropped little) in the deflation of mid-1920 to mid-1923, but also because their money wages increased in the 1923-1929 period. Although most of these groups lost heavily to the inflation of the war period, it is undeniable that in general, during the 1920s, they made up for those losses and did much better than most blue-collar workers. Table 2 shows six-year periods from 1914-1920 and 1920-1926 for eight groups of white-collar workers and, for the sake of comparison, Table 2a shows six categories of blue-collar workers in the same period.

Graph 2: Changes in Real Weekly Earnings of Manufacturing Workers, 1923-1929

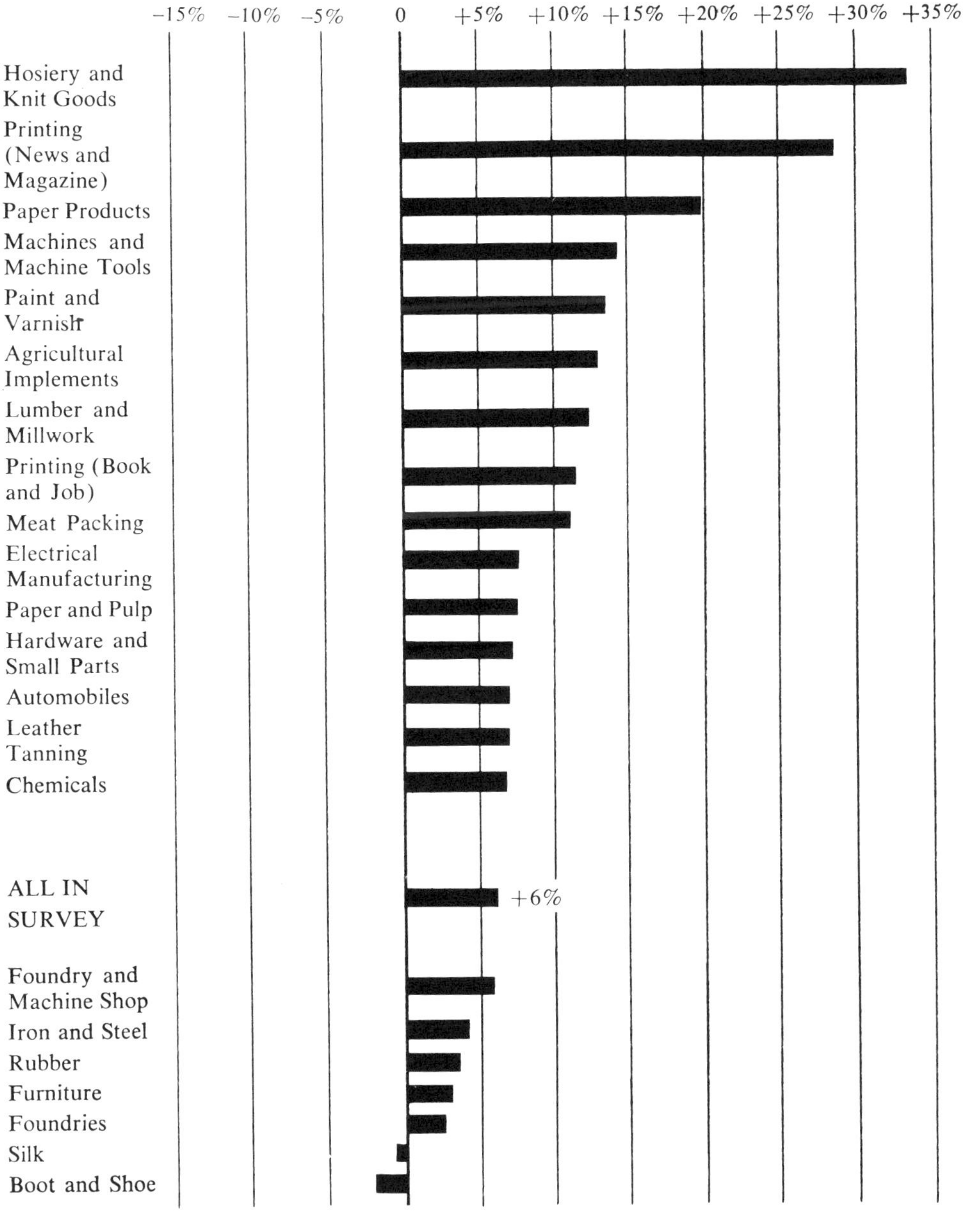

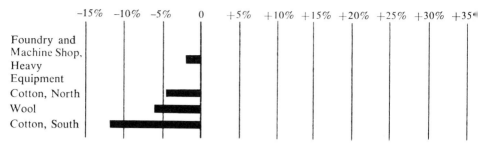

Source: National Industrial Conference Board, *Wages in the United States, 1914-
1929* (New York, 1930), 45; and Consumer Price Index in *Historical Statistics of the
United States*, I, 210.

What is the balance sheet on wages and annual real earnings?
Before we can finally be certain about changes and how they
affected the earnings of workers of different ages, skills, sexes,
and family responsibilities, we need studies of wages and earnings at particular workplaces. Estimates must be made of real
annual earnings after subtractions for time lost to layoffs, sickness, and shorter hours. Case-studies of particular industries can
fill this need.[24] We also need studies of white-collar occupations;
most of the samples from the period focus on blue-collar workers. This is especially unfortunate since the white-collar sector expanded rapidly in the 1920s. Finally, if we are to arrive at some
general estimation of the economic standards of the average person, we need studies of small proprietors, whose life-styles, class
backgrounds, and incomes were not always so different from
those of working-class persons.

In the meantime, we can offer tentative generalizations about
earnings in the 1920s. Samples of white-collar workers show
them doing well though their gains must be seen against a background of tremendous losses during the 1914-1920 period. Manual workers generally gained from 1914 to 1920, suffered in
the 1921 depression, gained in the 1922-1923 expansion, and
made moderate gains for the rest of the decade, the new era of
prosperity. By the end of the 1920s, their earnings were well
ahead of the pre-war period.[25]

---

[24] Ozanne's study of International Harvester, cited above, makes no attempt to estimate annual earnings; but it serves as an example of the kind of case study
needed.
[25] Based on Douglas, especially 316-364, 376.

Table 2: Changes in Real Annual Earnings for Selected Categories of White-Collar and Public Employees. (Six year periods unless otherwise noted)

Occupation	World War I Period	Total Change (%)	1920s Period	Total Change (%)
	1914-1915 to 1919-1920a		1919-1920 to 1926-1927b	
1. College Professors	1914-1915 to 1919-1920a	-35%	1919-1920 to 1926-1927b	+63.8%
2. School Teachers	1914 to 1920	-19%	1920 to 1926	+60.5%
3. Salaried in Manufacturing	1914 to 1920	-18%	1920 to 1926	+29.3%
4. Clerical on Railroads	1914 to 1920	-1%	1920 to 1926	+13.1%
5. Salespeople (Ohio)	1915 to 1920a	-16%	1920 to 1926	+31 %
6. Service Workers (Ohio)	1915 to 1920a	-3%	1920 to 1926	+25.7%
7. Government Workers (District of Columbia)	1914 to 1920	-30%	1920 to 1926	+30 %
8. U.S. Postal Clerks and Letter Carriers	1914 to 1920	-23%	1920 to 1926	+37.7%

Table 2a: Changes in Real Weekly Earnings for Selected Categories of Blue-Collar Workers.

	Period	Total Change (%)	Period	Total Change (%)
1. All Manufacturing Wage Earners	1914 to 1920	+20%	1920 to 1926	+ 8.3%
2. Male Unskilled, Manufacturing	1914 to 1920	+30%	1920 to 1926	+ 2.3%
3. Female, Manufacturing	1914 to 1920	+18%	1920 to 1926	+12.7%
4. All Railroad Wage Earners	1914 to 1920	+14%	1920 to 1926	+ 5.3%
5. Railroad Workers, Unskilled	1914 to 1920	+28%	1920 to 1926	- 10.9%
6. Railroad Shop, Skilled and Semi-skilled	1914 to 1920	+24%	1920 to 1926	0

a Five year period. b Seven year period.
Note: Post-war percentage gains exaggerate real gains because they are calculated on the lower 1920 base. Thus a 30 percent loss from $1000 to $700 between 1914 and 1920 would not be made up by a 30 percent gain to $910 from 1920 to 1926.
Sources Table 2: For college professors, Trevor Arnett, Teachers' Salaries in Certain Endowed and State Supported Colleges and Universities in the United States, With Special Reference to Colleges of Arts, Literature and Science, 1926-1927 (New York, 1928), 18. For 2-8, Paul H. Douglas, Real Wages in the United States, 1890-1926 (Boston and New York, 1930), 382, 364, 370, 371, 376, 378.
Source Table 2a: For 1-6, NICB, Wages in the United States, 1914-1929 (New York, 1930), 104, 180, 182, 183. For these categories the 1920s data run from the fourth quarter of 1920 to the fourth quarter of 1926.

But such generalizations hide the poor showing of millions of blue-collar workers. In many cases the unskilled gained little in the 1920s, either in absolute terms, or—continuing a pre-war trend—relative to "the labor aristocracy." Auto workers, printers, workers in the building trades, and the railroad operating crafts did well. Women workers in manufacturing, common labor on the railroads, in the steel industry, in road construction, and at International Harvester, foundry workers, farm laborers, and in general, workers in New England and the South, lost or gained little during the prosperity period from 1923 to 1929. Furthermore, wage differentials widened. While real weekly earnings in the building trades advanced 51.6 percent from 1920 to 1926, those of unskilled laborers increased only 7.9 percent and those of farm labor, steel workers, and cotton workers declined respectively 12.9 percent, 14.8 percent, and 14.6 percent.[26]

For the average manual worker without special skills or union protection, the good news of the 1920s was not that wages shot up or that unemployment disappeared, but that workers had higher incomes than before the war and that after the 1921 slump there were no major depressions to slash wages and cause widespread layoffs. The new era from 1923 to 1929 was indeed better than the depression periods of the 1870s, 1890s, and 1930s, but this relative prosperity must be seen for what it is.[27]

Even in the 1920s, the difference between poverty and minimum comfort for many working-class families was quite simply whether the head of household had work. Although social agencies could give minimal help to some of the unemployed, there was nothing equivalent to our present system of unemployment compensation, food stamps, and social security. Unemployment may have been lower than in the pre-war period, but it was not insignificant during the 1920s.[28]

In that decade there were no annual national unemployment censuses by the Federal government such as we have today, and

[26] Based on Douglas, *passim* and especially 637 ff. On the widening of wage differentials and the "Labor Aristocracy" in the pre-war period, see Andrew Dawson, "The Paradox of Dynamic Technological Change and the Labor Aristocracy in the United States, 1880-1914," *Labor History*, 20 (1979), 325-351.

[27] See Summer H. Slichter, "The Current Labor Policies of American Industries," *The Quarterly Journal of Economics*, 42 (May 1929), 393-435.

[28] For the assumption that unemployment all but disappeared, see Hawley, 81. Bernstein, 55-63, gives the best short summary of relevant data on unemployment.

it is unlikely that we will ever have completely satisfactory statistics.[29] However, available evidence casts doubt on the common view that unemployment was negligible in the 1920s, and
suggests that the most commonly used figures, those developed
by Stanley Lebergott and reproduced in *Historical Statistics of
the United States*, underestimate the extent of unemployment
and disguise its severe impact on particular groups. Table 3
shows four series of unemployment rates. Series A, perhaps the
most commonly used, shows a remarkably low average rate of
3.3 percent during 1923 to 1929. The low 1.8 percent rate for
1926, if true, would be close to a modern peacetime record for
the US.[30] Series C, Robert Coen's new estimates for Series A, result in an average unemployment rate of 5.1 percent for 1923
to 1929, considerably higher than Lebergott's estimates. With a
labor force of about 45,000,000 in the mid-1920s, Coen's estimates mean that an average of 810,000 more people were unemployed each month than Lebergott's figures yield.[31] Coen did
not calculate new figures for non-farm employees (corresponding to Series B), but had the difference been as great as between
Series A and Series C, the unemployment rates for non-farm
workers must have averaged more than 7 percent in the prosperous years from 1923 to 1929.

   Series D shatters the notion of low unemployment. Douglas'
figures for unemployed wage-earners in manufacturing, transportation, mining, and building average 12.95 percent from 1921
to 1926 and even the best three years (1923, 1925, 1926) average 8.1 percent. It is reasonable to add to these figures one or
two percent for the time lost by part-time workers who wanted full-time work. An analysis of unemployment in early 1975
showed that adding to the unemployment rates the equivalent
of that portion of the work week lost by part-time workers who
wanted a full week raised the number of unemployed from 8.2
million to 9.9 million and the unemployment rate from 8.9 per-

---

[29] On the poor quality of data on unemployment, see John A. Garraty, *Unemployment in History: Economic Thought and Public Policy* (New York, 1979), 166 ff.
[30] In the 20th century, only one other peacetime year recorded an unemployment
   rate below 2 percent and that was 1906. See *HS*, I, 126.
[31] The labor force in 1925 was 45,432,000, according to *HS*, I, 126.
   Thus Coen: 5.1% × 45,000,000 = 2,295,000
   Lebergott: 3.3% × 45,000,000 = 1,485,000
                                    ─────────
                                    810,000

Table 3:   Unemployment in the 1920s

	A	B	C	D
	As Per Cent of Civilian Labor Force	As Per Cent of Non-farm Employees	As Per Cent of Civilian Labor Force (Coen)	Wage-earners in Transportation, Mining, Building, and Manufacturing
1921	11.7%	19.5%	–	23.1%
1922	6.7%	11.4%	7.3%	18.3%
1923	2.4%	4.1%	4.5%	7.9%
1924	5.0%	8.3%	6.0%	12.0%
1925	3.2%	5.4%	4.9%	8.9%
1926	1.8%	2.9%	4.1%	7.5%
1927	3.3%	5.4%	5.0%	–
1928	4.2%	6.9%	5.5%	–
1929	3.2%	5.3%	5.5%	–

Sources: Series A and B, *Historical Statistics of the United States*, I, 126. Series C, Robert M. Coen, "Labor Force and Unemployment in the 1920's and 1930's: A Re-Examination Based on Postwar Experience," *The Review of Economics and Statistics*, 55 (1973), 52. Series D, Paul H. Douglas, *Real Wages in the United States, 1890-1926* (Boston and New York, 1930), 460.

cent to 10.7 percent. Certainly in the 1920s, without the supports people have today during unemployment, part-time work brought hardship to many. In fact, it made it more difficult to save for periods of total unemployment. As one writer noted in 1928, "due to the amount of part-time work during the past year or two, they have found it impossible to accumulate a financial reserve to fall back on when out of a job." [32]

Evidence from several samples shows the prevalence of unemployment among blue-collar families. In 1924, of a sample of Chicago's unskilled and semi-skilled workers, 31 percent lost up to six weeks of work due to layoffs and sickness. In Muncie, Indiana ("Middletown") in the same year, 43 percent of one sample of heads of working-class families lost at least a month of work and half of these, 24.2 percent of the total sample, lost three or more months of work. For the first nine months of 1924, these families experienced an average unemployment rate

[32] Caroline Manning, *The Immigrant Woman and Her Job*, Bulletin of the Women's Bureau, US Dept. of Labor, No. 74 (Washington, DC, 1930), 100 ff.; for the quotation, J. F. Bogardus, "Unemployment Among Organized Labor in Philadelphia," *American Federationist* 35 (Aug. 1928), 939. For a discussion of groups excluded from the most highly publicized and widely used unemployment figures, see "Capitalism and Unemployment," *Monthly Review*, 27 (June 1975), 1-14, especially 11 on part-timers wanting full-time work.

of 17.5 percent. A survey of employment in Philadelphia in April 1929 showed 10.4 percent out of work because there was no work to be found (7.8 percent) or because of sickness, old age, and similar causes (2.6 percent). In the industrial neighborhoods investigators found 18.9 percent of the workers unemployed. A Cincinnati survey in May 1929 discovered that 5.9 percent of the employables (not counting the sick and aged) were out of work and in the six poorest wards the rates ranged from 10 to 26.8 percent.[33]

Even in the best of times, economic insecurity clouded the hopes of working-class families. As Frederick Croxton put it at the end of the decade, the burden of unemployment, whether from slack work, sickness, or old age, was heavy "even when industrial conditions are considered approximately normal."[34] Many working-class families were poor when employed. Unemployment pushed them over the brink. Said the wife of an unemployed roofer: "When my husband's working steady I can just manage, but when he's out, things go back. First I stop on the damp wash, then on the food, and then the rent goes behind."[35] Some families nearly starved rather than seek charity from social agencies; one lived on tea and bread for six weeks. A devoted father stood on the street-corner at lunch-time "for fear if he came home he would be tempted to eat what they have been able to put on the table for the children." With malnutrition came disease, especially pneumonia. In extreme cases, adults had nervous breakdowns or turned on the gas.[36]

---

[33] Leila Houghteling, *The Income and Standard of Living of Unskilled Laborers in Chicago* (Chicago, 1927), 30-31; Robert S. Lynd and Helen Merrell Lynd, *Middletown: A Study in American Culture* (New York, 1929), 512; J. Frederick Dewhurst and Ernest A. Tupper, *Social and Economic Character of Unemployment in Philadelphia, April, 1929*, BLS Bull. No. 520 (1930); "Unemp'oyment in Cincinnati," *Monthly Labor Review*, 29 (Dec. 1929), 192; and also Fred C. Croxton and Frederick E. Croxton, "Unemployment in Buffalo, NY, in 1929, with Comparison of Conditions in Columbus, Ohio, in 1921 to 1925," *Monthly Labor Review*, 30 (Feb. 1930), 25-39. The percentage for Middletown was calculated as follows from the figures which the Lynds give only in terms of groups of workers losing 1-2 months, 3-4 months, and so on. Those who lost under a month were dropped. Those who lost 1-2 months were assumed to have lost 1½ months, those losing 2-3 months, 2½ months, and so on. The total losses for the nine months were 260.5 months, or 28.9 months per month. The total number of workers in the sample was 165. Hence 28.9 divided by 165 = 17.5 per cent.

[34] Croxton and Croxton, 37.

[35] Clinch Caulkins, *Some Folks Won't Work* (New York, 1930), 37.

[36] *Ibid.*, 37, 123, 137, and *passim*. See also Lynd and Lynd, 59, ff., and Manning, 100-103, 110 and 137.

These examples might seem like isolated ones. In a large country, one can find desperate cases no matter how low the unemployment rates. But a mathematical example can demostrate how serious unemployment was even with a low national rate for the total labor force. The year 1929 was a good one. The GNP increased almost 7 percent over the previous year.[37] Unemployment for the non-farm sector, according to Lebergott's estimates, was only 5.3 percent. Unemployment is usually higher for blue-collar workers than for all non-farm workers. Assume a rate of unemployment for male blue-collar workers of 10 percent, not unreasonable in light of figures given above for the industrial areas of Philadelphia and Cincinnati. Assume that half the blue-collar families stand on the line between poverty and minimum comfort. A 10 percent annual average of unemployment means that each month 10 percent of the blue-collar workers are without jobs. This might mean, for the sake of argument, that if the duration of unemployment averages two months, 60 percent of the blue-collar workers lose two months or 1/6 of their annual earnings. Without recourse to charity or sending other members of the family out to work or substantial savings—and often even with those supports—these families fall into poverty. Thirty percent of the blue-collar families (60 percent multiplied by the 50 percent on the edge of poverty with employment) fall into poverty with an unemployment rate of 10 percent. This imaginary example demonstrates how an apparently modest national unemployment rate, averaged over a year, hides what was happening to blue-collar workers on a month-to-month basis.

Despite the decline in European immigration and except for specific skills and rare months of high demand, there was a glut in the market for industrial workers after 1923. The decade opened with a sharp contraction, but even the prosperity period of 1923 to 1929 was punctuated by brief recessions in 1924 and 1927. As the decade progressed, workers had a harder time finding jobs. It is true that European immigration tapered off, but this was "more than counteracted by the enlarged flow from farm to city." Except for a few months early in 1923, it was an employers' market.[38]

---

[37] Gordon, 24.
[38] Quotation from Slichter, 396; see also *ibid.*, 425-431, and Manning, 100-103, 110

As the flow from rural areas to industrial areas continued and as the labor force continued to grow from natural causes (despite declining birth rates), there was little increase in employment in basic industry. Productivity zoomed upward and increasing output was possible with the same number of or fewer workers. It is a striking fact that, even with the enormous increases in American industry's output in the 1920s, there was almost the same number of production workers in manufacturing in 1928 and 1929 (8.1 and 8.6 million) as there had been in 1919 and 1920 (8.6 million).[39] As some lines of production increased their demand for labor, others, through mechanization and the reorganization of work, displaced workers. Of these many suffered months of unemployment before finding work.[40]

Even if unemployment were low relative to the pre-war period and even if, as we have seen, earnings were probably higher than in the pre-war period, working-class incomes were not very high in an absolute sense. It is not easy to determine what people needed for a decent life. As one expert put it in 1928, "there is little knowledge about human needs, real or custom made." [41] Nor is it easy to weigh changes in the quality of life. For exam-

---

and Ralph J. Watkins, *Ohio Employment Studies* (Columbus, 1927), 46, which shows lower employment in 1924, 1925, and 1926 than 1923.

[39] Figures from *HS*, I, 43, rounded off.

[40] David Weintraub, "Unemployment and Increasing Productivity," in National Resources Committee, *Technological Trends and National Policy* (Washington, 1937), 74, 79-80, 83, 87; Calkins, 89-91 and *passim*. Isador Lubin, *The Absorption of the Unemployed by American Industry* (Washington, DC, 1929), offers evidence on how hard it was for workers displaced from old jobs to find new ones.

[41] Jessica B. Peixotto, "Family Budgets of University Faculty Members," *Science*, 68 (Nov. 23, 1928), 500. The determination of standards of minimum comfort and levels of poverty is obviously difficult. Always in the 1920s investigators developed standards to fit specific social groups. Thus there was a "professional standard" for professors and there was a special standard for clerical workers and a different one for skilled workers. Standards developed for workers were usually very low. The Bureau of Municipal Research in Philadelphia determined that a "workingman's" family of five needed $1,994.06 in 1925 to stay out of poverty. See Karl De Schweinitz, "Are the Poor Really Poor?" *The Survey*, 59 (Jan. 15, 1928), 517-519. Paul H. Douglas, in *Wages and the Family* (Chicago, 1927), argued that workers should have the "subsistence-plus, or the minimum health-and-decency budget," which demanded $1500 to $1800 for urban working-class families. This was not "the American standard of living," which would have demanded $2000-2400, but Douglas feared that at the higher level, workers would lose "a large part of their incentive to work." See pp. 5-6, 192-193. In view of the austere levels of living even at the $2000 level, this is a remarkable statement. Douglas himself contradicted its assumption when later, arguing that guaranteed income levels would not lead to higher birth rates, he asserted that with "democratized consumption," in most economic classes, "men's wants greatly exceed their income" (see 245-255).

ple, store-bought bread and canned goods saved labor time in the home, but sometimes meant a loss of taste and nutrition.[42] However, using standards developed in the 1920s and examining the expenditures of families at specific income levels, we can estimate what people could afford and, in monetary terms at least, how well they lived. Obviously this material emphasis is only part of the texture of daily life, but it is an important one, about which much has been assumed in the historiography of the period. People may not live on bread alone, but they cannot live without it.

The proportion of families living in poverty in 1929, at the end of the decade of prosperity, was large. The following table lists four estimates of poverty lines in 1929. While the determination of poverty lines and changes in the cost of living over time is less exact than one might wish, a 1929 income of about $1550 for a non-farm family of four roughly equals the poverty line of $5500 set for the same group in 1977 by the Federal Government. It seems safe to conclude—after discounting Smolensky's high estimate—that 35 to 40 percent of the non-farm families in 1929 were poor.[43]

These figures about poverty seem abstract. What could work-

Table 4:   Poverty Levels in 1929

Source	Poverty Levels For Families	Per Cent of All U.S. Families Under Poverty Level	Per Cent of All U.S. Non-Farm Families Under Poverty Level
Brookings	$1500	42.3%	34.5%
Smolensky[a]	$1912	56.5%	50.1%
Smolensky[b]	$1574	44.9%	37.3%
Smolensky[c]	$1694	50.0%	42.0%

Sources: Brookings, *America's Capacity to Consume*, 87, 54, 231; Eugene Smolensky, "The Past and Present Poor," in Robert Fogel and Stanley L. Engerman, eds., *The Reinterpretation of American Economic History* (New York, 1971), 87-92. Smolensky[a] is based on the 1929 equivalent of $3000 in 1964; Smolensky[b] on the 1929 equivalent of the Works Progress Administration's 1935 estimate for an urban family of four; Smolensky[c] is my calculation from his finding that New York City minimum comfort levels averaged 50 per cent of real per capita Gross National Product from 1903 to 1935. GNP data from *Historical Statistics of the United States*, I, 224 and income distribution from Brookings, 52.

[42] On food losses, see Richard Osborn Cummings, *The American and His Food: A History of Food Habits in the United States* (Chicago, 1941), 111 ff.
[43] For the 1977 poverty line, Gary M. Walton and Roger LeRoy Miller, *Economic Issues in American History* (San Francisco, 1978), 169. The business-oriented National Industrial Conference Board's *The Cost of Living in Twelve Industrial Cities* (New York, 1928), 3, 9, 51, set the "fair, minimum, American standard

ers afford? How well did they live? Although historians must examine all elements of expenditure in family budgets before they can arrive at a well-rounded judgment about living standards, consumption patterns, and personal choices, for this review two items have been singled out: 1) food, because it is so basic to human existence and, for the vast majority of families, the largest single expenditure in the budget during the 1920s, and 2) automobiles, because they seemed so characteristic of what was new, exciting, and prosperous in the decade.

Could the average working-class family afford a nourishing diet? That depended on three things: the definition of a nourishing diet, the kinds of foods purchased within a given income, and the total family income. For the purposes of this broad survey, we can ignore the second factor, assuming that the most important determinant of adequate nutrition was the size of the family income. Careful, knowledgeable purchasing and preparation could stretch a given amount of food dollars and vice versa. But on the whole, income level was the most important determinant of nutritional level. A sample of the families of Chicago's semi-skilled and unskilled workers from a variety of ethnic backgrounds confirmed that "although because of faulty selection of individual items of food, a standard expenditure does not always insure an adequate diet, generally speaking, it was found that as expenditure for food increased, the diet became more adequate." Nor is it surprising that of all family groups whose food patterns were studied during the 1920s, there was only one in which no single family was undernourished and that was a sample of twelve professional families each spending what was, as we shall see, the princely sum of $1000 a year for food.[44]

of living" for an urban wage-earner's family of four at around $1500 to $1600. This allowed very little for emergencies, no large furniture purchases, and no automobile. It seems clear that the poverty standards referred to in this paper are not high.

[44] Houghteling, *The Income and Standard of Living of Unskilled Laborers in Chicago*, 90, 191; quotation from Leila Houghteling, "The Budget of the Unskilled Laborer," *Social Service Review*, 1 (Mar. 1927), 30; Mary Gorringe Luck and Sybil Woodruff, *Cost of Living Studies, III: The Food of Twelve Families of the Professional Class*, Univ. of California Publications in Economics, 5 (1931), 277. See also Cummings, 165; and Heller Committee for Research in Social Economics and Constantine Panunzio *Cost of Living Studies, V: How Mexicans Earn and Live: A Study of the Incomes and Expenditures of One Hundred Mexican Families in San Diego, California*, Univ. of California Publications in Economics, 13 (1933), 32, 34.

What then was an adequate diet and could working-class families afford it? Social workers, dieticians, and social economists in the 1920s developed menus and budgets for minimum levels of calories, protein, and essential minerals such as calcium and iron. In the late 1920s, this scientifically developed minimum cost about 41 cents a day, for a moderately active adult male or, for a family of five, about $500 a year. To get the minimum nourishment for this expenditure demanded "exceeding great care" in the selection of foods and left "little variety and very little margin of safety in respect to vitamins and minerals." That this was not in the least a liberal diet which allowed flexibility and variety in purchasing foods, can be inferred from the fact that it was the standard allowed for families dependent on charity, and for families of the unemployed in the depression of the 1930s.[45]

Could working-class families afford this poverty diet of 41 cents a day per adult male or $500 a year for a family of five? The following table shows that more prosperous groups among the working class spent much more than $500 and for families of fewer than five members.

Table 5: Food Expenditures of "Prosperous" Workers' Families

Sample and Year	Average Annual Family Incomes	Average Actual Family Size	Total Annual Food Expenditures
Typographers (San Francisco), 1920-1921	$2600.00	3.4	$893.30
Streetcarmen (San Francisco), 1925	$1886.00	4.2	$789.80
Federal Employees (New York, Boston, Baltimore, Chicago, New Orleans), 1928	$2433.91	4.56	$810.64

Sources: Jessica B. Peixotto, *Cost of Living Studies II: How Workers Spend a Living Wage: A Study of the Incomes and Expenditures of Eight-Two Typographers' Families in San Francisco*, University of California Publications in Economics, 5 (1929), 161-245; Heller Committee for Research in Social Economics, *Cost of Living Studies, IV: Spending Ways of a Semi-Skilled Group: A Study of the Incomes and Expenditures of Ninety-Eight Street-car Men's Families in the San Francisco East Bay Region*, University of California Publications in Economics, 5 (1931), 295-365; and "Cost of Living of Federal Employees in Five Cities," *Monthly Labor Review*, 29 (Aug., 1929), 41-69.

---

[45] Quotation from Brookings, 122. Other material from Luck and Woodruff, 256; Florence Nesbitt, *A Study of a Minimum Standard of Living for Dependent Families in Los Angeles* (Los Angeles, 1927), 36, which set the adult male

We can assume that these families, with total incomes well above the poverty line and food expenditures much higher than the $500 minimum were well fed.

What about the millions of families of manufacturing workers and especially of unskilled workers in manufacturing and other sectors of the economy? Were wages sufficient for an adequate diet? The better paid manufacturing workers employed for a full year were able to purchase the minimum diet. The families of one hundred Ford employees with incomes averaging around $1700 a year in 1929, spent $556.12 on food, or the equivalent of 46.6 cents per adult male per day. These families had a margin of safety for waste in cooking and preparation and for some variety in their diet, and they were able to do it on income derived almost totally from the chief wage-earner. But the Ford workers included in the survey were unrepresentative; they averaged 250 days of work a year which was just below a full year of 260 days at Ford. For auto workers—as for workers in other industries—unemployment for a month or two a year was quite common and could have pushed them down to or below the level of minimum nutritional standards. And the wages of auto workers were near the top of the ranks among industrial workers.[46]

Table 6 creates a model to estimate the adequacy of the earnings of the chief wage worker to a family's food needs. It begins with actual weekly earnings of two groups, production workers in manufacturing and unskilled railroad workers. It multiplies this by two proportions of the weekly wage spent for food (35 percent and 40 percent) which were typical at those income lev-

---

equivalent for Los Angeles in 1927 at 42 cents; Ruth Okey and Emily H. Huntington, "Adequate Food at Low Cost," *The Pacific Coast Journal of Nursing*, 28 (May 1932), 279-283, allowed about 30 cents for an unemployed male in San Francisco in Nov., 1931; using the figures on changes in food costs in M. Ada Beney, *Cost of Living in the United States, 1914-1936* (New York, 1936), 59-61, we find that this was the equivalent of 40.1 cents in 1929. See also Erle F. Young, *Social Statistical Summary of Los Angeles* (Los Angeles, 1931), 28, and Hazel K. Stiebeling and Medora M. Ward, "Diets at Four Levels of Nutritive Content and Cost," U.S. Dept. of Agriculture Circular No. 296 (Washington, DC, 1933), 1-58.

46 "Standard of Living of Employees of Ford Motor Co. in Detroit," *Monthly Labor Review*, 30 (June 1930), 15-25; "Instability of Employment in the Automobile Industry," *Monthly Labor Review*, 28 (June 1929), 20-23. For estimates of more typical earnings of Ford workers than those in the *Monthly Labor Review* sample, see two articles by Reinhold Niebuhr, "How Philanthropic is Henry Ford?" and "Ford's Five Day Week," *Christian Century* (Dec. 9, 1926), 1516-1517 and (June 9, 1927), 713-714.

Table 6: Model for Estimating the Adequacy of the Wages of Manufacturing Workers and Unskilled Railroad Workers to Food Needs, 1929

		I	II	III	IV	V	VI
		Average Weekly Wage	Per Cent of Wage Spent on Food	Family Size in Adult Male Equivalents	Daily Expenditures Per Adult Male Equivalent	Minimum Daily Standard for Adult Male	Per Cent Above or Below Adult Male Standard
	A	$24.76	35%	2.45	50.5¢	41¢	+23.1%
	B	$24.76	40%	2.45	57.7¢	41¢	+40.7%
Production	C	$24.76	35%	3.35	37.0¢	41¢	− 9.8%
Workers in	D	$24.76	40%	3.35	42.2¢	41¢	+ 2.9%
Manufacturing	E	$24.76	35%	3.8	32.6¢	41¢	−20.5%
	F	$24.76	40%	3.8	37.2¢	41¢	− 9.3%
	G	$17.97	35%	2.45	36.7¢	41¢	−10.5%
	H	$17.97	40%	2.45	41.9¢	41¢	+ 2.2%
Unskilled	I	$17.97	35%	3.35	26.8¢	41¢	−34.6%
Railroad	J	$17.97	40%	3.35	30.7¢	41¢	−25.1%
Workers	K	$17.97	35%	3.8	23.6¢	41¢	−42.4%
	L	$17.97	40%	3.8	27.0¢	41¢	−34.1%

Sources: For manufacturing wages, *Historical Statistics of the United States*, I, 170, and railroad unskilled, NICB, *Wages in the United States, 1914-1929* (New York, 1930), 183. The budget proportions spent for food are based on Brookings, *America's Capacity to Consume*, 257. Column III reduces the food needs of different ages and sexes to their equivalent in adult male requirements, a standard practice in the 1920s. Thus an adult male counted as 1, an adult female as .9, children ages 3, 5, and 13 as .15, .4, and .9. The 3.35 family = Brookings' model family of five: adult male and adult female, children ages 13, 5, and 3. The 2.45 family = the same minus the teenager. The 3.8 family = adult male and adult female, two teenage children.

els. Finally it divides that sum by seven days of the week and by three possible family sizes (reduced to equivalents in adult males) to discover how close to the minimum adult male standard the families could have come on the wages of the chief wage-earner.

In three of six possibilities (C, E, and F) manufacturing wages could not buy an adequate diet; in a fourth case (D), the food expenditure was dangerously close to the minimum. In only one case (H) was the wage of unskilled railroad workers sufficient to reach the minimum. From these theoretical possibilities, it seems clear that despite rhetoric about high wage policies in the 1920s, employers were not, in many cases, paying workers enough to support their families even at the most minimal levels. Moreover, a stretch of sickness or layoffs could push even better paid workers into poverty. Additional income, from children and spouses, and lodgers and boarders, was often necessary to reach even the minimally adequate diet.[47]

Additions to the family income beyond the chief wage-earner's wages were, while life-saving for the family, often not enough to raise the family's living standard to the minimum level. The annual family incomes of unskilled and semi-skilled workers in Chicago in 1924 averaged around $1700; many included income in addition to that of the primary wage-earner. Yet as many as 43 percent of these families spent less than was needed for the minimum diet.[48] In respect to the adequacy of family incomes, the following table summarizes data on non-farm family incomes in 1929, using the Brookings tables on incomes and budget allocations for the five lowest income groups, the Ford sample as typical of the size of lower income families, and a subtraction for waste in preparation and cooking—a common deduction in studies of that era which gives us a figure that suggests how much the typical family, without a dietician's knowledge and without extreme care in selection, was probably getting for their food expenditures.

---

[47] This point is shown very graphically in Caroline F. Ware, *Greenwich Village, 1920-1930: A Comment on American Civilization in the Post-War Years* (New York, 1965), 72-73. See also, note 48, below.

[48] Houghteling, *Income and Standard*, especially 52-103, and Houghteling, "The Budget of the Unskilled Laborer." In 55.1% of these families, the chief breadwinner earned less than $1400 a year.

Table 7: Food Expenditures of Non-Farm Families, 1929: Family Income from $0-3000

A Per Cent of All Non-Farm Families	B Income Range	C Average Food Expenditure		D Average Daily Adult Male Equivalent	E After 10 Per Cent Deduction for Waste
12.6%	$0-1000	$360	÷ by 3.27, Ford families, in adult male equivalents ÷ by 365 days	30.2¢	27.2¢
21.9%	$1000-1500	$490		41.1¢	36.9¢
18.9%	$1500-2000	$610		51.1¢	45.9¢
13.0%	$2000-2500	$700		58.6¢	52.8¢
8.1%	$2500-3000	$770		64.5¢	58.1¢

Sources: Columns A-C from Brookings, *America's Capacity to Consume*, 257, 231. The Ford families were the equivalent of 3.27 adult males. See "Standard of Living of Employees of Ford Motor Co. in Detroit," *Monthly Labor Review*, 30 (June 1930), 4.

Probably most of the families in the lowest two income groups and some in the third group ($1500-2000) had insufficient incomes to buy the minimum diet. Some families were better off and some worse off than the averages, depending on family size and the kinds of foods purchased, but a rough estimate would be that 40 percent of the non-farm families in the United States had insufficient incomes to buy an adequate diet at the end of the decade of prosperity. This percentage is close to our earlier estimate that about 35 to 40 percent of all non-farm families in the United States had incomes below the poverty line.

Perhaps, after all, it was people's fault if they ate poorly; careful analysis of family budgets might show that poor families "wasted" their money on radios and automobiles. Certainly it was and is a major assumption of writings about the 1920s that almost everyone had a car. As early as 1927 French observer André Siegfried asserted that "it is quite common to find a working-class family in which the father has his own car, and the grown-up sons have one apiece as well." Later historians have followed the same line.[49] To be sure, Americans loved their automobiles. Said the wife of an unemployed worker in Middletown, "I'll never cut on gas! I'd go without a meal before I'd cut down on using the car."[50]

49 Siegfried, *America Comes of Age* (New York, 1927), 162; Potter, 47; Hicks, 112; and Leuchtenburg, 194.
50 Lynd and Lynd, *Middletown*, 63.

Total automobile registrations in the United States leaped from 6,679,000 in 1919 to 23,120,800 in 1929.[51] Simple arithmetic seems to demonstrate that of the 29,582,000 households in 1929, just over 6,000,000 lacked cars, and 78 percent had them.[52] This would indeed be remarkable, because only 55 percent of all families had them in 1950.[53]

As a matter of fact, total registrations are not a good indicator of private ownership. Many automobiles were owned by businesses; some families had more than one car even in 1929; and there were many unattached individuals counted neither as families nor households who presumably had the same American birthright to the automobile. In 1929 there were 36,100,000 consumer units (adding families and unattached individuals). Using Lebergott's estimate that 78 percent of all cars were available for private use after subtracting business vehicles leaves 18,034,222 cars. In 1927, a survey by the General Federation of Women's Clubs indicated that 18 percent of the car-owning families possessed two or more cars. This must have been an exaggeration based on a sample biased toward upper-income groups and including some business cars. In 1950, 7 percent of all families had more than one car. A conservative estimate would use the latter figure for 1929. This leaves 16,771,826 automobiles for 36,100,000 consumer units; about 46 percent of the units had cars—rather less than "everyone."[54]

Using a different approach the Brookings study estimated that after subtracting for duplicate registrations, cars scrapped during the year, cars used for business, and cars owned by farmers, there were 14-15,000,000 cars available to 22,000,000 non-farm families and 9,000,000 non-farm unattached individuals; by this count, just under 50 percent of all non-farm units owned cars in 1929.[55]

The distribution of automobile ownership varied by state, type of community, and income level. California had a higher per-

[51] *HS*, I, 716.
[52] Roughly Potter's position, 68.
[53] Margaret G. Reid, *Consumers and the Market* (New York, 1938), 24; and *HS*, II, 717.
[54] Data on consumer units, *HS*, I, 301; Lebergott, *The American Economy*, 289; for a summary of the General Federation of Women's Clubs survey, James J. Flink, *The Car Culture* (Cambridge, MA, 1975), 142; for 1950 figures on two car families, *HS*, II, 717.
[55] Brookings, 252. See also Lebergott, *The American Economy*, 290.

centage of car owners than any other state; farmers and people in small communities had higher rates of ownership than
people in large communities; towns dependent on automobile
manufacturing seemed to have had a higher than average working-class ownership of autos. Almost half of one sample of Middletown's working-class families, already in 1924, and 47 percent
of a sample of Ford workers in 1929 owned cars. But generally,
working-class families were less likely to have cars than upper-
income groups. The Brookings authors guessed that a third of
all wage-earners and "lower-salaried men" owned cars in 1929.
While 57 percent of a sample of Univ. of California professors
already owned cars in 1922 and 56 percent of the Yale faculty
in 1928, only 3 percent of Chicago's unskilled in 1924, 26.5
percent of San Francisco's streetcar workers in 1925, 22.5 percent of urban federal workers in 1928 (ranging from 5.9 percent in New York City to 33.3 percent in Chicago), and 26 percent of a small sample of Mexican workers in 1929-1930 had
cars.[56]

The car was enormously important in American culture and
in the American economy in the 1920s, but most working-class
families did not own automobiles. Nor did car ownership indicate a family budget bursting with affluence—not when a used
car could be had for $60 ($5 down and $5 a month).[57] More
work needs to be done on family finances, installment credit,
and workers' attitudes toward the car. At this point we can say
that Americans were much more likely than Europeans to have
cars, that the average non-farm family in 1929 probably had
a 50 percent chance of owning a car, and that the average work-

[56] Flink, 142; Lynd and Lynd, 254-255; "Standard of Living of Employees of Ford,"
49; Brookings, 252; Jessica B. Peixotto, *Getting and Spending at the Professional
Standard of Living: A Study of the Costs of Living an Academic Life* (New York,
1927), 225; Yandell Henderson and Maurice R. Davie, *Incomes and Living Costs of
a University Faculty* (New Haven, 1928), 50; Houghteling, *The Income and Standard of Living of Unskilled Laborers in Chicago*, 120; Heller Committee, *Cost
of Living Studies*, IV, 332; "Cost of Living of Federal Employees in Five Cities:
Miscellaneous Expenditures," *Monthly Labor Review*, 29 (Oct. 1929), 243, 248;
Heller Committee and Panunzio, *Cost of Living Studies*, V, 52-53. In the lower
half of the incomes (under $1000) in 1934, about 38 percent had one or more
cars; in the upper half of the incomes ($1000 and over), almost 73 percent had
one or more cars. These figures covered only urban families (see Reid, 24).
[57] Archie Chadbourne, "Debt is the Only Adventure a Poor Man Can Count On,"
American Magazine, 104 (Dec. 1927), 45. Chadbourne's annual income was
about $1300 if he worked steadily. He estimated that he had about $681.39 in
debts, but he did have a vehicle. See also Harold Cary, "Can Every Family Have
a Car?" *Colliers* (Jan. 5, 1924), 6-7, 29.

ing-class family had perhaps a 30 percent chance of owning a car. These are all educated guesses, but they are more educated than those which appear in many treatments of the 1920s.

      ✳   ✳   ✳   ✳   ✳   ✳

Contemporaries such as Sinclair Lewis and recent writers such as Stuart Ewen have drawn marvelous portraits of the culture of consumerism that blossomed in the 1920s. But each author has served us badly by directing our attention away from bread-and-butter issues. George Babbitt's psyche may have been invaded by the new materialism, but George could afford it at an annual income of $8000. No doubt Ewen's advertisers made aggressive efforts to channel human needs into commercial consumption, and divert workers from their discontents, but it matters very much whether the workers being pacified could afford the goods and whether novel items or more basic human needs were uppermost in their minds.[58]

The outpouring of goods and the creation of needs in the 1920s supports the decade's reputation as the first excursion into mass affluence. But the masses were not affluent enough to worry much about clean-smelling breath and fancy cars. Wages were higher than in the pre-war period, but for many increased little after 1923. Unemployment did not disappear and the annual earnings of many workers were inadequate to support basic needs. Perhaps 40 percent of the population was poor in the 1920s.[59] So many unskilled workers had to use social agencies and free services that contemporaries found it hard to delineate a poverty line separating independent families from dependent ones.[60]

For the majority of those below the median family income of $1700 in 1929, security rather than affluence or profligate expenditure lay at the core of the American dream. Economic necessity drove people. An immigrant working wife explained why she worked outside the home: "Husband work—I'm stay home. Husband sick; nobody give me eat, I work." And another: "Just

---

[58] Lewis, *Babbitt* (New York, 1961, Signet Edition), 46. Stuart Ewen, *Captains of Consciousness: Advertising and the Social Roots of the Consumer Culture* (New York, 1976). Ewen does not do much with the wage-and-income figures he occasionally throws in (see 19, 28-30, 122-123).

[59] See the text above.

[60] Houghteling, *Income and Standard of Living of Unskilled Laborers in Chicago*, 27.

as well to work—never know when sickness comes."[61] The desire for security motivated many workers more than ambition. A New York cab driver claimed that if any of his co-workers were offered a steady job at $25 a week, he would "leave his car standing in the street" to grab it.[62] When asked what they would do with extra income, the streetcar workers' families usually mentioned house payments, medical care, more clothing, more furniture, vacations for over-worked husbands and sickly children, more insurance, paying cash to avoid installment charges, and savings for emergencies and the future. Even the families of these relatively secure workers suffered from a lack of adequate medical care and the inability to provide against death and old age.[63] Theirs were hardly unusual needs.

Material living standards probably did rise in the 1920s; incomes were higher than before the war. But the struggle for economic security, not the struggle to keep up with the Joneses dominated working-class life in the prosperity decade.

---

[61] Manning, 54, 56.

[62] Calkins, 74-76.

[63] Heller Committee, *Cost of Living Studies*, IV, 345. Also see data in "Why Workers Borrow: A Study of Four Thousand Credit Union Loans," Mildred John, *Monthly Labor Review*, 25 (July 1927), 6-16, especially 12. Although not conclusive evidence because it gives no information about other loans and installment debts these families had, it is instructive that the most frequent purposes for loans were for medical and dental bills (23.2%) and for coal (15.5%), rather basic needs.

15

"United We Eat": The Creation and Organization of the Unemployed Councils in 1930

DANIEL J. LEAB

"Fight!—Don't Starve." Utilizing this slogan the American Communists, even before widespread unemployment began late in 1929, had atempted to organize the jobless. The party, while still in its underground stage, had called an "Unemployment Conference for Greater New York" in March of 1921. Thirty-four A.F. of L. and independent unions as well as the I.W.W. had sent representatives to the conference, which established the Unemployed Council of Greater New York with Israel Amter, a communist leader, as Secretary.[1] Among its "immediate demands," the Council listed public works, unemployment insurance, low-cost housing, and resumption of trade with Russia (which according to the American Communists would, because of the Soviet Union's many needs, re-employ great numbers of men).[2] To publicize and support these demands, and to give substance to the Council, Amter tried to form local neighborhood groups to be known as Councils of Action.[3] At sparsely attended "mass" meetings, to which the party attemped to lure the out-of-work with false promises of free soup and sandwiches, Amter would declare "the unemployed must organize and take action."[4] Hoping to capitalize on the hard times, the party expected to attract an army of jobless, though at best it enlisted a corporal's guard. Attempts to develop the group nationally as the Worker's Unemployed Council

---

[1] Theodore Draper, *American Communism and Soviet Russia* (New York, 1960), 175-176. Draper calls the Unemployed Council of Greater New York "one of the first real membership fronts."
[2] *The Toiler*, December 31, 1921; *The New York Times*, November 27, 1921, 16.
[3] *The Toiler*, April 9, 1921.
[4] *The New York Times*, February 5, 1922, 21. The action demanded by Amter could mean many things. In this instance it meant admission by the unemployed to the empty homes (on Fifth Avenue and Riverside Drive) of the rich who had gone away for the winter.

Reprinted from *Labor History* 8 (1967), 300-315.

of America came to naught. In New York, where fear of communism and a fairly harsh winter had enabled the Council to achieve some local notoriety, the group faded rapidly into oblivion once economic conditions improved.[5]

Despite this initial failure, the Communists continued trying to organize the jobless during the 1920s, especially in those chronically depressed areas which did not share in the prosperity of the times. Periodically, the party would announce new organizational drives among the unemployed. It again declared in 1923 that one of its major tasks in the American labor movement would be "the organization of groups of unemployed . . . to force resolute action for the improvement of their position."[6] A few years later the party's Central Executive Committee issued a "Program on Unemployment" which concluded with instructions for the party "to set up Councils of Unemployed everywhere. . . ."[7] Communists efforts during this period, however, had almost no success, and invariably their organizational drives among the unemployed resulted in nothing but paper groups.[8] In 1929 the newly organized Trade Union Unity League (T.U.U.L.)—the Communist Party labor group— determined to try once again to organize the jobless.[9]

The first T.U.U.L. convention took place on August 31-September 1 —about the time the collapse of the American economy began. During the winter of 1929-30, the first large numbers of previously employed persons were idled, and began to discover the scarcity of jobs and the inadequacies of relief.[10] From the Communists' point of view, it is hard to imagine how the unemployment situation initially could have developed along lines more favorable to them. Most people had become

---

[5] Louis Eisman, "The First Decade of the Communist Party" (Unpublished Master's Thesis, Department of Political Science, University of California, 1935), 100. During February 1922, *The New York Times*, which had previously ignored the group, devoted a number of reports to the movement, one (February 14, 1922) even appearing on the front page. However, most New York newspapers continued to ignore the group.

[6] Quoted in *Resolutions and Decisions of the Second World Congress of the Red International of Labor Unions* (Chicago: Trade Union Educational League, 1923), 8; Eisman quotes a Communist at this time asserting that groups of unemployed should be formed to "ask for legislation compelling the capitalists to pay wages to the workers to whom they cannot give employment." (Eisman, *op. cit.*, 101-102.)

[7] Quoted in Eisman, *op. cit.*, 221-222.

[8] Eleanor Kahn, "Organizations of the Unemployed as a Factor in the American Labor Movement," (unpublished Master's thesis, Department of History, University of Wisconsin, 1934), 103.

[9] The new union, in fact, specifically declared in its statement of purpose that "the Trade Union Unity League organizes the unemployed." (As quoted in David Carpenter, "The Communist Party: Leader in the Struggle of the Unemployed," *Political Affairs*, XXIX (September, 1949), 83).

[10] By the end of 1929 close to 3,000,000 fewer persons held jobs than in September.

accustomed to the prosperity of the boom years of the 1920s. The sudden economic collapse in 1929 came as a shock; but it did not leave the jobless disspirited. The dull apathy which characterized so many of the unemployed as the Depression dragged on had not yet set in. Under Communist leadership people expressed their anger at the turn of economic events, and their frustration at being unable to help themselves. As Howe and Coser have pointed out "the Communist Party [in the winter of 1929-30] managed to seize upon a highly explosive issue and to rally a considerable number of non-Communist workers under its banners."[11] The party, once again utilizing the slogan "Fight—Don't Starve," set out to take organizational advantage of the increasing distress caused by decreasing means of support.[12] Working through the T.U.U.L., the Communist Party intensified its efforts to organize the jobless into groups that ultimately became known as Unemployed Councils.

These Councils, like the earlier "front" instruments used by the Party in its attempts to win over the jobless, were patterned in structure and philosophy on the Saint Petersburg Councils of the Unemployed, which during the 1905 uprising in Czarist Russia had been revolutionary units formed by the displaced factory workers.[13] The Communists had intended that these American counterparts should also be "revolutionary centers," in which "the unemployed by participation in the class struggle on a mass action basis would gain political insight into the historical destiny of the proletariat and join the Party."[14] The Communist Party,"

---

[11] Irving Howe and Lewis Coser, *The American Communist Party* (Boston, 1957), 192. An example of this would be the activities of John Pace, who at one time led the Communist veterans' group. Testifying before the Dies Committee in 1938, after he had abjured his earlier Communist position, Pace recalled that "when the crash came in 1929, I lost my business and what money I had in a bank that closed. I lost that and the money that I had gone into business with which I had figured pretty hard to earn. Well, I just got sore, that is all. I got sore at myself and everybody else, and got connected with an unemployed group." (U. S. Congress, House of Representatives, Special Committee on Un-American Activities, *Hearings, Investigation of Un-American Propaganda Activities in the United States*, 75th Congress, 3d session, 1938, 2267, hereafter referred to as House Un-American Activities Committee, 1938.)

[12] *Fight! Don't Starve, Organize—Demands for Unemployment Insurance Made Upon the United States Congress* (New York: Trade Union Unity League, 1931), 1. This was but the first of a long line of belligerently defiant slogans which the Councils hurled at society. Perhaps the crassest of the lot was the one which Council members shouted at Mayor La Guardia during a public hearing in 1934 concerning relief in New York City, namely, "Feed us or shoot us." (*New York Post*, June 22, 1934, 1.)

[13] Helen Seymour, "Organization of the Unemployed" (unpublished Master's Thesis, Department of Sociology, Columbia University, 1940), 10; at this time the party press published a short history of the St. Petersburg Unemployed Councils, presumably so that it might serve as an example to the American jobless. See Sergei Malyshev, *Unemployed Councils in St. Petersburg in 1906* (New York: Workers' Library Publishers, 1930).

as Irving Bernstein points out, "had as one of its main goals the organization of the unemployed into a cadre of revolution."[15] In the radical changes of American social and economic conditions, the Communists thought they saw the beginnings of the objective revolutionary situation predicted by "third period" ideology. The United States, it was declared, abounded with "revolutionary potentialities" which the Councils might help to exploit.[16]

Under T.U.U.L. aegis, the Communist organizers—"hatless young men in simulated leather jackets," as Arthur Schlesinger Jr., described them[17]—sought out the jobless wherever the involuntary idle queued up. Council organizers hung out in parks, on breadlines, outside soup kitchens and flop-houses, among the groups of men loitering at factory gates or waiting in crowded relief offices. Using the rapidly spreading unemployment as a comon denominator, the organizers created and expanded Unemployed Councils all over the country. In city after city, Party-led groups of jobless men organized demonstrations, led marches, and created committees of protest—all demanding that something be done.[18]

At this early stage in their development, the Councils (also known as the Councils of the Unemployed) conducted their campaigns on a local basis. In each particular locality the Communist Party organizers would importune the out-of-work to elect or form a Committee of Action.[19] Usually some of the more dissatisfied or more militant among the listeners would give heed, and around this small core the local Council would form.[20] Steve Nelson, describing "How Unemployed Councils Were Built in Lackawanna County," recalled that he and his fellow organizers made contact with a few jobless they had heard complaining and induced them to come to a series of meetings, out of which eventually emerged one local group.[21] Joe Brandt reported to the *Party*

[14] Kahn, *op. cit.*, 102.
[15] Irving Bernstein, *The Lean Years* (Boston, 1960), 426.
[16] M. J. Olgin, "From March 6 to May 1," *Communist,* IX (May, 1930), 417-422.
[17] Arthur Schlesinger, Jr., *Crisis of the Old Order* (Boston, 1951), 219.
[18] Harold Lasswell and Dorothy Blumenstock, *World Revolutionary Propaganda* (New York, 1939), 192-193; Seymour, *op. cit.,* 11; Bernard Karsh and Phillips Garman, "The Political Left," in *Labor and the New Deal,* edited by Milton Derber and Edwin Young (Madison, 1957), 88-89.
[19] Herbert Benjamin, *A Manual for Hunger Fighters: How to Organize and Conduct United Action for the Right to Live* ("Unemployment Series No. 3," New York: Workers' Library Publishers, 1933), 4.
[20] Seymour, *op. cit.,* 9.
[21] Steve Nelson, "How Unemployed Councils Were Built in Lackawanna County," *Party Organizer,* VII (March, 1934), 7-9.

Organizer that he had been able to create a Council local by bringing housewives together to hold "empty pot and pan demonstrations."[22] Mrs. Mildred Olsen, a Council member from San Francisco, told the California State Unemployment Commission how she had been recruited by a housewife who had canvassed her apartment building.[23] In large cities and thickly populated areas, the organizers attempted to form committes or councils based on the neighborhood, the block, or even on one or two large apartment houses. In smaller towns and in sections where one-, or two-family dwellings prevailed, the organizers attempted to group together those locals which were in a larger area, such as the ward or the county.[24] In some areas the organizers attemped, with more success, to form groups built along language or ethnic lines, such as the all Yiddish-speaking locals in New York City.[25]

During this embryonic period the Councils existed on an extremely unstable basis. No real interaction existed between the separate components. Rarely did one Council act in unison with another. Indeed, the only points they had in common were their demands for more relief and more public works, their emphasis on the philosophy of class struggle, and their over-all Communist sponsorship. Despite Party urging that local Committees of Action "register all workers . . . willing to record themselves as supporters . . .," most Committees proved reluctant or unable to do so and remained loose entities without membership meetings or an integrated framework.[26] After a demonstration had ended, only the hard core of militants and Communists remained to continue the life of the local group until the next mass gathering.[27] But because of the temper of the times, this hard core managed to bring out ever-increasing numbers of people for the various protest demonstrations.

The early developments of these Unemployed Councils reached its apex in the country-wide demonstrations of March 6, 1930, while they

---

[22] Joe Brandt, "How Our Block Committee Works," *Party Organizer* V (May-June, 1932), 38-41.

[23] *Abstract of Hearings on Unemployment before the California State Unemployment Commission,* April and May 1932 (Sacramento: California State Printing Office, 1933), 161-162.

[24] "Self Help Among the Unemployed," *Information Service* XII (January 28, 1933), 4.

[25] Kahn, *op. cit.,* 106. Evictions helped in the formation of these Council locals. Miss Kahn reports how people who had come in contact with the Council would be evicted and in the new neighborhood, to which they often had moved by virtue of their ethnic or lingual relations, they would spread the news about the Councils.

[26] Benjamin, *op. cit.,* 12.

[27] Clarence Hathaway, "Our Failure to Organize the Unemployed," *Communist,* IX (September, 1930), 786-788.

were still linked directly to the Trade Union Unity League. March 6 had been designated "International Day for Struggle Against World-Wide Unemployment" by the Comintern, and marked the first successful Communist attempt to coordinate their activities among the unemployed on a national scale.[28] Originally scheduled for February 27, "the Day" had been postponed for a week because the Comintern, sensing from the initial response the possibility of a great international propaganda success, delayed the event in order "to enable all [Communist] Parties to thoroughly prepare . . . and carry on a broader campaign."[29]

On March 6, "International Unemployment Day" took place as planned. Throughout much of the world demonstrations duly protested "the exploitation of the unemployed," demanded an "end to hunger," and prophesied the imminent "failure of the capitalistic system."[30] In those countries such as the United States where no provisions for any form of employment insurance had been enacted, the demonstrators also clamored for "work or wages."[31]

The American Communist Party went to great lengths to insure the participation of large numbers of unemployed in its demonstrations. Not relying solely on the Councils organized through the T.U.U.L. it had marshalled all its forces. For example, a few days prior to March 6, the Agit-Prop Department of the Party's Chicago branch informed all Party members in the Chicago area that it had printed 50,000 stickers, 50,000 shop papers, and 200,000 leaflets which must be distributed. Agit-Prop also counted upon every Party member to hold meetings in his neighborhood, to recruit participants for the "International Unemployment Day" demonstrations under the Councils' banner, and whether employed or jobless, to take an active part in "the Day's" activities.[32] Similar instructions had been sent out by the local Agit-Prop Departments and Party groups across the country, so that in one way or another such instructions reached all Party members.[33]

While few in number (the Party had only about 10,000 dues-paying

[28] *Daily Worker,* March 6, 1930.
[29] Cable from the Executive Committee of the Communist International to the Executive Committee of the Communist Party of the United States, quoted in Lasswell and Blumenstock, *op. cit.,* 191-192.
[30] *The Times,* March 7, 1930, 12. In Germany, where the demonstration played a part in the bloody political war the Nazis and the Communists fought over who should inherit the Weimar Republic, "the Day's" activities resulted in a number of deaths.
[31] *The New York Times,* March 7, 1930, 1, 2, 5.
[32] Lasswell and Blumenstock, *op. cit.,* 192-193.
[33] *Ibid.,* 192.

members at the end of 1929), they did their job thoroughly and well.[34] Demonstrations took place in almost every important American industrial and commercial center on March 6. Although the *Daily Worker,* the press organ of the American Communist Party, exaggerated when it claimed that millions had participated in the demonstrations, large numbers did take part, many of them ostensibly at the instigation of the local Unemployed Councils under T.U.U.L. aegis.[35]

Many of the demonstrations were orderly, uneventful affairs. In San Francisco, some 2,000, joined en route by the chief of police, marched to the municipal office building, where Mayor James Rolph, Jr. listened to their petitions and addressed them.[36] In Chicago, despite anticipated police violence (which did not materialize), nearly 5,000 paraded through the streets while a committte of fifteen—headed by Nels Kjar, a prominent Communist leader and Chairman of the Chicago Unemployed Council—presented a petition at Mayor William Thompson's office.[37] The Baltimore Police Department treated the whole affair as a joke. Upon the Party's refusal to ask for a permit to march, a Negro named "Alexander Turnipseed" received one for them at his request, and on March 6, the acting Mayor met the demonstrators wearing a red tie and a red carnation.[38] In Trenton, where about a thousand marchers paraded to the State House, the Director of Public Safety asked the speakers at the unemployment rally to "speak up louder."[39]

But serious clashes between police and demonstrators took place in other localities. The Washington, D.C. police used tear-gas bombs to

---

[34] Statistical figures as to exact membership are one of the most obscured aspects of the Communist movement in America. After a thorough study, Theodore Draper has come to the following conclusions: there were about 7,000 members in October 1925, and the membership slowly rose from that point to about 9,500 in 1927 and hovered around that figure until the end of the decade. Not until 1932 did the C. P. have more than 15,000 members. (Draper, *op. cit,* 186-187.) Howe and Coser, relying on party records, quote the following figures for C. P. membership: 1930, 7,500; 1931, 9,527; 1932, 14,475; 1933, 19,165 (Howe and Coser, *op cit.,* 225).

[35] *Daily Worker,* March 7, 1930. This newspaper claimed that 110,000 people had marched in New York City, 100,000 in Detroit, 50,000 in Chicago, 20,000 in Pittsburgh, and appreciably large numbers elsewhere. The doubtfulness of these estimates is displayed by the *Daily Worker*'s assertions that 20,000 police attacked the marchers in New York. Had this actually happened, it would have meant that more policemen would have been present at the rally than were on the force at that time.

[36] *San Francisco Chronicle,* March 7, 1930, 1.

[37] *The New York Times,* March 7, 1930, 3. This is one of the relatively few peaceful demonstrations of the unemployed which took place in Chicago. Sandwiched in between were serious riots where police and unemployed had battled viciously. Violence was anticipated because of a rumor that thirteen men had been imported from New York City to kill John Stege, Deputy Police Commissioner, and Make Mills, Captain of the Red Squad.

[38] *New York World,* March 8, 1930, 3.

[39] *New York World,* March 8, 1930, 3.

disperse crowds which had gathered before the White House.[40] The Seattle police also had to use tear gas to break up the demonstrations.[41] The Boston Common became a battleground between police and demonstrators as the Communists attemped to hold their protest meeting there.[42] Serious conflict also occurred in Detroit when the marchers resisted atempts to disperse them.[43] But the most violent clash, and the one which gained the most notoriety, took place in New York. Some 35,000 persons had attended the "International Unemployment Day" rally in Union Square.[44] The police had permitted the meeting, but had expressly prohibited the Communist organizers from leading any protest marches away from the Square. The outburst came at the end of the rally when, despite police orders, the Communist leaders urged the crowd to march to City Hall and present their demands for work and relief to Mayor James Walker. When one of the speakers shouted "Let's go," the police charged and in the ensuing confusion, lashed out at demonstrators and spectators alike.[45] "Thousands of terrified people scattered," *The New York Times* reported, "rushing for safety from the flailing police, shouting, stumbling, stepping over one another in their fear and haste to get away."[46] Scores of citizens and two policemen sustained serious injuries.[47]

---

[40] *The Washington Evening Star* (March 7, 1930, 1) claimed that the Communists apparently were successful in holding off the police, and almost succeeded in driving them back until the police used tear gas. The *New York World* also reported that the fight had been apparently going against the patrolmen until they had used tear gas (*New York World*, March 7, 1930, 2).

[41] Walter O'Dale of the Detective Bureau of the Seattle Police Department testified that the March 6 demonstration had been "the largest single Communist meeting" until that time, and one of the "most difficult" to handle. (U. S. Congress, House of Representatives, Special Committee to Investigate Communist Activities in the United States, *Hearings, Investigation of Communist Propaganda*, 71st Congress, 2nd session, 1930, hereafter referred to as House Committee to investigate Communist Activity in the U. S., 1930).

[42] *Christian Science Monitor*, March 7, 1930, 1.

[43] *New York Times*, March 7, 1930, 2.

[44] Many of them may have been just passers-by. The rally had been called in an industrial district during the lunch hour. By the time the riot broke out the crowd had been reduced since many people had returned to their jobs. But one newspaper estimated that many thousands were still in the Square. (*New York World*, March 7, 1930, 1-2.)

[45] Israel Amter, "William Z. Foster: Leader of the Unemployed," *Political Affairs*, XXX (March, 1951) 82.

[46] *The New York Times*, March 7, 1930, 1.

[47] There are complexities to the rally which space precludes discussing. But it is difficult to understand the actions of the Communist leaders. There is no doubt that they provoked the police and caused the riot. Then they left by taxi for the Mayor's office, thus escaping entirely the violence which they had incited. There is, to be sure, no excuse for the police actions. "Hundreds of policemen and detectives, swinging nightsticks, blackjacks, and bare fists, rushed into the crowd, hitting out all with whom they came in contact, chasing many across the street and adjacent thoroughfares. . . . A score of men with bloody heads and faces sprawled over the Square with policemen pummeling them. The pounding continued as the men, and some women, sought refuge in flight."

News of the March 6 clashes, especially in New York, screamed out in the headlines of the nation's press the next day. Any form of mass demonstration, such as the Communists had envisaged, would have been newsworthy. But the riots brought them much added publicity which, while not of the most favorable sort, did serve their cause and that of the Unemployed Councils.[48] The March 6 demonstrations had been the first concerted, large-scale protest in this country against the downward economic trend. They had broken through the generally optimistic, cheerful tone of a press which had talked of little but quick recovery and happy days.[49] Many people had been persuaded by the events of March 6 that the Communists and their adjuncts, such as the Unemployed Councils, could help people face the deteriorating economic situation.

The Party, still working through the Councils organized under T.U.U.L. aegis, tried quickly to capitalize on the success of the demonstrations. A conference was called to meet in New York City on March 29-30, 1930. Known as "the First Preliminary National Conference on Unemployment," this gathering, according to Communist sources, supposedly brought together "215 delegates from 13 states representing 19 industries . . . speaking for millions of unemployed workers."[50] In reality, it assembled most of the Party's leaders in unemployed work.[51] Under banners which bore such slogans as "Down with [William] Green-[Herbert] Hoover-[Norman] Thomas—the Holy Trinity of Capitalism," John Schimes, assistant National Secretary of the T.U.U.L., called the meeting to order to discuss the unemployment situation.[52]

This matter-of-fact report of police brutality comes not from some portion of the Left-wing press, but from *The New York Times* (March 7, 1930, 1) which, while not openly condoning the police action, did not condemn it. The *New York World* carried a report about a policeman who kicked an inspector who was trying to pull him off a youth he was pummeling (*New York World*, March 7, 1930, 2). Both papers prominently displayed front-page pictures showing a dapper Grover Whalen, then Police Commissioner of New York, attended by an equally dapper Deputy Commissioner, and a bodyguard, in the midst of the riot, looking on as the police attacked the crowd.

[48] Bernstein, *op. cit.*, 430. Louis Adamic believed that "these demonstrations became sensational front-page news all over the country—not because they were demonstrations of the unemployed, or because the Communists had organized them, but because they produced bleeding heads." Louis Adamic, *Dynamite* (New York, 1935), revised edition, 458.

[49] Almost immediately after the riots of March 6 President Hoover predicted "the worst effects . . . of the Crash . . . will have passed during the next sixty days." (*The New York Times,* March 8, 1930).

[50] *Daily Worker,* March 31, 1960; *Labor Unity,* March 24, 1930.

[51] Howe and Coser, *op. cit.,* 192.

[52] House Committee to Investigate Communist Activity in the U. S., 1930, *op cit.,* 232-236.

The speakers who followed him, including William Z. Foster (the 1928 Party presidential candidate), Israel Amter (New York District Organizer for the Party), and Robert Minor (editor of the *Daily Worker*), declared that the Councils could now stand independently of the T.U.U.L., and should do so. They urged the formation of an autonomous national unemployed organization.[53] Accepting this view, the conference delegates laid plans for another meeting, to be held in Chicago during July, which would bring such an organization to life.[54]

The conference also adopted a preliminary program which, though it underwent revisions, became the general platform of the Unemployed Councils, and remained so for some years. Its demands included federal unemployment insurance; federal appropriations for relief; no discrimination against rehiring workers because of race, religion, or sex; exemption from taxes and mortgage payments for the jobless; and a fair distribution of all available employment.[55] This last differed sharply from the "share-the-work" proposals of industry in that it called for a curtailment of the working day without any reduction in wages.[56] To this program the various local organizations added their own immediate demands: such as free hot school lunches in New York City,[57] or free milk for babies in Detroit.[58] Before adjourning, the conference also selected Pat Devine, a Pittsburgh party functionary, to serve as interim National Secretary.[59]

Three months later, on July 4-5, 1930, 1,320 delegates attended the Chicago meeting which, acting as a convention, transformed the old T.U.U.L.-sponsored groups, and established a new national organization —"the Unemployed Councils of the U.S.A."[60] The new group adopted as its main task, to use words of Nels Kjar, chairman of the convention, "immediate organization of all unemployed."[61] To coordinate the activities of the various local Councils, the convention elected Bill Mathieson,

[53] *Ibid.* That not all the speakers limited their remarks to the matter at hand is evidenced by the chairman's repeated cautions to confine themselves more to the unemployed and less to extraneous matters such as racial discrimination.

[54] *Ibid; Labor Unity*, April 8, 1930.

[55] *Daily Worker*, March 31, 1930.

[56] *Labor Unity*, April 8, 1930.

[57] *New York Hunger Fighter*, March 4, 1932.

[58] A. Gerlach, "How Unemployment Formed Block Committees and Organized in Detroit," *Daily Worker*, August 13, 1932, 3.

[59] House Committee to Investigate Communist Propaganda Activity in the U. S., 1930, *op. cit.*, 236.

[60] *Labor Unity*, July 16, 1930; *Daily Worker*, July 7, 1930; much of the impressiveness of the delegate figure is lost when it is noted that at least 500 of the delegates came from Chicago. (Howe and Coser, *op. cit.*, 193.)

[61] *Daily Worker*, July 7, 1930.

a Party leader, National Secretary, and chose a National Committe of thirty-eight. Elected as honorary members were Minor, Foster, and Amter—at that time all serving prison sentences for their part in the New York riot of March 6.[62]

The convention in Chicago, while adopting the preliminary program prepared by the New York conference, also added a number of refinements. It demanded, among other things, that all relief be administered by representatives of the unemployed. Again calling for immediate action by Congress, the convention also insisted that federal expenditures for relief should be allocated "now" from funds already appropriated for military purposes. At the same time, the new organization declared that the United States ought to recognize the Soviet Union.[63] One proposed plank for the Council's platform had even gone so far as to call for "Defense of the Chinese Soviets."[64] The statement of purpose resulting from the convention's deliberations has been described, according to Howe and Coser, as one wherein "immediate demands pertaining to the needs of the unemployed jostled political slogans reflecting Communist ideology."[65]

Whatever else the Unemployed Councils achieved for the jobless, the Communist Party hoped they would serve as "transmission belts" to bring in new members.[66] It looked upon the day-to-day economic action of the Councils as "meaty bait" to attract the workers.[67]

As its organizational structure for "the Unemployed Councils of the U.S.A.," the convention adopted that which T.U.U.L. Councils used in their attempts to mobilize the unemployed. The new group claimed only

---

[62] These three (plus Harry Raymond who claimed to represent unemployed maritime workers) had been charged by the City of New York, because of their actions on March 6, with urging "unlawful assembly" and "creating a public nuisance." Found guilty, they served six months before being released. At the time of the Chicago meeting, Foster, Amter, and Minor were all on Blackwell's Island, the New York City prison. Upon their release, at the end of October 1930, all four were welcomed by a rally in Madison Square Garden (*Daily Worker,* October 22, 1930).

[63] *Labor Unity,* July 16, 1930.

[64] U. S. Congress, House of Representatives, Committee on Un-American Activities, *Hearings, Communist Metthods of Infiltration,* 83rd Congress, 2d session, 1954, 4527.

[65] Howe and Coser, *op. cit.,* 193.

[66] Clarence Hathaway, "On the Use of 'Transmission Belts' in Our Struggle for the Masses," *Communist,* X (May, 1931), 409-413. "Through these organizations . . . the Party must necessarily find its best training and recruiting ground" (p. 413) is how Hathaway described the Party's aims; Max Kampelman (*Communist Party versus the C.I.O.* (New York, 1957), 109), quotes a union official as saying "these organizations were created to capitalize on the misery and grief of the unemployed . . . merely to use these organizations as a transmission belt to the Party. . . ."

[67] Karsh and Garman, *op. cit.,* 90.

to have expanded the framework and supposedly used it with but few changes (except in name) until a merger of unemployed organizations in 1936 ended the Councils' separate identity.

Ideally, as in the Councils formed by the T.U.U.L., the basic unit remained the local—the Committee of Action—as Party organizers called it. The Unemployed Councils were to be made up of delegates selected by the Committees of Action. In the larger cities, the locals were expected to combine first on a ward, precinct, or borough basis, and then these lesser Councils would form a City Unemployed Council. In the smaller towns, where the organizers anticipated less success and a limited turnout, the locals were expected to form a County Council. Theoretically, these City and County Councils together, through their appointed delegates, formed the basis for the state and national organization.

As outlined by the Chicago convention, the local was expected to be the active force through which the Councils would demonstrate their militancy and effectiveness. It would create "listening posts" where its leaders could be found at fixed times by those unemployed who had grievances or other problems. It would set up committees—a food commitee, a housing commitee, an emergency relief commitee, and whatever other committees might be necessary to deal with the problems of the jobless. If "direct action" had to be undertaken, these measures would be carried out by the local. The Committee of Action also served "to popularize . . . [the Party] point of view through meetings, discussions, lectures, etc. . . ."[68] But primarily the local served as an instrument to bring the unemployed into the revolutionary ranks of the Party. No requirements for the number of persons needed to form a local existed until 1934, when the remnants of the organization adopted a written constitution which set the minimum membership in a single unit at twenty-five.[69]

The supreme governing body of the Councils was announced to be the National Convention. Between meetings the ultimate authority over

---

[68] Benjamin, *op. cit.,* 20.

[69] *Constitution and Regulations of the National Unemployment Council of the U. S. A.* with a foreword by Herbert Benjamin (Unemployment Series No. 10) (New York: Workers Library Publishers, 1934), 8. (hereafter referred to as Unemployed Council Constitution.) The hey-day of the Councils had long since past by the time the constitution had been adopted. This absence of any requirement during their most flourishing period, coupled with an almost complete lack of registration records for those involved in Council activity, makes it very difficult to judge Communist estimates of membership. A claim of 100 locals in an area could mean only 100 interested people, or it could mean 100 locals with fifty members each.

the locals would rest with a national executive body. Throughout the Councils' existence the form and name taken by this body varied; only its supposed function remained the same—to coordinate the activities of the different Councils, and to speak for them nationally. Decisions in each local would be achieved by majority vote in an Assembly that met periodically and that would be composed of those who had registered as supporters of the group. So, too, the delegates to the various city, state, and national Councils should express the views of the locals.[70] Presumably, it should be added, the governing procedures of these Councils had been established according to democratic principles. But, as in most Communist fronts, behind the fiction of rank-and-file democracy, the Party caucus in each local held control. Joe Brandt mentions how Party members at local meetings should "inject very subtly certain suggestions."[71] Clyde Morrow told the House Un-American Activities Committee that for some locals the Party would choose "innocents" as its leaders, knowing that Communist members would have no difficulty keeping them in line.[72] Testifying before the same committee, John Pace recalled how the Party fraction in his group "would come together before a meeting. . . ."[73]

Initially, neither the national nor the local groups levied any dues. Finances were to be handled in a number of ways. The creators of the Councils had planned that the jobless adherents of Committees of Action should be registered every three months, and that upon registration each would pay a five cents fee. Another source of revenue was expected to come from the sale of "Penny Contribution" tickets. The locals, which would buy these tickets in bulk at reduced rates from the state or national organization, were to sell them at Council functions, unemployed gatherings, etc. The income of "the Unemployed Councils of the U.S.A." supposedly would come from the tickets and other items it might sell to the local groups.[74]

---

[70] Benjamin, op. cit., passim; organizational set-up outlined by Carl Winters, New York Unemployed Council leader, in the New York Hunger Fighter, March 7, 1932; "For Clarity in the Forms of Organization of the Unemployed," Party Organizer, IV (November, 1930) 1-5, passim; Seymour, op. cit., 11-12; Brandt, op. cit., 38-41; "Resolution on Work Among the Unemployed," Communist, X (October, 1931), 838-850, passim.; Unemployed Council Constitution, op. cit., passim.

[71] Brandt, op. cit., 39.

[72] House Un-American Activities Committee, 1938, op. cit., 1489.

[73] Ibid., 2269.

[74] Other items the national organization sold included printed petition lists, Council buttons and stickers.

Between March 6 and July 5, 1930, the Unemployed Council movement had mushroomed. Previously, the American laborer had been adverse to the Councils because of their revolutionary bent; in 1930, however, the worsening times favored their formation. By mid-summer, the Councils had twelve locals in Chicago alone with over 1,000 people registered. Both Milwaukee and Indianapolis had active Councils which also were growing rapidly.[75] Seven flourishing locals existed in Philadelphia. A Council in Minneapolis had 375 jobless workers listed on its rolls; and Duluth's was vigorous and expanding.[76]

Yet the Councils proved unable to exploit these gains. For the most part, this failure resulted from their avowal of policies dictated by "third period" doctrine. The economic situation had not yet deteriorated so badly during the summer and fall of 1930 that the American working class, traditionally non-revolutionary, would accept a policy of gratuitous violence against society predicated on the belief that a dying capitalism must be dealt the death blow.[77] The jobless could not comprehend the Councils' attempts, as part of this policy, to assail other groups offering help to the unemployed, as in New York when a Council rally in August 1930 ended in a march on a free employment agency maintained by Tammany Hall.[78] Further dissatisfaction by the jobless with Councils' policies came from the continued call for demonstrations which often had nothing to do with issues arising out of unemployment. In Detroit, for example, a fairly serious riot ensued after an Unemployed Council protest march against the British bombing of Indian frontier rebels.[79] Louis Adamic believed that the average workingman,

[75] "Weekly Organizational Letter of District No. 8," cited in his exhibit by Captain Make Mills, Chief of the Red Squad of the Chicago Police Department. House Committee to Investigate Communist Activity in the U. S., 1930, *op. cit.,* 550.
[76] John Schmiess and Carl Miller, Council organizers, quoted in a report by Jacob Spolansky. House Committee to Investigate Communist Activities in the U. S., 1930, *op. cit.,* 234-235.
[77] "Self Help Among the Unemployed," 4. The general Communist attitude during these years (until the advent of the Popular Front) is made clear by this exchange at a Congressional hearing between Senator Hugo Black and an official of the T.U.U.L. who had helped in the formation of the first Unemployed Councils in 1929-30. The Senator asked William F. Dunne if it was true that "the Party does say the only way to accomplish anything is by force. . . ."
   MR. DUNNE: Our Party believes that no ruling class . . . ever . . . has surrendered voluntarily or peaceably its powers . . . and . . . is going to. . . .
   SEN. BLACK: Does your organization set that out as its objective?
   MR. DUNNE: It says that the capitalist system will only be overturned by a forcible struggle.
   (U. S. Congress, Senate, Subcommittee of the Committee on the Judiciary, *Hearings, Thirty Hour Week,* 72d Congress, 2d session, 1933, 115-116.)
[78] *Daily Worker,* August 22, 1930.
[79] *Daily Worker,* October 25, 1930.

even the jobless one, considered the policies practiced by the Councils at this time to be "too radical, too violent."[80] Many of those who, after March 6, had enlisted in the Councils abandoned them when they found that instead of a larger relief ticket or a settlement of their grievances, all their "radical militancy" got them was a crack on the skull from a police club.[81]

As long as it had seemed that the Unemployed Councils would help the out-of-work, and as long as they had no competition, the Councils retained many of their members, and even gained new adherents. But the continued call for demonstrations during the summer of 1930, many of them on abstract issues which the jobless did not understand—such as support of revolutionary action abroad—exhausted much of the popular support that the Councils had gained after March 6. The Councils came to be "politically branded," and less radical organizations began to appear, competing with them for the support of the unemployed.[82] The new groups attracted both those moved to action by the economic failure of society, and those disillusioned by the crude violence so often perpetrated by the Councils.

Only two months after the Chicago convention, some of the Communist leadership recognized the existence of trends away from the Councils. Clarence Hathaway, a Chicago Party leader active among the unemployed, complained in September 1930 about "organizational weaknesses," and "the failure to organize the unemployed."[83] One Communist official described these months as "an initial period of adventurism and confusion";[84] another, looking back to these early days, asserted that the Party and the Councils had brought large numbers to "action," but had failed to retain them in "permanent" organization.[85]

In November 1930, shortly after the appearance of Hathaway's article, the Party's Central Committee, in a sharply self-critical evaluation of its activities among the unemployed, took note of the shortcomings of its unemployed policy.[86] Although reaffirming its faith in the prin-

---

[80] Louis Adamic, *Dynamite* (New York, 1930), 422.
[81] Kahn, *op. cit.*, 103.
[82] Seldon Rodman, "Lasser and the Workers' Alliance," *Nation*, CXLVII (September 10, 1938), 242.
[83] Clarence Hathaway, "Our Failure to Organize the Unemployed," *Communist*, IX (September, 1930), 788-795.
[84] Howe and Coser, *op. cit.*, 184.
[85] Herbert Benjamin, "Unity in the Unemployment Field," *Communist*, XV (April, 1936), 332.
[86] "Communication from the Central Committee of the Communist Party of the United States of America," published in the *Daily Worker*, November 8, 1930. The com-

ciples of the "third period," the Commitee determined to reorient the activities of the Unemployed Councils toward more direct work among the jobless; the Councils, in other words, would not abandon their revolutionary aspects, only de-emphasize them. It had also been decided that the Councils would operate on two levels: nationally, they would campaign for direct federal aid to the out-of-work, which in effect meant that the national organization was comatose except when revived by the Party for a supposed national demonstration, such as the Hunger Marches to Washington, D.C., in 1931 and 1932; locally, they would adopt as their main task "the protection of the unemployed," representing the jobless in their relations with relief authorities. The Committees of Action were to serve as representative agencies of the out-of-work, publicizing and settling their grievances.[87] However, the subsequent history of the Unemployed Councils is not that of a unified organization. Nor did they fulfill the expectations of their Party organizers. Notwithstanding their later notoriety, the Unemployed Councils never again duplicated for the Communists their success of March 6.

---

munication is entitled "From November to January," and after referring to the July convention, and what should have occurred thereafter, went on to describe what the Councils should do in the next few months. The "Communication" did not deal only in generalities. For example, it specifically suggested that the Councils take jobless persons into courtrooms so that they might view eviction cases and see how these were decided, the implication being that exposure to "the capitalistic law" would turn them toward the Councils.

[87] Ossip Piatnitsky, secretary of the Commintern, wrote a pamphlet at this time that indicates the line for the Councils. Piatnitsky, addressing himself to all the Communist unemployed organizations, those in Europe as well as the Councils in America, wrote that the Councils must be "centers both in the sphere of strugle—the organization of processions, hunger marchers, demonstrations, etc.; and also in . . . ideological and political activities." At the same time, he also referred to such specific tasks as fighting "against incivility on the part of . . . officials. . . ." (Ossip Piatnitsky, *Unemployment and the Tasks of the Communists* (New York: Workers' Library Publishers, 1931), *passim.*)

16

Origins of the Sit-Down Era: Worker Militancy and Innovation in the Rubber Industry, 1934-1938

DANIEL NELSON

On June 8, 1937, Byron H. Larabee, former assistant city law director of Akron, Ohio and executive secretary of the Greater Akron Association, a business organization recently investigated by the LaFollette Committee, spoke knowingly to the local Rotary. In a nation convulsed by worker unrest, labor management confrontation, and that novel, often frightening phenomenon, the sit-down strike, Akron, he said, "has a civic and industrial stability that many Akron citizens would have considered . . . impossible twelve months ago." He believed that Akron had passed through a cycle . . . which practically all industrial sections of the United States are destined to pass through before the present . . . unrest has reached a stopping point."[1] Larabee's analysis was overly optimistic, particularly in proclaiming the return of "industrial stability," but it contained a valuable insight. For reasons distinctive to the rubber industry and its employees, Akron played a key role in the labor upheaval of the mid-1930s. Rubber workers pioneered the sit-down strike and helped ignite the wave of unrest that engulfed American industry between 1936 and 1938. Most important, their experiences anticipated the complex process of initiative and reaction that characterized industry generally in the late 1930s and made the

---

[1] *Akron Beacon Journal*, June 8, 1937.

Reprinted from *Labor History* 23 (Spring 1982), 198-225. An earlier version of this paper was read at the 1979 meeting of the Organization of American Historians. I am indebted to David Brody, Sidney Fine, and Maureen Greenwald for their comments and suggestions.

sit-down era the decisive phase in the turbulent years of labor dynamism and innovation inaugurated by the Great Depression.

The decade after 1933 was a critical period in American labor history. Spurred on by Section 7A of the National Industrial Recovery Act, hundreds of thousands of hitherto unorganized industrial workers formed local and national organizations in 1933-34 and became a force in and out of the plant. Initially, however, their external impact exceeded their effect on the factory or mine. Worker militancy was a major force in the rise and decline of the NRA, the breakup of the early New Deal coalition, and the fragmentation of the AFL, but it had only a fleeting effect on the operation of most industries.[2] Between 1936 and 1938 workers and unions once again seized the initiative, with far more profound and permanent results. Together with the NLRB they inaugurated the modern era of industrial relations and labor politics. Public hostility and the recession of 1937-38 curbed the workers' activities but did not restore the pre-1936 status quo. The sit-down movement, the most prominent symbol of the resurgent militancy of the mid-1930s, was thus the critical link between New Deal labor initiatives and the wartime period of consolidation, the final phase of the turbulent years.

The dynamics of reemergent worker militancy were first apparent in the rubber industry and the city where it was peculiarly concentrated—Akron, Ohio. In 1936-37 sit-down strikes overshadowed more familiar contemporary events—the lingering depression, the New Deal, even the union organizing campaigns and the AFL-CIO split—and brought far reaching, even revolutionary changes to industry and community alike. First, they accelerated the process of industrial evolution that was a major effect of the labor unrest of the 1930s. More than in any previous period, production workers became the principal agents of change. Their actions profoundly, irreversibly influenced the operation of the factory. Second, worker militancy had an ambiguous impact on the labor movement, alternately stimulating and retarding it. To union officials, particularly those at the

---

[2] See William E. Leuchtenburg, *Franklin D. Roosevelt and The New Deal* (New York, 1963), Ch. 5; Irving Bernstein, *Turbulent Years* (Boston, 1970), Chs. 4-6; Sidney Fine, *The Automobile Under the Blue Eagle: Labor, Management, and the Automobile Manufacturing Code* (Ann Arbor, 1963), *passim.*

higher levels, the effect was highly unsatisfactory. Long before the sit-down had spread from Akron to Detroit, Flint, and the nation, the leadership had resolved to curb rank and file activism. Finally, labor militancy had a disruptive effect outside the factory and union hall. It polarized the local community, unleashed virulent anti-union forces, and persuaded manufacturers to flee. Militancy and "decentralization"—the movement of the industry to other, usually non-union towns, were two sides of a common coin.

*   *   *   *

Since the turn of the century the rubber industry had consisted of two contrasting elements. The first, embracing a majority of firms, produced traditional industrial and consumer products—mechanical goods, footwear, and rubber sundries. Most of these firms were small, family-owned operations; the exception was the DuPonts' United States Rubber Company, a late 19th century trust that had combined the largest and most efficient companies of that era.[3] In this sector of the industry technology was simple and labor intensive. Working conditions were disagreeable, often dangerous, and wages were among the lowest in all northern manufacturing. Nearly half the employees were women.[4] Clustered in Boston, central Connecticut, New Jersey, and scattered midwestern towns, these manufacturers and their employees left little mark on the industry or the United Rubber Workers before World War II. The plants were relatively easy to organize, but the tangible benefits of union membership were slight. The very marginality of the firms acted as a deterrent to militancy and innovation.

The other sector of the industry, the manufacture of automobile tires, could not have been more dissimilar. With few exceptions the tire companies were products of the auto era. Survivors of a harsh winnowing process, they were large and efficient; by the 1920s and 1930s tire manufacturing was probably the most

---

[3] Glenn D. Babcock, *History of the United States Rubber Company: A Case Study in Corporate Management* (Bloomington, 1966), Ch. 2.
[4] See US Dept. of Commerce. Bureau of the Census, *Biennial Census of Manufactures, 1935* (Washington, DC, 1938), 757, 764. Low wages and women workers were also the rule in the non-tire divisions of the tire plants in Akron and other cities. For a similar situation in another industry see Robert H. Zieger, "The Limits of Militancy: Organizing Paper Workers, 1933-35," *Journal of American History*, 63 (1976), 638-57.

highly concentrated major industry in the United States.[5] Goodyear Tire & Rubber, the industry leader with a market share of more than 30 percent, Firestone, B. F. Goodrich, General Tire, and the tire division of U.S. Rubber accounted for 96 percent of US production.[6] Geographical concentration was almost as great. In 1935 two thirds of the tires manufactured in the US were made in Akron.[7] Mechanized, conveyorized, meticulously organized, the Akron tire factories were tributes to the ingenuity of the engineer and the transforming influence of the automobile.

The aura of centralization, power, and modernity that impressed visitors to the factories was nevertheless misleading. The extension of the automobile market led to the establishment of regional manufacturing facilities in Los Angeles, Gadsden, Alabama, and other sites in the 1920s. In the factory itself, the development of the Banbury mixer drastically altered the economics of tire production.[8] A capital and labor saving invention, the Banbury eliminated the slower roller method of "milling" the rubber, the first major step in the production process. But it also affected the entire manufacturing process. Because of the Banbury, optimum plant size fell to as little as 1000 casings per day, approximately 2 percent of the capacity of the giant Goodyear or Firestone plants.[9] By the mid-1930s the competitive edge of the large Akron plants had disappeared. Manufacturers faced new challenges and opportunities. In time the Banbury became an important anti-union weapon.

The work of the tire plants revolved around a few key tasks. In essence chemical reactions transformed a natural material into a complex consumer good. Machines guided these processes and men supplemented the machines, overseeing their operation and performing tasks that resisted mechanization. In a large tire plant nearly 20 percent of the employees were tire builders—assemblers—and 15 percent were vulcanizers or "pit" workers.[10] Most

[5] See Alfred D. Chandler, Jr., "The Structure of American Industry in the Twentieth Century: A Historical Overview," *Business History Review,* 43 (1969), 258-59.
[6] "The Rolling Tire," *Fortune,* 14 (Nov., 1936), 99.
[7] *Census of Manufactures, 1935,* 757.
[8] Ralph William Frank, "The Rubber Industry of the Akron-Barberton Area: A Study of the Factors Related to Its Development, Distribution and Localization (unpublished PhD Diss., Northwestern Univ., 1952), 27; D. H. Killeffer, *Banbury the Master Mixer* (New York, 1952).
[9] Frank, 27; Lloyd G. Reynolds, "Competition in the Rubber-Tire Industry," *American Economic Review,* 28 (1938), 466.
[10] See "Statements of Enrollment," NLRB Files, RG 25, Box 2116, File 1832, National Archives.

tire workers facilitated machine operations; tire builders performed manual tasks with the aid of machines. Yet unlike assembly line workers in the mechanical industries they made the entire product. The essential attributes of a tire builder were agility and quickness. Any reduction in his pace immediately affected work in the pit and eventually in other departments. To maintain production schedules, foremen "drove" the tire builders, who responded with informal production limits.[11] The pit or curing room worker was also a select employee. Because of the heavy work and debilitating heat of the pit, he had to be strong and durable. The rule of thumb was that pit workers had to weigh at least two hundred pounds. Like the tire builders, they were aggressive, self-confident individuals, proud of their abilities and awesome duties.

Tire employees in general were an elite element of the industrial labor force. Their work was not skilled in the usual sense; manufacturers classified only 10-15 percent of their employees, principally machine repairmen, as skilled operatives.[12] But tire manufacturing was responsible work. The slightest dereliction could destroy the casing or tire. Competence and diligence if not manual dexterity, experience, and creativity were essential. This characteristic of tire production coupled with rapid technological change accounted for the industry's high wage rates. In the 1920s and 1930s tire workers were among the best paid mass production workers.[13] Despite the trials of the following years, they maintained that distinction; at the time of the sit-downs they earned on the average 10 percent more than the typical auto worker.[14]

These features of the industry made Akron a mecca for ambitious young men in the pre-Depression years. During the World War I boom, manufacturers had turned to the South for their workers. Perhaps to their surprise, the employers liked what they found. By 1920 they had a clear conception of the ideal worker. He was a product of Appalachia, had the rudiments of a formal education, and took hard physical labor for granted.[15]

---

[11] Interview with John D. House, April 5, 1972.
[12] Frank, 83-101.
[13] John Dean Gaffey, *The Productivity of Labor in the Rubber Tire Manufacturing Industry* (New York, 1940), 138-39.
[14] *Akron Beacon Journal,* July 13, 1937.
[15] Howard and Ralph Wolf, *Rubber A Story of Glory and Greed* (New York, 1936),

The fact that he was willing to undertake an uncertain trek to a distant city testified to his ambition. Eschewing elaborate interview procedures. IQ tests, and other accoutrements of wartime personnel management, personnel officials at Goodyear and Firestone asked to see the prospective employees' hands. The uncalloused applicant had little future in the tire shops.[16] Though Akron, like most cities, had immigrant enclaves, the rubber plants were known for their strapping young "Snakes"—the local pejorative for West Virginians.[17]

To retain their employees, manufacturers introduced extensive welfare plans during and after the war. They emphasized insurance and athletic programs, the types of benefits that supposedly appealed to a predominantly male labor force. Goodyear supplemented its efforts with an Industrial Assembly, an elaborate "congressional-style company union.[18] Although the Industrial Assembly had limited powers, it performed useful services and commanded the sympathies of a substantial group of workers. Moreover, it was a symbol of the advanced state of tire company management. By 1930 Goodyear and Firestone were notable examples of firms that had stripped the foreman of most of his traditional powers in production and personnel management, and had created a direct link between the corporation and the worker.[19]

The Depression had a devastating impact on the social system of the tire plants. Production and employment declined precipitously; short hours became the rule for those who remained. To preserve the labor force, manufacturers went to four six-hour shifts in 1931, but this move only partially offset the downward spiral. By 1933 the surviving workers were veteran employees, individuals with five or more years service. Of this group the men most sensitive to their plight were the instigators of the

---

435-37; Hugh Allen, *The House of Goodyear* (Akron, 1949), 167, 175, 178.

[16] This is a frequent observation of retired workers. See references to oral history interviews.

[17] Alfred Winslow Jones, *Life, Liberty and Property* (Philadelphia, 1941), 59, 64-5.

[18] Paul W. Litchfield, *Industrial Voyage* (New York, 1954), 183-86; Paul W. Litchfield, *The Industrial Republic* (Akron, 1919).

[19] See Allen, *The House of Goodyear*, 181-191; Alfred Lief, *The Firestone Story* (New York, 1951), Ch. 5. For welfare capitalism in the 1920s see David Brody, "The Rise and Decline of Welfare Capitalism" in John Braeman, Robert H. Bremner, and David Brody, eds., *Change and Continuity in Twentieth Century America: the 1920s* (Columbus, 1968), and Stuart D. Brandes, *American Welfare Capitalism* (Chicago, 1976).

union movement. At Goodyear, where a systematic survey was made in the late 1930s, United Rubber Workers officers had been the upwardly mobile young men of the 1920s. Nearly every union official had been a delegate to the Industrial Assembly or a member of the "flying squadron," an elite corps of versatile workers that supplied a large proportion of Goodyear supervisors.[20] In the other locals a similar pattern was evident. Rarely did such men have trade union experience; even more rarely were they committed agitators or ideologues. They were, on the contrary, men closely identified with the pre-1929 status quo.[21]

The early history of the Rubber Workers reflected the industry dichotomy and the larger trends of the NRA period. Spontaneous organization occurred in rubber factories throughout the country during the summer and fall of 1933. In the eastern plants local leadership was the decisive factor. Where a strong individual or group appeared, organization was rapid and successful; the employer's position was usually too precarious for an extended contest. However, where union leadership was weak or divided, the organization languished and died. The net result was a handful of enclaves and several thousand dedicated members. The eastern plants had little or no impact on the early development of the union.[22]

In Akron organization closely followed the pattern of the auto and other "mass production" industries.[23] With the passage of the NIRA tire workers rushed to join the AFL federal union locals, creating unprecedented challenges for the manufacturers and the AFL. By late 1933, 85 percent of Akron area rubber workers were union members.[24] Led by the tire builders and pit employees, the locals negotiated grievances and pressed for the recognition of seniority in layoffs and transfers. Their fates depended

[20] "List of Officers, U.R.W.A. Local 2 from 1937 to Date," NLRB Files, G 25, Box 1873, #1578. For a similar pattern in the electrical industry see Ronald Schatz, "American Electrical Workers: Work, Struggles, Aspiration, 1930-1950" (unpublished PhD diss., Univ. of Pittsburgh, 1977), 88.

[21] Radical writers have greatly exaggerated the role of Communists in the early URW. See Ruth McKenney, *Industrial Valley* (New York, 1939) and John Williamson, *Dangerous Scot* (New York, 1969), Ch. 9.

[22] See Harold S. Roberts, *The Rubber Workers* (New York, 1944), 100-104.

[23] See Roberts, Ch. 5; Irving Bernstein, Chs. 2-4; Sidney Fine, *Sit-Down: The General Motors Strike of 1936-37* (Ann Arbor, 1969) Chs. 2-3; Walter Galenson, *The CIO Challenge to the AFL* (Cambridge, 1960), Ch. 6.

[24] W. W. Thompson, "History of the Labor Movement in Akron, Ohio," CIO Papers, National and International (Catholic University)..

less on local leadership than on AFL policy—a policy that soon proved deficient. AFL organizers emphasized craft organization and the negotiation of collective bargaining contracts, neither of which was feasible in 1933-35. When the locals urged strikes to break the manufacturers' resistance, AFL officials counseled patience. With considerable difficulty local leaders restrained their charges. Finally, the General Tire local, the strongest of the federal unions, rebelled. Rejecting AFL leadership, the local officers waged a successful strike, including the nation's first important sit-down, in June and July 1934. The settlement provided for an informal bargaining arrangement with the General Tire management. Meanwhile, the other Akron locals declined rapidly.[25] By late 1935, when they rebelled and formed an international only nominally tied to the AFL, the locals retained only a fraction of their former strength.

The revival of the Rubber Workers did not await favorable political developments, outside leadership, or elaborate organizing campaigns.[26] For the tire workers the business revival of late 1935 and 1936 had an effect similar to the boom of the 1920s and the passage of Section 7A. The increase in hours, income, and employment opportunities that swelled the factory throngs revived the sense of opportunity that had been missing in the early 1930s and again in 1934-35. However, there was no parallel resurgence of faith in the industry or its employers. Energies that in earlier years had been devoted to personal advancement now were devoted to the reconstruction of the union, the improvement of the workers' status in the plant, and acts of defiance. Prosperity reignited the forces of worker militancy that made the industry a model for unionization in American manufacturing in 1936.

*　*　*　*

The strike "started when I walked through the plant and gave the signal to shut it down."[27] In this fashion Rex Murray, pres-

[25] "Report of General President Sherman H. Dalrymple, September 14, 1936," *Report of Executive Officers and Research Director to the First Convention, URWA, September 14, 1936* (Akron, 1936), 4.

[26] Compare this situation with the union resurgence in the auto, steel and other mass production industries. See for example, Bernstein, Chs. 10-12.

[27] Daniel Nelson, "The Beginning of the Sit-Down Era: The Reminiscences of Rex Murray," *Labor History*, 15 (1974), 94; *Akron Beacon Journal*, Mar. 29, 1937. Larry Englemann exposes the myth of the 1934 sitdown at Hormel Co. in " 'We were the Poor People' The Hormel Strike of 1933," *Labor History*, 15 (1974),

ident of the General Tire local, inaugurated the sit-down era in June 1934. The next sit-downs occurred in November 1935 as conditions improved. Between early 1936 and late 1937 at least sixty-two sit-downs, including forty in the critical months before the great General Motors strike, in December 1936, provided a focus for the expanding influence of the workers and the URW in the industry. There were three distinct phases to the Akron sit-down movement. The first covered the period from June 1934 to February 18, 1936, and culminated in the five week Goodyear strike of February-March, the "first CIO strike." The second extended from March to December 1936, when the sit-down emerged as a popular protest technique in other industries. The third stage lasted from December 1936 to June 1938; during this period worker militancy took other forms and the sit-downs declined, casualties of the reactions they had set in motion and the return of depression conditions.

The 1934 General Tire sit-down was a model for the sit-down movement of 1936-37. It was a planned, possibly rehearsed move by local union leaders. It lasted approximately eighteen hours, was non-violent, and ended when union officials decided to evacuate the plant and conduct a conventional strike.[28] In later years no union president or executive board ever called a sit-down (though critics frequently charged that they acquiesced in the actions of unruly followers). Otherwise, the General Tire strike serves as a useful guide to the Akron sit-downs.[29] Just as it reflected the militancy of the NRA period, so the sit-downs were expressions of the resurgent activism of the mid-1930s. The sit-downs of 1936-37 were diverse, embracing four of the five categories of sit-downs the Bureau of Labor Statistics identified in 1937.[30] They lasted anywhere from a few minutes to nearly three days, and they involved anywhere from a single individual to several thousand employees. They were generally non-violent. Although strikers made no formal arrangements to avoid the destruction of machines or tires, property damage was negligible.

497-99, 507-08.

[28] Nelson, 93-7.

[29] The following analysis of the Akron sit-downs is based on newspaper accounts, oral history interviews, and government documents. I have only footnoted quotations and references to sources of special importance.

[30] "Sit-Down Strikes During 1936," *Monthly Labor Review*, 44 (1937), 1233-34. URW strikers did not use the "third" technique, sitting for the length of a shift only.

Pit workers, who might have destroyed tires simply by not tending their machines, scrupulously synchronized their work with
their protests. Personal injuries were somewhat more frequent,
particularly at Goodyear, where a large anti-union group added
special turbulence to the sit-downs. But with one possible exception, the injuries were not serious. Violence was a common
feature of conventional URW strikes and organizing campaigns,
but not the sit-downs.

There was another similarity with the General Tire strike.
Whatever the causes of the sit-downs, they did not result in efforts to control factory operations. There were few explicit challenges to the foreman's realm, no reports of shared power, no
efforts to redefine the managerial role except in the personnel
area. Tire builders had traditionally attempted to limit production; their sit-downs against renegade workers in 1936-37 were
simply a new phase of an old contest. The one exception was
the workers' efforts to control the labor force. But even this
activity was confined to discrimination against non-union workers. Once a man became a URW member in good standing, he
became immune from attack. In this area, as in others, the sit-
down was an act of censure rather than a step toward a new
type of industrial management.[31] As a result the sit-downs had a
greater impact on the distribution of power and authority among
managers than they did on the duties of workers.

The General Tire strike also foreshadowed the employer's role
in the sit-downs. No manager ever attempted to expel strikers.
Even after August 1936, when city police were available for
strikebreaking duty, there was no effort to forcibly remove the
workers, presumably because of danger to the plant. Nor was
there any attempt to invoke the law against participants in sit-
downs. The only instance when workers were prosecuted was
an unusual case; the charge was not that they sat down, but that
they held their supervisors hostage. In general manufacturers
were remarkably accommodating. They kept cafeteria and jan-
itorial employees on the job and maintained heat and light in
occupied departments. By the summer of 1936 they concluded

---

[31] In this respect the rubber workers were apparently like other CIO militants. See
David Brody, "Radical Labor History and Rank and File Militancy," *Labor
History*, 16 (1975), 123.

that the most effective response to the sit-downs was simply to close the plant until the dispute ended. By this tactic they insured that non-striking workers and townspeople, frightened by the specter of a silent factory, would pressure union leaders and strikers for a settlement.

The five sit-downs that occurred at Firestone, Goodyear, and Goodrich between January 28 and February 18, 1936, built on the pioneering General Tire strike.[32] They reflected the improving economic environment, the managers' determination to return to "normal" operations, the workers' familiarity with the sit-down tactic, the decline of URW effectiveness, and the impotence of the company unions. In every case tire builders were the leaders. By trade union standards the sit-downs accomplished little. By the historian's gauge, however, they were a social innovation of the greatest significance. At a time when New Deal initiatives in the labor area had stalled and manufacturers were recapturing their customary prerogatives, successful acts of defiance were more meaningful than the settlement of any grievance.

The Firestone sit-down of January 28-30 was probably the single most important event in the history of the sit-down movement. In late January the company cut piece work rates in the tire room. When the tire builders, all URW Local 7 members, slowed their pace in protest, the company assigned a non-union man named Godfrey to the tire room, presumably to act as a "pacemaker." Godfrey proceeded to disregard the disapproving looks of his fellow workers and traded insults with Clay Dicks, the Local 7 committeeman. At one point Godfrey suggested that Dicks would be more circumspect without a "gang" to back him and Dicks accepted the challenge. The two men met at the plant gate after work and exchanged blows; Godfrey was knocked unconscious. He promptly complained to his supervisor who suspended Dicks for a week. When Local 7 officials objected, W. R. Murphy, Firestone's personnel manager, agreed to meet them.

---

[32] There was also a sitdown on November 8 by Goodyear first shift tire builders. It lasted less than an hour and resulted in a delay in a wage cut. Its most interesting feature, however, was the fact that first shift workers instigated it. In the following months first shift tire builders, the oldest, most secure employees, led the anti-URW, anti-sit-down effort at Goodyear. The November 8 incident was quickly forgotten, perhaps because the memory of the first Goodyear sit-down embarrassed first shift workers and URW militants alike. *Akron Beacon Journal,* Nov. 8, 1935.

However, before the local officials had an opportunity to plead Dicks' case, the tire builders stopped work and refused to resume their duties until Dicks was reinstated. Their action was spontaneous, as surprising to union officials as it was to the management. The protest spread to the auto tire room and other departments. "In place of feverish work a carnival spirit pervaded the shop." The workers "clustered in groups and talked. Some played cards. Others played checkers with the tops of pop bottles." [33] After a day of fruitless negotiations the local leaders turned to the International union for assistance. Sherman H. Dalrymple, the International president, henceforth led the union negotiators. "Our main effort," he explained on January 30, "is to get all those men back to work as soon as possible." [34]

The key incident in the dispute occurred later that evening. Murphy offered to pay the workers half their customary wages for the time they had lost if the union would drop the Dicks' case. Dalrymple and the Local 7 negotiators rejected this offer, insisting that Dicks be reinstated. As the meeting broke up a superintendent suggested to a Local 7 executive committee member that Murphy might pay Dicks too. Dalrymple immediately reconvened the conference and settled the strike on that basis.[35] The reason for this remarkable concession—paying the suspended man for his lost time—is unclear. Whatever Murphy's motive, "union men were unanimous in their declarations that the outcome of the protest was a 'victory.'" Dicks called the settlement "the finest thing in the world." [36] In his official statement Dalrymple asserted that the incident would "teach the men what an organization can do to settle their grievances." [37] In fact, the sit-down taught the men what they could do for themselves. The Firestone "victory" rekindled the optimism of 1933-34 and confirmed the lesson of the General Tire experience. Progress did not have to await a formal contract.

The sit-downs of the next two weeks bore the imprint of the Firestone strike. On Friday January 31 non-union Goodyear Plant 1 pit and tire workers sat down to demand the restoration

---

[33] *Akron Times Press,* Jan. 30, 1936.
[34] *Akron Beacon Journal,* Jan. 30, 1936.
[35] *Akron Times Press,* Jan. 31, 1936; *Akron Beacon Journal,* Jan. 31, 1936.
[36] *Akron Beacon Journal,* Jan. 31, 1936.
[37] *Akron Times Press,* Jan. 31, 1936.

of a piece rate cut. The head of the company union dismissed the sit-down as a reaction to the Firestone incident and maintained a "hands off attitude."[38] URW Local 2 officers were equally unenthusiastic at first. Secretary E. E. White told the press that "It isn't our baby and we're paying no attention to it."[39] Over the weekend, however, they did pay attention to a sudden resurgence of interest in the union. Men who had left in disgust paid back dues and others joined for the first time. On Sunday the union endorsed the protest and on Monday union members gathered at the gates to urge workers to continue the sit-down. First shift employees sat down briefly at 6 am and second shift workers sat down from noon to 2 pm, until the personnel manager threatened to discharge them. Work resumed but negotiations, with Local 2 representing the workers, continued through the week. In the meantime Goodrich tire builders sat down on February 7 to protest wage losses due to minor changes in the piece rate system. Negotiations followed and the company, as one committeeman reported, gave "more than had been asked for." But when the settlement was announced, the men sat down again demanding half pay—à la Firestone—for the time they had been on strike. Only when Dalrymple explained in the strongest possible terms that "they could not expect the company to pay them 'strike defense funds'" did they agree to leave the plant. On the following Sunday the International held a mass meeting for tire workers. Dalrymple led a parade of union officials, including Adolph Germer of the CIO, in condemning the sit-downs. "Such cessation of work does not demonstrate efficiency," he declared. "On the other hand it does demonstrate a dual movement. The proper way to handle grievances is through your union officers...."[40]

Five days later another major sit-down occurred at Goodyear Plant 2. At 3 am on February 14 the fourth shift truck tire department foreman began to notify between fifty-five and seventy non-union tire builders that they were to be furloughed as the company returned to the eight-hour day. As he went from machine to machine the men stopped their work to watch. Soon

[38] Ibid., Feb. 5, 1936.
[39] Ibid., Feb. 1, 1936.
[40] Akron Beacon Journal, Feb. 10, 1936.

they gathered around him. The news was disheartening; fourth shift workers were low seniority employees who had been recalled in late 1935. Pleading that he was simply the bearer of bad news, the foreman suggested that the tire builders choose a committee to talk to the shift foreman.[41] This move proved to be a turning point in the history of the sit-down. The committee members—notably C. D. "Chuck" Lesley, George Boyer, and James W. "Jimmy" Jones—became leading figures in the sit-downs of the following transitional months. If the Firestone strike provided the spark that ignited the movement, Lesley—a large, tough National Guardsman and former anti-union militant who "spoke well," Boyer—a spare family man who had weathered the worst of the Depression on a hard scrabble southern Ohio farm, and Jones—a small "dapper" Georgian and union zealot, provided the fuel that sustained it.

From that point the Goodyear dispute escalated rapidly. The Lesley committee received no satisfaction from the shift foreman and returned to the tire department at 5 am. When asked to leave the plant Lesley supposedly challenged his coworkers: "What are we, mice or men? If we're going to be men, let's stick with it." The men responded: "We're going to be men!"[42] They sat down for the rest of their shift and half of the morning shift. When they left at 9 am, having been promised a meeting with the plant manager and personnel manager later that day, John D. House, Local 2 president, was waiting at the gate. He offered support and the use of the union hall. Local 2 thus became a factor in the protest. Sit-downs on the afternoon and evening shifts closed the plant—as it turned out, for more than a month. On the evening of February 17, Local 2 held a rally for tire workers. After several hours of increasingly strident speeches, a union officer, without prior warning, seized a flag from the podium and led a motley army to the plant gates. The great Goodyear strike had begun.[43]

The Goodyear conflict, famous for reviving the URW and inaugurating the CIO, was also important as a gauge of public attitudes toward the union and its tactics. Local 2 was hardly a formidable contestant; it had a paid-up membership of less than six hundred, perhaps 5 percent of the Goodyear labor force, when the strike began.[44] It succeeded because it commanded a much larger informal following, both in Goodyear and in the community at large. This support reflected widespread disillusionment with the corporation and a feeling that the strikers were merely demanding what they deserved. Many local residents, non-union workers and others, undoubtedly saw the sit-downs as appropriate responses to the company's intransigent approach to New Deal labor initiatives, including the union. As a result local businessmen contributed more than $25,000 to the strike relief fund.[45] The two local newspapers maintained a careful neutrality, and most important, the city administration of Republican Lee D. Schroy refused to allow the police to be suborned into a strike breaking force. The concessions the union ultimately won seemed just rewards for what had been a broad-based public undertaking.

The settlement of the Goodyear strike on March 21 marked the beginning of the second, more innovative and disruptive phase of the sit-down movement. In January and February worker militancy revived the union; between April and the Fall it had a far more profound impact on factory operations and public attitudes toward the union and labor issues. By the time of the General Motors strike, the process of innovation and adjustment was largely complete. The subsequent history of the sit-down movement in the industry and the nation was largely an extension of the experiences of the turbulent spring and summer of 1936.

Between April and November periodic waves of sit-downs convulsed the rubber factories. Typically a sit-down in one plant would spark a rash of sit-downs in other plants. There was no apparent pattern to the waves nor any indication of coordinated activity. Even the workers' most vocal critics never detected a conspiracy of militants.[46] Indeed, they agonized over the opposite tendency, the "chaotic," "anarchistic," and "syndicalistic"

---

[44] Local 2 Membership Record.
[45] *United Rubber Worker*, 1 (May, 1936), 1. For public opinion, see Jones.
[46] The Goodyear management suggested that "communistic" or "radical" influences were behind the sit-downs on several occasions, but with little effect.

character of the sit-downs.[47] In January and February workers sat down in response to managerial initiatives, wage cuts and layoffs; after April they sat down for varied, occasionally frivolous reasons. The most common substantive grievance, a reflection of the Goodyear role and the growth of the URW in 1936, was the presence of non-union workers in a department. This complaint accounted for approximately one-third of the sit-downs. Other grievances included wage adjustments, layoffs and transfers, and the refusal of a worker or group of workers, often non-union employees, to adhere to production limitations. However, external concerns—the beating of Dalrymple by local toughs in Gadsden, Alabama, a cross-burning near the Goodyear plant, and the supposed abduction of a Goodyear committeeman—also prompted sit-downs. Others were responses to rumors; still others seem to have had no reason at all. A common management complaint was that it was impossible to negotiate because no grievances had been presented. Charles L. Skinner, Local 2 vice president, recalled that "sometimes it was laughable. I've been so damn mad I could have killed them all."[48] Clearly, the workers' new outlook rather than any shop problem or group of problems provided the principal stimulus for the sit-down movement.[49]

If there was a central theme to the sit-downs of mid-1936, it was their association with night work. Of the 35 sit-downs that occurred during this period (and the Goodyear management claimed a dozen more), at least twenty-two started between 6 pm and 6 am. At first this tendency surprised observers who assumed that the low seniority night employees, the principal beneficiaries of the economic boom and the men most vulnerable to layoff, would be least troublesome of all the workers. But two factors appear to have offset their insecurity. First, night shifts workers were younger and freer. Though industry veterans, they

[47] See for example Akron Times Press, Feb. 9, 1936; Akron Beacon Journal, May 8, May 20, May 23, 1936.

[48] Interview with Charles L. Skinner, April 23, 1976.

[49] A similar perspective fueled Detroit area sit-downs after the General Motors strike. Carlos A. Schwantes writes that Michigan sit-downs "cannot be linked solely to the mode of production, but must also be considered a psychological phenomenon. . . ." Carlos A. Schwantes, " 'We've Got 'em on the Run, Brothers;' The 1937 Non-Automotive Sit Down Strikes in Detroit," Michigan History, 56 (1972), 190.

were less likely to have mortgages and other inhibiting commitments. Second and possibly more important, the euphoria of the sit-down era militated against a long-term outlook or a rational calculation of costs and benefits. To many workers the possibilities of the moment were all that counted. "We didn't care" is a common recollection of the sit-down veterans.[50]

Of the night shift employees, the Goodyear Plant 2 tire builders were by far the most belligerent and irrepressible. Between May and July, the period during which more than half the sit-downs occurred, the Lesley group was the major irritant in the industry. They struck at least 10 times, set off three waves of sit-downs, and insured that the sit-down strike remained a major topic of discussion in and out of the plant.

The group's most controversial acts occurred in late May. During a sit-down in the Plant 2 tire department on May 6, the shop supervisors had remained in one of the plant offices. The reason for their action is unclear, but Lesley and his followers observed the supervisors' behavior, possibly encouraged it, and certainly learned from it. On May 20, Plant 2 third and fourth shift tire builders and pit men sat down to protest the transfer of a non-union man to the fourth shift pit crew. Lesley and Jones took control of the tire room and herded supervisors into a "bullpen," an area of the room they set off by arranging tire racks in a rectangular shape. A crude poster identified the men as "red apples"—friends of the management. The strikers kept the supervisors in the bullpen for the duration of the strike.

A foreman recalled his experience:

> I had been in the office not more than five minutes when I was informed by — — — that I was to go with a number of other supervisors. I asked where we were to go and — — — replied, 'Come on, get out of here, don't ask questions.'
>
> We were marched to the south end of building 73 and told to stay in the location of the repair section. The section was guarded by quite a large number of men varying from 15 to 50 at various times. . . .
>
> I walked to the windows once to look out and was told by — — — to get back in my place. He was armed with an iron pipe about two feet long in one hand and home-made black jack in the other hand.

---

[50] Interview with George Boyer, July 1, 1976.

Practically all the guards were armed with clubs, tomahawks, shears and one man carried a rubber mallet.

When the prisoners wanted to go to the lunch room, the guards would permit only three to go at one time. —— —— would pick the three prisoners and appoint three or four guards to accompany them.

The same condition existed when one of us wanted to go to the toilet or get a drink of water.

During the morning, the group of tire builders, assisted by some men from the pit, would bring in more prisoners. A pit man, who I later learned was Steve Friday [the non-union man] was brought back and told in very unpleasant words to stay with the rest of the 'red apple' bunch.

—— —— told the group at this time not to bother Friday if he stayed in his place but if he got out of place to give him the works— that he didn't give a damn.

Later on another pit man was brought in who showed evidence of having been handled rather roughly. His forehead was cut and he also looked bruised about his face, head and shoulders.

Some of the gang said 'Stand this —— —— against a post and don't let him sit down.' He stood for 10 minutes and then two guards were appointed to take him to the hospital.[51]

The sit-down ended at noon on May 21 when the management agreed to transfer the non-union man to another shift.

The next morning at the 6 am shift change, Jones and other fourth shift tire builders confronted Lyle Carruthers, a first shift worker who was a leader of the anti-union group. Blandishing "tomahawks," heavy knife like tools, they attacked Carruthers, chased him through the plant, surrounded him, and beat him unmercifully. When another worker came to his aid, he too, felt the militants' wrath.[52]

The bullpen and tomahawk episode impressed many observers as revolutionary acts, efforts to use the sit-down to control the plant rather than to "veto" company policies. To John N. Knight, local newspaper editor, the bullpen incident was "guerilla warfare,—undeclared, ruthless, uncontrollable."[53] Company officials, who pressed riot charges against the men, and the local prosecutor apparently took a similar view. In retrospect, however, these accusations seem unduly melodramatic. If the strikers had a larger objective, they never mentioned it, either during the

[51] *Akron Beacon Journal*, May 25, 1936.
[52] *Ibid.*, May 22, 1936; *Akron Times Press*, May 22, 1936.
[53] *Ibid.*, May 21, 1936.

sit-down or afterward.[54] During the bullpen episode Jones, Les-ley,' and Boyer assigned the participants to various tasks but made no effort to lecture the supervisors, bargain with them, or sug-gest that the workers would not tolerate certain activities. At his trial in June, Jones described the incident as an attempt to protect supervisors from marauding workers and, more credibly, as a lark. Despite considerable bitterness at their treatment, the foremen subscribed to the latter view. As a result Jones' jury deadlocked and the other tire builders were never tried.[55] Local 2 officials, on the other hand, were less tolerant. They viewed the bullpen episode as an irresponsible act of terrorism, directed as much against the union as the company. Publicly they de-fended the exuberant tire builders; privately they resolved to put an end to the antics of Lesley and his followers.

Spurred by the tire builders, the Lesley group in particular, workers in the non-tire divisions of the Akron factories and in other local industries also began to sit down in the spring of 1936.[56] During a strike by Goodyear Plant 2 tire and pit work-ers on May 7, footware employees stopped work for fifteen min-utes. Two weeks later Goodrich mechanical goods employees sat down for more than five hours to protest the layoff of three co-workers. This was the first sit-down conducted independently of the tire workers. And on August 18 Firestone mechanical goods employees sat down for twelve hours over a wage dispute. This was the first sit-down involving large numbers of women workers.' Although tire builders and pit workers remained at the forefront of the movement, they no longer monopolized it. After May, a sit-down could occur in any department in any plant.

The Akron sit-downs greatly accelerated the process of indus-trial change that the advent of unions had inaugurated. In the short term, at least, they speeded the organization of the plant, as non-union workers were forced to commit themselves. At Goodyear, where the largest company union group remained, Local 2 grew rapidly. The third and fourth shifts were soon one

---

[54] Goodyear attorneys questioned the defendants after they had been arrested, very likely to obtain such admissions. Although the men spoke freely their statements were of little value to the prosecution. *Akron Beacon Journal,* May 25, 1936.

[55] *Ibid.,* July 2, 1936.

[56] The first local sit-down outside the rubber industry occurred on Feb. 18, 1936, at the Pittsburgh Plate Glass plant in Barberton.

hundred percent URW. "We put everybody in," Boyer recalled, "of course, some of them joined the union just out of fear." [57] At the other companies the process was less dramatic but the results were similar. By late 1936 the Goodrich and General factories were almost completely organized; even the appearance of a "red apple" would shut down many departments.

The sit-downs also had a profound effect on the day-to-day operation of the plants. Most important, apart from the greater number of workers who looked to the union as well as to the management for direction, were the appearance of large numbers of worker litigants and the steady erosion of the supervisors' already tenuous position. Before 1936 union officers and committeemen had negotiated disputes with company officials. But these sessions had been infrequent due to the uncertain membership of the locals and the presence of company unions. And they had little if any impact on the roles of the foreman and other shop officials.[58] In 1936 this situation changed rapidly. Negotiations became a way of life.[59] The surviving documents do not permit an accurate comparison of the pre and post-Goodyear strike periods, but the number of hours and individuals involved must have risen dramatically. At Goodyear, formal negotiating sessions were nearly daily occurrences.[60] They often began in the affected departments and focused on the foreman's role and behavior. Whatever their cause, the sit-downs raised doubts about the supervisor's competence if not the powers he should exercise. The "bullpen" incident was an isolated event, but it symbolized the degradation of the foremen that may have been the most important long-term effect of the sit-downs. Supervisory morale plummeted in 1936-37. At Goodyear foremen complained bitterly of "insubordination," a "peace at any price policy," "giving undeserving men too many chances," and the "inability to get rid of men that are no good." [61]

As the foremen's confidence and self-esteem declined, the de facto role of the personnel department and its managers grew.

[57] Interview with George Boyer, July 1, 1976.
[58] This conclusion is based on the statements of various union officials.
[59] Interview with A. A. Wilson, May 17, 1973.
[60] Local 2 Plant Legislative Committee records, 1936-37.
[61] "Supervisory Conference, 1937-38," Goodyear Tire & Rubber Co., NLRB Files, RG 25, Box 1873, File 157B. John D. House recalls foremen who welcomed the sit-downs (interview, April 5, 1972).

Foremen and committeemen seldom were able to end sit-downs. If nothing else, the strikers demanded the attention of higher-level managers and union officials. The supervisor necessarily called in the personnel manager and union officers. After that point he had little part in the negotiations. When foremen complained of a "peace at any price policy," they referred to the staff specialists whose paramount objectives were to end disputes and maintain reasonable harmony with the union officials. The personnel experts, the foremen objected, did not have to live with the results of their agreements. Historians have often noted the managerial response to New Deal labor legislation and bureaucratized collective bargaining.[62] In Akron, at least, these adjustments preceded the advent of union contracts and formal negotiating procedures. Earlier stages of the factory revolution, so apparent in the rubber plants, had circumscribed the foreman's role in the personnel area; the sit-downs introduced a second, more decisive phase of that process.

The waves of sit-downs between April and December were sporadic and unpredictable, but the public response to the sit-downs, particularly as measured by newspaper statements and the actions of community officials, the "public" most critical to the welfare of the union movement, followed a clearer course. In April Goodyear, Goodrich, and General made their first "decentralization" announcements. By implication the sit-downs and the Goodyear strike were the cause, or at least one major cause. The exact reasons are impossible to ascertain—the Banbury mixer and marketing considerations made the establishment of additional branch plants inevitable. But labor militancy, by creating uncertainty among the executives and their customers, was also a factor. Most likely it encouraged manufacturers to confront the challenges of technological change, automobile marketing, and low wage competition in non-tire product markets by moving at least part of their operations elsewhere. Public officials sensed the executives' wariness.[63] With each wave of sit-

---

[62] See e.g., Thomas C. Cochran, *Business in American Life: A History* (New York, 1972), Chs. 16-17.

[63] Though manufacturers were ambitious about the effects of labor unrest on their plans, city fathers perceived it as one factor they could influence and therefore accorded it great, perhaps undue, significance. See *Akron Beacon Journal,* July 22, Aug. 19, 1936.

downs their concern grew. Regardless of the cause of the sit-down, the number of workers idled, or the immediate consequences, the officials antipathy toward the sit-down and the URW, which they believed had the power to halt the sit-downs, increased. By the Fall the process of polarization was complete. The newspapers, the business community, and the city administration, neutral as late as March, became bulwarks of the anti-union camp. The Greater Akron Association, formed in July to combat decentralization, signified this transformation.

URW International and local union leaders resisted these trends to little avail. Pragmatic politicians, they fought to enhance the union and their authority. This dictated a policy of opposing both the sit-downs and the managers' efforts to deal decisively with men like Lesley. Union news releases at the conclusion of a sit-down typically celebrated the workers' "victory" and condemned their lack of discipline. Dalrymple was the most direct and forthright of the URW officials. As early as May he threatened to expel sit-down leaders.[64] He continued to urge local leaders to take a firmer stand and was probably responsible for the 1936 URW convention resolution authorizing the expulsion of members who caused "a stoppage of work . . . without having the consent of the local union or its executive board."[65] By virtue of his position, moreover, he had another resource that proved more valuable. As the head of one of the early CIO organizations, he had a substantial claim on the Committee. Dalrymple soon turned to John L. Lewis and his United Mine Workers assistants for help in combatting the sit-downs.

In early July Thomas Burns, the URW vice president, met Lewis and other CIO leaders to plan organizing strategies.[66] As a result of these discussions URW leaders pledged a more vigorous effort to recruit members in the East and in other non-union centers. Lewis, on the other hand, agreed to pay the salaries of three rubber industry organizers, two of whom were to be

[64] *Ibid.*, May 9, 1936.
[65] *Proceedings of the First Convention of the URW of A, Sept. 13-21, 1936,* 429-31.
[66] Dalrymple had been severely beaten by anti-union workers in Gadsden, Alabama several weeks before. For the CIO action see "Report of Director to CIO Meeting on July 2, 1936," Minutes of CIO Meeting, July 2, 1936. Katherine Pollak Ellickson Papers (Franklin D. Roosevelt Library, Hyde Park), Reel 1; *Akron Times Press,* July 8, 1936; Melvyn Dubofsky and Warren Van Tine, *John L. Lewis: A Biography* (New York, 1977), Ch. 11.

URW men. The latter included William Carney, a Goodyear Plant 1 militant, who·was dispatched to Detroit to devote his abundant energies to organizing the U.S. Rubber Company. (Lesley, who was sent to Gadsden on an organizing mission in June, joined the ranks of URW organizers in September.[67]) The other organizer, Allen Haywood of the UMW, arrived in Akron in late July and spent nine months taming the sit-down monster. Described in the local press as the CIO "disciplinarian," Haywood had a marked effect.[68] In speeches, negotiations, and informal discussions with workers he preached the virtues of routinized grievance procedures, union rules, and group responsibility. In December he became a full-time advisor to House at Local 2, still the source of most of the turmoil.

Local union officials were necessarily more circumspect. The sit-downs had helped revive their organizations and had attracted considerable rank and file support. Nevertheless, the stoppages reflected adversely on their leadership and threatened to discredit their organizations. L. S. Buckmaster, of the Firestone local, often considered the most conservative of the local presidents, was the first of the Akron leaders to attack the sit-downs. Speaking to striking tire builders on May 8, he ordered an end to "unsanctioned stoppages of work."[69] Thus chastened, the men returned to work. Firestone experienced only three other sit-downs and Local 7 soon became the least militant of the major locals. House was the next to act. As a result of a July 14 sit-down, during which a "roving squadron" of fourth shift tire builders closed other departments and drove non-union men out of the plant, House called a mass meeting. After heated discussion, he and other executive board members pushed through a resolution threatening the expulsion of sit-down leaders.[70] In early August L. L. Callahan, the fiery president of the giant Goodrich local, won acceptance of a similar resolution. When workers in the braided hose department sat down in September, local officers, spurred

[67] URW General Executive Board Minutes, Sept. 21, 1936.
[68] *Akron Times Press*, July 22, 1936; Lorin Lee Cary, "Institutionalized Conservatism in the Early CIO; Adolph Germer, A Case Study," *Labor History*, 13 (1972), 483-84, 487-92.
[69] *Akron Times Press*, May 9, 1936. As early as March 29, Adolph Germer had received a sympathetic response from Local 7 leaders when he condemned the sit-downs. Germer Diary, Mar. 29, 1936, Adolph Germer Papers (State Historical Society of Wisconsin).
[70] *Akron Times Press*, July 20, 1936.

by Dalrymple, urged the management to close the plant and discussed sanctions against the men.[71]

Union efforts against the sit-down did little to restore the URW's public standing, however. The city's newspapers occasionally praised Dalrymple, Haywood, and the local presidents for their courage, but more frequently condemned them for weak leadership and "chaotic" labor relations. Resolutions, statements of policy, and threats obviously were not enough to reassure community leaders. Only an end to the sit-downs and evidence that union discipline would end the "decentralization" threat would redeem the union's reputation.

The most serious external effect of the sit-downs was the alienation of the Schroy administration. Faced with decentralization and a restive business community on the one hand and a militant union movement on the other, the mayor found it increasingly difficult to maintain his impartial stance. In late May he called for union-management conferences to deal with the sit-downs, but retreated when Goodyear and Local 2 indicated little enthusiasm for the proposal. He renewed his call at the time of the July 13-14 sit-down. However, when Lesley and the fourth shift tire builders drove non-union men out of the plant, the mayor exploded:

> The city is absolutely through with sit-downs.
> I issued orders to the police department to muster every available member . . . to go in and clean out the plants as soon as Goodyear officials saw fit to call us.
> We are going to keep the factories running at all costs.[72]

Possibly to his chagrin, the sit-down had ended by the time the police arrived at the plant and the crisis passed without further incident.

The final break between Schroy and the URW occurred three weeks later when municipal employees struck the water department and URW members from Goodyear and General Tire joined the picket line. Though House and Rex Murray, the General local president, rushed to the scene to keep order and the police reported no incidents, the mayor insisted that the police disperse the pickets. A journalist noted: "At one point Schroy

---

[71] *Akron Beacon Journal,* Aug. 3, Sept. 23, Sept. 24, 1936.
[72] *Ibid.,* July 14, 1936.

said that if the police department would admit to him it could not clear the grounds 'a group of citizens will go out and show those people they cannot tie up the city.' The mayor called the strikers and strike sympathizers communists."[73] Schroy was more candid in a conference with the president of the central labor union. "You know . . . how far I stuck my neck out for the unions last winter [during the Goodyear strike]," he raged, "and now I'm getting it cut off in nice fashion."[74] The riot that followed the mayor's order also eliminated the last vestiges of impartiality in other quarters. Henceforth Akron consisted of pro and anti-union factions.[75]

By the fall of 1936 an astute observer of the Akron rubber workers could have forecast the effects of the nationwide labor upheavals of 1937 with reasonable success. Months before Roosevelt's reelection, the General Motors strike, the national sit-down movement, the Little Steel strike, and other events associated with militant unionism, Akron residents had had abundant opportunity to examine the new labor activism. In January 1937 the *Akron Beacon Journal* sent its veteran labor reporter James S. Jackson to Flint to cover the General Motors conflict. He found a "stage setting almost identical, a plot that is similar and many leading characters who are the same"—the last a reference to the URW militants who made a similar trek. "The chief difference," he added, "was that events which took a year to transpire in the rubber capital have here been telescoped into a few brief weeks. . . ."[76] Largely as a result of that "telescoping" process, labor activism and the sit-down emerged as national phenomena. Workers, organized and unorganized, instigated far reaching changes in industrial relations. Union leaders labored often frantically, to contain and direct the new activism and the public divided into pro and anti-union factions.[77] Labor militancy became an innovative force in factory and society alike.

*   *   *   *

[73] *Ibid.*, Aug. 7, 1936.
[74] *Ibid.*
[75] See Jones, Part II.
[76] *Akron Beacon Journal*, Jan. 4, 1937.
[77] See "Sit Down Strikes During 1936," *Monthly Labor Review*, 44 (May 1937); Joel Seidman, *"Sit Down"* (New York, 1937). For the critical Michigan situation see Fine, *Sit Down*; Fine, *Frank Murphy: The New Deal Years* (Chicago, 1979), Chs. 8-9; Schwantes; and Roy Boryczka, "Militancy and Factionalism in The

After December 1936 militancy in the rubber industry became inseparable from larger trends in labor and union affairs. Though the local situation remained as turbulent as before, the roles of managers and workers became more conventional. Manufacturers made important concessions in principle—formal collective bargaining contracts at Firestone in 1937 and Goodrich in 1938 for example—but they also regained the initiative in the industry. Their enlarged personnel and legal staffs, the continued "decentralization" of production, and the anti-union sentiment of business and government leaders in Akron were important, perhaps decisive, factors in the new equilibrium. On the other hand, URW leaders diverted rank and file militancy to more "positive" ends and increasingly relied on the NLRB to preserve their position in the plants. URW legions supported CIO strikers in the auto and steel industries and in numerous local disputes. In the fall of 1937 the URW and other CIO organizations waged an aggressive but unsuccessful effort to capture the city government. These activities were highly controversial, occasionally as controversial as the sit-downs.[78] In addition, union leaders mounted vigorous organizing efforts in the eastern plants. On the eve of the recession they were preparing similar campaigns for new "decentralized" plants in Michigan, Indiana, Pennsylvania, Vermont, and Tennessee.

In this new atmosphere the sit-downs declined in number and consequence. There were 17 in the Akron rubber factories in 1937 and five in 1938, approximately one-half the total that occurred in the city during that period. At Goodrich, Firestone, and General they were shorter and more peaceful than they had been in 1936. A January 1937 strike at Goodrich, called "the most friendly sit-down ever conducted in American industry," ended with the protesters singing "Happy Birthday" to the plant manager who, because of the disturbance, had missed the party his family had planned.[79] Even at Goodyear there were important changes. As a result of a February 1937 sit-down, Local 2 and the management formed a joint council—"supreme court" was

United Auto Workers Union, 1937-1941," *The Maryland Historian,* 8 (Fall 1977), 13-25.
[78] URW confrontations with Youngstown deputies during the Little Steel strike and with Akron Police during the Enterprise Manufacturing Company strike in July, 1937, are excellent examples.
[79] *Akron Times Press,* Jan. 31, 1937.

the workers' euphemism—to arbitrate grievances that might lead to sit-downs. In the following months the council resolved numerous disputes, and personal relations between plant officials and union leaders improved.[80] Conceivably a permanent relationship might have evolved. Yet a variety of factors in the summer and fall, periodic sit-downs, NLRB litigation, the company's refusal to sign a collective bargaining contract, and the onset of recession, underminded the atmosphere of early 1937. A mass layoff in November provoked an extended sit-down that embittered relations between the union and the company. The last Goodyear sit-down, in May 1938, sparked a three-hour battle between police and militants, the most violent incident in the history of the industry.[81]

With these exceptions the sit-downs of 1937-38 did not have the kinds of effects they had had in 1936. The Goodyear joint council was the only sit-down induced managerial innovation of the period. The protests may have contributed to the growth of anti-union sentiment and ultimately to the URW's difficulties in 1937-38, but other factors, national and local, likely would have had the same effects, given the precedents of 1936. In most respects the creative phases of the sit-down movement in the rubber industry had ended, well before the collapse of the economic "boom" and the revived opportunities that accompanied it.

The legacy of the era was nevertheless substantial. Between mid-1934 and late 1936 the rubber workers inaugurated a new stage in the development of American industry and the public perception of the union and industrial relations. Spurred by economic fluctuations and the signal victories at General in 1934 and Firestone in early 1936 they briefly held the initiative in the industry. Managers, union leaders and public officials recaptured their customary powers in 1937, but the sit-down experience left a permanent imprint on the industry. The workers' actions radically altered the duties of shop managers, the executives' conception of personnel management, and the role of union officials in the day-to-day operation of the plant. They likewise redefined the relationship between components of the union; a loosely organized coalition of locals embarked on the path to centralized

[80] Minutes of Joint Council, NLRB Files, RG 25, Box 350, Folder 8.
[81] Roberts, 169-72.

leadership and bureaucratic structure. Worker initiatives similarly disabused many local citizens of the notion, popular during the NRA years, that union expansion and local economic growth could occur simultaneously. Similar trends were apparent in other industries in the late 1930s. The extent, timing, and specific circumstances of the militant upsurge varied but it was a factor, often the decisive factor, in most of the union initiatives of 1937. The reactions of employers and union leaders also paralleled those of the rubber manufacturers and URW officers. As Byron H. Larabee told the Akron Rotary, "virtually all industrial sections" of the United States were "destined to pass through" the "cycle" that Akron had experienced. The rubber workers, particularly that responsible elite that created and assembled the nation's tires, ignited the labor revolution of the mid-1930s; it remained for others to carry it to fruition.

17

Frank Murphy, the Thornhill Decision, and Picketing as Free Speech

SIDNEY FINE

The United States Supreme Court decision of 1940 in the case of *Thornhill* v. *Alabama*[1] has been described as "the high water mark in the constitutional rights of labor" and as "the most significant . . . majority opinion" rendered by Justice Frank Murphy during his more than nine years on the nation's highest tribunal.[2] The decision equated peaceful picketing, to a degree, with free speech and extended to the discussion aspect of picketing the protection of both the First and Fourteenth Amendments of the federal Constitution. In picketing cases since 1940 the Supreme Court has considerably narrowed the definition of peaceful picketing as a form of speech, but it has not seen fit to overrule the Thornhill doctrine.

Mr. Justice Murphy's opinion in the Thornhill case raised more questions than it answered, and what the Michigan Justice intended and what his words actually meant quickly became, and have remained, matters of some controversy. It is still difficult to dispel all the fog that hovers about the picketing-free speech decision, but the Frank Murphy Papers,[3] which have recently been made available, and the abundant literature on the subject of picketing and the courts enable one, at least, to place the Thornhill case in its historical context and to explain more adequately than was previously possible the evolution and the meaning of Murphy's opinion.

From 1880, when a labor picketing case was first reported, until

---

[1] 310 U.S. 88.

[2] Eugene Gressman, "Mr. Justice Murphy—A Preliminary Appraisal," *Columbia Law Review*, L (Jan. 1950), 45; John P. Frank, "Justice Murphy: The Goals Attempted," *Yale Law Journal*, LIX (Dec. 1949), 23.

[3] The Frank Murphy Papers are located in the Michigan Historical Collections, Ann Arbor, Michigan.

Reprinted from *Labor History* 6 (Spring 1965), 99-120. The preparation of this article was facilitated by a grant to the author from the Horace H. Rackham School of Gradute Studies of the University of Michigan.

1940, "the story of picketing . . .," in Joseph Tanenhaus' words, "was a chapter in the law of torts."[4] In a minority of cases, the courts had held that picketing was illegal *per se,* but the more common view was that the legality of picketing, like the legality of strikes, depended on the manner in which the picketing was conducted and the purpose or purposes for which it was intended. When the means-and-ends test was applied, the burden of proving that picketing was legally justified rested on the picketers; their activities carried a presumption of illegality since they had sought to bring pressure on employers by interfering with their normal business relationships. Some courts, viewing all picketing as coercive or as simply a nuisance, refused to distinguish peaceful from other types of picketing and hence to provide it with some measure of protection. "There is and can be no such thing as peaceful picketing," declared Judge Smith McPherson for the Circuit Court for the Southern District of Iowa in 1905, "any more than there can be chaste vulgarity, or peaceful mobbing, or lawful lynching. When men want to converse or persuade they do not organize a picket line." Some states and municipalities, not content to leave the matter to the courts, banned all forms of picketing, but even where peaceful picketing was permitted by statute, the courts generally hedged so about its practice as to restrain all but the most nominal sort of picketing.[5]

Insofar as it had spoken on the subject before 1937, the United States Supreme Court had held that only nominal picketing was entitled to any legal protection. It had stated in 1921, in *American Steel Foundries* v. *Tri-City Trades Council,* that single pickets could be posted at each gate of a struck plant who would have "the right of observation, communication and persuasion but with special admonition that their communication, arguments and appeals shall not be abusive, libelous or threatening, and that they shall not approach individuals together but singly, and shall not in their single efforts at communication or persuasion obstruct an unwilling listener by importunate following or dogging his steps." In the same opinion, the Court made reference to "the sinister name of 'picketing' " and observed that the

4 Tanenhaus, "Picketing as a Tort: The Development of the Law of Picketing from 1880 to 1940," *University of Pittsburgh Law Review,* XIV (Winter 1953), 197.
5 The best discussion of the law of picketing before 1940 is in *ibid.,* 170-98. See also Archibald Cox, "The Influence of Mr. Justice Murphy on Labor Law," *Michigan Law Review,* XLVIII (Apr. 1950), 775-76; Charles O. Gregory, *Labor and the Law* (Second Revised Edition; New York, 1958), 293; and 139 Fed. 582, 584.

very word "'picket' indicated a militant purpose inconsistent with peaceable persuasion."[6] Two weeks after the American Steel Foundries decision the Court, in *Truax* v. *Corrigan*, overturned an Arizona statute that forbade the enjoining of peaceful picketing.[7]

The adoption in 1940 by the Court of a far more tolerant view of picketing than had previously characterized its opinions and the identification of peaceful picketing with free speech, although regarded by some as "astonishing,"[8] do not seem so strange when viewed against the background of the New Deal years. Governmental and public acceptance of a strong labor movement as a desirable element in American life, the Court's increasing concern for the protection of free speech from legislative interference, and the impact on the lower courts of the ambiguous words of Justice Louis D. Brandeis, in an opinion involving labor picketing, all helped to prepare the way for Murphy's celebrated Thornhill opinion.

By accepting Section 7(a) of the National Industrial Recovery Act in 1933 and the provisions of the National Labor Relations Act in 1935, Congress and the President had, in effect, concluded that it was in the interests of the nation to have a strong labor movement whose bargaining power was roughly equivalent to that of management. State governments joined the federal government in placing their stamp of approval on organized labor and in removing some of the obstacles in the path of union growth. Partly as the result of the protection afforded by legislation, and partly because of its own militancy, the labor movement grew in strength after 1933 and by 1940 had become a major force on the American scene.

Frank Murphy had played no small part in these developments. As governor of Michigan in 1937, he had refused to use state troops to evict auto workers who had sat down in some of General Motors' Flint plants, and in this way he had helped the United Automobile Workers of America to win a victory of crucial significance to the future growth of automobile unionism in particular and industrial unionism in general. He had also urged the state legislature to enact a labor-relations law that explicitly legalized picketing in Michigan for the first time in the state's history. When the legislature passed a measure that did not, how-

---

[6] 257 U.S. 184, 205, 206-7.
[7] 257 U.S. 312.
[8] See Gregory, *op. cit.,* 296.

ever, entirely satisfy him, Murphy vetoed the bill, and Michigan's labor-relations act was not placed on the statute books until after Murphy's term as governor had come to an end.[9] In view of the labor develop-opments of the 1930s, it was possible for Murphy to state in a draft of his Thornhill opinion that "it is recognized now that satisfactory hours and wages and working conditions in industry and a bargaining posi-tion which makes these possible have an importance which *transcends* the interests of those in the business or industry directly concerned."[10] It followed from this policy statement that the courts should view with greater tolerance than they previously had the tactics employed by unions in pursuit of their goals.

The path was opened to Thornhill not only by the more favorable view of organized labor in the 1930s as compared to previous years but also by a series of Supreme Court decisions, beginning with *Lov-ell* v. *Griffin*[11] in 1938, that dealt with the power of state and local governments to impose limitations on freedom of speech and of the press. In these so-called "handbill" cases, the Court had held that localities were without constitutional power to prohibit the distribution of religious, political, or labor handbills or to require a person to ob-tain a license before he could disseminate such literature. In *Lovell* v. *Griffin*, a unanimous Court had found a municipal licensing ordinance of this type to be "invalid on its face."[12] It required no great stretch of the imagination for one who was already well-disposed toward organ-ized labor to conclude upon reading this and similar cases that the Fourteenth Amendment might also serve as a barrier to state and local measures that unduly restricted labor picketing.

It was not, however, necessary to turn to non-labor free speech cases in 1940 to surmise that peaceful picketing might be regarded as a form of speech and thus entitled to the protection of the First and Four-teenth Amendments. As Joseph Tanenhaus has observed, *Thornhill* v.

---

9 Detroit *News*, May 29, 1937; Murphy, "The Shaping of a Labor Policy," *Survey Graphic*, XXVI, (Aug. 1937), 411.
10 Draft of Thornhill opinion, *Thornhill* v. *Alabama* folder, Box 129, Murphy Papers. My italics. All other references to the Murphy Papers, unless otherwise noted, are to items in this folder.
11 303 U.S. 444.
12 William K. Sherwood, "The Picketing Cases and How They Grew," *George Washing-ton Law Review*, X (May 1942), 781-82; E. Merrick Dodd, "Picketing and Free Speech, A Dissent," *Harvard Law Review*, LVI (Jan. 1943), 522-23; Barbara Nachtrieb Armstrong, "Where Are We Going with Picketing?" *California Law Review*, XXXVI (Mar. 1948), 13; *Schneider* v. *State*, 308 U.S. 147 (1939); *Lovell* v. *Griffin*, 303 U.S. 444.

Alabama "did not lack ancestry of a sort." Although their opinions—
majority, concurring, and dissenting—constituted only a small percentage of the opinions dealing with picketing, state court judges in more
than a score of cases before April 1937 had found picketing to be a
form of speech.[13] The association of picketing and free speech became
even more common after April 1937 because of the enigmatic words
of Justice Brandeis in *Senn* v. *Tile Layers Protective Union.* Upholding
a Wisconsin anti-injunction law, Brandeis, after observing that "picketing and publicity" were not prohibited by the Fourteenth Amendment,
stated that "members of a union might, without special statutory au-
thorization by a State, make known the facts of a labor dispute, for
freedom of speech is guaranteed by the Federal Constitution."[14]
Opinion differs as to whether Brandeis here meant to imply that picketing was a form of free speech that was constitutionally protected or
was simply stating the truism that a union did not require legislative
permission to publicize the facts of a labor dispute because union members, like other persons, were entitled to speak freely.[15] Whatever
Brandeis had intended, however, the state court judges, who in more
than thirty cases between Senn and Thornhill paid some heed to his
words, concluded that he had indeed found picketing to be a species
of speech.[16] It was thus possible for a writer in the *New York University Law Quarterly Review* in March 1940, one month before the
Thornhill opinion was delivered, to refer to "the modern view of peaceful picketing as an informative agent."[17]

When the Colorado Supreme Court in 1939 struck down a state

---

[13] Tanenhaus, "Picketing as Free Speech: Early Stages in the Growth of the New Law
of Picketing," *University of Pittsburgh Law Review,* XIV (Spring 1953), 397-98,
401-2.
[14] 301 U.S. 468, 478.
[15] On the meaning of Brandeis' words, see Tanenhaus, "Picketing as Free Speech,"
403-4; Charles O. Gregory, "Peaceful Picketing and Freedom of Speech," *American
Bar Association Journal,* XXVI (Sept. 1940), 712; Charles O. Gregory, "Constitutional Limitations on the Regulation of Union and Employer Conduct," *Michigan
Law Review,* XLIX (Dec. 1950), 199; Archibald Cox, "Strikes, Picketing and
the Constitution," *Vanderbilt Law Review,* IV (Apr. 1951), 592; and Milton R.
Konvitz, *Fundamental Liberties of a Free People: Religion, Speech, Press, Assembly*
(Ithaca, 1957), 196-97.
[16] Tanenhaus, "Picketing as Free Speech," 404-10. This did not mean that these judges
had also concluded that picketing was no longer subject to legislative or equitable
regulation but only that it was no longer permissible to impose an outright ban
on picketing regardless of the manner in which it was conducted and the purposes
for which it was intended.
[17] Irving Robert Feinberg, "Picketing, Free Speech, and Labor Disputes," *New York
University Law Quarterly Review,* XVII (Mar. 1940), 404.

statute that prohibited all picketing, Alabama alone among the forty-eight states still had on its statute books a law which, by court interpretation, forbade all picketing at the scene of a labor dispute regardless of the manner in which it was conducted and the purpose for which it was intended.

> Any person or persons [declared the Alabama law], who, without a just cause or legal excuse therefor, go near to or loiter about the premises or place of business of any other person, firm, corporation, or association of people, engaged in a lawful business, for the purpose, or with the intent of influencing, or inducing other persons not to trade with, buy from, sell to, have business dealings with, or be employed by such persons, firm, corporation, or association, or who picket the works or place of business of such other persons, firms, corporations, or associations of persons, for the purpose of hindering, delaying, or interfering with or injuring any lawful business or enterprise of another, shall be guilty of a misdemeanor; but nothing herein shall prevent any person from soliciting trade or business for a competitive business.[18]

It was this sweeping Alabama law that led directly to the Thornhill case.

The Brown Wood Preserving Company, a small firm located in Brownville, Alabama, was engaged in the business of treating lumber with creosote and other substances to prevent rotting. Dissatisfied with working conditions, the union in the plant, whose members included all but four of the company's approximately one hundred employees, struck the concern and set up two picket posts of six to eight persons each on an around-the-clock basis. At first the company suspended operations, but then it decided to resume work. On the day the plant reopened Clarence Simpson, one of the non-union men who was reporting to the plant for work, was approached by Byron Thornhill, the union president, and was told that the men were on strike and "did not want anybody to go up there to work." Simpson later testified that Thornhill had approached him "in a peaceful manner, and did not put me in fear; he did not appear to be mad." Thornhill, after standing trial twice, was sentenced by the Circuit Court of Tuscaloosa County to seventy-three days imprisonment in default of payment of a fine of $100 and costs. The United States Supreme Court granted *certiorari*

---

18 *Thornhill* v. *Alabama,* 310 U.S. 88, 91-92, 98-99; Tanenhaus, "Picketing as Free Speech," p. 410. There were, to be sure, local ordinances in effect in 1940 of the same character as the Alabama statute.

to review the affirmance of the conviction by the Alabama Court of Appeals.[19]

According to the notes taken by Justice Murphy, the peaceful character of the picketing and its relation to free speech were the principal issues discussed by the Justices at the Court conference on the Thornhill case. Justice Harlan F. Stone viewed the Alabama statute as "a cloak for suppressing free speech." One of the justices contended that a portion of the Alabama statute interfered with free speech and that it was invalid to this extent; but he did not wish to reverse the law on the basis of the Fourteenth Amendment, nor did he desire the Court to take the position that a state might not prohibit picketing. He thought that the Court should not "do anymore than we have to do in this case." Chief Justice Charles Evans Hughes noted that the case posed the difficult question of the power of a state to preserve the peace by the suppression of peaceful picketing. Unlike the justice just referred to, however, Hughes thought that since the statute had to be classified as "arbitrary legislation," the Court had a duty to strike it down under the Fourteenth Amendment.[20] Justice Murphy's notes on the conference do not indicate what he may have contributed to the discussion, but, judging from the opinion that he later wrote, it is safe to assume that he did not take exception to the judgment that the right of free speech was at issue in the case.

In view of his life-long commitment to the cause of civil liberties and his strong ties with organized labor, it is not surprising that Murphy, availing himself of the privilege generally granted a new Justice, selected Thornhill as the first Supreme Court case for which he was to write the opinion.[21] After stressing the importance of freedom of speech as "essential to free government," Murphy contended in his opinion, which was handed down on April 22, 1940, that the Alabama picketing statute had to be "judged upon its face" since the complaint against the petitioner had been phrased "substantially" in the words of the statute itself and the lower courts had made no effort to narrow the construction placed upon the law in earlier court deci-

---

[19] For the facts in the Thornhill case, see *Thornhill* v. *Alabama,* 310 U.S. 88, 91-95, and Elias Lieberman, *Unions before the Bar* (New York, 1950), 219-20.

[20] Conference notes, *Thornhill* v. *Alabama* folder, Murphy Papers. It is possible that the Thornhill case was discussed at two Court conferences.

[21] Gressman, "Mr. Justice Murphy," 45. Although Thornhill was the first case assigned to Murphy, the first opinion that he actually delivered was in *Tradesmen's National Bank of Oklahoma City* v. *Oklahoma Tax Commission,* 309 U.S. 560 (1940).

sions. There was, consequently, "no occasion to go behind the face of the statute or of the complaint for the purpose of determining whether the evidence, together with the permissible inferences to be drawn from it, could ever support a conviction founded upon different and more precise charges." Also, citing *Lovell* v. *Griffin* and related cases, Murphy noted that "proof of an abuse of power in the particular case has never been deemed a requisite for attack on the constitutionality of a statute purporting to license the dissemination of ideas." The penal statute before the Court posed a threat similar to that inherent in a licensing system because it "does not aim specifically at evils within the allowable area of state control but, on the contrary, sweeps within its ambit other activities that in ordinary circumstances constitute an exercise of freedom of speech or of the press."

Murphy noted that the Alabama statute, as construed by the state's courts, applied regardless of the number of pickets involved, the peaceful character of their behavior, the nature of the dispute, and the truthfulness of the information conveyed to the public. "The vague contours of the term 'picket' " were not defined in the law. The conduct proscribed comprehended "every practicable method whereby the facts of a labor dispute may be publicized in the vicinity of the place of business of an employer."

Having decided that the Alabama statute would have to be judged "upon its face," Murphy concluded that it was "invalid on its face." If freedom of discussion were to fulfill "its historic function" in the United States, he wrote, it "must embrace all issues about which information is needed or appropriate to enable the members of society to cope with the exigencies of their period." Labor disputes, in the year 1940, had to be included among the issues about which information was required.

> In the circumstances of our times the dissemination of information concerning the facts of a labor dispute must be regarded as within the area of free discussion that is guaranteed by the Constitution. . . . It is recognized now that satisfactory hours and wages and working conditions in industry and a bargaining position which makes them possible have an importance which is not less than the interests of those in the business directly concerned. . . . Free discussion concerning the conditions in industry and the causes of labor disputes appears to us indispensable to the effective and intelligent use of the processes of popular government to shape the destiny of modern industrial society.

As Murphy saw it, the issues raised by statutes such as that of Alabama, which infringed upon the right of workers "effectively to inform the public of the facts of a labor dispute," were "part of this larger problem." He indicated in this connection his concurrence with the views concerning free speech and labor disputes expressed by Brandeis in the Senn case, although he had previously wondered whether the Senn dictum really met "the specific question here."[22]

Murphy conceded that the expression of opinion on matters of importance might induce action that benefited one group rather than another, but he also contended that this did not mean that "the group in power at any moment" might proscribe "peaceful and truthful discussion of matters of public interest" merely because such discussion might persuade others to act in a manner inconsistent with the interests of the ruling group. Echoing the language of Holmes and suggesting the applicability of the clear and present danger test to the speech element of peaceful picketing, Murphy stated that discussion of this sort could be abridged "only where the clear danger of substantive evils arises under circumstances affording no opportunity to test the merits of ideas by competition for acceptance in the market of public opinion. We hold that the danger of injury to an industrial concern is neither so serious nor so imminent as to justify the sweeping proscription of freedom of discussion" embodied in the Alabama statute.

The state, Murphy observed, declared that the statute's purpose was to protect the community from violence and breaches of the peace, which it held to be concomitants of picketing. Murphy made it clear that he had no doubts concerning the "power and the duty" of the state to protect the public from these dangers, but he found "no clear and present danger of destruction of life or property, or invasion of the right of privacy, or breach of the peace . . . to be inherent in the activities of every person who approaches the premises of an employer and publicizes the facts of a labor dispute involving the latter." Murphy carefully noted that the Court was not dealing in this case with mass picketing or with picketing conducted in such a way as to occasion "such imminent and aggravated danger to these interests as to justify a statute narrowly drawn to cover the precise situation giving rise to the danger." He thought that "the danger of breach of the

---

22 Marginal note by Murphy on Draft #2 of Thornhill opinion, Murphy Papers.

peace or serious invasion of rights of property or privacy at the scene of a labor dispute" was not so imminent in all instances as to warrant the legislative determination that the entire range of activities specified in the Alabama statute should be outlawed. With only Justice James C. McReynolds dissenting, Murphy therefore held for the majority that the decision of the lower court should be reversed.[23]

Murphy's opinion has been hailed as "a great milestone in labor's long struggle to safeguard the Bill of Rights from being whittled away by reactionary and anti-labor forces,"[24] and criticized as "one of the greatest pieces of folly the Supreme Court ever perpetrated."[25] Critics of the opinion complained that it denied to state and local governments the right to prevent public disorder and that it made all regulation of peaceful picketing impossible. Fears were widely expressed that the right of free speech extended to labor pickets would not also be extended to employers who urged their employees not to join labor unions. Some commentators have insisted that Murphy's association of picketing with free speech was altogether in error since the purpose of peaceful picketing was not to inform but to coerce. Edward S. Corwin expressed a common view when he characterized Murphy's opinion as "unguarded," and the Michigan Justice's language has been criticized for its "impulsiveness" and for being too sweeping in scope to serve as good precedent. Although Archibald Cox thought that the gains derived from the opinion outweighed its shortcomings, he commented that Murphy was "more concerned with speaking out against intolerance and oppression than with legal craftsmanship."[26]

23 *Thornhill v. Alabama*, 310 U.S. 88, 95-106.
24 Harvey W. Brown, president of the International Association of Machinists, as quoted in *Progressive*, May 4, 1940, clipping in Murphy Papers.
25 Gregory, *Labor and the Law*, 328.
26 For newspaper opinion on the case, see the file of clippings in the *Thornhill v. Alabama* folder, Murphy Papers, and Murphy Scrapbooks, Vol. XVII, *ibid.* See also Gregory, "Peaceful Picketing and Freedom of Speech," 714; Gregory, *Labor and the Law*, 299-305; Ludwig Teller, "Picketing and Free Speech," *Harvard Law Review*, LVI (Oct. 1942), 180, 200-2; Corwin, Book Review, *ibid.*, LVI (Nov. 1942), 486; J. Woodford Howard, Jr., "Frank Murphy: A Liberal's Creed" (Ph.D. thesis, Princeton University, 1959), 191; Mary Margaret Clarke, "Justice Murphy and the Problem of Civil Liberties" (Ph.D. thesis, Johns Hopkins University, 1951), 229; Cox, "The Influence of Mr. Justice Murphy," 782. That Murphy's opinion was not altogether "unguarded" is recognized in the following: Eugene T. Kinder, in *Michigan Law Review*, XXXIX (Nov. 1940), 117-18; Armstrong, *op. cit.*, 12-13; Charles M. Rehmus, "Picketing and Freedom of Speech," *Oregon Law Review*, XXX (Feb. 1951), 117-18; Edgar A. Jones, "The Right to Picket—Twilight Zone of the Constitution," *University of Pennsylvania Law Review*, CII (June 1954), 998-99;

If the Thornhill opinion was "unguarded," it must be said that only Justice McReynolds among Murphy's brethren on the Court found it necessary to disagree with him and that there was no concurring opinions to qualify the degree of acceptance of any of those who voted with the majority. With regard to the language of the draft opinion that he had submitted to the Court, only two questions of any moment were raised by Murphy's colleagues. In his draft, Murphy, as noted above, had stated that "satisfactory hours and wages and working conditions in industry and a bargaining position which makes these possible have an importance which transcends the interests of those in the business or industry directly concerned." It is interesting to note that only Justice Stone, Chief Justice Hughes, and possibly Justice William O. Douglas or Justice Felix Frankfurter raised objections to the inclusion in the opinion of the statement in this form. "This may be, and probably is true," Stone wrote Murphy, "but I think it is a serious tactical error to invite a certain kind of criticism which will result from stating the matter in comparative form." He advised Murphy that he did not have to appraise the rights of employers and employees "relatively" and that he could justify his position "without rubbing the fur of the employers the wrong way." Chief Justice Hughes suggested that Murphy change the word "transcends" to "is not less than," and Murphy circumspectly followed this advice.[27]

Justice Stone, who in *Lovell* v. *Griffin* had agreed with his brethren that a handbill licensing ordinance was invalid on its face, was troubled that Murphy had made a similar finding with regard to the Alabama statute. He wondered, he wrote Murphy, whether the statute should be treated as void on its face or void only as applied to the particular petitioner. If, for example, the defendant had visited the employer's factory and thrown a brick at the machinery, the issue of free speech would not have been involved, and it could not have been said that the statute was void and did not apply. "Perhaps," said Stone, "it all

---

and Guy Farmer and Charles G. Williamson, Jr., "Picketing and the Injunctive Power of State Courts—From Thornhill to Vogt," *University of Detroit Law Journal,* XXXV (Apr. 1958), 453.

[27] Stone to Murphy, Apr. 19, 1940, Murphy Papers; comment by Hughes on draft of Murphy's Thornhill opinion, *ibid.* In the margin of the copies of the opinion sent to Justices Douglas and Frankfurter, the statement is amended to read: "an importance which transcends the business or industry directly concerned and touches upon the interest of the general public." The emendation is not in the handwriting of either of the two Justices. Copies of draft of Thornhill opinion, *ibid.*

comes down to a matter of use of words, but as I understand it when a statute is said to be void on its face we mean that it can never be applied to anyone under any circumstances." Stone indicated that he was "inclined to go along" with Murphy, but before he decided to do so he wished to see whether any of the other Justices "have this difficulty."[28] When none of his colleagues appeared to be troubled by the point, Stone did not press his objection.

Although Stone had some reservations about Murphy's opinion, he regarded it as "a very thorough and painstaking piece of work," and Murphy's colleagues other than McReynolds, who wrote him that "I cannot agree! but I do not care to express dissent," concurred in this judgment. Justice Owen J. Roberts regarded the opinion as "a carefully balanced and discriminating treatment of this troublesome subject"; Chief Justice Hughes wrote Murphy that he had "disposed of the case very thoroughly"; Justice William O. Douglas thought the opinion "a very excellent job"; and Justice Frankfurter, not generally regarded as an admirer of Murphy's craftsmanship, commented that the opinion was "an altogether skilful, wise and delicate performance, worthy of the difficulties and importance of the theme."[29] When Murphy, in the companion case of *Carlson* v. *California*,[30] struck down a Shasta County, California, ordinance as sweeping in character as the Alabama statute at issue in the Thornhill case, his colleagues other than Mc-Reynolds once again found no reason to object to language similar to that of the Thornhill opinion. Frankfurter now wrote Murphy: "This gives me a chance to say what I put very inadequately on the *Thornhill* opinion—that this is work of the very best judicial quality. It decides extremely important issues fearlessly but also circumspectly, in language that rises to the heights of the great argument, appropriate to the profound issues canvassed and the best traditions of the Court. I warmly congratulate you and rejoice to be with you."[31]

The very general language of Murphy's opinion was undoubtedly dictated by the sweeping character of the statute that was before the Court. As Felix Frankfurter wrote of Thornhill many years later: "As the statute dealt at large with all picketing, so the Court broadly as-

---

28 Stone to Murphy, Apr. 19, 1940, *ibid.*
29 *Ibid.;* the comments by the other justices are on the copies of the draft opinion circulated by Murphy, *ibid.*
30 310 U.S. 106 (1940).
31 *Carlson* v. *People of California* folder, Box 129, Murphy Papers.

similated peaceful picketing in general to freedom of speech. . . ."[32]
The statute's ban on loitering and picketing allowed for no exceptions,
and it had been interpreted by the state's courts to prohibit even a
single individual from walking slowly back and forth on a public side-
walk in front of the premises of an employer, speaking to no one and
carrying a sign which stated that the employer did not engage union
men. "The trouble with this statute," Murphy privately noted, "is that
you may be acting legitimately and come within it." As he observed to
his law clerk, "*part* of the answer " in the case lay in "insistence"
[*sic*] on statutes precisely framed and free from nebulousness when
they undertake to set limits on a citizen's right of expression."[33]

The facts of the Thornhill case also lent themselves to the interpretation that the right of free speech was at issue. Although the
picketing had been carried on continuously for several weeks, public
authorities apparently made no attempt to interfere with the picket line
until Thornhill made his brief statement to Simpson. Thornhill, it appeared, was "being punished not for picketing, but for speaking," and
it was not illogical to conclude that the statute actually banned free
speech at the scene of a labor dispute.[34] Murphy, however, reached
this conclusion rather cautiously. Before he finally made up his mind
on the point, he wondered whether it was the mere act of speaking
that had been Thornhill's offense or whether speech was only inci-
dental to the real offense, which was loitering and picketing to interfere
with or injure the employer's business. Murphy expressed his doubts on
this matter to his law clerk and advised him that "we ought to answer
this in our own minds before we get on to the wrong track"[35] But in
the end Murphy apparently concluded that the picketing had not unduly interfered with others in the enjoyment of their rights, that it had
threatened neither injury nor disorder, and that no one had been intimidated or libeled.[36]

---

[32] *International Brotherhood of Teamsters* v. *Vogt,* 354 U.S. 284 (1957), 288-89.

[33] *Thornhill* v. *Alabama,* 310 U.S. 88, 98-99; undated note in Murphy's handwriting,
Murphy Papers; Murphy to E.E. Huddleson, Jr., undated, *ibid.*

[34] For the development of this point, see an unsigned and undated statement in the
Thornhill v. *Alabama* folder, Murphy Papers.

[35] Murphy to Huddleson, Jr., undated, *ibid.* Murphy may have been reacting to an
unsigned memorandum on the case submitted to him on March 30, 1940, which
was critical of the point of view expressed in the Thornhill opinion. The author
may have been Murphy's long-time friend and legal advisor, Edward G. Kemp.
The memorandum is in *ibid.*

[36] This point is developed in the statement referred to in n. 34.

Murphy was conscious from the outset of the need to balance the right of the state to preserve order as against the right of the individual to speak freely. As he informed his law clerk when the task of framing the opinion began: "Our job as I see it is to write a reversal without serious prejudice to the police power of the state which I believe is imperative to safeguard without unduly curtailing the right of free expression."[37] In another memorandum, Murphy advised his clerk that he was impressed with the words of Brandeis, in *Duplex* v. *Deering*,[38] that it is for the legislature and not the courts "to declare the limits of permissible contest" in industrial disputes.

> To go so far [Murphy wrote] as to say that legislatures may not regulate the practices of picketing in the public interest because of an *incidental* infringement on free speech and assembly in an area of dispute may be to extend constitutional guarantees far beyond reasonable limits. I am not at all sure of this but we must think straight and clear about it. Are we moving—in our desire to maintain free speech and assembly—the freedom concerning which in my own thoughts and actions I place above nearly every other consideration—in the direction of paralyzing popular government and making democracy if we go the full length of such logic, ridiculous and impotent?[39]

Murphy's defense of Thornhill's right to speak freely was thus arrived at only after he had carefully weighed this right against the admitted power of the state to preserve order in industrial disputes. He expressly acknowledged in his written opinion the authority and obligation of state governments to act to preserve peace and order and "to set the limits of permissible contest open to industrial combatants,"[40] and his opinion was not intended to place peaceful picketing beyond the scope of state power.

Murphy was clearly seeking to protect only the kind of picketing at issue in the Thornhill case, not all picketing nor even all peaceful picketing. The difficulty with the Alabama statute, he privately observed, was that it was not directed at the "substantial evils" that might result from picketing, such as "molestation, annoyance, intimidation,

---

[37] Murphy to Huddleson, Jr., undated, Murphy Papers.
[38] 254 U.S. 443 (1921).
[39] Murphy to Huddleson, Jr., undated, Murphy Papers. Murphy's italics. It is difficult to decipher the punctuation marks used by Murphy in this handwritten note. Murphy considered but rejected the contention of the defense that the right of assembly as well as of free speech was at issue in the case. Murphy to Huddleson, Jr., two undated notes, Huddleson, Jr., to Murphy, Mar. 30, 1940, *ibid*.
[40] 310 U.S. 88, 103-4.

[and] other forms of coercion or wrong." Murphy regarded picketing as a "variable term" which might sometimes mean one thing, sometimes another. In a footnote to his opinion, he called attention to a law-review article that listed the types of activities which the term picketing might encompass, ranging from the mere observation of workers or customers to the use of violence, the destruction of property, etc.; and in the body of his opinion he noted that the Court was not concerned in the instant case with mass picketing or with picketing that might occasion "imminent and aggravated danger" to life, property, and the public peace.[41] In the process of editing one of the drafts of the opinion, he had proposed as a substitute for the reference to mass picketing noted above a statement that the Court was not saying that a state might not regulate "picketing in such numbers or otherwise conducted as to present a threat of violence or injury or [which] constitutes annoyance or substantial interference with the right of privacy or free exercise of other rights."[42] Murphy did not say that peaceful picketing was under all circumstances immune from regulation but only that insofar as it involved the dissemination of truthful information concerning the facts of a labor dispute, it was protected by the Constitution and could be abridged only in accordance with the clear and present danger test. Murphy established the same criterion for the judgment of the validity of peaceful picketing in the companion Carlson case.[43]

Murphy might have been more explicit in dealing with the subject, but it is reasonable to conclude from his opinion and from the documents on the Thornhill case in his Papers that he did not regard picketing as being merely a form of speech and nothing more. He had concentrated on the free-speech aspect of picketing in his opinion because the facts in the case appeared to him to make this the central issue, but he was well aware that picketing might have an altogether different character from that presented in Thornhill. It was, however, the indicated relationship of picketing and free speech that attracted attention and made the opinion such a controversial one. Peaceful picketing, declared Charles O. Gregory, who insisted that the Court

---

[41] Undated note in Murphy's handwriting, Murphy Papers; 310 U.S. 88, 101 n., 105. The article cited by Murphy was Jerome R. Hellerstein, "Picketing Legislation and the Courts," *North Carolina Law Review*, X (1931-32), 186-87 n.

[42] Draft #2 of Thornhill opinion, Murphy Papers.

[43] 310 U.S. 106, 113. On this point, see Jones, Jr., "The Right to Picket," 998-99.

had said that peaceful picketing was speech and nothing more, is not "an argument intended to achieve an intellectual conquest" but is rather "a type of coercion." It is "a sort of psychological embargo around the picketed premises, depending for its persuasiveness on the associations most people have in mind when they think about picketing." The Supreme Court's description of coercion of this sort as free speech was "ridiculous" and constituted a "sheer misunderstanding of the concept." Gregory thought that the Court had been swayed "more by political pressures and its economic and social predilections than by dispassionate considerations of the correct use of political power within the states, regardless of what values local legislatures may entertain."[44]

Ludwig Teller feared that the identification of picketing with free speech posed "a threat to the role of courts in labor controversies since it injects into such controversies a constitutional issue which narrows the usual scope of judicial control." He described picketing as "the exercise of economic pressure" and thought that the question of its legality and enjoinability was properly "solved under the law of torts."[45] Corwin was also more than a little dubious that picketing was in any way similar to free speech. "In many circumstances," he wrote in an oft-quoted statement, "picketing, even when unaccompanied by actual violence or fraud, is coercive and intended so to be; and when it is, it is related to freedom of speech to about the same extent and in the same sense as the right to tote a gun is related to the right to move from place to place."[46]

Other commentators, however, rejected the argument that all peaceful picketing was *ipso facto* coercive. Edgar A. Jones, Jr., thought that there was "no sustainable ground" for this view and that those who took this position understood neither the connotations nor the nature of picketing. Coercion, he declared, involved "some kind of a forceable substitution of the coercer's will for that of an unsuccessfully resistant person," and he did not find this "iron rodded control of another's will" present in peaceful picketing.[47]

---

[44] Gregory, "Peaceful Picketing and Freedom of Speech," 714; Gregory, *Labor and the Law*, 301-4.
[45] Teller, "Picketing and Free Speech," 180, 204; Teller, "Picketing and Free Speech: A Reply," *Harvard Law Review*, LVI (Jan. 1943), 534, 537, 539.
[46] Corwin, Review, *ibid.*, LVI (Nov. 1942), 486.
[47] Edgar A. Jones, Jr., "Picketing and Coercion: A Jurisprudence of Epithets," *Virginia Law Review*, XXXIX (Dec. 1953), 1039, 1042, 1050.

E. Merrick Dodd believed that the Thornhill opinion "somewhat overstates" the extent to which the sort of picketing at issue in the case was designed to inform rather than to induce employees to remain away from work, but he nevertheless thought the Supreme Court wise to regard picketing as "a form of free speech," albeit a form that was subject to delimitation:

> To hold that labor unions and others have a constitutionally protected privilege of engaging in peaceful picketing [he asserted] is to accord them a privilege which is broader than the privilege of free expression. It is to accord them the privilege of attempting to influence the conduct of A in a manner detrimental to B by means which are only in part the communication of ideas. On the other hand, to hold that no such privilege exists is to hold that labor unions may be denied what is generally the only practicable method of communicating the ideas which they wish to express to the persons to whom they wish to express them."[48]

This same view—that peaceful picketing was more than speech but nevertheless had, or at least might have, a speech element in it—was expressed by others[49] and was the position taken by the Supreme Court itself in the 1940s. Frank Murphy, it should be noted, found no reason to quarrel with this judgment.

Murphy himself provided the answer for those who questioned whether the right of free speech extended to labor pickets under certain circumstances would also be extended to employers who urged their workers not to join labor unions. In *N.L.R.B.* v. *Virginia Electric Power Company* Murphy, in what has been described as "perhaps his most remarkable evaluation of the importance of freedom of speech," held for the Court that employers, without violating the National Labor Relations Act, could speak frankly to their employees about the merits of labor unions provided that the statements were not coercive on their face or were so closely associated with other employer acts that contravened the statute as to be part of a pattern of coercion.[50]

The Thornhill opinion left unanswered a good many questions concerning the scope and meaning of the Court's new doctrine. Did

[48] Dodd, *op. cit.*, 517-18, 526-27.
[49] See Cox, "The Influence of Mr. Justice Murphy," 788-89; Cox, "Strikes, Picketing and the Constitution," 592-96; Louis L. Jaffe, "In Defense of the Supreme Court's Picketing Doctrine," *Michigan Law Review*, XLI (June 1943), 1039, 1044, 1054; Armstrong, *op. cit.*, 31-33; Francis E. Jones, Jr., "Free Speech . . ." *Southern California Law Review*, XXIX (Feb. 1956), 175.
[50] 314 U.S. 469 (1941); Clarke, *op. cit.*, 236.

the free-speech interpretation of picketing extend to both stranger and secondary picketing?[51] What was the meaning of "peaceful"? Was the purpose of picketing irrelevant in judging its legality? The Supreme Court in the 1940s was to provide the answer to these questions, and in the process to indicate that there were definite limits on the applicability of the Thornhill doctrine.[52] "The Court," Felix Frankfurter declared in 1957, "came to realize that the broad pronouncements, but not the specific holding, of *Thornhill* had to yield 'to the impact of facts unforeseen,' or at least not sufficiently appreciated."[53] In *Milk Wagon Drivers Union* v. *Meadowmoor Dairies,* on February 10, 1941, a Court majority, speaking through Frankfurter, held that a state may authorize its courts to enjoin "acts of picketing in themselves peaceful when they are enmeshed with contemporaneously violent conduct which is concededly outlawed." Although Frankfurter, following Thornhill, described peaceful picketing as "the workingman's means of communication," he also stated that "utterance in a context of violence can lose its significance as appeal to reason and become part of an instrument of force." He noted that "entanglement with violence was expressly out" of Thornhill and Carlson. Justices Black, Douglas, and Reed dissented in Meadowmoor,[54] but Justice Murphy did not regard the decision as inconsistent with his Thornhill and Carlson opinions. He did for a time consider writing a separate opinion because he believed the original versions of the Frankfurter and Black opinions to be unsatisfactory and possibly because he was piqued that the case had not been assigned to him, but in the end he went along with Frankfurter, who had revised his opinion to accommodate Murphy's views.[55]

In *American Federation of Labor* v. *Swing,* with Frankfurter again writing the opinion, the Court, on the same day that the Meadowmoor decision was handed down, extended the Thornhill doctrine to apply

---

[51] Stranger picketing is picketing by persons who are not employees of the firm picketed but are from the same industry or occupation as the company's workers. Secondary picketing is picketing at the premises of an employer who is one step removed from the dispute.

[52] The cases are conveniently summarized, among other places, in Tanenhaus, "Picketing-Free Speech: The Growth of the New Law of Picketing from 1940 to 1952," *Cornell Law Quarterly,* XXXVIII (Fall 1952), 1-50.

[53] *International Brotherhood of Teamsters* v. *Vogt,* 354 U.S. 284, 289.

[54] 312 U.S. 287, 292, 293, 297, 299-321.

[55] Murphy to John J. Adams, undated, Adams to Murphy, Feb. 7, 1941, Frankfurter to Murphy, Feb. 7, 1941, *Milk Wagon Drivers Union* v. *Meadowmoor Dairies* folder, Box 130, Murphy Papers.

to stranger picketing. "A state," the majority held, "cannot exclude workingmen from peacefully exercising the right of free communication by drawing the circle of economic competition between employers and workers so small as to contain only an employer and those directly employed by him. The interdependence of economic interest of all engaged in the same industry has become a commonplace."[56]

With regard to secondary picketing, the Court, in *Carpenters and Joiners Union* v. *Ritter's Cafe,* ruled on March 30, 1942, that the freedom of speech guaranteed by the due process clause of the Fourteenth Amendment was not infringed by a state court decree enjoining, as a violation of the state's antitrust law, the picketing of a restaurant by union carpenters and painters who had no grievance against the restaurant owner except that he had engaged a contractor who had employed non-union labor to construct a building that was not connected with the restaurant business. The state, Frankfurter declared for the majority, had the power to forbid the "conscription of neutrals" and "to insulate from the dispute an establishment which industrially has no connection" with it. "Peaceful picketing," he asserted, "may be a phase of the constitutional right of free utterance," but this did not mean that the state was without power "to confine the sphere of communication to that directly related to the dispute." This effort of the Court to limit the constitutional protection afforded to secondary picketing on the basis of the proximity of the economic relationship of the picketers and the picketed was challenged in a dissenting opinion by Black, in which Murphy and Douglas joined, and in a separate dissenting opinion by Reed. Black thought that Thornhill "settled the question," and Reed stated that "until today, orderly, regulated picketing has been within the protection of the Fourteenth Amendment."[57]

On the same day as the Ritter opinion the Court, in *Bakery and Pastry Drivers* v. *Wohl,* indicated that secondary picketing, at least in some circumstances, was protected by Thornhill. "One need not be in a 'labor dispute' as defined by state law," declared Justice Robert H. Jackson, "to have a right under the Fourteenth Amendment to express a grievance in a labor matter by publication unattended by violence, coercion, or conduct otherwise unlawful or oppressive." In a con-

[56] 312 U.S. 321, 326.
[57] 315 U.S. 722, 727, 728, 730, 738.

curring opinion, in which Justices Murphy and Black joined, Justice Douglas significantly declared that "picketing by an organized group is more than free speech, since it involves patrol of a particular locality and since the very presence of a picket line may induce action of one kind or another, quite irrespective of the nature of the ideas which are being disseminated."[58]

In *Cafeteria Employees Union* v. *Angelos*, on November 22, 1943, the Court, on the basis of *Swing*, upheld the picketing of self-employers,[59] but for the next several years it had no occasion to elucidate further the meaning of the picketing-free speech doctrine. In addressing themselves to this question during these years, state courts sought to determine the validity of the picketing at issue in the cases before them on the basis of the proximity of the economic relationship of the picketers and the picketed and the objective toward which the picketing was directed. As an authority in this field has pointed out, the finding that picketing was being conducted for an unlawful objective was "a convenient way of circumventing the rigorous limitations" of the Thornhill doctrine.[60] In *Giboney* v. *Empire Storage and Ice Company*, on April 4, 1949, the Supreme Court itself followed the unlawful objective approach in upholding an injunction against peaceful picketing on the ground that it was part of a course of action whose objective was to cause the violation of a valid state law. Thornhill and Carlson, Justice Black declared for the Court, could not be used to support the contention that "conduct otherwise unlawful is always immune from state regulation because an integral part of that conduct is carried on by display of placards by peaceful picketers."[61] It is noteworthy that Frank Murphy, then only a little more than three months away from death, did not dissent from the Court's use of the unlawful objective test.

In three important picketing cases decided on May 8, 1950,[62] after Murphy's death, the Court sanctioned the use of the injunctive power against picketing designed to induce action not consistent with the

---

[58] 315 U.S. 769, 774, 776.
[59] 320, U.S. 293.
[60] Tanenhaus, "Picketing-Free Speech," 22-32.
[61] 336 U.S. 490, 499.
[62] *Hughes* v. *Superior Court of California*, 339 U.S. 460; *International Brotherhood of Teamsters* v. *Hanke*, 339 U.S. 470; *Building Service Employees* v. *Gazzam*, 339 U.S. 532.

public policy of a state as defined either by its legislature or its courts. In one of these cases, Frankfurter stated that "while picketing is a mode of communication it is inseparably something more and different." Citing Gregory and Teller among others, he observed that the purpose of a picket line is "to exert influences, and it produces consequences different from other modes of communication." It had been "amply recognized," he declared, "that picketing, not being the equivalent of speech as a matter of fact, is not its inevitable legal equivalent."[63] In another of the cases, Frankfurter asserted that Court decisions, as Paul Freund had noted, had reflected the view that picketing was a " 'hybrid.' " The Court, he observed, was attempting to strike a balance between "the element of communication" in picketing and "the power of the State," as Thornhill declared, "to set the limits of permissible contest open to industrial combatants."[64] These opinions led some writers to conclude that Thornhill was "no longer the prevailing rule" and that it existed "only as a historical footnote,"[65] and it is true that the Court had imposed restrictions on peaceful picketing that it did not place on other forms of speech.[66] It must be remembered, however, that Murphy had not said that picketing and free speech were synonymous.

When the Supreme Court in 1957, in *International Brotherhood of Teamsters* v. *Vogt,* upheld the legality of an injunction against picketing whose purpose was to coerce an employer to force his employees to join a union in violation of a state policy making such employer conduct an unfair labor practice, Justice Douglas stated in a dissenting opinion that the decision marked the "formal surrender" of the Thornhill doctrine;[67] but this was hyperbole. Since 1940 the Supreme Court had upheld restrictions on picketing that some thought inconsistent with Thornhill, but as Douglas himself conceded, state courts and legislatures were no longer free as they had been before 1940 to impose a ban on all picketing. Also, despite the qualification of the

[63] *Hughes* v. *Superior Court of California,* 339 U.S. 460, 464-65.
[64] *International Brotherhood of Teamsters* v. *Hanke,* 339 U.S. 470, 474.
[65] Arthur M. Weis, "From Thornhill to Hanke," *Labor Law Journal,* II (Aug. 1951), 594; Herbert Burstein, "Picketing and Speech," *ibid.,* IV (Dec. 1953), 803.
[66] The unlawful-objective doctrine has, of course, been applied in recent years to peaceful picketing which supports an illegal secondary boycott as defined in the Taft-Hartley Act and the Landrum-Griffin Act. See the analysis of this problem in *Local 761* v. *N.L.R.B.,* 366 U.S. 667 (1961).
[67] 354 U.S. 284, 297.

very general language of Thornhill, the doctrine of torts as applied to picketing had not been resuscitated. "Tort doctrine," Joseph Tanenhaus wrote in 1952, "regarded picketing as illegal unless justified; free speech doctrine considers restraints upon picketing unconstitutional unless justified. The burden of proof rests, as it has since *Thornhill's* case, on the shoulders of those who seek to limit picketing."[68] Thornhill *had* made a difference, and Murphy, were he alive today, would no doubt be pleased with the durability of his picketing-free speech opinion.

---

[68] *Ibid.;* Tanenhaus, "Picketing-Free Speech," 48-49.

18

Delivering the Goods:
Industrial Unionism during World War II

JOSHUA FREEMAN

The content and significance of militancy among industrial
workers has long been a central concern of American labor historians. The struggles of the 1930s, leading to the creation of the
CIO, have been extensively studied in an effort to understand
the nature of upsurges in labor activity. The late 1940s and 1950s
have been examined as a contrasting period, when union combat-
iveness was seemingly replaced by more stable, but more conservative, patterns of industrial relations. Surprisingly, little has
been written about the transition between these eras, particularly
about labor during World War II. Yet the war years, when militancy and conservatism co-existed in a complex and dynamic
relationship, can help in understanding both why and how basic
changes in the labor movement occurred and, more fundamentally, the meaning of militancy itself.

Until recently, the standard account of wartime labor had
been Joel Seidman's *American Labor from Defense to Reconversion,* a narrative study of the problems of economic conversion,
government policy, and union reaction. In addition, there were
contemporary labor relations studies, a few general works containing relevant material, and primary sources.[1] In the last few

---

[1] Joel Seidman, *American Labor from Defense to Reconversion* (Chicago: Univ. of
Chicago Press, 1953). A valuable older labor relations study is Colston E. Warne,
et al., Yearbook of American Labor, Vol. I, *War Labor Policies* (Brooklyn:
Remsen Press, 1945). Among general histories of US labor, Thomas Brooks'

Reprinted from *Labor History* 19 (Fall 1978), 570-93. The author wishes to thank Steve
Fraser, Nelson Lichtenstein, and Paul Milkman for helping shape his understanding of this
period, and David Oshinsky for his criticism and assistance in preparing this paper.

years, however, a number of new scholarly works, memoirs, and polemical tracts have appeared that greatly enrich our knowledge of workers during World War II.

Although the recent literature is diverse in perspective and approach, certain general themes emerge that distinguish it from Seidman's work. Writing in the early 1950s, Seidman focused on traditional concerns: unions as institutions, contractual arrangements between unions and employers, work stoppages, economic conditions, and government labor policy. Labor history from this perspective is in a sense a branch of the history of American business. Missing from the picture were the war workers themselves. Recent authors have tried to rectify this situation by placing the rank and file in the center of the story, where they rightly belong.[2] In doing so, they have gone beyond many of the limitations inherent in Seidman's approach. But as we shall see, this alone does not guarantee a full understanding of the changes in unionism and working class life. In fact, by narrowly focusing on certain types of rank and file activity, without placing them in a larger political and social context, the recent literature is encouraging a revised image of wartime labor that is in many ways as narrow as Seidman's.

Two related issues have been at the core of most historical writing on the union movement during World War II. First, there has been a continuing debate over the wisdom of the no-strike pledge and related union policies. Second, there has been an ongoing effort to chronicle and analyze violations of the pledge, especially the so-called wildcat strikes.[3]

Seidman, writing from a liberal perspective, endorsed the no-strike pledge, and in general supported the wartime policies of both the government and the major union federations. While

---

Toil and Trouble: A History of American Labor, 2nd ed. (NY: Delacorte Press, 1971) has a particularly good account of labor during World War II. Other specific works will be cited as discussed. For a good recent bibliography, see James Green, "Working-Class History in the 1940s: A Bibliographical Essay," in a special issue of *Radical America,* 9 (July- Oct. 1975), devoted to American labor in the 1940s.

[2] See, for example, Ed Jennings, "Wildcat! The Wartime Strike Wave in Auto"; James Green, "Fighting on Two Fronts: Working Class Militancy in the 1940s"; Stan Weir, "American Labor on the Defensive: A 1940's Odyssey"; and Nelson Lichtenstein, "Defending the No-Strike Pledge: CIO Politics during World War II," all in *Radical America,* 9 (July-Oct. 1975).

[3] In addition there has been considerable discussion of unions and racial discrimination during the war, an issue that will be touched on later in this essay.

sympathetic to labor, he stressed the necessity for unions, and industry, to subordinate their immediate interests to the requirements of a nation at war. Eleven years later, Art Preis, using a methodology not fundamentally different from Seidman's, reached opposite conclusions. He bitterly criticized the wartime policy of both the government and most labor leaders, while praising wildcat strikes. In the war years, Preis saw the seeds of post-war conservatism and bureaucratization.[4] During the last five years, Preis' point of view has become increasingly popular. Its most recent and most sophisticated expression has been in the work of Nelson Lichtenstein, who has shown in considerable detail just how government labor policy contributed to basic changes in the major CIO unions.[5]

In March 1941, as both defense production and a major industrial strike wave accelerated, President Roosevelt established the National Defense Mediation Board (NDMB) to prevent interruptions in defense production stemming from labor disputes. Although the Board's formal powers were limited, behind it were the varied resources of the federal government and the weight of public opinion. Through mediation and occasional settlement recommendations, the NDMB succeeded in sharply reducing strike activity, but eventually collapsed in November 1941 during the captive coal mine dispute.

After Pearl Harbor, the NDMB was replaced by the more powerful War Labor Board (WLB). Although labor and business leaders had voluntarily agreed at a Washington conference in mid-December to end all strikes and lockouts for the duration of the war, the federal government sought to further ensure uninterrupted production by imposing what was in effect a system of compulsory arbitration administered by the WLB. Rather than resolving disputes referred to it on a case by case basis, which had been the general policy of the NDMB, the WLB began to develop guidelines to be used in settling the most important collective bargaining issues. After a period of experimentation,

---

[4] Art Press, *Labor's Giant Step* (NY: Pioneer, 1964).
[5] Nelson Lichtenstein, "Ambiguous Legacy: The Union Security Problem During World War II," *Labor History,* 18 (1977), 214-238. For a fuller version of Lichtenstein's argument, see his "Industrial Unionism Under the No-Strike Pledge: A Study of the CIO During the Second World War" (unpublished Ph.D. diss., Univ. of Calif., Berkeley, 1974).

these guidelines were formalized in a July 1942 decision ending the Little Steel dispute.

In an effort to control inflation, the WLB devised the so-called "Little Steel formula": only those pay hikes necessary to bring wages up to a level equal to January 1941 rates, re-calculated to include the intervening rise in the cost-of-living, would be permitted. Once this level was reached. no further general wage hikes would be allowed. (In April 1943 wage increases were further restricted by FDR's "hold-the-line" Executive Order 9328.) Recognizing the problems this new wage stabilization policy would create for the union movement, the WLB also evolved a union security policy, designed to help unions maintain and expand their membership under wartime conditions. In general, such assistance was provided through maintenance of membership clauses in union contracts, a device which had been used on several occasions by the NDMB. The no-strike, no-lockout agreement, the WLB mechanism for resolving labor-management disputes, and the Little Steel formula together formed a new framework for industrial relations that was to endure for the remainder of the war.[6]

As Lichtenstein shows, the consequences for the CIO of these new arrangements were complex and pervasive. The loss of the strike weapon and the creation of new government channels to resolve labor disputes forced most unions in effect to stop relying on traditional collective bargaining to determine wages, hours, and working conditions, and instead to depend on decisions by government agencies. This pattern of dependency became increasingly generalized to all labor issues as the war went on. As a result, the CIO had an ever deeper interest in the political composition and direction of the administration. This in turn drew it

---

[6] Maintenance of membership was a modified union shop. Employees had 15 days after being hired, or after a new contract was signed, to indicate that they did not want to join the union. After that period ended, all members of the union had to maintain union membership for the life of the contract in order to retain their jobs. Lichtenstein, "Ambiguous Legacy," 215-232, Seidman, 44-45, 55-73, 96-108. The most complete account of the activities of the WLB is *The Termination Report of the National War Labor Board: Industrial Disputes and Wage Stabilization in Wartime, January 12, 1942-December 31, 1945,* Vols. I-III (Washington, D.C., 1947). See especially Vol. I, xii-xv, 81-91. The text of the Little Steel decision is in Vol. II, 288-322. For an interesting account of the thinking behind the WLB union security policy, written by a public member of the Board, see Frank P. Graham, "The Union Maintenance Policy of the War Labor Board," in Warne, *et al.,* 145-161.

into an ever closer relationship with the Democratic Party, culminating in the creation of CIO-PAC and in Sidney Hillman's largely successful efforts in 1943 and 1944 to deflect or coopt any movement towards a third party. For all the CIO effort, however, union influence in the major wartime agencies decreased as the fighting continued, and was always overshadowed by the power of the corporate executives who streamed into Washington.[7]

The labor movement expanded tremendously during the war, going from 10.5 to 14.7 million members, partially as a result of maintenance of membership. In some unions the gains were spectacular. The UE, for example, grew from 154,000 members in September 1940 to a wartime high of over 600,000.[8] But, if maintenance of membership could be given to a union by the WLB, it could also be taken away. The NDMB and the WLB developed a policy whereby the economic and political attitudes of a union would determine whether or not maintenance of membership would be granted. The most important criterion was the willingness of a union's leadership to enforce the no-strike pledge.

The new wartime arrangements themselves, however, tended to encourage violations of the pledge. Since corporations no longer had to fear strikes, they could take a hard line on labor issues, including grievances. The WLB, charged with resolving deadlocked disputes, lacked the procedures or staff to speedily settle all the presented cases, and avoided involvement in the myriad local grievances that arise out of even normal production. This situation led in the latter half of the war to the widespread use of short work stoppages to settle outstanding grievances, and speed the resolution of stalled disputes.

By tying union security to the question of strikes, the WLB shrewdly used the unions themselves as the chief instrument of wartime labor discipline. When, as in the case of a major strike in 1943 at the Detroit Chrysler plants, the WLB felt that a union was not vigorously acting to suppress strikes, it did not hesitate

---

[7] Lichtenstein, "Industrial Unionism," 522-571; Seidman, 28-29, 173-174; John Morton Blum, *V was for Victory: Politics and American Culture During World War II* (NY: Harcourt, Brace, Jovanovich, 1976), 117-140.

[8] Green, "Fighting on Two Fronts," 14; Ronald Schatz, "The End of Corporate Liberalism: Class Struggle in the Electrical Manufacturing Industry, 1933-1950," *Radical America*, 9 (July-Oct. 1975), 194-195; Warne, *et al.*, 109-110, 543.

to deny maintenance of membership. Other WLB sanctions included the withdrawal of seniority rights, shift premiums, vacation pay, and the right of a union to handle grievances. In one
case, involving New York City newspaper deliverers, the WLB
went as far as freeing the employers of any obligation at all to
deal with the union in question.[9]

As wildcat strikes became more frequent, the WLB policy became a powerful pressure on international union officers to exercise tight controls over locals that failed to suppress strikes. This
led to centralization, bureaucratization, and a decrease in democracy in the CIO unions. By simultaneously promoting wildcat strikes by union members and the suppression of such strikes
by union officers, government policy had important effects on
the atmosphere inside unions. Leadership became more distant
from the rank and file, while subtle WLB intercessions in internal union politics set dangerous precedents for future government action. Meanwhile, debates over the no-strike pledge, the
Little Steel formula, premium and incentive pay, and other related issues led to a revival of CIO, and particularly UAW and
URW, factionalism, and helped set the stage for the post-war faction fights.

Wartime labor arrangements were to a great extent imposed
on the labor movement from the outside. The CIO had only a
limited degree of freedom in which to shape its response. However, even within the given limits, most CIO leaders chose to accept federal labor policy, and rarely questioned its basic premises.
The no-strike pledge was voluntarily offered even before the
WLB was established; the CIO generally cooperated with WLB
procedures until the very end of the war; and CIO leaders served
as board members. Even when there were disagreements with
specific WLB policies—a frequent occurrence as wages remained

[9] Warne, *et al.,* 149-156; Lichtenstein, "Industrial Unionism," 353-363; Seidman,
104-105, 149; *NWLB Termination Report,* Vol. I, 93-98. In his opinion in the
Little Steel cases, Frank P. Graham wrote: "By and large, the maintenance of
a stable union membership . . . makes for faithfully keeping the terms of the
contract. . . . If the union leadership is responsible and cooperative, then irresponsible and uncooperative members cannot escape discipline by getting out of
the union and thus disrupt relations and hamper production. If the union leadership should prove unworthy, demagogic and irresponsible, then worthy and
responsible members of the union still remain inside the union to correct abuses,
select better leaders, and improve production." *NWLB Termination Report,* Vol.
II, 300-301.

stabilized and living costs increased—the CIO position was often presented as an alternative way of interpreting the basic principles promulgated by the Board, not as an attack on them.[10] Since some elements in the labor movement *did* severely criticize and even openly defy the WLB, it is important to see just why the CIO leadership largely acquiesced to a rather restrictive government labor policy.

One factor, which Lichtenstein stresses, is the degree to which the WLB union security policy helped to solve a growing crisis within the industrial unions. It is easy to forget how new and shaky the CIO was on the eve of the war. As late as 1939-40, in each basic industry there was at least one important component that did not nationally recognize any union (Ford, Goodyear, Westinghouse, Little Steel, southern textiles, etc.). In some industries, such as meatpacking, the major producers did not sign their first contracts with the CIO until 1940. Even where unions had been recognized as bargaining agents, locals were often only beginning to develop as coherent and stable organization. By June 1941, among the major industrial unions, only the UMW, the ACWA, and the UAW at Ford had union shops. SWOC, for example, had constant difficulties in the late thirties and early forties collecting dues from members it had under contract, and to avoid insolvency it often had to resort to coercion in the form of dues picket lines.[11]

Defense mobilization created new problems for the CIO, including the disruption of production and high turnover in organized plants, the influx of large numbers of unorganized workers into war industries, an increasingly conservative political atmosphere, and the anticipation of a post-war depression. So when the war began, with control over wages lost, strikes suspended,

---

[10] See, for example, "Labor's Wartime Wage Policy,"by UE economist Russ Nixon, in Warne, *et al.*, 447-452.

[11] Lichtenstein, "Industrial Unionism," 2-4, 146, 72-91; David Brody, *The Butcher Workmen: A Study in Unionization* (Cambridge, MA: Harvard Univ. Press, 1964), 194-195, 203-205. As Brody points out in his introduction, and Peter Friendlander illustrates in great detail in *The Emergence of a UAW Local, 1936-1939: A Study in Class and Culture* (Pittsburgh: Univ. of Pittsburgh Press, 1975), signing a contract may be only an initial step in developing a local union into an ongoing and meaningful institution. Many CIO locals in the late 1930s had won recognition, but were still at only a primitive level of internal development. For a description of dues picket lines at Inland Steel plants in 1941 and early 1942, see Inland Steel Company, *Facts on the Dollar-A-Day Increase, Closed Shop and Check-Off Demanded by Steel Workers Organizing Committee From Inland Steel* (Chicago, 1942), 92-131.

and few union security clauses written into contracts, CIO leaders realistically feared that their unions would disintegrate as workers found little reason to join or maintain their membership. Their reaction was to turn to the government for protection, and they found it in the maintenance of membership section of the Little Steel decision. The CIO's willingness to live with the principles of that decision thus can not be explained simply as treachery or ideological capitulation. Rather, to the extent that it was voluntary, the turn towards "corporatism" and government dependence was partially an outgrowth of the failures of the previous decade, particularly the Little Steel strike. If the CIO had independently completed its project of organizing all major US industry before the war, the situation might have been quite different.[12]

Of course the weakness of the CIO and its desire for security were not the only reasons why the CIO leadership offered the no-strike pledge and cooperated with the WLB. By late 1941 virtually all CIO leaders—John L. Lewis being the main exception—whole-heartedly supported the US defense mobilization. These men believed that some kind of labor and wages policy such as the WLB eventually arrived at was an inevitable and even necessary part of a win-the-war program. The no-strike pledge was not offered primarily as a result of government pressure. The CIO leadership itself had a firm, independent belief in the need for uninterrupted and increasing war production.[13]

Could the CIO leadership have followed a radically different policy even if they had so desired? It is difficult to say, but the constraints upon them were numerous. The degree to which wartime labor arrrangements were voluntary reflected the government's success in winning cooperation from labor leaders, not its lack of power. The Administration always had the option of seeking a severe mandatory labor code. The passage of the Smith-Connally Act, over Administration objections, was a clear indi-

---

[12] In an excellent recent article, cited above, Ronald Schatz has shown how both the pre-World War II "corporate liberalism" of Westinghouse and General Electric, and their post-war switch to "Boulwarism," resulted not from strictly ideological inclinations but also reflected changing competitive and productive conditions in the electrical industry. It is a parallel argument to the effort here to understand changes in union policy as reflective of material conditions, and not solely ideological in origin.

[13] See, for example, Lichtenstein, "Industrial Unionism," 227.

cation of the likelihood of Congressional approval for any such request. Throughout the war, the threat of legislative action, on both the state and national levels, was a Damoclean sword hanging over labor and limiting its options. The Army was also an important conservative pressure. It was used as early as the North American Aviation strike of June 1941 to break strikes (in that case with the initial approval of some CIO leaders), and continued to serve that function throughout the war. From the start the Army also pushed for national service legislation, and Lichtenstein argues that only the collapse of Germany prevented the passage of some sort of labor draft.[14]

Any radically different CIO policy would have entailed a confrontation with much of the public as well. It is convenient at times to forget just how unpopular wartime strikes were. The reaction to the 1943 coal strikes makes the situation perfectly clear. According to Seidman, they "aroused public opinion against the striking union and its leader to a degree that our history had seldom witnessed." In arguing against such strikes, UAW President R. J. Thomas said: "Our union cannot survive if the nation and our soldiers believe that we are obstructing the war effort." [15]

The point here is not that the CIO leadership could not or should not have explored alternatives to the policies that they endorsed. The fact is they made very few efforts in that direction. Once their early initiatives, Phillip Murray's Industrial Council Plan and Walter Reuther's Equality of Sacrifice Program, were essentially ignored by the government, they continued to publicize them largely for internal union consumption, but made no serious effort to build a political coalition around these or other alternative mobilization, production, or economic stabilization

[14] Lichtenstein, "Industrial Unionism," 134, 590-596; Seidman, 69-80, 107, 141, 159-164, 191-194; Warne, et al., 72-78.
[15] Seidman, 133, 142. Lichtenstein, in "Industrial Unionism," 530-560, implies that independent political action was one possible alternative for the labor movement. This was true only within narrow limits. The existing third party movements, such as the American Labor Party, were small and geographically restricted, and the upsurge of sentiment among Michigan rank and filers for forming a new third party exceptional. An indication of how tentative all these movements were is the fact that they could exist at all only by making it clear that they would support Roosevelt in the 1944 election. With the organized working class firmly behind the President, independent political action represented a long-range strategy that might have come to fruition in the post-war period, but would not have helped solve immediate problems.

schemes. Inertia and passivity developed instead, and effective responses were never offered to various government and business programs. Still, any critique of the CIO leadership must be made in the context of the specific constellation of forces they confronted, and not revolve around completely abstracted ideological issues.

*   *   *

While sharp questioning of CIO policy is a thread that runs through most recent historical work, it is accompanied by a noticeable lack of proposed alternatives.[16] Instead, the common response of those critical of that policy has been to dwell on and glorify those elements of the labor movement that defied it: Lewis and the UMW, some AFL unions, and CIO wildcatters. The results, however, have not always been very enlightening. The wartime coal strikes, for example, have been extensively recounted, often sympathetically counterposed to the actions of other industrial unions. However, it remains unclear why the UMW was willing and able to conduct its tenacious campaign at a time when no other union undertook any similar struggle. Finding an answer will require a new approach—one moving away from chronicling the complex maneuvering by union, business, and government leaders, and focusing instead on the social composition of the UMW and the distinctive, and seemingly timeless, culture of the mines and mining towns. Wartime conditions in the coal industry will also have to be examined, including the relative stability of the work force compared to other industries, the existence of coal surpluses at a time when there were no equivalent stockpiles of tanks, steel, rifles, or ships, and the difficulty in using troops to break a national coal strike. Failing to examine these areas, accounts of the coal strikes have generally fallen back on Lewis' stature, outlook, tactical ability, and courage to explain the stoppages. While Lewis' personality and worldview are undoubtedly important, they are not sufficient as an explanation, particularly since many of the stoppages began without Lewis' endorsement.[17]

---

[16] In addition to Lichtenstein and Preis, authors explicitly or implicitly critical of CIO policy include Irving Howe and B. J. Widick, *The UAW and Walter Reuther* (NY: Random House, 1949); Jennings, "Wildcat!"; and Green, "Fighting on Two Fronts."

[17] See, for example, Lichtenstein, "Industrial Unionism," 448-521; Preis, 174-197;

Far less has been written about AFL unions during the war, despite the fact that they comprised the biggest single section of organized labor. Many federation unions were far less enthusiastic than the CIO about the greatly increased government role in labor relations. AFL leaders particularly opposed the wage stabilization program, but their attitude extended to non-monetary issues as well. Many AFL affiliates, for example, objected to the activities, and in some cases the very existence of the Fair Employment Practices Committee (FEPC). The AFL also sponsored the "Frey rider," which prevented the NLRB from invalidating contracts more than three months old.

To some extent this wartime AFL stance was simply a continuation of pre-war "voluntarism." However, it was also a way of defending long-standing AFL policies, often not at all progressive, from challenges arising from the conditions of war production and the new framework of industrial relations. Thus the AFL unions that criticized the FEPC often themselves had dismal records in the area of job discrimination. Local and national unions repeatedly collaborated with employers, or acted independently, to exclude blacks from all but the most menial jobs. Likewise, the "Frey rider," while limiting government intervention in labor relations, was intended primarily to protect narrow AFL interests, and in practice diminished workers' democratic rights. AFL unions would sometimes sign contracts at a shop just before a major defense contract was to begin. In effect a handful of men would make an agreement that would be binding on thousands soon to be hired. The "Frey rider" protected this practice, and forestalled CIO efforts for new recognition elections once the work force was assembled.[18]

Green, "Fighting on Two Fronts," 15-19. For a detailed chronology of the coal strikes, see Colston E. Warne, "Coal—The First Major Test of the Little Steel Formula," in Warne, et al., 278-303. In a thoughtful account of the 1943 events, Melvyn Dubofsky and Warren Van Tine in their recent *John L. Lewis: A Biography* (NY: Quadrangle, 1977), point out that Lewis was frequently following the lead of his rank and file both in the formulation of demands and the use of the strike weapon. However, the very nature of their study once again keeps the focus on Lewis, and not on the coalfields.

[18] On AFL unions and job discrimination, see Merle Reed, "The F.E.P.C., the Black Worker, and Southern Shipyards," *South Atlantic Quarterly*, 74 (1975) 446-467; Philip S. Foner, *Organized Labor and the Black Worker, 1619-1973* (NY: Praeger, 1974), 238-268; and Warne, et al., 359-360, 370. For a comparison of the attitudes towards racial discrimination of the CIO-affiliated NMU and the AFL-affiliated SIU-SUP, see Donald T. Critchlow, "Communist Unions and Racism: A Comparative Study of the Response of the United Electrical Workers

AFL unions were sometimes more aggressive than their CIO counterparts in defending their members' economic interests, and their own organizational autonomy, as a result of a worldview that was critical of the expanding role of the federal government. But this opposition to government interference must be evaluated in concrete terms, and in relation to the underlying issues at hand. Thus while AFL "voluntarism" protected certain rights of labor, it also could, and was, used to protect some of the more reactionary policies of the labor movement itself.

*   *   *

The area in which there has been the greatest amount of recent work is the study of wartime wildcat strikes. Here the literature has moved away from Seidman's narrow perspective, which saw the strikes as essentially a problem of policy enforcement, and has begun to focus on the work force itself. A rich record of rank and file activity has been uncovered and some of the largest wildcats have been described.

What is peculiar about this literature is that so many of those writing about wartime wildcat strikers see them as the most politically advanced, most class-conscious, and ultimately most admirable working class element of the era, a remarkable reversal of contemporary popular opinion. In part, this reflects the continuing influence of the left-wing factional debates that took place during the war itself. Many of those who have written about this period—including Preis, Martin Glaberman, Irving Howe and B. J. Widick, Stan Weir, and Lichtenstein—identify with one side of those controversies, sharing a Trotskyist political perspective highly critical of the no-strike pledge and its backers. Several identify with the views of a very specific Trotskyist formation, the Workers Party, which was one of the few organizations active in the labor movement that opposed US participation in World War II, arguing that it was an imperialist war in which US workers had no stake or interest. Although quite small, the Workers Party played an active role in several wildcat strikes, and helped form the UAW Rank and File Caucus. For the

---

and the National Maritime Union to the Black Question During World War II," *Labor History*, 17 (1976), 237-244. The "Frey Rider" is discussed in Seidman, 179-182, and Warne, *et al.*, 184-186.

Workers Party, and American Trotskyists in general, the war was the period of their greatest potential influence in the labor movement. With the possible exception of the Minneapolis General Strike of 1934, it was their one moment on something approaching center stage. It is not surprising then that authors sympathetic to this tendency, or who themselves participated in it, should devote so much energy to studying the war years, and thus become a major presence in the historiography of the period.[19]

For the Trotskyists' factional opponents, the Communist Party, the wartime labor policies of the CIO and the Party itself were not their proudest moment. The enthusiastic support of the Party, and some labor leaders close to it, for an end to premium pay, the introduction of incentive plans, national service legislation, and a post-war no-strike pledge was politically costly both during the war itself and in the post-war faction fights. Internally, the Party was thrown into turmoil by its dissolution in May 1944 and its reconstitution fourteen months later following the publication of the Duclos letter. Writers sympathetic to the Communists, particularly those who themselves were once active in union affairs, generally deal with wartime labor by trying to avoid the whole subject.[20]

It would be a mistake, however, to conclude that the war was uniformly a disaster for the Party's working class strength. In spite of its problems, the Party grew in size during the war to a

[19] In their work on this period, Howe and Widick, Glaberman, Weir, and Lichtenstein all to some extent sympathize with the Workers Party. Oddly enough, none of these authors gives any information on what the Workers Party itself was publicly advocating during this period, particularly whether or not it openly presented its position on the war in the shops. For a brief account of the organization, see Lichtenstein, "Industrial Unionism," 380-383. Harvey Swados' novel about a group of Workers Party members, *Standing Fast* (NY: Ballentine, 1970), captures both the wartime exhilaration of the group and their lurking fear at the war's end that their historical moment might be rapidly ending.

[20] John Williamson, wartime national organizational secretary of the Communist Party, and a long-time party leader in labor affairs, fails to even mention the no-strike pledge, wildcats, or wartime CP labor policy in his autobiography, *Dangerous Scot: The Life and Work of an American "Undesirable"* (NY: International, 1969). James J. Matles and James Higgins, in *Them and Us: Struggles of a Rank-and-File Union* (Englewood, NJ: Prentice-Hall, 1974), deal with those issues in one paragraph, and cover the whole war period in four pages. For another view of the wartime UE, see Schatz, 194-195. Philip Foner deals more extensively with the war years in *The Fur and Leather Workers Union* (Newark, NJ: Nordan Press, 1950). Victor Reuther, writing from a quite different political perspective, also avoids most of the key wartime issues in his recent *The Brothers Reuther and the Story of the UAW: A Memoir* (Boston: Houghton, Mifflin, Co., 1976).

membership of 80,000. In September 1941, shortly after the Communists adopted their no-strike, productionist, patriotic stance, Albert Fitzgerald defeated James B. Carey for the UE presidency with the backing of the Party. In New York City two Communist city councilmen were elected with working class support.[21] The late war years did see "a decline in the industrial and trade union composition of the party," but exactly how the CP's wartime policies affected its shop-floor strength is still unclear.[22]

Although together the Trotskyists and the Communists represented only a distinct minority of CIO workers, they were the two poles of the wartime intraunion debates, and to a large extent shaped the terms of discussion during and after the war. The legacy of this partisanship has carried over to the historical literature, and is one reason that there is not yet a complete and balanced account of the wartime wildcat strikes.

Another problem is the indiscriminate use of the phrase "wildcat" to describe all wartime strikes. Work stoppages during the war varied greatly in size, cause, and character. Altogether over 14,000 strikes occurred, involving 6¾ million strikers. In both 1943 and 1944 the number of individuals involved in work stoppages exceeded the comparable figures for all other years after 1916 except 1941. The *typical* wartime strike, according to Ed Jennings, was initiated without union involvement, might include the use of picketing, would last at most a few days, and generally ended as a result of union mediation. Some strikes were brief stoppages by a few workers with no union involvement at all. On the other hand, there were also massive, coordinated walkouts led by official local union leaders, such as the May 1943 strike of 50,000 Akron rubber workers or the May 1944 strike of 10,000 Chrysler workers at six Michigan plants.[23]

It is conceptually confusing to lump together strikes conducted locally within the official union structure with those that

---

[21] Williamson, 145-148; Lichtenstein, "Defending the No-Strike Pledge," 68: Matles and Higgins, 133-134.

[22] Williamson, 147.

[23] Seidman, 135; National Industrial Conference Board, *The Management Almanac, 1945* (NY: National Industrial Conference Board, 1945), 130; Jennings, 83-95; Lichtenstein, "Industrial Unionism," 475-481. For statistical overviews and short chronologies of wartime strikes, see, Warne, *et al.,* 140-142, 567-571; National Industrial Conference Board, *The Management Almanac, 1944* (NY: National Industrial Conference Board, 1944), 115-117, and *The Management Almanac, 1945,* 129-133.

took place outside of and even in opposition to that structure. Labelling both "wildcats" deprives that term of any significance. Some local union leaders felt that openly or covertly they had to lead strikes in violation of the no-strike pledge (and sometimes contractual agreements as well), when other efforts to resolve serious grievances or win new benefits failed. Many of these officials were rewarded with removal from office, and occasionally were even expelled from their unions by international officers (who at the same time used the stoppages as levers to win concessions from government agencies). Still, these strikes were essentially a continuation of pre-war activity and not fundamentally a new phase of working-class activity.

At the same time many strikes were taking place outside of union structures. The most frequent causes of these true wildcats included disciplinary action—particularly the firing of union officials or militant workers, working and safety conditions, long hours, and speed-ups. Some strikes were openly anti-union. Only infrequently were wages a cause of wildcats. In a few cases, including a strike of 11,000 Reynolds Tobacco workers, the main issue was union recognition. Generally, however, wildcats were defensive in nature, attempts at preventing the erosion of hard-won rights or protests against the worst corporate excesses in a situation where no other effective grievance procedure existed.[24]

What was the historical character of these wildcat strikes? One historian says: "[They] resembled those work stoppages which flared in the auto industry before the organization of the international union: uncoordinated except on the department or plant-wide level, short in duration, led by a shifting and semi-spontaneous leadership."[25] In other words, organizationally and politically these strikes were a throwback to an earlier and more primitive stage of historical development. Although somewhat more developed, they bear a strong resemblance to the wildcat tendency described by Friedlander in his study of the origins of a Hamtramck UAW local in the late 1930s, which he shows "though volatile and militant . . . existed on a low level of historico-political activity."[26]

---

[24] Jennings, 85; Lichtenstein, "Industrial Unionism," 355, 364-367; Foner, *Organized Labor*, 261-262.
[25] Lichtenstein, "Industrial Unionism," 367.
[26] Friedlander, 77.

Although on a completely different scale, the wartime wildcats, like those described by Friedlander, failed to produce an
articulated social vision, a political program, an organizational
form, or a prominent leadership. The highest political expression
achieved was the Rank and File Caucus of the UAW, which was
a coalition of quite disparate elements, whose program simply
called for rescinding the no-strike pledge, independent political
action by labor, and the election of UAW leaders pledged to
these goals. Although it remained small, the caucus did succeed
in forcing the September 1944 UAW convention to schedule a
referendum on the no-strike pledge, but the pledge was upheld
by a two-to-one membership vote. The caucus was always in the
shadow of the larger and more established Reuther caucus. At
the same 1944 convention, a Rank and File candidate running
against Walter Reuther and Richard Leonard for second vice
president received only 4% of the vote, as most of the caucus'
own membership deserted to Reuther. After the war, the caucus
rapidly disintegrated since its only basis for existence was opposition to the no-strike pledge.[27]

The question, then, is why did the wildcat strikes and the associated militancy fail to produce a more substantial challenge
to either CIO policy or the general rightward drift of national
politics? In looking for an answer, we can find some clues in a
category of wildcat strikes not yet discussed, walkouts by white
workers protesting the hiring or upgrading of blacks. In Detroit
there was a whole series of such stoppages from 1941 on, culminating in June 1943 with a strike of 25,000 white Packard
workers who refused to work beside upgraded blacks. The
Packard strike was part of a national wave of racist wildcats that
began in the spring of 1943, and coincided with a general outbreak of interracial violence. Shipyards were the site of some of
the worst incidents. At the Sun Shipbuilding Yard in Chester,
PA, black and white workers battled violently, while in Mobile,
AL, 20,000 white shipyard workers struck and rioted, successfully forcing the FEPC to abandon its attempt to provide non-
discriminatory advancement for blacks. At the Bethlehem shipyard at Sparrows Point, MD, a wave of "hate strikes" occurred
in July 1943. Other CIO-organized industries that had such

---

[27] Howe and Widick, 121-124; Lichtenstein, "Industrial Unionism," 659-672.

strikes included aircraft construction and electrical manufacturing. Perhaps the best publicized incident of the war was a wildcat strike of Philadelphia transit workers in August 1944. Protesting the upgrading of eight blacks to positions as trolley motormen, the strike shut down the city's transit system for several days. It ended only after 5,000 federal troops were brought in and strikers were threatened with immediate loss of draft deferments, and criminal penalties under the Smith-Connally Act.

In most cases, CIO leaders worked hard to prevent or end such strikes. In early 1942 the CIO set up the Committee to Abolish Discrimination in an effort to win over its own membership to opposition to job segregation. During the 1943 Packard strike, R. J. Thomas unsuccessfully pleaded with a rally of strikers to return to work. In another incident he suspended a local union official who had led a racist wildcat. Sometimes union leaders, unable to end such strikes themselves, turned to the government. When UE officials failed to end a wildcat at the Western Electric Company plant in Breeze Point, MD, where white workers demanded segregated toilet facilities, they asked Roosevelt to intervene, which he did in the form of an army takeover. During the Philadelphia transit strike, the TWU, which had just won a recognition election, first tried itself to end the strike, and then called for army intervention.[28]

Wartime racist strikes present a sticky problem for those historians who uncritically extol all militant labor action in and of itself. In fact, most of the research on these incidents has been done not in the context of general studies of labor activity, but in studies focusing specifically on race relations. But this historiographic separation masks a certain essential similarity among all wildcat strikes that can serve as an important analytic clue. The relationships in "hate strikes" among rank and file workers, var-

[28] Howe and Widick, 220-222; Howard Sitkoff, "Racial Militancy and Interracial Violence in the Second World War," *Journal of American History*, 58 (1971), 671-675; Reed, 449-462; Foner, *Organized Labor*, 255-257, 265-268; Allen Winkler, "The Philadelphia Transit Strike of 1944," *Journal of American History*, 59 (1972) 74-89. In 1942 the Klu Klux Klan had an estimated Detroit membership of 18,000 (Howe and Widick, 8). While the UAW hierarchy supported black occupancy for the controversial Detroit Sojourner Truth Housing Project, white UAW members were among the leaders of the opposition to the project (Foner, *Organized Labor*, 258). For an interesting example of international leaders interceding against local racially exclusionary practices, see Charles P. Larrowe, *Harry Bridges: The Rise and Fall of Radical Labor in the United States* (NY, Westport, CT: Lawrence Hill, 1972), 270.

ious levels of union leadership, and the government were similar
to those that emerged in the larger number of wildcats over non-
racial issues. Now clearly it would be wrong to label the racist
wildcats as the most politically advanced activity of the working
class. Yet the very similarity in form between the two types of
wildcat strikes indicates that caution is needed before applying
such a designation to any part of the trend.

For a fuller understanding to emerge we will need to know
more. Were the same workers, or types of workers, involved in
the racial and non-racial strikes? What were the social backgrounds of the wildcat strikers? Were they primarily skilled or
unskilled; old or young? Had they been pre-war union activists,
or were they new to industrial work? Yet even without these
questions fully answered, we can start to look at certain social
developments which may help to explain both the full range of
wildcat activity and its failure to develop politically.

In a sense, the CIO moved back in time during the war. As the
country mobilized, an ever greater percentage of the CIO membership resembled more the industrial workers of 1930 than the
workers of 1939. Most important was the massive influx of new
workers into the industrial work force. Many of these workers
came from non-union, rural, conservative backgrounds. Millions
of women and teenagers with no previous industrial experience
also entered the labor force. At the same time, millions of veteran
unionists were leaving the shops for the armed services. Thus
the large industrial unions were increasingly becoming composed
of workers who had never participated in the deeply transforming process of creating those unions. Many of the new workers
had negative or passive attitudes towards unions. Some were
still deeply immersed in rural, preindustrial cultures. Many had
racial attitudes formed in the South.[29]

With the work force dramatically changing, and many ex-

---

[29] Blum, 102; Seidman, 154-155; Warne, *et al.*, 414-415, 420. There is no satisfactory
general account of the influx of new workers into the industrial work force during World War II, although there has been a considerable amount written on the
creation of new job opportunities for women and blacks. Perhaps the best
sources for a sense of the atmosphere created by this massive migration are
Katherine Archibald's *Wartime Shipyard: A Study in Social Disunity* (Berkeley
and Los Angeles: Univ. of California Press, 1947) and two excellent novels
about wartime industrial communities, Harriet Arnow's *The Dollmaker* (NY:
Macmillan, 1954) and Chester Himes' *If He Hollers Let Him Go* (1945; reprinted NY: New American Library, 1971).

perienced union leaders trying to suppress wildcats, not lead them, it is not surprising that much of the wartime activity of CIO workers had an undeveloped and at times even reactionary quality to it. Militancy tended to be spontaneous, unchannelled, uncoordinated, and untempered by larger political or union concerns. Related was the high level of violence that observers noticed in wartime plants, especially in Detroit. Supervisors were on occasion terrorized, assaulted, and even stabbed, and in one well-publicized incident, workers at the Ford River Rouge complex completely demolished a company labor relations office.[30] This type of violence is clearly a more primitive form of activity than strikes, unions, rallies, or political action.

The new industrial workers were a major source of instability for the CIO unions. Organizing drives and maintenance of membership clauses helped get them into the unions and keep their dues flowing. But with many experienced organizers and unionists in the service, and with industries expanding at extraordinary rates, the internationals were hard pressed to incorporate these new workers in a socially meaningful sense. This is most obvious in relation to interracial solidarity, but was by no means restricted to that issue. This situation was a major impetus, independent of the need to suppress strikes, towards bureaucratization and centralization. Again we see on a large scale an approximation of a process that Friedlander describes on the local level in an earlier period. As a union expands to bring in large numbers of workers passive or hostile to it, the more active and experienced unionists begin to increasingly structure and bureaucratize the union to prevent its disintegration or drift to the right. As Friedlander argues, bureaucratization is not just the result of bureaucrats and opportunism, although both are present and important, but is also a natural outgrowth of the very success of unions in organizing new, less politically advanced sections of the working class.[31] Thus both the changing composition of the union membership, and the resulting response of various union hierarchies,

[30] Jennings, 91, 94-95.
[31] Friedlander, 93-97. Companies were not unaware of the destabilizing effect of rapid union growth. One UAW leader suggested that it was with this in mind that Ford granted a union shop in all of its plants in June, 1941, and not just the heavily unionized River Rouge complex. Ford also agreed to grant dues check-off, apparently believing that it would give the company some influence over the union. See Lichtenstein, "Industrial Unionism," 146fn; Reuther, 212.

tended to retard the development of any politically articulate challenge to CIO war policy.

It also must be remembered that under wartime arrangements unions were able to win significant victories for their members. The government labor mechanism served not only as a damper and constraint on the union movement, it also protected the movement and granted it some contractual gains that unions had been previously unable to achieve on their own. Wartime wage *rates* increased more slowly than the cost of living as a result of government controls, but because of the steadiness of war production and extensive overtime, average weekly *earnings* of manufacturing employees rose 70% between January 1941 and July 1945. Additionally, government labor boards often rationalized wage structures in ways that helped unions achieve goals that they had failed to achieve in the pre-war period. The UE, for example, which had an unusually high percentage of female members, was able to win through the WLB equal pay for equivalent work by men and women. In the New York City fur industry, the Fur and Leather Workers Union was able to use Roosevelt's Wage Stabilization Order to eliminate traditional wage differentials between slack and busy seasons, and used WLB cases to win health insurance, job security with ten months shared work, and in some locals equal pay for women. These were all long-standing unachieved aims of the union. Other unions were able to eliminate interracial, intraplant, and intraregional wage differentials through WLB cases. In addition, many unions won unprecedented fringe benefits.[32]

Although wartime living conditions were often difficult and sometimes as in Detroit atrocious, "at the peak of the war effort, in 1944", according to John Morton Blum, "the total goods and services available to civilians was actually larger than it had been in 1940." Kate Archibald's observation about her fellow shipyard workers can well be applied to the industrial workforce as a whole: "For the majority of the workers the war was an ex-

[32] Seidman, 111-112, 115, 128; Schatz, 195; Matles and Higgins, 138; Foner, *Fur and Leather*, 618-619; Foner, *Organized Labor*, 261; *NWLB Termination Report*, Vol. I, 150-155, 226-259, 290-297: Brody, 214-215; Warne, *et al*, 120-125. On November 24, 1942 the WLB issued General Order No. 16 which permitted, without prior Board approval, wage increases designed to equalize female and male wage rates for equal work. *NWLB Termination Report*, Vol. II, 191.

perience of opportunity rather than limitation. Their wartime income was larger than ever before, and they ate more abundantly and lived more agreeably. The men of draft age were also aware that every day in the shipyard was a day not spent in a barracks or a foxhole, and were properly grateful."[33] For many workers, the war was the most prosperous time they had ever known. If the policies of the industrial unions were to some extent responsible, there was that much less reason to challenge those policies.

If this helps explain why the wartime wildcat tendency remained politically incoherent, we still have not touched on the most important factor of all, the war itself. And it is here that the literature is at its weakest. For most recent writers on wartime labor, the war is little more than a labor shortage, a new set of bargaining conditions, and the expanded production of war materials. There is little interest in the political and psychological meaning of the war for union members, or the larger social and moral implications of the fighting.[34]

The vast majority of US workers supported World War II, although the grounds on which they did so varied. For many, the war was not only a patriotic war, but was a war against fascism, against totalitarianism, in defense of democracy. It was a war that was both a culmination and a defense of the spirit and very real gains of the New Deal era. More politically conscious workers, except on the Trotskyist left, saw the war as a worldwide struggle against reaction, a struggle that might plant the seeds of a whole new progressive world order.[35] Victor Reuther recalls that for him: "[World War II] was just another phase of the long historical struggle of people to free themselves from authoritarian rule and win a measure of individual freedom. . . . we could not afford to forget the subjugated colonial countries that would soon be fighting for national sovereignty and social and economic justice."[36] National political figures, such as Wendell Willkie and Henry Wallace, union and political educational

---

[33] Blum, 90-100, 141 (see 91 for quoted passage); Archibald, 188.
[34] This narrow view of the meaning of the war characterizes the work of Preis, Lichtenstein, Jennings, Green, and Weir among others.
[35] Lawrence Wittner, *Rebels Against War: The American Peace Movement, 1941-1960* (NY and London, 1969), 47-48; Lichtenstein, "Defending the No-Strike Pledge," 67, Jennings, 78.
[36] Reuther, 244.

campaigns, and some government propaganda served to reinforce this perception of the meaning and possibilities of the war.[37]

Undoubtedly, this vision, and the mood carried with it, was strongest and most articulated among those involved in the popular front, but it was certainly not restricted to them. Rightly or wrongly, a broad spectrum of unionists and workers felt that the nation was involved in what the November 1943 CIO convention called a "people's war of national liberation," a war to defend and expand economic and political democracy at home and abroad.[38] Even among less politically conscious workers, support for the war was genuine and widespread, although frequently based on more traditional, nationalistic grounds, and sometimes on anti-Japanese racism. Only among non-white workers, particularly in the early days of the war, was there significant ambiguity or outright disdain for the US war effort.[39]

Given the experiences of the last two decades, it is easy to disbelieve the sincerity of US workers' support for the war, or to sneer at them for that attitude. But it certainly was genuine. There is no other way to explain the extraordinary efforts made by union members for the war effort. Furriers, for example, not only bought tens of millions of dollars of war bonds, gave money for British, Russian, Greek, and Chinese war relief, organized relief committees and blood drives, but 20,000 workers even volunteered 150,000 hours of labor to make fur vests for British and later American sailors.[40] The Furriers Union, heavily communist and Jewish, may have been somewhat unusual, but it was not totally atypical either. Many unions had large numbers of members whose families or origins were in the war zones of Europe, and for them the war had a special meaning.

It is only in this context of broad support for the war effort that we can fully understand the behavior of workers in the war years. In spite of the loss of the strike weapon, workers continued to join unions in record numbers, often following patriotic, productionist organizing campaigns. The UE, for example, one of

---

[37] On wartime social liberalism, see Norman Morkowitz, *The Rise and Fall of the People's Century: Henry Wallace and American Liberalism, 1941-1948* (NY, 1973).
[38] Warne, *et al.*, 506.
[39] Wittner, 46-47; Archibald, 102-104, 191; Sitkoff, 664-667; Blum, 183.
[40] Foner, *Fur and Leather,* 611-615.

the fastest growing unions, won 831 separate recognition elections during the war, in plants employing a total of 335,000 workers. In the year ending June 30, 1943 alone, the NLRB conducted over 4000 recognition elections in which over a million ballots were cast—82% for a union.[41] Likewise, the majority of workers did not violate the no-strike pledge in spite of constant provocation, the deterioration of the collective bargaining process, and the transparent war profiteering of the major corporations. And if most workers supported the no-strike pledge in their actions, by not striking, a larger majority—including many wildcatters—supported the pledge in principle. Even in the UAW, where a majority of all members at some time participated in a wildcat strike, the pledge was upheld in a referendum by a two-to-one margin.[42] If workers were unwilling to always abide with the CIO-AFL-CP-WLB line, and abstain from any defense of their rights and conditions, they were also unwilling to repudiate the principle underlying that line, that the war was a positive national effort for which all must sacrifice. It was the blatant, almost arrogant refusal of the business corporate producers to make even a gesture towards equal sacrifice that set the psychological background for the stoppages that did occur.[43]

Similarly, the ever-strengthening hold of the Democratic Party on US workers can partially be explained by the strong backing for the war. Roosevelt was as popular as "Dr. Win-the-War" as he had been as "Dr. New Deal." In this regard the political stance of the CIO leadership reflected the inclination of the ranks.

*   *   *

In the work of those left historians who see in the wildcat tendency the most developed expression of working-class consciousness, there is an underlying set of political and psychologi-

---

[41] Lichtenstein, "Industrial Unionism," 262-266; Matles and Higgins, 138; Warne, *et al.*, 181.
[42] Jennings, 78, 83-84, 97.
[43] Workers perceptions that the war was their war as well as that of the corporations also provided the ideological basis for the often strained popular front efforts to defend the no-strike pledge. For example, the Weavers song "Deliver the Goods" contained the following verse:
    "Now, me and my boss, we never could agree,
    If a thing help'd him it didn't help me;
    But when a burglar tries to break into my house
    You stop fighting with the landlord and throw him out."
Highlander Folk School, *Songs: Labor, Folk, War* (Monteagle, Tenn., n.d.), 29.

cal assumptions. For them, left-wing trade unionism is essentially just militancy combined with political independence.[44] Working class support of the war, when acknowledged at all, is seen as at best quaint, touching but slightly embarrasing, and at worst deplorable and worthy of contempt. For this school, workers, regardless of skill, cultural background, ideological inclination, or historical context, are essentially economic rationalists, out to protect and extend their material standing.[45] This perceived narrow economism, rather than being criticized, is celebrated.[46]

Labor militancy is a form of working class activity, but only a form. Its presence or absence can tell us a great deal about the state of development of industrial workers. But we must also go beyond the form of activity to look at the political worldview that explicitly or implicitly informs it.

The history of American workers has repeatedly shown that outbursts of labor activity may or may not contain the seeds of fundamental change. The measure to be applied cannot be solely aggressiveness. Equally important is the political content of labor struggles, particularly the degree to which they transcend exclusively addressing the immediate problems of specific groups of workers and begin confronting the general condition of workers as a whole, not only as economic beings, but as complete people. If we fail to apply this test, we may find ourselves once again glorifying what in the end is nothing other than Samuel Gompers' "more."

---

[44] The most explicit expression of this position is by Lichtenstein, in "Industrial Unionism," xvi-xvii, 531.

[45] This is expressed most openly, and with the greatest sophistication, by Paddy Quick, in her essay on women during the war, "Rosie the Riveter: Myths and Realities," *Radical America*, 9 (July/Oct. 1975), 115-131. Quick assumes that women throughout this period were family-loving economic rationalists, whose entry into war industry was primarily the result of their private calculations of what would be most economically advantageous for their families. Quick is making enormous assumptions about the culture, personality, and outlook of these women. As Friedlander and others have argued, these attributes should be the object of study for labor historians, not assumed to be universal. Virginia Yans, in fact, has shown how precisely these traits can play a crucial role in determining patterns of female entry into the work force, in "Patterns of Work and Family Organization: Buffalo's Italians," *Journal of Inter-Disciplinary History*, 2 (1971), 299-314.

[46] For an example of this, see Martin Glaberman, "Epilogue," *Radical America*, 9 (July/Oct. 1975), 106-107.

19

Women Workers and the UAW in the Post–World War II Period: 1945-1954

NANCY GABIN

Josephine DiChiera could not understand "why if the company says we'd have to go after we were married . . . the membership and the union wouldn't fight for us also. To all of us girls, it seems as though they are waiting for us all to get married so they can get rid of us. . . . There are some shady deals being pulled somewhere down the line. . . . We all want reimbursed on our Union dues we've paid. . . . It appears as though they're taking our money for nothing and fighting against us." DiChiera's angry challenge to the men in her United Automobile Workers (UAW) local union reveals the problems that many women in the union confronted in the post-World War II period. Her statement describes the efforts made by management to remove women from the jobs they held during the war; it indicates that men in the union not only shared management's attitudes toward women but often actively assisted in its efforts to deprive them of employment; and it further illustrates the degree of frustration and bitterness women could feel when the union, which claimed to defend its members regardless of sex, acted against the interests of women members.[1]

The auto industry had not been eager to employ women during the war's first years. When management complained of labor shortages, the UAW and other unions responded that

[1] Josepnine DiChiera to Ray Ross, May 18, 1953, Emil Mazey Collection, Box 35, Local 1020 Folder, Archives of Labor History and Urban Affairs, Walter P. Reuther Library, Wayne State Univ., Detroit (hereafter cited as WSU Archives).

Reprinted from *Labor History* 21 (Winter 1979-1980), 5-30. I would like to thank Sidney Fine, Robin Jacoby, and Jacqueline Jones for their helpful comments and suggestions on earlier drafts of this paper. Whatever errors remain are, of course, my own.

the cause was the employers' refusal to hire qualified women and blacks. By 1943, however, it was apparent to management everywhere that women would have to be employed to meet the nation's wartime needs. The number of women in the total labor force jumped from 12,090,000 in the week before Pearl Harbor to 18,740,000 in March 1944. Most dramatic was the increase in the number of women newly employed in manufacturing industries. In 1939, there were an estimated 31,330 female production workers in the transportation equipment and automobile industries; in November 1943 there were 777,400 women in these industries, an increase of nearly 2,400 per cent. Substantial occupational shifts accompanied the expansion of the female labor force; although 43.2 per cent of the women employed in March 1944 in manufacturing came from outside the labor force, 16.6 per cent came from other industry groups, most often the traditionally female trade and service sectors.[2]

By 1941, the Big Three automobile companies—General Motors, Chrysler and Ford—which were soon to convert to war production and to hire great numbers of women, had all recognized the UAW as the bargaining agent for their plant workers. The UAW like other unions benefitted from its wartime no-strike pledge. In return for pledging not to strike, government granted the unions the maintenance-of-union membership formula, which provided that after a grace period of fifteen days, workers had to retain their union membership for the life of the contract. By 1945, the UAW had one million members, 28 per cent (280,000) of whom were women.[3]

[2] *UAW International Convention Proceedings, 1943,* 97-114; Mary Elizabeth Pidgeon, *Changes in Women's Employment During the War-Special Bulletin No. 20, U.S. Women's Bureau* (Washington: Government Printing Office, 1944), 2-3; Pidgeon, "Women Workers and Recent Economic Change," *Monthly Labor Review,* 65 1947), 667; and Pidgeon, *Changes in Women's Employment,* 12, 26. The remaining 38 per cent were those women who had formerly been employed in manufacturing industries (Pidgeon, *Changes in Women's Employment,* 12).

[3] Nelson N. Lichtenstein, "Industrial Unionism Under the No-Strike Pledge: A Study of the CIO during the Second World War" (unpublished Ph.D. diss., Univ. of California, Berkeley, 1974), 225; Gladys Dickason, "Women in Labor Unions," *Annals of the American Academy of Political and Social Science,* 251 (May 1947), 72. Figures for female membership in the UAW before World War II are unavailable. Women, however, represented 6.2 per cent of all automobile and transportation equipment workers in Oct., 1939; this figure can serve for comparison with the 1945 female membership figure (Pidgeon, "Women Workers and Recent Economic Change," 669).

The UAW responded to its new female members in an ambivalent manner. During the war, the public's perception of women workers was at odds with the fact that the majority of women employed between 1941-1945 had worked before Pearl Harbor and presumably would continue to work after the war. The glamorized image of Rosie the Riveter, whose commitment to her job was allegedly due more to her sense of patriotism than to her economic need, confirmed the popular belief that women belonged in the home. Women workers were seen as temporarily employed until brothers, sweethearts, and husbands returned home. There was a conflict within the UAW between those who agreed with this popular sentiment and those who feared that management would take advantage of it after the war to justify the replacement of women workers with men.[4]

The problem of discrimination against women workers by both management and organized labor had long been an issue for the labor movement. The American Federation of Labor (AFL) had a history of hostility to women that was the result not only of its refusal to organize the industrial semi- and unskilled labor force (many of whom were female) but also of its adherence to the popular myths about working women. The AFL rationalized its policies by declaring women both unorganizable and unworthy of organization. Women's low pay, lack of skill, and temporary tenure in the labor force were seen as proof of their disinterest in organization rather than as conditions brought about by a sex-biased and class-biased cultural ideology.[5]

The Congress of Industrial Organization (CIO), formed

---

[4] For the story of women during World War II and the image of Rosie the Riveter, see William Chafe, *The American Woman* (London: Oxford Univ. Press, 1972), 135-195; Paddy Quick, "Rosie the Riveter: Myths and Realities," *Radical America,* 9 (1975), 115-132; Eleanor Straub, "U.S. Government Policy Toward Civilian Women during World War II," *Prologue,* 5 (1973), 240-254; and Joan Ellen Trey, "Women in the War Economy—World War II," *Review of Radical Political Economics,* 4 (July 1972), 40-57.

[5] For the background on women workers and the labor movement prior to the formation of the CIO, see Chafe, 66-89; Nancy S. Dye, "Feminism or Unionism? The New York Women's Trade Union League and the Labor Movement," *Feminist Studies,* 3 (Fall 1975), 111-125; Robin Jacoby, "Feminism and Class Consciousness in the British and American Women's Trade Union Leagues, 1890-1925," in Berenice Carroll, ed., *Liberating Women's History* (Urbana: Univ. of Illinois Press, 1976), 137-160; Alice Kessler-Harris, "Organizing the Unorganizable," in Milton Cantor and Bruce Laurie, eds., *Class, Sex and the Woman Worker* (Westport: Greenwood Press, 1977), 144-165; and Kessler-Harris, "Where are the Organized Women Workers?" *Feminist Studies,* 3 (1975), 92-110.

during the middle and late 1930s as a result of a conflict within the AFL over the principles of industrial and craft organization, could have been the force for challenging and changing attitudes toward, and thus the conditions of, women's work. As opposed to craft unionism, industrial unionism was theoretically committed to the organization of all workers regardless of race, national origin, or sex. If workers were organized by the industry in which they worked, management, it was thought, would be less able to divide them according to their ascribed characteristics and would be forced to treat them equally and fairly. The possible benefits for women, who had generally been restricted to occupations simply because of their sex, loomed as considerable.

The advocates of the UAW's female membership wanted the union to fulfill the promise of industrial unionism and to make an effort to secure gains for working women in anticipation of the post-war period when reconversion would eliminate many of the new wartime jobs. Responding to these demands, the UAW created its Women's Bureau in 1944 as a department of the union's War Policy Division, to meet both the wartime and the post-war needs of women members. R. J. Thomas, president of the UAW, explained in a letter to the local unions that the bureau was designed to deal with the special employment problems of the union's female membership, such as day care, the enforcement of state and federal laws regulating the hours and conditions of women's work, equal pay for equal work, and the hostility of management and male workers toward the idea of women working.[6]

Thomas also noted in this letter that the bureau would "develop techniques for interesting women in general union activities." This aspect of the bureau was intended for those who were more interested in the union's welfare and wanted to avoid a conflict after the war. "If a long-range policy covering female workers cannot be worked out before peace is declared abroad," C. G. Edelin, president of Local Union 51, providently warned, "we may find ourselves in some very warm water." Implicit in Edelin's comment was the assumption that women workers

---

[6] R. J. Thomas to All Regional Directors and Local Union Presidents, April 22, 1944, UAW War Policy Division-Women's Bureau Collection, Bqx 5, Folder 10, WSU Archives.

would not willingly leave their jobs after the war.[7]

The placing of the bureau in the War Policy Division, however, indicates the limited and short-range character of the UAW's commitment to its female members. The UAW's position on equal pay for equal work further illustrates how shallow was the union's concern for women. Emphasizing that women's employment was expected to "significantly decline" in the postwar period, Thomas stated in his report to the 1942 International Convention that it was necessary to incorporate the principle of equal pay for equal work in bargaining agreements and legislation in order to protect the wage standards of male workers against management attempts to establish lower wage levels for women in jobs previously held by men. Similarly, when the War Policy Division in 1944 issued its suggested policy for filling job openings, it strongly urged the elimination of job classifications by sex "so management can't claim any job or classification strictly for women and use this, especially after the war."[8]

The UAW defined its post-war membership as male, not as both female and male. When, contrary to expectation, 85.5 per cent of female UAW members said they wanted to keep their jobs in industry because they were better-paying and better-protected than the traditionally female jobs in the retail, clerical, and service occupational sectors, the union reacted unfavorably. Fearing that the reduction of wages and a decrease in the availability of jobs would threaten the solidarity of the workers and their faith in the UAW, the male unionists viewed the women in auto plants as competitors for jobs and as a threat to wage standards. During the reconversion process and continuing well into the post-war period, women complained of discrimination in layoffs and in job grading, but the male leadership and membership of the UAW, in the main, did not respond with sympathy or concern. Women discovered that management was not alone in wanting to exclude them from post-war jobs as a variety of jointly negotiated contract clauses served to deny them the ben-

---

[7] *Ibid;* C. G. Edelin to International Union Executive Board, Feb. 7, 1944, UAW Local 51 Collection, Box 28, Folder 9, WSU Archives.
[8] Thomas, *Automobile Unionism* (Detroit: n.p., 1942), 81-82; UAW War Policy Division, "Recommended Policy on Transfers and Filling Openings with Female Help," n.d. [1944], UAW Local 51 Collection, Box 28, Folder 8, WSU Archives.

efits that industrial organization was supposed to offer.[9]

Women were not without supporters within the union during the post-war period. In June 1946 the union leadership made the Women's Bureau part of the newly established Fair Practices and Anti-Discrimination Department. William Oliver, co-director of the Department, explained that, although the unit was principally concerned with the employment problems of black workers, it would give "[s]pecial emphasis . . . [to] women's problems in the automobile industry since it is unquestionably the largest single minority group within the jurisdiction of the UAW-CIO." It is to the credit of the union that it identified racism and sexism as specific problems in the auto industry and established the Fair Practices Department and the Women's Bureau to deal with them. The difficulties that the two offices experienced in working with the union leadership and membership, however, confirmed the fact that it was not only the employers who discriminated against women in the post-war period.[10]

The Women's Bureau and the Fair Practices Department attempted to counteract male antagonism to women workers by means of educational materials, International Convention resolutions, and policy statements issued to the membership and leadership which stressed the danger that discrimination posed for the union. A pamphlet published by the Fair Practices Department

---

[9] "Women's Postwar Plans," *UAW Research Department Research Report*, 4 (March 1944), 3, UAW War Policy Division Collection, Series I, Box 21, WSU Archives. With the exception of Lyn Goldfarb, *Separated and Unequal: Discrimination Against Women Workers After World War II* (The Women's Work Project, A Union for Radical Political Economics Political Education Project, n.d.), there are no studies of women workers in trade unions during the immediate post-World War II period. Goldfarb uses the experience of female UAW members in the Detroit area to illustrate the problems that women workers confronted in the post-war era. Although she is not consistent in her use of Detroit materials, and her analysis is suggestive rather than conclusive, Goldfarb makes several important insights into the dynamics of sexual discrimination in unions.

[10] "Second Quarterly Report of the Fair Practices and Anti-Discrimination Department, 1946," UAW Fair Practices and Anti-Discrimination Department-Women's Bureau Collection, Box 2, Folder 17, WSU Archives. The Fair Practices Department and the Women's Bureau acknowledged the special problems of black women, whose status was one of double jeopardy. Convention resolution and Department reports and policy statements referred specifically to black women workers as the group against whom management and the union most often discriminated. The two offices jointly handled cases involving discrimination against black women on the basis of either their sex or race. *UAW International Convention Proceedings, 1946*, 328; "Second Quarterly Report, 1946," 15; and William Oliver to Lillian Hatcher, May 4, 1948, Fair Practices and Anti-Discrimination Department-Women's Bureau Collection, Box 5, Folder 7, WSU Archives.

in 1946 stressed the need for increased vigilance against management's efforts to exclude women from post-war employment and pointed to the UAW's opposition to such practices. "The catch phrase, a woman's place is in the kitchen," the pamphlet stated, "is a silly slander, a cover slogan for tricky attacks on everyone's standard of living and everyone's political rights."[11]

Resolutions submitted for membership approval at the 1946 and 1949 International Conventions underscored the idea that an attack on one worker was a threat to all workers. The 1946 convention adopted a resolution condemning the layoff of women as well as management's efforts to down-grade and reclassify jobs, and the convention resolved that the UAW "must use [its] full collective bargaining power to defeat these moves of management to undermine the workers' condition." A resolution approved at the 1949 convention observed that, contrary to the popular conception, women worked for the same reasons men did, to support themselves and their families. "We are going into a period of job scarcity," the resolution noted, "when management will use every effort to take advantage of working women and create disunity among our members by spreading propaganda against women working. This is an attempt to weaken and finally break down our seniority structure."[12]

In an effort to combat discrimination against women, the Women's Bureau and Fair Practices Department, with the approval of the International Executive Board (IEB), dispatched fair practice, anti-discrimination, and seniority policy statements to the UAW membership. These statements were issued with instructions that they serve as guides in the negotiation of contracts and the filing of grievances. Referring to the Fair Practices Model Contract Clause prepared by the department, William Oliver stated, "The real test of fair practices is understanding by the union and management with respect to equal opportunities at the employment gate and equal opportunities for all jobs within the plant or seniority unit. This phase of fair practice is the most vital and most beneficial to our entire membership."[13]

---

[11] *Equal Pay for Equal Work* (Detroit: Fair Practices and Anti-Discrimination Department, n.d. [1946]), Women Employment Vertical File, WSU Archives.

[12] *UAW International Convention Proceedings, 1946*, 46; *UAW International Convention Proceedings, 1949*, 8.

[13] "Fourth Quarterly Report of the Fair Practices and Anti-Discrimination Depart-

In a much more strongly worded statement on the Department's seniority policy, Oliver explained that, "[i]n many local seniority agreements, industrial minority groups . . . are traditionally remained [sic] there; and are continuously identified with certain types of work in the shops because of their minority characteristics. . . . [T]hese traditional patterns have often reflected themselves in the form of written agreement which tends to sanction historically prejudicial patterns." The statement concluded with a directive to local unions and regional directors to work to eliminate these patterns so as to be consistent with the basic principle of industrial unionism." [14]

Although the policies and activities of the Women's Bureau and the Fair Practices Department carried International approval, the Department expressed frustration at the inaction of the International. A report prepared by the Fair Practices Department in 1947 on women foundry workers in the UAW stated the problem clearly and explicitly. *"The Fair Practices and Anti-Discrimination Department alone cannot solve all of these problems,"* the report stated. "It will take the united support and mobilization of all forces within our union to change the one factor which is most difficult—the question of *changing human nature."* The report concluded with the comment, "No one but a blind fool would believe that in the UAW-CIO prejudice against women . . . has been eliminated." In a plea to the IEB, the Department urged the Board to "recognize the difficulties incumbent upon this department when, on one hand clearly defined policies are to be observed as they appear in the constitution and official records of the Union; and on the other hand observances of these policies are ignored and even flaunted in the absence of appropriate enforcement machinery." The petition closed with a reminder to the IEB of the fundamental principle of the UAW-CIO: "It behooves the International Executive Board to give serious consideration to this aspect of our internal discipline in order that democracy and fair play will be something more than window dressing." [15]

ment, 1947," 19, Fair Practices and Anti-Discrimination Department-Women's Bureau Collection, Box 2, Folder 18, WSU Archives.

[14] *Ibid.,* 3-4.

[15] Fair Practices and Anti-Discrimination Department, "Report-Conditions Affecting the Equal Status of Women Foundry Workers in the UAW-CIO," n.d. [April

Conflict within the UAW over the issue of "special privileges" for minority groups undermined the authority of the Women's Bureau and the Fair Practices Department in making and enforcing policy. The conflict can be traced to 1943, when the creation of a Minorities Department within the International was proposed at the International convention. Supporters of the defeated proposal stressed the lack of representation of minority members in leadership positions. Opponents claimed that the proposed department would divide workers into discrete categories, discourage the union's collective consideration of the problems of minorities, and encourage tokenism. Pat Sexton, a UAW member and plant steward at the time, recalls that the establishment of the Women's Bureau in 1944 also met with opposition from unionists. "Some," she noted, "thought it would increase the segregation of women, limit rather than broaden the attention given them, and pacify their demand for general representation. Supporters thought that women needed a staff to perform an advocate's role in the union." [16]

Although opposition to special privileges or affirmative action would appear to be a corollary of the principle of industrial unionism, it seems that, in this instance, opposition was due more to a defensive refusal to confront the problem of discrimination than to any commitment to ideological consistency. This was reflected in the manner in which union officials questioned the influence and power of the Fair Practices Department. When William Oliver offered Richard Leonard, head of the UAW's Ford Department, assistance in dealing with company discrimination against women at the Detroit River Rouge and Highland Park plants in 1946, Leonard politely but firmly refused. In so many words, Leonard scolded Oliver for presuming to interfere and for implying that the local unions would act in a discriminatory manner. In replying to Oliver, Leonard wrote:

1947], 3, 15, Walter P. Reuther Collection, Box 21, Fair Practices Department 1946-47 Folder, WSU Archives; "Fourth Quarterly Report, 1947," 1-2.

[16] *UAW International Convention Proceedings, 1943*, 369-389; Patricia Sexton, "A Feminist Union Perspective," in B. J. Widick, ed., *Auto Work and Its Discontents* (Baltimore: Johns Hopkins Univ. Press, 1976), 27-28. The conflict over special privileges also reflected the political factionalism within the UAW. The Minority Report on the Minorities Department proposal in 1943, which was supported by the Frankensteen-Addes wing, proposed that the director of the department be black. The Majority Report, which opposed the potential Jim Crowism of the Minority Report demand, was coauthored by Victor Reuther.

I am happy to have had your interest in this matter. However, I think
you will agree that seniority is a contractual matter and that policing
of the contract is a responsibility of the local unions and the Ford
Department, and that it is unfair to your department to be involved
unless definite proof is advanced that either local unions or the Ford
Department have been remiss in their duties.[17]

Although the International Convention established the Fair
Practices Department, the International leadership remained
mute regarding the extent of the department's sphere of influence and authority. One explanation for the silence of the executive leadership could be that it was reluctant to dictate an unpopular policy to its constituency for fear of risking the loss of a
battle over local union autonomy, a highly valued UAW tradition. If this was the fact, the degree of hostility to women among
the rank-and-file is confirmed. It has also been argued, however,
that the UAW leadership actually consolidated its powers over
the locals in this period. If so, the International's silence on the
authority of the Women's Bureau and the Fair Practices Department reflected the ambivalence of the leadership itself in regard
to discrimination against minorities. Whatever the explanation,
the leadership did not pay sufficient heed to the need for anti-
discriminatory action.[18]

The UAW did advocate governmental action on the problem
of discrimination against minorities. In 1946, Walter Reuther,
newly elected president of the UAW, claimed that "the answer
to this post-war problem lies not in special privileges but in the
creation of 60,000,000 peacetime jobs in America." To this end,
the UAW strongly urged the passage of a Full Employment Act
and supported national efforts to secure equal pay for equal work
legislation and the institution of government-supported day care
centers. Although the Women's Bureau and the female membership agreed that the government had an obligation to aid women
workers, they were suspicious of the International's motives in
advocating federal and state action against discrimination. Helen
McLean, a delegate to the 1946 convention from the Ford Highland Park plant local union, denounced a resolution invoking

---

[17] Richard Leonard to William Oliver, Aug. 19, 1946, Walter P. Reuther Collection,
Box 21, Fair Practices Department 1945-47 Folder, WSU Archives.
[18] Alan Gale Clive, "The Society and Economy of Wartime Michigan, 1939-1945"
(unpublished Ph.D. diss., Univ. of Michigan, 1976), 612-613.

government responsibility to women workers as an attempt "to pass the buck on to the United States Government rather than setting a policy with our own union." [19]

Despite the efforts of the Fair Practices Department and the Women's Bureau to challenge prejudice against women on the part of management and the union, there was rampant discrimination against women on the local union level. The discrimination took the form of local union toleration of inequitable hiring practices, layoffs of women workers, discriminatory pay scales, and transfers by management. The hostility of male unionists toward female employees was expressed through the harassment and intimidation of women who pressed grievances against management or complained of local union inequities, the obstruction of grievance procedures, and the negotiation of contracts, supplemental agreements and verbal agreements that sanctioned discriminatory practices. The collusion between management and the union limited women's employment opportunities in plants under UAW contract.

Evidence of discrimination against women on the local union level is available in the reports of cases brought to the attention of the Women's Bureau, in unsolicited letters found in the papers of various International leaders, and in the case files of the IEB Appeals Committees. The dates of these documents range from 1945 to 1954; the majority of the IEB appeal hearing cases took place between 1950 and 1954. Although the early 1950s would seem to lie beyond what can appropriately be called the post-World War II period, the substance of these cases indicates that the effort to exclude women from the jobs they held during the war was based on the terms of contracts written during the war and in the immediate post-war period and extended well beyond the initial period of demobilization and reconversion.

Until a systematic analysis of all grievances submitted to management is undertaken, we cannot know for certain how many women protested their treatment in the post-war period. Evidence of the role the local unions played in suppressing grievances and appeals suggests, however, that the number of docu-

---

[19] Reuther, quoted in Chester W. Gregory, *Women in Defense Work During World War II* (NY: Exposition Press, 1974), 185; *UAW International Convention Proceedings, 1946,* 52.

mented cases of rank-and-file discrimination is only the tip of the iceberg. It has been argued that the limited number of protests filed by women indicates the extent to which, in the postwar period, they willingly acquiesced in their treatment at the hands of management and membership. The evidence of harassment and intimidation, on the other hand, suggests that such a conclusion is erroneous.[20]

Local union hostility to women was for the most part a function of the male workers' view of women as threats to their jobs. The male view that women belonged in the home helped to justify their approval of a variety of discriminatory plant practices. Although married women were the object of some of the most blatantly discriminatory practices, single women were also victimized by inequitable seniority agreements that gave men the right to "bump" women in the event of transfers or lay offs (but did not accord women the same right) and by unequal wage rates on similar jobs performed by men and women. And both married and single women were subject to verbal harassment and intimidation by fellow workers, stewards, and local union officers. Tactics of this sort were used both to coerce women into leaving their jobs and to prevent them from filing grievances against management for sexual discrimination. To the extent that local unionists succeeded in the latter effort, they helped to conceal both to outside observers and sometimes to international officers the extent of their collusion with management in discriminating against female employees.

In a case heard by the IEB Appeals Committee, the appellant, Nettie Bennett, accused Johnnie Kallos, a steward, of conspiring to remove women from jobs improperly and of using verbal harassment and threats to prevent the women from protesting. One witness for the appellant who had also been laid off reported that, because she had refused to date Kallos, he had told her that she would not be recalled to work at the Hudson Motor Car Company as long as he was chief steward in the department.

---

[20] Clive, 539-547. Clive's statement that, "[i]f female workers were outraged by the treatment accorded them, they made no public show of their displeasure" is clearly at odds with even the minimal coverage of female UAW members' protests in the labor press and statements of women delegates during the International conventions (Clive, 542). *Michigan Chronicle, United Automobile Worker,* and *Ammunition* clippings in the Vertical Files-Women, WSU Archives, and the 1944, 1946, 1949 *UAW International Convention Proceedings.*

Another woman testified that after she had submitted a request for a pregnancy leave, Kallos "had the gall to walk up and down the line with his stomach stuck out pretending he was me on the job." Kallos told Mildred Westbrook that there would be no women in his department as long as he was steward and that it would be best for her to find employment elsewhere.[21]

In the Bennett case, the local union ordered the steward to reinstate the women against whom he had discriminated in a transfer action. Other UAW locals were less willing to come to the aid of female members victimized by discrimination. Josephine DiChiera, a member of Local Union 1020 in Homewood, Pennsylvania, discussed with her steward her desire to continue working even though she was about to get married. The steward brought her intention to a vote at a local union membership meeting. "Naturally, when you have about 70 or so girls up against a membership of 1,100, with the rest as man [sic], they wouldn't vote to keep us there," DiChiera reported to regional director Ray Ross. "I feel that this should never have been brought up for the membership to vote on because I feel they were voting Union members against Union members. . . . It appears as though they're taking our money for nothing and fighting against us." Dominic Dornetto, an UAW international representative who supported DiChiera, explained to Ross that the motion at the meeting to keep married women on the payroll "was overwhelmingly defeated with many slurs and other improper behavior of the members." Dornetto later reported to Ross that management refused to answer DiChiera's charge that she had been dismissed without cause, a grievance which she had filed in spite of the steward's lack of support, because the local union did not recognize her complaint as a grievance.[22]

Since the Bureau's major strategy for combatting discrimination on the basis of sex was through the negotiating and grievance machinery on the local level, its efforts required the support

---

[21] Grace Curcuri to To Whom it May Concern, Sept. 16, 1952, Nina Fuston Maynard to Richard Gosser, Sept. 16, 1952, Mildred Westbrook to Dear Sirs, Sept. 16, 1952, Mazey Collection. Box 37, Local 154 Folder, WSU Archives.

[22] Josephine DiChiera to Ray Ross, May 18, 1953, Dominic Dornetto to Ross, June 4, 1953, and Dornetto to Ross, June 17, 1953, Mazey Collection, Box 35, Local 1020 Folder, WSU Archives. The local union did not recognize DiChiera's grievance because of the existence of a verbal agreement dating back to 1946 that forbade the employment of married women (Ida Seibert and Josephine Jurinko [DiChiera] to Ray Ross, Nov. 10, 1953, ibid).

of stewards and local union committeemen and officers. When that support was not forthcoming, female employees could easily be victimized. A 1947 report of the Fair Practices Department to the IEB noted that women often waited months or years before filing a complaint against discriminatory practices which, the report emphasized, should have been originally handled through the regular grievance machinery. The report suggested that this was "due to [women's] lack of information and proper understanding of the collective bargaining procedures of their local unions." The authors of the report might, in all fairness, have added that the ignorance of women concerning these procedures might have been due to male efforts to conceal the information from them or to suppress their protests.[23]

If procedural and verbal restraints were not effective in silencing women, discriminatory contract clauses and supplemental and verbal agreements often served this purpose. Three types of discrimination were sanctioned by various union and management agreements. There were, first of all, local agreements prohibiting the employment of married women and providing for the discharge of single women who married. Secondly, agreements providing for unequal hiring-in rates for men and women and unequal wage rates on similar jobs discriminated against single and married women. Thirdly, women, under some agreements, were not permitted to exercise seniority rights equal to those of men in transfers and lay offs. These three practices not only conflicted with post-war UAW policies calling for the protection of the rights of women workers but, by dividing workers according to sex, subverted the theory of industrial unionism. Without a systematic analysis of contracts and supplementary agreements negotiated in this period, it is difficult to determine

---

[23] "Report of the UAW-CIO Fair Practices and Anti-Discrimination Department to the International Executive Board, September 8, 1947," 7, Fair Practices Department-Women's Bureau Collection, Box 2, Folder 18. WSU Archives. When Leona Frifeldt complained to the International's Fair Practices Department that her local union bargaining committee had not heard her grievance against an improper transfer because of her sex, she was advised to exhaust the local union grievance machinery before appealing to the International. Shortly thereafter, she requested the Department to withdraw her appeal "due to incomplete utilization of grievance machinery." Exactly what happened to Frifeldt is unknown, but it is possible that, because of the lack of support from local officers, either the membership or the company rejected her grievance or she ran afoul of the time limits placed on the filing and processing of grievances ("Third Quarterly Report of the Fair Practices and Anti-Discrimination Department, 1947," 4, *ibid*).

the extent of this type of discrimination. The fact, however, that the union's records refer to practices of the sort indicated as a widespread problem, suggests that the examples noted were not isolated phenomena.

The codification in UAW contracts and agreements of hostility against married women employees originated in the war period when labor shortages demanded the employment of women to fill essential positions. Management and the UAW agreed that married women, who it was assumed were all adequately supported by their husbands, should not accumulate any seniority and should be the first fired in the event of lay offs. These wartime agreements were continued in post-war contracts. Because John Fernandes, a shop committeeman, supported the seniority rights of all workers regardless of sex, management did not fire married women in his plant after the war, and allowed women who married to continue working. Since recent job cutbacks had resulted in the layoff of a number of men with families, local union members criticized Fernandes for protecting the seniority of married women. One union member voiced his unhappiness in a letter to the city newspaper:

> My main gripe against Local no. 76 [he wrote] is that they are doing nothing about getting rid of 15 women who persist in hanging on to their jobs . . . while veterans with children are being laid off. It's about time these women realized that the war is over, and that they should stay home and tend to their knitting. All of them are married and I believe that the husband's salary should be enough to tide them through.

Fernandes informed Walter Reuther that the local union was "being torn apart over this question." [24]

A 1953 case involving Local Union 85 that was heard by the International Executive Board illustrates not only union and management collusion in denying married women employment but the extent to which such practices were not even recognized as discriminatory. The Walker Manufacturing Company in Racine, Wisconsin, discharged both Bertha French and Grace Fairless because they had married. In defending the discharges, the management and the leadership of the local cited a verbal

[24] John Fernandes to Walter Reuther, April 19, 1949, Mazey Collection, Box 21, Local Union 1031 Folder, WSU Archives; newspaper clipping, *Oakland Tribune* (California), n.d., *ibid.*

agreement, supplemental to the 1948 written contract, that forbade the hiring of married women. The local union's Fair Practices Committee, to whom the women appealed the local executive board's decision to reject their grievance and request for reinstatement with back pay, stated the local union's position on the matter: "There was no intention of discrimination then nor is there now. It is simply a working agreement which until this time has been satisfactory to all parties concerned. . . . [W]e cannot see where Mrs. Fairless has been treated unfairly, nor has she been discriminated against. Her request to be re-instated on her job was refused because it was merely in keeping with this local's present agreement with management." [25]

The IEB appeal hearing report concluded that the local union was ignorant of the discriminatory nature of its agreement and that the local union, in negotiating the supplemental agreement, had believed "since 1947 that they were conforming to area practice consistent with Local autonomous rights and not in violation of policies of the International Union." Local 85 must have known, however, that the International Fair Practices Department in 1946 compelled Racine Local 642 to delete the section of its 1946 contract that denied married women seniority rights. And in 1948 the IEB ordered Local Union 391 of Racine to delete its discriminatory by-laws providing for unequal hiring-in rates for men and women, but the local union refused to comply and proceeded to operate under a contract that was not approved by the International. Between 1946 and 1949 the Fair Practices Department negotiated with three other Racine area locals in an effort to remove discriminatory contract clauses then being renegotiated with management. The fact that Local 85's agreement with the Walker Manufacturing Co. was a verbal, rather than a written, agreement perhaps indicates some awareness on the part of both management and the local union that the agreement was in violation of UAW policy. In attributing the local's actions to ignorance, the IEB was indicating its own unwillingness to take forceful action to curb sex discrimination. [26]

[25] "Agreement between Local 85 and Walker Manufacturing Company," June 1, 1948, Mazey Collection, Box 32, Local 85 Folder, WSU Archive; Walker Manufacturing Company to Local 85, May 28, 1953, ibid.; and "Report Form, Local Union Fair Practices Committee," Oct. 1, 1953, ibid.
[26] "Appeal Hearing Report," April 28, 1954, ibid.; William Oliver to Caroline Davis

In 1952, during the course of an IEB appeal hearing dealing with four married women from Local Union 206, the local union officers admitted that, although this was the first time one of the local's married women had appealed a case to the International level, a number of married women had taken grievances to the membership in the early post-war period only to have the membership deny the women the right to work. Other women had been laid off without filing formal complaints, although several women had discussed the problem with the local bargaining committee. In late 1951, the officers testified, women employees "had become aware" of International policy forbidding discrimination on the basis of marital status. When the women notified the UAW regional director of sex discrimination in their local union, he convinced the local's bargaining committee to inform the company that the union would no longer tolerate the discharge of married women.[27]

Fearing that it might have to reinstate the women with back pay in the event of an appeal, the company insisted that the local union assume its share of the responsibility for the discriminatory agreements. The local union leadership therefore raised the issue at a membership meeting. Advised that if it approved the layoff of married women it would be in violation of International policy and the mandate of the International Convention, the membership nevertheless approved a motion not only to continue to support the layoff of married women but to require women to

---

and Lillian Hatcher, April 12, 1949, Fair Practices Department-Women's Bureau Collection, Box 5, Folder 8; William Oliver to Frank Sahorske, May 19, 1949, Walter P. Reuther Collection, Box 20, Fair Practices Department 1948-49 Folder; and George Addes to Local Union 391, n.d. [1948?], Fair Practices Department-Women's Bureau Collection, Box 5, Folder 1, WSU Archive. Under such agreements, the hiring of married women was left to the discretion of the local union and the company. If a married woman could show cause for employment—for example, if her husband was incapacitated or in the service—she might be allowed to work, but only under certain onerous constraints. Local Union 72 in Racine allowed married women thus hired to accumulate seniority only in the department in which they worked rather than in accordance with the contract's principle of plant-wide seniority. They were, however, the first to be laid off, regardless of any seniority they might have accumulated. The notorious Local Union 391 had a particularly insulting way of ensuring a married woman's gratitude: she had to pay the local union one dollar per week for permission to work. (W.G. Kult to R.J. Thomas, June 22, 1944, UAW War Policy Division-Women's Bureau Collection, Box 5, Folder 12, WSU Archives: George Addes to Local Union 391, n.d. [1948?], Fair Practices Department-Women's Bureau Collection, Ibid).

27 "Appeal Hearing Report," May 20, 1952, Mazey Collection, Box 40, Local 206-2 Folder, WSU Archives.

sign a statment when they were hired that they would voluntarily resign if they married. The membership approved this decision a second time at a meeting one month later against the advice of Leonard Woodcock, the regional director, who attended the meeting in order to inform the local union of the implications of its actions. During the appeal hearing one male witness arrogantly explained that the International Union could continue to follow its policy without complaint from the local union as long as the local was allowed to follow its own policy.[28]

In April 1953, William McKenna, chairman of the Fair Practices Committee of Local Union 1020, wrote to Caroline Davis, head of the UAW Women's Bureau, requesting advice regarding a grievance that two women from the local had filed to protest their discharge. The women had been dismissed in accordance with a verbal agreement between the local union and management dating from 1946 which provided for the discharge of married women. McKenna acknowledged that the agreement was in violation of International policy but he was not at all certain that this was of any significance. "Exactly what is *insisted* upon and what is *desired* by the International" he asked. "In a sense such a practice is unfair, but it is *not* contrary to the local constitution or contract. . . . Violation of 'policy' and violation of contract or constitution, to our way of thinking are two different things." Claiming that the local union executive board and membership did not want to change the terms of the agreement, Tom Nolan, the president of the local, bluntly challenged the International Union to act.[29]

The International submitted the grievance against the company to an arbitrator selected by the American Arbitration Association. But it was Tom Nolan who presented the case for the women and the union. Not only did the appellants note his ineffectiveness, but so, too, did the neutral arbitrator, who said, "What am I doing here if the Company and the Union agree to lay off the married women?" Following this farcical hearing, an IEB Appeal Committee directed the local union officers and membership to end their discrimination against married women:

---

[28] Paul Luckett to Emil Mazey, April 21, 1952, *ibid.;* "Appeal Hearing Report," May 20, 1952, *ibid.*

[29] William McKenna to Carolina Davis, April 27, 1953, Mazey Collection, Box 35, Local 1021 Folder, *Ibid.;* Tom Nolan to Ray Ross, June 15, 1953, *ibid.*

"This type of agreement denies rights to members of the Union who are part of the collective bargaining group and provides hiring opportunities to people who have no rights under the collective bargaining agreement." [30]

The continuation of practices initiated during the war to limit and restrict the rights of newly hired women caused employment problems during the post-war period not only for married women workers but also for single women. When the UAW Research Department conducted a survey of wartime contract clauses, it discovered provisions requiring that, in the event of layoff, women were to be laid off before men regardless of their greater seniority and that women hired after July 7, 1942 on what were considered male jobs would be placed on a special list and granted no seniority. The latter clause limited their employment to the duration of the war or whenever a man was available to replace them. The Local Union 217 contract, the Research Department discovered, stated that when a man was transferred to a woman's job, he would receive the male rate, but when a woman resumed the job, she would receive the lower female rate. This practice also worked in reverse: when a woman was placed on a job classified as male, she received the lower female rate. These practices continued in the post-war period and were incorporated in new contracts. The practice of differentiating workers on the basis of sex penetrated all the aspects of work that the union was supposed to protect. The classification of jobs as male or female permitted unequal wage rates regardless of equal job content. The practice of separate male and female seniority lists, based on the principle of separate, non-interchangeable occupational groups, compounded this problem. Practices of this sort restricted women to jobs which, because they supposedly required less skill, were not as highly paid. [31]

Disputed cases in which management reclassified a female job as male without any change in the nature of the job reveal the extent to which the labelling of jobs as male or female was entirely arbitrary. In late 1950, women on the 8 a.m. to 4 p.m.

---

[30] Josephine Jurinko to Caroline Davis, Dec. 3, 1953, Mazey Collection, Box 35, Local 1021 Folder, *ibid.;* "Appeal Hearing Report," April 29, 1954, *ibid.*

[31] "Clauses Pertaining to Seniority of Women," enclosed with R. J. Thomas to Officers and Regional Directors, Nov. 13, 1944, Mazey Collection, Box 13, Women's Division 1941-47 Folder, *ibid.*

and 4 p.m. to midnight shifts of the punch press operation at the
Auto-Lite Battery Corporation in Vincennes, Indiana (UAW
Local Union 675) filed a grievance with the company demanding equal pay with the men on the midnight to 8 a.m. shift—
the women were receiving $1.05 an hour while the men on the
same operation, but on a different shift, were receiving $1.25
an hour. The company rejected the complaint and, instead, offered to pay male rates on the punch press job only if the local
union agreed to put men on all the shifts. If the local union refused, the job was to remain in the "female" classification and
receive the lower rate.[32]

The local union membership accepted the company's proposal
to place men on the early shifts in spite of the advice of an
International representative, who informed the membership of
the International's equal pay for equal work policy. The result
was that the women on the two shifts were laid off. Because of
the agreement between the local union and the company providing not only for differential pay rates for "male" and "female"
jobs but also for separate male and female seniority lists, the only
alternative for the women who had been laid off was to replace
other women in lower-paid job classifications. To add insult to
injury, the local union refused to follow the mandate of the International Fair Practices Department and the Women's Bureau
to negotiate with the company for the reinstatement of the wom-
en on the jobs on the early shifts at the higher rate of pay. Ignoring the International's conclusion that the women should have
had their grievance processed to a successful conclusion with
the full support of the local membership, the local union permitted the company to place men with less seniority on the jobs
the women had held. In a letter to Caroline Davis, head of the
Women's Bureau, the women expressed their frustration and said
in desperation that they would accept the lower rate of pay if
only they could get their jobs back.[33]

The non-discriminatory intent of a contract provision for plant
wide seniority without reference to sex was sometimes nullified

[32] "Fair Practices and Anti-Discrimination Department-Women's Bureau Appeal Hearing," Oct. 15, 1951, Mazey Collection, Box 39, Local 675 Folder, *ibid.*
[33] *Ibid.;* Dorothy Williams to Caroline Davis, Nov. 1, 1951, *Ibid.* To reduce the number of female classified jobs in a plant with separate seniority lists was an effective means of limiting the number of women workers.

by other provisions within the same contract. The September 1950 agreement between the Newport Steel Corporation-Universal Cooler Division and Local Union 750 in Marion, Ohio, thus provided for plant wide seniority but also provided for the classification of jobs by sex. When, five months later, the Tecumseh Products Company bought Newport Steel, the new president of the company, which was still under UAW contract, made it clear to the local union that he did not approve of women working, stating that he thought women "should be home in the kitchen." He told the local union that he wanted to eliminate the female employees, a proposal with which the male leadership of the union agreed. A supplemental agreement was therefore drawn up which arbitrarily, and without reference to job content, revised the classifications of some female jobs to male, with corresponding rate increases. The remaining female classified jobs were to "constitute the job classifications to which all female employees shall be limited." The women working on the jobs newly classified as male were laid off.[34]

The women then filed grievances with the company to protest what had occurred. Rachel Shaffstall, a woman working on one of the few remaining female classified jobs, demanded a rate of pay equivalent to that paid men on male classified jobs. The arbitrariness of job classifications had restricted her to the lower "female" pay rate although her job was as heavy and demanding of skill as some of the men's jobs. Betty Delaney claimed that the installation of conveyor belts had actually made one of the reclassified soldering jobs less burdensome than when it had been classified as a female position. Glenna Clements claimed she had been laid off without regard to her seniority and requested reinstatement with back pay. In defense of her demand, she cited the 1950 agreement, which provided for plant wide seniority. The company and the local union rejected Clements' grievance, claiming that "past practice and precedent have always dealt with female classifications independently of male classification";

[34] "Agreement between Universal Cooler Division, Newport Steel Corporation and Local 750," Sept. 20, 1950, Mazey Collection, Box 39, Local 750 Folder; Florence Butcher to Caroline Davis, August 28, 1951, Mazey Collection, Box 31, Local Union 750-6/51-5/52 Folder, *ibid.;* "Supplemental Agreement between Universal Cooler Division, Tecumseh Products Company and Local 750," *ibid.;* and "Schedule A of New Hourly Rates," March 26, 1951, Mazey Collection, Box 39, Local 750 Folder, *ibid.*

they referred Clements to the negotiated supplemental agreement of January 1951. Evading the women's complaints of violations of the contract, the local union grievance committee superciliously advised all the female grievants to "thoroughly acquaint yourself with the contract and the supplement in regards to female classifications." [35]

The male membership, which outnumbered the women seven to one, sanctioned the behavior of the local union's grievance committee. At a local union meeting, the membership voted down a motion to classify all jobs which women were able to perform according to state law as either male or female so that women could continue working in line with their seniority. In her report of the investigation she conducted at the plant, Caroline Davis noted that the male workers had submitted a petition in 1946 demanding the elimination of female employees. The local union's claim that the management was responsible for the discrimination against the women in 1951 seems rather dubious given the date of the hostile petition. The report of the Fair Practices Department and the Women's Bureau Appeal Committee condemned the illegality of the local union's attitude and actions: "There is . . . little question," the report stated, "that the . . . women . . . were dealt a serious injustice since their inability to return to work is brought about not by a lack of seniority but by the manipulation of jobs which deprived them of employment." [36]

The principle of the contract was at the heart of the theory of labor organization; without a contract, workers were powerless to challenge the whims of management. For women workers in the post-war period, the contract, however, often offered no protection. Because of the complicity of their union representatives, the contract simply codified their separate and unequal status.

Discrimination against women in the UAW occurred not only because of the hostility toward women at the local union level but because of the complicity of regional directors and International representatives. These officials were certainly aware of

---

[35] "Rachel Shaffstall Grievance," *ibid.*; "Fair Practices and Anti-Discrimination Department-Women's Bureau Appeal Hearing," n.d. [August, 1952?], Mazey Collection, Box 31, *ibid.*; "Glenna Clements Grievance," Box 39, Local 750 Folder, *ibid.*; and Form Letter from Local Union 750 Grievance Committee, Oct. 30, 1951, *ibid.*

[36] Minutes of Local 750 membership meeting, Dec., 1951, *ibid.*; "Appeal Hearing," n.d. [Aug., 1952?], Mazey Collection, Box 31, *ibid.*

the UAW's policies on discrimination; much of the out-going correspondence in the files of the Fair Practices Department and the Women's Bureau was addressed to International officials outside the Detroit headquarters in an effort to alert them to the problem of the protection of the rights of the women workers. If an International official approved a discriminatory contract and was sufficiently hostile to a woman's attempt to appeal the practices of either management or her local union, the grievant would have to go over his head to the International Fair Practices Department or the Women's Bureau. The same regional officials, however, often challenged the authority of these units.

The behavior of regional directors regarding the contracts written at the Electric Auto-Lite Company and the Newport Steel Corporation illustrates the role played by these officials in furthering discrimination against women. The Electric Auto-Lite Company and the UAW-CIO agreed in 1950 to a company-wide contract that incorporated fair practice and anti-discrimination principles. The Local Union 675 agreement, however, provided for separate seniority lists, differential job listings, and differential wage rates. The Local 675 agreement and the equitable national agreement were signed by Ray Berndt, the regional director. Protesting to the IEB, a number of women who had been laid off after requesting equal pay for equal work referred to the national agreement as justification for their request that the IEB grant their appeal. The IEB appointed Berndt to oversee the local union's negotiations with the company to reinstate the women. There is no reference in the minutes of the appeal hearing or of the IEB meeting to Berndt's participation in the negotiation of the offensive local union agreement.[37]

Regional director Charles Ballard signed a 1950 agreement between the Newport Steel Corporation and Local Union 750 that provided for separate job classifications. When several women protested the supplemental agreement, which further reclassified as male jobs many jobs previously allotted to women

---

[37] "National Agreement between the Electric Auto-Lite Company and UAW-CIO (12 Locals in Burt Foundry Unit)," n.d. [1950-1951?], Mazey Collection, Box 39, Local 675 Folder, *ibid.;* "Agreement Between Auto-Lite Battery Corporation, Vincennes, Indiana and UAW-CIO Local 675," March 7, 1951, *ibid.:* "Appeal Hearing Report," Sept. 9, 1952, *ibid.;* and Emily Mazey to Richard Gosser and Ray Berndt, Sept. 24, 1952, *ibid.*

and explicitly limited women to the remaining female classifications regardless of the original agreement's provision for plant wide seniority, Ballard expressed his disapproval of their protest. Florence Butcher was unable to meet with Ballard to discuss the grievance and appeal procedures as Caroline Davis had directed her to do. Davis herself encountered difficulty in dealing with Ballard. In a letter to Emil Mazey, the secretary-treasurer of the International, Davis said that she had been "unable to impress him [Ballard] sufficiently" with the seriousness of the women's charges and could not get him to arrange a date for a meeting between the local union and the Women's Bureau to investigate the problem. Davis asked Mazey to use "the good influence" of his position to arrange the meeting. Mazey's "influence" apparently was effective since the Women's Bureau did conduct an investigation three months later. As in the Local Union 675 case, the IEB Appeal Committee directed Ballard (with Davis' assistance) to negotiate with the company for the elimination of the contract clauses that discriminated against women. Again, however, the IEB failed to chastise the regional director for his previous behavior.[38]

The regional directors, International representatives, local union officials and the UAW membership were, of course, all subject to the authority of the IEB. In failing to exercise its power, as for instance when it did not criticize Berndt and Ballard for their behavior, the IEB, in effect, sanctioned discrimination against women. It must be granted that in the appeal cases that were referred to it, the IEB nearly always ruled in favor of the appellants, and it usually condemned blatantly discriminatory behavior that was brought to its attention. But the IEB did not use its full authority to force recalcitrant locals to adhere either to its recommendations or its policies.

Thus, the initial IEB ruling on an appeal of four women requesting reinstatement with restoration of seniority and pay for time lost was in favor of the appellants. The local union was successful in negotiating their reinstatement with seniority, but management refused to reimburse the women for lost wages. The

[38] "Agreement between Newport Steel and Local 750," ibid.; Caroline Davis to Charles Ballard, Sept. 6, 1951, Mazey Collection, Box 31; Davis to Emil Mazey, Oct. 29, 1951, ibid.; and "Appeal Hearing Report," Jan. 23, 1953, Mazey Collection, Box 39, Local 750 Folder, WSU Archives.

company claimed that, since the local union was responsible for the appealed practice of firing married women, it should be responsible for the back pay. Leonard Woodcock, chairman of the IEB Appeal Committee for the case, advised the IEB that it should close the case because the local union was liable for the lost wages of the four women and to force it to pay "would be just rubbing salt in the wound." Woodcock did not extend his sensitivity regarding the local union's injured pride to the economic distress of the four women workers.[39]

In the case of a Marion, Ohio local union, the IEB ordered the local union to negotiate the reinstatement of nineteen women who had been laid off despite their seniority. When the union failed in its efforts to secure the restoration of the appellants' seniority, Woodcock, who was also the chairman of this IEB Appeal Committee, explained to the members of the IEB that only a strike could achieve the restoration of seniority, but that a successful strike vote from the predominantly male membership on this question was "not a practical possibility." Woodcock requested the IEB to close the case "because of the practical trade union considerations involved." [40]

"Practical trade union considerations," however, did not interfere with the IEB's decision in 1952 to revoke the charter of the Braniff-UAW local union in Dallas, Texas, for racial discrimination against UAW members. The fact that the IEB used its power in this instance but not in cases of discrimination against women workers indicates the extent to which the UAW leadership simply did not take the issue of discrimination against women workers or its female membership as seriously as did the women or the Women's Bureau. In numerous instances, the IEB surrendered to the demands of the male membership rather than assuming its responsibility to uphold and execute the anti-discrimination policy resolutions approved by the delegates at International Conventions. Clearly, the issue of sexual discrimination caused conflict within the union and among the rank-and-file. The rights of its female membership, however, deserved and re-

[39] Minutes of IEB meeting, Sept. 15-18, 1952, 323-324, UAW International Executive Board Minutes Collection, Box 6, WSU Archives. It must be noted that although the company was justified in its refusal to accept full moral responsibility for the discriminatory practice, it never objected to the procedure.
[40] Minutes of IEB meeting, Jan. 18-21, 1954, 338, *ibid.*

quired the same protection offered the male rank-and-file.[41]

The experience of women in the UAW during the post-war period suggests that women workers did not necessarily acquiesce in the treatment accorded them by management and that the role played by male unionists in obstructing the protests of women workers and in excluding women from employment in industry needs further exploration. In an effort to exclude women from the industrial labor force after World War II, the UAW—despite its image as an especially progressive union—denied women rights that organized labor considered fundamental, such as the principle of seniority and unrestricted access to the grievance machinery. Certain individuals within the UAW condemned the violation of these rights and the division of workers according to sex. Upholding the principle of industrial unionism, these individuals tried to show how threatening such practices were to the goals of the labor movement. The ambivalence with which the UAW responded to such arguments suggests that industrial organization alone was insufficient to change negative attitudes regarding women employees and to end sexual discrimination. This is not to say that women workers gained nothing from organization; their effective organization among themselves enabled them to impress at least the International leadership with the validity of their demands. The degree of hostility that women workers confronted in demanding their rights from their union demonstrates, however, that the problem of discrimination against women workers was not simply the by-product of management prejudice or a particular method of labor organization but was much more deeply rooted in social ideology.

[41] "Appeal Hearing," May 20, 1952, Mazey Collection, Box 40, Local 206-2 Folder, WSU Archives.

20

Work and Community Life in a Southern Textile Town

DALE NEWMAN

Study of a rural-industrial county in Piedmont North Carolina reveals that white cotton mill operatives exercised less control over their daily activities during this century than did their black neighbors. By examining the power and prestige of employer paternalism,[1] one is able to understand why collective action by white textile workers was slow to come and quick to fail; by examining the values and culture patterns of the black community within the rigidities of the caste system,[2] one can understand why black operatives undertake collective action only nine years after racial integration of the mill occurs, and are largely successful.

The LeClay Mill[3] began spinning cotton yarn in 1908. It was the second plant to be constructed by Roseville Cotton Mills in Carol County, North Carolina. Located two miles from the town of Roseville, the community which developed around the second mill became known as LeClay after the founder Lee Edward Clay. For the 100 workers who operated the 10,000 spindles, the Company built 45 houses. The mill hands worshiped in a grist mill

---

[1] "Paternalism" is used to denote the Company's ownership of the land and structures (including mill, houses, stores, and churches) in the unincorporated village as well as their sponsorship of goods and services (coal, credit, electric and limited medical). For detailed discussions of Southern textile mill village paternalism, see Harriet L. Herring, *Welfare Work in Mill Villages: The Story of Extra-Mill Activities in North Carolina* (Chapel Hill, 1929); James A. Hodges, "The New Deal Labor Policy and the Southern Cotton Textile Industry: 1933-1941" (unpublished Ph.D. diss., Vanderbilt Univ., 1963); and Melton A. McLaurin, *Paternalism and Protest: Southern Cotton Mill Workers and Organized Labor, 1875-1905* (Westport, 1971).

[2] "Caste" is used to denote the racial segregation of socio-economic life that relegated blacks to a subordinate position in society. John Dollard's classic *Caste and Class in a Southern Town* (New York, 1937) continues to be a useful introduction to Southern *mores*.

[3] Pseudonyms have been used for all proper names of people and places; and numbers and statistics have been rounded off to protect the identity of respondents. See the Appendix for an abbreviated methodological statement.

Reprinted from *Labor History* 19 (Spring 1978), 204-25. This paper is a revised draft of one presented at the Organization of American Historians' annual convention in St. Louis on April 9, 1976. The author gratefully acknowledges the advice and encouragement of David Montgomery and Milton Cantor.

on Sundays. A 1925 map of LeClay Village showed a 25,000 spindle plant, 96 dwellings, a post office, drugstore, company store, theatre, bank, Baptist and Methodist churches, and a 7-grade mill school.[4] Reflecting the short-lived prosperity of the early twenties, bank and theatre had disappeared before 1930.

In addition to these facilities, the Roseville Cotton Mills also provided LeClay residents with a host of services: The Company sold coal with which to heat the houses; extended credit for medical debts and other causes it deemed worthy; deducted church building-fund contributions, charges for the company stores, rent and electric current for the houses.[5] Since these expenses were deducted from wages before workers received their pay, there was no "robbing Peter to pay Paul." As one female winder phrased it, "money just went all way 'round."

Three generations of employer paternalism had produced an hereditary work force of poorly educated, economically insecure, and socially isolated individuals. While most of the circumstances which contributed to producing an hereditary work force are integrally related to life in the mill community, a predisposing element is the initial labor recruitment of large families in which females were predominant. The textile industry's preference for female-headed households and female operatives is usually explained as the desire for a tractable work force with nimble fingers.[6]

---

[4] The data in this paragraph are compiled from published and unpublished histories of the cotton mill and Baptist church.

[5] A 1922 pay envelope listed the following items as potential deductions: Wood, Cotton, Docks, Store, Coal, Cash, and Rent. The wood and coal were sold for heating and cooking, and the cotton for making quilts. There has been no indication that Roseville Cotton Mills employees were under any compulsion to trade at the Company store, but the conclusion of a special committee appointed in 1934 by the Administrator of the National Recovery Administration is analogous to the LeClay operatives' circumstances: "The economic status of many employees forces them to seek credit. The extension of credit by the employer, under a charge over pay roll arrangement, obliges these employees to patronize the company store." See "Industrial and Labor Conditions: Company Stores and the Scrip System," *Monthly Labor Review* (July, 1935), 53.

[6] Re the use of children, see Andrew Ure, *Philosophy of Manufactures or an Exposition of the Scientific, Moral, and Commercial Economy of the Factory System of Great Britain; Continued in Its Details to the Present Time* (New York, 1969), 301; re the use of women, see Karl Marx, *Capital: A Critique of Political Economy*, Volume I: "The Process of Capitalist Production," ed. Frederick Engels (New York, 1967), fn402 quoting from "Ten Hours' Factory Bill," the Speech of Lord Ashley, March 15th, Lond., 1844; the manufacturer cited " . . . gives a decided preference to married females, especially those who have families at home dependent on them for support; they are attentive, docile, more so than unmarried females. . . !" Note the similarity in employer rationale cited by Richard Rowan more than 100 years later: "Our best production employee is the Negro female, age 27 to 30, who has worked formerly as a domestic. She many times bears the

The attraction which cotton mill labor held for white tobacco farm families with large numbers of females and males of small stature can best be understood by examining the labor requirements of tobacco agriculture in Carol County. During the first quarter of this century, tobacco was harvested by cutting the whole stalk of the three-feet high (or taller) plant; the practice of successive strippings of leaves did not become prevalent until about 1930.[7] The cutting of the full stalk, heavy with dew; the holding of four-feet long sticks upon which a half-dozen or more plants would be hung before they were transported from the field to the barn; the passing of these heavily-laden sticks, weighing as much as twenty-five pounds, from the ground up a human ladder to the top-most tier of the eighteen-feet high barn required considerable strength and was considered men's work.[8]

Frequently, white workers who began their labors in the mill as children answered the question, "Why did your parents leave the farm for the mill?" in words similar to these: "Papa decided he would come because he didn't have nothing much but girls and they had to get out and work like men."[9] The physical difficulty of meeting the heavy labor requirements of tobacco harvesting resulted in a self-selection process that reproduced itself in the mill village. In 1933, a Public Health Service study of males in a Southern carding, spinning, and weaving mill noted the striking tendency for the workers to be under the average weight of other industrial employees by about ten pounds.[10]

major responsibility for her family at home and is therefore a responsible person at work." ("The Negro in the Textile Industry," *Negro Employment in Southern Industry: A Study of Racial Policies in Five Industries* [Philadelphia, 1970], 130). McLaurin found no evidence of Southern employers expressing such motivation regarding white women and children however, and indicates the lower wages paid to women and children are a more dominant motive in recruitment (McLaurin, 22-23).

[7] *The Roseville Messenger* [pseudonym] August 5, 1941, Sec. A, 12. Interviews with black and white, male and female tobacco farmers and former farmers. The transition to priming occurred later in Carol County than it did in much of the Old Tobacco Belt. See Nannie May Tilley, *The Bright Tobacco Industry 1860-1927* (Chapel Hill, 1948), 57-58, 71-81, for comparisons between the two methods. For a detailed description of children's contributions to tobacco agriculture under both systems of harvesting, consult Harriet A. Byrne, *Child Labor in Representative Tobacco-Growing Areas* (Washington, 1926); the data pertaining to Halifax, Virginia, are analogous to Carol County procedures before 1930; the data relating to Florence, South Carolina would correspond to the priming era.

[8] Women and young children have helped hang tobacco, however, by standing on a platform laid across the tiers in the barn. Interviews with farm operators.

[9] Interview with white female, hereafter designated WF, winder who came to the village in 1916 with her parents and seven siblings. (White male, black male, or black female will be referred to respectively as WM, BM, BF to indicate race and sex).

[10] Rollo Britten, *et al.* "The Health of Workers in a Textile Plant," *Public Health Bulletin,*

The inability to succeed at farming undoubtedly accounts in part for the feeling of inferiority which many students of Southern textile workers have observed and which is very pronounced among LeClay mill hands.[11] More important in encouraging such feeling, however, was the low esteem in which cotton mill workers were held. To leave the farm for the factory was to sink so low in social status that often families were severed by the transition. A widow who brought her seven children and her mother to LeClay Village in 1914 was so criticized for the move that she never notified her brothers and sisters of her mother's death many years later. A family who came in 1918 was told by country relatives that they might as well be going to a "whore house" as to the mill. And a young man who went to work in the mill in the late twenties and decided to marry a fellow employee was instructed by his parents: "If you marry that woman from the cotton mill, don't ever come to our house again. Don't come home no more." (But he notes they came to love her as their own daughter.)

LeClay mill hands lived, learned, worked and worshipped in the village—physically and socially isolated from the nearby town of Roseville.[12] Town boys and girls did not date those from the village—known as "cotton mill trash." So the operatives met their spouses in the mill, and mill workers begot mill workers. Class lines between mill and town were still quite clear to the minister of the LeClay Baptist Church who assumed his pastorate in 1960. He recalled, "There was a distinctive social line . . . . There was quite a dividing line socially."

While these lines have blurred, the feelings of inferiority which were engendered continue. Born in 1916, a woman who was one

No. 207 (Washington, 1933), 13,20.

[11] See Jennings J. Rhyne, *Some Southern Cotton Mill Workers and Their Villages* (Chapel Hill, 1930), 197; Broadus Mitchell, "Why Cheap Labor Down South?" *The Virginia Quarterly Review*, October, 1929, 486; Herbert J. Lahne, *The Cotton Mill Worker* (New York, 1944), 65-66; and Ralph M. Lyon, *The Basis for Constructing Curricular Materials in Adult Education for Carolina Cotton Mill Workers* (New York, 1937). 17-19.

[12] The social isolation of Le Clay is not atypical. A Senate study of women and children in the cotton textile industry published in 1910 found the low social status of cotton mill workers to be general throughout the South; see U.S., Senate, Document. No. 645. *Women and Child Wage Earners in the United States, Volume I: Cotton Textile Industry* (Washington, 1910), 585-587. The Women's Bureau discovered Northern operatives suffered less from class distinctions than Southern ones who lived "in a world apart," though the former had language barriers. See "Lost Time and Labor Turnover in Cotton Mills: A Study of Cause and Extent," *Bulletin of the Women's Bureau*, No. 52 (Washington, 1926), 21. According to J.G. Van Osdell, mill workers were "a class not so much cast out as never admitted into a society in which there was no place for them"; see "Cotton Mills, Labor, and the Southern Mind: 1880-1930" (unpublished Ph.D. diss., Tulane Univ., 1966), 37.

of the few Roseville Cotton Mills children to attend high school before the mid-century describes her emotions:

> Even to this day [1975], I do not like to tell anyone that I ever worked in a mill . . . . In school, I always had a feeling of inferiority because my family worked there, and I was very conscious of the fact that we were very poor and that I did not have the kind of clothing to wear that other kids . . . had . . . . Later in life . . . my sense of shame was even greater . . . . To be a cotton mill employee can never really degrade one, but it can cause one to feel degraded in spite of all that he knows to be the truth.[13]

The majority of the white employees at LeClay never attended high school. For most of them, formal education was obtained only from the 7-grade mill school and ended sometime between the fourth and seventh grades. The age at which they quit attending school approximates the minimum age requirements for working in a mill in North Carolina. The following narrative by a woman born in 1909 and still working as a winder in 1974 illustrates the procedure for training workers—whose labors contributed to family income but who do *not* appear on the payrolls until they reach the legal age for employment:[14]

> That coming June, I was eight years old . . . I went to the mill . . . I wasn't getting paid for it, now. I was going in and helping my sisters . . . I never started getting paid until I was twelve years old. I'd go in at 6:30 and work until 8, getting to school just in time to get in line; I'd come after aschool and work until 6, and I'd come in on Saturday and work until 12.

Fourteen was the minimum age when George Yancy began in 1925 to "sweep the big alley down the middle of the spinning room." Hired two days before his birthday by his uncle who said, "Two days don't make no difference," George was the second generation of Yancys to be employed in the mill. With few ex-

---

[13] The depth and persistence of such feelings are not peculiar to LeClay and were vividly illustrated during an interview with a union employee at a TWUA Convention in Pittsburgh in 1972. As he tried to recall the words of a union song, the former weaver was overcome with tears. When he had regained his composure, he explained: "Back when I was coming up [in Southeastern North Carolina] where the mill was. . . everybody was looked down upon . . . And we as workers didn't think much of ourselves . . . I had a hard time when I got in the Union to get over the inferiority complex I had . . . It is all cotton-mill village environment."

[14] The Senate investigation of women and child wage earners published in 1910 found the child-labor laws most flagrantly violated in the Carolinas. The "helper system" under which many children assisted in the mill while drawing no wages was, according to the study, "merely a subterfuge whereby a law which prohibits the employment of children under a certain age is evaded." U.S., Senate, Document No. 645, 189-190.

ceptions, the boys and girls who quit school to begin work at ages twelve, fourteen, or sixteen as the minimum age is raised, did so for economic reasons.[15] Having begun in 1940, one winder explained: "All of the children had to quit school when they were sixteen and go to work . . . I finished eighth grade . . . and I never got to go back. . . . I cried for two weeks, I wanted to go to school so bad, but back then times were hard . . . ."[16]

The few children from the village who graduated Roseville High School before 1960 were usually sons and daughters of overseers and foremen.[17] An investigation of North Carolina mill schools published in 1925 concluded: "As a rule, the children of mill-workers would have had three times as much chance for a high school education had the father remained in the rural districts rather than moved to a mill village which maintains schools of only seven grades."[18] A 1960 survey of school plants and facilities in Carol County assigned a rating of 296 points out of a possible 1000 to the LeClay School.[19] The study recommended that any school scoring below 300 points should be abandoned or put to other use, but the mill school functioned through the academic year 1969-70.[20]

The reasons for the economic insecurity which compelled children to quit school, mothers to work the second shift,[21] and all able-bodied members of the family to labor are numerous: Textile wages have historically ranked lower than those of other industries, and Southern wages have been lower than those of the North.[22] More important to LeClay operatives was their lack of

[15] A larger proportion of Southern women began work when very young than did Northern ones, according to the "Study of Lost Time and Labor Turnover," 29. A partial listing of interviews includes: WF Roping (or Roving) Frame Tender; WM Draw Frame Tender; WF Sparehand; WM Electrician; WF Winder; WM Roping Frame Tender.

[16] Interview with WF Sparehand.

[17] Interviews with WM Foreman of the Card Room; WM Overseer of the Card Room; WF Winder; WF Postmistress of LeClay Post Office; WM Supervisor of Spinning. Noteworthy among operatives whose children *did* graduate was the tendency for these families to have very few children—usually one—and an attitude of firm commitment for the child to complete high school as expressed in such statements as: "You going to finish if you forty years old!"

[18] John Harrison Cook, *A Study of the Mill Schools of North Carolina* (New York, 1925), 38.

[19] *Survey of School Plants and Facilities Carol* [pseudonym] *County Schools* (Chapel Hill, 1960), 32.

[20] *The Roseville Messenger* (April 13, 1972), 1.

[21] Most women who worked on second shift felt it was preferable when their children were school age; they were able to get domestic chores done during the day, as well as rest before going to work. But few respondents had any choice as to which shift they would work. "Seniority" has become relevant only with racial integration.

[22] On the basis of data compiled by the Department of Labor and averaged by the National

occupational alternatives. Farm work was not a viable option. While there was another textile firm in the county, the two companies had an agreement not to hire each other's help.[23]. This agreement was observed until the 1960s. A family was expected to provide at least two workers for the mill or be subject to eviction from the company house.[24]

The wages received by the operatives were not only low, but they were very irregular. Several practices contributed to the irregularity of income. First, the mill would run only part-time during recessions, depressions, and seasonal slumps.[25] Second, a practice of hiring "spare hands"—more people than there are

---

Association of Cotton Manufacturers, Southern cotton mill operatives earned 28.8 cents per hour in 1926, while Northern operatives averaged 44.8 cents per hour; the latter was 55.5 per cent greater. "Working Conditions of the Textile Industry in North Carolina, South Carolina, and Tennessee," *Hearings Before the Committee on Manufactures United States Senate,* 71st Cong. 1st Sess. on Senate Res. 49 (May 8, 9, and 20, 1928), 38. Prior to 1929, the annual earnings in textiles were $700-800 compared with $1,200-1,300 for all manufactures. See "Cotton Textile Industry," Message from the President of the U.S. transmitting a *Report on the Conditions and Problems of the Cotton Textile Industry. . .* (Washington, 1935), 74th Congress, 1st Sess., Senate Document No. 126, 28. Lower wages have been a primary factor in the migration of Northern textiles in the South. See Richard Woods Edmonds, "Yankee Thrift and Southern Progress: Some Yankee Views of the South's Industrial Awakening and its Bearing on the Future Prosperity of New England," in *Cotton Mill Labor Conditions in the South and New England* (Baltimore, 1925), 40; John Sheridan, "Industry's View of the South . . . Fruitful but Flawed," *Industry Week* (February 28, 1977), 49-58. Textile weekly wages in February, 1977 were $150, which is $63 below the general factory wage of $213. Southern and national averages have been and are meaningless to LeClay workers, however. In 1925, the operatives worked 60 hours and 40 minutes each week (10 hours, 55 minutes Monday-Friday, or 6:30-6:00 with 35 minutes for "dinner;" and 6 hours, 15 minutes Saturday, or 6:30 a.m. to twenty minutes to 1:00 p.m.). Men who received a daily wage of $1.35 at that time would have received $8.10 per week, or $421.20 per year. But with the exception of war years and those immediately following racial integration when rapid industrial expansion occurred in the County, Roseville Cotton Mills always had too many workers for the number of jobs and employees had to "rest" regularly.

[23] Interviews with WF Spooler; WF Winder; WM Draw Frame Tender; WM Card Room Foreman. Cooperation among employers was not limited to the textile industry, as the foreman of a construction gang learned when he was compelled by his employer to fire a former operative from LeClay (interview with WM Construction Foreman); also interview with personnel manager of another industry who requests that the type of industry not be identified.

[24] Both local textile companies owned houses, but a larger percentage of LeClay workers occupied company dwellings. The employer in the village of residence had the first "say so" about where one worked. Interviews with WM Draw Frame Tender; WM Twister Room Fixer/Foreman; WF Spooler; WM Doffer; WF Winder; WF Spinner.

[25] For a most thorough analysis of the economics of the textile industry, see "To Rehabilitate and Stabilize Labor Conditions in the Textile Industry of the United States," *Hearings on H.R. 9072,* January 27, 28, 29, 30, 31 and February 3, 4, 5 and 6, 1936, 74th Congress, 2nd Sess. (Washington, D.C., 1936). Illustrative of the irregularity are the partial contents of two letters written by a grandmother in 1924 to her daughter who had gone to Advance, NC to tend her sick husband who was working in a mill there. In one letter, the grandmother writes of the grandchildren: "The children are *all* working this morning." (italics added.) In the other, she writes: "The head ones at the mill think the prospect is getting better[,] they think they will work four or five days this week. _____ and _____ both out today."

jobs—meant the company regularly sent the extra ones home;[26] employees were never certain if they would work or be sent home "to rest" after they arrived at the mill.[27] Third, workers were docked for poor work or for soiling the materials.[28] Fourth. Operatives paid by "production" were unable to control all of the conditions which affected their output.[29] Fifth. Some departments would be shut down and workers sent home to allow other divisions to catch up.[30] Sixth. The white mill hands were "laid off" for periods ranging from one night to two weeks for infractions of company rules. These rules included: being late for work; failing to call in or send word if too sick to come in; any misbehavior or misconduct on the job, in the village, or town, such as getting drunk or fighting.[31] Workers were not allowed to "cuss" on the job or "talk back" to foremen.[32]

The poorly-educated, ill-paid men, women and children who lived in one-half of a four or five-room company house which was arbitrarily and preferentially assigned,[33] subsisted on a diet consisting primarily of cornbread, fatback meat and pinto beans.[34]

---

[26] See "Lost Time and Labor Turnover," 43-43; and Lahne, 151. Also interviews with WF Spooler; WF Winder; WM Roping Frame Tender; WM Card Room Foreman; BM Card Room Foreman; BF Winder.

[27] Interview with WF Winder. The uncertainty of work discouraged operatives from buying on credit from the town stores.

[28] Interviews with WF Spooler; WM Inspector.

[29] WM Doffers; BM Doffers; WF Spinners; BF Spinners; BF Winder; WF Winders; Executive Vice-president; WM Card Room Foreman.

[30] WM Cardroom Supervisor; WF Spinner.

[31] WM Carpenter was laid off for two weeks for riding a mule into an uptown barber shop on a Saturday. A WM Doffer managed to circumvent the superintendent's intent to lay him off (as well as get promoted to fixer) by producing a news clipping from another town which showed the superintendent had been arrested for drunk driving in that town.

[32] WM Cardgrinder.

[33] "Roseville [pseudonym] Cotton Mills and Textile Workers Union of America—CIO" Case No. [withheld]. Decisions of National Labor Relations Board. Also interviews with WM Sweeper; WM Card Room Supervisor.

[34] Interviews with WF Spinner; WF Winder; WF Spooler. The pellagra-producing three-M diet (meal, molasses, meat—"Fat back"—a cheap grade of fat pork) was the usual bill of fare. See also Lyon, 26. In an unpublished study of the village based on three years of participant observation during the mid-thirties, there were seven known cases of pellagra in LeClay. While some of the dietary deficiency of cotton mill workers might be attributed to nutritional ignorance, the most thorough studies of pellagra reveal an inverse relationship with income. As income increases, the incidence of pellagra decreases. See Joseph Goldberger, et. al, "A Study of Endemic Pellagra in Some Cotton Mill Villages of South Carolina," Hygienic Laboratory Bulletin No. 153 (January, 1929), 44-52. Low in the B vitamins as well as protein, the three-M diet suggests that the suspicions, mistrust, and hostility exhibited by cotton mill workers toward "outsiders" may be a product of biological needs as well as class distinctions. For a broader coverage of the subject, see Elizabeth W. Etheridge, The Butterfly Caste: A Social History of Pellagra in the South (Westport, 1972). The argument that the cost of living in the South is lower and thus compensates for the low wages received by the cotton mill workers is refuted by Senate

Several large families dominated second-level management, but marriages criss-crossed between operatives, fixers, second hands, and overseers.[35] These kinship ties and the company's promotional policies of advancing the most loyal and reliable employees fostered the fear that even one's own family might report one's unapproved activities—not just in the mill or village—but in the home as well.[36] One warp room worker used to place bottles of liquor on the window ledge outside the room he and his wife occupied in a four-room house they shared with his parents, his two sisters, and their husbands. Once inside the privacy of the room, he would retrieve the bottle.[37]

To insure its knowledge of employees' behavior, the Roseville Cotton Mills assigned the first five houses leading into the village to the superintendent and the overseers who could see who came and went, and employed a deputy sheriff who reported "not of his own knowledge, but what people would tell him."[38] He was assisted in his moral policing by the superintendent who would not allow women to smoke on their porches, or wear shorts in public, and who evicted any family whose daughter got pregnant out of wedlock.[39] As one former worker phrased it:

> *You didn't have no private life at all* . . . I used to pull a high/lonesome once in a while, and I go back in Monday morning; first thing boss would say: 'You drunk Friday, Saturday, and Sunday—'
>
> Who told you?
>
> Oh, I heard it . . .
>
> That's the way it was . . . What was done on the weekends was carried back to them. . . . You could come home and take your pants off and leave one leg on, and they'd tell you about it at the mill.[40]

Mill influence in community life extended to the religious institutions. The Company was very generous with the Baptists and provided them acreage for their church, educational building,

Doc. No. 645 "Family Budgets of Typical Cotton-Mill Workers," *Report on Condition of Women and Child Wage-Earners in the United States,* Volume XVI, 61st Congress, 2nd Sess. (Washington, 1911), 36; Abraham Berglund, George T. Starnes, Frank DeVyver, *Labor in the Industrial South* (Charlottesville, 1930), 154; Lois MacDonald, "The Labor Scene," in *Southern Workers Outside the Legislative Pale,* ed. by H. C. Nixon (New York, 1942), 12.

[35] WM Creeler; WF Winder; WF Spinner.
[36] *Ibid.*
[37] Interview with WF Winder.
[38] Interview with WM Overseer's Assistant/Spinning Department.
[39] Interviews with WF Spooler; WM Doffer; WM Draw Frame Tender.
[40] Interview with WM Card Room Operative.

and parsonage. Each Christmas, a "love-gift" ranging from $500 to $2000 was given to the pastors of the Baptist and Methodist churches.[41] The reflection of the mill management in the Baptist Church hierarchy motivated some employees to join the Methodists. As a male yarn packer explained: "At the Baptist Church, the superintendent of the Mill was the superintendent of the Sunday School; the foremen were the teachers; section men/fixers were ushers; deacons were foremen. One thing I didn't like about it. . . . It was run like the mill."[42] Occupational divisions between the churches hardened, and the Baptist managerial workers and their families did not visit in the homes of the Methodist operatives.[43]

The Roseville Cotton Mills were a regular sponsor of "Come to Church" ads which appeared in the twice-weekly newspaper. Themes and texts of the ads were good for business as well as for men's souls, as the following selection illustrates:

> *Time and God* . . . It is no accident that men, the world over, have built clocks into the steeples of their churches. Reduce life to its simplest components and what have you? Time and God . . .
>
> A parable then: The Clock in the Steeple . . .
>
> Man finds material security and temporal happiness as he learns to respect time. . .
>
> Man finds spiritual security and external happiness as he learns to love God.[44]

The mutuality of interests between Christianity and the Company are mirrored in the Sunday Bulletins of the Baptist Church which encourage faith and strength to endure life's adversities.[45] The LeClay workers' prayers echo their Sunday morning bulletins: "Lord, we do not ask you to remove our difficulties and sorrows; we just pray you will give us grace to bear them in a manner that will honor you."[46] And the hymns they sing reflect a similar desire to submit to God's will: "Have Thine Own Way, Lord!" "Take My Life and Let It Be."

Not surprisingly, employee initiative was limited primarily to

[41] Interviews with LeClay Baptist Church Pastor; LeClay Baptist Church Pulpit Committee Chairman.
[42] Interview with WM Shipping Department Employee.
[43] *The Roseville Messenger*, April 24, 1952, 7.
[44] Interview with WM Fixer; WM Card Room Supervisor; WM Inspector.
[45] The largest collection of bulletins examined is in the possession of a woman who began teaching in the Sunday School in 1917 and still attends services faithfully.
[46] May 23, 1965.

individual acts and job control.[47] The community acted as a whole only in times of crisis—sickness, accident, or death. And then, only in order to cope, not control. Sometimes this meant taking up a collection in the mill, or asking the manager of the store to put up a sign by a box for donations saying, "So and so needs such and such." The custom of giving food goods to those in need was called a "pounding,"[48] meaning a pound of coffee, or sugar, or whatever the donor could spare.

In one case where the father of a family had been confined to bed for eight months with terminal cancer, the school served as agent for aid. His son, the third generation of the family to be employed by the Mill, recalls the incident which occurred in 1946:

> I was in the fourth grade; they asked us all to bring something, even if it won't nothing but a piece of soap . . . . Mama found one or two taters [potatoes] . . . the onliest thing . . . that we had . . . . And she put it in a bag, and I carried it to school thinking they was going to give it to somebody else. And all the time, they was fixing us a box . . . . The Mills have give a lot of people a place to work, and well, it raised me, [but] they like to let us starve to death . . . . The people . . . kept us going.[49]

When thirty-seven—years-old Nathan Yancy, with a second grade education, a wife and three children, attempted to organize a union in 1950, he was acting contrary to the philosophy expressed in the hymns he sang at LeClay Baptist Church and contrary to community practice. But he was desparate; he explained: "I had athelete's foot . . .It was bleeding and I stopped to rest . . . I was using two home-made brooms to sweep. My Uncle [Overseer] whistled and motioned me to come up, and he chewed me out. There was two little balls of cotton under the frame. He said if [the Superintendent] was to come up, we'd both be fired . . . . Two little balls of cotton running around.... That was the beginning of the union."[50]

It was March when he, his brother and their wives began to organize. During spring and early summer, they held meetings in the village and established contact with the Textile Workers' Union of America in a nearby city. Before summer ended, both

[47] Interview data.
[48] WF Winder; WF Spooler; WM Carpenter, WM Card Room Operator; WM Draw Frame Tender; WM Warper Hand.
[49] WM Draw Frame Tender.
[50] WM Sweeper.

men and two other union supporters were fired.[51] No mention of
these activites ever appeared in the local newspaper. But the press
reported Company activities and enhanced the prestige of the
Roseville Cotton Mills in Carol County. In April, 1950 the Mills
gave five feet of land to the City, and the editor extolled, "Would
that we had more Santa Clauses like them." In August, the city
manager announced that the Mills had paid seventy-five per cent
of new street work costs of almost $34,000. On October 2, 1950
the newspaper reported on page 1 a 10-cent hourly increase in
pay for the workers and noted, "It has been the policy of the . . .
company . . . [heretofore] to make no public announcement
concerning increases in pay." Press praise continued into January,
1951 with the news that LeClay homes were to be modernized,
including the installation of water and sewage lines. About one-
half of the 100 houses were without inside plumbing and dependent upon outside privies and water pumps; the houses with
toilet facilities had no bathtub or shower equipment. An editorial
based on a tour of the mills soon followed which noted the good
ventilation, modern machinery, and "floors comparable to those
of many dance halls [with] a trace of lint on the floors [that] is
kept to a minimum."

The first press acknowledgement of efforts to form a union is
an article covering the National Labor Relations Board hearings
in early May, 1951. A few days later, an editorial on the trial
concluded: "We are proud of the cordial relations . . . between
employees and management . . . They are the same sort of folks
and they do not need any outside organizers or any National Labor Relations Board to tell them how to handle their affairs."
Roseville Cotton Mills were found guilty of unfair labor practices
and ordered to pay back wages to the employees[52] who had since
obtained employment in other towns. But no union was formed,
and the people known to have supported the effort were laid off
for other reasons and remain blacklisted at LeClay.[53]

During the organizing attempt, the Company's response was

---

[51] Interviews with the two brothers, one of their wives, the brother of one of the older men who
was fired but died before research was undertaken; and with one woman who was subsequently fired—though the cause cited was her separation from her husband. The Company did not condone divorce. Also NLRB Trial Examiner's Report.

[52] *Decisions of National Labor Relations Board.*

[53] WF Winder. The wives of one of the men could never acquire work even with two different
subsequent owners of the mill.

classic: spies at meetings, surveillance which included following workers to the union office in another town, interrogation of employees, eviction from company houses, promises of easier jobs, and threats of harder job assignments and speed-up.[54] More painful than the Company's response to the principals involved, however, were the family members who asked them not to visit, the friends who quickly entered their houses and shut the doors when they passed, the minister who never came to "call" again, and the anonymous letter telling them to leave town.[55] The crisis in interpersonal relationships precipitated by the unsuccessful effort to unionize in 1950 culminated in the sale of the mill houses in 1961.[56]

The long range trend in the Mill has been toward an increased work load: more machines to operate at a faster speed with greater output on larger packages. In spite of this trend, however, LeClay operatives exerted considerable control on the job. Employee control is greatest on second and third shifts when there is a minimum of supervisory personnel around. The hiring of spare-hands, male and female, has enabled workers to learn a variety of jobs, which vitiates the monotony present in doing the same one all the time.[57] The Company's policy of promoting the most loyal employees to fixer and foreman has often produced personnel who know much less about the machines they are supposed to repair than the operatives running them. Since many of these bossmen began their employment in the mill as children, they had little or no formal education. Of one supervisor, it was joked that all he could write was: "Hired. Fired. and K. C. Hicks [his name]."

Operative control of working conditions has been strengthened since the mid-sixties under new ownership and the appearance of a managerial staff well-versed in textbook technology but ig-

---

[54] Interviews and Trial Examiner's Report.
[55] Interview data.
[56] Interviews and County Deed Transfers.
[57] Robert Blauner concluded that Southern textile workers found their work interesting because of their traditional backgrounds, limited education, and low skill level; see "The Textile Worker: Integration Without Freedom in a Traditional Community," in *Alienation and Freedom: The Factory Worker and His Industry* (Chicago, 1964), 82-83. This study concludes that LeClay operatives found the monotony of their work reduced by the variety of jobs, unpredictability of how the work would run because of operations preceding the one at which one is engaged, the different yarns being run, the different quality of cotton being used, the number of fires which cause shutdowns, machinery breakdowns, considerable horseplay and courting activities which take place in the mill.

norant of machine idiosyncrasies. As a machine installer explained:
"I remember when personnel was president, manager, and foremen. They have eighteen-to-twenty supervisors now—trying to do
it on paper. If fixer and supervisors listened to the help more,
they'd find out more about the machinery . . . If a spinner says
to me, 'something is wrong with rack,' it usually is." Employee
initiative and resistance to management are most apparent in
frequent machinery breakdowns, oft-occurring fires, restriction
of output, and abuse of company property.

No amount of employee control of working conditions, however, compensates for the mill environment. Cotton lint and dust
permeate the air:[58] old white men chew tobacco; old white women dip snuff; young males suck on Certs; and young females
chew gum to counter its effects. Moisture added to the 80-100
degree temperature creates a year-round hothouse atmosphere.
The noise is deafening. A 1973 survey of the plant registered noise
levels of 90 decibels or over on the A scale in six departments—
Spinning: 92-98 dbAs; Roving: 90-96 dbAs; Drawing: 89-92
dbAs; Pickers: 92-95 dbAs; Unicones [a type of winder]: 92-98
dbAs; and Opening: 75-100 dbAs.[59]

Until 1964, the LeClay operatives spinning cotton yarn were as
white as the fibre they processed. With the Civil Rights Act, the
Mill doors opened to the black men and women who constituted
thirty-five percent of the county's 26,000 population. Moreover,
rapid industrialization in the area opened other doors to whites
and made room for blacks— 1964: new valve core plant employing 600; 1965: new synthetic yarn plant employing 125 and a
metal fabrication plant employing 100; 1966: new electric energy
power plant employing 100; 1968: storm windows and doors plant
employing 150.[60]

Before the integration of the mills, migration had provided the
major alternative to agricultural labor for the black community.
Blacks comprised forty-two percent of the population in 1900

[58] The Women's Bureau found female cotton mill workers lost more time through sickness than
women in other industries and noted Perry's finding that the death rate per 1000 women
between the ages of 15-44 was 82 per cent higher for cotton mill operatives than for non-
operatives. Deaths for tuberculosis exceeded non-operatives by 142 per cent ("Lost Time
and Labor Turnover," 70-71).
[59] Copy of survey in author's possession.
[60] Interviews with the personnel managers of the firms; also county data reports.

and thirty-three percent in 1970.[61] The black operatives in LeClay Plant in 1974 comprised forty-two percent of the 387 workers.[62] They possessed diverse backgrounds. Their formal education is greater than that of the older whites, ranging from fourth grade through highschool graduation. Almost one-half of the fifty black LeClay employees interviewed had completed highschool. Of those who did not, the age at which schooling was discontinued was usually higher than that for whites, being 16-18 years for blacks rather than 12-16 for whites. The reasons blacks gave for quitting school were also different: I got too grown; I got married; I got tired of it.[63]

Previous occupational experiences are similarly varied and include farm work; logging, lumbering, sawmilling; domestic, business and hospital service; and factory work in auto and textiles. Much of this experience was obtained in Southern and Northern cities and indicates the complex network of relationships maintained between migrants and Carol County residents. Some of these connections were established before World War I and solidified during peak labor demands at Aliquippa, Braddock, Donora, Pennsylvania, and Sparrow's Point, Baltimore, Maryland. Most of the traffic between Carol County and the points of outward migration has been incoming: for vacations, holidays, harvest season, funerals, graduations, births and marriages. The patterns of migration have been ritualized in annual celebrations hosted by various local churches—such as Baltimore Day—when dozens of men and women return to the county of their American origin. Some of the Northern churches reciprocate by celebrating North Carolina Day. The ties between migrants and residents have provided assistance at each end and in a variety of ways: lodging, work, money, and knowledge—of politics, unions, Federal legislation, or just how to get by.[64]

All of the black operatives have worked on tobacco farms. For the landowners and children of landowners, mill work sometimes provides their first employment by whites.[65] The former

[61] U. S. Census Data for 1900, 1960, and 1970. The percentage decline in black population since 1900 has been gradual.

[62] Interviews with LeClay Executive Vice-president and Personnel Manager.

[63] BM Card Room Operative; BF Winder; BF Spinner.

[64] Interviews with black workers and non-mill residents.

[65] Interviews with BM Card Room Operative; BM Card Room Foreman; BM Doffer in Spinning.

sharecropper is most analogous to the first generation of white mill workers, but there are many differences between them. The black sharecropper has not failed at farming; mill work represents a rung *up* on the occupational ladder for him. Though he was economically and materially usually worse off than the white mill village resident, black sharecroppers had wielded greater personal initiative over their individual and institutional activities within the caste system than whites under paternalism. Agricultural landlords did not interfere in the personal and familial affairs of tenants. One black respondent with many years of agricultural extension work testified: "Landlord had nothing to do with what tenants did on Saturday, and Sunday, or in the home. That was their own time." Unlike the white mill supervisors, farm-owner employers did not concern themselves with the personal lives of their laborers. One seventy-five-year-old Baptist landlord states: "As long as they did the work . . . I didn't *ever* want to know [about tenant's private lives]!" As a former tenant summed up, ". . . since slavery broke, people didn't let them go that deep." Agricultural landlords did not interfere in the familial affairs of tenants; they did not own, staff, and direct the policies of the schools and churches attended by their employees, and they did not impose a restrictive code of moral and social behavior on their landed laborers.

Black sharecroppers could and did make frequent moves to improve income and working or living conditions.[66] No *blanket* agreement existed among agricultural employers to refuse tenancy to croppers who wished to change landlords.[67] The croppers' family income—unlike the millworkers'—derived from a variety of sources, most of which were independent of each other: For himself and older sons, there was sawmilling, lumbering, and handywork in the winters; for his wife and daughters, there was domestic work: cleaning, washing, ironing, cooking and child-tending. Tobacco sacks were strung by the women and children in the "putting out system" through the first third of this century, and tobacco warehouses continue to provide seasonal la-

[66] Tobacco tenants appear to have averaged moving every two years just as cotton croppers have and for much the same reasons: better land, house, working arrangements, smaller/larger acreage/house; "to better ourselves."

[67] In fact, landlords would on occasion "buy out" the indebtedness of a tenant to persuade him to move.

bor.[68] And the cropper family was able to earn additional income with agricultural day work when its tenant obligations were fulfilled.[69]

Black sharecroppers were not socially isolated from the rest of their community. Croppers, businessmen, professionals—doctors, teachers, midwives—farmers, and domestics attended churches, schools, and the events sponsored by black institutions together.[70] The predominant values of institutional life and individual acknowledgement are self-help and racial cohesion. One of the first organizations formed to uplift the race dates to 1875 and was originally named the Carol County Emancipation Association; it is now called the Carol County Improvement Association and seeks to effect changes in the political, social, educational and economic arenas.[71]

Within the caste system, the inadequately-funded black schools consistently engaged citizens in the many rural districts in advancing the cause of education during this century—1916: Oak Grove Community parents cut logs to make timber for a new school; 1917: parents in Pine Hill Community, anxious for a new school, began raising money by having box parties and each pledged $10.00; 1918 was a good tobacco year, and parents built another room onto the school; 1921: patrons of Hillview got together and built a small room on their school; 1944; Friends for a Negro Branch Library circulated a petition for money which brought in pledges ranging from ten cents to two dollars; 1951: the summary report of Jonah Majors School revealed that parents took the lead in building four of the six classsrooms.[72]

Black cooperative effort turned to agricultural problems in 1933. Sixty-one local farmers with the aid of a professor from another county organized an agricultural office. Pooling their

[68] White mill workers (primarily women and children) used to string sacks also, as did some white families in the landowning class. The LeClay families used their "sack money" to buy coffee, sugar, and other staples. According to Margaret J. Hagood, this sweatshop industry in North Carolina terminated with the Wages and Hours Bill in 1938 (see her *Mothers of the South* [New York], 52).
[69] White mill families and town blacks also "farmed out" their children in the summer for room, board, and small amounts of money which would be used for buying fall school clothes.
[70] Interviews with black mill operatives, landowners, sharecroppers, teachers, ministers and domestics.
[71] Interview with President of the Association.
[72] Copies of the Negro School Reports in author's possession. The expenditure per Negro child in 1930 was about one-third of that for whites, according to Charles S. Johnson, *Statistical Atlas of Southern Counties: Listing and Analysis of Socio-Economic Indices of 1104 Southern Counties* (Chapel Hill, 1941).

resources, they hired a Negro agent for $65 a month until he be-
came funded by the government. The agent acquired a building
for his organization by going to individual landowners and getting them to contribute ten, twenty logs, a window, or door, and
by getting several people to donate the roof. His former colleague
says he motivated people through the philosophy of "your little
mite put together . . . for the common good." In concert with
others, the agent established a cooperative store in 1936 which
lasted three years. Under his direction, the community was divided into thirty-one neighborhoods with each headed by a chairman who was assisted by two to five subchairmen. The effectiveness of the procedure and the programs instituted would eventually
win for the county the state's annual award for rural progress.
In explaining the Negro communities' success, the agent said:
"Groups of family representatives numbering from seven or eight
to 35 or 40 got together and decided what they wanted to do and
could do. They won assistance from all kinds of agencies, but
they also worked for themselves and each other." Among their
accomplishments that year: per farm income increased $620 over
the previous year; 650 gardens were planted at a value of $500-
900 each; bread gave way to meat as the leading food in a representative survey; milk and dairy products moved from fourth to
second place; green vegetables from seventh to fifth; 300 families
participated in a kitchen and yard improvement program, and
100 toilets were built. A ninth grade health project reached 1900
homes, and sixty-five percent of the boys and girls age ten to
twenty (1184 of 1857) were enrolled in 4-H Clubs at the time of
the award; those boys and girls completed 712 projects in garden-
ing, food, field crops, food conservation, and clothing that
equalled $76,000 in value during the year preceding the award.[73]

The collective activities of the Emancipation Association, the
schools, churches, and agricultural agency were often led by and
always included the ministers of the churches. The predominant
value of black religious life was hope—hope for change in the

---

[73] *The Roseville Messenger* and interviews with principals involved. Also news story from
The Durham Morning Herald. The collective efforts of Carol County blacks to improve
the conditions of their race are not peculiar to the Piedmont area. See Frances Sage
Bradley and Margaretta Williamson, "Rural Children in Selected Counties of North
Carolina," *Rural Child Welfare Series No. 2,* Bureau Publication No. 33 (Washington,
1918), 16-18.

present—not resignation to life's inequities in hopes of salvation in the hereafter. And black operatives brought the beliefs of their religious institutions to the mill. The new employees brought the attitudes of agricultural laborers toward time and work, captured in the words of a song recalled by an eighty-one year-old black farmer: "I work all the summer. I work all the fall. Christmas come and catch me in overalls. Take it easy. Take it easy. Take it easy." His recommendation that you not push too hard because you are not going to get anywhere is heeded by an operative who times his machines to run until he can go home so someone else will have to empty them. The recognition that everything but acts of God are controlled by the Man in Charge is acknowledged by a young black spinner who says she could increase her speed, but the foreman would just give her more to do.[74]

When black operatives undertake collective action to improve their working conditions only nine years after racial integration of the mill, they are reflecting attitudes and engaging in activities of self-help and cooperative effort to which they are long accustomed. In 1973, two black male cardhands carried a petition to the executive vice-president of the mill which requested that the second shift pay be changed from Friday night to Thursday night because the banks were closed on Saturdays. The petition was signed by all the black workers and an estimated 90 percent of the white. In presenting the petition to the vice-president, one of the men said: "We brought the petition because we knew everybody couldn't come to the office, and we are representing them." During the course of their one and a half-hour interview, the two men expressed to the executive sensitivity to the possibility their actions might result in losing their jobs but as they were both landowners, they and their wives were willing to take the chance. In addition, the cardhands asked the official to "look into some other matters" that were of concern to the black employees. These "matters" related to operatives' dignity, safety, and earnings. The vice-president was asked to check on the way older white foremen spoke to the young highschool boys and girls on second shift; the length of time it took for breakdowns to be repaired; the absence of covers and guards on the machinery.

---

[74] Interview.

Changes began to occur immediately. The pay day was changed
to Thursday night the next week. A new plant manager was acquired. Parts began to appear more quickly when machines broke
down, and covers and guard rails were replaced sooner than the
three weeks it had taken previously. Two of the most abusive
foremen were demoted. Less than six months later, two black
women from the winding department circulated a petition requesting that the Company observe all legal holidays by shutting
down. Again, all but a few white employees signed. The Mill
granted the holidays, but began to institute new policies. One of
the men who had carried the first petition to the front office was
promoted to foreman of the second shift cardroom; the other appeared on a summer 1974 supervisor's memo as a *farmer* (italics
added) whose employment should be discontinued; it was. Other
black males have since been promoted to fixers, and foremen,
and for the first time in its seventy-year history, women—only
black, however—are being told they are being considered for a
fixer's job (but they are told not to tell anyone they are being
groomed for these promotions).[75] A system of regular breaks has
been introduced, and everyone is required to take them at the assigned time. Foremen use the breaks to talk with employees who
are no longer allowed to leave their respective departments without the foreman's permission; anyone who does is subject to
termination.[76]

Since early 1974, the economy of Carol County has been so
depressed that there is little likelihood of workers forming a union
in the near future.[77] But it is the new work force that offers the
greatest hope for organization. And more importantly, the

---

[75] Interviews with both men and one of the wives; also interviews with WM fixer/sharecropper
who assisted one of the black operatives in the planning stages; BF Draw Frame Tender
and 2 BF Roving Frame Tenders.

[76] Interviews with employees, supervisors; copies of break schedules in author's possession.
Because these breaks interfere with production and affect wages adversely, some operatives
have arranged with foremen to take breaks when it is "more convenient." In view of the
noise levels in many departments, it is clear that workers following scheduled breaks would
not be exposed for the maximum allowable time and thus relieve the company from being
in technical violation of OSHA regulations.

[77] F. Ray Marshall has noted the support of unions by Southern blacks as has Bruce Raynor
of the TWUA. See Marshall, *Labor in the South* (Cambridge, 1967), 239; Raynor,
"Unionism in the Southern Textile Industry: An Overview" (unpublished ms. n.d. presented at the Southern Labor History Conference at Atlanta, April, 1976), 20. The favorable union vote at the Roanoke Rapids Stevens' plants is attributed to a 70 percent black
vote (see Frank Guillory, "N. C. Textile Firm Finally Unionized," *The Washington Post*
September 2, 1974, A1, A9). The failure of white mill workers to unionize has often been

values and heritage brought to the LeClay Mill by black operatives have gained a recognition for that working class which
promises an end to the epithet "cotton mill trash."

Appendix

The bulk of the data examined during the course of this inves-
tigation is documentary in nature and includes U. S. Census
Data on Commerce, Agriculture, Vital Statistics, Social and
Economic Characteristics of the County; City and County Data
Books; State and County Educational, Agricultural, Economic
and Health Reports; local newspapers, church records, histories,
Chamber of Commerce Data Sheets, National Labor Relations
Board Trial Examiner's Report, and available company records.
Because of the inadequacy and incompleteness of written evi-
dence, however, oral data has provided a major resource for
learning about people's experiences, perceptions, purposes, mo-
tives, and goals.

Childhood, adolescent, and continuing adult experiences in
the community under study have enabled the writer to return to
the county and assume the position of a person with the right
to learn, to observe, and to inquire casually about others. Northern residence, education, and institutional affiliation provided
the entree to the black community. While acting as a participant
observer and interviewer on eighteen visits between Fall, 1971
and Spring, 1977, the writer has conducted over two hundred
interviews with residents of Carol County. Pseudonyms have been
used for all proper names of people and places; and numbers
and statistics have been rounded off to protect the identity of
respondents. The interviews were a combination of open-ended,
focused, and structured format. The format was determined by
the amount of time available for the initial interview, the occupational status and area(s) of respondent expertise, and the nature of the relationship established between the interviewer and

---

attributed to "individualism" rooted in agricultural origins (see G. T. Schwenning,
"Prospects of Southern Textile Unionism," *Journal of Political Economy*. XXXIX [Decem-
ber, 1931], 802-803). The strongest support for the LeClay collective action, however, was
from white and black with ties to the land. The government's study of part-time farmers
in the Southeast also found more members of unions on the land than in the villages (R. H.
Allen, *et al, Part-Time Farming in the Southeast*, Works Progress Administration,
Research Monograph IX [Washington, 1937], 67-68).

the respondent. The length of the interviews ranged from less than an hour to six hours in length at a time. Many respondents have been interviewed several different times and since have corresponded with the writer.

As of June, 1974, the LeClay plants employed 387 people: 55 percent male; 45 percent female. Sixty percent of the employees were white and forty percent were black as of that year, when most employee interviews were conducted. The writer has interviewed 150 workers and former workers in the Roseville Cotton Mills, most of whom have been employees of the LeClay Plant. These interviews include the executive vice-president, personnel manager, superintendent, fourteen foremen/supervisors, six fixers (in Southern yarn mills, the position of fixer has often been the first step up the mill hierarchy.), and employees from every department and every shift. Of these 150 interviews, 90 were with whites: 51 male; 39 female. The remaining 60 were with blacks: 25 male; 35 female.

Seventy-four interviews were conducted with farmers, agricultural day laborers, sharecroppers, domestic workers, teachers, school administrators, city and county officials, ministers, personnel managers, other professional employees, and workers in other industries and businesses, agricultural agents, and lumber men, along with the spouses of these various individuals where possible. Approximately one-third of these interviews were with blacks. Twelve respondents reside in other towns or states.

The numbers of respondents in particular age, sex and racial groups are indicated below: (The total is less than the number of individuals interviewed because life histories were not collected from everyone.)

Birth Date	White Females	White Males	Black Females	Black Males
Before 1900	7	6	4	5
1900-1909	6	11	4	6
1910-1919	11	14	5	—
1920-1929	5	8	2	2
1930-1939	4	8	9	—
1940-1949	2	2	12	12
1950-1959	—	2	15	14
Totals	35	51	51	39

Afterthoughts

JAMES A. HENRETTA

In the mid-1980s it is clearly apparent that the study of social mobility was the product of a particular time and ideological mood. For some years now scholars have shunned mobility studies and have explored the life experiences of ordinary Americans in other ways. What is the significance of this relatively impoverished intellectual legacy? Is it unique, or the fate of most scholarly fads? Other recent approaches to the American past — such as those focusing on particular communities, on the lives of blacks and of women, and on republican ideology — seem to me to have produced more interesting and more complex historical insights. For this reason I remain critical of social mobility studies and the intellectual and ideological assumptions on which they were based.

GARY B. NASH

When I wrote this article, studies of poor relief and early manufactory labor were relatively new to social historians. The link between the rise of poverty and the development of manufactories in England and America, not sufficiently noticed by historians, was well known in the eighteenth century. "Manufactures," wrote Benjamin Franklin in 1760, "are founded in poverty."

The leaders of America's maritime centers waited no longer than their first experience with severe economic depression and the impoverishment it produced to copy the English example of working the poor. This involved a fundamental change in attitudes toward the "deserving poor" — those who through injury, decrepitude, or widowhood found themselves destitute. The customary way of maintaining such persons had been through outrelief, which allowed the indigent to subsist at home. But as their numbers grew, especially through the rise of widowhood caused by war, the respectable poor were victimized by the drive to economize on poor relief through institutionalizing charitable support.

Public officials experimented with working the poor in all the seaport capitals before and after the Revolution. They focused particularly on textile production. As in England, where early textile manufactories were closely associated with prisons, workhouses, and orphanages, the American textile industry grew up amid a rationale that viewed the poor as idle, undisciplined, and frail persons. Boston's leading men had started a linen factory in the 1740s to lower poor rates and instill what they regarded as a waning love of labor among the poor. By the early nineteenth century, long before Lowell, poor relief officials were directing some of the country's largest textile operations.

ALFRED YOUNG

My article originally appeared in tandem with one by Staughton Lynd on the mechanics from 1774 to 1788 and a preface in which we attempted to locate mechanics in late eighteenth-century society. Lynd elaborated some of these themes in *Class Conflict, Slavery, and the United States Constitution* (Indianapolis, 1967) and I in *The Democratic Republicans of New York: The Origins, 1763-1797* (Chapel Hill, N.C., 1968). The arguments, now apparently widely accepted, then challenged orthodoxies of several schools. Mechanics were a decided presence in a city's political life. They were in quest of personal independence and respect and not merely "belly" issues. There was not one mechanic vote; they divided, they became Federalist, then became Republican. And they expressed themselves not only at the polls but also in societies, fraternal, political, and economic, and in crowd actions, mass meetings, and parades.

For New York these themes have since been extended forward by Howard Rock, Richard Twomey, and Sean Wilentz, and backward, most noticeably by Edward Countryman and Gary B. Nash. For other cities these themes have been developed with variations: for Philadelphia by Charles Olten, Eric Foner, Steve Rosswurm, and Roland Baumann; for Boston by Dirk Hoerder and Jesse Lemisch; for Baltimore by Charles Steffen. Collectively this scholarship points to a mechanic culture as well as an artisan republicanism — themes I attempt to bring together in a book in progress I call "The Craftsman as Citizen: Mechanics and Laborers in the Shaping of the Nation, 1760-1820."

EDWARD PESSEN

When I wrote this essay fifteen years ago, I sought to point out some of the limitations of the quantitative method that was becoming increasingly the vogue among American historians. The achievements of American historical scholarship since that time suggest the wisdom of not thinking in terms of "either/or." Quantifiers have thrown important new light on such significant matters as the distribution of wealth, transiency, the extent of upward mobility, the life-styles of diverse social classes, the slave family and black society, and the comparative economic circumstances of different ethnic groups. And yet the most interesting recent work on American labor before the Civil War is a tribute not to the glories of statistical methodologies but to the imaginative powers of creative historians. To cite only two examples: Bruce Laurie's study of the moods, values, and ideologies competing for favor among Philadelphia working people and Paul E. Johnson's analysis of the interrelationship between industrial and religious developments in Rochester, N.Y., remind us that good work depends not on whether the historian uses one rather than another methodology but on the originality of the historian's mind.

DAVID MONTGOMERY

Since this article was written, many historians have greatly enriched our knowledge and understanding of the questions it broached. Important new insights have emerged concerning work culture, the transformation of work processes and relations at the turn of the century, and the meaning of what has been variously called the "deskilling" and the "degradation" of work.

The diversity of workplace customs has been emphasized: Susan P. Benson has sketched the variety of work cultures within large department stores; David Bensman has portrayed resilient ethical codes obeyed by hat finishers; Patricia Ann Cooper has contrasted the behavioral norms of skilled cigar makers with those rolling five-cent stogies in factories; Bruce Nelson has analyzed the unique work culture of merchant seamen.[1]

Moreover, all these studies (and others) have suggested paradoxical conclusions concerning the historical role of work cultures. First, these cultures have provided both a wellspring of working-class cohesiveness and struggle, and a network of informal relationships created by workers for their own benefit, but without which employers could not run their enterprises. Second, it was the context of industrial conflict and of formidable rewards and punishments available to employers that provoked workers to transform workplace custom into explicit union rules with codified sanctions (fines and expulsions, for example) against those who succumbed to the blandishments of acquisitive individualism. This process has been demonstrated by the researches of Shelton Stromquist (nineteenth-century railroad workers), James Barrett (packinghouse workers at the turn of the century), John Bennett and Mary Freifield (iron and steel workers), and Richard Oestreicher (the Detroit Knights of Labor). Their work underscores the notion that workers' control was a struggle endemic to industrial life, which was given a distinctive shape in the late nineteenth century by the way in which production itself was organized.[2]

Further, the character of the transformation of work process and relations between the 1880s and the 1920s has been subjected to close scrutiny, especially due to the influence of Harry Braverman. Among those who have dealt with various aspects of the influence of Frederick Taylor and his disciples are Stephen Meyer III (who devoted himself to mechanization and personnel management), Maurine Greenwald (whose analysis of telephone operators and of

1. Susan Porter Benson, " 'A Great Threat': Saleswomen, Customers, and Managers in American Department Stores, 1890-1940" (Ph.D. diss., Brown University, 1983); David H. Bensman, *The Practice of Solidarity: American Hat Finishers in the Nineteenth Century* (Urbana, 1985); Patricia Ann Cooper, "From Hand Craft to Mass Production: Men, Women, and Work Culture in American Cigar Factories, 1900-1919" (Ph.D. diss., University of Maryland, 1981); Joseph Bruce Nelson, "Maritime Unionism and Class Consciousness in the 1930s" (Ph.D. diss., University of California, Berkeley, 1982).
2. R. Shelton Stromquist, "A Generation of Boomers: Work, Community Structure, and the Pattern of Industrial Conflict on Late 19th Century American Railroads" (Ph.D. diss., University of Pittsburgh, 1981); John W. Bennett, "The Workers of Woods Run and Johnstown: The Union Era" (Ph.D. diss., University of Pittsburgh, 1977); Richard J. Oestreicher, "Solidarity and Fragmentation: Working People and Class Consciousness in Detroit, 1877-1895" (Ph.D. diss., Michigan State University, 1979).

women in wartime railroad repair shops demonstrated that reorganization of work not only far outran the direct influence of Taylor and colleagues but also suggested that for many women these changes entailed opportunity as much as degradation), and Cecilia Bucki (her essay on Bridgeport munitions strikes points out that important wartime labor struggles were criss-crossed by mutually contradictory reactions of different kinds of workers). Moreover, the historical typology offered by economists David Gordon, Michael Reich, and Richard Edwards, and the comprehensive history of American management by Alfred D. Chandler have enabled us to formulate a broader conception of managerial innovations and a more precise periodization of their development.[3]

Finally, the whole process by which the autonomy, ethical code, and craft organization of skilled workers were undermined now needs to be elaborated in ways that both confirm the seminal importance of Braverman's analysis and avoid his unidimensional model of craftsmen's hegemony yielding to the degradation of work. Common laborers had long experienced industrial life in very different ways than craftsmen. Mechanization, detailed division of labor, and piecework had become standard fare for operatives in textile and shoe establishments decades before the advent of Taylor's ideas.[4] What is suggested by this article is that the industrial role of skilled trades was changed by the restructuring of management, and with it the internal dynamics of the workers' movement.

The nineteenth-century craftsman was a production worker; his twentieth-century counterpart performs ancilliary tasks (such as tool and die making, set-up, supervision) to the operatives, who fashion

---

3. Stephen Meyer III, *The Five Dollar Day: Labor Management and Social Control in the Ford Motor Company, 1919-1921* (Albany, 1981); Maurine Weiner Greenwald, *Women, War and Work: The Impact of World War I on Women Workers in the United States* (Westport, Conn., 1980); Cecilia F. Bucki, "Dilution and Craft Traditions," *Social Science History* 4 (1980), 105-24; David Gordon, Richard Edwards, and Michael Reich, *Segmented Work, Divided Workers: The Historical Transformation of Labor in the United States* (New York, 1982); Alfred D. Chandler, *The Visible Hand: The Managerial Revolution in American Business* (Cambridge, Mass., 1977).

4. Andreas Graziosi, "Common Laborers, Unskilled Workers, 1890-1915," *Labor History* 22 (1981), 512-44; Leslie Woodcock Tentler, *Wage Earning Women: Industrial Work and Family Life in the United States, 1900-1930* (New York, 1979); Susan Levine, "Their Own Sphere: Women's Work, the Knights of Labor, and the Transformation of the Carpet Trade" (Ph.D. diss., Columbia University, 1979); Tamara Hareven, *Family Time and Industrial Time: The Relationship between the Family and Work in a New England Industrial Community* (Cambridge, Mass., 1982).

and assemble the parts. Consequently, any future study of workers'
control struggles and their evolution must take these changes in
industrial relations into account.[5]

HERBERT G. GUTMAN

My essay dealt with a brief moment in the history of American
railroad workers. Recent scholarship has not convinced me to alter
its essential arguments. What we need is a study of strike patterns
among railroad workers prior to 1873. And we need a full study
of the great 1877 railroad strikes. Such research and publication
might cause a reconsideration of the agruments in this essay. And
I welcome such work.

H. M. GITELMAN

As far as I know, no new evidence has come to light that would
lead to changes in the information or interpretation as originally
presented. Unfortunately, students continue to credit Samuel Gompers with much of Adolph Strasser's intellectual achievements. An
extant body of untapped material dealing with Strasser's career
remains unavailable at this writing.

JAMES HOLT

If I were writing this article today, I would revise what I said
about the comparative level of real wages and wage differentials
between the skilled and the unskilled in the light of Peter R. Sher-
gold's *Working Class Life: The "American Standard" in Comparative Perspective, 1899-1913* (Pittsburgh, 1982). However, I would
see no reason to modify the article's major themes.

PAUL B. WORTHMAN

While American society has made some significant strides toward
integration in the fourteen years since I wrote about black and white
workers in Birmingham, the national leadership of the American

---

5. For elaboration of these arguments, see David Montgomery, "Introduction," in Im-
manual Wallerstein, ed., *Labor in the World Social Structure* (Beverly Hills, 1983), and
David Montgomery, "Labor and the Republic in Industrial America," *Le Movement
Social* 111 (1980), 201-15.

labor movement has regrettably lagged behind. Although work sites are far more racially integrated today than fourteen years ago, and a higher proportion of black workers than white workers are unionized in the workforce, the top echelons of national unions and most local bureaucracies remain almost entirely white (and male). Influenced by the "new social history" of the 1970s, labor historians have shifted their concentration from labor elites to ordinary workingmen and women. The rise and resurgence of militant rank-and-file movements in the 1970s and the growing independence of local unions formed an important historical link between the period when this article was first published and the time period it described. Today a more integrated working class confronts demands from bosses for concessions and collaboration, which are often supported by fearful trade union elites. Since workers occasionally hear about the "new social history" in schools, community colleges, and universities, perhaps the lessons of resistance and interracial working-class cooperation from Alabama eighty years ago can provide inspiration to workers still struggling to gain control over their working lives and the society in which they live.

MELVYN DUBOFSKY

In the twenty years since I wrote this article, a veritable explosion of research and publication has transformed the field of labor history. Yet, however much I have learned from the new scholarship, I see no reason to revise the article's central themes. I still believe that the origins of western working-class radicalism must be located within the general history of capitalism both as a national and a world system, and not as a consequence of a mythic American frontier spirit or U.S. exceptionalism. But we have since learned much more about the earlier history of miners' unionism (Richard Lingenfelter, *The Hardrock Miners* [Berkeley, 1974]) and the more conventional, less radical aspect of worker behavior in the mountain West in the era of radicalism (Mark Wyman, *Hard Rock Epic: Western Miners and the Industrial Revolution, 1860-1910* [Berkeley, 1979] and James Foster's occasional articles and statistical data collections on the Western Federation of Miners).

MICHAEL H. EBNER

When I wrote this article, my main interest was more the I.W.W. than the labor history of Passaic. In retrospect I have learned that to understand a single strike — however important — the circumstances must be placed in a broader context, not unlike the community society suggested by Samuel P. Hays. Hence the appearance of my article "Strikes and Society: Civil Behavior in Passaic, 1875-1926" in *New Jersey History* 97 (Spring 1979), 7-24. I am indebted to Herbert G. Gutman's articles on working-class protest in specific settings — most notably those in Paterson, N.J. — for enhancing my appreciation of such circumstances.

ALICE KESSLER-HARRIS

In light of the recent work in labor history, and of changes in my own direction, I would probably change this article in two ways. First, I would frame the discussion of women in their community in terms of what is now commonly called women's culture. That is, in addition to acknowledging the values that emerge from the immigrant tradition in general, I would provide a fuller and more coherent pattern of values and norms among union women as they emerged from the particular relationships of family life and of women with each other. Second, I would make a sharp distinction between women's relationships to unionism in the organizing process and their relationships to unionism once organization was complete. I have come to believe that the dynamics of male/female relationships change dramatically once women become part of institutional structures, particularly when the social environment is hostile.

FRANK STRICKER

In an international context the United States in the 1920s looks very prosperous indeed; I should have acknowledged the contrasts (Great Britain and Germany are good examples). But I have no second thoughts about the basic tenor of "affluence for whom." My article may have been overly empiricist in its focus on statistical data. I should have made clear that people's past and their expectations shape the meaning of wage levels and living standards. To what extent did specific groups in the working class view the 1920s as prosperous years? Were unskilled workers content with their incomes, even if those were extremely low? These questions must be answered, but in analyzing workers' attitudes we must not ignore the simple bread-and-butter issues. Perceptions do shape reality, but the amount of the paycheck and the regularity of employment are a chunk of reality that shapes perception.

Three additional points: (1) General cost-of-living indices hide a great deal; they leave unanswered many of the most important questions, for example, did the quality of automobiles go up, so that consumers got more for the same or even fewer dollars? (2) Were I rewriting the article, I would spend more time on those who made big wage gains in the 1920s, and I would directly analyze income divisions within the working class between union and non-union workers, blue- and white-collar workers, and skilled and un-skilled workers. (3) Finally, in a rewrite I would highlight the situation of minorities. The inclusion of specific information, for example, about Pullman porters, black and Mexican industrial and farm workers, and southern sharecroppers would, I think, strengthen the basic arguments of the article.

DANIEL J. LEAB

At the time this article appeared (as well as another one by me on the barter and self-help groups active in 1932-1933 in *Midcontinent American Studies Journal* 7 [1966], 15-24), little scholarly work had been undertaken on the unemployed organizations of the 1930s. Since then Roy Rosenzweig has intelligently delved into the problem in a series of fine articles: "Radicals and the Jobless: The Musteites and the Unemployed Leagues, 1932-1936," *Labor History* 16 (1975), 52-77; "Organizing the Unemployed: The Early Years of the Great Depression, 1929-1933," *Radical America* 10 (July-Aug. 1976), 37-60; "Socialism in Our Time: The Socialist Party and the Unemployed, 1929-1936," *Labor History,* 20 (1979), 485-509. Less satisfactory but still useful is Al Prago's Ph.D. dissertation (Union Graduate School, 1976) on "The Organization of the Un-employed and the Role of the Radicals, 1929-1935." My judgments on the failings of the Communist party notwithstanding, the vital and indeed noble efforts of individual party members are reinforced by Harvey Klehr, *The Heyday of American Communism: The Depression Decade* (New York, 1984), ch. 3. I am currently at work on a study of all the unemployed movements in the 1930s.

DANIEL NELSON

Worker militancy is hardly a new theme in historical writing on the labor upheavals of the 1930s and 1940s. What is comparatively new is the treatment of rank-and-file militancy as a phenomenon separate from the rise of industrial unionism, the CIO, and government involvement in collective bargaining. In recent years studies focusing explicitly on worker behavior have proliferated and become an important feature of the historical literature of the Depression era. As a result it is possible to see the actions of workers as a phase of the social history of the American labor force rather than as an adjunct, and a rather unimportant and unwelcome one at that, to the history of the New Deal. Thus far, most books and articles have emphasized the so-called mass production industries, the automobile industry in particular. In the future there is reason to anticipate similarly valuable accounts of workers in transportation, mining, and the service fields. For other examples of the new approach to worker militancy, see Nelson Lichtenstein's "Auto-Worker Militancy and the Structure of Factory Life, 1937-1955," *Journal of American History* 67 (1980), 335-53, which was prepared for the same session of the 1979 Organization of American Historians meeting as "Origins of the Sit-Down Era" and the citations in Bernard Sternsher's "Great Depression Labor Historiography in the 1970s: Middle Range Questions, Ethnocultures, and Levels of Generalization," *Reviews in American History* 2 (1983), 300-317.

SIDNEY FINE

In *Frank Murphy: The Washington Years*, I deal somewhat more fully with the drafting of Murphy's *Thornhill* opinion. The papers of most of Murphy's brethren have become available since I wrote the article, but they do not alter the argument of the piece. The unidentified justice referred to in the paragraph dealing with the Court's *Thornhill* conference was Hugo Black, a sitting justice at the time I wrote the article. In addition to its longevity as a precedent in labor picketing cases, *Thornhill* served as a precedent for the Warren Court in deciding free-speech and nonlabor picketing cases.

JOSHUA FREEMAN

Since this review essay was first published, the trickle of writing on labor during World War II has turned into a steady stream. Several of the authors discussed herein have published books that deal in part or in whole with the wartime period, including Martin Glaberman, Ronald Schatz, and Nelson Lichtenstein, whose *Labor's War at Home: The CIO in World War II* (New York, 1982) now stands as the most important work on the subject. Excellent new studies have also appeared on managerial practices and on the massive entrance of women and nonwhites into the industrial work force. There remains, however, much to be done; we still lack, for example, a comprehensive treatment of the AFL during the war. Although I believe that the main thrust of my essay is still valid, some of my views have certainly changed in the light of more recent scholarship.

NANCY GABIN

This article has become part of a broader study of women automotive workers and the UAW-CIO. Focusing on the period from 1935 to 1955, this study examines the historically marginal status of women in the automobile industry, a result of the sexual division of labor. Codified in seniority agreements, job classifications, and wage standards, occupational segregation by sex limited women's employment opportunities in automobile plants. The attempt by women unionists to expose the dynamics of sexual inequality and to mount a challenge to this discrimination demonstrates the importance of the union as an arena for female activism and the way in which union membership may serve not only as a constraint upon but also as a resource for women's collective action.

DALE NEWMAN

Major changes have occurred at LeClay Mill since the publication of this article in 1978. The company no longer manufactures all-cotton yarns, but produces synthetics or combinations of cotton and synthetics.[1] More efficient machinery has been installed in every department with a resultant decrease in the work force and an increase in production from 150,000 pounds of yarn per week to 240,000 pounds.[2]

The composition and attitudes of the work force have also altered with the deteriorating economy and the company's more rigorous screening procedure in hiring. While labor became increasingly black during the late 1970s, it is becoming whiter with the depression of the 1980s. As one foreman noted, "They are hiring as many whites as they can." Before anyone is hired, the personnel manager phones previous employers to find out if the applicant has been a "trouble maker" of any sort — a procedure, which according to management, has resulted in a "lot better help."[3]

For the nearly one-third fewer employees at the mill, the above changes have brought steadier work and higher wages. These improvements, along with the legacy of activists during the early integration of the mill, have given workers a greater status in the community. Asked if LeClay operatives were still looked down on, a white male card room employee with thirty-two years experience replied: "I think to a certain extent people will always look down on you, but people do get the respect now... for two reasons: One, they demand more respect; and two, they make enough money to get the respect. The Mill is paying almost as much as other places.... We are on the same level with other firms... years ago, we weren't."[4]

---

1. *Roseville Messenger,* Aug. 26, 1979, p. 1, indicates that concern over cotton dust was an important factor in product and machine changes.
2. Interview with a white male card room foreman, June 1, 1983.
3. Ibid.
4. Interview with a white male card room employee, May 30, 1983.

Notes on Contributors

DAVID BRODY is professor of history at the University of California, Davis. His books include *Steelworkers in America: The Nonunion Era* (1960) and *Workers in Industrial America: Essays on the Twentieth-Century Struggle* (1980).

MELVYN DUBOFSKY is professor of history and sociology at the State University of New York at Binghamton. His books include *We Shall Be All: A History of the Industrial Workers of the World.* He is the co-author of a biography of John L. Lewis (1977) and of *Labor in America: A History* (4th ed., 1984).

MICHAEL H. EBNER is chair of the department of history at Lake Forest College. He is co-chair of the urban history seminar of the Chicago Historical Society, is on the national advisory board of the *History Teacher,* and recently completed service on the national council of the American Association of University Professors. His writings include "Urban History: Retrospect and Prospect," *Journal of American History* 68 (1981), 69-84.

SIDNEY FINE is Andrew Dickson White Distinguished Professor of History at the University of Michigan and has been the chair of the editorial board of *Labor History* since 1976. His books include a multivolume biography of Frank Murphy (vol. 1, 1975; vol. 2, 1979; vol. 3, 1984) and *Sit Down: The General Motors Strike of 1936-1937* (1969).

JOSHUA FREEMAN is a senior research scholar at the City University of New York and on the staff of the American Working Class History project. He has taught at New York University, Yale University, and the College at Old Westbury, State University of New York. His publications include "Catholics, Communists, and Republicans: Irish Workers and the Organization of the Transport Workers Union," in Michael Frisch and Daniel Walkowitz, eds., *Working-Class America: Essays on Labor, Com-*

munity, and American Society (1983), 256-83. He is currently writing a
book on the Transport Workers Union between 1933 and 1950.

NANCY GABIN is assistant professor of history at Purdue University.
She received her Ph.D. from the University of Michigan in 1984, and her
dissertation dealt with "Women Auto Workers and the United Automobile
Workers, 1935-1955." Her publications include " 'They Have Placed a
Penalty on Womanhood': The Protest Actions of Women Auto Workers
in Detroit Area UAW Locals, 1945-1947," *Feminist Studies* 8 (1982), 373-
98.

H. M. GITELMAN is professor of economics at Adelphi University. His
writings include *Workingmen of Waltham: Mobility in American Urban
Industrial Development, 1850-1890* (1974) and "Being of Two Minds:
American Employers Confront the Labor Problem, 1915-1919," *Labor
History* 25 (1984), 185-212.

HERBERT G. GUTMAN is Distinguished Professor of History at the
Graduate Center, City University of New York. His writings include *Work,
Culture and Society in Industrializing America* (1976) and, with Ira Berlin,
"Natives and Immigrants, Free Men and Slaves: Urban Workingmen in
the Antebellum South," *American Historical Review* 88 (1983), 1175-1200.
He is the supervisor of the American Working-Class History Project and
is completing a book entitled "Gilded Age Workers and the Remaking of
American Society, 1865-1880."

JAMES A. HENRETTA is professor of history at Boston University. His
writings include *The Evolution of American Society, 1700-1815: An Interdisciplinary Analysis* (1973). He is joint author of the textbook *The
American People: A New History of the United States* (1985).

The late LAURENCE JAMES HOLT was chief historian of the New
Zealand Historical Publications. His writings include *The Emergence of
Modern America, 1890-1920* (1972) and "The Trade Unions and Socialism
in the United States," *Journal of American Studies* 7 (1973), 321-28.

ALICE KESSLER-HARRIS is professor of history and co-director of the
Center for the Study of Work and Leisure at Hofstra University. She is
the author of *Out to Work: A History of Wage-Earning Women in the
United States* (1982) and *Women Have Always Worked* (1980) and editor
of Anzia Yezierska's *The Open Cage: A Collection* (1980).

DANIEL J. LEAB has been the editor of *Labor History* since 1974. His books include *A Union of Individuals: The Formation of the American Newspaper Guild* (1970) and *From Sambo to Superspade: The Black Image in American Films* (1975). He is co-compiler with Maurice Neufeld and Dorothy Swanson of *American Working-Class History: A Representative Bibliography* (1984).

DAVID MONTGOMERY is Farnam Professor of History at Yale University. His books include *Beyond Equality: Labor and the Radical Republicans, 1862-1872* (1967) and *Workers Control in America* (1979).

RICHARD B. MORRIS, a co-founder of *Labor History*, is Gouverneur Morris Professor of History Emeritus at Columbia University. He is the author of numerous articles and several books, including his Bancroft Prize–winning *The Peacemakers: The Great Powers and American Independence*. He is now engaged in research on labor in the Confederation years.

GARY B. NASH is professor of history at the University of California, Los Angeles. His books include *Red, White, and Black: The Peoples of Early America* (1974) and *The Urban Crucible: Social Change, Political Consciousness, and the Origins of the American Revolution* (1979).

DANIEL NELSON is professor of history at the University of Akron. His writings include *Managers and Workers: Origins of the New Factory System in the United States, 1880-1920* (1975) and *Frederick W. Taylor and the Rise of Scientific Management* (1980) as well as various articles on the establishment of the United Rubber Workers.

DALE NEWMAN teaches labor history courses in Pittsburgh-area colleges. She is a political activist in the feminist movement, is chair of the Pennsylvania labor task force for the National Organization for Women, and serves on the executive board of the Pennsylvania Labor History Society. Her publications include "Culture, Class, and Christianity in a Cotton Mill Village," *Oral History* 8 (1980), 36-46, and "Labor Struggles in the American South," *International Labor and Working Class History* 14/15 (1979), 42-47.

EDWARD PESSEN is Distinguished Professor of History at Baruch College and the Graduate Center, City University of New York. Among his writings are *Most Uncommon Jacksonians: The Radical Leaders of the Early Labor Movement* (1967) and "Social Structure and Politics in American History," *American Historial Review* 87 (1982), 1290-1345.

FRANK STRICKER teaches history and labor studies at California State University at Dominguez Hills. He has published articles and reviews on women's history, labor history, and economics in *Mid-America, New Labor Review,* the *Journal of Social History,* and *Economic Forum.*

PAUL B. WORTHMAN, having taught history at various colleges, is now executive director of L.E.A.R.N. (Labor Relations, Economic Analysis, Advocacy, Research, Negotiations Services), which assists local unions and independent employee associations with negotiations, research, and public affairs. His other publications include "Working Class Mobility in Birmingham, Alabama, 1880-1914," in Tamara Hareven, ed., *Anonymous Americans* (1970).

ALFRED YOUNG is professor of history at Northern Illinois University. His writings include *The Democratic Republicans of New York: The Origins, 1763-1797* (1968) and "George Robert Twelves Hughes, 1742-1840: A Boston Shoemaker and the Memory of the American Revolution," *William and Mary Quarterly,* 3d Ser., 38 (1981), 561-623. Among his edited works is *The American Heritage Series* (1963-73), 50 vols.